DAYS OF OPPORTUNITY

Global America

GLOBAL AMERICA
Edited by Jay Sexton and Sarah B. Snyder

Columbia University Press's Global America series pushes the history of U.S. foreign relations in new directions, sharpening and diversifying our understanding of the global dimensions of American history from the colonial era to the twenty-first century. Books in the series explore America's global encounters, including how external forces have shaped the development of the United States and vice versa; why American encounters with the wider world have produced volatility, ruptures, and crises; the shifting contours of U.S. power over time; and the impact of hierarchical attitudes regarding identity in shaping U.S. foreign relations. Taken together, the series analyzes the global history of the United States; its authors employ a diverse range of methodological, chronological, disciplinary, geographical, and ideological perspectives.

M. Todd Bennett, *Neither Confirm Nor Deny: How the Glomar Mission Shielded the CIA from Transparency*

Days of Opportunity

THE UNITED STATES AND AFGHANISTAN
BEFORE THE SOVIET INVASION

Robert B. Rakove

Columbia University Press
New York

Columbia University Press
Publishers Since 1893
New York   Chichester, West Sussex
cup.columbia.edu

Copyright © 2023 Columbia University Press
All rights reserved

Library of Congress Cataloging-in-Publication Data
Names: Rakove, Robert B., 1977– author.
Title: Days of opportunity : the United States and Afghanistan before the Soviet invasion / Robert Rakove.
Other titles: United States and Afghanistan before the Soviet invasion
Description: New York : Columbia University Press, 2023. | Includes bibliographical references and index. |
Identifiers: LCCN 2022056937 | ISBN 9780231210447 (hardback) | ISBN 9780231210454 (trade paperback) | ISBN 9780231558426 (ebook)
Subjects: LCSH: United States—Foreign relations—Afghanistan. | Afghanistan—Foreign relations—United States. | Afghanistan—Foreign relations—20th century. | United States—Foreign relations—20th century. | Afghanistan—History—20th century.
Classification: LCC E183.8.A3 R356 2023 | DDC 327.730581—dc23/eng/20221214
LC record available at https://lccn.loc.gov/2022056937

Cover design: Milenda Nan Ok Lee
Cover image: Afghans awaiting Eisenhower's motorcade, December 9, 1959.
Source: United States National Archives, College Park, Record Group 306

To Alex and Elliot, and in memory of Stephen Scharf

Contents

Notes for the Reader   ix

Introduction: "A Day of Opportunity"   1

1 A Game of Hide-and-Seek: The Afghan Pursuit of Diplomatic Relations, 1921–1938   13

2 "We Have a Rare Opportunity": U.S.-Afghan Relations Amid the World Crisis, 1938–1945   33

3 Preeminence and Peril: The American Influx and the Coming of the Afghan Cold War, 1945–1952   63

4 "We Might Be Willing to Take a Chance": The Choice to Contest Afghanistan, 1953–1956   100

5 Anxious Coexistence: The Aid Contest, 1956–1959   135

6 The Crisis Era, 1959–1963   171

7 Reform and Retrenchment, 1963–1968   205

8 The Fall of the Monarchy, 1968–1973   239

9 Return to Engagement, 1973–1976   272

10 The End of Diplomacy, 1977–1979   306

Conclusion: "Into the Jaws of Catastrophe"   343

Acknowledgments   357
List of Abbreviations   363
Notes   365
List of Archives   445
Index   449

Notes for the Reader

During the course of my research for this book, I encountered alternative spellings of Afghan names in both documents and the historical literature; therefore, in the text I have used the most common forms of Afghan names, assisted by Ludwig Adamec's *Historical Dictionary of Afghanistan*.

Some confusion might arise due to individuals having similar names, although they generally are not discussed in close proximity. Wali Khan, an intrepid Afghan diplomat, leads off the first chapter. Another Wali Khan headed the Pakistani National Awami Party during the 1970s and appears in chapter 9. Shah Wali, the longest lived of King Zahir's uncles, features in the first nine chapters, until his death in 1977, which is mentioned in chapter 10. His sons, Wali Shah and Abdul Wali, appear in chapters 6 and 9. An unrelated Shah Wali served as foreign minister to the Democratic Republic of Afghanistan and appears toward the end of chapter 10. Confusion may also attend the dual appearance of King Mohammed Zahir Shah and Prime Minister Abdul Zahir within chapter 8. Both are fully named in their overlapping section.

Brothers John Foster Dulles and Allen W. Dulles appear in chapters 4 and 5, the former far more often than the latter. Unless otherwise indicated, the Dulles in question is John (Allen briefly appears in chapter 1).

Until 1948, British, French, and U.S. representation in Afghanistan was maintained at the ministerial level. Acting in relative conjunction that year, the three countries elevated their diplomatic representatives to the rank of ambassador and, accordingly, their diplomatic missions from legations to embassies. The Afghan government reciprocated.

State Department cables often omitted words, chiefly articles and prepositions, for the sake of telegraphic brevity. To improve general readability, they are added here in square brackets.

Capital cities are employed as metonyms for the governments that they house. In Pakistan's case, the same city cannot be used continuously. Karachi served as the national capital from independence in 1947 until 1959. After an interregnum, during which time Rawalpindi constituted the seat of government, Islamabad assumed its current status in 1967.

The administration of U.S. foreign assistance changed with greater, more dizzying rapidity. President Harry S Truman's Point Four Program brought the Technical Cooperation Administration into being in 1950. President Dwight D. Eisenhower christened the International Cooperation Administration as its effective successor in 1955. Fundamental reforms within the 1961 Foreign Assistance Act established the overarching Agency for International Development (AID), alternatively known as USAID.

The term Third World is employed in its political, Cold War context, connoting nonaligned states.

Figure 0.1 Map of Afghanistan. NWFP, North West Frontier Province

DAYS OF OPPORTUNITY

Introduction

"A Day of Opportunity"

The extraordinary pastness of our story results from its having taken place *before* a certain turning point, on the far side of a rift that has cut deeply through our lives and consciousness.
—THOMAS MANN, *THE MAGIC MOUNTAIN*

Henry Kissinger: From what I know of Afghan history, you always gave a lot of difficulties to whoever came in here. [*Laughter*]

Mohammed Daoud Khan: In fact, they created difficulties for us! Others came to our house, not we to theirs! [*Laughter*]
—KABUL, AUGUST 8, 1976

On April 15, 1965, U.S. ambassador John Milton Steeves drafted an impassioned letter to his government from his office in Kabul. Painstakingly courteous and dignified, Steeves could summon righteous anger when circumstances demanded. He had grappled with conflicting notions of service all his life. As a young Seventh Day Adventist missionary in India, Steeves broke with his church to enlist in the struggle against fascism. A stalwart anticommunist, he counted the Soviet ambassador in Afghanistan as one of his closest friends. His superiors often disagreed with him yet liked him personally and respected his views when set to paper. So, too, did they read carefully Steeves's lamentation of the halting implementation of aid programs in Afghanistan. Written sharply in 1965, his words take on a haunting resonance in the current century: "It may be that, in the larger arena of world strategy, Afghanistan doesn't really matter. If it doesn't, then, of course, my argument falls, but if it does and we never have admitted that it doesn't, I fancy that we may have to pay a much higher price one day to try and retrieve what we are losing in a day of opportunity."[1]

If Steeves entertained some specific notion of that price, he did not express it. Had he lived to witness the attacks of September 11, 2001, and the ensuing twenty-year U.S. war in Afghanistan, he would have rejected any prophetic mantle. Striking as his prediction of calamity is, another, more mundane statement demands attention: that Afghanistan mattered to the United States, well before the 1979 Soviet invasion, the ensuing war, or the conflicts of the twenty-first century.

That suggestion may be startling. Leading histories of the Cold War tend to begin their coverage of Afghanistan in the late 1970s.[2] Accounts more specifically concerned with the country offer a story of American neglect. Afghanistan, it is true, was not incorporated into Washington's regional alliances, unlike its eastern and western neighbors, Pakistan and Iran. Within the country, the Soviet bloc substantially outspent its capitalist foes, paving roads, building airports at Kabul and Bagram, and—in an impressive feat of engineering—blasting a high-altitude tunnel through the mountains north of Kabul at the Salang Pass. Beside these monumental feats of socialist construction, U.S. efforts can appear paltry or nominal. Afghan officials regularly appealed for more U.S. assistance and at times a formal alliance, proclaiming their desire to remain independent of their powerful northern neighbor. In the wake of the Soviet invasion, their entreaties assumed a tragic character, and a narrative of neglect quickly took form, reflected in early scholarship.[3]

This book contends otherwise: that the story of the U.S.-Afghan relationship before 1979 is one of consequential involvement, not of abandonment. Measured by comparative yardsticks—either alongside the aid furnished by Washington to treaty allies or against the programs deployed by the communist bloc—it is easy to dismiss the U.S. role in pre-cataclysm Afghanistan. Close investigation of U.S. diplomacy and aid within and around Afghanistan across four decades, however, reveals a different story. Small, remote, often poorly understood, Afghanistan nevertheless assumed real significance to successive administrations in Washington. Afghan leaders, in turn, attached considerable importance to their country's relationship with the North American superpower. Successive U.S. administrations identified an interest in preserving Afghan independence and nonalignment and pursued it doggedly, despite budgetary and geopolitical constraints. Afghans capitalized on the bilateral bond, meanwhile, in the pursuit of national, personal, or factional objectives.

Days of Opportunity joins a growing field of scholarship rethinking the extent of Washington's role in pre-cataclysm Afghanistan. Recent histories by Nick Cullather, Timothy Nunan, Jenifer Van Vleck, Daniel Weimer, and James Tharin Bradford study the ambitious Helmand Valley project, collaboration between Pan American Airways and its Afghan counterpart Ariana, and expansive U.S. antinarcotics efforts within Afghanistan.[4] Benefiting from these individual studies of development and collaboration, and working chronologically, this book strives to situate these episodes within the bilateral relationship and the global Cold War, discussing their broader causal implications. It explores the emergence, evolution, and undoing of the Afghan-American relationship, positing that one cannot understand Afghanistan's tragic emergence as a violent Cold War battleground without closely examining this bilateral history.

The Afghan Cold War

The Cold War described here is, of course, the global struggle between the blocs led by the United States and the Soviet Union. This designation does not reject other such concurrent conflicts, described by Lorenz Lüthi, or reduce the contest within Afghanistan to a strictly bipolar affair.[5] The People's Republic of China took an active interest in Afghanistan, rendering Kabul a site of the Sino-American and Sino-Soviet competitions chronicled by Gregg Brazinsky and Jeremy Friedman.[6] After the Soviet invasion, the KGB and its Afghan allies hunted local Maoists with deadly avidity.[7] Afghanistan witnessed other contests for influence. Both German states vied for Afghan recognition with promises of aid, and a comparable inter-Korean contest began in the 1970s. A Malaysian diplomatic delegation staged an emergency trip to Kabul in June 1965, seeking Afghan assistance against Indonesian efforts to exclude their country from an upcoming Afro-Asian summit.[8] Yet none of these other conflicts posed the same peril to the Afghan state as the rivalry between Washington and Moscow, its two largest benefactors. No other external parties matched the two superpowers in their willingness to contest Afghanistan and in the resources they could bring to bear.

That does not mean, however, that the Cold War necessarily constituted the principal foreign policy concern for Afghanistan. A long-standing campaign for the self-determination of Pakistani Pashtuns—a primarily but not exclusively cold war in its own right—preoccupied Afghan elites to a greater degree. Another nettlesome dispute with Iran over the distribution of the Helmand River waters stirred greater domestic passions than the status of Berlin or Cuba. Kabul noted the onset of U.S.-Soviet tensions in the late

1940s and took specific steps to avoid hostilities with its northern neighbor. Afghan leaders addressed Cold War questions cautiously but also discerned possibilities in this latest great power competition. The onset of the aid contest within Afghanistan confirmed the success of Afghan nonalignment, affording Kabul greater leeway to pursue its own regional agenda—to the frequent consternation of Washington.

Several paradoxes confronted U.S. policy toward Afghanistan: of commitment, alignment, and mediation. Pre-cataclysm Afghanistan represented a crucial site of the peaceful battle for influence between the United States and the Soviet Union, alongside other sites such as India, Indonesia, and Egypt. Afghanistan, however, presented unique challenges to the West: its distance, landlocked location, and proximity to the Soviet Union placed Americans at a clear disadvantage. Consequently, although the Afghan Cold War was often spirited, Washington could not compete to win—indeed, doing so might draw a disproportionate Soviet response. It was obligated, instead, to mount a substantial effort that could, at least, stand in symbolic contrast to the ambitious programs of the communist bloc. The novelist Joseph Heller could have appreciated the ensuing dilemma: the United States both dared not bid too much and feared that it was not bidding enough.

Alongside the commitment problem, Cold War policymakers grappled with the paradox of alignment. Early in the Cold War, Afghanistan expressed interest in admission into the Western alliance system. Pessimistic U.S. assessments of the country's defensibility and Afghanistan's persistent disputes with Pakistan and Iran precluded formal enlistment. Yet neither could Washington allow Afghanistan to be absorbed into the communist bloc, thereby menacing two vital allies. The United States instead sought to maintain Afghan nonalignment. With striking frequency, a policy adopted to shield allies instead sparked further friction within those bilateral relationships. Treaty commitments notwithstanding, U.S. policymakers read Afghan developments differently than their allies did and strove to balance appeals to a nonaligned government with the obligations owed to Cold War partners. Iranian and Pakistani complaints thus offer a helpful, albeit inconvenient, index of the value Washington ascribed to Afghanistan, at times influencing a broader disaffection toward their superpower ally.

Mediation constituted the final paradox within Afghanistan policy. Clashes between Afghanistan and its noncommunist neighbors threatened to thrust Kabul into Moscow's embrace—especially in 1955 and in 1961–1963 when they brought the curtailment of overland access to the port of Karachi.

Left unaddressed, Kabul's dispute over the waters of the Helmand or its challenge to Pakistan's post-partition borders might assume Cold War implications. As a friend and ally to the disputants, the United States could potentially play a constructive mediating role—but not without some risk. Too close an effort might link Washington to one side or the other or arouse Soviet suspicions of a broader regional agenda.

Thus, Afghanistan policy before the 1978 coup represented a continual balancing act. The difficulties presented by Afghanistan to Washington's regional strategy could be managed but resisted resolution. Their intractability had little to do with any innate Afghan qualities but rather spoke to fundamental flaws in the U.S. alliance system constructed during the 1950s. Afghanistan had, unsurprisingly, not received emphasis in the major strategic doctrines commissioned by President Dwight D. Eisenhower. Yet Eisenhower and his successors worked to reconcile the peculiar problem it posed with their broader vision, through a diverse and sometimes ambitious aid program, vigorous frontline diplomacy, and direct interpersonal appeals to Afghan leaders.

U.S. geostrategic choices influenced Afghanistan, while diplomacy and aid sometimes worked to considerable effect within the country. If Americans were not the dominant foreign actors within pre-1978 Afghanistan, they still could not claim to be marginal observers. The country witnessed a frenzied aid competition during the 1950s, followed by a period of localized détente that checked Afghanistan's ability to garner aid from either side. The Soviet diplomat Anatoly Dobrynin described a "modus vivendi" between the blocs within Afghanistan during the middle Cold War years; Americans discerned the same dynamic.[9] The Marxist coup of 1978 and an ensuing spiral of action and reaction helped to propel the superpowers toward an unprecedented, profoundly destructive contest within Afghanistan at the end of the 1970s. While principal blame for the Soviet invasion must ultimately rest with its initiators, General Secretary Leonid Brezhnev and his chief advisors, U.S. choices necessarily contributed to that outcome.

Not advertently, however. This book does not endorse the notion of a U.S. effort to entrap the Soviet Union in Afghanistan, which has been methodically and effectively refuted by Conor Tobin.[10] Nor does it ascribe a grand design to Soviet policy. East German, Czechoslovak, and Soviet records illuminate instead a relatively cautious communist bloc policy, marred at times by paranoia. The same criticism, of course, could be leveled against the United States, for which fervid myths of a centuries-long Russian drive south—purportedly dating back to the reign of Tsar Peter the Great—offered convenient if reductive explanations for Soviet policy.[11] Rather, in chronicling Washington's decades-long engagement in Afghanistan, this book is a story of adaptive policies but not grand strategies—certainly not a "Great Game"—culminating in a tragic cycle of fearmongering, miscommunication, and mutual escalation. Once somewhat peripheral, Afghanistan needlessly became a central battleground of the Cold War, testifying powerfully to the fundamental influence of misperception and inadvertency in the East-West struggle.[12]

Defining Threads

No Cold War battleground can be perfectly representative of the conflict, and Afghanistan, while not exceptional, boasted some of its own idiosyncrasies. It had regained full independence earlier than most of its Afro-Asian peers, practicing a distinctive form of nonalignment before the term gained currency (the Dari equivalent is *bi-tarafi*, meaning "without sides"). For this and for the vigor and range of its diplomacy, Afghanistan enjoyed the esteem of its Islamic and postcolonial peers; to the Indian journalist G. H. Jansen, it was "perhaps the doyen of the non-aligned."[13] Dire proximity to one superpower and distance from the sea further set it apart. Afghan governments spoke with exquisite care about the Cold War, differing at times from some of their less reticent counterparts in the Third World. They never felt the freedom to burn their bridges with either camp. To antagonize Moscow might invite aggression; pushing away Washington could produce a dangerous dependence on their northern neighbor.

Consequently, Afghan diplomacy was persistent, personal, and skillful: a dynamic program undertaken by a cosmopolitan elite. Afghan representatives forged interpersonal bonds with foreign hosts and counterparts as a necessary step toward meaningful intergovernmental ties. Afghan hospitality and stunning local scenery endeared the country to many a guest. U.S. officials and diplomats received special emphasis and appeared to be especially susceptible to Afghan charms. "Nowhere in the world," wrote the well-traveled geologist (and later diplomat) Ernest Fox in 1943, "have I met those whom I esteem more highly than the Afghans. . . . Their honor is their bond; their hospitality is full and generous; and their tolerance is more honest than our own."[14] "They're very good at convincing you that you really need to help them," Ambassador Theodore Eliot recalled wistfully of his hosts in 2014.[15]

Afghans actively cultivated such sentiments. The skill of their diplomacy thus constitutes an important argumentative thread—but with a vital qualification. To an extent, this book joins others depicting the agency of small states in the international system.[16] A lengthy history of balancing between great powers bequeathed Afghan leaders shared methods, if not consistently shared objectives. The coordination of their efforts should not be assumed; this book treats neither state as a unitary actor. Individual Afghan officials could pivot between powers, but not in harmony or with equal agility. Their efforts sometimes advanced personal or factional goals at the expense of the Afghan state or its people. In its discussion of the cumulative, often negative effects of this competition, this book was substantially influenced by David Engerman's rich, insightful study of the corrosive consequences of the Cold War aid battle within India.[17] It joins others positing the central symbolic importance of development within the Cold War, even as the superpower protagonists depicted here often committed to projects grudgingly amid an incessant competition or engaged in uncertain efforts to salvage foundering schemes.[18]

Their remarkable persistence impels us to consider how Afghan diplomacy and events were experienced. Drawing upon recent arguments by Barbara Keys and Frank Costigliola, the role of emotion in diplomacy constitutes the second of the book's central threads.[19] The affinity felt by Americans for Afghanistan emerges as its prevalent strand. With some caveats, Americans liked Afghanistan and its people. They did not travel extensively within it, and their perspective was skewed by interactions with a Westernized Kabul-based elite, which did not always encourage trips outside the capital. The first cohorts posted there faced difficult living conditions, unfriendly microorganisms, unfamiliar cuisine, and unsympathetic landlords. A bulging folder in the U.S. National Archives contains complaints gathered by the U.S. mission in the 1940s to argue for an increased cost-of-living allowance to compensate for the difficulties of Kabul life. The political officer David Wharton composed a six-page mock-Dickensian screed including a litany of ailments he and his family had experienced.[20] The following year, however, Wharton wrote fondly about a visit to the famed Buddhas of Bamiyan, of the "tranquil, haunted magnificence of the place."[21] By the late 1950s, improved living conditions and esprit de corps fostered a distinctive enthusiasm for the post. "There's something about the place you just love," recalled Ambassador Henry Byroade.[22]

The importance of local, embassy-level diplomacy constitutes a third, related thread. In this, the book joins other works emphasizing the salience of lower and mid-level officials.[23] A formidable if not famous assemblage of diplomats waged a decades-long struggle in pursuit of U.S. objectives in Afghanistan, usually believing them to be compatible with Afghan aspirations. Persistent advocacy from Kabul influenced a State Department generally bereft of expertise on the country. Presidential attention to the country before 1978 was, at most, sporadic. "It makes a lot of difference whom we place in difficult spots like Afghanistan," President John F. Kennedy told Steeves in 1962. His successor, Lyndon B. Johnson, confessed to Prime Minister Mohammed Hashim Maiwandwal, "I gotta be honest with ya. Days go by when I don't think of Afghanistan at all." U.S. representatives waged a dual struggle: reporting Afghan conditions to their colleagues in Washington while explaining sudden, even capricious doctrinal changes to their hosts. At times the latter task proved the more difficult one. The Kabul diplomats did not win every argument—indeed, angry correspondence speckles the ensuing pages—but they succeeded often enough, and some of their heated prose should be taken as calculated bureaucratic gamesmanship.[24]

Some of it, however, reflected real frustration. Afghanistan, of course, offered significant difficulties to effective diplomacy and aid. Poor road conditions delayed and damaged goods. A dearth of experienced Afghan officials and administrative turnover brought similar frustration. The grandiose modernization schemes of Afghan elites presented their own challenges, although U.S. officials encouraged or abetted them much of the time. Still, another, more crippling set of difficulties stemmed from domestic, not Afghan, origins. Afghanistan enjoyed considerable leverage as a nonaligned state, but it could not easily overcome fundamental changes in the domestic or bureaucratic politics of its superpower patrons.

The salience of domestic factors to policymaking, recently argued by Daniel Bessner and Fredrik Logevall, thus constitutes a crucial fourth thread, applicable to both the United States and its Soviet rival.[25] Although the preservation of Afghan independence and nonalignment remained a consistent diplomatic policy goal, abrupt changes in the purposes, means, and politics of U.S. foreign assistance, driven primarily by domestic and bureaucratic politics, greatly complicated that pursuit. So, for that matter, did a deepening Soviet weariness with the aid contest. Afghans had little capacity to influence these factors and could suffer greatly if they changed in adverse ways.

In close parallel, broader perceptions of Cold War danger influenced the superpower competition within Afghanistan. So, necessarily, did fundamental beliefs held in each capital about the opposing power and its agenda, and a shared proclivity to imagine Afghanistan as the object of adversarial designs. Afghans and other regional actors could influence such perceptions, but only if their arguments resonated within existing strategic debates. Ill-timed appeals could appear hyperbolic or manipulative to strategists attempting to reconcile goals with available resources. Waning Cold War tensions reduced the persuasive power of Afghan entreaties in the mid-1960s. Even in more propitious circumstances, the internal balance within a White House, the outlooks and relative influence of its principal policymakers, could be determinative. The role of superpower beliefs, chiefly alarmist misperception, constitutes a powerful, albeit intermittent, fifth thread.

Lastly, as conveyed by the title, opportunity—more specifically, its pursuit—constitutes the sixth and final argumentative thread, serving to interweave the others. Afghans and Americans alike perceived potential in the bilateral relationship. Businessmen surveyed the resources of Afghanistan in the interwar years. Before the Cold War, U.S. officials envisioned Afghanistan as a potential showcase for their ideals, a transit route, or a listening post on the Soviet border. Aided by Washington, the Morrison-Knudsen construction firm captured a lucrative postwar contract. For their part, Afghan leaders seized upon the geopolitics of the Second World War and Cold War to pursue a beneficial relationship that might advance various domestic projects or perhaps enable the attainment of regional goals. Others, not in power, employed contacts with Washington to support their own objectives. This shared pursuit greatly complicated efforts to preserve Afghan nonalignment and independence from the Soviet bloc, enduring long after both efforts failed.

Across Six Decades

An overarching history of U.S. engagement in Afghanistan before 1979 requires consideration of myriad bilateral interactions: economic aid, business ventures, regular and high-level diplomacy, conflict mediation, human rights, disaster relief, espionage, cultural outreach, and ultimately confrontation.

It also requires consideration of the perspectives and activities of various third countries: European allies, world war and Cold War antagonists, and other states in Afghanistan's region. Fittingly, for its role in modern history, the study of Afghanistan is inescapably an international endeavor. Alongside U.S. records, archives in Britain, France, Germany, and the Czech Republic, along with Soviet records held by the Cold War International History Project and the National Security Archive, proved especially useful. Among the communist bloc records consulted, the former Czechoslovak archives were particularly helpful and comprehensive.

Caution should, of course, be exercised in assembling an account from the perspectives of foreign observers, but as independent sources in a country where a free press only operated intermittently, diplomatic records are indispensable. They are often voluminous, reflecting the diplomat's less celebrated role as beat reporter. They also contain documents otherwise lost. At the very least, consulted in combination, they can assist in charting the outer contours of Afghan foreign policy: telling us what Afghans said, if not always why.

An introduction is the place to acknowledge historiographical debts and topical limitations. Crucial accounts of modern Afghanistan by Amin Saikal, Robert Crews, Barnett Rubin, Faiz Ahmed, Louis Dupree, Elisabeth Leake, Faridullah Bezhan, Jonathan Lee, and Ludwig Adamec, among others, have been essential to my own depiction.[26] Studies of development in Afghanistan by Cullather, Van Vleck, Bradford, and Weimer have also been invaluable. The ensuing chapters will necessarily discuss the same episodes—particularly the Helmand project, aviation aid, and the counter-narcotics campaign—in ways intended to complement and build upon these vital contributions. Accounts of the Soviet intervention by Artemy Kalinovsky, Vasily Mitrokhin, Odd Arne Westad, Rodric Braithwaite, and Vladislav Zubok have been similarly helpful, as have depictions of Moscow's earlier Afghan policy by Timothy Nunan, Paul Robinson, and Jay Dixon.[27] My own use of communist bloc sources does not facilitate a comprehensive account but does enable periodic comparisons between the blocs. The striking mundanity of pre-coup communist records belies more ominous accounts of Moscow's agenda within the country. Lastly, although this account departs significantly in its interpretation, I gratefully acknowledge the pioneering works of Leon Poullada, Leila Poullada, and Jeffery Roberts.[28]

As is so often the case, writing a Cold War story requires consideration of prior events. My first two chapters cover the early years of U.S.-Afghan relations. Chapter 1 depicts an era of distant relations, between the world wars. Although President Warren G. Harding's reception of a visiting Afghan delegation in 1921 conferred recognition upon the Afghan kingdom, his State Department rebuffed Afghan requests to establish a resident mission in Kabul. Persistent efforts by Afghan envoys and the allure of business opportunities in the kingdom gradually and subtly undermined Washington's efforts to maintain distance. Chapter 2 examines the opening of relations against the backdrop of the Second World War and the far-reaching efforts of Minister Cornelius Engert to aid neutral Afghanistan, which paved the way for a broader U.S. role in the country after the peace.

Chapter 3 depicts an era of relative U.S. preeminence within Afghanistan in the immediate postwar years. A contract to construct an irrigation system in the Helmand Valley by the Morrison-Knudsen firm—arranged to fulfill promises made during the war—effectively committed Washington to the project of Afghan development. The U.S.-Soviet Cold War, however, cast Washington's presence within Afghanistan in an ominous light, and the departure of the British Empire from South Asia reopened historic Afghan complaints about the partitioning of Pashtun territories. U.S. efforts to assist Afghanistan and the floundering Helmand project instead drew the kingdom into the Cold War.

Chapters 4 and 5 consider the Eisenhower administration's choices in Afghanistan. Chapter 4 examines the U.S. response to the mounting Soviet aid program within Afghanistan while Washington moved hastily to establish its own alliance system. Although President Eisenhower contemplated undermining Afghanistan's nationalist prime minister, Mohammed Daoud Khan, he opted instead to counter the Kremlin with his own aid program, whose ebbs and flows are depicted broadly in chapter 5. Chapter 6 examines the height of Afghan-Pakistani tensions, against the backdrop of recurrent Cold War crises. The effective closure of the border threatened to link the Durand Line conflict to the superpower struggle, but effective local and regional diplomacy by the Kennedy administration contributed to the March 1963 ouster of Daoud and the subsequent reopening of the border.

Chapters 7 and 8 depict U.S. policy during the years of Afghanistan's constitutional experiment, set into motion by King Zahir after Daoud's dismissal, amid the relaxation of Cold War tensions within the kingdom. Washington welcomed the pluralization of Afghan governance, but a sharp domestic reaction against foreign assistance limited what it was able to provide the new Kabul government. The Vietnam War distracted President Johnson and divided the two countries as LBJ sought to punish the Kabul government for a stray expression of mild criticism. Chapter 8 examines Nixon-era policy up to the overthrow of the monarchy and constitutional regime in July 1973. As the constitutional project struggled, Afghan officials grappled with a worsening drought, U.S. exhortations to practice "self-help," and Washington's escalating concern with curbing opium cultivation. The ensuing famine in 1971–1972, although somewhat alleviated by emergency U.S. food aid, gravely undermined the Afghan state, providing Daoud with his opportunity to seize power again.

The final chapters chronicle the period following Daoud's coup, up to the Soviet invasion. Chapter 9 examines the interplay between Afghan events and the détente system, through the end of the Ford administration. Washington worked to engage Daoud anew while also reassuring its allies, who feared a broader Soviet design lay behind events in Kabul. Benefiting from a relative lull in Cold War tensions, U.S. and Iranian diplomacy helped to achieve a tenuous Afghan-Pakistani détente by the end of 1976. Chapter 10 depicts the final years of the diplomatic relationship and Afghanistan's emergence as a violent battleground bearing global implications. Daoud's violent overthrow in April 1978 came amid a general fraying of the détente system. The emergence of a Marxist regime in Kabul reinforced a narrative of Soviet advances around the periphery of the Indian Ocean, gradually strengthening the hands of hawkish advisors within the Carter administration. Acting from anxiety and perceiving opportunity—yet bereft of any grand design—Washington sought to extract a cost from its Soviet adversary. The ensuing cycle of reaction and misperception, centered on Afghanistan, undermined the détente system at the great and enduring expense of that country and the wider world.

The importance of 1979 as a point of rupture for Afghanistan cannot be overstated—especially in the current century. For this reason, several closing caveats should be offered. This book does not treat Afghanistan as an exceptional country, and it rejects the pejorative moniker "graveyard of empires."[29] It does not treat Afghanistan as timeless or static. Rather, its chronological structure and use of narrative represent an effort to glimpse the experiences, hopes, and fears of Afghanistan's Cold War combatants over time. For this reason, it largely refrains from reference to events outside of its stated timeframe. Such foreshadowing distracts, and the pre-cataclysm era of U.S.-Afghan relations should be understood on its own terms, not ours. Steeves wrote presciently: choices made in and about Afghanistan held grave and lasting implications for the United States and the world.

CHAPTER 1

A Game of Hide-and-Seek

The Afghan Pursuit of Diplomatic Relations, 1921–1938

Amid midsummer rains, Afghanistan's first diplomatic mission to the United States entered New York Harbor on July 11, 1921, aboard the French passenger liner *La Savoie*. Disembarking was a young, seemingly inexhaustible Afghan diplomat named Mohammed Wali Khan. Afghanistan's roving envoy had already traveled thousands of miles, securing recognition from governments in Moscow, Rome, Tehran, and Istanbul. The imposing New York skyline must have impressed him as *La Savoie* edged into its dock. Accompanied by a small delegation, Wali sought an audience with Secretary of State Charles Evans Hughes and President Warren G. Harding. He hoped to obtain U.S. recognition before sailing to London for the culmination of negotiations with his kingdom's diplomatic adversary.

Almost nothing proceeded according to plan. A press conference in New York was dominated by inane questions about an unknown Afghan woman named "Princess Fatima," polygamy, and whether Wali had been surprised by the skirts worn by American women ("We have been in Paris," answered his aide, Faiz Mohammed).[1] In Washington, incessant streetcar noise drove a sleep-deprived Wali to decamp from his Pennsylvania Avenue hotel.[2] Above all, the Harding administration was prepared to receive the Afghans courteously—but to do little else.[3]

The kingdom of Afghanistan held a precarious position after the Great War. Having boldly attained its independence in 1919, it still faced serious threats from both north and south. Far more than martial valor, Afghan elites relied upon diplomatic outreach and the allure of commercial opportunity to provide for their long-term safety. Constrained by geography and budgetary limitations, Afghan diplomacy was nevertheless omnidirectional, balancing between imperial neighbors while fostering deeper political and economic connections with other, noncontiguous powers. The latter included France, Germany, Italy, Turkey, and Japan, yet no distant country appears to have been more enticing to successive Afghan governments than the United States—the richest and most disinterested victor.

Washington did not reciprocate. Courted repeatedly by Kabul's envoys, the State Department—which operated free of any White House interest in the distant kingdom—kept Afghanistan at arm's length. Harding's reception of Wali Khan afforded basic recognition, but the United States declined to establish a diplomatic mission in Kabul. Perceiving little commercial opportunity in the country, regarding it as volatile and backward, the State Department responded to Afghan entreaties politely but noncommittally. It remained aloof from Afghanistan well into the following decade. Stymied for two decades by the State Department's rigidly cautious Near East Division, the Afghan government nevertheless succeeded in cultivating American friends in expectation of a better day.

Afghanistan in the World, 1747–1921

Defined by external actors, its autonomy famously asserted through sustained resistance, Afghanistan evades easy description. Its name describes no single ethnicity, although it is often conflated with the identity of Pashtuns, the country's largest group. The presence in Pakistan of a larger Pashtun population confounds any claim by the Kabul government to represent that people internationally. So, too, do divisions among the Pashtuns: linguistic and genealogical. Like most urban Pashtuns, the Mohammedzai dynasty, which reigned over Afghanistan, spoke Dari, a close relative of Persian. Pashto could be heard more readily outside of cities and towns, especially on both sides of the current Afghan-Pakistan border, the Durand Line. Large populations of Uzbeks, Turkmen, and Tajiks reside in northern Afghanistan, kin to peoples found in neighboring Central Asian states. In the mountainous center of Afghanistan live the Hazaras. Sunni Islam is prevalent within Afghanistan, but the Hazaras, as Shiites, are the principal exception to the rule. For this and other reasons, they have faced sustained persecution, continuing to the present day.[4] The heterogeneity of identity within Afghanistan poses a continued challenge to its rulers, who have responded variously with cooptation, repression, and resettlement programs. Nationalization campaigns have ranged from efforts to foster a shared Afghan identity to the cultivation of Pashtun chauvinism.[5] In the twentieth century, development projects offered a new, tantalizing means to bind distant, distinct regions to Kabul.

Afghanistan's geography impedes the exercise of state power. It is a land of dizzying topographical extremes, raised by the ancient collision of the Indian subcontinent with Asia. Road building was a leading objective of Afghan elites—so long as it did not facilitate foreign invasion. Poor communications frustrated foreign trade, hindered the creation of a national market, and worsened famine in times of drought. A limited road network allowed rural lords to hold preponderant authority and also amplified distance from the capital.[6] The population remained overwhelmingly rural through the 1970s, with subsistence agriculture prevalent in the countryside. Government figures, published in 1976, estimated a national population of 16.67 million, with only 14.3 percent (2.39 million) classified as urban. Alongside the 11.87 million classified as rural were perhaps 2.4 million nomadic peoples. Understandably, these numbers should be regarded as somewhat speculative—especially the latter two figures. Yet urban growth far outpaced rural growth.[7] Kabul had become a city of a half million, and one scholar extrapolated in 1975 that the capital would boast between 2.13 and 3.66 million inhabitants by 2000.[8] Afghanistan was agrarian, but far from static.

Afghanistan entered the twentieth century neither a colony nor entirely independent. Its experience in the preceding century illustrates both the explicit and implicit forms of European colonialism. Decades after its 1747 founding by Ahmad Shah Abdali, a cavalry commander who exploited a succession struggle within the Persian Empire, the Afghan kingdom encountered the expanding might of the British Empire. Britain famously conquered Afghanistan in 1839, only to lose—save a single man—its entire occupying garrison. Deepening competition within Afghanistan between Britain and Tsarist Russia led to a second invasion in 1878. Although it suffered a costly defeat at Maiwand, Britain did not conclude the Second Anglo-Afghan War empty-handed. Scant harm was done to London's hold on India by the two Afghan wars, and the second, although costly, yielded a satisfactory outcome. Lurid accounts of Afghan resistance obscure this fundamental truth and the devastation suffered by Afghanistan during both invasions.[9]

In other ways, the rise of British power in India held transformative implications for Ahmad Shah's polity. As Robert Crews writes, the First Anglo-Afghan War set a precedent for Afghans seeking the throne: to harness the aid of one or another foreign power.[10] Concurrently, European notions of strictly defined territoriality displaced local conceptions of overlapping authority. Whereas Ahmad Shah in his heyday could maintain his authority through plunder, the Afghan state now relied on doubtful forms of internal taxation—a development that spurred urbanization, particularly in Kabul. Commercial ties increasingly bound Afghanistan to India, even as overland commerce withered. Acting as purportedly impartial arbiters, a British commission demarcated the border between Afghanistan and Persia in 1872 to the satisfaction of the former.[11] British models of governance influenced Afghan rulers, notably Sher Ali, who ruled from 1869 to 1879.[12]

The Second Anglo-Afghan War facilitated the rise of Abdur Rahman Khan as king of Afghanistan. Abdur Rahman accepted the terms of the earlier Treaty of Gandamak, which bound him to maintain exclusive diplomatic relations with the United Kingdom. Afghanistan emerged from the war as a British suzerainty and a buffer state against further Russian expansion. Extensive British subsidies aided Abdur Rahman in his project of state building and the centralization of power in Kabul. In some ways, Afghanistan retained considerable freedom of action. Gandamak notwithstanding, the kingdom conducted its own foreign policy. Abdur Rahman's successors dealt quietly, albeit warily, with Russia and strictly limited the activities of British officials in Kabul. Internally he waged brutal, successful campaigns against his adversaries: rival Pashtuns, Hazaras, and Turkic peoples in the north. As Francesca Fuoli argues, Abdur Rahman drew upon administrative changes implemented by the British in his centralization of power. Nevertheless, survival came at a cost. Entanglement with the British authorities in India led to the formal demarcation of the Afghan-Indian frontier in 1893 by the Durand Line, which divided neighboring settlements and lay astride the traditional paths of nomadic peoples. The price of Afghan autonomy was a tenuous, circumscribed existence between two empires, the cooptation of its sovereignty, dependence on foreign subsidies, and de facto acceptance of reduced borders.[13]

Abdur Rahman's son, Habibullah, continued his father's state-building project and proved more receptive of outside influences. Within Kabul, rival factions headed by the Tarzi and Musahiban families advocated different modernization projects: the former drawing upon the example of the Young

Turk movement in the Ottoman Empire; the latter, the more conservative tenets of Indian Muslim thinkers. Habibullah's reign witnessed the opening of Habibia College, the kingdom's first secondary school, in 1904; the arrival of automobiles in Kabul the following year; and the opening of the first state hospital in 1913.[14] Among the foreign consultants Habibullah hired was A. C. Jewett, an American engineer contracted to construct a hydroelectric project near Jalalabad.[15]

The First World War posed serious complications for the cautious Habibullah, as Afghan opinion strongly favored entry alongside the Ottoman Empire. He welcomed a delegation of German and Ottoman envoys in autumn 1915 but hesitated to accept their proposal for a military alliance. A German delegate later complained, "One day the Amir says he is for us, and the next against us." Ultimately Habibullah had to give his hawks something. He and his guests signed a draft treaty in January 1916. Habibullah promised to enter the war upon the arrival of German or Turkish soldiers in Afghanistan. Neither Central Power had surplus soldiers to dispatch on an arduous march across neutral Iran, and the delegation departed in May. Habibullah's finesse under pressure was admirable and prudent, but subsequent upheaval in Russia only deepened his domestic predicament. With the former Tsarist empire in turmoil, nationalists demanded that he pursue full independence. Britain refused to concede fully, and Habibullah appeared unable to capitalize on the moment.[16]

Habibullah was assassinated on February 20, 1919, during a hunting trip near Jalalabad. After a brief, intense power struggle, Habibullah's third son, Amanullah, emerged as his successor. Amanullah aligned with the Tarzi faction and had backed entry into the war. Habibullah's death nullified existing agreements with the United Kingdom, and London delayed in recognizing Amanullah's succession. The impasse encouraged the young monarch toward dramatic action. On April 13, 1919, during a public trial of Habibullah's accused assassins, Amanullah declared his country's independence. Politely turning to the British agent in Kabul, he asked, "O Safir, have you understood what I have said?" The envoy had, but his government proved unwilling to accept a fait accompli, particularly amid rising unrest in India. The third and final Anglo-Afghan War erupted in May. Distracted by Indian upheaval, London was disinclined to invade Afghanistan yet again, although it did bomb Kabul from the air. Amanullah concluded a treaty with Britain at Rawalpindi in August 1919, yet this, too, was subject to divergent interpretations. The Afghans felt they had attained full independence; Britain contended that Afghanistan still lay within its sphere of influence and discouraged other powers from opening relations.

Amanullah benefited greatly from a transformed relationship with Russia, now under Bolshevik rule. In a personal letter, Amanullah termed Lenin "the greatest hope of the Afghan people." This was no flowery exaggeration. Successful resistance by Red Army units in Turkistan had shielded Afghanistan from a northern attack during the recent war. The Bolsheviks, meanwhile, perceived the kingdom as a bulwark of anti-imperial resistance—or at least a vital buffer. Amanullah's contested regime was the first to extend them diplomatic recognition. To an extent others seldom recognized, Moscow's relationship with Afghanistan represented a pilot program in diplomacy toward the noncommunist world. Amanullah's envoy, Wali Khan, received a warm welcome in Moscow upon arriving in October 1919. Mirsaid Sultan-Galiev, the foremost Muslim revolutionary, lauded Wali's "small but heroic country" and explicitly linked the Soviet and Afghan struggles against imperialism. A subsequent Bolshevik mission to Kabul promised funds, training, and weaponry in exchange for collaborative efforts against the British.[17]

Wali Khan's conference with the Bolsheviks represented just the first leg of a wildly ambitious itinerary. In Tashkent, the envoy had dispatched a telegram to President Woodrow Wilson, reporting his intention to represent Afghanistan at the Paris Peace Conference and requesting a meeting. Wali may be added to the ranks of envoys from subjugated lands who sought Wilson's assistance—but only just barely. He reached Tashkent one month before Wilson sailed back home, and a rapid journey across war-torn lands to the gilded halls of Versailles stretches the limits of counterfactual plausibility. As it happened, Wali had business in Moscow for much of the autumn, and it is hard to consider that time ill spent. Finally voyaging westward, he and his delegation were turned around at the Estonian frontier—Britain had prevailed upon the young, vulnerable Baltic state to deny the Afghans passage. The envoy retreated to Tashkent.[18]

Negotiations with Britain remained deadlocked, and Amanullah clearly hoped to outflank London. Wali returned to Moscow in autumn 1920. The Bolshevik state remained marginalized within the international community, but some opportunities still presented themselves. In addition to a treaty of friendship with the Soviet Union, the industrious Afghan concluded pacts with Turkey and Iran while beginning conversations with an unofficial representative of the German government. Germany in defeat was now far less eager to involve itself in Afghan affairs. Wali received a courteous but cautious welcome in Berlin from a government wary of inciting British anger. Italy, in a sour mood after the war, proved indifferent to British sentiment and negotiated a treaty in short order. France initiated discussions but was unwilling to conclude a treaty before its British ally.[19]

Wali hoped to cap his travels by concluding a treaty with the United States. Before his departure, he met with Hugh Wallace, the U.S. ambassador in Paris. Wallace received Wali civilly but not before clearing the meeting with Lord Hardinge, his British counterpart. Hardinge offered no objection, but advised that his government did not "look with favor" on the Afghan mission. He wrote: "We consider Afghanistan, though ostensibly independent, as still within our sphere of political influence."[20]

The British government monitored Wali's movements and read his telegraphed messages to Kabul. His departure aboard *La Savoie* was noted, and a cable to Washington preceded his arrival. British ambassador A. C. Geddes received instructions to avoid defining Afghanistan's international status but not to object to any official reception of the Afghans. London could accept Afghan independence, so long as it retained preeminence in Kabul, but sought to maintain its leverage before the final round of negotiations.[21] In Washington, Geddes discerned "little interest" in the Afghan delegation.[22]

Wali Khan arrived in New York on July 11, only to find his mission overshadowed through a bizarre coincidence. A middle-aged Afghan woman who fancied herself "Princess Fatima" had preceded him by two weeks, disembarking in San Francisco. Fatima claimed to be Amanullah's sister and brought three teenaged sons—all purportedly bound for school in Britain. Press attention fixated on her impressive collection of jewels. Glowing, wild-eyed coverage, rich with personal descriptions of the exotic, bejeweled Afghan woman followed the Fatima party during its travels. Probably unintentionally, the faux princess—she was not Amanullah's sister but could claim a distant link to the royal family—managed to overshadow her country's first modern embassy.

Before meeting with Wali, Hughes advised Harding, "I think it would be well, if you approve, that you should also receive them," but counseled going no further.[23] Hughes's July 20 meeting with the Afghan delegation reinforced that assessment. "My inquiry as to the commercial opportunities for our people in Afghanistan indicates that they are extremely limited," he wrote, also noting some lingering British "sensitiveness" on the question.[24] Harding hosted Wali Khan on July 26, accepting a letter from Amanullah. Harding's reply letter to Amanullah extended warm wishes and the hope that bilateral relations "may always be of a friendly character" but observed that he would be unable to establish a diplomatic mission without a corresponding act of Congress.[25] Adding insult to injury, "Princess Fatima" had already visited the White House, escorted by an ersatz "naval officer"—in fact a serial impostor named Stanley Clifford Weyman who had felt strangely compelled to aid her.[26] Years later, Faiz Mohammed recalled the humiliation of the Fatima affair, describing his delegation's muted White House reception as "disappointing and heartbreaking."[27]

The press was informed that while the U.S. government had welcomed the delegation, this did not constitute recognition of the Afghan kingdom.[28] Most likely, the Harding administration intended this message for British consumption, but its language conflated recognition with the establishment of sustained, routine diplomatic relations. One had been conferred by the Wali Khan meetings, however Hughes or Harding cared to think about them. The other had been denied to the Afghans—and would be for the ensuing two decades.

Recognition Without Relations, 1921–1934

Wali Khan had intended to broaden Afghanistan's diplomatic horizons, apply pressure against Britain, and hopefully foster partnerships that would abet economic modernization. The development of relations with Bolshevik Russia lessened London's leverage, and British negotiators proved unable to sunder them. The November 1921 Treaty of Kabul, personally negotiated by Amanullah, established Afghan independence and the kingdom's right to conduct its own diplomacy. British disfavor limited the accord to a treaty of neighborly relations, rather than one of friendship.[29]

After the nullification of Afghan suzerainty, several powers established diplomatic missions in Kabul, as Amanullah embarked upon an ambitious and accelerating program of modernization. Wary of Britain and especially alarmed by the violent subjugation of Central Asian lands by the Red Army and the ensuing flow of refugees across its northern border, Afghanistan sought distant friends. Germany and Italy offered technical assistance, and Germans rapidly constituted the largest European community in Kabul. Kemalist Turkey proved a welcome source of technicians and educators. France dispatched an archaeological mission. Anomalously, the United States stood aloof.[30]

This did not occur as a consequence of Afghan disinterest. Well after attaining independence, Kabul avidly pursued relations with Washington, especially the reciprocal establishment of diplomatic missions. Afghan diplomats in third countries—typically Britain, France, Iran, Turkey, and Italy—sought out their U.S. counterparts, inquiring about the possibility of broadening relations.[31] They were not turned away, nor were their credentials questioned. Civility and hospitality remained the rule. Their questions, however, drew hazy, elliptical replies. Professions of good wishes for Amanullah's kingdom came accompanied by reminders that the opening of a new mission required a congressional appropriation.[32]

The State Department's Near East Division assumed almost exclusive responsibility for policy toward Afghanistan during the interwar years; cabinet- or White House–level interest in the kingdom was effectively nonexistent. Hughes's policy of distance continued during the directorships of Allen Dulles (1922–1925) and G. Howland Shaw (1925–1929). Wallace Murray, who succeeded Shaw in November 1929, maintained the policy but brought a singular vehemence to its implementation. While the policy remained rigid, three distinctive phases of Afghan-American interactions can be observed. In the first phase, Dulles and Shaw, carrying forward the logic of Hughes's response to Wali, politely rebuffed Amanullah's third-country entreaties. Amanullah's 1928–1929 overthrow and the promotion of Murray initiated the second phase, as King Nadir Shah sought both to restore recognition—lost with Amanullah's overthrow—and achieve full representation. Murray resisted these entreaties but, exceeding his predecessors, contrived to deny recognition as long as possible. His ultimate failure brought the third phase, which followed the 1934 restoration of intergovernmental relations.

Like the policy, the rationales undergirding it remained consistent. Absent from the interwar years were explicit security concerns. In their stead, successive administrations sought to promote overseas commerce.[33] Dulles, Shaw, and Murray often cited the lack of substantial trade with Afghanistan, but an unspoken corollary of that statement was their perceived need to develop and protect economic interests elsewhere in the region. Britain still asserted that Afghanistan lay within its sphere of influence. Washington and London confronted serious disputes over lucrative oil concessions in Iran, Mesopotamia, and Palestine.[34] So long as commercial imperatives prevailed, some vestige of Hughes's hesitancy to trespass in a traditionally British zone endured in Washington.

The division's second rationale emerged when its leadership fielded inquiries about the lack of representation. The safety of foreigners in Afghanistan appeared questionable. Two notorious episodes in the 1920s allowed Dulles, Shaw, and Murray to contend that Americans could not be safely stationed in Kabul and that they should not promote commerce with Afghanistan. The arrests of the Italian engineer Dario Piperno and the German geographer Gustav Stratil-Sauer on murder charges and the summary trial and execution of the former raised for the department fundamental concerns about the legal protections afforded to foreigners. Both episodes had the incidental effect of debilitating the diplomatic mission of the state involved: acrimony over Piperno's death instigated an exodus of Italians from Kabul, and Berlin recalled its minister to obtain Stratil-Sauer's release.[35]

Distance did not constitute total disinterest. Washington could notice Afghanistan when the kingdom's choices affected broader questions of international law or commerce. The State Department protested in Paris in 1924 after Afghanistan awarded an exclusive archaeological concession to a French professor. Under Secretary of State William Phillips reasoned: "I believe we should stand on the theory of the Open Door, not only in commercial enterprise, but also in the interests of international scholarship and research."[36] Four years later, Washington discreetly sought and obtained Afghan ratification of the Kellogg-Briand Pact, which renounced military force as a tool of statecraft.[37] The State Department meanwhile solicited news about Afghan affairs, placing an added reporting burden on missions in Tehran, Karachi, and Calcutta. Diplomats from those posts advocated opening a Kabul legation, describing contact with friendly Afghan peers, but likely also considering the task of reporting on their host country a sufficient burden.

Contacts from Afghan diplomats occurred throughout the decade but seemingly spiked in 1924–1925, attesting to Amanullah's dissatisfaction with his kingdom's diplomatic profile. Afghanistan's immediate neighborhood remained uncertain. Imperial wars raged to the kingdom's north and south. Relations with London remained strained as British and Indian troops battled Pashtuns in neighboring Waziristan. The British government distrusted Amanullah and suspected Afghan incitement lay behind unrest in the border areas. The Red Army, while suppressing Basmachi rebels, occupied an island in the Amu Darya River, triggering a brief war scare between the two countries. The Piperno and Stratil-Sauer episodes, meanwhile, shook relations with Italy and Germany.[38]

Thus eager to broaden his country's diplomatic relations, demonstrate Afghan independence, and support his modernization program, Amanullah embarked upon an ambitious world tour near the end of 1927. It encompassed a wide array of destinations: major European powers such as Britain, France, the Soviet Union, and Germany; neighbors Iran and Turkey; and smaller powers such as Belgium, Poland, and Switzerland.[39] His minister in Italy anxiously conveyed a request for an invitation to visit the United States. The State Department's reply, crafted by Shaw, struck a remarkable balance. Invoking the 1921 exchange between Harding and Amanullah, which was "still recalled with pleasure and satisfaction by the Government of the United States," the State Department still sought to turn him away. Falsely claiming that the United States had no custom of inviting foreign monarchs, it postulated that an Amanullah visit would "present serious practical difficulties," as well as the "further possibility of misunderstanding and disappointment," lest the king seek a diplomatic mission in Kabul.[40] Stopping short of a firm rejection, the message promised that should Amanullah and his queen *still* wish to visit, they would be welcomed by President Calvin Coolidge at the White House.[41] Amanullah got the hint.

While the rebuff deprived the king of a scintillating conversation with Coolidge, Amanullah would have been well advised to cut his trip short. His grand tour lasted seven months, and he only returned to his country in late June. Intended to advance Afghan modernization, Amanullah's sustained tour instead weakened his domestic authority, allowing his opponents time and space to plan against him. Worse, upon his return, the brash young monarch sought to accelerate the pace of his reforms, which he announced in a succession of August speeches. Particularly noxious to the clergy were proposed laws requiring Western dress in Kabul, allowing women to remove the headscarf, and providing for free education to both genders. Amanullah soon faced upheaval in both Kabul and the countryside. Improbably, a Tajik bandit named Habibullah Kalakani drove the king from the capital in January 1929, thereafter ruling in his stead until another branch of the ruling family rallied to defeat and execute the usurper.[42]

General Nadir Khan came from the Musahiban family, traditionally opposed to the modernizing doctrines of Amanullah (his third cousin) and the Tarzis. With their cousin ousted, Nadir and his brothers succeeded in rallying Pashtun opinion against Habibullah Kalakani. An army led by one brother, Shah Wali Khan entered Kabul on October 13; two days later Nadir was elected king through an extraordinary tribal assembly, a *loya jirga*. Nadir and his brothers pursued a more cautious course of modernization, one more considerate of conservative religious opinion. They sought to reassure the great powers to the north and south while continuing to court distant patrons. The ousted king—now in Italian exile—retained loyalists who objected to Nadir's rule and remained a threatening figure to his ascendant cousins. Wali Khan, widely seen as Amanullah's most faithful deputy, could not escape Musahiban suspicion. Imprisoned in 1929, he was executed in 1933. His former aide and translator, Faiz Mohammed, succeeded him as Afghanistan's foreign minister.[43]

Despite the animus between Nadir Shah and his ousted cousin, Afghan foreign policy witnessed no sharp pivots under the Musahibans. In a public policy declaration, the new king pledged the continuation of Amanullah's foreign policy, the expansion of foreign trade, and the initiation of irrigation, mining, agricultural, and railroad construction projects. Afghan relations with the Soviet Union remained civil if not overly warm. Nadir declined to support the Basmachi rebels, while Afghan-Soviet commerce increased. London had somewhat greater cause to welcome Nadir and provided his regime with modest financial and military assistance—yet British efforts to consolidate control in the Indian borderlands remained a source of friction. Kabul dared not grow too close to either neighbor, and Nadir's efforts to cultivate beneficial relationships with third countries reveal a further continuity with Amanullah. His short reign witnessed the signing of more than a dozen treaties of friendship or nonaggression with European powers. Despite suspicions of pro-Amanullah sentiment in Berlin, he pursued ties with Germany. A November 1930 treaty of friendship opened full relations with Japan. To Nadir's frustration, one power ignored his diplomatic entreaties.[44]

To the State Department, Amanullah's ouster and the ensuing anarchy had seemingly vindicated the policy of distance while incidentally undoing Wali Khan's earlier accomplishment. Washington no longer recognized the government in Kabul and felt no need to do so. Nadir Shah shared his predecessor's assessment of the United States—indeed as minister to France, he had attempted to advance a draft treaty of friendship—but made no headway during his short reign. Increased Afghan entreaties in the early 1930s suggest a sense of urgency, as Nadir sought to restore stability and refute the politically dangerous charge that he relied on British support. Addressing a visiting *New York Herald Tribune* correspondent, the king remarked, "We prefer to be exploited by a nation that has no colonial ambitions. We, therefore, look to America, whom we all admire, for help." With evident impatience, he added, "You tell me now why America does not recognize Afghanistan."[45]

It was a good question, not immediately explicable by the lack of commercial interests, frugality, or safety concerns. Instead, Near East Division chief Wallace Murray single-handedly blocked the restoration of relations. Whereas his predecessors had been content with recognition without representation, Murray drew the line more restrictively, defending it when colleagues and superiors looked askance. Some of his fervor likely stemmed from personal experience. Murray had been stationed in Tehran during the Piperno episode, which apparently made a deep impression upon him. Years later, he specifically cited the young Italian's "horrible death" as an argument against Americans entering Afghanistan.[46] At another point, he dubiously invoked the fates of British invaders in the previous century.[47] Repeated inquiries by Afghan diplomats and by Americans whom he regarded as their tacit proxies further exasperated him. Afghanistan was, he explained to his superior, Under Secretary of State William Castle, "the most fanatic Moslem country in the world."[48]

That explanation sufficed in autumn 1929, with the year's upheaval fresh in mind. Two years later, however, the conspicuous failure to extend recognition appeared odd. Castle remarked that he saw no reason why recognition should not be extended, thereby prompting Murray to defend his stance at length:

> I am of the opinion that we could seize the present opportunity to recognize the present regime of Afghanistan if we so desired. The question is, have we anything to gain by such action? . . . I can't for the life of me see any useful purpose in encouraging Americans to become involved in such a hopeless part of the world as Afghanistan. Not even the rudiments of a proper banking system exist there and Heaven help American business representatives who might have the misfortune to fall into the toils of Afghan law.

Were recognition to be granted, "I fear that we shall at once have a new gang of adventurers on our neck" demanding the establishment of official relations. Castle deferred to his vehement subordinate.[49]

Thus, Murray evaded and misled the Afghans. Cleverly and disingenuously, he later attributed the five-year lapse in recognition to the absence of an official Afghan request. Murray had served long enough in the region to discern that the Afghans were unlikely to phrase the request directly, lest they invite open embarrassment. Crucially, none of his division's authorized replies to Afghan entreaties contained that helpful suggestion. In May 1931, the Afghan minister in London asked U.S. ambassador Charles G. Dawes which specific preconditions his government should fulfill to obtain recognition. Dawes could only offer general criteria and a useless promise to forward the inquiry to Washington. Murray privately admitted that he was "not particularly anxious" to inform the Afghans how recognition might be obtained.[50]

Murray successfully delayed the issue through the Hoover presidency, but signs of a potential shift became apparent during 1933 as his office fielded several inquiries from Americans, including Arizona senator Henry Ashurst. A New York attorney, apparently employed by the Kabul government, wrote directly to President Franklin D. Roosevelt. Nonrecognition, moreover, obstructed Roosevelt's global initiatives. Afghanistan had been omitted from a May 1933 presidential message on disarmament, yet the kingdom had emerged as an active participant at the World Disarmament Conference in Geneva. Noting the kingdom's "war-like past" and crucial strategic position, Murray grudgingly observed, "Afghanistan cannot be regarded as a negligible factor in the question of world disarmament." He finally admitted that there was "no compelling reason why, if properly approached" his government should continue to withhold recognition.[51]

Next to inquire was U.S. ambassador Joseph Grew in Tokyo, who wrote to Washington after a conversation with the local Afghan minister, Habibullah Tarzi. The inquiry had been routine, but Grew held great standing in the department, and Murray saw some need to shift to a more defensible position.[52] Writing to his superior, William Phillips, Murray described "an excellent opportunity to put an end to the game of hide-and-seek that we have been playing with the Afghans for a number of years in the matter of recognition."[53] Murray irritably asked Grew to communicate to Tarzi that his department was "not at all impressed" by efforts to obtain recognition made through U.S. citizens.[54] He thus placed the onus entirely on the Afghans, even as he held preponderant responsibility for the long standoff.

By then, Afghanistan had sustained yet another violent change of leadership. While Nadir and his brothers had restored a degree of order, factions associated with Amanullah targeted the royal family over the summer and autumn of 1933. An Afghan student in Germany, purportedly devoted to Amanullah, assassinated the king's brother, Mohammed Aziz, then serving as minister in Berlin. Another loyalist attempted to murder the British minister in Kabul. On the afternoon of November 8, the king was assassinated by a student. His young son, Zahir, ascended to the throne within a few hours, backed by his father's three surviving brothers: Hashim, Shah Mahmud, and Shah Wali.[55]

Relations Renewed

In sharp contrast to the kingdom's descent into anarchy four years earlier, Afghanistan weathered the trauma surprisingly well. The elder Musahibans maintained Nadir Shah's policies while employing his son as a figurehead. The kingdom's peaceful transition, wrote the U.S. consul in Karachi, "has been one of the most remarkable features of contemporary history."[56] Afghan diplomats continued their appeals for relations. From Moscow, U.S. ambassador William Bullitt reported one such conversation, pointedly adding that he had "not been able to discover any reason" why recognition should not be extended to Zahir's government.[57] Favorable trade reports about the sales of U.S.-made goods on the Afghan market bolstered his argument. Ford cars and Caterpillar tractors sold with some regularity in Afghanistan; the latter firm hired a sales representative in Kabul. An Afghan industrial fair in August 1934 drew exhibitions from Ford, General Motors, and the Singer Sewing Machine company. Washington's consul in Calcutta noted a "high esteem" for U.S.-made goods, predicting "moderate but worthwhile opportunities" for trade with the kingdom.[58]

Such arguments carried greater weight amid the Great Depression, and the State Department's influence had waned under the new Roosevelt administration. Diplomats stationed in the region increasingly questioned the policy of distance, sometimes volunteering their own suggestions to Kabul's emissaries. Disdaining the "back door," Murray nonetheless insisted upon a direct appeal from Kabul. U.S. diplomats received authorization to illuminate the front door, and Bullitt did so in his March 1934 exchange. "We have been afraid to make a formal request," remarked the Afghan ambassador in Tehran, "for fear that the American government would decline," embarrassing Afghanistan before countries that had already accorded it recognition. Wali Khan had, after all, visited the White House, to no great consequence. No such guarantee reached them, but the Afghans evidently decided to gamble.[59]

On June 30, 1934, the Afghan minister in Paris, Shah Wali, transmitted a letter from King Zahir, announcing his father's death, his own accession, and expressing the desire for closer relations. The Near East Division deemed the communication "not exactly what we had in mind as the proper approach," but, "Afghanistan being what it is," acceptable. Writing to Roosevelt, Phillips noted the stability of Zahir's regime, writing, "I can see no reason why we should withhold recognition." Neither could Roosevelt, who promptly signed a reply letter, thereby extending recognition.[60]

The exchange restored only the pre-Amanullah status quo that had dissatisfied Kabul. Yet the ice was clearly breaking. Roosevelt subsequently nominated the U.S. minister to Iran, William Hornibrook, to serve concurrently as a nonresident envoy to Afghanistan. The arrangement gave Hornibrook—a staunch advocate of broader ties—greater leeway to make his case. Hornibrook paid his first official trip to Kabul in spring 1935, presenting his credentials on May 4 and staying nearly a month. Upon his return, he argued emphatically for opening a legation, noting a variety of commercial opportunities available to Americans: in the exploitation of minerals, the export of U.S. goods, and the development of Afghan infrastructure. These were familiar arguments, but both Hornibrook and, subsequently, Bullitt offered a new and compelling case for a diplomatic mission: Afghanistan's proximity to Soviet Central Asia and its potential to serve as a "listening post" on its northern neighbor.[61]

Simultaneously, Zahir's government proved eager to consolidate its achievement. Shah Wali in Paris notified U.S. ambassador Jesse Isidor Straus that he had been authorized to negotiate a treaty of friendship. Here, suddenly, the State Department's preferences veered away from formality. Wary of crowding another treaty vote onto the legislative calendar, the Near East Division recommended an executive agreement. Straus informed Shah Wali that a less formal agreement stood to achieve Afghan purposes "more expeditiously and satisfactorily." Clearly impatient, Shah Wali assented, but by June 1935 a serious, albeit semantic snarl had emerged. The United States insisted upon an explicit most-favored-nation trading clause in the agreement; Afghanistan, wary of facing British and Soviet demands for equivalent concessions, resisted.[62]

Earlier in the decade, that might have been the end of it, but efforts toward an even more modest agreement recommenced in early 1936. Quietly, the State Department had discovered yet another flaw with the 1935 draft: language on the equal treatment of nationals would conflict with 1924 immigration legislation that barred Afghans (among many other peoples) from gaining U.S. citizenship. Apprehending that the core Afghan concern remained relations, it pared back the draft to a simple agreement affirming bilateral friendship and rights of diplomatic and consular representation. Never especially invested in the commercial article and disinterested in immigration, the Afghans quickly signaled their approval. The two parties signed the provisional agreement on March 26, 1936.[63]

Afghan diplomats expressed elation. The Near East Division held less enthusiasm. Raymond Hare wrote that the dropping of the commercial article left "little to be gained" from the remaining "generalities"; indeed, the division "should not be disappointed in the least if the whole affair could be brought to an amicable termination."Yet a hitherto absent concern for Afghan feelings had emerged within the State Department.[64] Afghanistan's recent emergence as a potential petroleum exporter and the avid pursuit of a concession by a U.S. firm could not have been wholly unrelated developments.

Even before Wali Khan reached Washington, Afghan diplomats had attempted to interest Americans in their country's oil reserves. Afghanistan's minister in Iran suggested in February 1921 that Americans might receive an oil concession.[65] Four years later, Afghan diplomats in London furnished their American colleagues with a report on oil deposits near Herat.[66] While serving as minister in Paris, Nadir Khan again proposed a U.S. oil concession the following year, claiming that his country already entertained offers from British, Soviet, and Italian firms, but would prefer to contract with an American firm.[67] The competition was not nearly so fierce, nor were the Afghans solely courting U.S. firms. Entreated by the Afghans the same year, the Anglo-Persian Oil Company concluded that Herat lay too close to the Soviet border and too far from the nearest port, rendering it "entirely unattractive from a commercial point of view."[68]

Others proved more bullish—particularly Charles Calmer Hart, the impetuous U.S. minister (and onetime journalist) stationed in Tehran in the early 1930s. Afghan ambassador Azizullah Khan had enticed him to visit Herat in 1930, pointedly directing his attention to the nearby oil.[69] From Washington, Murray scolded his Tehran envoy for undertaking an unauthorized trip.[70] Nonetheless, the short visit made a deep impression, and Hart continued to report on Afghan events. "I admit to finding myself becoming . . . 'Afghan-minded,'" he wrote in 1931.[71] Increasingly disaffected, Hart resigned his post in 1933, but not before using it as a lever for

Figure 1.1 Afghan laborers and officials examine oil seepage near Tir Pol, 1934
Source: Photograph by Frederick Clapp. University of Wisconsin-Milwaukee

professional reinvention.[72] He reappeared in Tehran months later, followed by his new business partner, the esteemed petroleum geologist Frederick Clapp.[73] The two men surveyed the Herat oil sites in summer 1934, notifying the State Department only afterward.[74]

Hart and Clapp now represented a significant and credible petroleum enterprise: the Inland Exploration Company. Inland had been chartered by the Seaboard Oil Company, a recognized and profitable midsize oil firm. Former secretary of the treasury Ogden Mills sat on its board, as did several senior officers of the Texas Company (subsequently Texaco).[75] Seaboard had to be taken seriously, but the firm lacked experience outside of the Western Hemisphere. Nonetheless, its agents Hart and Clapp unfolded an ambitious plan to obtain oil concessions in both Afghanistan and Iran. Difficult, sometimes acrimonious negotiations ensued, which nearly foundered after the Afghans attempted to bring a French firm into the bidding. Forging onward, the American duo reached terms on an extensive, exclusive oil concession with the Afghan government in November 1936.[76]

To his growing consternation, Murray now confronted persistent lobbying by Seaboard and its backers for a Kabul legation. He remained adamant

[30] A GAME OF HIDE-AND-SEEK

that his government had been "well-advised" in its prior stance, but the matter could no longer be postponed. Outpaced by events, contemplating the arrival of hundreds of rowdy oil workers in the kingdom, he conceded, "I do not see how we can avoid much longer establishing a permanent legation at the Afghan capital." The State Department initiated budgetary planning for a Kabul mission.[77]

Murray need not have worried, as the concession imploded. An inadequately staffed, poorly planned Inland exploratory mission began shakily in October 1937 and never recovered, hampered by illness and winter conditions.[78] By spring 1938, Seaboard and its backers had lost heart, having failed to locate oil in southern Afghanistan while deeming the transportation costs of the northern oil prohibitive. A sharp downturn in the U.S. economy, anxiety about foreign concessions after Mexico's oil nationalization, and looming war clouds in Europe further dampened Seaboard's interest in an already doubtful venture.[79] Hart's belated, clumsy, and peremptory delivery of the news to his Afghan hosts in June completed the fiasco. Murray was able to defer the opening of a Kabul legation for a while longer.[80]

Waning Distance

Seventeen years after Wali Khan had reached New York Harbor, his government's diplomatic outreach to the United States remained unfulfilled. In part, this reflected the failure of its commercial argument. The problems of geography and infrastructure, coupled with the kingdom's geopolitical predicament and periodic instability, limited the opportunities perceived by Americans while they pursued numerous, more obviously lucrative markets during the 1920s. Afghan efforts at salesmanship were slow to bear fruit and exasperated the already skeptical Near East Division.

The United States had not been the sole target of Afghan entreaties, and Afghan offers to U.S. diplomats and business representatives must be assessed in a comparative light. Kabul was often less single-minded than its envoys claimed. Nonetheless, the rationales behind persistent Afghan inquiries after the Great War are readily discernible. The United States represented a third country par excellence: geographically distant, uniquely affluent, and the producer of appealing consumer goods. Visibly removed from either imperial neighbor, its own empire notwithstanding, Washington appeared likely to place the fewest impositions on Afghanistan. Most likely, the Afghans underestimated U.S. cooptation into the European imperial system and the consequent willingness of senior officials to place their country within London's sphere of influence. The prejudices of Wallace Murray also remained veiled to them.

Yet, improbably, years of persistent outreach by Kabul's diplomats slowly yielded results. Contacts in other capitals and inquiries by American intermediaries and other interested parties regularly forced the leadership of the Near East Division to justify its policy to others. By the end of Nadir's brief reign, those explanations had developed a defensive tenor. Diplomats within and outside of the region challenged the ongoing rationale for the policy, perceiving Afghan affairs as bearing some importance for U.S. diplomacy. Bullitt, Grew, Hornibrook, and—despite it all—Hart represented success stories for their Afghan interlocutors. This accomplishment emerged not only in their advocacy for a substantial relationship but also in the apparent warmth with which they described their Afghan counterparts.[81] Sustained interpersonal engagement won the kingdom much-needed friends within the U.S. diplomatic service—demonstrating the importance of emotion and rapport in the conduct of foreign relations. In 1942, with the arrival of Cornelius Engert in Kabul, the dividend would grow beyond anything Amanullah could have expected.

At the moment of attaining independence, Afghanistan had been profoundly alien and unfamiliar to Americans. Its distance, instability, and obscurity deterred conventionally minded businessmen and formalistic diplomats while offering fodder to adventurers and, at times, fabulists. That dynamic still held at the end of the 1930s, but fundamental and gradual shifts in U.S. geostrategic thought, coupled with the worsening of international tensions, encouraged Americans to ascribe strategic value to the remote kingdom. Amid the ensuing global cataclysm, a small but dedicated number of Americans applied their own sense of mission to Afghanistan.

CHAPTER 2

"We Have a Rare Opportunity"

U.S.-Afghan Relations Amid the World Crisis, 1938–1945

Wilbur Harlan's troubles began somewhere in northern Afghanistan. The twenty-five-year-old American schoolteacher had departed Kabul in late August 1939, first motoring west to see the famous Buddhas of Bamiyan. Misfortune subsequently attended him in the far north. Suspicious authorities in Mazar-i-Sharif briefly detained Harlan on the grounds of the local governor's palace. Intermittent car difficulties after his release forced a stop in the town of Kholm. There, Harlan was offered a room in the abandoned Bagh-i-Jehan Nama Palace, built during the reign of Abdur Rahman. His misfortunes continued the following day. His rear spring broke, and Harlan waited eight hours for a bus to the nearest town, where he spent the night on a bench. A bridge collapse imposed further delays, but Harlan, unconcerned, passed the time composing a letter to his father. He was not lonely, writing: "A nice old man has taken me under his wing and at intervals we carry on a conversation of sorts until we are exhausted." Their chief topic was the German invasion of Poland.[1]

Harlan's account resembles those of other Westerners who visited Afghanistan during the interwar years. Swiss writers Ella Maillart and Annemarie Schwarzenbach had driven much the same route days before, at the culmination of an automotive journey from Geneva—the two women even slept in the same palace in Kholm.[2] Yet whereas Maillart later wrote an indelible book about the tragic journey, which had been marred by her companion's descent into addiction, Harlan's plain-spoken account traveled a stranger path. Responding to a request from the State Department, which lacked firsthand accounts of Afghanistan, Harlan's father, a government employee, forwarded his son's correspondence. Wilbur was no diplomat, but, without a U.S. mission in Kabul, his whimsical observations of life there would have to do.[3]

Travel accounts from Afghanistan almost invariably recount difficult road conditions, breathtaking natural scenery, evocative ruins, and local hospitality. Taken together, these elements seemingly distance Afghanistan from the chaos then engulfing the industrialized world. Yet Harlan and Maillart, traveling separately in the summer of 1939, beheld a country profoundly concerned with the coming European war. A sudden ban on foreign travel, imposed after its outbreak, stranded Maillart and Schwarzenbach in Kabul, to the latter's great misfortune. Harlan's arrest in Mazar-i-Sharif also attested to Afghan anxieties about the European war. The kindly old man whom he encountered somewhere east of Kholm likely shared those concerns.

Also present in these accounts are depictions of Afghanistan's influential German colony. Geologist Ernest Fox, who surveyed the country for the Inland Exploration Company, observed numerous signs of Germany's "forceful, peaceful penetration into Afghanistan." Just before his detention, Harlan learned of the war from two Germans in Kunduz. At Pul-i-Khumri, Maillart and Schwarzenbach encountered a German engineer who invited them to tea at his residence. Maillart subsequently wrote: "A portrait of Hitler watched over the coffee-table, the pet dog, the cushions, the fair-haired lady of the house. Were we still in Asia?"[4]

Germans appeared omnipresent, whereas Harlan and a fellow teacher constituted the entire American colony in Afghanistan. Yet within six years, the German presence had been liquidated, and a small but energetic U.S. diplomatic mission stood in Kabul, the spearhead of unprecedented, expanding American influence in Afghanistan. This outcome came as a consequence of both Afghan vulnerability and Allied victory in the Second World War. While Afghanistan enjoyed some room to maneuver in the war's early years, Hitler's invasion of the Soviet Union led to the dramatic curtailment of the German and Italian presence in the kingdom. The defeat of the Third Reich in 1945 completed the process.

This is only half the story, however. While an Anglo-Soviet ultimatum and battlefield victories created a vacuum in Afghanistan, the U.S. choice to fill that void was not preordained. Changing conceptions of U.S. security drove policymakers in Washington to ascribe strategic value to the obscure, remote kingdom. The outbreak of war and President Franklin D. Roosevelt's choice to support Britain and the Soviet Union undermined prior rationales for avoiding direct relations.

Even so, choices made in Washington could hardly prove determinative. The promotion of Allied interests and the maintenance of a friendly Afghan neutrality required active, effective representation in Kabul. Cornelius Engert, the first U.S. minister to Afghanistan, acted decisively toward this end. Aided by his unequaled familiarity with Afghanistan, actively cultivated by the Kabul government, and believing in a special U.S. role in the country, Engert worked to transform the bilateral relationship: lobbying for a subsistence level of Afghan commerce, promoting U.S. culture, and positioning his government as the kingdom's chief benefactor. With the aid of receptive officials in Washington, he succeeded. Absent from Kabul when the war broke out, the United States had become Afghanistan's principal foreign partner as the guns fell silent.

Afghanistan Between the Great Powers

To understand the beginning of U.S. diplomacy within Afghanistan, some attention to the kingdom's changing stance toward the other major powers during the final prewar and early war years is necessary. In the mid-1930s, Afghans perceived the United States as a potentially powerful new actor within a complex multipolar contest in Kabul. Washington's aloofness endured past the outbreak of war, however. Sudden shocks, such as the fall of France and the German invasion of the Soviet Union, influenced a heated internal debate on foreign policy, while the war fundamentally disrupted Afghan commerce.

Afghanistan's mid-1930s drive for a direct relationship with the United States occurred as the kingdom perceived growing threats to its security. Upheaval in the Pashtun borderlands complicated relations with Britain and the Indian colonial government. Diplomatic communications intercepted by the British, meanwhile, attested to a pervasive Afghan fear of the Soviet Union, validated by periodic killings of Afghan soldiers along the northern border.[5] Nadir Shah's brother and effective successor, Prime Minister Mohammed Hashim Khan, endeavored to maintain correct relations with both imperial neighbors. As a pious conservative, he nursed a greater distrust of the Soviets and a concern that Moscow might subvert his government's authority in the far north. Hashim authorized policies to bind restive regions to the center. His interior minister settled Pashtuns in the north while forcibly relocating Central Asian refugees elsewhere. The government promoted Pashto as a national language while advancing the myth of a common Aryan ancestry for all of Afghanistan's peoples. With Hashim's sanction, Abdul Majid Zabuli, a wealthy financier and later minister of the economy, established a national bank and a series of state-authorized monopolies, known as *shirkat*—thereby marginalizing Hindu, Sikh, and Jewish merchants who had traditionally played an essential role in the kingdom's foreign commerce. Afghan modernization assumed a nationalist cast.[6]

Such policies attested, at least partly, to a growing sense of insecurity, amid a worsening international climate. Japan's campaign in Manchuria evoked ambivalence in Kabul: underscoring the weakness of the League of Nations, but visibly unnerving the Soviet Union. Afghanistan only joined the league in 1934, shortly before Italy's invasion of Ethiopia effectively discredited the body, seemingly portending similar inaction in the event of Soviet aggression. "Who, ten years ago, would have looked on Italy as a menace to the integrity of Abyssinia?" a clearly distressed Hashim asked British minister William Fraser-Tytler.[7] Thus discouraged, Afghanistan maintained a low profile in Geneva, using its membership to widen its diplomatic outreach.[8] Kabul concluded a nonaggression treaty in 1937 with Turkey, Iran, and Iraq, the Saadabad Pact, but placed little stock in it. None of the four signatories was likely to provide meaningful aid to the others. French involvement in Afghanistan remained limited to an archaeological mission. Ties with Tokyo remained largely commercial, and the activities of Japanese intelligence officers in northern Afghanistan provoked a stern rebuke, as Eunan O'Halpin chronicles.[9] Italy's choice to host Amanullah made it a dubious partner. Renewed efforts to forge meaningful commercial ties with Washington foundered with the Inland Exploration Company expedition. Only one state appeared both capable and willing to play a major role in the kingdom: Nazi Germany.[10]

Thus, German influence within Afghanistan grew dramatically during the 1930s. Hashim's policies, predicated on the construction of a strong Afghan nation-state, bore certain parallels to doctrines emerging from Hitler's Third Reich. A rising generation of Afghans, similar in outlook to

Amanullah, favored ties to Berlin, regarding it as a capable and willing patron and a potential ally against Soviet aggression. These included Hashim's nephews and protégés Mohammed Daoud Khan and Mohammed Naim Khan, as well as Abdul Majid Zabuli. Their elders beheld the Third Reich more warily, recalling German ties to Amanullah. Hashim personally regarded Nazism as subversive. Yet Berlin lent at low interest rates, and German experts seemed atypically amenable to the modest wages and difficult living conditions associated with Afghan contracts. "Beggars," Fraser-Tytler reasoned, "cannot be choosers."[11] The partnership deepened after Foreign Minister Faiz Mohammed and Majid visited Berlin in 1936. A confidential loan agreement provided Afghanistan 15 million reichsmarks toward arms purchases. Other agreements promised the education of Afghans in German universities and the dispatch of German flying instructors and training aircraft to the kingdom. Lufthansa opened a highly unprofitable route to Kabul in spring 1938, conveying an estimated four passengers per trip.[12] To French minister Jean-Baptiste Barbier, the preeminent position of German technicians within Afghanistan appeared unassailable.[13]

Before 1938, Britain regarded the Soviet Union as its most serious rival within Afghanistan, fearing that communist agents might foment unrest among Pashtuns in the borderlands. Inasmuch as it helped the kingdom resist Soviet pressure, German assistance to Afghanistan served British interests as well. Yet mounting European tensions in the summer of 1938 prodded Fraser-Tytler to reconsider the implications of Germany's extensive Afghan colony. He grimly estimated that "upwards of 100 unofficial Nazi Agents" now operated throughout the country, against only a handful of Britons. Noting continued, unabated Afghan fear of the Soviet Union, the British minister counseled some combination of military and technical assistance to bolster London's influence.[14]

British officials strove to undo the Reich's gains. They received mixed messages from Kabul. When Hashim complained to Fraser-Tytler about British policy, he could not be placated by promises of enhanced assistance. The absence of a security guarantee left the kingdom, in his words, "neglected and friendless, a small ill-armed state surrounded by dangers and difficulties."[15] The outbreak of war in September effectively severed Afghan-German commerce—bringing, weeks later, a surprising appeal from Berlin's closest Afghan ally. Zabuli requested a long-term loan toward a ten-year plan of development. Fraser-Tytler responded noncommittally, but wrote afterward that his government should consider the request. Suggesting the contours of the coming contests for Afghanistan, he concluded:

> I cannot help feeling that the problem of Afghanistan should . . . not [be] divided into its political and economic components as hitherto. We have in the past . . . regard[ed] the economic side of the question as one to be treated on strictly "business lines," . . . without taking fully into account the fact that the political stability of this country depends just as much, or even more, on its economic prosperity as on its armaments. I believe that we should be well advised . . . to associate ourselves . . . with the cultural and economic development of this country and to look on the outlay required for this purpose as a political investment which, with all its risks, should repay us in the end.[16]

Even as British conceptions of the geopolitical struggle for Afghanistan evolved, developments in the European theater altered Afghan views of the war and the opportunities it might afford.

So long as the Western Front remained quiet, the most immediate effects of the war, as experienced in Afghanistan, were the disruption of German commerce and the apparent emergence of an unsettling Berlin-Moscow axis. The brutal partitioning of Poland and Moscow's subsequent invasion of Finland reinforced Afghan concerns about Soviet aggression.[17] When the war appeared stalemated, Hashim's outward reliance upon Britain and acquiescence in London's broader defense strategy appeared justifiable. Kabul hosted a visiting British military mission in December 1939. After months of internal debate, the British government directed Fraser-Tytler to provide a secret, verbal guarantee of support in the event of a Soviet attack.[18]

In December 1939, Fraser-Tytler admitted that, to the Afghans, "We are nearly always reluctant and late in our offers of assistance."[19] The belated security guarantee confirmed this pattern, reaching Kabul on the eve of Germany's May invasion of the Low Countries and France. The ensuing French collapse signaled Germany's apparent mastery of the European continent and raised the possibility of British defeat. In Kabul, it deprived the British diplomatic mission of their sole ally while formally adding Italy, which had belatedly invaded France, as an adversary. The Afghans took note. Four days after the French armistice, Zabuli informed German minister Hans Pilger that Germany could enjoy Afghan support in the war, in exchange for a guarantee against Soviet attack and access to the sea. Hashim's government grew less receptive to British offers of assistance while making guarded inquiries about the future of India and the possibility of revised borders.[20]

The example of Habibullah should be recalled when considering wartime Afghan diplomacy. Afghans predicated their belligerency on unlikely if not infeasible conditions. While individual Afghans—notably Zabuli and the Afghan minister in Berlin—professed enthusiasm for an Axis victory, they consistently sought a German security guarantee against hypothetical Soviet aggression. This is not to suggest that different Afghan actors read from the same script during the uncertain year following the fall of France. Faridullah Bezhan describes an intergenerational wartime debate, pitting a conservative elder generation, wary of and indebted to British power, against a rising, nationalistic generation, impressed by the German model. Hashim, a cautious, suspicious monarchist, personified the former, Zabuli the latter. Uniting the two factions was a shared suspicion of the Soviet Union, coupled with a profound sense of the kingdom's weakness.[21]

Meanwhile, without the permission of the Kabul government, German and Italian spies sought to foment unrest in British India. In their most notorious wartime feat, agents of the German *Abwehr* spirited the Indian nationalist Subhas Chandra Bose through Afghanistan, to eventual exile in Berlin. Principally, they directed their efforts at restive Pashtun tribes, seeking contact with the Fakir of Ipi, among other known rebels. Debate raged in Berlin, meanwhile, over Afghan policy. Early in the war the Foreign Ministry bickered with the Nazi Party's international arm over a proposal to oust Zahir and restore Amanullah to the throne—thus validating Hashim's suspicions.[22]

Paradoxically, even as Allied fortunes worsened during 1941, a combination of events rendered Afghan support of the Axis less feasible. Britain's suppression of a pro-Axis revolt in Iraq, followed by another successful campaign in neighboring Syria, illustrated Germany's relative weakness in the Middle East and seemed to dampen Zabuli's eagerness to support subversive operations in the borderlands. Most decisively, the June 22 Axis invasion of the Soviet Union, Operation Barbarossa, forged a united front between Afghanistan's two neighbors. Fraser-Tytler had repeatedly complained about the activities of the German colony. In a testy March exchange with the British minister, Hashim pledged to curtail further subversion. A strange episode in the summer suggests that Hashim spoke sincerely. Two Germans in turbans, searching for the Fakir of Ipi, had a lethal encounter with an Afghan army patrol. Hashim later claimed that the Germans had been led into a trap. Finally, the German Foreign Ministry heedlessly proposed to dispatch Werner Otto von Hentig to serve as military attaché in Kabul.[23]

A quarter-century earlier, von Hentig had accompanied Germany's wartime mission to Afghanistan. Kabul's initial acceptance of the appointment brought nearly two years of accumulated British frustration to the fore. Fraser-Tytler informed Faiz Mohammed that no act, short of flying the German flag above the royal palace, could be more calculated to disturb Anglo-Afghan relations. London and Moscow, sudden allies in Kabul and elsewhere, jointly made their displeasure clear. Fraser-Tytler counseled applying an economic blockade against the kingdom; against his objections, London adopted a more gradual course. Kabul retracted von Hentig's approval, but some economic sanctions had already taken effect, including a reduction in petroleum exports into Afghanistan. Stricken by gasoline shortages, the government imposed a drastic rationing regime.[24]

Berlin advised its Kabul mission to avoid rash action, but Afghanistan's German colony faced a bleak future. Even as the German army advanced deeper into the Soviet Union, London and Moscow, acting in tandem, enjoyed unprecedented leverage in Kabul. Fraser-Tytler and his Soviet counterpart commenced serious discussions on the elimination of the German and Italian colonies. Perceiving a more urgent threat from the estimated 2,000 Germans residing in Iran, and greater recalcitrance on the part of the government in Tehran, London and Moscow acted militarily, commencing a joint occupation of the country on August 25. Afterward, they turned their attention to Afghanistan. "Let us get rid of them now," wrote Prime Minister Winston Churchill of Kabul's Axis colonies, "while all this part of the world is under the impression of our Persian success." Joint ultimatums, delivered by the British and Soviet representatives in Kabul in October, secured the expulsion of all nondiplomatic German and Italian residents. Anxious about the domestic fallout, Hashim convened a *loya jirga*, which endorsed the action while affirming Afghan neutrality and warning against any further infringements upon it.[25]

The departure of the Germans and Italians, aboard Peshawar-bound buses in late October, terminated their countries' sizable assistance programs. Some replacement specialists could be found amid the odd assortment of émigrés and refugees who now resided in Kabul. Nonetheless, the expulsions had dealt a severe blow to Afghan economic aspirations, leaving the kingdom at the mercy of its two imperial neighbors, as the world war raged on toward an uncertain outcome.

A Legation in Kabul

Fatefully, the Axis expulsions narrowly preceded formal U.S. entry into the war. When Fraser-Tytler warned Hashim about the risks of close association with Germany, he included the United States among the countries Afghanistan risked antagonizing. By the summer of 1941, a collision course between the United States and Germany was apparent—in Kabul and elsewhere.[26]

Afghanistan still sought a closer relationship with the United States. Early in 1940, Roosevelt had dispatched Undersecretary of State Sumner Welles on a mediation mission to Europe. In Rome, the local Afghan minister somehow obtained an audience with the envoy. Upon his return, Welles became the latest senior official to inquire about a Kabul legation. He accepted Wallace Murray's rote reply, which dramatically invoked the fates of nineteenth-century British invaders alongside more relevant, contemporaneous contentions. Yet contacts continued, and wartime changes to the global economy had furnished the Afghans with a new argument.[27]

By then, the war had forged a fateful economic connection between the two states. Afghanistan's most lucrative export, karakul lamb hides, had lost their traditional market in Western Europe while selling lucratively in North America. By 1941, the United States drew virtually all of Afghanistan's annual karakul output. The kingdom, meanwhile, continued to import automobiles and related goods, and wartime commercial disruptions only strengthened General Motors and Ford's grip on the market. Murray pondered ways to formalize the trade relationship.[28]

Wartime commerce augured a deepening of the bilateral relationship. So did the first ministerial visit to Kabul in several years. The U.S. minister to Iran, Louis Dreyfus, spent three weeks in the capital, meeting virtually the entire cabinet. In grand form, he concluded his visit with an Afghan feast, treating the assembled guests to a whole roasted lamb, rice pilau, and—in lieu of alcohol—dugh, a beverage made from yogurt. Dreyfus returned with an Afghan proposal for a formal treaty of relations. He strongly advised opening a legation, writing: "I do not see where we stand anything to lose," rather "it may be of considerable benefit to us to take part in the development of this virgin country." Alongside this familiar tenet, the minister also voiced a newer, more potent argument, observing that his government, "in keeping with its world responsibilities" should accept Afghanistan's proffered friendship and thus "[establish] itself solidly and in a preferred position in what may eventually become a strategic spot in Asia."[29]

Dreyfus's perceptions of the kingdom's potential strategic utility as well as of his own country's newfound global role illuminate an unfolding sea change in U.S. conceptions of security. When he began the long drive to Kabul, Roosevelt's Lend-Lease program had been in effect for nearly two months, rendering the United States a de facto ally of Britain. Dreyfus returned to Tehran on June 22, in time to learn of Barbarossa. The subsequent extension of Lend-Lease aid to Moscow—some of which would be transported via a southern route—magnified the importance of countries in the immediate region.

Apprehending these currents, Murray bowed to the inevitable. In a December 2 memorandum, acknowledging that "recent developments in the Near East have increased the geographical importance of Afghanistan," he endorsed a Kabul legation. The German advance risked severing Soviet supply lines through the Caucasus, necessitating consideration of an alternate route through Afghanistan. Planning for that contingency required the local reporting only a dedicated diplomatic mission could provide. Indeed, the Navy and War Departments had already inquired about conditions in the kingdom.[30]

Figure 2.1 The roads of the Khyber Pass, looking into Afghanistan
Source: Photograph by Cornelius Engert. Georgetown University

Murray also wrote vaguely about "the importance of Afghanistan as a source of political information" that would be unavailable without a Kabul mission. It is an unusually nebulous passage from a bureaucrat who was habitually explicit, but one possibility suggests itself. Afghanistan's ambassador in Moscow had befriended U.S. diplomats, providing rare information on events in Soviet Central Asia. There, Ambassador William Bullitt had earlier complained that it was impossible to ascertain conditions in the Soviet Union's southernmost regions.[31] A Kabul legation could enable systematic intelligence gathering in that area. Tellingly, Bullitt advised Roosevelt to dispatch a Russian speaker to Kabul.[32]

Fittingly, one final obstacle delayed the full establishment of relations. Dreyfus received instructions to ask his Afghan colleague whether his government would assent to the establishment of a legation led by a resident minister: a diplomat of junior rank. He reported that Afghanistan "preferred" a U.S. envoy with the higher rank of ambassador or minister plenipotentiary. Once again, the roles had been reversed: the Afghans favored formality and equality, and the State Department pursued expediency. In successive conversations with Turkish ambassador Mehmet Münir Ertegun, who represented Afghan interests in Washington, Murray proposed sending a third secretary immediately and a minister eventually. Faiz Mohammed insisted on a ministerial appointment. His minister in Tehran added that his government viewed the proposed appointment of a junior officer as "belittling the importance of Afghanistan."[33]

What explains the impasse? By itself, an explanation centered upon the Afghan need for respect, after the accumulated humiliation of two decades of U.S. avoidance, might suffice. Yet the kingdom's political and economic situation remained precarious, and the arrival of U.S. diplomats clearly served Afghan interests. Ertegun's initial response to Murray's proposal is suggestive. The Turkish ambassador observed that it would be "regrettable" if the U.S. representative in Kabul held a lower rank than his peers. A junior officer, inferior to his British or Soviet counterparts, would be unlikely to serve as a check on their ambitions or persuade his superiors in Washington to do so.[34]

Here, at last, Afghan persistence triumphed. Perhaps through Bullitt's intervention, the standoff attracted the attention of President Roosevelt, who impatiently asked Welles, "Why not name the regular Minister to Afghanistan now and get it over with? Perhaps you can find someone from a demobilized Embassy or Legation."[35] Thus overruled, the State Department identified a candidate: Cornelius Engert, then serving as consul general in

Beirut. Citing Engert's role in local negotiations, the Near East Division sought to delay his departure. Welles curtly vetoed the proposal. His patience with that office's prevarications had run out.[36]

Events in Lebanon and wartime travel difficulties conspired, however, to delay Engert. Consequently, the Afghans grudgingly agreed to admit Charles Thayer, a junior diplomat. Originally intended to serve as resident minister, Thayer had been effectively stranded in Tehran amid the dispute over rank. Finally receiving permission to proceed, Thayer and two colleagues began an often-bizarre journey to Kabul. Informed of the scarcity of fuel in Afghanistan, they hired a motorbus and loaded nearly 200 gallons of gasoline aboard. Lavish Afghan hospitality imposed unplanned delays after they crossed the border. Difficult road conditions and spring floods added others. Near Farah, when the approaches to a bridge proved impassable, some 150 workmen pulled the bus up an improvised ramp. At Girishk, the bus crossed the Helmand River aboard a rickety ferry, sharing the passage with several bemused Afghans and a herd of goats. The trio reached Kabul on May 31. The Afghan government had already set aside a building for the legation and a villa as a ministerial residence. Thayer opened the legation on June 6, 1942. His hosts still impatiently awaited Engert's arrival.[37]

Mr. Engert Goes to Kabul

Why did the Afghans attach such significance to Engert? In accepting his eventual posting, they had compromised on the rank issue, allowing Thayer to head the mission for seven weeks. Within the State Department, Cornelius Engert was Afghanistan's oldest friend, and his appointment represented a much-belated dividend from Amanullah's policy of outreach. Engert played a singular role in the development of the U.S.-Afghan relationship and yet remains a little-known figure in the history of American foreign relations. Some biographical attention is therefore warranted.[38]

Across two decades, Engert had improbably established himself as the State Department's leading expert on Afghanistan. In 1920, while Engert was posted at the Tehran legation, the local Afghan minister avidly sought his acquaintance, convincing him to visit Kabul. The State Department assented—but only on the condition that Engert personally fund the trip. Amanullah, ever eager to court Engert's superiors, hosted him in a royal guesthouse for several weeks, serving his visitor food from his own kitchen.[39] After his departure,

Engert composed an extensive report on the kingdom's governance, environment, economy, and peoples. He listed commercial opportunities present in Afghanistan: the development of mineral resources, the banking sector, or physical infrastructure. Above all, he argued, "The most important consequence of American diplomatic relations with Afghanistan would be their moral effect on Central Asia." Revolution in Russia and the waning of British influence presented the United States with an opportunity to reap material benefits "as the only politically disinterested" power in the region.[40] In later years, as he advanced to posts in El Salvador and China, Engert continued monitoring Afghan events. He resumed reporting regularly on the kingdom in the mid-1930s, when he returned to Tehran. At the height of the Inland Exploration Company venture, when the establishment of a Kabul legation appeared necessary, Murray recommended Engert for the post.[41]

Engert nursed a considerable independent streak and thrived most at some distance from authority. His career was adventurous, even by the standards of his day—but not usually by design. He experienced the 1906 San Francisco earthquake, witnessed the Chinese Civil War, and endured three harrowing days in Ethiopia in 1936 while harboring a small group of Americans and others within the U.S. legation during the Italian invasion. Asked about his capacity to deal with mortal peril, Engert observed: "I had played polo and climbed mountains. A person who has frequently had to make sure he would not be swallowed up by a crevice or killed by a pony falling on top of him learns to sort things out."[42] In distant capitals, often under arduous conditions, he acquired a talent for strong advocacy: for his mission, and often for his host country.

Afghan impatience for Engert's arrival stemmed from uncertainty about the war's course. Viewed from Kabul, the auguries of the summer of 1942 suggested that an Axis victory remained probable. Japan's entry into the war and the subsequent collapse of the British Empire in Southeast Asia disheartened Hashim's faction. The subsequent American naval victory at Midway—in its closing stages as the Stars and Stripes was hoisted above the legation—could not undo the appearance of Japanese preeminence in East Asia.[43] Mounting agitation against British rule in India added to Hashim's trepidation. Axis victories in North Africa cast a further shadow. Even more ominously, Germany renewed its offensive into the Soviet Union, this time driving toward the oil-rich Caucasus. Outside of the Central Pacific, the Axis appeared to be prevailing. "Allied stock has gone down considerably," British minister Francis Wylie wrote in late April.[44]

Within Afghanistan, a certain stability had emerged. While Axis propaganda continued to circulate, the three enemy legations now operated under tighter scrutiny, with the German and Italian missions largely debilitated by the expulsions. A final set of Afghan entreaties to the Germans took shape a few weeks after the U.S. legation opened. Naim suggested to Pilger that his country would enter the war should Axis armies reach Afghanistan's vicinity and pledge support for the liberation of Muslim peoples. Word of these conversations reached the British almost immediately. Under other circumstances it might have prompted further Anglo-Soviet pressure on Afghanistan, perhaps even consideration of a joint occupation. Stalin's government was especially hard-pressed by the new German offensive, however, and Britain contended with unrest in India.[45] Yet the kingdom also fundamentally depended on Allied imports, especially American industrial goods, and its earnings from karakul sales lay within U.S. banks.

Engert reached Kabul on July 18 and acted quickly to assess Afghan elite opinion. Hashim made a profound impression upon Engert, who admiringly termed the Afghan "one of the outstanding personalities not only of his country but of the political world today." German advances on the Eastern Front fostered an evident "feeling of despondency" among the legation's contacts, while popular sentiment seemingly celebrated the reduction of the Soviet threat. Within the kingdom, elements friendlier to the Reich maneuvered, perhaps in anticipation of a coup attempt against Hashim. Hashim and his government clearly feared the Axis advance, as Rome and Berlin appeared to favor the restoration of Amanullah.[46]

This suggested an opening. Discerning an Afghan crisis of confidence, Engert opted for the carrot over the stick. "In my wanderings from the Bosphorus to the Indus," he wrote, "I have never found a community where the external stimulus of a financial character [did not] fall on fruitful soil." Believing that the German advance could soon necessitate development of an alternate supply route into the Soviet Union, Engert advised immediate actions to improve the Afghan economy: a credit to finance karakul exports or perhaps Lend-Lease assistance.[47]

While creative, such measures would not have allayed Hashim's fears, had Axis armies reached the Caspian Sea. Autumn battlefield developments seemingly shored up the morale of the kingdom's leadership, however. Obdurate Soviet resistance in the city of Stalingrad as well as British success in suppressing the "Quit India" revolt elicited relief from Hashim's government. After Allied victories in North Africa in November, Kabul received a cable from its Berlin mission, later passed to Engert, reporting a sharp decline in German morale.[48] The Soviet counteroffensive at Stalingrad followed within days, trapping 250,000 Axis soldiers within the shattered city.

Victory at Stalingrad confirmed that Soviet power would survive the war, dealing irreparable harm to German prestige within Afghanistan. Yet Axis propaganda and subversive efforts continued, and Afghan political and economic conditions merited close attention. Disorder in the kingdom could easily spread across the Durand Line. Preserving stability within Afghanistan drove Engert and State Department colleagues to support Kabul's longstanding pursuit of modernization while waging an incessant bureaucratic battle to prevent economic breakdown: a battle with profound consequences for the postwar relationship.

The Problem of Supply

The early material struggles of the nascent U.S. legation illustrate the economic predicament of wartime Afghanistan. Unlike colleagues in other neutral capitals, Engert faced the challenge of establishing a mission in short order. Shipping shortages and the depredations of German U-boats forced the legation to operate on a shoestring, with items borrowed from sister missions or rented within Kabul. To the grief of the Engert family, some forty-seven cases of household items had been lost in transit—sent to the bottom of the eastern Mediterranean by a German submarine. Upon his arrival, Engert found the legation and ministerial residence devoid of furniture and office equipment. Items ordered in February had not arrived, and supply problems persisted into the autumn. Finding the department unresponsive, Engert dramatically proposed closing the legation, "as there is literally no place to live." Furniture and office supplies ultimately arrived, but often damaged, in inadequate quantities, and mismatched. Some of the damage had been inflicted by overzealous Indian customs officials.[49]

Engert's logistical woes illustrate the difficulties the world war posed for the Afghan economy. Afghanistan relied heavily upon imported goods: from lightbulbs and copper wire to gasoline and vehicles. The same wartime delays and the shortages that plagued the U.S. legation limited the inflow of goods into Afghanistan. So, too, did logistical and administrative delays in British India, where officials were not inclined to expedite overland shipment into the kingdom. The same hurdles applied equally to Afghanistan's exports, particularly karakul skins. Maintaining a subsistence level of Afghan commerce represented Engert's principal challenge. His ultimate successes in improving the inflow and outflow of goods laid the foundation for a meaningful U.S.-Afghan relationship.

Of the two problems, Afghanistan's export bottleneck presented itself more immediately. Shortly after his arrival, the Afghan Foreign Ministry sought Engert's assistance in securing shipping space for 900 bales of karakul, stranded at the port of Karachi for lack of available hull space. Engert emphatically recommended making space available on ships returning from India. He obtained the State Department's support, but this alone could not decide the matter. Another agency declined to term karakul a high-priority import, worthy of hull space. State Department efforts to purchase the skins, and thereby obtain passage, failed before another bureaucratic impediment. The matter dragged into 1943, to Engert's frustration. "The whole idea," he wrote, "is to prove to the Afghan Government that the United Nations are in a position to and willing to render material assistance provided Afghanistan behaves herself." Only when hull space became more abundant, in the summer, did the War Production Board (WPB) grant karakul a 1,500-ton quota on the shipping list.[50] The kingdom's principal export could now be transported to its one viable wartime market.

"It is reported that the Department of State is charged with the formulation and execution of American foreign policy," one of Engert's colleagues lamented about the karakul problem, "but here, as is so often the case, we have to go about with cup in hand begging a handout from some other agency of the Government to enable us to do what we think ought to be done."[51] This complaint applied equally to the far more extensive problem of obtaining Afghanistan's import requirements. By volume, the kingdom's needs were not overwhelming. Yet listing and evaluating the necessities of Afghan economic life was a formidable task, requiring the young U.S. legation to deal with numerous government and private actors while laboring to make their claims legible to a skeptical Washington bureaucracy. "It gives one a very proprietary interest in every detail of the native life," Thayer reflected.[52]

Understaffed and liaising with an array of Afghan ministries and companies, the legation produced an extensive but very rough list of necessary goods in October 1942. The ministries often failed to provide full specifications, precise quantities, or effective justifications for their requirements. Unable to articulate the merits of each request, the legation articulated broader arguments: that the United States was the only exporter able to meet Afghan needs, that those needs were comparatively modest, and that the specified goods would serve fundamental needs including education, public health, and the production of primary necessities.[53]

Compared to the logistical demands of the U.S. military or Lend-Lease aid, Afghan demands appear slight. The outgoing 1942 karakul crop occupied 894 tons of storage space. Engert placed the kingdom's automotive needs, in 1942, at 480 vehicles.[54] Yet, while Afghanistan's requirements were moderate, they were notably diverse. Some, inevitably, would entail the diversion of strategic materials from the war effort. All would necessitate the reservation of scarce hull space, and then transshipment via rail and road. Where volume alone did not offer complexity, variety, distance, economics, and bureaucracy more than compensated.

From conception to fulfillment, Afghan material requests traveled a labyrinthine path. After transmission from Kabul, they awaited review by the Bureau of Economic Warfare (BEW), which aggregated overseas requests before sending them to the WPB. The latter agency oversaw all material distribution, weighing BEW requests alongside others from the U.S. military, the Lend-Lease administration, and civilian authorities. BEW requests were evaluated collectively and then divided between applicant countries, ensuring cuts in allocations. Afghan representatives, meanwhile, needed to file timely applications for export licenses. The complexity of the system, cobbled together to serve much of the non-Axis world, all but guaranteed frustration for the Afghan government.[55]

Transportation presented a final problem. By joint Allied agreement, Britain oversaw shipping within the Indian Ocean, and the India Supply Mission governed the allocation of hull space within Karachi-bound vessels. Shipping availability worsened in early 1943, as Churchill diverted vessels from Indian Ocean routes, worsening scarcities throughout the entire region. The colonial government in New Delhi looked askance at the diversion of precious hull space away from its own necessities, toward those of its distrusted neighbor. It also enjoyed preferential treatment as a supplier of goods to Afghanistan and controlled transshipment across its territory. This intermediate layer of skeptical bureaucracy increased the frequency of delays. In December 1942, Indian officials in Washington abruptly barred the loading of all Afghanistan-bound goods, claiming that the kingdom needed to obtain import licenses. They relented more than a month later, but the maddening delay had needlessly impeded a shipment of medicinal chemicals ordered by the Afghan Health Ministry.[56]

U.S. authorities proved more receptive of Afghan requests, but denials and delays in 1943 elicited deep frustration from Mohammed Omar, the kingdom's purchasing agent. A rejected application to acquire two scientific microscopes provoked an especially anguished letter to the State Department. Omar noted that the kingdom's prior application, submitted in 1941, had been lost by the BEW. After the request was renewed, a patronizing reply from the WPB, terming the microscopes a "want," rather than a necessity, brought Omar's frustration to the surface. "For years," he wrote, "Afghanistan has gone along without the things she wants." Each Afghan application addressed a necessity. Grasping the symbolism of this request, the State Department succeeded in procuring two less advanced microscopes—ten months later. Discouragingly, one reached Kabul in damaged condition and the other vanished somewhere in transit.[57]

Shipping and administrative delays threatened the Allied position in Kabul. Even as the German threat receded, Engert warned of deteriorating economic conditions. "The general outlook," he wrote, "is extremely gloomy and the entire economic structure is undergoing a very severe strain."[58] Trucks held a singular importance to the Afghan economy, which depended utterly upon automotive transport. The kingdom had imported several hundred trucks annually before the war; deliveries of new vehicles ceased after 1940. Before transmitting the comprehensive import list, Engert telegraphed Afghanistan's request for 480 vehicles. Here, however, was an item vital to the war effort, requiring considerable shipping space. Repeated entreaties from Engert in 1943 belatedly yielded a meager offer of fifty-two trucks. No further vehicles could be procured unless they were diverted from the U.S. Army or Lend-Lease. Hoping to defuse the matter, Engert's superiors asked him to reevaluate the kingdom's transportation requirements.[59]

Reevaluation could not banish the problem; internal communication within Afghanistan was breaking down. Engert estimated that only 150 Afghan trucks remained in good repair—roughly half the number required to keep Kabul supplied with essentials. The transportation crisis added inflationary pressure; flour cost four times as much in Kabul as in the wheat-producing regions. Engert placed the kingdom's minimum requirement at 450 light trucks and obtained a promise from Washington to locate the necessary vehicles. The State Department proposed shipping trucks in disassembled condition, to be pieced together in India. As a further measure, the Indian government agreed to advance 200 trucks to Afghanistan, to be replaced out of the kingdom's forthcoming U.S. allotment.[60]

Progress could be discerned, as the British and U.S. governments became more responsive to Afghan requests, and as the U-boat threat eased by summer 1943. Even so, Afghan officials remained frustrated by delays. The Afghan minister in Washington inquired why Britain should regulate India-bound cargo, when many of the ships reaching Karachi were U.S.-flagged. Shipping delays struck him as only the latest manifestation of British malevolence. Accordingly, Engert and his British colleagues recommended fundamental revisions to the shipping system. The two legations pledged to assist the Afghans in creating accurate lists, addressing economic necessities up to a year in advance. In vain, Engert also suggested removing the India Supply Mission's veto authority over shipments. In other respects, his government responded supportively. To assist in the creation of accurate, comprehensive import lists, the Office (formerly Bureau) of Economic Warfare dispatched a specialist, Eric Beecroft, to Kabul in early 1944.[61]

The problems confronting Afghanistan and its would-be suppliers were complex, stemming from wartime circumstance, bureaucracy, and conditions specific to the kingdom. Beecroft helped to identify many of them, even as solutions were not always available. Wartime Afghanistan lacked dedicated sales or technical representatives from foreign firms. Prewar procurement had often come from continental European suppliers, employing different specifications from British and American producers. A predilection for secrecy also hamstrung the Afghans. Applications for export licenses required some demonstration of urgency, yet Afghan officials often seemed "more willing to risk leaving their requests unsupported than to reveal what they believe to be vital information."[62] Other difficulties stemmed from turbulent wartime economics, magnified by the vast distances between Afghanistan and its suppliers. Prices frequently shifted dramatically between the formulation of cost estimates and the actual submission of orders.[63]

Administrative factors impeded all parties involved. Afghan representatives in the United States repeatedly failed to obtain export licenses. Within Kabul, numerous ministers lacked adequate technical knowledge. Assembling and consolidating the requirements of diverse government entities proved an especially vexing challenge, and the lists presented by Afghans in New York or Washington did not always match those delivered to Engert. Yet the kingdom had no monopoly on bureaucratic impediments. At the insistence of the British legation, all lists were first submitted to the government in India. While this procedure identified items available regionally, thus conserving hull space, it also added weeks of delay. The U.S. legation, meanwhile, struggled to advise the Afghans on how to clear the hurdles before them. Well into 1943, Engert's mission lacked basic information on the export control regime: its procedures, criteria, and the complex terrain of the wartime bureaucracy.[64]

Beecroft worked extensively with the Allied legations and Afghan government during his month-long stay. His ensuing report highlighted the need for closer coordination between the two but also noted the serious delay imposed by the requirement to investigate available supply in India. Beecroft wrote later that he was "struck by the directness and sincerity with which many Afghan officials expressed their special desire to deal directly with the United States," and by their interest in planning for the postwar future. He seconded Engert's argument about the ongoing need for trucks. Perhaps desiring to refute a potential counterargument or perhaps acting out of simple curiosity, Beecroft reported that "from careful timing" he had ascertained that the speed of Afghanistan's camels "remains a steady 1 1/2 miles per hour."[65]

Beecroft expressed alarm at the worsening shortage of medicines in Afghanistan.[66] His conclusions validated, in Washington and in Kabul, the belief that Indian concerns had unnecessarily impeded Afghan imports. Engert's efforts to meet Afghan economic requirements fostered a degree of tension between his government and its British ally. Initially the junior partner in Kabul, the United States increasingly looked to act independently of London. U.S. policymakers, noting the improved availability of shipping space, questioned the utility of the existing arrangement. Exasperation grew within the State Department toward the convoluted list review system. One official observed that the arrangement gave Britain the "right of refusal" on all Afghan trade, even as Afghans had an avowed, entirely welcome preference for U.S.-made goods.[67] A subtle divergence between Washington and London's Afghan agendas was under way, as the former emerged as the kingdom's chief foreign benefactor.

Spreading the American Dream

Engert's success in maintaining the kingdom's economic lifeline hinged entirely on the support he received from his colleagues in Washington. In a remarkable volte-face, the Near East Division emerged as a consistent ally to the Kabul legation. Much of this stemmed from the division's organizational imperative to support its newest diplomatic mission. Even so, division officials looked well past wartime necessity, envisioning a distinct postwar U.S. role in the kingdom's development. This ultimately entailed standing apart from Washington's senior partner in Afghanistan, the United Kingdom.

This outlook emerged as early as August 1942. During the debate about karakul shipping, another State Department division contended that Britain should purchase the stranded lamb hides. Calvin Oakes of the Near East Division argued strenuously against "placing [the problem] in Great Britain's lap." London appeared unlikely to help. Most significantly, Oakes reasoned, "British and American interests in the area concerned are not always identical and are likely to be antagonistic after the war." Allowing Britain to aid the Afghans could place the United States at a disadvantage, should Anglo-American tensions emerge after the war.[68] With one major caveat—he was an avid Anglophile—Engert shared this view. His belief in the potential U.S. role in Afghan development, forged in 1921, had only deepened over time. Wartime exigencies concerned him, but so too did postwar possibilities. Even as his legation battled to maintain the kingdom's commerce, it also sought, by various means, to advance U.S. cultural influence.

Personally, Engert accorded the greatest significance to educational assistance. In March 1943, the Afghan government sought his assistance in hiring seven new teachers. Forwarding the request, the minister wrote, with characteristic fervor:

> We therefore have a rare opportunity not only of access to a new nation in the making but of helping and guiding it in connection with the intimate problems of mental and moral adjustment which the pressure of modern forces have created. If the presence of tactful and intelligent teachers can add to the merely superficial modernization of the country a sincere effort to adapt the old Islamic creed and tradition to a new way of living we shall not only render a great service to Afghanistan but we shall make American idealism and justice and vision a positive and constructive force in the whole of Central Asia.[69]

Two highly qualified American instructors were already present in Kabul, but they presented a separate problem for the legation. Daniel Ingalls and Richard Frye, both teaching at Habibia College, were also spying for the Office of Strategic Services (OSS). Engert and Thayer quietly opposed this arrangement and welcomed their eventual departures from Kabul, warning against the dispatch of other OSS personnel. "There is really no useful work they can do," Engert wrote, "and if Afghans suspected connection it would involve grave danger to themselves and most serious embarrassment to Legation and Department."[70]

This was not the legation's only brush with the OSS. In 1943, Engert received word that Charles Calmer Hart—formerly of the Inland Exploration Company—wished to travel to Kabul to negotiate a new oil concession.[71] Engert advised against the visit. Raising the issue risked more immediate wartime priorities, and the Soviet reaction to any oil concession in the north could not be predicted.[72] Engert acted with better reason than he knew. The OSS was, in fact, encouraging U.S. oil firms to seek concessions in Afghanistan to facilitate the infiltration of U.S. agents into the country.[73] The dangers of mixing wartime diplomacy, espionage, and postwar concession-hunting were more readily discernible in Kabul than in Washington.

Meanwhile, the Near East Division struggled to locate additional teachers. The U.S. military had first claim on the nation's manpower, greatly thinning the field. The State Department made the dubious choice of turning away conscientious objectors—one potentially rich pool of applicants. The department also felt obligated to reject teachers with missionary backgrounds, even if they pledged to eschew evangelical work. Concerns about wages likely influenced several prospective hires. Engert received word in November 1943 that the department's "best efforts" to hire teachers had met with "little success."[74]

Candidates eventually emerged. J. Robert Fluker had actually been recruited by the OSS to replace the outgoing Ingalls in Kabul, until the State Department succeeded in convincing its counterpart to pursue greener pastures elsewhere. Fluker proved a dedicated instructor, subsequently advising the Ministry of Education. Three other Americans taught in Kabul by spring 1944, although maintaining even that number proved vexing.[75]

Similar challenges confronted the State Department as it sought qualified engineers for Afghanistan. The 1941 expulsions had left numerous specialist positions vacant. Under British pressure in 1943, the Afghan government also declined to renew the contracts of four Japanese engineers. The quartet had worked on the Boghra Canal, an irrigation project along the Helmand River, which had initially been undertaken by German specialists. Their effective ouster attached special symbolism to this project. The Allies promised to find specialists to replace the departed Axis personnel, but unemployed engineers proved especially scarce in wartime.[76]

Perceiving Allied credibility to be at stake, the State Department secured a visit by the Bureau of Reclamation's chief designing engineer, John Lucian Savage. Britain dispatched its own specialist, T. A. W. Foy, an employee of the government of Punjab with prior experience in Afghanistan. Foy and Savage collaborated collegially but reached differing conclusions. Savage endorsed hiring a team of U.S. engineers to pursue the Boghra project. Foy recommended proceeding slowly, concerned about the dearth of Afghans able to act as overseers. Rushing ahead without effective middle management risked the entire project.[77]

The British government hoped that the Afghans would heed the local experience of its engineers and hire personnel based in India. Long-standing Afghan suspicions and Savage's apparent optimism led Kabul elsewhere. Two American specialists arrived to pursue work on the Boghra Canal during the summer, followed by John B. Alexander, an experienced engineer charged with supervising the project. Work proceeded slowly, but the Boghra Canal marked an especially consequential avenue for U.S. penetration of Afghanistan.[78]

Public diplomacy, meanwhile, constituted another front in the contest for Afghan opinion. Although ostensibly simpler than the legation's other efforts, it posed its own distinct challenges. Information warfare in Afghanistan, Engert wrote, presented "a special problem." The kingdom's rural population was largely inaccessible to propaganda, rendering the royal family and government officials the only meaningful target audience. Yet an overtly political campaign appeared hazardous. The Afghan government regarded direct propaganda as a violation of its sovereignty, and elite audiences tended to ignore it. Instead, Engert recommended a subtle approach: selling Afghans not on the Allied war effort, but on the United States. He suggested the distribution of prominent U.S. magazines, including *Life* and the *Saturday Evening Post*, and requested "high class literature depicting the best side of American life."[79]

Engert also endeavored to screen American films in the kingdom's sole movie theater. Government censors barred war films, newsreels, and titles likely to offend devout Muslims. "Afghan standards," one diplomat observed, "are even more rigorous than those of the Hays Organization." This left the field open to crime dramas, comedies, sports films, and especially Westerns. Engert again sought positive depictions of American life. "Our program here should be long-term in character," he wrote. Historical and educational movies appeared especially effective. A double feature of a Louis Pasteur biography and *The Winged Scourge*—in which Disney's Seven Dwarves battle malarial mosquitoes—was "received with great enthusiasm" by a large student audience.[80]

The overall impact of these campaigns is unknowable. Engert at least avoided annoying his hosts by flouting their ban on outright propaganda, and his extensive experience in Islamic societies alerted him to other potential pitfalls. Growing Afghan interest in U.S. firms, methods, and products suggests that Engert's soft-power offensive further bolstered his country's standing within Afghanistan.

Finally, presaging efforts by his Cold War–era successors, Engert employed humanitarian aid as another lever of influence. In summer 1944, flash floods in Kabul Province killed at least 600 people. Foreign Minister Ali Mohammed described it as Afghanistan's worst natural catastrophe in living memory. Engert and his colleagues successfully persuaded the reluctant American Red Cross to donate $2,000 to Afghan flood relief. This was the third-largest international donation, behind those proffered by Britain and the Soviet Union, each looking to their postwar standing in the Afghan kingdom.[81]

Victories and Anxieties

Deepening U.S. inroads into Afghanistan indisputably served the Allied cause. Washington's unparalleled industrial capacity made it the one ally able to trade meaningfully with the kingdom, limiting, although not averting, serious disruption of the local economy. Afghan-American interactions were unburdened by the apprehensions held in Kabul toward the other Allies. The extent of postwar U.S. interest in Afghanistan remained questionable, and Washington could hardly appear as a greater evil to either of the kingdom's imperial neighbors. Even so, during the war's final years, flickers of unease and acrimony occasionally marred inter-Allied cooperation in Kabul. The anxiety of the Afghan government, meanwhile, grew more palpable, as the probable contours of the peace came into view.

In April 1943, the Afghan government arrested several dozen individuals, largely refugees from the former Emirate of Bukhara, on conspiracy charges. British sources confirmed that German diplomats had liaised with the Bukharans, seeking to foment unrest in both the Soviet Union and India. The episode usefully reopened the question of the Axis legations in

Kabul. While the danger posed by the Bukharan conspiracy was debatable, the opportunity to further reduce the Axis diplomatic presence struck the government in India as "too good to miss."[82]

At this point, a fateful miscommunication occurred. London directed Wylie to request the reduction of the three Axis legations. After reporting his instructions to Engert, the British minister executed them during an acrimonious meeting with Hashim. Engert, meanwhile, reported that his colleague would demand the reduction of the Italian and German legations to two diplomats, each—a far more drastic step than what London actually contemplated. Responding to Engert, the State Department opted to stand apart from its allies. Engert received instructions to, if necessary, inform Hashim's government that the United States did not "associate itself" with any Allied effort to force it to break relations with Rome and Berlin or expel their diplomats.[83]

The State Department response alarmed London. Washington's proposed message would undermine Anglo-Soviet efforts in Afghanistan while alerting Kabul to a significant split in the alliance. Engert expressed the same concern. After further consultation, Washington retracted its earlier instructions but advised its ally that "embarrassment might well be avoided in the future" if London consulted it before undertaking action. It also questioned British assertions that the security of Afghanistan's frontiers did not affect U.S. interests, suggesting that its ally had "failed to give due consideration to the indivisibility of the United Nations' war effort."[84] This message conveyed far less than the deference London had traditionally received from its ally on Afghan affairs.

Britain prevailed on the substance of the dispute—such as it was—yet the assertion of U.S. interests in Afghanistan rankled. "The Americans had no representative in Kabul until a year ago, and their interests in Afghanistan are only imaginary," wrote one analyst. "Surely we do not expect them to consult us before they start an approach to Nicaragua or Panama?" The Afghan response, in any case, proved fundamentally satisfactory. It included the arrests of several individuals implicated in the Bukharan conspiracy and the withdrawal of three Axis diplomats (additionally, the departure of the four aforementioned Japanese engineers).[85]

Wylie and Engert might have celebrated this outcome, but the episode represented a final straw in their fraying relationship. Nearing the end of his short tenure in Kabul, the British minister penned a furious, rambling letter to his superiors, attempting to explain his frustrations with his U.S.

counterpart. "I don't know," Wylie confessed, "All I can say is that I do not like his technique." His unmoved superiors sided with Engert. "Exasperating idiot," one wrote. Denigration and exasperation came easily to Wylie, and much of his antipathy toward Engert was personal and idiosyncratic. Yet he also expressed a belief, shared by his superiors, that the ultimate purpose of the U.S. legation was to "muscle in" on postwar trade with Afghanistan. In the near term, however, success in Afghanistan required close Anglo-American coordination. Wylie's successor, Giles Squire, received instructions to collaborate closely with Engert.[86]

Whether the Axis legations still posed a meaningful threat by 1943 is questionable. Engert reported in September that there "is little room for doubt left in the minds of thinking Afghans that the Axis is losing the war." Even "normally Germanophile circles" hoped for a speedy Allied victory, if only to restore the kingdom's peacetime trade. The Bukharan affair attested more to London and Moscow's anxieties than any Afghan culpability in Axis schemes. Whatever danger Axis diplomats posed was further reduced by Italy's September 1943 defection. Pietro Quaroni, Rome's minister in Kabul, supplied the Allies with information on Axis activities in the country. To British personnel, the Italian painted a scathing picture of Axis ineptitude. Of his German colleagues, especially Pilger, he declared himself "astonished" to have had to work with "such a set of fools."[87]

Whatever the extent or efficacy of Axis activities, the Kabul government clearly perceived scant room for maneuver. Hashim and his allies watched the Soviet advance apprehensively. The spring 1943 rupture of relations between Moscow and the Polish government in exile and reports of Soviet subversive campaigns in Iran compounded their anxieties. Afghan officials closely scrutinized statements emanating from major Allied conferences. The absence of any explicit mention of the kingdom or any relevant discussion of the postwar fate of small states furthered their unease.[88]

Thus, by late 1943, Engert perceived a clear Afghan preference for a postwar bond with his government—its "ideal friend"—even as Kabul had "comparatively little to offer" in return. The suppression of subversive activity directed at either neighbor represented its only meaningful gesture. To the U.S. minister, Afghanistan appeared ready to "exercise a stabilizing influence" in its immediate region, "provided only she can be reasonably certain that she will not be ground between the upper and nether millstones of rival powers striving for supremacy." Would U.S. interest in the kingdom endure past victory over the Axis, however?[89]

A surprising telegram that reached the Kabul legation on Christmas Eve 1943 announcing the impending visit of Gen. Patrick Hurley suggested that it would. Formerly secretary of war during the Hoover administration, now a special envoy for Roosevelt, Hurley drove to Kabul from Peshawar in early January 1944. The envoy remained for nearly a week, meeting with nearly the entire government, including King Zahir. He promised U.S. support for the kingdom's postwar economic development while seeking no special privileges. The scope of the welcome accorded to Hurley led Squire to observe that "for the time being" the Afghan government had "forgotten all about their neutrality." Hurley's visit seemingly left them "reassured and far more confident in their outlook on world affairs."[90]

If the bilateral implications of the Hurley visit appear straightforward, its underlying motivations are somewhat more ambiguous. Roosevelt had expressly included Afghanistan within Hurley's ambit, asking his emissary to report "upon general conditions" there and furnishing him with a letter of introduction addressed to King Zahir. Hurley may have received further instructions from Roosevelt at either the Tehran or Cairo conferences. Close contact with British governance in the wider region led Hurley to imagine a postwar conflict with London. "We are approaching the irrepressible conflict between world-wide imperialism and world-wide democracy," he warned Roosevelt in a letter from Tehran. He urged FDR to adopt a global policy of "building associated free nations." Hurley's Afghan sojourn supported this vision while serving immediate wartime ends: investigating the availability of Afghan transit facilities.[91]

The envoy may have been pursuing other, narrower aims as well. While serving the White House, he continued correspondence with a prior client, the Sinclair Oil Company, which had long sought an oil concession in Iran. Hurley's files contain extensive records from the earlier Inland Exploration Company mission, and British observers speculated with good reason that he sought to reopen the question of an oil concession.[92]

Whatever the case, Hurley departed triumphantly. Hurley assured Roosevelt that the Afghan authorities would "accept and support enthusiastically a plan for national development" along the lines he also envisioned for Iran. He was far from alone in foreseeing a substantial postwar relationship. An August 1944 memorandum by Paul Alling, director of the Near East Division, revealed the great distance traveled by official opinion on Afghanistan and the emergence of his government as the preeminent foreign actor within the country. U.S. aid to the kingdom would redound to Washington's benefit throughout the Islamic world while positioning American firms favorably for the future development of the kingdom's petroleum and mineral resources. For these reasons, Alling predicted, U.S. interest in Afghanistan would *not* decline "after the war, to the very minor role we occupied there prior to 1939." Washington had responded favorably to Afghan requests out of "our desire to befriend a weak and underdeveloped country," while it pursued postwar opportunities. Thus, U.S. interests favored the establishment of "a strong Afghanistan, capable of maintaining internal order and stability."[93] For the moment, Kabul and Washington had achieved consensus.

The Beginning of a Beautiful Friendship?

Radio broadcasts from India transmitted word of President Roosevelt's death to Kabul early on April 13, 1945. First to pay their condolences at the U.S. legation were Soviet diplomats. Ambassador Ivan Bakulin, with "evident sincerity," spoke of his "admiration and respect" for the departed president, expressing the hope that others would carry on the work Roosevelt had undertaken. The following day, virtually the entire Afghan government presented itself. Hashim expressed his "profound personal regret" and lauded Roosevelt's promotion of peace, equality among nations, and freedom for all peoples. Recounting the visits, diplomat Elbert Mathews noted their heartfelt quality and their implied message: that Afghanistan hoped to align with the United States "in the settlement of post-war problems." Three days of official mourning followed.[94]

Weeks later, news of the German surrender reached the Afghan capital. The British legation, by chance, had scheduled a film screening for the evening. Soviet attendance at such affairs was typically modest, but the gathering proved exceptional. Squire reported "a most enjoyable evening," with much singing and dancing, and an atmosphere of "genuine friendliness." Public commemoration of victory in Europe could have been a more delicate affair. Japan fought on and the Afghan government might have frowned upon too public a display, as infringing upon the kingdom's neutrality. Instead, the British festivities were graced by the appearance of the Afghan minister of war, Shah Mahmud, and his nephews, Daoud and Naim—both formerly members of the pro-Axis faction. The government permitted the celebrants to set off fireworks, and even loaned out some decorative materials and illumination.[95]

Visitors to Kabul in the spring could have been forgiven for believing that the kingdom had joined the Allies. Like other neutral countries, it had continually adjusted its stance toward the war, as battlefield circumstances changed, and as questions about the postwar order loomed. Neutrality spared Afghanistan the horrors of total war, and also the sudden dislocation experienced by so many lands in the spring and summer of 1945. The changes wrought by the end of the wars in Europe and Asia were felt more gradually within the kingdom, as wartime disruptions and restrictions eased.

The war years forced economic deprivation upon Afghans, through shortages of gasoline, transportation breakdowns, deteriorating industrial capital, and faltering export revenue. The expulsions of 1941 abruptly halted major development projects. The stresses of wartime diplomacy showed clearly on the Afghan elite, which clung to a tenuous—sometimes opportunistic—neutrality. Neither Axis nor Allied victory came free from unwanted complications and worrisome prospects.[96]

Nor was the war's final year free from domestic conflict. A government effort in the summer, led by Daoud, to enforce centralized conscription against a small tribe in the Kunar Valley, the Safis, backfired badly, provoking a brief but pitched revolt. The kingdom's economy remained bedeviled by wartime inflation and shortages of gasoline, kerosene, and cotton goods.[97] The expected retirement of Hashim, in poor health near the end of the war, added a fundamental element of uncertainty. His genial, less forceful brother Shah Mahmud stood in the wings—but so did their ambitious nephews. Within the ruling family, the specter of intergenerational conflict loomed, if not immediately, then inevitably.

Nevertheless, viewed against the experiences of so many others, Afghanistan proved fortunate. It did not experience terror bombing, genocide, or the mass dislocations of peoples. It faced neither the terrible famine experienced in India, nor the dispiriting occupation that befell Iran. As the war's end loomed, so did the promise of a postwar partnership with the United States within an international order that would accord greater protection and rights to smaller states.

Over the preceding four years, Americans had—in contrast to the two preceding decades—proved surprisingly responsive to Afghan aspirations. New York emerged as the world's leading karakul market. As shipping availability improved and bureaucratic obstacles gradually crumbled, U.S.-made goods made the long voyage to Karachi for transshipment into the kingdom. A small yet visible cohort of American teachers and engineers applied themselves in classrooms and in the Afghan countryside. American businesses inquired discreetly about postwar opportunities in the kingdom.

The rationales for U.S. involvement in Afghanistan may appear fleeting or far-fetched: stemming from short-lived wartime imperatives. The notion that the kingdom could have served as a supply route may seem risible—but only if the war's other convoluted, often nightmarish journeys are banished from mind. Next to Arctic convoys or flights over the Himalayan "Hump," Afghanistan's bumpy roads verged on the mundane. The same may be said of professed Afghan fears of the Wehrmacht's advance. Hindsight may deem them exaggerated or opportunistic, but U.S. Army intelligence had predicted that the Germans would reach Lake Baikal.[98]

Waging a global conflict required contesting Afghanistan in myriad ways. Wartime support of Britain and the Soviet Union necessitated attaining familiarity with the willful buffer state that perplexed both empires. Engert's extraordinary shoestring efforts in a capital once regarded by his superiors as one of the world's least desirable sites for a diplomatic mission reveal the globalization of U.S. interests wrought by the war. They also attest to the successful efforts of Mohammed Hashim Khan—generally regarded as a ruthless, even cruel man—to cultivate his sympathies as a "benevolent despot."[99] Afghans had not caused the sea change in U.S. perceptions, but they pivoted adroitly to receive it.

The durability of perceived national interests and affinities, beyond wartime exigency, also revealed the distinct way by which Engert and his colleagues understood Afghanistan. Approaching the kingdom, Americans pursued opportunities invisible or obscure to others. Afghans, in turn, welcomed them heartily, forging a bond with tremendous but perilous implications in the immediate wake of the world war. The inter-Allied amity experienced that spring would pass more rapidly than any of its celebrants in Kabul could have expected.

CHAPTER 3

Preeminence and Peril

The American Influx and the Coming of the Afghan Cold War, 1945–1952

By any telling, Myles and Ruth Walsh had an eventful journey to Afghanistan. The young mining engineer and his pregnant wife set sail aboard a Karachi-bound freighter in New York. A stop in Alexandria afforded a chance to see the pyramids via camel—and to expedite the delivery of their son. With no doctor aboard, Walsh oversaw the birth. In tumultuous pre-partition Karachi, the family boarded a train without intact windows. Rioting in Rawalpindi led the Walshes to lock themselves inside their compartment for twelve hours. "Eventfully," Walsh later wrote, "we reached the Khyber Pass and peaceful Afghanistan."[1]

Walsh exemplified the postwar influx of American expertise into Afghanistan. He came recommended by the State Department, which suggested to the Morrison-Knudsen construction firm—now at work in the Helmand Valley—that Walsh might assist in identifying local mineral reserves. Former Inland Exploration Company petroleum geologist Ernest Fox, now the State Department's principal Afghanistan expert, recommended Walsh, a Harvard classmate and friend experienced in overseas work.[2]

Walsh began his work without delay, surveying Kandahar, seeking gold in Badakhshan, and revisiting sites noted by the Inland team. In winter 1948, Walsh ventured into the Panjshir Valley, seeking silver mines described by ninth-century Arab travelers. Heavy snowfall checked his progress, but his ancient predecessors proved accurate guides. Walsh located a substantial complex of ruins. The intrepid engineer did not confine his survey to the surface, walking, sometimes crawling deep into long-abandoned passageways. He returned with abundant samples, which he dispatched to both the Afghan Ministry of Mines and the State Department.[3]

Walsh's expertise and industry impressed observers, but the local and international politics of development proved a far greater challenge in postwar Afghanistan. His efforts and those of other Americans in Afghanistan interacted unpredictably with Afghan politics, the Cold War, and the postcolonial conflicts of South Asia. U.S. connections to Afghanistan deepened as the Cold War took root: not through the implementation of grand strategy, but haphazardly, as Afghans and Americans pursued postwar opportunities. Direction from Washington was limited. A State Department preoccupied with postwar reconstruction and concerned by the rise of Soviet power could offer only sporadic guidance toward such a remote, unfamiliar country.

Kabul nursed its own bilateral aspirations. Less authoritarian and conservative than his brother and predecessor, Prime Minister Shah Mahmud Ghazi pursued Afghanistan's postwar development, seeking the assistance of its wartime benefactor. Younger, ambitious ministers such as Abdul Majid Zabuli and Mohammed Kabir Ludin staked their positions on the burgeoning relationship with Washington, retaining Shah Mahmud's ear and adapting their appeals to changed geopolitical circumstances. Exploiting the emerging U.S.-Soviet Cold War, Shah Mahmud, Zabuli, and Ludin could enlist the sympathies of U.S. diplomats, but Washington's ability to help proved limited.

Into that space stepped private actors—especially the Morrison-Knudsen construction firm. Acting as a chosen instrument, enjoying unconditional support from the U.S. government, Morrison-Knudsen Afghanistan (MKA) could theoretically operate with versatility and independence while freeing Washington from direct responsibility. Yet from its inception, MKA encountered myriad difficulties: some specific to the tumultuous circumstances of partition-era South Asia, others testifying to its negligence and opportunism. Rather than freeing government actors from responsibility, MKA's travails drew them further into Afghanistan.

Geopolitical turmoil further complicated the designs of Americans and Afghans. A postwar divergence in Afghan priorities between the United States and its European allies fostered suspicion and hindered coordination. The division of British India reopened the question of the Durand Line for Afghan elites. Acrimony with Pakistan led to repeated disruptions of Afghan commerce and periodic energy crises. The eruption of the Cold War made U.S.-supported development a dangerous proposition for Afghanistan, as

Moscow signaled its mounting disapproval. Simultaneously, it also enabled Afghans to threaten that they would seek Soviet aid if Washington proved unhelpful.

Upheaval in Kabul generated further uncertainty. Shah Mahmud's experiment in political liberalization yielded its own unintended consequences. Open elections in 1949 and the relaxation of censorship in 1951 allowed frank, fractious discourse on the Afghan future. The aging prime minister faced challenges from a rising generation of Afghan elites—most notably his nephew Mohammed Daoud Khan—who assailed his modernization program and questioned the ardency of his Pashtunistan agitation.

Development aspirations, national agitation, and the superpower contest became irrevocably entangled. The troubled Helmand project, Pashtunistan, Cold War pressures, and recurring energy shortages spurred fateful choices in the early 1950s, as the Afghan government reopened the fraught question of petroleum development. Washington, while declining to arm the Afghan military, pursued other means of maintaining the kingdom's independence. These included financial support, technical assistance, and diplomatic mediation of Afghanistan's quarrels with Iran and Pakistan. Perceiving a global Cold War against a totalitarian adversary intent on dominating the Eurasian landmass, Americans naturally regarded Afghanistan as a potential, albeit inopportune battleground. They did not wish to confront Moscow there, but inclusion of Afghanistan and its region within their own conceived Cold War drew an ominous Soviet response, bringing the kingdom inexorably, irrevocably into the conflict in summer 1952.

At War's End, 1945

As elsewhere, the roots of the Cold War in Afghanistan can be found within the preceding conflict. The Afghan government visibly sought to discern the contours of the postwar international system, as the guns fell silent. Afghan leaders dealt carefully with the victorious Allies. Resigned to the strengthening of Soviet power, the kingdom sought to avoid conflict with its northern neighbor. Friendly relations with London enabled cooperation against restive border peoples, while British military aid helped Kabul to exert authority in its northern, non-Pashtun provinces. Lastly, the delayed project of economic modernization made cooperation with the United States essential.

On that front, the war's final year presented mixed indications. U.S. diplomats continued to grapple with Afghanistan's import lists. Afghan lobbying in Washington finally succeeded in removing the shipping quota, obtaining a monthly hundred-ton allocation, and freeing Afghan imports from the scrutiny and potential veto of the India Supply Mission. After the Japanese surrender, the Afghans received greater leeway to purchase a range of less restricted goods. These revisions eased but did not entirely resolve the kingdom's supply problems.[4] Facing unrest in the Pashtun borderlands, the Afghan government sought unsuccessfully to purchase surplus U.S. trucks.[5] Another application to import tin for hospital and kitchen use was repeatedly rejected.[6] The end of hostilities promised an eventual easing of commercial restrictions, but not on a timetable suitable for Kabul.

American engineers working on the Boghra Canal in 1945 confronted a different scarcity: a lack of trained personnel. In vain, the project manager, John Alexander, sought to hire or borrow additional engineers. Bereft of additional supervisory personnel, the two U.S. engineers on site found themselves overwhelmed with managerial work, and thus unable to fulfill their planning responsibilities. Cornelius Engert, soon to depart Kabul, appealed for assistance, but Alexander's professional network proved more responsive.[7]

A Morrison-Knudsen (M-K) representative visited the State Department in June inquiring about projects in Afghanistan. John Lucian Savage, whose spring 1944 visit had facilitated U.S. involvement with the Boghra project, was a close friend and mentor of the company's president, Harry Morrison, and endeavored to provide M-K with foreign contracts. "I will bring you the business," he reportedly promised Morrison.[8] Alexander wrote to the firm on May 16; Savage likely facilitated the contact. Already prominent for numerous ventures in the West, including the Boulder Canyon (Hoover) Dam, M-K enjoyed a close wartime association with the U.S. government. The firm dispatched two engineers to Afghanistan, where discussions about future projects quickly ranged well beyond the Boghra Canal, encompassing bridges, roads, and dams.[9]

The final months of the war also witnessed renewed dialogue about an oil concession, as Kabul resumed earlier efforts to court U.S. firms—and their government by extension. A representative of the Standard-Vacuum Oil Company spent three weeks in Afghanistan in the spring of 1945 investigating a possible concession.[10] On August 9, Deputy Prime Minister Mohammed Naim Khan expressed the hope that U.S. oil companies would seek a concession. The State Department promptly notified major U.S. firms of the opportunity.[11]

Evidence soon emerged, however, that Moscow nursed a quasi-possessive interest in Afghan oil. Soviet ambassador Ivan Bakulin bluntly told Prime Minister Mohammed Hashim Khan in July that Soviet firms should receive prospecting rights in Afghanistan. The U.S. military attaché Ernest Fox discussed the issue in October with his gregarious Soviet counterpart, Col. Georgi Mylnikov. Outwardly supportive of U.S. aid to Afghanistan, Mylnikov inquired whether Kabul sought U.S. petroleum development assistance. Feigning ignorance, Fox asked how Moscow might respond to such a request. "For the first time during the conversation," Fox recounted, "the Colonel had to search for words." Mylnikov finally replied that he could not say: his government would have to consider the regional context.[12]

Kabul's anxieties could be exaggerated for effect, but Afghan leaders had good reason to wonder what the peace portended for them. Neither Hashim nor Shah Mahmud cared to be consigned to a Soviet sphere of influence. As unrest continued in the borderlands, and vital imports remained scarce, Afghan officials invoked promises made by Engert and his peers in wartime. While U.S. responses presented an ambiguous picture, Washington's postwar policy toward the kingdom incorporated assumptions and inclinations developed during the war. Well before the division of Europe became irreversible, Americans began the pursuit of relative preeminence within Afghanistan.

The United States, Afghanistan, and the Postwar Order

As before, postwar Afghanistan policy did not flow from explicit choices by senior officials. President Harry S Truman and his chief advisors left, at most, soft imprints on the U.S. approach to the kingdom. South Asia, itself, received only sporadic scrutiny from the White House, and the preponderance of that addressed India and Pakistan. Afghanistan sought U.S. assistance by depicting itself as a model citizen of the postwar order, committed to the promotion of peace and regional stability. The eulogies offered to President Roosevelt by the Afghan elite had an aspirational quality. Afghans wanted to live in the proposed Rooseveltian order: with peace, unrestrained commerce, and justice for all states.

This messaging succeeded to a reasonable degree. Those policymakers concerned with Afghanistan's immediate region perceived it as a friendly and responsible actor—and as a site of postwar opportunity for U.S. firms. Kabul's anxieties about postwar Soviet designs scarcely needed explaining to a State Department brimming with suspicion of Stalin's regime. Wartime concerns with the maintenance of regional stability carried over into the postwar era. One March 1946 policy statement called for supporting a government "capable of controlling the tribes and maintaining internal security" even allowing that arms sales might be authorized, subject to British approval.[13]

London's assent was not guaranteed, however, as the allies had drifted apart within Afghanistan. Some disharmony was inevitable, as the three had necessarily assumed distinct roles during the war. Blessed by material abundance and unfettered by history, Washington had played a largely beneficent "good cop" role in Kabul. Beset by the Nazi invasion and long-standing Afghan suspicions, the Soviets held the "bad cop" role. Britain stood somewhere in between, alternating between threatening the Afghans and assisting on supply issues. London's diplomats in Kabul sought to reestablish British preeminence, maintaining the kingdom as a buffer state for the foreseeable future. A 1944 understanding committed London to supplying the Afghan military, while Washington attended to economic questions.[14]

Postwar programs led the allies onto different paths, and one U.S. analyst detected "quite a divergence" between the British and U.S. visions of postwar cooperation in the region. Washington felt free to espouse an open door: "free competition" in the fields of trade and communication, the "complete independence" of Middle Eastern states to choose between patrons, leading to a "friendly vying" between British and American concepts of development and sovereignty.[15] Contemplating rising disorder in India, as independence sentiment intensified, London could not treat the postwar contest in Kabul as an amicable competition.

Washington's response to an Afghan appeal for emergency food aid in 1946 revealed the growing Anglo-American division. In April, citing drought conditions, Kabul requested the sale of 100,000 tons of wheat. Afghanistan was hardly alone in facing hunger the Truman administration and the United Nations had been battling starvation in Europe and Asia for months. Days earlier, Truman had implored Americans to consume less food, thus freeing domestic stocks for emergency relief.[16] The scale of the global problem initially left scant hope that the Afghan request could be met. Nevertheless, the State Department supported the Afghan request, obtaining a grudging promise of 8,000 tons of flour from the Department of Agriculture.[17] Hoping to expand the sale, the Near East Division enlisted Acting Secretary of State Dean Acheson. A letter signed by Acheson articulated the postwar rationale for aid: "Afghanistan, while not a war devastated country, has claims upon the interest and support of this country which are unique. I refer to its devotion to peace for many years, to its meticulous observance of its neutral obligations during the war, its announced belief in the efficacy of international cooperation, its strong faith in the reality of United States leadership and technical and cultural assistance." Failing to validate Afghan trust would, in turn, forfeit "a magnificent constructive opportunity to promote order and welfare in a strategic area."[18]

The appeal succeeded, but the colonial government in India now objected. U.S.-Afghan discussions of the grain shipment had unfolded without any British input. An Indian representative noted that grain shipments would pass through the restive, also drought-ridden North West Frontier Province. British diplomats in Kabul argued that India faced a worse shortfall. Washington dismissed the objection, and the grain reached Afghanistan without incident in early 1947. Zabuli subsequently reported that the crisis had passed.[19]

Differences between the allies within Afghanistan became apparent to both by the end of 1946. Some of this divergence was interpersonal: Engert had been atypically Anglophilic, unlike his successor, Ely Palmer. British minister Giles Squire found Palmer to be "secretive, suspicious, and non-cooperative" and "too inclined to accept as true anything that the Afghans tell him."[20] Palmer, meanwhile, labored to demonstrate his country's independence of London. "We leave no doubt as to our conception of Afghanistan as a proud and independent nation," he wrote. "The British, on the other hand, often appear to regard it as a projection of India."[21]

Such analyses smacked of self-congratulation, as London's perspective also derived from far greater experience. The two allies disagreed fundamentally in their assessments of the Afghan elite. Discerning U.S. suspicions of London's policy, the British diplomat J. H. Watson posited that his American counterparts viewed Afghanistan as "another Turkey or Persia": a sovereign state whose independence should be strengthened. He and his peers beheld a far more fragile polity, and he worried: "Ignorance of the country's history and the temper of her peoples (and the Americans are very new to Afghanistan) might lead to impractical advice about modernisation." Circulated in Washington, Watson's report drew a sharp rebuke. Autocratic and unpopular as the monarchy might be, Ernest Fox argued, "the present Government in

Kabul is more enlightened and popular than any other Afghan Government has been in recent history," and its plans for modernization were "the surest and soundest means of elevating the Afghan population generally."[22]

Both allies desired a stable, independent Afghanistan but differed fundamentally on how to attain it. While London regarded the kingdom's politics and potential for modernization pessimistically, Americans raced ahead. Morrison-Knudsen initiated a project of unprecedented scope in southern Afghanistan. The prewar scramble for Afghan resources resumed. Above all, the shocks of 1947—the violent partitioning of India and the beginning of the Cold War—ended the postwar idyll and greatly complicated the kingdom's postwar drive for economic sufficiency, ultimately straining the bilateral relationship.

Into the Helmand

The most profound U.S. entry into Afghanistan occurred in early 1946, when Morrison-Knudsen and the Afghan government signed an extensive construction contract. Two visiting engineers affiliated with M-K had discussed seven major projects bearing an estimated total cost of $16 million with their hosts the previous year. Kabul instructed its U.S. legation to reach terms with M-K, and negotiations advanced quickly in early 1946. Mohammed Kabir Ludin, the Afghan minister of public works, had studied engineering at Cornell University and expressly preferred to contract with a U.S. firm.[23]

One late snag imperiled the negotiations. Recalling the shortcomings of prior foreign specialists, the Afghan government sought a contractual clause guaranteeing the work for five years. Morrison balked at this and enlisted another friend, Robert J. Lynch, who had served as special assistant to Secretary of State Edward Stettinius, to lobby on M-K's behalf. The State Department assisted as well, convincing the Afghans to drop their demand. Perhaps State Department impartiality was unlikely, but Afghanistan deserved better counsel. Sometime in early 1946, its lawyer divulged confidential information about the politics behind the guarantee clause to Lynch.[24]

Morrison-Knudsen was a trusted partner of the U.S. government, boasting a broad range of competencies. Its arrival elicited relief within the State Department, which had struggled to find specialists for Afghanistan. M-K could act with greater agility, but Washington's esteem for the firm rested on two contradictory premises: it could both convince the Afghan government "of our sincerity and ability to give effective aid," yet remain more "acceptable" than an official entity.[25]

Ominously, this understanding overstated M-K's distance from the government. The firm had initially been referred to Afghanistan by Savage, a senior official. The State Department had lobbied on M-K's behalf when the contract negotiations deadlocked, directing its representatives in Kabul to use their "good offices" to support the firm's position. Afterward, U.S. diplomats inevitably felt obligated to assist M-K. Indeed, after the conclusion of the contract, the State Department intensified its intragovernmental advocacy: seeking to expedite the acquisition of equipment, the movement of personnel, and the approval of export licenses for Afghanistan. At the behest of the firm and its Afghan employers, Washington refrained from discussing the contract with the British government until the scope of M-K's activity became undeniable.[26]

Other parties were free to draw their own conclusions by noting M-K's uncanny knack for obtaining foreign contracts or from different conceptions of political economy. Afghans would not necessarily distinguish broadly

Figure 3.1 John Lucian Savage (second from right) and Morrison-Knudsen employees in Afghanistan, 1948
Source: Boise State University

between corporate entities and governments; their own approach to commerce did not entail one. Zabuli's *shirkat* system comprised semiofficial companies that enjoyed state-sanctioned monopolies. Indeed, he and Ludin later informed Palmer that they had selected M-K on the assumption that it would enjoy the full backing of its government.[27] Nor would Moscow make that distinction. To Joseph Stalin, M-K could only constitute an unmasked manifestation of the same capitalist interests intent on impeding the Soviet Union throughout the world.

By the late autumn, an unprecedented American colony of roughly eighty M-K employees had taken root in Afghanistan, mostly stationed in either Kandahar or Girishk, the site of the planned Boghra Canal. The firm concurrently entertained constructing a cement plant and perhaps building a new capital outside of Kabul. The cement plant proposal prompted the firm to consider coal and limestone extraction (thus bringing the Walshes to Afghanistan). Considerable and escalating transportation requirements led M-K to inquire about the establishment of aerial routes to Kabul.[28]

M-K had far more immediate concerns, however. A September 1946 dockworkers strike delayed the loading of heavy equipment. A further bottleneck awaited in Karachi, as a local fuel shortage impeded further shipment. The fuel crisis impeded work on M-K's projects, but the resulting scarcity of U.S.-shipped foodstuffs posed immediate dangers, fueling employee complaints about living conditions. Washington gamely secured a loan of gasoline from the Indian government.[29]

Shipping delays could be attributed to simple misfortune, but M-K's other difficulties revealed fundamental planning failures. Much of its heavy equipment had been acquired, at prodigious cost, from wartime construction sites in the South Pacific and shipped to Seattle for repair and renovation before departing for Karachi. Inexperienced in Indian transshipment, the firm was flummoxed when the New Delhi government only accorded it a fraction of the required railcar space: three weekly railcars instead of the necessary twenty-five. M-K likely paid a price for withholding its plans from the British authorities.[30]

M-K consistently made costly decisions while falling well behind its initial schedule. Construction of comfortable camps for American workers constituted a further expense. M-K and its diplomatic boosters rationalized these expenses by claiming that camps and equipment would ultimately be turned over to the Afghans. Yet the inherited Boghra Canal project was itself questionable. Although initially supportive, the engineer John

Alexander came to doubt its feasibility; by his estimates, the canal would render arable less than a third of the promised 80,000 acres. Having failed to convince the Afghan government to abandon the project, Alexander resigned his post.[31]

Objections from Afghanistan's downriver neighbor, Iran, further complicated the Helmand endeavor. Fearful that the canals would deprive eastern Iranian farmers of water, Prime Minister Ahmad Qavam expressed disbelief that a U.S. firm, backed by Washington, would undertake such a project. Afghan officials countered that they had the right to undertake projects on their own soil. Atypically dry years on the Helmand in 1946 and 1947 heightened the conflict. Iranian farmers claimed that water had already been diverted into the (yet unfinished) Boghra Canal. Complicating the dispute further was the unruly nature of the Helmand itself. The river's flow varied wildly from drought to flood-level volume, while it remained susceptible to, as a 1905 arbitration commission wrote, "sudden and important changes in its course."[32]

U.S. diplomats investigated conditions in the western borderlands, confirming drought conditions, without addressing the inflammatory question of whether water had been diverted. Iranian concerns could not be dismissed, not least because a conflict over the Helmand seemingly offered the increasingly unfriendly Soviet Union a chance "to fish in troubled waters." Afghan development was no longer a purely local question.[33] As partition and the Cold War heightened conflict around Afghanistan, the Helmand project attained far greater symbolism, inside and outside the kingdom.

Afghanistan in a Partitioning World

For a brief interregnum, Afghanistan contended with a seemingly multipolar world, as cohesion between the three allies waned. Geopolitical fluidity abetted Afghan aspirations. Drawing from foreign currency reserves amassed from karakul exports, Afghanistan could bring foreign experts into the country. Britain continued exporting arms to the Afghan military. France reopened its legation, shuttered in 1943, and resumed its archaeological mission. Soviet-Afghan cooperation, largely focused on combating rinderpest and locusts, proceeded in the north. The liberation of Czechoslovakia allowed commercial contacts between Kabul and the Škoda firm to resume. "To anyone with pre-war knowledge of Afghanistan, there is a familiar ring to all this," mused W. K. Fraser-Tytler, formerly London's minister in Kabul, about the various foreign specialists once again roaming the country.[34]

Two different shocks, however—one gradual and global, the other regional, sudden, and calamitous—erupted in 1947. The breakdown of U.S.-Soviet relations complicated the Afghan pursuit of American aid. The partitioning of British India into two successor states, meanwhile, reopened the question of the Durand Line, pitting Afghanistan against its new neighbor, Pakistan. The chaos of partition, compounded by Pakistani retaliation against its neighbor, produced debilitating shortages within the kingdom and the further disruption of Morrison-Knudsen's troubled enterprise.

Soviet unease with the U.S. presence in Afghanistan extended back to the final years of the war. Bakulin had long complained about the presence of American experts. In summer 1945, Moscow blocked the engineer John Alexander from joining a commission to demarcate Afghanistan's northern border. The following year, it protested M-K's use of a hotel in Kandahar. Deteriorating bilateral relations intensified Moscow's suspicions. Autumn 1946 Soviet radio broadcasts charged that Washington's Afghan aid projects constituted preparations for war. Soviet diplomats pressed Afghan officials to explain the presence of so many Americans within the country. Their incessant inquiries left the Afghans visibly wary of employing too many Americans in an official capacity.[35]

The sharpest expression of Soviet disapproval came in early 1947, after Afghanistan moved forward with plans to develop a national airline. A U.S. diplomat in Cairo arranged a contact between the Afghans and Transcontinental & Western Air (TWA), which expressed interest in the project. In a subsequent meeting in Herat, Zabuli and Shah Mahmud contracted with TWA to operate and supply an airline service, serving airports throughout the country. Like the Morrison-Knudsen contract, the kingdom's agreement with TWA portended deeper U.S. involvement in the Afghan economy. The envisioned Afghanistan Airline Company required modern airports, communications equipment, and meteorological stations. Kabul anticipated asking Washington for a loan of $7 million.[36]

An intemperate Soviet reaction quashed the entire scheme. In April, Bakulin interrogated Foreign Minister Ali Mohammed about the TWA agreement. Why, he asked heatedly, had Afghanistan sought U.S. assistance when Soviet aid was readily available? He termed the development of Afghan airports a further Anglo-American step toward the total "encirclement" of his country. His government regarded northern Afghanistan as lying within its sphere of influence. Ali Mohammed angrily replied that his country could not be subdivided by others. Attempting to lighten the mood, he joked that the Soviets should be able to occupy the northern airfields quickly in wartime and find them useful thereafter. Bakulin was not amused. Kabul quietly abandoned the contract. Promptly informed of the exchange, Palmer neglected to notify his colleague, Squire.[37]

What was at stake for the Kremlin in Afghanistan? Washington and Moscow had already clashed over Iran in 1946, after Stalin refused to remove his soldiers. He had attempted to pry an oil concession from Qavam's government and pressed the Iranians even after agreeing to a withdrawal.[38] The Soviet Union resented and feared the influx of Americans into Afghanistan. Otherwise, Stalin attached modest importance to the kingdom and ascribed scant revolutionary potential to it. Meeting the Afghan ambassador in 1946, he advised pursuing cautious reform policies while placating progressive religious leaders. Amanullah, he declared, was a fool.[39] While friction within the kingdom was not a major cause of the Cold War, the emerging contest cast U.S. and Soviet choices within and around Afghanistan in a more ominous light.

The emergence of the Cold War, lastly, drove London and Washington to coordinate more closely. Comprehensive staff talks, held in Washington in October 1947, considered policy in the greater Middle East. In a joint statement, the allies assigned Afghanistan intermediate strategic importance. They noted its "position on the flank of Iran and athwart the approach to India," yet described its potential loss—although "fraught with serious consequences"—as less calamitous to regional security than setbacks in existing battlegrounds: Greece, Turkey, and Iran. Accordingly, the kingdom's defense should be bolstered through the framework of the United Nations. Some hatchets were buried. Britain affirmed that it welcomed U.S. assistance in Afghan development, while both allies pledged to coordinate in the future.[40] However constructive, these conclusions could not entirely bridge the gulf between the allies.

Events in Afghanistan's vicinity were already testing Anglo-American collaboration. From the spring of 1947 onward, Kabul fervently advocated for the self-determination of Pashtuns in pre-partition India. Pashtuns in the North West Frontier Province were offered, in a July referendum, only a stark choice between joining India or Pakistan. Kabul and like-minded Pashtuns in the borderlands argued that a third option, Pashtunistan, should have been on the ballot. Yet the nature of Pashtunistan, as envisioned by the Afghan government, remained nebulous, ranging from autonomy to outright independence. British officials accused Afghanistan of engaging in territorial revanchism. The motivation behind Kabul's stance also sparked speculation. Some Afghans, especially Shah Mahmud's nephew Mohammed Daoud Khan, appeared wholly sincere in their nationalism. To skeptical observers, however, Pashtunistan appeared a reckless ploy by the Dari-speaking Kabul elite to bolster its legitimacy among restive border peoples or to distract the population from economic difficulties. Shah Mahmud likely acted from some combination of sincere sentiment and political necessity: disliking the stark choice imposed on the borderlands and reluctant to open himself to attacks by Pashtun nationalists.[41]

Whatever its purpose, the Pashtunistan campaign aggravated an inherently combustible situation. Under the 1944 Lancaster Plan, Britain had assumed the responsibility of training and arming the Afghan military. London's withdrawal from the subcontinent unbalanced Kabul's earlier geopolitical calculations. Marred by mutual suspicions, prejudices, and bitter history, the Anglo-Afghan relationship had nevertheless served the interests of both countries, providing the latter with military assistance and a counterbalance against Soviet power.[42] Emerging within, but scarcely filling the vacuum left by British retreat were two successor states, wracked by the violence and upheaval of partition.

The Afghan campaign for Pashtun self-determination—expressed through incendiary radio broadcasts and a vote by Kabul's UN delegation against the admission of Pakistan—also tested Anglo-American cooperation. Britain vocally defended the Durand Line's legitimacy. Washington proved more reticent. Palmer declined to join his British colleague's protests, quietly counseling restraint to the Afghans instead. "Palmer seems to think that by soft soaping the Afghans he will get more out of them," Squire reported. In Washington, State Department officials informed British diplomats that they feared inflaming Afghan suspicions.[43]

No actual difference existed between the allies. Inquiries in Washington quelled any serious British concern. Through 1948, Afghans attempted to invoke Cold War imperatives: contending that an independent Pashtun state would better serve the defense of South Asia than a weakly governed Pakistan. The response of U.S. regional specialists was instructive. Fox and a colleague wrote in April 1948 that while they accorded great strategic importance to South Asia, they could not accept the Afghan thesis on Pashtunistan. Nor could they disregard Pakistan's "great strategic value," noting its accessible terrain, port facilities, transport routes, airfields, greater population and food resources, and more advanced state of modernization. The two neighbors were "complementary," and regional defense hinged upon their cooperation.[44] The litany of attributes ascribed to Pakistan also suggested the future direction of U.S. preferences in the region.

Above all, the chaos of partition, magnified by some degree of punitive action by the Pakistani authorities, wrought economic havoc within Afghanistan. The transition undermined an already shaky arrangement for the provision of gasoline to the kingdom. A preexisting 1946 agreement with the government in New Delhi afforded Kabul a monthly supply of 180,000 gallons of gasoline. While Afghanistan was free to purchase additional gasoline, outside of the arrangement, participating firms believed themselves bound to import and store it at facilities in Karachi, and to obtain the approval of local authorities before transporting it north. Nor did the kingdom possess the requisite infrastructure for the shipment and storage of fuel from other neighbors.[45]

Under normal circumstances, this arrangement imposed a straitjacket on Afghan gasoline requirements; partition laid bare the kingdom's economic vulnerability. Shipping permits became difficult to procure, as familiar colonial officials vanished. In July, only 80,000 gallons reached the kingdom. The human upheaval of partition, with its consequent disruption of rail networks, surely caused much of the delay. Yet authorities in newly independent Pakistan, angered by the Pashtunistan campaign, wondered aloud why they should aid a troublesome neighbor.[46]

The effects of the gasoline shortage were felt throughout Afghanistan. Food prices, already elevated by poor harvests, shot upward by a third. The government curtailed bus services and instituted a gasoline rationing system even stricter than that of the war years. Private cars became ineligible for gasoline, while trucks received an inadequate allotment. Cruelly, the effects of the shortage were magnified by Afghanistan's partial recovery from wartime scarcity. Trucks had finally returned in substantial numbers to the kingdom's roads, and a substantial construction boom had followed the end of the war.[47]

One consumer of gasoline stood out prominently within Afghanistan: Morrison-Knudsen. Backed by Washington, the firm contrived a separate import arrangement, but faced the same bottlenecks bedeviling the kingdom's shipments, especially a shortage of fuel cars. In their absence, the U.S. government obtained storage for the fuel, likely at the expense of other

Pakistani regions experiencing shortages. While M-K awaited its shipments, it drew its fuel from Afghanistan's national quota, receiving 120,000 gallons out of the kingdom's allotment by November. Embittered and facing its own petroleum scarcity, the Pakistani government withheld shipping permits. M-K's supply of petroleum remained uncertain well into 1948, jeopardizing its Afghan projects.[48]

Partition and the Cold War presented Washington and Kabul with difficult choices. Afghanistan's pursuit of U.S. assistance now risked Soviet ire. Partition brought the end of Britain's long-standing role in South Asia and precipitated a clash between Afghanistan and Pakistan. In turn, Afghanistan endured the further disruption of its commerce. By themselves, these developments threatened U.S. aspirations within Afghanistan, but the undeniable deficiencies of the M-K operation and the clear limits of U.S. beneficence called the benefits of the relationship further into question.

The Relationship at a Crossroads, 1947–1948

Like Wali Khan before him, Shah Mahmud had a nondescript journey to New York, arriving by commercial flight on August 3, 1947. The trip was unofficial in character. He chiefly intended to visit his ailing son, a Harvard University undergraduate, but also hoped to meet with Truman and Secretary of State George Marshall. Both were happy to oblige. Shah Mahmud's August 8 conversation with Truman largely consisted of shared pleasantries, but the prime minister had a more substantial message for Marshall. Noting the recently announced Marshall Plan, as well as aid to Greece, Turkey, and Iran, Shah Mahmud expressed the hope that the United States would consider assisting Afghanistan. Afterward, State Department officials realized that, yet again, a concrete request had been misread as something less pressing.[49]

In subsequent Washington conversations, Shah Mahmud requested a $100 million loan to finance a wide array of projects. These included existing Morrison-Knudsen schemes, but also extended to the paving of roads, reforestation, various industrial plants, domestic airlines, petroleum and mineral exploitation, and national defense. His State Department hosts directed him to apply to the Export-Import Bank (Eximbank).[50]

Afghan officials had sought a loan since 1945, but their inquiries became more urgent over time, invoking Cold War considerations. In Kabul, Ludin presented to Palmer an essay by Zabuli soliciting a U.S. loan. Zabuli argued that the wartime devastation of Europe obligated the United States to look farther afield. This, naturally, drew it into conflict with Moscow. Alongside Greece, Iran, China, and Turkey, Afghanistan was at "the forefront of any struggle" between the Western democracies and the Soviet Union—and yet, unlike the other four, it had not received U.S. assistance. Afghan development, aided by a loan, stood to prevent the country's fall to communism, transforming it into a robust market for U.S. exports and an employer of American firms and specialists.[51]

Unable to lend, and doubtful that the Eximbank would respond positively, the State Department sought other means to abet Afghan development. One crucial, albeit low-key initiative began in Washington in October 1947, as Iranian and Afghan diplomats commenced negotiations on the Helmand waters question. The State Department declined to mediate the matter outright, but its efforts—characterized as "informal good offices"—entailed acting as a de facto go-between. U.S. diplomats hoped to prepare the way for the establishment of an impartial international commission and obtained preliminary Afghan and Iranian assent to the proposal.[52]

By then, however, worse problems confronted the Helmand project. The mood among the "Em-kayans" had been visibly fraying, even before the gasoline crisis. Complaints about poor housing and food mounted through 1947—M-K reneged on earlier promises to provide furniture or allow spouses to visit. Employees appeared psychologically unprepared for the difficulties of Afghan life.[53]

The Afghan government, meanwhile, had cause for exasperation. Before the gasoline crisis, shipping delays left the MKA employees with little to do besides surveying work. By June 1948, the firm had spent $12 million, largely on procuring machinery and constructing work camps. Few projects had commenced, and none had been completed. Burning through its $17 million budget, which it now expected to exhaust by March 1949, MKA elected to close two camps and focus its efforts on fewer projects. Heavy personnel turnover and steep equipment maintenance expenses compounded the costs. The firm argued that initial estimates, based on earlier surveys by John Alexander, had been too low; the envisioned projects would cost $34 million. The irate government in Kabul began an audit of the firm.[54]

Afghan officials voiced their frustration. Ali Mohammed declared himself "appalled" by the skyrocketing costs. Particularly galling was the Em-kayans' carefree use of gasoline and company vehicles while Afghans coped with drought and the energy crisis. Hashim, now retired, asked why the contractors "should live in air-conditioned houses with electric light when we ourselves have to put up with ordinary oil lamps?" Chastened, M-K representatives admitted that they had failed to "sell themselves to the Afghan public."[55]

Afghan complaints about MKA reached a crescendo in early 1949. Ludin and Naim, the latter now Afghanistan's ambassador in Washington, submitted extensive critiques of the firm's operations. "The logic and sequence of the works to be done seem to be obvious," Ludin reasoned, "Surveys should have been completed first." MKA employees admitted as much in confidential conversations with U.S. diplomats. Instead, at great expense, the firm had acquired and transported heavy equipment, which sat inert in Afghanistan, accumulating dust. So, too, had disaffected MKA work crews, who had been set to building camps. Both Ludin and Naim described an alarming lack of cost control. The Kabul-Torkham Highway had grown from $2.4 million in the contract to $14.5 million in November 1948; the Kandahar-Girishk Highway increased from $600,000 to $4.1 million; and the Saraj Storage Dam, forecast at $225,000, had risen to $1.75 million. "It would be useless to deny," Palmer's successor, Louis Dreyfus, later wrote, "that in those early days the MK organization was not a paragon of efficiency."[56]

Plainly put, the Afghans were being bilked. In successive conversations at the State Department, Harry Morrison and his representatives expressed regret, admitting that they had "gotten off on the wrong foot," but largely attributing delays and expenses to Afghan desires to launch multiple projects immediately, leading to a dispersal of equipment and personnel. Morrison defended exorbitant expenditures on living conditions as a necessity of employing Americans abroad. He allowed that the hiring of other nationals should be considered. Naim's key criticism remained unanswered, however: that MKA had failed to give prompt notification of escalating costs, when it surely had "at least a moral obligation" to do so. His mission had received no updates before January 1948. MKA repeatedly failed to present timely or consistent information on its expenditures, attesting to a comprehensive failure to log its expenses. None of the engineers roaming southern Afghanistan specialized in cost control.[57]

Certainly, MKA had been unlucky. It had confronted equipment shortages, transportation bottlenecks, fuel scarcity, labor disruptions, political upheaval, and malicious interference. Nevertheless, some of these difficulties attested to the firm's haste and imprudence, rushing into a volatile, unfamiliar region. If Afghan expectations had been unrealistic, they had been founded on estimates that M-K had been free to discard outright. M-K claimed that it had never regarded Alexander's initial estimates as accurate and that it had repeatedly criticized them in the contract negotiations.[58] Yet M-K had already moved beyond the Alexander estimates in a revised December 1947 statement—which still fell well below projections presented the following year.[59] Nor had the State Department received significant notice of escalating costs from Morrison-Knudsen before the end of 1947.[60] The firm likely expected that additional funding would become available: either from Afghan export earnings or through a loan from the U.S. government.

Neither source could be taken for granted, however. Karakul prices fell precipitously in early 1947, undermining Afghanistan's foreign currency earnings. The Eximbank, meanwhile, held only a meager $500 million in reserve. With mounting horror, Afghan observers apprehended that they had expended much of their foreign currency reserves, to no effect. Naim wrote bitterly, "We feel certain that even a country as wealthy as the United States could not afford to spend such a large amount of money with so little results being shown."[61]

Afghan entreaties to the United States had yet to bear significant fruit. Bereft of news about a loan, Shah Mahmud complained that the United States appeared to be helping every country in the world—except for his own.[62] Aided by Ludin and Zabuli, he continued to seek assistance from Washington. British withdrawal and Pakistani hostility left the United States the kingdom's most obvious noncontiguous patron: perhaps as an arms supplier. Other American endeavors within Afghanistan, while hardly trouble-free, held their own promise.

For its part, the Truman administration still regarded the kingdom's continued independence as desirable, if not essential to the broader project of containment. As during the war, Afghan requests had been directed into a bewildering bureaucratic labyrinth, attesting to the real dearth of established, routine assistance programs. Like Lend-Lease before them, the Marshall Plan and postwar food relief constituted specially tailored responses to extraordinary circumstances. Envisioning a protracted global struggle with Soviet power, the White House sought to devise programs to meet the development aspirations of rural peoples. These programs offered distinctive new opportunities to the kingdom.

Struggling Forward, 1948–1949

To an unprecedented degree, the U.S.-Afghan relationship bore the scars of disappointment and frustration. Pashtunistan raised fundamental questions about Afghanistan's commitment to regional stability. Soviet disapproval rendered uncertain the wisdom of close Afghan ties to the United States. The troubled Helmand project lent itself to mutual recriminations. Nevertheless, the politics of the late 1940s bolstered renewed Afghan entreaties: for military aid and an Eximbank loan. Washington, meanwhile, attempted to bolster other U.S. endeavors within the kingdom.

One of these was the work of Myles Walsh, who impressed Americans and Afghans alike with his studies of the country's mineral wealth. Walsh hoped that Afghanistan could one day export strategically vital minerals to the United States, but another endeavor held greater urgency. Having witnessed Afghanistan's energy crisis, Walsh wrote: "For raising the standard of living in Afghanistan, I know of no single mineral development more beneficial than the development of Afghanistan's petroleum reserves." Properly extracted, they would provide Afghans with affordable kerosene, gasoline, and asphalt, easing local construction costs. He advised Minister of Mines Ghulam Mohammed to begin test drilling at Sheberghan, a site fifty miles south of the Soviet border.[63]

For all his industry, Walsh could not evade deepening Cold War tensions or changing political tides within Kabul. Overruling his consultant, Ghulam Mohammed engaged the services of French experts to survey the northern oil fields. He also entertained a competing French offer for mineral exploitation, and delayed extending Walsh's advisory contract. Walsh had run afoul of several countervailing trends within the Kabul government. U.S. firms did not enjoy quite their former prestige. Nor had the Afghans abandoned their traditional, sensible habit of seeking competing bids. Deepening U.S.-Soviet tensions rendered French consultants preferable—particularly for a project in the north. Lastly, Ghulam Mohammed, a member of the royal family, had allied with Daoud, and visibly detested Zabuli (an outsider). As it happened, the French foreign ministry expressed only mild interest in another Afghan oil concession while noting the "difficulties" posed by the "proximity of the Russian border."[64]

Walsh's difficulties were emblematic of a growing ambivalence within Kabul toward the United States. Besides the Helmand, no issue aroused as much Afghan frustration as military aid. Britain's withdrawal from South Asia rendered the Lancaster arrangement defunct, theoretically passing responsibility for arming Afghanistan to India (or Pakistan, had it been willing). Convulsed by post-partition chaos, India was unable to aid Afghanistan, while an overstretched Britain could only act to encourage others. The most obvious surrogate supplier was unfortunately the most problematic. The eponymous Colonel A. S. Lancaster, himself, had warned that U.S. arms deliveries to Afghanistan would "greatly increase Soviet suspicions and endanger Soviet-Afghan relations."[65]

Afghanistan attempted to keep its options open. In 1947, it renewed a prewar relationship with the Škoda firm through a covert purchase of artillery shells. In summer 1948, Kabul opened discussions with the U.S. military attaché on the acquisition of military equipment, expressing interest in light tanks and aircraft. Zabuli argued that the arms would both help the kingdom maintain internal security and enable a "delaying action" in the event of a Soviet invasion.[66] The Afghan arms request met with its own delaying action. Washington pondered it at length through 1949. A frustrated Zabuli complained in June that he had yet to learn how the United States regarded his country. Several factors lengthened the delay. The deepening Pashtunistan conflict fostered hesitance: arms delivered to Kabul would surely anger its eastern neighbor. The year's Mutual Security Act (MSA) limited the allowable recipients of military aid to treaty allies and a handful of named exceptions. Accordingly, to the dismay of senior Afghan military officials, the State Department directed its Kabul embassy to discourage its hosts from seeking an official arms sale.[67]

To some, this episode marks a key early abandonment of Afghanistan, enabling the expansion of Soviet influence.[68] Some of the confusion stemmed from the fact that the Afghans never submitted a finalized aid request. The paramount fact remains that Washington had not defined Afghanistan as it had the other non-allied exceptions to the MSA: Iran, Greece, Turkey, South Korea, and the Philippines. The first three represented familiar bulwarks against Soviet expansion and sites of postwar crises, while the Philippines and South Korea battled leftist insurrections. Afghanistan faced neither a rebellion, nor Soviet territorial demands, nor a Red Army overstaying its welcome. Its border dispute with the Soviet Union had been peacefully resolved by treaty in 1947.[69] Zabuli's elaborate efforts to link Afghanistan with other recipients of Cold War aid had failed.

Events in Afghanistan had not elicited alarm in Washington—not out of contemptuous ignorance, but because the Cold War had not meaningfully involved the kingdom. Afghans understandably feared their northern neighbor, but evidence of sustained Soviet efforts against them eluded even vigilant observers. A 1948 CIA report observed: "In contrast to its activities vis-à-vis other Near and Middle East neighbors, the USSR has made no formal demands upon Afghanistan, has issued no threats, and has not carried on an organized propaganda campaign against the people or the government, although it has been critical of current US activity in Afghanistan. This lack of interest probably arises from the fact that Afghanistan itself contains little of immediate value to the USSR and could be readily occupied by the Soviet Army should the need arise."[70] Squire detected "no proof of any undue [Soviet] interest . . . in Afghan affairs."[71]

Simultaneously, Washington rated Afghanistan's military potential poorly. A 1948 study concluded that establishing a modern Afghan army would be "expensive and difficult": beyond its expected utility as a "delaying force" against Soviet aggression. Intermediate steps, such as sending an advisory mission, would "proclaim Afghanistan's alliance with the West and its latent antagonism to the USSR," thereby provoking some form of Soviet retaliation. Truly effective Afghan resistance would hinge upon the unlikely cooperation of both India and Pakistan.[72]

Fortunately, other instrumentalities were emerging, able to offer Afghanistan assistance short of military aid. In his 1949 inaugural address, Truman unveiled an expansive global technical assistance program, subsequently known as Point Four. He promised to share "the benefits of our scientific advances and industrial progress" to promote "the improvement and growth of underdeveloped areas." Notably, he promised to work through the United Nations "whenever practical." Truman's enthusiasm for the Point Four Program far outpaced the vital work of designing and funding it. To his frustration, the legislature did not share his fervor. A bill for a technical assistance program only reached Congress in July, belatedly gaining passage the following June.[73]

In this instance, the United Nations proved a more agile actor. Articles in its Charter provided for the advancement of living standards, and UN discussion of technical assistance preceded Truman's inaugural address. At the UN headquarters, then at Lake Success, New York, Truman's diplomats pressed for the creation of a technical assistance program, finding willing collaborators within the organization's secretariat. Communist delegations expressed misgivings, but the General Assembly approved the creation of an Expanded Program for Technical Assistance unanimously in November 1949. The UN program preceded Point Four by nearly a year, yet the two were recognizably siblings.[74] Scarcely a month later, the Afghan government formally requested a UN technical assistance program.[75]

Any Afghan aid program required reliable overland access to the kingdom—a questionable prospect in 1949. Amid incendiary Afghan broadcasts, the Pakistani military pursued an aggressive counterinsurgency campaign in the borderlands. The Truman administration remained wary of stepping into the melee. The Kabul embassy received instructions to avoid commenting on the merits of either disputant's position while urging caution and dialogue on its host government. The accidental bombing of Afghan territory by Pakistani warplanes in June highlighted the possibility of conflict, however, suggesting the need for a more direct approach.[76]

Even so, Washington's leverage in Kabul was clearly waning. Ali Mohammed spoke with frustration about the still unresolved question of an Eximbank loan. His government had applied for a $55 million loan in February, as funds for the MKA operation neared exhaustion. Contributing to the application, M-K agronomists offered wildly optimistic estimates of the future value of lands around the Boghra Canal. The Eximbank deliberated into the spring as a panicked, embattled Ludin warned that his government would have to reduce MKA-related expenditures. In May, the bank rejected the application, counseling the Afghans to focus on fewer projects. Aided by MKA, Zabuli hurriedly filed a revised loan application.[77]

Recalling the earlier drought, the Eximbank's report endorsed southern irrigation schemes. Yet the bank nursed serious reservations about the Helmand project, noting the lack of fundamental data and agricultural surveys. Its engineer wrote: "No responsible engineer would risk his reputation" on projects of such magnitude in the United States "on the basis of such meager data."[78] While the bank pondered the second application, MKA withdrew a third of its personnel. Dreyfus implored his government to grant the loan: to salvage the Helmand project, U.S. prestige, and the positions of Ludin and Zabuli. Abandoned work camps, he warned, would serve as "monuments of American inefficiency." Still, the bank's review process could not be circumvented.[79] The impasse dragged into November, as Dreyfus observed that the delay had already wrought "irreparable damage" to the bilateral relationship. State Department lobbying and the assurances of Harry Morrison overcame the bank's misgivings. The Eximbank approved a $21 million loan, but not before the beleaguered Ludin lost his ministry to Naim in a dramatic cabinet shuffle. Zabuli's calculus had changed, meanwhile. He inquired tentatively about a loan at the Czechoslovak legation, claiming that his country faced overwhelming Western pressure to join the "imperialist bloc."[80]

The perilous politics of development reflected wider changes in Afghan life. Shah Mahmud governed Afghanistan with comparative leniency. Upon taking office, he had freed numerous imprisoned supporters of the former king Amanullah, hoping to enlist them in his reformist program. Relatively free elections unfolded in 1949. A spirited new parliament and the gradual relaxation of censorship enabled criticism of faltering, expensive modernization programs. After obtaining the loan, the government faced sustained parliamentary scrutiny. Insisting that the loan should be subject to their approval, legislators questioned the kingdom's capacity to repay it. Pashtunistan advocacy offered a useful lever to Daoud as he maneuvered against his uncle, in temporary concert with Zabuli.[81] Shah Mahmud appeared politically weakened—"almost powerless" in Dreyfus's estimation.[82] Afghanistan's growing internal volatility prodded U.S. diplomats toward efforts to ease local conflicts, as they struggled to develop a coherent Cold War strategy for the region.

Afghanistan Amid the Global Cold War, 1950–1951

Afghanistan entered the 1950s once again unable to obtain gasoline. Amid heightened tensions in 1949, Pakistan informed its neighbor that Afghan gasoline trucks did not comply with existing safety regulations. By Pakistani accounts—regarded as credible by Western observers—the relevant Afghan *shirkat* had received repeated notice but neglected to upgrade its tanker fleet. The ban took effect in January 1950. Once again, the Afghan government adopted gasoline rationing while appealing its case in Washington and London.[83]

Foreign observers perceived the act as an act of retaliation for the Pashtunistan campaign. Tellingly, when five newly compliant Afghan trucks reached Peshawar, the local authorities proved uncooperative. Dreyfus reported that "practically all top Afghan officials" had threatened to turn toward the Soviet Union if the United States did not aid the kingdom against its neighbor. News reached Washington in March of authorities in

Karachi halting the shipment of petroleum and blasting caps ordered by MKA, risking further delays.[84]

Three years after its inception, the Pashtunistan problem still mystified the Truman administration. Bereft of additional economic carrots after extending the Eximbank loan, Washington opted for high-level diplomacy. Ambassador-at-Large Philip Jessup had embarked upon an extensive tour of Asia in mid-December to assess the local prospects for containment after the collapse of the Republic of China. Afghanistan had not originally featured on Jessup's itinerary—Pakistan had—but an improvised thirty-six-hour trip to Kabul quickly took form.[85]

Jessup represented the kingdom's most prominent U.S. guest since Patrick Hurley. Superficially, the visit appeared to go well. Shah Mahmud treated Jessup and his wife to an honorary dinner. Jessup detected a "considerable" and shared Afghan and Pakistani "reliance on and friendship for the United States." His visit and subsequent Anglo-American efforts resolved the latest gasoline crisis. Shortly after Jessup's departure, modified Afghan trucks received permission to refuel in Peshawar.[86] Yet Daoud bitterly noted the brevity of Jessup's Afghan sojourn and questioned the envoy's impartiality. Indeed, Jessup subsequently described the Afghan position as "utterly devoid of logic." To the French ambassador in Kabul, he appeared chiefly interested in investigating Soviet activities within Afghanistan.[87]

A bizarre, highly unfortunate circumstantial bond linked Jessup with the next prominent American to visit Afghanistan. On March 8, days after the diplomat's car left Kabul, he ran afoul of Senator Joseph McCarthy's demagogic campaign. The same ordeal awaited Owen Lattimore, a distinguished scholar of Asian affairs dispatched by the United Nations to head its technical assistance mission in Afghanistan. Shortly after his March 12 arrival, Lattimore received a press inquiry requesting comment on McCarthy's characterization of him as a security risk. Upon the advice of his colleagues and thoroughly perplexed hosts, Lattimore stayed in Kabul for nearly three weeks, completing his initial investigative mission.[88]

Lattimore's misfortune had only begun, and McCarthy's malign attentions precluded him from further involvement with the UN's program in Afghanistan. His March trip had merely explored possibilities for technical assistance in the kingdom, with a longer summer visit intended to elucidate specific projects. In Lattimore's stead, the United Nations dispatched an American agricultural expert, Edwin Henson, to supervise the second mission. New to the kingdom, lacking, in Dreyfus's assessment, "background [in the] intricacies [of the] Afghan scene," Henson visibly struggled. In fairness, the task could have bedeviled anyone, as disorder within Shah Mahmud's government limited possibilities for coordination. Authorities quashed a purported coup plot in March, and the embattled Zabuli had resigned his ministry, after clashing with the prime minister.[89] Henson was, himself, only intended to serve in a temporary capacity. He and most of his personnel departed in the autumn, passing their blueprints to yet another group of newcomers.[90]

Concurrently, Washington quietly sought to resolve the Helmand waters dispute. These efforts culminated in a State Department conference room in August 1950, as Afghan and Iranian representatives debated the parameters of an international commission to arbitrate the issue. Opening the proceedings, Richard Leach of the State Department's South Asian Division declared his intention to act solely as an observer. Both parties, while emphasizing their desire to reach an agreement, deadlocked on the scope of a commission. Iran favored a broad commission. Afghanistan, wary of restrictions on further development, preferred a narrow body.[91]

Negotiations remained stymied for two weeks, threatening to break down. Stretching the definition of "informal good offices," George McGhee, the energetic head of the State Department's newly created Bureau of Near Eastern, South Asian, and African Affairs, entered the room and implored the parties to reach an understanding. "In light of the world situation we face," he declared, his government felt obligated to "stick to people as close together as you two nations are." McGhee's admonishment and a shift by Leach toward active mediation seemingly galvanized the two delegations, leading them to reach agreement at the beginning of September.[92]

That "world situation" scarcely needed elaboration. As the Afghan and Iranian delegations parted amicably, the Korean War neared the end of its third month. War on the Korean Peninsula confirmed the fundamentally global nature of the Cold War, thereby galvanizing the Truman administration to refine its strategy for the defeat of Soviet power. NSC 68, approved after the war's outbreak, defined the Soviet adversary as "animated by a new fanatic faith, antithetical to our own," and intent on imposing "its absolute authority over the rest of the world," beginning with the subordination of the Eurasian landmass.[93]

After years of intermittent consideration, U.S. policy toward Afghanistan's broader region—if not the kingdom itself—gained added urgency.

In January 1951, the National Security Council adopted NSC 98/1, its first comprehensive policy statement addressing South Asia. "India and Pakistan," the statement began, "are the key nations of the area." India's loss to communism would entail that "for all practical purposes all of Asia will have been lost." Prior strategic statements had recognized the vast human potential in the subcontinent; the fall of the Republic of China elevated the importance ascribed to the region's two largest, most populous states. Tellingly, NSC 98/1 scarcely mentioned Afghanistan, as did other regional policy discussions in early 1951.[94]

Always to be found on one imagined periphery or another, Afghanistan had moved yet again. Its dependence on Pakistani ports and the incessant Pashtunistan problem rendered South Asia a relevant geographic category for the kingdom. A country-specific State Department policy statement, issued in February, affirmed U.S. interest in Afghanistan's independence, stability, and, crucially, improved relations with Iran and Pakistan. The Pashtunistan problem overshadowed all facets of Afghanistan policy, jeopardizing U.S. regional interests if it continued to fester. In other respects, the outlook remained hopeful. Acknowledging earlier difficulties, the statement endorsed further economic assistance programs within Afghanistan while identifying local fuel shortages as a "most serious handicap." Lastly, military aid could be proffered to the kingdom if progress was made toward resolving the Pashtunistan problem; indeed, it might serve as an "inducement toward a further rapprochement" between the fractious neighbors.[95]

Strategic planners in early 1951 took the possibility of a world war seriously. Analysts gauged the likelihood of further communist aggression and the capacity of states to resist assault. Here, again, the kingdom received mixed marks. Afghanistan maintained "an attitude of cautious correctness" toward its northern neighbor, "combined with firm resistance to Soviet efforts at penetration." Thus far, "Soviet pressure has not been severe," nor was Soviet influence in the kingdom's northern regions visibly "extensive." The State Department expected Afghanistan to adopt neutrality should global tensions worsen. In the event of war, "a period of watchfulness" would follow, as Kabul awaited "a suitable opportunity to align with the winning side." Tellingly, the document did not propose enlisting Afghanistan, positing at most that Kabul might be induced to shelve its quarrels with Iran and Pakistan. Soviet "encroachment" upon Afghanistan, itself would necessitate consultation with Afghan, Pakistani, and Indian leaders to facilitate "guerrilla resistance" within the kingdom, which otherwise lacked significant conventional military capability.[96]

These assessments durably consolidated earlier appraisals of Afghanistan's place in the global Cold War. Close Soviet scrutiny, economic weakness, political fragility, and Pashtunistan all militated against establishing Afghanistan as a frontline ally. Yet geography and affinity argued for continued economic and diplomatic support. If the kingdom could not contribute greatly to the anti-Soviet struggle, its loss could undermine the security of its neighbors, whose own importance was clearly growing. Adapted to serve Soviet objectives, the Pashtunistan campaign could be wielded against Pakistan. Afghan entreaties, the continued role of Morrison-Knudsen, the prospects of quiet mediation, and the new possibilities of technical assistance all argued for maintaining Washington's current course. Afghanistan could not become an ally, but it should remain friendly.

Consequently, Washington attempted to prod Afghanistan and Pakistan toward negotiations. In November 1950, the State Department instructed its Kabul and Karachi embassies to communicate that the dispute had created a "situation favorable [to] Soviet intrigues and subversion." The department offered to act as an "informal 'go-between' " in arranging direct, bilateral talks, urging that both states cease inflammatory rhetoric. Kabul welcomed the proposal; its neighbor proved more suspicious. Visiting Washington, Pakistani foreign minister Zafrullah Khan sought explicit U.S. recognition of the Durand Line. McGhee and his colleagues offered private assurances but declined to issue so fundamental a declaration before the two neighbors met. Zafrullah remained unpersuaded.[97]

From these hesitant beginnings emerged Washington's first significant effort to address the Pashtunistan problem. The November initiative endured well into 1951, as Kabul professed its eagerness for dialogue and Karachi remained reluctant. Ironically, neither Afghan enthusiasm nor Pakistani unease were merited. Washington accepted the Durand Line but balked at providing Karachi assurances that would prejudice any negotiated outcomes. McGhee and his colleagues hoped that the two states would limit their propaganda in advance of talks, perhaps fostering mutual concessions once dialogue began.

Timing and circumstance did not favor the U.S. initiative. Shah Mahmud, in faltering health, spent much of the year seeking treatment in the United States, appointing Foreign Minister Ali Mohammed to govern in his stead. Dreyfus's retirement in February left the Kabul embassy without an ambassador for much of the year. Tensions between the two neighbors festered, especially after May clashes near Chaman and Kandahar.[98] Nevertheless, encouraged by the previous summer's Helmand waters breakthrough, McGhee and his colleagues forged ahead. Their endeavor was less consequential for the Pashtunistan problem than it was for the signals it sent—to allies and adversaries alike—about Washington's regional agenda.

McGhee's March 1951 visits to Kabul and Karachi represented the most visible aspect of his government's initiative. He ascribed some value to Afghanistan but regarded Pakistan as a bulwark of regional defense, able to shield the subcontinent and the Middle East. In Kabul, McGhee implored his hosts to consider the dispute "in light of the expansionist policy of Soviet Russia," which stood poised to exploit the conflict. He gave no ground on Pashtunistan, opining that the principle of self-determination was "not applicable in the present world," and doubting that the borderlands could be politically or economically viable. Despite hearing impassioned Afghan advocacy, McGhee departed believing that they hoped to reach a meaningful compromise.[99]

Paradoxically, while McGhee negotiated in Kabul, Shah Mahmud stayed in the United States. After a successful operation, he visited Washington for meetings with Truman and Secretary of State Dean Acheson. In June, McGhee hosted the Afghan leader at his historic northern Virginia farm. Guest and host angled for bass on an adjoining lake but settled for catching bluegills. The Americans presented Pakistan's belated reply: a limited acceptance of the November proposal. Yet while Shah Mahmud declared his gratitude for U.S. assistance, he suggested that nothing less than an independent Pashtunistan would suffice. Somewhat rashly, McGhee pressed his guest: Did the Afghans truly believe in their advocacy for Pashtunistan or had the matter been raised for domestic consumption? Shah Mahmud's tearful response convinced him.[100]

At another point during the farm visit, Shah Mahmud inquired whether Pakistan was buying weapons in the United States. McGhee termed Pakistani purchases insignificant, to which the Afghan prime minister "good-naturedly" replied that something was better than nothing. His government formally requested arms in August and grew increasingly impatient as it awaited a reply. Shah Mahmud complained that, unlike Turkey and Pakistan, Afghanistan had not received "a single cartridge," ruminating that he might soon have to turn to Czechoslovakia. Washington assented three weeks later but added significant caveats: requiring cash payments and refusing to take responsibility for shipping the arms. Shah Mahmud "laughed heartily," terming the response "a political refusal."[101]

Such disagreements failed to dampen Shah Mahmud's apparent affinity for the United States. Indeed, for much of 1951, a different problem presented itself: the recuperating Afghan was in no hurry to depart, leaving his government effectively paralyzed, under the cautious interim leadership of Ali Mohammed. Shah Mahmud was unwilling to act on the U.S. mediation initiative without consulting his cabinet; nor would the cabinet move without him. The U.S. embassy noted an "extreme fluidity and drift" in Kabul. Western observers fretted that Daoud's nationalist faction was gaining strength while the prime minister lingered.[102]

Concurrently, the kingdom's experiment in liberalization continued. A new press law abolished preliminary censorship and legalized privately owned publications. Afghans advocating constitutional reform—a largely urban, intellectual group—began publishing the newspaper *Watan* (Homeland), named after their political grouping. While *Watan* endorsed Pashtun self-determination, it did not emphasize the issue or endorse militant solutions.[103] Yet others, linked to Daoud, centralized Pashtunistan. In May, dozens of students stoned the Pakistani embassy. Blaming Daoud for the disturbances, and fearing he might seize power, the British government hoped its ally would encourage Shah Mahmud's departure. Even so, he did not return to Kabul before mid-September. In his absence, foreign observers contemplated an inevitable confrontation between the prime minister, Daoud, and perhaps the ousted Zabuli.[104]

A relationship that appeared healthy in Washington exhibited signs of mutual fatigue in Kabul. Weariness toward the Pashtunistan conflict jaundiced diplomats against the government; a quiet sympathy for the Watan faction emerged within the U.S. embassy. Simultaneously, apparent U.S. recklessness compounded Afghan anxieties about the Cold War. Having earlier endorsed the UN defense of South Korea, Kabul shifted to support Indian efforts to mediate the conflict. Ali Mohammed privately termed the U.S. decision to advance beyond the 38th parallel a grave mistake. For Afghanistan, the prolongation of the war risked a broader conflagration—raising the specter of Soviet intervention. This limited the aid Kabul was willing to accept. Shah Mahmud opined that accepting grant aid from Washington would be "politically unwise."[105] His government sought less provocative options.

Oil, UNTAM, and the Coming of the Afghan Cold War, 1951–1952

Other opportunities—mutually palatable and notionally less conspicuous—appeared viable. Building upon earlier survey missions, Afghanistan's United Nations Technical Assistance Mission (UNTAM) commenced operations. Afghans preferred international assistance, yet most UNTAM personnel came from the Free World, including its director, a former State Department agricultural specialist named Philip Beck. The collaborative capacity of the Afghan government had diminished, meanwhile, under interim leadership and amid rising political upheaval. Itself bereft of ambassadorial leadership, the U.S. embassy labored to fill the vacuum, reasoning that close coordination with UNTAM could facilitate dialogue with the Afghan government while avoiding duplication of effort.[106]

Coordination and limiting redundancy represented legitimate concerns, and UNTAM was not the first international development mission to reach Afghanistan. It joined the World Health Organization (WHO), which had begun a malaria control project in early 1950, an expert from the United Nations Educational, Scientific and Cultural Organization surveying Afghan education, and a group from the United Nations International Children's Emergency Fund endeavoring to improve prenatal care and child nutrition. UNTAM included specialists from the Food and Agriculture Organization (FAO), whose projects ranged from introducing new farm tools to livestock disease eradication. These efforts won UNTAM recognition from journalists and scholars.[107]

Nonetheless, from its inception, UNTAM evoked deep unease among Western diplomats in Kabul. While its FAO personnel made considerable headway, other projects faltered without effective coordination with the Afghan government. Beck fell seriously ill and departed Afghanistan for several months, fostering a general lack of cohesion. Above all, UNTAM reopened the dangerous question of Afghan oil development.[108]

No knowledgeable observer could begrudge Afghanistan's interest in energy security. Pakistan had demonstrated, creatively and extensively, its willingness to wage economic warfare, while development projects drove up Afghan demand for fuel. Yet that same heightened demand suggested new possibilities for the kingdom's known reserves. Domestic requirements alone might justify development of the petroleum-rich north while binding it to Kabul.

Questions of cost and feasibility remained, but Soviet hostility presented the greatest obstacle. Moscow had demonstrated a clear, consistent postwar interest in securing oil resources, from neighboring Iran to distant Austria. Soviet forbearance toward a UN development project just below its territory could hardly be expected—especially if oil was involved.[109] Amid the Korean War, Stalin's government regarded the United Nations, as historian Ilya Gaiduk writes, to be "an American organization, an appendix to NATO, and an auxiliary to the U.S. State Department used for the realization of objectives of American foreign policy."[110]

Notably, during his March 1950 survey, Lattimore had evaluated oil development skeptically—for both political and economic reasons. He had also briefed Soviet diplomats on his mission's objectives and introduced his team to them before departing.[111] His UNTAM successors behaved less prudently. In early February, the acting mission head proposed flying heavy equipment into the Sheberghan area and paving airstrips for that express purpose. More experienced officials deemed the proposal wildly infeasible; one U.S. diplomat warned that the Soviet reaction could scarcely be predicted. Myles Walsh, soon to depart, termed the proposal "ridiculous." Still a staunch advocate of Afghan petroleum development, Walsh now preferred investigating potential deposits in the southwest, solely because they had the "distinct advantage in being far from Russia."[112]

British and French diplomats in Kabul already felt anxious about the increasingly conspicuous U.S. presence within Afghanistan. Taken together, the sizable U.S. diplomatic mission, MKA's activities, the Eximbank loan, conspicuous efforts at regional mediation, and the Jessup and McGhee visits risked, in British ambassador John Gardener's words, "needlessly arousing Soviet suspicions about Western intentions in Afghanistan." UNTAM's fraternal relationship with the U.S. embassy only compounded the problem. U.S. diplomats, Gardener wrote, regarded UNTAM with "an obvious proprietorial air." Worse, Beck and other Americans on the mission "scarcely bother to pay lip service to their international status." "The Americans," Gardener wrote, "unconsciously do their best to lend colour to the Soviet accusation that the U.N. is a creation of U.S. national policy."[113]

Moscow's suspicions mounted. Soviet ambassador Artemy Fedorov speculated wryly during the Jessup visit that the envoy intended to "rally Asia and provoke a war against communism." He repeated the remark, mirthlessly, during McGhee's trip.[114] The Czechoslovak foreign ministry directed its representatives to monitor the activities of MKA in Kandahar. Its legation in Kabul, which collaborated closely with its Soviet comrades, described U.S. efforts to resolve the Pashtunistan conflict as serving the broader objective of establishing a southern base from which to attack the Soviet Union.[115] The Soviets, French ambassador Marcel Berthelot noted, had already voiced suspicions about the WHO and FAO personnel.[116] Further expansion of the U.S. role in Afghanistan bore terrible risks: "The restraint that the Soviets presently display is in danger of ending. There is no guarantee that an intervention on their part against the Afghan government would not be followed rapidly by unimaginable international complications."[117]

Gardener perceived those dangers in the oil mission. In March, he urged his government to seek a postponement of UNTAM's petroleum project. His superiors demurred; London could hardly be seen trying to thwart a project undertaken at the request of the host country. Sharing Gardener's trepidation, the British sought instead to intercede with the State Department. In Washington, a British diplomat advised adopting a "go slow" policy in Afghanistan. His hosts rebuffed him, contending that such a reversal would contravene U.S. promises to assist underdeveloped countries. The oil in question was likely too meager to tempt Soviet action. Surely, one American reasoned, the political dimensions of oil exploration had already received ample consideration in New York. The meeting only produced an elliptical promise that the matter would receive consideration from "higher authorities."[118]

Rationalizations that sufficed in Washington held less traction in Kabul. Zabuli, now president of the Afghan National Bank, questioned the wisdom of the petroleum project. George Merrell, a South Asia veteran who replaced Dreyfus in June, quickly apprehended the danger of rushing ahead. Cabling Gardener's objections to Washington, Merrell added that his embassy was "in full agreement." He doubted, moreover, that any of the precautionary steps undertaken and contemplated by the Afghan government—the use of a UN mission or the establishment of a national oil development firm employing foreign technicians—would preclude "strong Soviet suspicion." Hoping to stall the project, Merrell advised imposing procedural hurdles on the Afghans.[119]

Considerable disquiet could be discerned among various Westerners and Afghans, yet the project advanced. Circumstantial and political factors prevented its critics from successfully opposing it. Merrell faced a sudden health emergency and resigned less than a year after his arrival. Zabuli also left Afghanistan that year. Britain opposed the project most consistently but had little meaningful capacity to impede it. Explicit efforts to do so risked antagonizing Afghanistan or annoying the United States. Berthelot repeatedly expressed his own concerns, but his government only gingerly inquired about the issue in Washington. Paris may have entertained the possibility of a French firm winning an exploration contract.[120]

Concurrent developments galvanized proponents of the petroleum project. Iranian prime minister Mohammed Mossadegh's nationalization of the Anglo-Iranian Oil Company and the consequent closure of the Abadan oil refinery produced regional shortages of gasoline, once again threatening MKA projects. Anticipating scarcity, Pakistan initially refused to reexport fuel to the kingdom and then relented somewhat, setting a maximum quota that still fell short of estimated Afghan requirements. An Afghan mission, headed by Naim, now the minister for mines, reportedly negotiated the purchase of fuel from Iran, but poor road conditions, a shortage of trucks, and the dearth of storage facilities along the route made its fulfillment unlikely.[121]

Under such trying circumstances, UNTAM's determination and optimism must have provided considerable encouragement to the beleaguered Afghan government. Upon his return, Shah Mahmud took a personal interest in UNTAM. Beck met with King Zahir, and UNTAM's rapport with Afghan ministries visibly improved. Kabul media celebrated the accomplishments of the mission and its sibling organizations. Speaking for his ministry—and probably for his brother—Naim endorsed the oil project. Anton DeLaive, UNTAM's Dutch petroleum specialist, evinced "something approximating missionary fervor" for the northern oil. He and his Afghan interlocutors acknowledged the risk of a Soviet reaction but believed that employing non-American personnel might forestall it. French firms expressed interest in the project, and, in this instance, neither British nor U.S. diplomats begrudged the loss of commerce.[122]

Such safeguards held questionable value—France was, after all, a member of NATO. Yet Soviet apprehensions did not appear keyed to oil development alone. One Afghan diplomat reported that the Soviets had demanded lists of foreigners present in the north. With diminishing amity, the Soviets asked why Afghans had not turned first to them for development assistance. UNTAM's choices only added to their suspicion, as the mission continued to collaborate closely with the U.S. embassy while embracing a wide array of additional projects, including a national road system and a development bank. Not all Afghans were comfortable with the arrangement. British ambassador Eric Lingeman wrote of a growing Afghan unease with

UNTAM's frenetic pace and decidedly American character. Nor did the UN mission hold a monopoly on U.S. activity within the kingdom. In the spring, an Eximbank delegation visited the Helmand Valley in anticipation of a further Afghan loan application.[123]

Long-standing communist suspicions coalesced as the tempo of U.S. activity quickened. František Zachystal, Czechoslovakia's representative in Kabul, described the Eximbank visit as demonstrating "the interest of American imperialism in Afghanistan," reporting that it had met with DeLaive. Recalling the Jessup and Lattimore visits, Zachystal termed UNTAM conclusive evidence that technical assistance constituted "a form of U.S. imperial infiltration" designed to exploit Afghanistan's resources and strategic location.[124] His Soviet colleagues expressed particular alarm at the ubiquity of foreign experts in the north. "If you dig deep enough," one Russian asked rhetorically, "do you not occasionally strike oil?"[125]

In June, the Afghan government awarded the contract for extracting the northern oil to a French firm. "This whole scheme is a gamble," Beck admitted on August 7, "but it might pay off." That month, the Soviet Union finally acted. In both Kabul and Moscow, the Soviets delivered a démarche warning Afghanistan that development of the northern oil would represent "an unfriendly act." Lingeman received word on August 30 when he dined with Shah Mahmud and a visibly depressed Ali Mohammed. Only on September 9 did the Afghans notify the U.S. embassy, claiming to have rejected the Soviet demand.[126]

Outwardly defiant, the Afghan position was only symbolic. Kabul had no stomach for brinksmanship, and the UNTAM oil venture died quietly that autumn. While the mission continued, both Beck and DeLaive departed the country by year's end. It remained for Western observers to interpret the most serious Soviet intervention in the kingdom since 1941, and, consequently, Afghanistan's new place within the Cold War.

"What a Great Responsibility Is Ours"

In June 1945, when Allied solidarity remained strong in Kabul, Ernest Fox laboriously recorded his frank recollections of the Inland Exploration Company expedition. Expecting a renewed postwar competition for Afghan oil, he closed his account with a prescient warning: "It should be noted that all of the potential Afghan oil fields lie in the north, near the Soviet Frontier, and that the Soviets can be expected to view any new American penetration in this area much as Americans would look upon similar Russian penetration in Mexico adjacent to the Rio Grande."[127]

Why did they forge ahead? Why did Americans continue the pursuit of northern oil, despite the warnings of allies and Afghans that the effort would draw a dangerous response from Moscow? Several reasons may be posited, illuminating political, institutional, and ideological factors—revealing, in turn, the nature of U.S. engagement with Afghanistan after the world war.

Americans embraced M-K because it promised to do what official actors could not, and because it stood apart from the government. Yet, the ambitious firm soon found itself out of its depth, appealing for aid from Washington. U.S. officials could not cut their losses; MKA needed rescue. This, in turn, necessitated the Eximbank loan, diplomatic visits, and visible efforts to mediate Afghanistan's various conflicts. Lastly, it made the development of a stable source of petroleum, free from Pakistani caprice, highly desirable.

Institutionally, the postwar years witnessed considerable churn in Kabul within both the Afghan government and the U.S. mission. Ambassadors Palmer, Dreyfus, and Merrell were each capable, but only Palmer lasted more than two years at his post. Trying conditions in Kabul shortened tours of duty and caused the occasional death. Health and logistical difficulties complicated the task of coordination with allies and international actors. The chaotic atmosphere of 1951–1952 helped to ensure that highly motivated newcomers in UNTAM would forge ahead, despite the palpable unease of their diplomatic counterparts.

Differences in outlook also enabled Americans to pursue a more ambitious, sometimes reckless path. Engert's immediate successors felt the same sense of mission within Afghanistan. Confidence in the applicability of U.S. methods to Afghan soil bolstered them and rendered British or French criticism sour grapes. Another fundamental perceptual difference between allies is worth noting: the U.S. conception of the Cold War itself was far starker. "What a great responsibility is MKA's!" wrote Palmer in 1949, "And what a responsibility likewise is ours. . . . Each time we let the Afghans down we make it that much easier for the USSR to get in a blow back at us—and a deserved one."[128] He had not been an alarmist, but Palmer and others understood the Cold War as a global phenomenon. Consequently, it would inevitably encompass Afghanistan. NSC 68 effectively endorsed that conception of Soviet ambitions. British and French observers, who had monitored Moscow's policy toward the kingdom since the days of Amanullah, did not agree.

That is not to say that U.S. policymakers did not perceive risks in Afghanistan. Undeniably, they did. Nor did they nurse some early–Cold War notion of entrapping the Soviet Union there. Attention to the kingdom and its broader region was sporadic at most, and assessments of local military capabilities were invariably pessimistic. A strain of scholarship on the early postwar years faults the Truman administration for rebuffing Afghan entreaties for military aid or an alliance while engaging Pakistan. The latter indeed proved a problematic ally, but the fault lay not in Washington's choice of South Asian partners but rather in its panicked rush to include the region in the project of containment.

In fairness, Afghan leaders had encouraged that process. Shah Mahmud and his ministers had framed their appeals within a Cold War context. Less conservative and authoritarian than his brother, the prime minister clearly preferred some form of association with Washington. He retained, however, a traditional Afghan caution and evinced greater concern about a Soviet reaction as the Cold War deepened. Increasingly, perhaps reluctantly, he played the Soviet card in his dealings with Washington, anticipating a strategy employed more famously by his nephew. Development, political liberalization, and Pashtunistan agitation each appealed to him yet could not easily be reconciled with each other. The unresolved conflict between these imperatives facilitated the rise of Daoud's nationalists and led Kabul to embrace UNTAM's oil mission.

Yet, having declined other entreaties, U.S. officials still could have backed away. Instead, an enduring sense of mission, a fundamentally global conception of the Cold War, and the corresponding political imperative of salvaging the troubled Helmand project converged in the early 1950s, motivating the renewed and dangerous pursuit of Afghanistan's northern oil. A lack of sustained attention to Afghanistan in Washington and high turnover within the kingdom allowed the plan to proceed.

Thus, even in the absence of presidential policy, the early postwar years witnessed the zenith of U.S. influence within Afghanistan, with transformative consequences. Amid the escalating Cold War, Americans, encouraged by Afghans, pursued opportunities within the kingdom—but managed, in the process, to bring the global conflict with them. Not long thereafter, they confronted with growing apprehension the prospect of Afghanistan's loss to communism.

CHAPTER 4

"We Might Be Willing to Take a Chance"

The Choice to Contest Afghanistan, 1953–1956

First Secretary Nikita Khrushchev reached Kabul on a frigid afternoon on December 15, 1955. Traveling alongside Marshal Nikolai Bulganin, the notional Soviet head of state, Khrushchev had already, with much fanfare, visited two other nonaligned capitals: New Delhi and Rangoon. Prime Minister Mohammed Daoud Khan and his brother, Foreign Minister Mohammed Naim Khan, received Khrushchev and Bulganin, accompanied by an honor guard of Afghan soldiers inconveniently clad in old German-issue helmets. The incongruity may explain the somber expressions on the faces of Soviet guests and Afghan hosts alike.

Western observers took some solace from the muted welcome received by the Soviet leaders. U.S. diplomat Armin Meyer termed the reception at Kabul Airport "short and lukewarm." British ambassador Daniel Lascelles and his French counterpart, François Briere, posited that the sizable crowd lining the airport road was "unmistakably there by order." Indeed, thousands of Afghans had been waiting along the roadside with paper Soviet flags for more than four hours in cold, windy weather. Small wonder, then, that the public response appeared paltry. "It just shows," joked Indian ambassador Bhagwat Dayal, "what you can do when you administer an anesthetic beforehand."[1]

Such satisfaction proved fleeting. Despite a surprisingly limited public presentation, including a "remarkably mild" speech by Khrushchev at Ghazi Stadium, the Soviets appeared to depart triumphantly. The announcement of an unprecedented, massive $100 million loan to Daoud's government came leavened with additional acts of generosity: the gift of fifteen buses and a promise to equip a Kabul hospital. Bulganin endorsed a "just settlement of the Pashtunistan question," visibly pleasing his hosts. Reports of a secret Soviet arms deal circulated within the Afghan capital. The U.S. embassy glumly described the visit as "virtually [a] clean sweep" for Moscow and a sharp blow to U.S. efforts to forge a regional barrier against Soviet expansionism. The loan, coupled with expanding commerce with Moscow, rendered Afghanistan effectively "a satellite of [the] USSR." Daoud and Naim, wrote Lascelles, had "brought their country into peril of extinction." Briere predicted that the Afghans would find the loan to be a "Trojan Horse."[2]

Such dire prophecies would have amused Khrushchev, whose recollections ascribed far less grandiose ambitions to the trip. Khrushchev remembered Kabul as a strange, discomfiting place. He and Bulganin struggled with altitude sickness, which left the latter effectively bedridden. Afghan poverty disturbed him. Kabul's residential buildings "made a miserable impression," and Afghan garments "couldn't have been any poorer." Conservative Afghan mores led the Soviets to curtail a cultural presentation that featured female performers. "What did we need any extra problems for?" Khrushchev rationalized. The sight of veiled women upset him. So did the engagement at Ghazi Stadium. He had been invited to watch *buzkashi*: a famously rough sport wherein riders vie, sometimes battle, to place a goat carcass in a circle. Not known for his fastidiousness, Khrushchev found the game "coarse and boorish."[3]

Khrushchev also believed that his trip had been successful but defined its objectives far less expansively. Conscious of behaving as a good neighbor, he wrote with satisfaction that he had achieved "the warmest and friendliest possible relations" with the Afghan monarchy. Demonstrating Soviet benevolence appealed to Khrushchev: both symbolizing his policy toward the developing world and, more urgently, forestalling Afghan enlistment in the expanding U.S. alliance network. He, too, described a race against time, as he sought to surmount traditional Afghan suspicions of his country. Otherwise, he reflected later, Moscow might well find Afghanistan enmeshed within an anti-Soviet alliance and U.S. forces ensconced along its southern border: "The United States was courting Afghanistan, had provided credits to it, had built roads and done other construction there, and had offered its services in extracting and processing the country's natural riches. In short, they were making every effort to draw Afghanistan into the pro-U.S. bloc." His suspicions of U.S. policy in the kingdom were limitless. Had he refrained from countering U.S. outreach to Afghanistan, "They would have put in their missile base!"[4]

The two blocs assigned greater strategic significance to Afghanistan by the mid-1950s. Each ascribed hostile designs to the other: of converting the kingdom into a base for anti-Soviet activity or into a communist satellite. Deepening tensions over Afghanistan reflected the globalization of the Cold War, strategic choices by its combatants, and the greater willingness of Afghanistan's new leadership to exploit the contest. Four fateful changes in leadership across a ten-month span intensified the Cold War within Afghanistan: Dwight D. Eisenhower's November 1952 election to the presidency, Ambassador Angus Ward's concurrent arrival in Kabul, the March 1953 death of Joseph Stalin, and Daoud's appointment as prime minister in September. In sum, these transitions increased the propensity of the superpowers to contest Afghanistan, as well as the kingdom's willingness to court competing offers from both blocs.

Three years after the Soviet démarche of August 1952, stark warnings of the impending fall of Afghanistan became routine. Washington and its allies agreed on the strategic utility of Afghan independence but struggled to meet Moscow's political offensive. As Eisenhower sought to ring the Soviet Union with allies, Afghanistan held a paradoxical significance. Its persistent quarrel with Pakistan and military weakness precluded its enlistment as an ally. Yet neither could Afghanistan be safely consigned to the Soviet bloc—which appeared increasingly intent on its absorption. Across Eisenhower's first term, as Daoud's contacts with the Soviet bloc deepened, U.S. policy veered between diplomatic suasion and confrontation. First contemplating a grand federation encompassing Afghanistan and Pakistan, and then facing a border crisis provoked by Kabul's inflammatory rhetoric, the White House entertained the possibility of overthrowing Daoud. Afghanistan ultimately forced a reckoning of ends and means within an administration that sought to wage the Cold War on fiscally sustainable bases. Inheriting questionable choices from its predecessors, it ultimately concluded that while Afghanistan might not be winnable, neither could it be lost.

After the Démarche, 1952–1953

Moscow's démarche sparked the first serious debate about Afghanistan policy within the State Department. John Evarts Horner, serving as the interim head of the Kabul embassy, termed the ultimatum part of a "total effort [to] block any economic progress" in northern Afghanistan, leaving the region "a ripe plum to be plucked at leisure." Noting Afghanistan's history as an invasion route into India, he sought a dramatic expansion of U.S. assistance, primarily focused on improving the capacity of the Kabul government to maintain its authority in the north. Afghanistan, he warned, faced an "imminent crisis which will determine for all time whether it leans toward the West or becomes a [Soviet] satellite."[5]

Horner's call for emergency assistance constituted a remarkable personal reversal. He had previously chronicled the dramatic collapse of the kingdom's experiment in political liberalization. Authorities targeted the newspaper *Watan* after it questioned the government's commitment to democracy. *Watan* was banned outright in February 1952. Dubious elections followed in April that produced a parliament without opposition legislators. Students demonstrated in Kabul when the results were announced. The arrest of seventeen opposition figures, including recent legislators, followed in May. Outraged, Horner suggested suspending aid to Kabul, arguing: "We cannot afford to give even the appearance of propping up a weak, corrupt and reactionary regime." He asked, "Are we to allow ourselves to be blackmailed into giving aid simply out of the fear of Soviet encroachment?"[6]

Afghan politics continued along their authoritarian trajectory, however, and the démarche jolted Horner away from solidarity with Kabul's jailed democrats. Yet his sense of urgency was not felt elsewhere. From Moscow, Ambassador George Kennan noted the near-total absence of Afghanistan coverage within the Soviet press. He posited that Stalin's government was unlikely to take military action.[7] Similarly, the British Foreign Office described the démarche as a "normal reaction to [the] extension of Western strategic influence" near the Soviet border, while suspecting the Kabul government of engaging in blackmail.[8] Washington was inclined to agree. Successive cables approved by Assistant Secretary Henry Byroade, who headed the Near East, South Asian, and African Affairs bureau, contended that the démarche did not pose "any substantially new" problem for Afghanistan. Increased aid for northern projects risked inflaming the matter further.[9] Protesting that his superiors "seriously" underestimated the dangers of Soviet pressure on the kingdom, a clearly frustrated Horner appealed in vain.[10]

Yet as the Truman administration prepared to depart office, some concern emerged in Washington. In November 1952, expecting shortages, the Afghan government requested funds to purchase 10,000 tons of grain. The Kabul embassy warned that a failure to meet the request would push Afghanistan into Moscow's arms.[11] Washington's response proved uncharacteristically prompt. Although the availability of funds was initially doubtful, Secretary of State Dean Acheson interceded with the Mutual Security Administration, arguing that, as the Soviet démarche "had been the most serious in years . . . I felt strongly now they had asked us for the wheat and we should get along with it."[12] Citing Cold War considerations, Director for Mutual Security Averell Harriman recommended extending a $1.5 million loan. President Truman approved it on December 31, 1952.[13]

An embassy review of the wheat loan deemed the entire episode to have provided a "timely opportunity to make a substantial political and propaganda gain" after the démarche. Washington had reaffirmed its willingness to feed Afghanistan in times of scarcity.[14] Yet the embassy's emphatic, effective advocacy for the loan also attested to its forceful new ambassador: a prominent senior diplomat named Angus Ward. Like Cornelius Engert, Ward exerted a powerful influence on U.S.-Afghan relations and on Washington's perceptions of the distant kingdom. Some attention to his earlier life is therefore warranted.

A native Canadian, Ward joined the State Department in 1925, after service in the U.S. Army and the American Relief Administration. Thereafter, he developed a specialization in Soviet and Chinese posts and an apparent affinity for hardship assignments. He served in Tianjin during the Japanese occupation. Afterward, he headed the U.S. consulate in Vladivostok during the war. Secret police ringed the consulate with high-power spotlights, which shone relentlessly at night. Women who socialized with U.S. diplomats risked imprisonment. Kennan likened assignment to Vladivostok to "a sentence of exile and solitary confinement." The experience was probably embittering, but Ward, with a characteristic combination of grim determination and poor luck, had worse ahead of him.[15]

Ward subsequently returned to China to head the consulate in Mukden (Shenyang), only to face the renewed civil war. The collapse of the Republic of China exposed Ward to the wrath of the triumphant communists, who placed his consulate under increasingly stringent restrictions: first a cordon of guards, then the suspension of electricity and hot water. In summer 1949, Ward and his staff were arrested and charged with subversive activities. He and four colleagues endured a month of imprisonment in unheated cells on a bread and water diet, before being deported in December 1949.

To the delight of American pet owners, Ward and his wife, Irmgard, brought their four cats out with them.

Ward's imprisonment in Communist China had made him a cause célèbre. Some of the attention related to the terrible circumstances of his captivity and release, but much else stemmed from the politics of the early 1950s. As Joe McCarthy assailed the State Department, Ward gained prominence as a demonstrably anticommunist diplomat. The influential Senator William Knowland (R-CA) urged Truman to appoint Ward ambassador to the Republic of China on Taiwan. Washington's decision to post Ward at the U.S. consulate in Nairobi, Kenya, instead drew audible howls. Senator Homer Capehart (R-IN) charged that Ward had been "exiled" for his anticommunism. Criticism continued into 1952, most prominently in the Scripps-Howard newspaper chain, echoed at times by Republican legislators. The beleaguered Truman administration evidently decided to deprive its domestic foes of a martyr, nominating Ward to fill the vacant Kabul ambassadorship.[16]

Kabul might have constituted exile. The Scripps-Howard campaign—which Ward was suspected to have encouraged—only reinforced existing reservations about him. Ward's courage in China was undeniable, but he boasted an independent streak, compounded by the belief that events there had vindicated him. Prior to his Nairobi assignment, he had publicly contradicted Acheson, receiving afterward an order to decline further speaking engagements.[17] Stories about his peculiarities, especially his temper, puritanical nature, and intolerance of disagreement, circulated widely. Deep-seated enmities with respected peers from the Soviet mission, Loy Henderson and Charles Bohlen, limited his career advancement, and assessments of his efficacy varied alarmingly. Three State Department selection boards had rated Ward in the lowest tenth of his class.[18]

Ward acted with his usual forcefulness to bring a decentralized country team to heel. Isolation in Kabul seemingly magnified his eccentricities. The Wards brought three cats to Kabul, along with urns conveying the ashes of their predecessors. The live cats assumed places of honor at the ambassadorial dinner table, which they defended fiercely, clawing several unfortunate guests for unwitting acts of trespass. Indulgent toward his pets, Ward proved a stern administrator. The understaffed, demoralized U.S. mission and crisis atmosphere likely called for drastic measures.[19] Increasingly Afghanistan demanded attention—if not in its own right, then for the implications of its alignment on U.S. regional strategy. Ward's embassy could not make the case for Afghan inclusion into regional defense pacts, but it did argue the kingdom's importance to regional security, as the Eisenhower administration embraced Iran and Pakistan.

Eisenhower, National Security, and Afghanistan, 1953–1954

Choices made in Washington in 1953 held fundamental, albeit inadvertent implications for Afghanistan. So did Joseph Stalin's March 5 death and Khrushchev's gradual emergence as his successor. Henceforth, to Washington's growing dismay, the Kremlin appeared to adopt a dynamic new policy in Asia, exploiting anticolonial sentiment and the growing trend of nonalignment.

From its inception, the Eisenhower administration confronted monumental, interrelated problems. Eisenhower and his secretary of state, John Foster Dulles, worried about growing Soviet power, the military weakness of Western Europe, and the vulnerability of Africa, Asia, and Latin America to communist penetration. Containment struck them as an ineffectual halfmeasure in the face of a relentless, resourceful adversary. Simultaneously, Eisenhower believed that his predecessor had made fiscally unsustainable commitments.[20]

Confronting such uncertainty, Eisenhower exhorted his advisors to devise a sustainable national security strategy for the United States. Yet the volatile Middle East demanded immediate attention. Anglo-American efforts to develop a Middle East Defense Organization (MEDO) had stalled in the face of Arab opposition. Abandoning the MEDO framework, building upon the strategic thinking of the previous administration, Dulles turned his gaze northward.[21] He visited Turkey and Pakistan in May; afterward, he declared himself "immensely impressed by the martial and religious characteristics of the Pakistanis." Their country "could be made a strong loyal point." He endorsed shifting the focus of regional defense to a "northern tier" of states, stretching from Turkey to Pakistan—and hopefully eventually encompassing Iran.[22]

The White House endorsed the northern tier concept on July 14, 1953, with the issuance of NSC 155/1. Ascribing "great strategic, political, and economic importance" to the Near East region, the document discerned "conditions and trends . . . inimical to Western interests." Rising Arab nationalism and distrust of European colonial powers called for a redirection of efforts northward and demonstrating independence from London and Paris. The statement identified as potential allies: states "most keenly aware of the [Soviet] threat" and "who are geographically located to stand in the way of possible Soviet aggression." Pakistan and Iran received specific mention.[23]

Concurrent acts of policy helped assemble the northern tier. Eisenhower hurriedly shipped a million tons of wheat to Pakistan after it requested emergency food aid in early 1953. In August, the CIA-backed overthrow of Iranian prime minister Mohammed Mossadegh presented another opportunity. With similar speed, the administration extended $68 million in economic assistance to Iran.[24] In both countries, U.S. efforts to develop bilateral relationships raced well ahead of the establishment of regional alliances. Generous aid provided immediate assurance of Washington's interest while the more exacting details of regional defense were ironed out.

That autumn, the Eisenhower administration's definitive foreign policy statement declared the importance of alliances to national security. Intense deliberations produced the landmark NSC 162/2, better known to history as the "New Look." While the document famously declared the centrality of nuclear weapons to the defense of the Free World, NSC 162/2 also observed: "The United States cannot . . . meet its defense needs, even at exorbitant costs, without the support of allies." This concern extended beyond the existing alliance system. The "vast manpower, essential raw materials," and "potential for growth" present in "underdeveloped areas" demanded close attention. Their loss to the Soviet bloc "would greatly, perhaps decisively, alter the world balance of power to our detriment." Accepting the infeasibility of a formal Middle Eastern defense pact, it advised: "The United States should build on Turkey, Pakistan and, if possible, Iran" while offering limited military and technical assistance to other countries in the region.[25]

Separate policy statements and acts in early 1954 articulated the centrality of Iran and Pakistan to Cold War strategy. NSC 5402, in January, termed the preservation of Iranian independence to be "of critical importance" and U.S. military aid as necessary for the new regime's survival. Three days later, Eisenhower approved military assistance for Pakistan. NSC 5409, issued in February and specifically addressing South Asia policy, called for enlisting Pakistan in "a common front against communism." After years of uncertainty, the contours of U.S. regional strategy in the Middle East and South Asia were emerging.[26]

Critical ambiguities endured, however, despite the deluge of analyses and policy statements. Neither Iran nor Pakistan represented pillars of stability in late 1953. Political unrest wracked the former following the August coup. Tensions festered between Prime Minister Fazlollah Zahedi and the Shah. A facsimile of calm only returned to Iran late in the following year. Pakistan presented its own baffling difficulties, as Karachi rivaled Tehran as a site of political upheaval. Prime Minister Liaquat Ali Khan had been assassinated in October 1951. His successor, Khawaja Nazimuddin, was ousted in April 1953 after endorsing a constitutional blueprint that granted—according to his opponents—too much power to the country's eastern (Bengali) wing and traditional religious authorities. Days after the May 1954 conclusion of a military assistance pact with the United States, the Pakistani government imposed central rule in the east. Pakistan had not become more stable. Rather, in their pursuit of containment, the policymakers of the Eisenhower administration proved able to look past factors that had troubled their predecessors.[27]

Unsurprisingly, Afghanistan did not feature extensively in Washington's northern tier concept. Its absence from the deliberations of 1953 and consequent omission from the regional alliance system have drawn considerable retrospective criticism. Afghan officials continued to seek U.S. military assistance afterward. Dulles did not visit Kabul, yet it is questionable whether doing so would have changed his thinking. Neither Jessup nor McGhee had returned from their earlier visits convinced that Afghanistan could be a bulwark of containment. Afghan wariness toward the Soviet Union was well known, but estimates of the kingdom's defensibility remained pessimistic. The implications of the Soviet démarche also bear consideration. Eisenhower and Dulles sought to establish a strategic perimeter around the Soviet Union, not to cross lines Moscow had already drawn.[28]

Above all, Pashtunistan precluded Afghanistan's incorporation into any regional pact. The kingdom's defense required Pakistani collaboration, which could hardly occur while Kabul dabbled with irredentism. Alliance creation, as Eisenhower knew from European experience, required the resolution of serious territorial disputes. Worse, proffering an early invitation to Kabul risked removing Afghanistan's incentive to de-escalate. Periodic post-démarche suggestions from Kabul that it was willing to negotiate seriously validated a strategy of patient suasion toward the kingdom.

In 1953, the Eisenhower administration placed two risky bets. It need not be faulted for declining to venture a third. Rather, ensuing events call the prudence of its entire alliance-building strategy into question. Embracing a postcoup regime in Iran headed by a mercurial monarch and the far-flung, volatile Pakistani state required Washington to monitor the headstrong kingdom between them. The logic of the northern tier proved elastic. Afghanistan could not be incorporated into the hastily constructed network, but neither could it be abandoned to the expanding designs of its northern neighbor.

Soviet policy toward the Afghan kingdom evolved visibly during 1953. The démarche reverberated through the winter, as Soviet publications denounced U.S. activities in Afghanistan, and the prospect of Afghan accession into MEDO. Stalin's death, however, offered both governments the opportunity to turn a page. Daoud headed his government's delegation to the funeral and spent five days in Moscow. The Soviets subsequently agreed to construct grain silos within Afghanistan, which, in a bitter twist for Washington, would be used to store wheat obtained in the United States. Ward's embassy unsuccessfully opposed the deal, imploring the Afghans to contract with Morrison-Knudsen Afghanistan (MKA). An August 8 speech by Georgi Malenkov—then Stalin's probable successor—praised "stable" relations between Moscow and Kabul. The Kabul daily *Islah* declared the speech proof of "great changes" in Soviet policy since Stalin's death, adding: "It is no longer true to say that Russia is 'behind the iron curtain.' "[29]

Tonally, Soviet policy had indeed changed, but the communists held the same suspicions of Western policy in Afghanistan. Czechoslovak diplomat František Zachystal reported in February that he and his Soviet colleagues believed that Washington sought to enlist Afghanistan in MEDO. Ongoing Anglo-American efforts to mediate the Pashtunistan problem provided further apparent evidence of bloc-building. So did the wheat loan, the Eximbank loan, and Ward's assignment to Kabul. Moscow remained ever vigilant. The Soviet newspaper *Izvestiya* denounced Morrison-Knudsen and the United Nations Technical Assistance Mission (UNTAM) as agents of U.S. imperialism in October.[30]

Communist denunciations of Morrison-Knudsen served a dual purpose. Pillorying the U.S. firm effectively warned Afghanistan against closer association with the West. Crucially, the bloc also capitalized upon evident Afghan disaffection with MKA. In 1952, Zachystal reported that Shah Mahmud was incensed by leakage along the Boghra Canal. Perceiving that MKA held a near-monopoly on major construction projects and believing that Washington sought a stranglehold on the Afghan economy, the communists resolved to undercut the competition. Moscow's silo-building bid benefited from promising a lower price than that proposed by MKA.[31] Pivotal changes in Kabul, meanwhile, elevated leaders more open to accepting Soviet offers.

The View from Kabul, 1953–1954

Afghanistan experienced a political earthquake on September 6, 1953, when Radio Kabul broke news of Shah Mahmud's resignation and his replacement by Daoud. Weeks earlier, the prime minister had proclaimed his determination to stay in office, but his nephew capitalized upon a growing sense of stagnation within the kingdom, after the crackdown of the previous year. Simultaneously, King Zahir resented two decades of marginalization by his uncles. A decisive alliance between the two cousins brought an end to the era of rule by their uncles.[32]

Figure 4.1 An irrigation dam near Girishk, 1951
Source: United States National Archives, College Park, Record Group 306-PSB

Daoud had been Hashim Khan's protégé and shared his uncle's ruthlessness—but not his caution. As prime minister, he pursued three objectives, identified by Amin Saikal: the centralization of political power in Kabul, rapid modernization, and the establishment of Pashtunistan.[33] Few direct accounts of Daoud can be found in diplomatic records of the late 1940s or early 1950s. Reserved, determined, and taciturn, he had not charmed many of his Western interlocutors—and little evidence exists that he sought to engage them before assuming office. Thus, they received his appointment warily. McGhee had distrusted him instinctively upon meeting him in 1951.[34] Lascelles termed him "a dangerous little man with Napoleonic hankerings."[35] Nor, however, had Daoud developed strong ties to the communist bloc. A 1951 Czechoslovak analysis posited that he and Shah Mahmud pursued the same reactionary agenda, only differing in terms of their political methods.[36] An earlier interest in German-style nationalism brought occasional accusations of Nazi sympathies. Both blocs knew something of his wartime sympathies.

These observations differ from later, kinder characterizations of Daoud, the dominant political figure of his era. Daoud ruled as an authoritarian and constructed a fearsome police apparatus.[37] Yet his hold on power only solidified over time. He lacked the personal prestige or legitimacy of his uncles among the restive, powerful Pashtuns of the borderlands. Rumors of Daoud's impending replacement by one or another uncle circulated in the early years of his government.[38] His initial cabinet retained political allies of Shah Mahmud, including Deputy Prime Minister Ali Mohammed and Defense Minister Mohammed Arif. Daoud's extensive ambitions faced initial constraints, which he gradually surmounted.

Like his predecessors, falling within a recognizable Afghan tradition, Daoud espoused neutrality in the Cold War. Western observers did not ascribe communist sympathies to him. Daoud shared the traditional Afghan distrust of Russian imperialism but remained confident in his ability to exploit Cold War tensions: to deal profitably with both blocs. He benefited from the emergence of nonalignment, as a rising group of postcolonial states declared their intent to avoid enlistment in the global conflict. Daoud's affinity for statist economics worried Westerners, however, as did the possibility that his courting of Soviet aid and commerce would economically enmesh Afghanistan within the communist bloc. Finance Minister Abdul Malik seemingly shared these tendencies. Conversely, Daoud's brother and foreign minister, Naim, represented the regime's friendliest face. Far more genial and extroverted than his brother—one American likened him to the actor Basil Rathbone—Naim continually solicited Western aid. In this, he and his U.S. counterparts faced an uphill challenge, as the Helmand project appeared to teeter on the brink of calamity.[39]

Stung by earlier Afghan criticism and forced austerity, MKA had begun to achieve greater efficiencies in the early 1950s as it constructed irrigation dams along the Helmand and Arghandab Rivers, as well as the Boghra Canal. A relieved U.S. embassy attributed MKA's progress to lessons learned, but the firm was again cutting corners. MKA completed the Arghandab Dam in January 1952, by which point the Boghra Canal was largely ready, drawing "extravagant" praise from Shah Mahmud. This should have enabled the settling of Pashtun nomads in the vicinity, but—ominously—housing construction lagged well behind. Superficial triumphs in the Helmand only further compounded a sequence of disastrous decisions, stemming back to the postwar months.[40]

Dizzy with success, the company and its Afghan employers planned to apply for a second Eximbank loan to cover further improvements in the valley, as well as other projects. Yet the Helmand constituted far more than moving earth. The successful harnessing of the river required comprehensive environmental assessments, while the settlement of nomads on newly irrigated lands constituted an unprecedented sociological experiment. Neither MKA, nor the Afghan government, nor the U.S. technical assistance mission in the country was remotely prepared for these tasks.

Administrative difficulties appeared especially daunting. Amid the disorder of Shah Mahmud's final years, the Afghan government lacked individuals or entities able to supervise the transformation of desert land into viable farmland, settle nomads, or manage resources. In 1951, Ambassador George Merrell reported he was "seriously perturbed" by the absence of Afghan planning for the Helmand Valley's water and electrical resources. Deputy Prime Minister Ali Mohammed admitted that his government lacked a plan for the valley. Confronting a divided, often unresponsive Afghan government, U.S. officials contemplated improbable workarounds. After an unsuccessful bid to attract former Tennessee Valley Authority (TVA) chairman David Lilienthal to "lay down the law" to the Kabul government, the U.S. country team obtained the services of another TVA alum, William J. Hayes, to head the technical assistance mission.[41]

Prodded by the embassy, the Afghan government agreed to establish a Helmand Valley Authority, appointing Herat's governor, Abdullah Khan, to lead it. Yet Afghan hesitance illuminated more than just the disarray of Shah Mahmud's final years. Elements affiliated with Abdul Majid Zabuli resented the focus on agriculture, preferring an industrial emphasis. Worsening export revenues and the necessity of another Eximbank loan fostered further anxiety.[42] Ward discerned a "basically defeatist" view toward the project, reporting: "This defeatism is in fairly direct proportion to the mental capacity and familiarity with conditions of the individual concerned. Many of these people feel . . . that the choice of the Helmand as the major channel for expenditure of foreign exchange was ill-advised and has been made without sufficient study, that the execution of the projects has been wasteful and extravagant by Afghan standards, and that the physical and social problems now emerging in the area may well be insoluble."[43]

Abdullah Khan vividly expressed the growing Afghan panic. Distraught, he asked aid officials in November 1952 whether his government should liquidate the project entirely, rather than sustain further losses. Abdullah cited a dismaying October soil study by MKA agronomist Claude Fly of 16,000 irrigated acres at Nad-i-Ali, where 125 families had recently settled. Few Afghan personnel were present to assist the settlers, who received conflicting instructions and waited impatiently for the construction of acceptable housing. Above all, the farms yielded anemic wheat harvests. Fly blamed "poor seed, salts and alkali, and over-irrigation."[44]

The latter factors indicted the entire project. Amid the struggle to administer the valley, another, graver problem was literally rising to the surface. Much of the irrigated area featured shallow soil layers, above thick clay or rock. The lower strata limited drainage and allowed water tables to float dangerously close to the topsoil. Normal irrigation, canal leakage, and overuse of water by inexperienced settlers elevated saline and alkaline concentrations, killing crops. A British diplomat wrote after an April 1953 visit to Nad-i-Ali, "I have seldom seen a more dismal sight than this tract of land, either barren and scarred with salt patches or bearing obviously stunted crops."[45]

All of this could have been avoided. Seven years earlier, in September 1945, Kaiser Engineering dispatched Sinclair O. Harper, the longtime chief engineer of the Bureau of Reclamation, to evaluate the Boghra Canal project. Even before his departure, Harper identified salinity and shallow soil as potential problems. Visiting Girishk on September 5, he noted, "Entire area should be classified by soil expert before conclusion can be reached as to feasibility of project." Appearing "somewhat discouraged" after the visit, Harper shared his concerns with the State Department and the Kabul legation. Noting the potential problem with soil quality, diplomat Elbert Mathews presciently wrote to Washington, "I hope that a thorough-going survey can be made in the near future, as it would be highly undesirable for an American contractor to become involved in this project before its economic value is established."[46]

MKA and its government boosters knew of the salinity problem but accorded it little discussion. Even so, what they knew should have raised fundamental doubts. Frank Youngs, another MKA agronomist, reconnoitered Nad-i-Ali in 1946, before construction commenced, noting poor drainage, mediocre soil quality, and visible salts. Surface salts were an open secret among MKA employees. A 1949 embassy report termed Boghra-area soils "in places poorly drained and saline." Yet consideration of the problem only belatedly crested in 1952, likely precipitated by settler discontentment and the Fly report.[47]

The aid mission met Abdullah's anxious inquiries with vigorous sophistry and positive thinking. Hayes defended MKA, contending that, without firm direction from Kabul, they had acted as any contractor would. The failure to anticipate waterlogging and salinity were "understandable" in the absence of systematic soil data. Nad-i-Ali was just one tract of land. It was premature, Hayes argued, to judge the project "in extreme terms of 'good and bad.'" Even if costs ran high, it might yield "benefits Afghanistan cannot afford not to provide." Privately, Hayes wrote far less forgivingly of Morrison-Knudsen, accusing it of "proceeding blindly without sufficient information on soils and drainage problems to know where they are going." MKA appeared either unwilling or unable to undertake the required studies. Yet Hayes felt compelled to defend the firm, convinced that his hosts would otherwise blame its mistakes on the U.S. government.[48]

Having written the disappointing Nad-i-Ali report, Fly proved bullish on the future of Helmand Valley agriculture. He advised repairing leaky canals, improving drainage, regulating water use, leaching salts from the soil, and regular crop rotation. Some of these prescriptions required additional funding—accordingly Afghanistan requested a second Eximbank loan in December 1952. Others, however, illuminated another major conceptual flaw: how well might neophyte farmers adapt to a schedule of crop rotation? To anthropologist Louis Dupree, neither Kabul nor MKA appeared interested in preparing nomads to cultivate difficult land. Reviewing the program, the rural anthropologist Carl Taylor observed that successful settlement and adaptation appeared to have been regarded "as something which would follow automatically after engineering and agricultural problems were solved." As Nick Cullather writes, the entire premise rested upon the denigration of nomadic peoples. Confronting meager harvests, deficient housing, and administrative confusion in a malarial environment, many simply walked away.[49]

MKA and its U.S. advocates described a promising project confronting a few inevitable, unanticipated setbacks. British observers perceived an unfolding disaster that jeopardized the entire Western position in Afghanistan. "I have never before seen major works carried out in such obviously questionable soil without pretty comprehensive preliminary enquiries," wrote a knowledgeable British member of UNTAM. Ambassador Eric Lingeman warned that, in the Helmand, "the immediate question is not so much one of achieving positive success as of averting disastrous failure." He noted the "technical ignorance" of the Afghans, but wrote damningly about Morrison-Knudsen: "It is impossible to resist the conclusion that the company have lured the Afghan Government into grossly excessive expenditure on the construction of dams and canals, and have failed to insist on the overriding need for soil surveys, agricultural research, and provision for the costly business of physically settling nomads on the new land. Morrison-Knudsen have in fact withheld a great deal of useful information and advice from the Afghan Government in order to make a large profit more easily." Appalled as he was, Lingeman could not contemplate abandoning the project, perceiving Anglo-American credibility to be "irrevocably committed" to it.[50]

Meanwhile, Afghanistan's second application for an Eximbank loan awaited a verdict. With the funds from the 1949 loan nearly exhausted by spring 1953, the bank held an effective veto over further action. Abdullah Khan's uncertainty and the known opposition of rival economic interests suggested weakening Afghan support for the project. Economist Peter Franck argued that U.S. aid might be better distributed among a variety of enterprises. Investments in local textile production stood to reduce imports. Simple improvements in agricultural production could have bolstered exports.[51] While northern oil exploration had been stalled by the Soviet démarche, irrigation projects in the region enjoyed far better prospects than in the south. Retreat from the Helmand would have been painful but not fatal while other opportunities loomed.

The U.S. mission grasped the extent of the problems confronting the Helmand project. Hayes observed that the endeavor would be "a difficult one, even if it were situated in the United States."[52] Murmurs of disaffection were sometimes audible. The embassy's chief economic officer remarked bitterly that MKA could convince itself of the necessity "of building a road diagonally across [Afghanistan]" if there was a profit to be made.[53] It was as good a moment as any to change course. Yet Hayes did not abandon the project, even as he contended with persistent staffing shortages, inadequate housing, poor coordination with the Kabul government, and fraying relations with MKA. As the Eximbank's review dragged on, Hayes and Ward worried that the bank contemplated abandoning the project.[54] Ward wrote dramatically: "The eyes not only of Afghanistan but of the entire area from the Mediterranean Ocean [sic] to the Bay of Bengal and from the Indian to the Arctic Oceans are on us, and I flinch when I think of the capital which could be created in Soviet propaganda if we fail to bring our phase of the Helmand Valley project to successful completion."[55]

Before the bank concluded its review, the implications of the Eisenhower administration's regional strategy had sharply curtailed the range of safe policy options. The formal assembly of the northern tier began on February 19, 1954, when Turkey and Pakistan announced a treaty of cooperation. Six days later, Eisenhower publicly affirmed his willingness to provide arms to Karachi.[56] Anxious Afghans considered the implications of exclusion from the regional defense system; communist diplomats worried about the converse prospect. Rumors reached Ward of an immediate Soviet reaction. A senior Afghan official confirmed that Moscow had offered a "fantastically large" aid package. Naim subsequently complained that Soviet ambassador Mikhail Degtyar was pestering him for a response.[57]

Soviet willingness to match its adversary, offer for offer, heralded a new phase of competition. Early in 1954, Moscow extended Kabul a $3.5 million credit, toward the construction of two silos, a flour mill, and a bakery. The credit featured a lower interest rate than Afghanistan's 1949 Eximbank loan and was repayable in terms of raw materials. Soviet aid appeared to flow freely, on easier terms, and with fewer strings attached.[58]

As late entrants in the aid contest, the communists enjoyed certain advantages but grappled with acute anxieties. Degtyar and Zachystal communicated their own sense of urgency, as they fought to prevent Afghanistan's political and economic absorption into the opposing camp. Nor did the communists approach the task without their own compelling sense of mission. MKA's missteps and Afghanistan's mounting debt burden presented a horrifying picture: of the rapacious capitalist exploitation of an impoverished country. They also offered an invaluable opportunity for the communists to distinguish themselves as prompt, respectful, and egalitarian benefactors to the Afghan people.[59]

By contrast, Washington appeared hamstrung. The United States responded expediently to another Afghan wheat shortage in 1954, purchasing 12,000 tons of wheat for distribution into the kingdom. Vice President Richard M. Nixon briefly visited Kabul in December 1953. The primary question overhanging the U.S.-Afghan aid relationship remained a second Eximbank loan. The Kabul government had submitted its application in January 1953 but waited more than a year for the bank's response.[60]

Much of the delay had nothing to do with Afghanistan. As the first Republican government to preside over the Eximbank since its establishment in 1934, the Eisenhower administration spent 1953 debating its mission, especially Eximbank loans toward development projects. While the debate ranged, such lending effectively ceased. Cold War imperatives ultimately

Figure 4.2 U.S. grain being distributed outside of Jalalabad, 1954
Source: United States National Archives, College Park, Record Group 306-PSB

preserved the bank's role in aiding development, just as the U.S. mission in Afghanistan and its State Department counterparts successfully argued for the paramount significance of the Helmand project. Acknowledging the political importance of the project, the bank authorized an $18.5 million loan in April.[61]

The new loan sufficed to keep MKA employed while expanding the scope of the Helmand project. Otherwise, it afforded scant reassurance to either government. Kabul complained about the loan's 4.5 percent interest rate, a full point above the level set in 1949. His own prior counsel notwithstanding, Ward felt a deepening ambivalence about the loan's recipients. Within Kabul a bitter struggle raged between Daoud's finance minister, Abdul Malik, and the National Bank (*Bank-i-Milli*), which remained tied to the ousted Abdul Majid Zabuli, over ownership of major assets and control over pricing.[62] As an apparent argument over the proper role of the state in the economy, the ministry-bank battle significantly colored Ward's assessments. Ward diagnosed in Malik a preference for statist economics that would "tend to play into the hands of the Soviets." An unnamed Bank-i-Milli officer suggested postponing the loan, lest Washington bolster the "madmen" running the government. On the eve of the loan's approval, Ward advised that it would "incidentally" strengthen Malik and Daoud, but added ambivalently that the State Department was better positioned to evaluate this factor.[63]

Paradox increasingly defined the bilateral relationship. Aid was needed to salvage the Helmand Valley project, even as it bolstered a regime that Ward distrusted. Washington's response to perennial Afghan inquiries about arms purchases or an alliance was similarly conflicted. NSC 5409 advised refraining "from encouraging Afghan expectations of military assistance" or enlisting Afghan participation in any regional defense arrangements. Yet Afghan requests for arms continued and Washington was loath to refuse outright.[64]

Amid rumors of a military assistance program for Pakistan, Afghan ambassador Mohammed Kabir Ludin—demoted after serving under Shah Mahmud—made a last-ditch appeal for the inclusion of his country in the regional security arrangement. Meeting with Dulles, he argued that Afghanistan constituted "the keystone in the arch between the Middle East and the Indian Subcontinent" and lay "within the perimeter of an area defense concept." He professed his government's willingness to support the defense of Pakistan, provided that the Pashtunistan question could be resolved. Ludin subsequently asked Byroade how the U.S. government might respond to an Afghan request for military aid. Byroade evasively pledged to give the question "serious thought," promising to contact Ludin "when he had something concrete to say." Further conversations ensured, but Byroade remained vague.[65]

Washington could not offer Afghanistan arms. Nor could it decline to do so outright. Pakistani concerns drove this ambiguity, as did fears of a Soviet reaction. Simultaneously, the kingdom could not be ceded entirely to its northern neighbor. Tellingly, Byroade expressed the hope that aid to Pakistan would impel Afghanistan to become "more realistic on the Pashtunistan question."[66] Daoud felt differently about the issue. Over the following year, the Cold War and the Durand Line became entangled, forcing Eisenhower to grapple with the problems of a willful, nonaligned Afghanistan.

Opportunity and Crisis, 1954–1955

Eisenhower's pursuit of global containment had enlisted Afghanistan's neighbors into the U.S. alliance system. Simultaneously, his reinvention of the National Security Council (NSC) led to an unprecedented level of executive engagement with regional issues. Eisenhower devised a comprehensive system for the creation and implementation of policy. He was, himself, a constant presence at NSC meetings, attending 339 of the 366 held during his presidency.[67] Afghanistan policy bore witness to this transformation. Eisenhower's reinvention of the council coincided with the rise of Soviet aid programs in the kingdom and preceded the eruption of a major crisis with Pakistan in 1955. For the first time in the history of the relationship, policy toward Afghanistan received close attention at the White House level. As the Soviet presence deepened and the kingdom's relationship with Karachi soured, Eisenhower and his advisors debated options ranging from an improbable Afghan-Pakistan confederation to Daoud's overthrow.

Concern about Soviet activities in Afghanistan crystallized by mid-spring. Noting recent Soviet-Afghan economic agreements, the State Department speculated that "active Soviet penetration or satellization" could be under way. Visiting Washington, Ward argued emphatically for partial Afghan inclusion in the regional defense system, describing a sense of abandonment in Kabul. Otherwise, the Soviets could be expected to advance to the Hindu Kush "within the foreseeable future." The core issue would be "whether we should enable the Afghans to oppose the Soviets at the Hindu Kush or permit the Soviets to advance practically unresisted to the Durand Line"—or beyond. "Determined Afghan resistance," Ward argued, "could upset the timetable of a Soviet drive to the Indian Ocean."[68]

Reports of new Soviet bloc endeavors continued to arrive: an oil pipeline to Soviet Uzbekistan, petroleum storage facilities in the north and—gallingly—a Soviet proposal to pave the streets of Kabul. Afghanistan had previously solicited U.S. assistance on the paving project; deeming it frivolous, Ward and his superiors had declined. Not to be outdone, in August Czechoslovakia negotiated a $5 million credit toward the construction of a cement factory, to be repaid at 3 percent interest in agricultural goods.[69] Noting the Soviet aid offensive, the NSC initiated its own study of the kingdom. While not predicting imminent Sovietization, a CIA assessment of Afghanistan forecast "continuing Soviet penetration of Afghanistan's economic and other internal affairs."[70]

The policies considered in Washington attested to its uncertainty about both Afghanistan and the wider region. The curious idea of an Afghan-Pakistan federation emerged as the earliest and most hopeful option, appealing to an improbable combination of U.S., Afghan, and Pakistani officials. In December 1953, an unnamed Afghan official proposed a compromise solution to the conflict to Pakistani ambassador A. S. B. Shah: renaming the North West Frontier Province as Pashtunistan, an array of trade, transit, border, and defense agreements, and Afghanistan renouncing any claim to Pakistani territory. Signals continued in 1954, as Afghanistan's representative in Karachi, Attik Rafik, suggested an alliance and customs union. Shah emerged as his government's leading proponent of pursuing détente with Kabul.[71]

The federation idea experienced a short life. It also illustrated the curious, autonomous nature of policymaking within Daoud's government. The proposal probably represented a semi-independent enterprise on Naim's part, rather than official state policy—Daoud did not appear interested in the idea. Western observers suspected Rafik of improvising, and Pakistanis found him maddeningly vague. Shah, meanwhile, lacked the confidence of his superiors, who thought he had been gulled by the Afghans. A sharp uptick in propaganda in the summer seemingly spelled the end of the notion. Even the patient Shah admitted defeat.[72]

Naim's autumn trip to New York, however, abruptly resurrected the idea. In conversations with Dulles and Byroade, he expressed anxiety about the "keen [Soviet] reaction" to U.S. regional policy. As a "member of the Free World," Afghanistan felt exposed to an array of Soviet pressures. Naim reiterated his interest in a federation, a security pact with Karachi, and U.S. military aid. Inclusion of Afghanistan into regional security and development programs would provide an "antidote to the despair and hopelessness now prevalent" in the kingdom. Likening Pashtunistan to the Franco-German dispute over the Saarland, Byroade wondered whether progress toward regional unity might resolve it. Taking heed, Naim subsequently emphasized the necessity of a federation when he met with Henry Cabot Lodge, the U.S. representative at the United Nations. When Lodge asked whether Naim contemplated an arrangement like Benelux, his guest proposed something "a good deal closer," placing the neighbors under the same flag.[73]

Impressed, Lodge emerged as the federation's main U.S. advocate, terming the idea "bold and statesmanlike" and "clearly in the best interest" of the United States. Yet the administration responded cautiously. Dulles argued that active support of any union would alarm the Soviet Union and India. Pakistanis who sought closer relations favored a cautious, incremental approach. The idea remained nebulous, and regional events once again dashed the project. Pakistan announced its "One Unit" plan to forge a single province out of its western wing. In response, Daoud declared that he did not regard the Pashtun territories part of Pakistan.[74]

For South Asian actors, the federation idea was dead. Yet it took on a strange afterlife on December 9, 1954, when Eisenhower's NSC considered Afghanistan policy. Chairman of the Joint Chiefs of Staff Arthur Radford declared that establishing a federation would constitute a "great stroke." Fondly recalling his welcome in Kabul a year earlier, Nixon seconded the notion, arguing that far more united the neighbors than divided them. Both men thought opposition to a federation rested solely within the royal family.[75] Eisenhower also found the notion intriguing. Countering arguments about its infeasibility, he opined that the consequences for Pakistan would be "much worse" if Afghanistan "fell into the Soviet orbit." Dulles contended that the kingdom remained indefensible; if Washington gave Moscow a pretext to invade, it would do so. Even if the Soviets exercised forbearance, the benefits would be dubious, as "two weak countries don't become any stronger by being joined together." This last point won Eisenhower's assent.[76]

This concluded the NSC's discussion of a federation, yet the conversation yielded one significant, albeit mysterious consequence. Shortly after Radford and Nixon denounced the royal family, Eisenhower "inquired whether the Director of Central Intelligence could not [redacted]." From December 1954 onward, the Eisenhower administration likely entertained the possibility of Daoud's overthrow. Concurrently, Eisenhower clearly affirmed Afghanistan's strategic value. Acknowledging its vulnerability and conceding "we do not want to pour money down a rathole," he posited that "if the Afghans really wished to be on the side of the free world . . . we might be willing to take a chance with increased assistance." To that, CIA director Allen Dulles cautioned that the "Soviets were inclined to look on Afghanistan much as the United States did on Guatemala" (an interesting analogy) and thus "were in a position to outbid us on any assistance programs."[77]

Eisenhower had affirmed Afghanistan's importance to regional defense. Yet the policy goal of maintaining Kabul's independence faced serious obstacles: Pashtunistan, Soviet responses, and the disheartening record of U.S. aid. Discussion of covert action and the moribund federation idea represented a search for alternatives amid a baffling situation. Failing to locate an ideal solution, the NSC opted for caution. Ludin subsequently received a definitive, disappointing answer to his inquiry about military aid: that Moscow's likely reaction made it impractical. Washington advised Kabul to improve its ties and communications with Pakistan, suggesting that aid would be available for that purpose. Should Afghanistan's relations with its eastern and western neighbors improve, military assistance would become feasible.[78]

Washington hoped that the consolidation of U.S.-Pakistani ties would compel the Afghans toward moderation. Tangible rewards, such as improved trade and communications, would reach the kingdom if it shelved its irredentist agenda. The White House gambled that traditional Afghan Russophobia outweighed the allure of Soviet aid or lingering anger over the Durand Line. Yet it failed to gauge Daoud's political investment in the Pashtunistan issue or to reconcile its strategy with regional developments. Pakistan's November announcement of the "One Unit" plan unbalanced Washington's calculations. To Daoud and his allies, it portended the absorption of the Pashtun lands into a Greater Punjab.[79]

Daoud's government redoubled its Pashtunistan rhetoric in early 1955, while continuing to solicit Soviet assistance. Expecting further trouble, Britain sought a tougher line from its ally: suggesting that Washington condition further aid on a cessation of propaganda and warn that the West would not rescue the Afghans from their ill-conceived Soviet policy.

The State Department was not prepared to go that far, believing that economic assistance might encourage Afghan moderation. The Foreign Office chafed at its ally providing aid without requiring "good behavior" from Kabul.[80]

The March 27 merger of Pakistan's western provinces drew a violent eruption in Kabul. Daoud denounced the act in a radio address. Possibly, he also authorized some form of retaliation. Early on March 30, while Afghan police stood by, a mostly student mob attacked the Pakistani embassy compound, ransacking the premises, and injuring four members of the staff. Similar attacks befell Pakistani consulates in Kandahar and Jalalabad, and a Peshawar crowd retaliated against the local Afghan mission.[81]

Lascelles wrote angrily, "There is no doubt about the full complicity of the Afghan Government in this disgraceful affair." Western missions in Kabul jointly protested the attack, while Pakistan demanded an apology, restitution, and a guarantee of protection for its diplomats. Naim's professed regrets did not impress the irate Pakistani head of mission, M. A. K. Khattak, who had narrowly escaped serious injury during the attack. Suspecting that Indian encouragement lay behind the Pashtunistan campaign, Karachi considered more drastic measures.[82]

Washington sympathized squarely with the aggrieved Pakistanis, but the episode risked a broader crisis. Pakistan might retaliate by invading or inciting restive border Pashtuns. Reports of Daoud meeting with Degtyar, meanwhile, drew speculation about the Soviets intervening in Afghanistan's defense. Pakistan retained a highly effective means of nonviolent retaliation: closing the Afghan border. Pakistani officials also spoke of instigating a change of government in Kabul. Unlike their nephews, the royal uncles, Shah Wali and Shah Mahmud, expressed contrition. Calling Daoud a "madman," Shah Wali reportedly promised Khattak that he would press Zahir for a change of government. The U.S. embassy in Karachi described prevailing sentiment that the "entire present Afghan ruling group must go." Lascelles concurred and hoped that a U.S. aid cutoff would accomplish that end: "Anti-communist forces here would then probably be strong enough to establish a more friendly regime—just as they were in Persia."[83]

Ejecting Daoud from office appealed to U.S., British, and Pakistani officials, to differing degrees, as the border crisis worsened. Lascelles chafed at seeming U.S. hesitancy to press for Daoud's ouster. Ward remained reticent, appearing, in the assessment of a French colleague, "too deeply imbued with the spirit of American philanthropy" to recommend an aid cutoff.

He received instructions to meet with Zahir, stressing U.S. concern over the crisis and growing Soviet influence within the kingdom. If he perceived the opportunity, Ward was also encouraged to suggest Daoud's dismissal. He fulfilled most, but not all, of that agenda in an April 26 meeting with a reticent Zahir, outlining his government's explicit concerns but declining to mention the monarch's cousin by name.[84]

If London and Washington agreed to blame Daoud, the two differed on how best to resolve the crisis. Pakistan and Britain held that the threat of an aid cutoff was required to force Daoud's resignation. The Eisenhower administration regarded that option warily, concerned it would drive Afghanistan into Moscow's arms, as would a Pakistani border closure. The allies believed Washington overrated the risk of a Sovietized Afghanistan; the White House lacked confidence Daoud could be driven from power. Cautioning that confronting Daoud entailed "substantial risks," Ward advised seeking his ouster.[85]

External events and the efforts of aspiring mediators delayed the full emergence of the crisis. For a critical week in April, Naim and his Pakistani counterpart attended the Bandung Asian-African conference in Indonesia. Amid a historic gathering dedicated to fostering postcolonial solidarity, neither government regarded further brinksmanship prudent. External efforts at mediation also exerted a delaying effect. A delegation of officials from five Islamic states, headed by a Saudi prince and including Egyptian minister of state Anwar al-Sadat, labored for weeks to reach an agreement. Talks stalemated over the question of whether the insults rendered in Peshawar merited the same form of apology as those perpetrated in Kabul and Jalalabad. Bedeviled by the impasse, the mediators withdrew in late June.[86]

By that point, Karachi had already acted. Beginning with a halt in visa issuances, an unofficial Pakistani blockade cohered during the spring, reducing cross-border traffic to a trickle. The government in Karachi wielded a broad array of bureaucratic pretexts for constricting Afghan commerce, without drawing the opprobrium of an official blockade. While Afghanistan could retaliate in kind, the kingdom's continued reliance on imported goods, especially gasoline, placed it at a clear disadvantage. Nor was Pakistan in any hurry to resolve the dispute, so long as some chance remained of forcing Daoud's resignation.[87]

Antipathy only partly explains Pakistani obduracy. Continued tumult in the country slowed policymaking in Karachi. One Unit remained far from an accomplished fact, the economy struggled, and the country's governing clique neared a delicate transition. The failing health of Governor-General Ghulam Mohammed, Pakistan's head of state, prompted speculation about the country's future in the event of his death. Daoud, of course, knew this, and Ghulam Mohammed's resignation in August seemingly heartened Afghan observers. His successor, Iskander Mirza, however, held no greater fondness for the Afghan government. Signs of disarray continually emanated from Karachi. Pakistani acceptance of the five-state mediation offer came suddenly and suggested less-than-maximal objectives. Describing one set of instructions as "confusion compounded," a frustrated Khattak remarked that allies and mediators should steer clear of the crisis until his government knew what it wanted.[88]

Pakistan's allies could not remain patient indefinitely, however. Weeks after endorsing Daoud's overthrow, Ward reversed course. Signs of Afghan economic distress were abundant, as industrial projects slowed, and potential fruit exports rotted on the ground. Ward warned that Daoud sought to open trade routes through Soviet territory. Unless Pakistan was certain that it could unseat him, it should compromise. His superiors still supported Daoud's ouster but identified the most important consideration as "preventing Afghans [from] falling under Soviet control." Washington remained wary of pressing Pakistan; if affronted, Karachi might refrain from joining the Baghdad Pact. News of an Afghan-Soviet trade agreement, however, compelled Dulles to approve a message asking the Pakistani government whether the blockade had become "counterproductive."[89]

One consideration forced the issue for Dulles: the Morrison-Knudsen operation in Afghanistan. By August, blockade-induced shortages of explosives, fuel, and parts threatened to halt all work in the Helmand. Ludin suggested that his government would, through force majeure clauses, cancel the contract and ask Czechoslovakia to complete the project. Abdul Malik affected disinterest, telling a U.S. diplomat, "That is your project and if work is stopped, it will be the Export-Import Bank who will lose." Dulles apparently felt similarly. The crisis lent chilling plausibility to Afghan complaints and threats to turn to the communist bloc. Dulles emphasized stranded MKA shipments in a message to the Pakistani government. He described the firm as "one of the chief influences which maintains Afghan connections with the West," predicting that its departure "would create [a] vacuum which the Soviets would be anxious to fill."[90]

Pakistani leaders had expected different counsel from their ally. Halting foreign projects in Afghanistan offered one powerful means of punishing Daoud. Karachi had already resisted West German and Japanese appeals on behalf of other endeavors and doubted the communist bloc could complete any abandoned Western projects. A senior official complained bitterly that Washington valued Morrison-Knudsen's interests over Pakistani security. Nor was the border crisis the sole problem dividing Washington and Karachi. The two governments differed over Pakistani military requirements and the slow pace of arms deliveries. An aspiring, anxious ally, Pakistan sought unequivocal support, especially against Afghan efforts to play the Soviet card.[91]

Yet by August, Pakistan's hard line had become untenable. Daoud remained entrenched. Prolonging the dispute and Afghanistan's economic distress risked forfeiting sympathy gained earlier. Little remained to separate the two disputants. Pakistani demands for the cessation of Pashtunistan propaganda appeared infeasible to friendly observers. Lascelles termed it "a position which cannot be adequately defended." Afghan media had long broadcast Pashtunistan appeals, without inciting anything like the embassy attack. Backed by Ward's embassy and Lascelles, Shah suggested distinguishing between ubiquitous appeals for Pashtun self-determination and those inciting violence. Washington endorsed that distinction in a message to Karachi. Ironing out an unwritten bilateral understanding on the proper limits of Pashtunistan advocacy consumed nearly another month.[92]

Early on September 13, a subdued Naim hoisted the Pakistani flag at Shah's embassy, departing soon after the formalities concluded. A similarly cheerless reciprocal ceremony followed in Peshawar. Until the last minute, semantic and protocol disputes threatened to derail choreographed gestures of regret and reconciliation. Naim attempted to dissuade diplomatic attendance at Afghanistan's ceremonies, which were also closed to the public.[93]

The curious flags crisis had ended. Pakistan could derive some satisfaction from the standoff. Its border closure had inflicted serious harm on the Afghan economy, while Kabul achieved no visible headway in obstructing the One Unit plan. Afghan propaganda diminished noticeably after the mid-September ceremonies, and Naim suggested a bilateral summit to negotiate the questions raised by One Unit. Afghanistan appeared wary of further confrontation.[94]

Yet the distrusted Daoud remained in power, having survived Karachi's blockade. During the crisis, his government had made a persuasive case that

Afghanistan could turn toward the Soviet bloc. Thus, although Washington sided with Karachi, it did not do so unconditionally. Earlier discussions of removing Daoud were followed by polite, insistent efforts to nudge Pakistan toward the negotiating table. Reassuring an ally at the expense of the Sovietization of Afghanistan would have represented a Pyrrhic victory to the White House. All the while, the crisis had pushed Kabul closer to Moscow, and its conclusion fundamentally left the paradox of the northern tier unresolved, while the Soviet presence in the kingdom grew ominously.

After the Flag-Raising, 1955–1956

Indeed, the sole beneficiaries of the border crisis had been the communist bloc. Its onset had represented a mixed blessing to them. Acrimony with Pakistan precluded Afghanistan's enlistment into the Western camp but also heightened the likelihood of Washington and Karachi pursuing Daoud's overthrow—and bloc diplomats detected Western efforts to unseat the Afghan leader.[95] Ironically, the communists also relied on Pakistani transit. Northern roads were no smoother than others in Afghanistan, and the Amu Darya River lacked modern freighters or port facilities. An Afghan-Soviet transit agreement in June only somewhat alleviated the kingdom's isolation. It could not aid southern fruit growers, who lost much of their crop to spoilage. Nevertheless, Soviet goods attained greater visibility. Fuel products reached the northern cities. In one ironic development, a West German hydroelectric project at Sarobi, threatened by a shortage of Pakistani cement, was rescued by shipments from Tashkent. Perhaps mischievously, Abdul Malik offered Soviet fuel and cement to MKA.[96]

Tenuous links forged in crisis offered Afghanistan a potential lifeline in future clashes with Pakistan. Within weeks, the post-closure lull dissipated. Daoud sought a summit with Mirza but also requested a postponement of the scheduled October 14 implementation of One Unit. The Pakistani authorities would brook no further delay. Daoud angrily retracted the offer and withdrew his representative in Karachi; Pakistan reciprocated, calling the long-suffering Shah home. Daoud, meanwhile, approved a visit by a Czechoslovak military mission to discuss future arms purchases. Western diplomats in Kabul received official word that Bulganin had been invited to visit; subsequent radio announcements noted that Khrushchev would accompany him.[97]

"Intensification of Soviet effort in [Afghanistan] appears to have begun," Ward wrote in late October. His State Department colleagues agreed. Describing the breadth of communist projects, one analyst perceived "the most comprehensive Soviet program of direct economic development aid in the free world." This observation preceded Khrushchev's trip by several months. Grandiose programs in India, Egypt, and Indonesia subsequently overshadowed the Afghan efforts in both scope and prominence. Yet in autumn 1955, Soviet programs within the kingdom appeared both novel and suggestive of the future course of Moscow's policy in the postcolonial world.[98]

No one believed this more than Ward and his subordinates. The ambassador enjoyed only intermittent contact with the Afghan government and reportedly was not on speaking terms with Daoud. Ward increasingly suspected he had been marooned in Kabul. Culturally, he was ill at ease. Invited to King Zahir's forty-second birthday festivities in October, Ward pointedly excused himself from the main spectacle, a *buzkashi* match, explaining to the monarch that he could not abide cruelty to animals.[99] "[He] makes little secret of the fact that he is completely disillusioned with the Afghans and is only filling in time until his retirement next March," reported Lascelles. Yet mounting signs of communist influence drove Ward and his embassy to appeal for an official response commensurate to the rising Soviet threat.[100]

In mid-October, Ward and his deputy, Leon Poullada, articulated Afghanistan's place in Soviet foreign policy and its centrality within a changing Cold War. Even as Moscow turned "a smiling countenance" westward, engaging in summitry at Geneva, it had unleashed an "aggressive . . . campaign aimed at economic penetration" of the Middle East and South Asia. Ward and Poullada cited Soviet assistance for Egypt's Aswan High Dam and India's Bhilai steel mill, adding that "the storm of Soviet economic activity which now looms so large . . . first appeared as a small cloud nearly two years ago in Afghanistan." Moscow regarded Afghanistan as the "geographic gateway to the area they wish to disrupt." Simultaneously, Afghanistan remained the "necessary key stone to any free world defensive arc bridging the Middle East and South Asia." By this account, it had moved from the Cold War's periphery toward its core, standing squarely along the main line of Soviet advance.[101]

Embassies, especially remote ones, regularly fret that their host country is being overlooked. Ward and Poullada's analysis might merely offer a striking example of a diplomatic mission appealing for attention. Yet the Eisenhower administration was inclined to agree. In Washington, Ambassador Ludin delivered a royal letter to Eisenhower protesting One Unit and soliciting U.S. mediation. Zahir's choice to call another *loya jirga* heightened the stakes of the exchange. As tensions in the borderlands worsened, Pakistan expected the assembly to endorse a return to hostilities. The Afghan authorities advised foreign firms to employ Soviet ports and rail for future shipments to the kingdom. Hoping to exert some moderating influence on the *loya jirga*, Ward sought and obtained a presidential message to Zahir. Daoud read it aloud to the assembled delegates.[102]

The prime minister emerged from the assembly triumphant and defiant. The gathering endorsed Daoud's appeal for Pashtun self-determination, called for a plebiscite in the Pakistani tribal lands, and supported the government's program of strengthening the Afghan military. The last provision endorsed Daoud's ongoing negotiations with Czechoslovakia. Thus strengthened, Daoud dismissed his defense minister, Mohammed Arif, who had reportedly opposed purchasing arms from the communist bloc.[103]

Washington took immediate notice. When the NSC met on December 1, CIA director Allen Dulles described the "dangerous situation in Afghanistan." Kabul insisted upon the shipment of goods through Soviet ports, imposing significant difficulties on MKA. Citing Arif's dismissal, Dulles offered an ominous and potent comparison: "the situation in Afghanistan was now very reminiscent of that which had prevailed in Iran not so long ago." Like Mossadegh, Daoud was "playing the Soviet game." Perhaps two dozen subsequent lines of text, still redacted decades later, suggest that the group subsequently considered covert action against Daoud.[104]

If so, days before Khrushchev's visit, Ward's embassy offered a frank, dispiriting prognosis for further efforts against Daoud. Since 1953, it wrote, "This Mission, Embassy Karachi and Department have indulged in [a] great deal [of] wishful thinking" about engineering his overthrow. Neither Zahir nor his uncles offered any meaningful opposition, whereas Daoud now enjoyed a "position of unprecedented strength." Afghanistan lacked a free press or opposition party, and Arif's dismissal afforded Daoud "virtual control" of the army. Predicating future policies on Daoud's susceptibility to a coup was "highly unrealistic." Nothing short of an "all-out campaign" would suffice and even that risked pushing Afghanistan toward Moscow. A case might be made for cutting U.S. losses. Nonetheless, the embassy wrote, revealing its own preferences, abandonment would undermine the northern tier, deal a "severe blow" to U.S. prestige, and "have severe repercussions" in the next presidential election.[105]

Whether Adlai Stevenson could have reaped electoral hay in 1956 by asking "Who lost Afghanistan?" is questionable. Nonetheless, after Khrushchev's dramatic visit, the Eisenhower administration resolved to prevent the kingdom's disappearance into the bloc. The previously established objective of achieving regional security provides a sufficient explanation for the choice. From late 1955 into the following year, the intricate policy-making apparatus of the Eisenhower administration sought to resolve a problem largely of its own inadvertent creation.

That Eisenhower and his aides attached value to Afghanistan is noteworthy, but not the sole point. Significantly, Afghanistan presented distinct and baffling problems to the administration. Its unusual circumstances forced Eisenhower and his aides to depart from principle and to contemplate the limits of their power, leading them toward solutions in which they lacked confidence, which strained already difficult relations with Pakistan.

Daoud's renewed postcrisis agitation for Pashtunistan and growing reliance on the Soviet Union fostered anger in Karachi. Western diplomats discerned a renewed Pakistani desire to confront Afghanistan, bolstered by the belief that they had compromised too soon the previous summer. Such recriminations fostered doubts in the Western governments that had urged negotiation. So did U.S. hesitancy toward the project of overthrowing Daoud. Moscow, meanwhile, appeared intent on punishing Pakistan by aiding its recalcitrant neighbor. Washington's apparent susceptibility to Afghan threats to turn to the Soviet Union led Pakistanis to question the benefits of alignment. Prime Minister Chaudhury Mohammed Ali chastised the Eisenhower administration for appearing to chase after "neutralists or worse-than-neutralists" like Afghanistan, citing the *loya jirga* message. This informed the world that "blackmail paid, and faithfulness did not pay." The U.S. ambassador in Karachi, Horace Hildreth, urged a tougher line toward Kabul. Failing to "call Daoud's bluff," he argued, would make it "impossible to work cooperatively" with the Pakistani government.[106]

These should have been potent arguments. Pakistan's September accession into the Baghdad Pact followed its earlier enlistment into the South East Asia Treaty Organization. Thus, Karachi could make an unusually compelling case in Washington. Its leadership enjoyed warm interpersonal relationships with their U.S. counterparts, nurtured through persistent early contacts, and subtly bolstered by shared cultural tenets. Lastly, Karachi remained dissatisfied with

Washington's military aid proposals. Afghanistan policy should have been one area for Eisenhower and Dulles to win sorely needed credit.[107]

Instead, when Dulles visited Karachi the following March, he rebuffed Pakistani calls to confront Afghanistan. Pakistani policy, he informed Mohammed Ali, would only ensure a "bad result." Rather than resigning himself to a Sovietized Afghanistan, Dulles declared that he "wanted a program to save Afghanistan from Soviet control." When Mohammed Ali implied that aiding Afghanistan rewarded blackmail, Dulles rejoined that "under certain circumstances" such aid made sense, invoking U.S. support of Yugoslavia. "Tell us what is wrong with the Pakistani position, and we will modify it," Mohammed Ali finally conceded.[108]

John Foster Dulles was never the inflexible zealot of popular lore. Close study of his career reveals a consistent pragmatism and a belief that any viable international system had to accommodate change. Nevertheless, he regarded the Cold War as a moral struggle and criticized states that eschewed alignment or exploited the conflict by drawing competing offers from the rival blocs. After his return from the subcontinent, he endorsed a punitive course against Egyptian president Gamal Abdel Nasser to demonstrate that countries could not "play both sides" in the Cold War. Nasser had, of course, also purchased arms from Czechoslovakia.[109]

That Dulles felt no similar inclination toward Daoud is striking. It attests to the dearth of choices available to the administration and the kingdom's continued, inescapable importance to the nascent regional defense system. A January 1956 intelligence analysis, NIE 53–56, described Daoud's hold on power as secure, especially after the *loya jirga* and Arif's dismissal. Efforts to unseat him risked some form of Soviet intervention. An aid cutoff hazarded pushing Afghanistan toward the bloc. Conversely, sustained U.S. aid could validate Daoud's continued course of playing the superpowers against each other. A November 1955 NSC report reached similar conclusions. Neither analysis posited an immediate Soviet threat to Afghanistan; both emphasized the intermediate risks posed by Moscow's growing economic influence after the border crisis.[110]

Such observations tended to eliminate old policy options, rather than reveal new ones. While portions of its transcript remain redacted, extant evidence suggests that the NSC's last substantive discussion of Afghanistan in 1956 shelved the idea of confronting or overthrowing Daoud. When the council met on May 17, Special Assistant Robert Anderson observed that "there were very severe limitations on the capability of the United States to counter Soviet maneuvers in Afghanistan." Within the group, Radford remained the most alarmist. Positing that the chances of keeping Afghanistan "out of the Soviet orbit" were less than even, he (following a redacted sentence) remarked that Daoud's elimination "from the scene . . . would probably change" the situation entirely. The recommendation does not appear to have been seconded. Dulles noted divided opinion on his recent Karachi trip; even the hawkish Mirza was willing to let the pursuit of a coup await an upcoming meeting with Daoud.[111]

The views of the other Dulles brother remain partially concealed yet can be posited from other documents, especially NIE 53–56. No available evidence suggests that the CIA had identified any viable opposition to Daoud. Nor had Ward's embassy, which deemed pursuing a coup a dangerous, futile act. Afghanistan in 1956 did not resemble 1953 Iran. Its military lacked independence, Daoud's regime monitored opponents closely, and Zahir showed no apparent inclination to follow the Shah's example.[112]

Instead, Eisenhower remarked that "if there was one sentiment universally abroad in the world today, it was the sentiment of nationalism." Thus, "the only course of action" available would be "to make clear to the Afghans that they will lose their national identity if they continue to go along with the plans of the Soviet Union." Nationalism and Islam constituted "the only real influences in Afghanistan on which we could base our hopes." The United States "could certainly not compete" against Moscow in the kingdom's "economic sphere."[113]

Striking a balance, Eisenhower invested his hopes in Afghan nationalism. In its conclusions, the NSC reiterated the need to promote ties between Afghanistan and Pakistan but did not predicate aid to the kingdom on any easing of tensions—as Pakistan clearly desired. New conclusions emerged, as the council amended its earlier policy statement for South Asia, NSC 5409. Paragraph 59—termed a "pious hope" by Allen Dulles—endorsed efforts to "discredit and make difficult increased Soviet activities in Afghanistan" while encouraging Afghan resistance to further penetration. In paragraph 56-A, a new guiding statement for U.S. aid emerged:

> Do not undertake an economic aid program aimed at matching in size and scope the credit and aid activities of the Soviet Union, but give assistance for a limited number of projects which will provide immediately visible evidence of continued U.S. friendship for and interest in Afghanistan.[114]

Paragraph 56-A articulated U.S. policy toward Afghanistan from 1956, past the fall of the monarchy in 1973, until the violent overthrow of Daoud's republic in April 1978. While they could not compete with Moscow, offer for offer, Eisenhower and his five immediate successors each sought to maintain the independence of the Afghan state. They thereby committed themselves to an extensive, evolving array of political, economic, and cultural programs within Afghanistan, with profound local and regional implications.

Strategy, Fear, and Hope

Undoubtedly the Eisenhower administration inherited a difficult situation in Afghanistan. Soviet suspicions had been triggered, critical, probably irreversible mistakes had been committed in the Helmand Valley, and Shah Mahmud's friendly but fractious government had little time remaining. Eisenhower might understandably have refrained from making further commitments—especially in the face of renewed Pashtunistan agitation under Daoud and complaints from Karachi. Yet he did not. His administration threw good money after what it believed to be bad, advancing the second Eximbank loan, the emergency wheat loan, and repeated efforts to prod Afghanistan and Pakistan toward compromise. While Washington sided with Karachi during the border crisis, its display of solidarity fell far short of Pakistani expectations. U.S. calls for restraint and negotiation added yet another irritant to a troubled alliance.

Global strategy partly suggested this course of action. Adopting the northern tier concept pushed Eisenhower to, as a second-order consequence, consider Afghanistan. Better to oppose a Soviet offensive amid the peaks of the Hindu Kush than along the Durand Line. Yet Eisenhower expressly embraced the notion that if the Afghans wanted to resist Soviet expansion, as a people deserving of freedom they should be assisted in doing so. Ultimately, he chose to bank on Afghan nationalism and its unassailable exponent, Daoud.

This decision afforded de facto validation to Daoud. Over two years, he had solidified his power, despite periodic rumors of his impending dismissal and nebulous foreign efforts to instigate his overthrow. He had confidently forged a new diplomatic path for the kingdom and strengthened his authority while inflaming tensions with his neighbor. Daoud successfully exploited the Cold War and usefully amplified U.S. anxieties about his country's direction. Always ambitious, he exuded a greater confidence after the first border crisis.

Shared alarmism and stunted analyses benefited Daoud above all. Ward and his deputies described the Soviet program in Afghanistan in ways calculated to galvanize attention. Incontestably, Ward engaged in alarmism—but then so did the communists. While Ward and his superiors endeavored to prevent Afghanistan's absorption into the Soviet bloc, his adversaries raced to halt Kabul's conscription in the anticommunist crusade. Each applied the metaphor of the Trojan Horse to the actions of the other. Missing, however, was meaningful dialogue over the minimum, reconcilable objectives each side sought within the kingdom. While the two blocs could negotiate productively elsewhere, they did not do so in Kabul. In the ambiguous period following Stalin's death, the hypothesis of a southward Soviet offensive went largely unchallenged, influencing the conversation within Eisenhower's NSC. Nor did the communists consider the difficulties Washington would face if it forced Afghanistan into alignment with its two neighbors.

Absent from Washington's deliberations—conducted by an administration that attached paramount importance to the development and refinement of strategy—was any real confidence in forestalling further Soviet progress in Afghanistan. Aid merely constituted the least worst option available, and it still held the drawback of angering Pakistan. Nor did the aid program have any guarantee of success, especially given the limitations placed by paragraph 56-A. Even as it dared not bid too much for the kingdom, the Eisenhower administration inevitably worried that it was not bidding enough. Nevertheless, the decision had been made. Eisenhower chose a course that some of his successors would recognize: to venture what he could in Afghanistan and hope for the best.

CHAPTER 5

Anxious Coexistence

The Aid Contest, 1956–1959

In places, the road from Baharak to Eshkashim was relatively straight. Other stretches severely tested the International Travelall truck. An unforgiving outcropping at one switchback knocked a side mirror off the vehicle. All along, the truck ascended into the mountains of northeast Afghanistan, reaching an estimated 9,380 feet above sea level. Although the August weather was bitterly cold, little snow lay on the ground. The driver, U.S. ambassador Henry Byroade, experienced a distinct thrill as the Travelall neared its destination. The Amu Darya River entered sight. Beyond it lay a rare glimpse of the Soviet Union. Advancing beyond Eshkashim the next day, Byroade could clearly view Soviet soldiers patrolling on the far side of the river.[1]

Byroade's purpose was not reconnaissance. Newly arrived in Kabul in March 1959, he had received a much-anticipated shipment: a collection of big-game trophies, accumulated during his previous posting in South Africa. These seemingly fascinated Afghan foreign minister Mohammed Naim Khan, an old acquaintance. After prying the story behind each mounted head out of Byroade, Naim suggested that his guest hunt the rare Marco Polo sheep: a species renowned for its long horns, whose range is limited to the high-altitude regions of Central Asia. Enthused, Byroade enlisted fellow sportsmen in the Kabul embassy, only to face an eleventh-hour hurdle. Naim's ministry informed him that, while he was welcome to visit the royal preserve, his subordinates could not. Crestfallen, Byroade pondered canceling the trip, which promised to be exceptionally arduous, but the allure of another trophy ultimately proved irresistible.[2]

Naim's ministry probably hoped to appear hospitable without actually hosting an American diplomat in the geopolitically sensitive Wakhan Corridor: the narrow finger of Afghan territory between Pakistan and Soviet Tajikistan. Failing to deflect Byroade, his hosts instead received him as near royalty. Along his arduous ascent and comparably slow descent, he received an unending stream of meals and gifts from local officials. Other challenges presented themselves. After Eshkashim, the Travelall's engine took an unplanned plunge into an Afghan stream of surprising depth, crippling it for the rest of the trip. Having ascended another 5,000 feet by horse, Byroade and his Afghan companions grappled with severe altitude sickness, an unresolved language barrier, and faltering marksmanship. Although Byroade shot two sheep, neither trophy met his exacting criteria. Such difficulties might have frustrated him, but Byroade's account of the expedition captures a sense of wonderment at his surroundings and gratitude toward his Afghan guides and hosts. "In the Pamirs, God is very close and very good—very good indeed," he wrote.[3]

Byroade's exuberance at his extraordinary, Quixotic journey emerges clearly from his account. So does his distance from the Afghans around him. The nature of rural Afghan life remained elusive. He visited villages but saw few of their inhabitants, and no women or children. "Food comes," he wrote, "but I don't know from where." Moved by local hospitality, he understandably regarded the Afghans as "the kindest people in the world." Yet, even far from Kabul, and as his counterparts elsewhere in Asia endeavored to measure popular opinion, Byroade could only interact with the Afghan elite and those few others it brought into his proximity. The kingdom presented a friendly face while evading deeper scrutiny. Savvy to Byroade's passions—typical among mid-century U.S. diplomats—Naim expertly employed his country's assets, in the service of furthering an ongoing superpower aid contest.[4]

Like his predecessor, Sheldon Mills, Byroade led the U.S. effort to contest Afghanistan. Beholding an unremitting Soviet economic and political campaign within the kingdom, and discarding notions of overthrowing the Afghan government, Washington initiated its own aid offensive. Diplomats and aid personnel attempted to wring a success story out of the Helmand Valley. Afghanistan received regular donations of surplus wheat. Kabul's international fairs drew competing exhibitions from the United States and its communist adversaries. Opening a new front, Americans sought new successes in the field of aviation.

Initial outcomes were promising. While second-wave U.S. aid programs enjoyed mixed results, often impeded by bureaucratic disunity, transportation difficulties, and insufficient funding, Afghanistan showed little sign of vanishing into the bloc. Bolstered by recent successes, Prime Minister Mohammed Daoud Khan successfully pivoted to engage Washington's envoys, expressing appreciation for aid and signaling that he understood the danger from the north. The dire predictions heard during President Dwight D. Eisenhower's first term went unfulfilled. Most hearteningly, encouraged by Washington, a fragile détente developed between the kingdom and Pakistan.

Afghanistan, however, retained its capacity to surprise, while its region remained volatile. Moscow answered the aid offensive in kind, as U.S. initiatives faltered. Pursuing an ambitious development agenda, Kabul labored to keep its patrons engaged, continually cultivating counterbids, and testing the outer limits of superpower largesse. An October 1958 coup d'état in Karachi dashed any prospects for rapprochement across the Durand Line. Problems elsewhere—the Suez invasion, the Iraqi revolution, and the nuclear arms race—affirmed Afghanistan's strategic value within the Cold War. Armed by the Soviet Union, distrusted by its other neighbors, the kingdom once again represented a source of anxiety in Western capitals as the decade concluded.

An "Economic Korea": The Aid Contest, 1956–1957

Just after the 1955 border crisis, the State Department and International Cooperation Administration (ICA) pondered the future of the aid program in Afghanistan, drawing extensive counsel from the Kabul embassy. As Ambassador Angus Ward became increasingly disengaged from his work, his deputies Armin Meyer and Leon Poullada offered their own assessments. The contours of a revitalized U.S. aid program cohered during this transitional phase—after the Wards and their cats departed for retirement in Spain—continuing under his energetic successor, Sheldon Mills. Under Mills's leadership, the U.S. mission approached the Afghan Cold War with renewed vigor, on an array of fronts, ranging from rural development to aviation to cultural diplomacy.

Poullada discerned two overarching challenges: ongoing Soviet economic penetration and the dismal record of the Helmand Valley project.

Moscow's efforts appeared both quantitatively and qualitatively superior to Washington's. "The Soviets have trained their heavy economic artillery on Afghanistan," he lamented, and his government had effectively "replied with technical advice on how to construct a pop-gun." Even before Khrushchev's $100 million credit, the Soviets had judiciously chosen conspicuous projects: the streets of Kabul, a bread factory, and oil tanks. If U.S. aid could not compete quantitatively, it should tangibly illustrate the benefits of association with the West while improving Afghanistan's commercial and political relations with its noncommunist neighbors. Poullada called for a focus on "small, highly visible short-range impact projects."[5] Afghanistan offered no shortage of potential development projects, yet two loomed prominently: the Helmand Valley and aviation. Acknowledging the Helmand project's troubled history, Poullada nonetheless considered it linked inextricably to the U.S. position in the country. Aviation development was also not a new issue, but Soviet advances and the border crisis lent it heightened importance.

Such advocacy hardly came free from reservations. Indeed, it is remarkable that the ensuing U.S. aid program to the kingdom happened at all, given the concerns felt in both Washington and the Kabul embassy. Shortly after Khrushchev's departure, a Soviet economic delegation arrived to discuss specific projects. The Soviets agreed to, among other endeavors, pave a road through the Salang Pass, linking Kabul to the north, renovate the capital's airport, and construct a new military airfield at Bagram. The Soviet lead seemed unassailable, raising the question whether further aid would, in Poullada's words, merely improve a house already mortgaged to Moscow. The embassy expressed comparable concern over the problem of "blackmail": the prospect of Kabul pitting U.S. and Soviet bids against each other. Afghan threats to seek assistance from Moscow were a wearisome feature of the bilateral relationship, and U.S. officials swore not to allow themselves to be so goaded.[6]

Kabul's economic agenda posed further cause for concern in Washington. Khrushchev's loan emboldened Daoud and his finance minister, Abdul Malik, to accelerate their development program. Their inaugural Five-Year Plan, described by Malik in March 1956, struck Poullada as "over-ambitious" and "beyond Afghan capabilities." Afghan plans, as assessed by Maxwell Fry, tended to be lists of projects rather than integrated economic policy statements. The 1956 document pledged further irrigation projects, the establishment of an aviation system including a national airline and airport construction, and the improvement of the national road network. It hinged upon optimistic assessments of foreign trade, internal revenue collection, and donor assistance. Poullada feared that the Soviets had encouraged its scope in an effort to prod the kingdom toward bankruptcy.[7]

Nevertheless, the administration reached consensus on the necessity of a renewed aid commitment. Eisenhower and Secretary of State John Foster Dulles believed the cost of conceding the kingdom to be prohibitive. To the embassy, Afghanistan's prominence within the Soviet aid offensive argued for a countereffort. The kingdom had received $120 million of an estimated $350 to $400 million in Soviet aid to noncommunist states. It represented a "key battleground," where Moscow hoped to demonstrate, to a far wider audience, the benefits of cooperation. In a telling and effective metaphor, the embassy termed the emerging contest an economic equivalent to the Korean War, adding, "As in Korea, we should not expect to rout [the] Soviets and gain total victory." Rather, the best possible outcome would be holding Moscow to a "standstill," thus frustrating Soviet plans to use Afghanistan as a "stepping-stone to [the] rest of Asia."[8]

Despite the peaceful nature of the contest, military metaphors dominated discussion of Afghanistan. They also suggested a solution: the maintenance of a "beachhead" within the landlocked kingdom. As in Korea, that beachhead lay in the south: in the Helmand Valley and nearby Kandahar. Redeeming the Helmand project promised not only to salvage Washington's reputation but also to establish a redoubt in a country otherwise at risk of Sovietization.[9] Yet the goal of forestalling Soviet advances could not coexist easily with the imperative of avoiding Afghan "blackmail." Even as it sought to fulfill past promises in the Helmand, the U.S. mission found itself leaping into other arenas, to decidedly mixed effect.

The Helmand Valley project, itself, remained a source of profound frustration. Dulles described it as "kind of a white elephant on our hands."[10] National prestige appeared inextricably committed, but bureaucratic actors had also embraced it. The Eximbank, although averse to extending further loans, worried about its reputation and the prospect of Afghan default, and therefore strongly endorsed additional aid to the project. Diplomats in the Kabul embassy, while sometimes frustrated with Morrison-Knudsen Afghanistan (MKA), argued similarly. There could be no walking away.[11]

Scant cause for optimism existed in the valley. Drainage problems persisted, especially at the vexed Nad-i-Ali settlement. Morrison-Knudsen president Harry Morrison estimated that 40 percent of the settlers had abandoned their farms and faulted the remainder for overusing water and failing to adopt a crop rotation schedule.[12] Administrative problems continued on the Afghan end, particularly on maintenance-related questions. A December 1955 canal break flooded hundreds of acres. Absent regular maintenance, the canal system might collapse, discrediting the entire project.[13]

Proper maintenance required close collaboration with the local authorities, but Afghan discontentment had become unavoidable. Daoud and Naim seemingly regarded the project as an unwelcome inheritance from their uncles. Naim lamented the kingdom's mounting debt burden and the meager results yielded to date. Tensions between Kabul and MKA rose during 1955, as the former withheld payments and demanded that MKA halt shipments through Pakistan.[14] Complicating matters further, the project continued to draw protests from Iran. Successive governments in Tehran had rejected the water allocation scheme suggested by the international commission earlier in the decade. Afghans, meanwhile, expressed interest in constructing dams downriver: an initiative likely to exacerbate the dispute. Lastly, the project, regarded as essential to U.S. objectives in Afghanistan, was one that few Afghans had ever personally encountered. Connected to the capital by what the U.S. embassy believed to be "some of the worst roads in the world," the Helmand project drew at best sporadic attention from Kabul officials. Its failures were excruciatingly well known; even if they occurred, successes risked remaining obscure.[15]

Diplomats, bankers, and aid officials each perceived the crisis. Poullada described an "atmosphere of defeatism and pessimism." The agencies in Washington called for a "fresh assessment" by experts to address immediate problems and chart a path forward. Afghan authorities welcomed the news. The ICA recommended the Tudor Engineering Company, a San Francisco–based consulting firm. Unknown to the Afghans, Tudor had a significant preexisting business relationship with Morrison-Knudsen and was unlikely to criticize the firm sharply. The consultants received the impossible charge of placing the project on a "sound operating basis" with a "minimum" additional expenditure of U.S. funds. The Tudor mission publicly signaled a broader U.S. commitment to development within Afghanistan, to be affirmed in other fields.[16]

U.S. aviation assistance exemplified the new approach. Afghan enthusiasm for aviation development was long-standing, yet had been stymied by war, Soviet scrutiny, and a lack of investment. From 1945 onward, successive Afghan governments sought flights by international carriers and improved aerial communications within the kingdom, including the development of regional airports. Indian-American Airlines (Indamer)—which was U.S.-owned but flagged in India—operated charter flights within Afghanistan. It conveyed cargo to neighboring countries and Afghan pilgrims on the annual Hajj but had a somewhat unsavory reputation, colored by rumors of black-market activities. Trans-Ocean, a U.S.-based carrier, engaged in two years of inconclusive negotiations with the Afghan authorities, to the latter's considerable frustration.[17]

Cold War competition greatly enhanced the kingdom's leverage, and the border crisis highlighted the importance of aerial communications. Kabul requested U.S. assistance in establishing a civil aviation authority in December 1954, as well as help in founding a domestic Afghan airline, Ariana, to be operated by Indamer. Ariana received its charter in January 1955, according Indamer control over 49 percent of its shares. Daoud also sought funding toward the construction of a major airport in Kandahar. Ward's embassy questioned the need for a Kandahar airport without assurances of sufficient demand or institutional support. Still, aviation appeared to be Daoud's "pet project," and he seemed determined to forge ahead, regardless. He asked MKA to construct an airport in Kandahar in June 1955. Daoud's enthusiasm was shared by Waclaw Makowski, a Polish émigré detailed by the International Civil Aviation Organization (ICAO) to advise the Afghan government.[18]

U.S. diplomats in Kabul only faintly endorsed the aviation project, uncertain of its economic utility. The best case for it appeared to be "preemptive": if Washington did not enter the field, Moscow surely would. Reports of a Soviet mission visiting Kandahar in February added to the sense of urgency. Some arguments supported a Kandahar airport. Kandahar's location and favorable climate potentially recommended it as a way station on flights between Kabul and other cities. Nevertheless, Washington hoped that the Kabul airport might still also be on the table and negotiated on that basis. The embassy received authorization to offer $10 million, half-loan and half-grant, toward the aviation project. Kabul, however, was spoken for, and Washington had to make do with Kandahar and perhaps some of the regional airports. Daoud hinted to Ambassador Sheldon Mills that some facets of the capital airport, such as navigational and communications facilities, could still be awarded to the United States.[19]

Washington enjoyed greater success in establishing an Afghan airline. As historian Jenifer Van Vleck writes, Pan American World Airways (Pan Am) already boasted considerable collaborative experience with Washington in developing national airlines. As Ariana's operating partner, it would be vastly preferable to Indamer, developing the carrier along U.S. lines. Washington and the Kabul embassy hastened not only to preclude Soviet encroachment but also to reap the publicity benefits of transporting summer pilgrims to Saudi Arabia.[20]

Serious negotiations began congenially in late April. Competing offers and the familiar prospect of "blackmail" soon surfaced, however. Abdul Hai Aziz, the former Watan Party dissident who headed the Afghan delegation, reported that the Soviets appeared interested in equipping and operating Ariana. More concretely, the Dutch airline KLM, uninterested in aviation development, also offered to buy Indamer's shares. Alarmed, Mills asked to raise the U.S. offer to $15 million, two-thirds of which would be a grant. Grumbling that it had not intended to "bargain with Soviets for Afghan favor," the ICA assented. Memoranda in Washington persuasively invoked paragraph 56-A of NSC 5409, deeming the project a suitably visible demonstration of U.S. friendship. Thus bolstered, U.S. negotiators reached an agreement with Kabul on June 27, and a Pan Am–leased aircraft subsequently conveyed thousands of Afghans on the annual Hajj.[21]

At this time, a predicament peculiar to Afghanistan began to surface. The United States had retained its southern beachhead but failed to dislodge the Soviets from Kabul's airport. Afghan aviation could not be partitioned, à la Korea. Ariana and its Pan Am advisors would make extensive use of that airport and other Soviet-built facilities. In other fields, U.S. personnel could easily encounter their Soviet counterparts—or perhaps even be asked to assist Soviet-funded projects. Among the economic battlegrounds of the Third World, this situation was atypical. Afghanistan, however, offered a narrow field of competition, and Daoud's government did not mind the adversaries working in awkward proximity if Soviet hackles were not raised. Anticipating this difficulty, the Kabul embassy sought to craft a "coexistence policy" that neither ceded the field to communist technicians nor rewarded Afghan opportunism.[22]

Aviation forced the coexistence issue, as the scramble for contracts had produced overlapping claims. While the Soviets bid successfully for the Kabul airport, the U.S. aviation agreement covered communications and navigational equipment across Afghanistan. The Soviet Union, meanwhile, remained outside of the ICAO, raising the question whether its airport design would meet international specifications. Kabul's climate and difficult location—the city is ringed by mountains—presented additional challenges.

Without Aziz and the ICAO advisor, Makowski, this combination of technical and political problems might have stymied the aviation project. A decorated veteran and a pioneering pilot in peacetime, Makowski pursued the project with singular determination. "You've got to speak to people," he counseled a U.S. diplomat.[23] With Afghan assistance, Makowski convened an extraordinary mid-August meeting. Two days of entirely technical dialogue between Soviet, U.S., and Afghan officials, tirelessly mediated and translated by Makowski, resolved the outstanding issues. The Soviets would build the airport to ICAO standards; the Americans would provide communication and navigational equipment. The U.S. aviation representative described the atmosphere as one of "extreme cordiality." ICA director Robert Snyder observed that the conversation was probably the first of its kind. Aziz closed the meeting observing that, having brought "our great friends together . . . we hope that they can also become friends."[24]

Perhaps he meant it, but Aziz's government clearly benefited from peaceful U.S.-Soviet competition. Kabul had avidly, profitably stoked the aviation contest, allowing neither superpower to attain predominance. The aviation negotiations also attested to a sea change in the Kabul embassy's relationship with Daoud's government. The newly arrived Mills sought close contacts with Afghan society, and Kabul officials eagerly reciprocated. "Unlike Ward, he has tried to befriend Afghans without regard to rank," the Czechoslovak minister wrote, "and he has had ample success thus far." Genial, attentive, and energetic, Mills proved a welcome replacement for the autocratic, aloof Ward. For his part, a more confident, outgoing Daoud sought a new relationship with the post-Ward embassy, emphatically declaring his distaste for communism and his determination to maintain Afghan independence. His appointment of the familiar Aziz to head the kingdom's aviation authority provided further encouragement.[25]

Even as U.S. and Soviet officials reached détente in the aviation field, the two prepared for another major contest. Afghanistan's annual independence celebration, Jeshyn, loomed in late August, and its accompanying trade fair offered Washington an ideal venue to advertise the American way of life. The Afghan government otherwise frowned upon the dissemination of propaganda. In February, Deputy Foreign Minister Mohammed Hashim Maiwandwal threatened to close the U.S. embassy's information section after it had distributed anticommunist literature.[26] In a subsequent episode, the Kabul authorities obliquely rebuffed a request by the U.S. mission to publish a nonpolitical cultural newsletter.[27]

Figure 5.1 Ambassador Mills (right) surveys the unfinished geodesic dome, August 1956
Source: United States National Archives, College Park, Record Group 286

Jeshyn, however, afforded a unique opportunity to practice public diplomacy. The border crisis had stymied the previous year's fair, but Moscow, Beijing, and Prague clearly planned extensive exhibitions for 1956. Despite early warnings, the U.S. exhibition only barely came together. Planner Jack Masey, who later devised the famous U.S. pavilion at the 1959 Moscow Exposition, recalled that it was pieced together from items

Figure 5.2 King Zahir and Daoud tour the U.S. Jeshyn exhibition, August 1956
Source: United States National Archives, College Park, Record Group 286

already used at other Asian trade fairs. The curious assemblage included a Lionel train set, Polaroid cameras, television sets, and (presumably advancing the cause of agriculture) mechanical livestock: a talking cow and chicken. The exhibition's most striking element was the structure housing it: an early geodesic dome created by designer R. Buckminster Fuller.[28] A shipping crisis erupted in August after summer floods severed connections to Karachi. As an emergency measure, Ariana airlifted the cow and chicken into Kabul. On the eve of Jeshyn, the U.S. pavilion space remained empty, until the dome—compact, lightweight, and itself flown into Kabul—took shape over forty-eight frenetic hours, as incredulous spectators looked on.[29]

Laudably, the exhibition opened on schedule. Unfortunately, Herculean feats of shipping and assembly could not remedy its core problems. As Mills reflected, the pavilion largely featured gadgetry, not products of U.S. industry. The dome itself and nighttime outdoor cinematic events captivated audiences, but Afghans found the daytime exhibition underwhelming, even frivolous. Beside ambitious, well-designed communist pavilions, the U.S. exhibition appeared a "puny effort." "Our great American allies have been beaten hollow," lamented a Pakistani diplomat. Afghan fairgoers ranked the exhibition fourth, well behind the Chinese, Soviet, and Czechoslovak pavilions, which had featured industrial achievements, consumer goods, and live cultural performances.[30]

The Jeshyn exhibition underscored the fundamental difficulties of competing in the Afghan Cold War. Aided by improved roads and port facilities in the north, Moscow and its allies now enjoyed something like a home field advantage in Afghanistan. In other fields, however, the United States retained a fundamental edge—especially food aid. The Kabul embassy and State Department had declined a request for wheat in spring 1955, wary of Daoud and skeptical that Afghanistan faced serious shortages.[31] The following year, after drought beset the far north and floods damaged crops around Kandahar and Jalalabad, Kabul requested a grant of 40,000 tons of wheat.[32]

Prior grain deliveries had occurred on a somewhat improvisational basis. By 1956, however, the Eisenhower administration had implemented a global program to supply the world with surplus grain. Public Law 480 (PL-480), passed in 1954, authorized the acquisition of surplus foodstuffs and their distribution overseas, thereby supporting prices at home while alleviating shortages abroad. Title I of the law, intended to cover most cases, allowed foreign governments to buy surplus foodstuffs at concession prices, paying in their own currency rather than scarce dollars.[33]

The ensuing negotiations and ultimate U.S. decision revealed much about the bilateral relationship. With trademark gusto, Finance Minister Abdul Malik requested a grain donation in successive conversations with Mills. Title II of PL-480 provided for charitable donations in humanitarian emergencies, but Mills and his staff, while aware of growing shortages, did not believe that Afghanistan faced famine. The ambassador attempted to steer Malik toward a Title I purchase, but the dialogue deadlocked. Throughout the exchange, Mills rebuffed Malik's efforts to invoke Cold War considerations. When Malik suggested that his government wanted to give Washington the "first opportunity to help Afghanistan," the ambassador delivered a "statement which I had been waiting to make at an opportune moment." Mills professed disinterest in "getting into a competitive race with the Soviets for Afghan favors," declaring that any agreement between Washington and Kabul should be based upon mutual benefit. If any of his subordinates supported an aid program on the basis of preempting Moscow, Mills would "throw that person out of my office."[34]

No doubt the declaration yielded some satisfaction. Mills had been saving it up—especially for Malik, who clearly relished playing the Cold War card. But the impasse continued, and his superiors grew anxious after Kabul requested a decision by mid-September. The State Department endorsed a Title II grant of 40,000 tons, reasoning that the Afghans *had* asked the United States first and Moscow would otherwise "act quickly." Thus, exploiting the anxieties of a superpower patron, Afghanistan received the first of several successive Title II grants.[35] It had little effect on bread prices, however. Afghan consumers deemed government-baked loaves, from the Soviet-built silo complex, inferior to local *naan*, while independent bakers profitably resold the flour.[36]

Lastly, and most remarkably, 1956 witnessed a thaw in relations between Afghanistan and Pakistan. Governor General (later President) Iskander Mirza pondered at length the merits of engaging Kabul. In January, Mirza endorsed measures to improve transit into Afghanistan while expressing concern about Soviet activities there and some regret about the previous year's blockade.[37] Mills and Ambassador Horace Hildreth in Karachi received instructions to approach both governments with proposals to improve transit while urging rhetorical restraint on Pashtun questions. Spring border clashes and the arrests of prominent Pakistani Pashtun leaders jeopardized the initiative, but Mirza visited Kabul in August. By all accounts, the trip was a tour de force. Mills described it as "very successful," and the normally pessimistic British ambassador Daniel Lascelles concurred. Mirza now believed that the kingdom was ready to negotiate in earnest. Washington instructed its envoys to "discreetly [prod] both sides to action."[38]

Much could be done to improve Afghanistan's commerce with the noncommunist world. Mirza contemplated providing the Afghans with Karachi warehouse space, reducing freight rates, improving roads, even extending Pakistani railroads to the Afghan border. Naim grandiosely hoped for rail links to Kandahar or Kabul. As elsewhere, delay risked Soviet preemption. Mills reported "many indications" that Moscow aspired to improve roads in the borderlands. As a reciprocal visit by Daoud to Karachi loomed in December, Mills opined that the "stage is as well set as it can be for reaching rapprochement." Such a prognosis would have been unimaginable the previous winter. An opening between the neighbors, moreover, offered new opportunities for the pursuit of Cold War objectives within Afghanistan.[39]

Holding Our Own: 1957–1958

The prospects of Afghanistan joining the communist bloc—vastly overrated in early 1956—appeared much diminished by the following winter. The Eisenhower administration credited its aid offensive for the turnaround. The autumn Anglo-French invasion of Egypt and the concurrent Soviet assault on Hungary also seemed to have influenced Daoud's calculus.[40] The former event drove the White House, once again, to contemplate Afghanistan's nebulous place in regional defense.

To the consternation of the Eisenhower administration, the disastrous Suez campaign created a power vacuum in the Middle East. Wary of Soviet influence filling the ensuing void, and distrustful of Arab nationalism, Eisenhower acted decisively. Addressing Congress on January 5, 1957, he announced a threefold commitment: to exclude Soviet power from the Middle East; to offer economic and military assistance to allied states; and to, if necessary, deploy U.S. forces to defend against communist aggression. The Eisenhower Doctrine is most often associated with U.S. policy in the eastern Mediterranean, particularly the 1958 intervention in Lebanon. Yet the peculiar problem of Afghanistan informed the doctrine's creation. In turn, Eisenhower's deepening concern for the broader region influenced Afghanistan policy.

First, as Salim Yaqub notes, Afghan considerations, alongside others, recommended keeping the doctrine's geographic boundaries blurry. Explicit inclusion would place Daoud's government in a difficult position; exclusion, however, could encourage outright Soviet aggression.[41] Second, Afghan officials showed surprising interest in the Eisenhower Doctrine. Aziz opined that his government should support the doctrine, even at the risk of antagonizing the Soviet Union. By his account, Moscow's intervention in Hungary had shaken the Afghan foreign ministry, which "could not help but see ourselves in the mirror." Was his government considering outright alignment? The State Department did not think so but regarded Kabul's interest in the doctrine and the easing of Afghan-Pakistani relations as heartening developments.[42]

In March, Eisenhower dispatched former congressman James Richards on a fifteen-country trip as a "traveling salesman" for the doctrine. Within an eclectic itinerary, Kabul easily qualified as his least likely destination. As the State Department admitted, Afghanistan presented a problem "of a different character from that in any other country" in the region. Excluding the kingdom would communicate disinterest, yet Washington had no desire to provoke Soviet retaliation. Richards would need to walk a fine line: keeping "Afghan expectations within bounds" while fostering Afghan confidence that closer ties were "possible and worthwhile."[43]

However ambiguous, this formulation precluded an open offer of support. Richards found the situation frustrating and remarked that if he had known he could not offer the Afghans military support, he would not have made the trip. If Richards sought to evade what Meyer nicknamed "The $64,000 Question," Daoud proved equally determined not to ask it. Likely discerning that a security guarantee was unavailable, the Afghans opted not to court embarrassment. Instead, the two governments tussled in crafting a joint statement. The Afghans required an affirmation of their "traditional independent policy of neutrality." Although it differed from his other public statements, Richards conceded the issue. Impressed by the Afghan determination to remain independent of Moscow and by the kingdom's vulnerability, the envoy could not fault his hosts for their caution. "I believe they are right in this stand," he wrote. Indeed, Richards carried the logic further, arguing, "What we should strive for is [a] really 'neutral' [Afghanistan] on Swiss model."[44]

Afghan circumstances convinced the Eisenhower Doctrine's chief salesman to accept a proclamation of neutrality. They did not, however, produce the level of U.S. aid that Daoud and Naim desired. Richards came bearing $5.36 million in new commitments: toward road maintenance, transportation services, mineral development, and equipping police. He also promised $2.95 million toward the Helmand Valley, consistent with the Tudor mission's recommendations. His promises to examine the prospects for regional transit, however, disappointed his hosts. Naim especially hoped for a U.S. commitment toward a railroad. "Do we have the means for reaching our Western friends or not?" he asked plaintively. Departing from his brother's stance, Naim had also sought a private assurance of military support.[45]

The crafting and selective deployment of the Eisenhower Doctrine confirmed Afghanistan's anomalous position outside of the formal alliance system. This reflected the kingdom's unique geopolitical circumstances, but it also attested to Eisenhower's partial acceptance of nonalignment. Since the border crisis, Daoud had succeeded in convincing Washington of his anticommunism and commitment to Afghan independence. Afghan nonalignment otherwise gave little offense. Daoud and Naim, pursuing a difficult rhetorical balancing act, erred on the side of reticence. Thus, U.S. analyses of

Afghan foreign policy convey little of the exasperation felt by Dulles toward other nonaligned powers. The kingdom's insecurity rendered its choices understandable. Tellingly, even as the administration's criticism of nonalignment reached its zenith in 1956—Dulles termed the stance "immoral" in a June speech—Washington renewed its bid for Afghanistan.

The remarkable, ongoing improvement in Afghan-Pakistani ties both facilitated Washington's aid offensive and lent it urgency. A visit by Daoud to Karachi in December 1956 further dispelled distrust between the two governments. The subsequent Pakistani release of the Pashtun dissident Abdul Ghaffar Khan in February afforded further grounds for optimism. Both Mills and Lascelles believed that Kabul sought an amicable resolution to the Pashtunistan conflict. Daoud and Pakistani prime minister Huseyn Shaheed Suhrawardy each visited the other's embassy on national holidays. Pashtunistan propaganda ebbed, while the Kabul press endorsed Karachi's stance in the Kashmir conflict. A Suhrawardy visit to Kabul culminated in pledges of solidarity and economic cooperation and an agreement to exchange ambassadors. The French embassy reported an atmosphere of "détente," while U.S. officials perceived an opportunity to deepen commercial ties between the neighbors.[46]

As the White House endeavored to appeal to uncommitted states, it also broadened its available policy tools. Afghanistan policy, alongside other bilateral programs, bore witness to this evolution. An administration initially skeptical of development assistance increasingly accepted such lending as necessary to the anticommunist cause. In August 1957, Eisenhower obtained grudging congressional authorization for the Development Loan Fund (DLF), designed to provide long-term loans toward development projects. Yet lending in the Afghan case threatened to expand the kingdom's onerous debt burden. Citing poor export revenues, Afghan officials increasingly sought grant aid. To a striking degree, Washington acted to accommodate them.[47]

The Helmand project remained central to U.S. efforts in the Afghan aid contest. The Tudor report, released in November 1956, offered a blueprint for further development of the valley. Predictably, the report dealt gently with Morrison-Knudsen while obliquely faulting the Afghans for holding "unrealistic expectations." The report proposed a new timeline for the construction of irrigation dams, canals, roads, and electrical generation capacity. It classified as "Phase I" projects those capable of being completed under MKA's existing contract, setting aside further irrigation, transportation, and hydroelectric works under "Phase II."[48]

The Tudor report held semiofficial implications, promising redoubled efforts in the valley. The $2.95 million promised by Richards confirmed Washington's commitment but fell well short of expected Phase I costs. It also signaled a fundamental transition in funding for the project as the second Eximbank loan drew down. Soon an acrimonious battle erupted within the U.S. expatriate community in Afghanistan, pitting the Eximbank and MKA against the embassy and aid mission, bringing long-submerged frustrations to the surface.

At issue were both authority over the expenditure of ICA funds and the upcoming Kandahar airport project. Backed by MKA and questioning the ICA's competence, the Eximbank argued that it should continue to oversee expenditures in the valley. The bank simultaneously supported MKA's efforts to secure the Kandahar contract—without a competitive bidding process and on a cost-plus basis. Diplomats and aid officials in Kabul formed an opposing coalition. The ICA and MKA clashed over the Kandahar project, and the aid agency maintained that it should administer the expenditure of its own funds after the Eximbank loan ran out. Seeking an open bidding process, Mills argued emphatically against giving MKA yet another "blank check." He wrote pointedly: "I am hopeful that the time has come about when the philosophy we believe in, or profess to, that is, competition, can start to play its beneficial part." Mills dramatically offered his resignation if his superiors disagreed.[49]

Cooler heads prevailed in Washington, and a bank-ICA compromise ultimately emerged. Haste remained a paramount consideration, and the Eximbank successfully argued that MKA could complete the airport before any potential competitor. As another olive branch, ICA, while administering post-loan spending, agreed to consult closely with the bank.[50] In all likelihood, the bank-MKA alliance stemmed from familiarity and broader political considerations. Like Tudor, the Eximbank had to consider its wider relationship with Morrison-Knudsen, extending well beyond Afghanistan.[51] Capitalizing upon hard-won experience and maintaining a fruitful partnership required looking past clear signs of worsening Afghan disaffection with MKA.

Construction work continued in the valley: extending the canal network, repairing the leaky Boghra Canal, and installing hydroelectric power generators. By the summer, however, relations between the firm and the Afghan government broke down amid disputes related to its performance on earlier contracts. Daoud's government withheld work orders for canal projects and made the conclusion of a new contract contingent on the firm yielding on the other issues. Mills discerned among Afghans a "lack of confidence in MK . . . so widespread" as to be irreparable. Projects elsewhere in Afghanistan allowed the government to draw damning contrasts between MKA's expenses and those of its competitors. "Perhaps it is time for a change" mused Abdul Kayeum, the acting president of the Helmand Valley Authority (HVA).[52]

Morrison-Knudsen's troubled tenure in the Helmand Valley was nearing its end, yet the aviation project afforded it further opportunities to make its imprint on the Afghan landscape. Yet this was no less complex an endeavor than the Helmand Valley project. Bureaucratic, technical, and administrative difficulties proved formidable. The Civil Aeronautics Board (CAB) in Washington, which needed to authorize Pan Am's acquisition of 49 percent of Ariana, posed one early hurdle. As Van Vleck chronicles, the CAB's antimonopolist outlook made it reluctant to approve the purchase. A financial dispute between Pan Am and the ICA caused further delays. Confusion reigned, meanwhile, over Ariana's legal status: whether it would constitute the kingdom's sole official airline. If not, future competition with a rival Soviet-backed airline remained a distinct possibility. With the reluctant assents of the CAB and ICA, Pan Am commenced negotiations with the Afghan government in January 1957, reaching terms on April 17. An ambiguous compromise rendered Ariana Afghanistan's only government-*funded* airline, but the specter of a second carrier lingered.[53]

However many airlines Afghanistan required, it still suffered from a dearth of modern airfields. Kandahar's future airport was intended to serve as both a way station on international flights and a domestic hub. Yet nearly a year after the June 1956 aviation agreement, construction had yet to commence, to Daoud's visible annoyance. The ICA–Pan Am dispute contributed to the delay, as had the still-unresolved question of MKA's involvement. Concerns about cost both impeded the selection of a contractor and required the completion of extensive surveys before breaking ground. Mills pleaded for action to "cut [the] red tape" and expedite the conclusion of a construction contract—almost certainly apprehending that this would deliver the project to Morrison-Knudsen. Abdul Karim Hakimi, the head of Afghanistan's civil aviation authority, warned that his government would cancel the project if no construction contract materialized and if work did not commence within a month of signing.[54]

Hakimi, the ICA, and Morrison-Knudsen reached terms on the Kandahar airport contract in late September, breaking ground a month later. The entire affair greatly strained working relationships within the U.S. mission. The aviation project required effective collaboration between the U.S. embassy, the aid mission, Pan Am, the CAB, Morrison-Knudsen, and the Afghan government. Mills grew frustrated with the ICA mission, which appeared hamstrung. Perceiving an "absence of timely planning, coordination, and execution," he wrote that the aid mission, as presently constituted was unable to "carry through [the] project with necessary speed."[55]

Some of Mills's complaints reflected frustrations specific to individual personnel—he believed that the quality of appointments to Afghan posts was uneven. His criticism of the aid mission suggests a deeper division, however. Mills, more than anyone, felt the imperative to keep pace with Afghan aspirations. The aviation project represented the new centerpiece of the U.S. aid offensive: a bid for the favor of Afghanistan's modernizing elite. Aid mission head Robert Snyder grasped the importance of the aviation project. "Hardly a day passes," he wrote, "that some Afghan official doesn't impress upon me the urgent necessity of . . . [assisting] with the airline." Yet the ICA could not sprint alongside the embassy in its project advocacy. Far more than its diplomatic peers, it faced scrutiny from a legislature highly skeptical of foreign aid. Initially bullish about the project—which he believed would "do more good for Afghanistan and for the United States" than any other conceivable expenditure—Snyder nevertheless could not improvise or act profligately. Repeated, mandatory inquiries to Washington imposed their own delays.[56]

Above all, Snyder nursed doubts about the Kandahar airport's economic feasibility. Speaking with Deputy Under Secretary of State Douglas Dillon in August 1958, he framed the U.S. dilemma starkly: between outright abandonment; maintenance of existing, insufficient assistance efforts; or an expanded program to bolster Afghan ties to the Free World and Pakistan. Aviation had been "the only possible project which could be developed at that time," even as Snyder allowed that "this project was not entirely justified on an economic basis"—particularly the Kandahar airport. Kandahar's utility as a refueling stop was questionable as aircraft gained greater range, and the city lacked hotels suitable for international travelers. Its role as a national hub required the future construction of airports elsewhere in Afghanistan. Dillon replied, tellingly: "Regardless of the merits or justifications of the

Air Project, we are in it and we must support it."[57] So it had been with the Helmand too.

U.S. choices in the field of petroleum development only reinforced the centrality of aviation. Afghanistan remained a prodigious importer of petroleum, while the border crisis heightened dependence on Soviet sources. Deterred from seeking U.S. or UN assistance and wary of bringing Soviet specialists into the north, Kabul sought a third option. To Moscow's consternation, the Afghan government enlisted a Swedish firm to conduct exploratory drilling at Sar-i-Pul. Afghanistan simultaneously sought to interest Western oil firms and the U.S. government in southern petroleum exploration.[58]

Afghan efforts to renew domestic petroleum development achieved mixed results. U.S. oil firms appeared uninterested, in the absence of a national petroleum law. Moscow, however, remained keen to develop the northern oil. Concerned that a northern concession might facilitate Soviet entry into the south, Mills sought funding for petroleum exploration. His government did not fund oil exploration, however, consigning that task to the private sector. Unhappy with the Swedish company, meanwhile, the Afghans reconsidered the Soviet bid. When Zahir visited Moscow in August, he accepted a Soviet offer to provide equipment and technicians to exploit the northern oil. Outraged, Mills confronted Naim afterward, describing the oil agreement as "utterly foolhardy and reckless." Dramatically, he asked whether his efforts in Afghanistan were not "a waste of time since the Afghan Government of its own volition is drawing ever closer to the Soviet Union." Unnerved, Naim replied that he had thought that U.S. assistance toward petroleum development was unavailable.[59]

Naim could hardly be faulted for thinking so. Little in the U.S. response to Afghan oil inquiries had communicated a sense of urgency. Reiterating the risk of a Soviet concession eventually penetrating the south, Mills warned against further "pussy-footing on this issue." Deference to oil firms stayed foremost in mind, however, illustrating the limits of the executive branch's leeway. Washington limited itself to dispatching Ralph Miller, an expert from the U.S. Geological Survey, to advise in drafting national oil legislation. U.S. oil companies stayed away.[60]

Naim and his government faced disappointment on another front as well. The Afghan foreign minister nursed a passion for trains—and an ardent desire to see Kabul connected by rail to Karachi. He had hoped that the Richards visit would bring a promise to fund the railroad and clung to that possibility afterward. Successive U.S. analyses concluded that the costs would be prohibitive, well above $100 million, and that the kingdom would be better served by road improvements. As ever, it fell to Mills to break the bad news.[61]

By that time, the Afghan authorities had delivered a shock of their own. Although a dearth of state statistics and a proclivity toward secrecy hampered efforts to track the Afghan economy, key officials appeared increasingly anxious about domestic inflation and a mounting debt burden. Kabul's revenue collection had not kept pace with spending, leading authorities to borrow from the central bank, while the latter issued new currency. In December, Afghan officials declared a moratorium on further borrowing, requesting that future assistance be provided on a grant basis. The decision held far-reaching ramifications for U.S. efforts, raising fundamental questions about whether the aviation project or Helmand work could continue to be funded. Remarkably, the U.S. mission, while concerned about securing grant aid and ever conscious of the possibility of "blackmail," accepted the change. Snyder wrote that the "decision to stop piling up of additional foreign debt and to limit internal inflation . . . cannot be quarreled with and should not be opposed."[62]

Indeed, the loan moratorium appeared to shift the contest onto terrain more favorable to the Western allies. Soviet aid came predominantly on a lending basis; indeed, it had never offered grant assistance outside of the communist bloc. Mills and Snyder perceived an opportunity to transform U.S. aid within Afghanistan, which had previously pursued defensive objectives, reacting to perceived Soviet thrusts. The shift would enable a "fundamental reorientation of Afghan policy." Even if the Soviets followed suit, they would hold less leverage as donors than as lenders. Grants faced greater hurdles domestically, but the administration had already changed the form of its Afghan aid to a remarkable degree. Development assistance expenditures for fiscal year 1958 had grown fivefold to $6.5 million from the previous year while the Kandahar airport and Pakistan transit initiatives remained largely idle.[63]

Thus, Washington stood poised to exploit the pivot in Afghanistan's economic policy. Meeting Daoud in January 1958, indulging in his penchant for melodrama, Mills declared that he and Snyder had put "our heads in nooses" by advocating for grant aid. They had obtained grants in the Helmand Valley, and—contingent on a transit agreement with Pakistan—additional funding for regional communications. Daoud expressed satisfaction and received the disappointing railroad news without protest.[64]

Afghanistan already possessed abundant motivation to improve its connections to Karachi. Feuds between Afghan and Pakistani truckers caused periodic traffic disruptions and highlighted the need for a comprehensive transit agreement. The two neighbors reached an agreement in May, containing mutual assurances of duty-free transit. Pakistan pledged to provide the kingdom with transit facilities in Karachi and to extend its railroad to Spin Baldak. The agreement conferred special significance on the Kabul-Peshawar road, the Afghan portion of which Washington had promised to improve.[65]

Immediately afterward, Daoud commenced his first-ever visit to the United States. Dulles and Vice President Richard Nixon received him at the airport. Eisenhower welcomed him to the White House, and Daoud delivered separate, much-applauded addresses before the House and Senate. After a lavish dinner hosted by Dulles, he embarked on a cross-country trip, visiting Niagara Falls, hydroelectric dams in the Tennessee Valley, and Yellowstone National Park. In Los Angeles, Daoud toured an aircraft factory and a missile test range, where he launched a battlefield rocket, before flying by helicopter to Disneyland. The combination might have been jarring, even discordant, but Daoud appeared especially moved by the Magic Kingdom. At a dinner with Hollywood stars, he conversed in French with his neighbor, Zsa Zsa Gabor. Screen Actors Guild president Ronald Reagan delivered a stirring toast speech to welcome the guest of honor.[66]

Sightseeing and hospitality superseded serious diplomacy on the visit. In official dialogue, Daoud and his hosts broke little new ground. Eisenhower and his aides professed their regard for their guest, their understanding of his neutrality, and their support of his development aspirations. Daoud, meanwhile, emphasized his determination to remain free of the Soviet bloc, as well as his gratitude for continued U.S. assistance. Neither party sought to confront the other. Daoud's inquiry with Dillon, at the State Department, about whether private Afghan enterprises might borrow from the new DLF represented the visit's most concrete discussion.[67] Perhaps consciously playing against type, Daoud also surprised his hosts with his candor, confidence, and occasional moments of levity. His "demeanor, manner of speaking and [personality] belied expected shyness or dourness," Mills and Poullada wrote.[68] Kabul embassy alumnus Armin Meyer, who had accompanied Daoud throughout the trip, described it as an "excellent investment." Mills wrote that his Afghan contacts were "simply delighted" by the visit. One Afghan diplomat reported that Daoud had been especially impressed by Eisenhower.[69]

A cautious optimism entered U.S. analyses after the visit, unrelated to the status of major aid projects. In late November, Mills described the U.S. position in Afghanistan as "one of just about holding its own," even as the U.S. "record of achievement in the technical and economic assistance fields has not been very impressive to date."[70] Assertions of an improved dynamic rested on three interconnected conditions. First, relations with the Afghan elite had improved profoundly since 1955. Daoud's warm welcome in the United States fostered goodwill within his government, but also, second, strengthened the credibility of U.S. aid projects. As one Afghan remarked, "This expression of friendship to our prime minister has convinced us that your interest is even deeper . . . that the U.S. does in fact want to help and assist the Afghan nation." Emotionally affective gestures compensated for the halting implementation of projects. Snyder postulated: "It is not necessarily the amount of aid that counts in Afghanistan. Rather it is the spirit in which it is given and the efficiency with which it is implemented."[71]

Third, and crucially, Afghan-Pakistani détente enabled improvements in bilateral ties. Reduced discord over Pashtunistan liberated U.S. officials from stark, zero-sum choices, while improvements in communications—feuding truckers notwithstanding—enabled work on major projects. Heartening progress continued into the late summer, when Pakistan, in an inspired gesture, sent Abdul Ghaffar Khan to attend Jeshyn in Kabul. Tacit U.S. diplomacy up to the spring transit accord had facilitated this rapprochement. Snyder justifiably termed the effort "one of our greatest successes that I am aware of."[72]

The thaw of 1956–1958 was impressive. Regrettably, it was also fragile. Its continuation hinged upon Daoud's calculations, the successful implementation of U.S. aid, and, pivotally, governmental stability in Karachi. In autumn 1958, that last pillar collapsed, thereby threatening the cross-border relationship and the U.S. agenda within Afghanistan.

The Trend Is Running Against Us, 1958–1959

On June 28, 1958, while flying to California, Daoud asked to speak with Armin Meyer. The previous day, while descending into the Niagara Falls area, Meyer had wished aloud that Afghan-Pakistani relations might someday resemble those between the United States and Canada. Whether by diplomatic design or fortuitous accident, Daoud's hotel room overlooked the falls and the customs posts, allowing him to watch cars cross the border with no more than a friendly wave. Recalling Meyer's remark, Daoud said that he shared the sentiment, but doubted it could be realized in the foreseeable future. Daoud expressed his regard for Mirza and the hope that Pakistan would negotiate with Pashtun dissidents, especially Abdul Ghaffar Khan.[73]

Autumn events precluded that possibility. Pakistan's shaky democracy collapsed on October 7, when Mirza placed the country under martial law. Amid a faltering economy, he acted to stave off defeat in upcoming February elections. Mirza had toyed with the notion of "controlled democracy" for years. The allure of control superseded Mirza's hope for friendly relations with Daoud. Within days, the Pakistani authorities imprisoned major opposition figures, including Abdul Ghaffar Khan. Yet Mirza's own hold on power was unstable, dependent upon his longtime ally, Gen. Mohammed Ayub Khan. Ayub's control of the Pakistani military enabled him to seize total power for himself, three weeks later, banishing Mirza from the country afterward.[74]

The Eisenhower administration deemed the coup lamentable yet understandable. The violent overthrow of the Iraqi government in July had shocked the White House. Upheaval in Pakistan jeopardized Karachi's continued adherence to the Western alliance system. Mirza and Ayub, whatever their other proclivities, remained stalwart Cold War allies. Eisenhower and Dulles offered their regrets that the coup had been necessary but remained intent on collaborating with the new dictatorship.[75]

By itself, Khan's arrest would have jeopardized relations between the two neighbors. Afghan representatives lost no time in protesting his detention. Left in office, Mirza might have contrived some compensating gesture, tending toward conciliation on Afghanistan policy. Ayub, however, brought entirely different instincts to bear. Himself a Pashtun, he despised Daoud and held his state in contempt. As Elisabeth Leake writes, Ayub envisioned tying frontier Pashtuns to the state through an ambitious project of development in the borderlands—all within the One Unit framework. The decisive extension of state power to the frontier would render Afghan objections moot.[76]

Although Ayub offered nominal assurances of neighborly goodwill after his coup, Afghan-Pakistani ties entered a sharp downward spiral. Ayub spoke of Afghanistan with growing hostility, suggesting in January 1959 that the entire royal family should be overthrown. Ayub's bellicosity undermined

U.S. assurances that Pakistan would not turn its American-made arsenal against Afghanistan, in turn heightening the risk of Kabul seeking further Soviet military aid. The Pakistani dictator appeared content to consign the kingdom to the bloc. Alarmed, the State Department directed its embassy in Karachi to urge restraint on Ayub. The Pakistani leader received the message civilly but replied that a Soviet takeover of Afghanistan was "only a matter of time."[77]

Although the Eisenhower administration rejected Ayub's assessment, its own anxiety about the direction of Afghan foreign policy mounted. Washington's seeming inability to restrain a newly hostile Pakistan—even as it furnished the Ayub regime with arms—altered Daoud's calculus. On December 28, the Afghan government suddenly announced Naim's departure on a weeklong trip to the Soviet Union.[78] Afghan officials responded furtively to repeated inquiries from Western diplomats, only fueling speculation that the trip entailed discussion of military aid or a fundamental realignment of Afghan foreign policy.[79] Mills doubted that Daoud had abandoned neutrality but noted that the invitation had apparently arrived at the last minute, as the Soviets moved to pursue a "target of opportunity."[80]

Reports of communist bloc weapons shipments into Afghanistan struck an already raw nerve. For years, the Western allies had traded reports and speculated avidly about the extent of Soviet bloc military assistance. London and Washington remained conservative in their assessments (although Ward once reported several flying saucer sightings), but regional allies professed greater concern. The Shah of Iran especially feared an Afghan-Soviet assault on his vulnerable eastern flank. Afghan secrecy compounded the mystery. Data only surfaced sporadically. One U.S. source, visiting the northern river port of Qizil Qala in early 1957, reported seeing extensive Soviet munitions shipments. Western observers painstakingly scrutinized the equipment on display in the 1958 Jeshyn parade. Amid this climate, Washington endeavored to calm its allies, contending that Kabul's purchases appeared moderate, that the Afghans remained independent of Moscow, and that adaptation to Soviet equipment could not occur easily.[81]

Up to this point, communist bloc observers had been equally attentive to the U.S. aid offensive. Czechoslovak minister Václav Havlin tellingly termed the contest an "aid race." Noting improved Afghan-Pakistani relations and the U.S. aviation project, Havlin warned in December 1956 that the United States was "now pursuing a shrewder policy." Yet U.S. objectives remained fundamentally unchanged in his eyes. Efforts to facilitate regional rapprochement betrayed Washington's interest in the accession of Afghanistan into an anti-Soviet alliance.[82]

To a striking, mutually unknown degree, communist objectives and perceptions in Afghanistan mirrored those of the West. The extensive Czechoslovak documentary record from this era offers no evidence of a subversive or confrontational agenda. Nor, as Paul Robinson and Jay Dixon write, did the communists seek to foster economic dependence on the bloc. Rather, they respected Daoud, found his neutrality agreeable, and endeavored to preserve Afghan independence against apparent insidious Western efforts to undermine it. Havlin repeatedly credited his hosts for their determination to resist U.S. pressure and urged his government to support them. Daoud's 1958 trip to the United States only reinforced this verdict. There, his forthright public defense of Afghanistan's friendship with its northern neighbor pleased Soviet diplomats. "The Afghans have not conceded their traditional policy [of neutrality], nor deviated from friendship with the USSR," Havlin wrote. Remarkably, Daoud gained Eisenhower's respect without sacrificing the bloc's esteem.[83]

Simultaneously, although their aid projects won plaudits from Afghans, who often compared them favorably to the Helmand enterprise, the communists experienced their own share of frustration. The East German government's provision of emergency aid to Afghanistan after a 1956 earthquake in Kabul failed to open relations between the kingdom and the German Democratic Republic. Daoud was unwilling to forfeit West German goodwill. The cultural and media terrain appeared especially forbidding. Havlin complained about the ubiquity of U.S. wire reports in the Kabul press, yielding "unfavorable" coverage during the Hungarian uprising in 1956. In the field of cinema, the situation was even worse. U.S.-made films with "sensational and crazy content" (Havlin had gangster and horror movies in mind) had captured the Afghan market. Afghan moviegoers showed comparatively little interest in the "serious art films" exported by the communist bloc.[84]

Nor did the bloc evade the economic, administrative, and cultural difficulties that baffled its foes. Hakimi, now deputy finance minister, complained to Meyer that the Soviet-built silo, mill, and bakery in Kabul operated at a substantial daily loss.[85] The Czechoslovak government found, to its dismay, that bilateral commerce was worsening Afghanistan's trade balance. "Our side has shown, albeit inadvertently, the same predatory commercial practices toward Afghanistan as other states," Havlin lamented. Although

Americans ascribed greater stoicism to their foes, Soviet and Czechoslovak experts surveying northern oil deposits complained vehemently about the failure of the Afghans to provide adequate accommodations, food, or medical care. Rather than abandon the project over a breach of contract, the communists rushed medical specialists to the site. Forfeiting the concession risked yet another U.S. oil mission in northern Afghanistan. Lastly, the quality of bloc personnel was not universally adequate. A major diplomatic incident almost ensued after one of Havlin's deputies made "coarse and ill-considered statements" about the wife of an Afghan employed by his legation. The aggrieved employee threatened violence, and Havlin reminded his staff that "the question of Afghan women is very sensitive."[86]

A sense of urgency afflicted the communists just as it did their Western adversaries—actively stoked by Afghan officials. Weeks after crediting Eisenhower for his American reception, Daoud confided to the visiting Czechoslovak prime minister Viliam Široký that Washington and London might seek his overthrow.[87] Communist anxieties fostered a pragmatic willingness to support an ideologically alien regime. In approving weapons deliveries to Kabul, Khrushchev overrode ideological objections from staunch Stalinists against arming a monarchy.[88] Haste also yielded failures that Americans could recognize. The paving of the Kabul streets constituted a crucial early propaganda success for the Soviets. Yet cracks began to appear by summer 1958, mere months after completion, and the streets deteriorated further with the onset of winter conditions. ICA engineers postulated that the Soviets had failed to prepare the roadbed thoroughly, used improper asphalt, and neglected the problem of drainage. Aziz inquired delicately in early 1959 whether DLF funds might be available to repave the capital's pockmarked streets.[89]

External events, meanwhile, heightened the perceived stakes of the Afghan Cold War, galvanizing both sides toward heightened efforts. The 1958 Iraqi revolution called the viability of the now ill-named Baghdad Pact into question. The accompanying murder of Iraq's King Faisal, years after Egypt's revolution, suggested a bleak future for monarchies amid a rising tide of nationalism in the Islamic world. Thirty years after Amanullah's downfall, observers weighed the possibility that Daoud, Naim, and Zahir might face a similar fate, creating a dangerous vacuum in Kabul.

Lastly, the accelerating superpower arms race intensified the contest in and around Afghanistan. Moscow's pavilion at the 1958 Jeshyn fair prominently displayed models of Sputnik, the satellite it had launched into orbit the previous autumn. A symbol of Soviet scientific prowess in Kabul, Sputnik assumed ominous implications in NATO capitals. Facing dramatic evidence that Moscow could now strike North America with nuclear weapons, Washington endeavored to demonstrate its continued commitment to its allies: ultimately through the deployment of medium- and intermediate-range missiles to Western Europe. The search for allies willing to host Thor or Jupiter missiles followed a long and convoluted path. Turkey ultimately emerged as a willing host, alongside Italy, but only in summer 1959.[90]

Long before the specter of Turkish missiles gained enough substance to vex Nikita Khrushchev, Soviet officials made their displeasure plain. Moscow simply did not know where the missiles would go and considered a wide range of potential sites along its southern border. Deputy Premier Anastas Mikoyan, visiting Washington, repeatedly termed such facilities inimical to peaceful relations between the superpowers, describing a greater uncertainty since the upheaval in Iraq.[91] Afghanistan escaped the suspect list but neither of its Western-allied neighbors could. Iran faced continual Soviet scrutiny on the missile question.[92] Brazenly exploiting the situation, Daoud's ambassador in Moscow informed Khrushchev that Americans were building rocket bases in northern Pakistan.[93] Thus, Moscow had every reason to maintain, even bolster, its efforts within Afghanistan.

Consequently, Americans in Afghanistan perceived a dismaying trend during 1959. Incoming ambassador Henry Byroade, who replaced Mills in March, initially struck a hopeful tenor. Before long, however, he became increasingly concerned. Daoud, convalescing in Switzerland for much of the spring, returned to Kabul after a five-day stop in Moscow, where he presented at length on the Helmand and Pashtunistan questions to a sympathetic Khrushchev. Days after his return, in early June, the Kabul press announced a major new Soviet project: the construction of a paved road from the border, through Herat, to Kandahar. Completion of the road would bring Soviet engineers into southern Afghanistan.[94]

Perceiving a serious reverse, Byroade requested an immediate audience with his old friend Naim. He sought an explanation for the road project, which, he wondered aloud, might not be "part of [the] plan conceived by Tsarist Russia long ago to reach for warm-water port areas." Naim informed the stunned Byroade that the Soviets had pledged to undertake it on a grant basis, with an estimated cost of $80 million. Moscow had answered the U.S. shift to grant aid in kind and once again raised the stakes.

Replying to Byroade's protests, Naim pointedly reminded Byroade of his proposed railroad.[95]

U.S. aid projects within the kingdom had progressed measurably during the decade's final years, but not always to Kabul's satisfaction. Aviation remained a principal concern, as both the U.S. country team and the Afghan government struggled to adapt to the loan moratorium and inevitable shipping and construction delays. Afghan and U.S. officials differed over the best aircraft for Ariana, which maintained a handful of venerable DC-3s and DC-4s. Naim sought advanced turboprop aircraft, which the U.S. aid mission contended would operate at a loss and require paved runways at regional airports. The Afghan government, meanwhile, refused to guarantee that Ariana would stay the sole national airline. The Soviet-built Bagram airfield, just north of Kabul, risked supplanting Kandahar as Afghanistan's premier international airport. Funding concerns remained paramount. Able to commit only an additional $8 million, the U.S. country team strove to keep the project from ballooning further, including dissuading the Afghans from developing a Kabul-Moscow route.[96]

A serious shortage of local currency confronted all significant development projects within Afghanistan by 1959. Largely dependent on export revenue and foreign assistance, Daoud's regime failed to improve its tax collection, which, as Barnett Rubin illustrates, composed an ever-shrinking percentage of state revenue. Foreign assistance could compensate for anemic domestic revenue, but not on pace with Daoud's development aspirations. Inevitably, shortfalls loomed within projects requiring the expenditure of both Afghan and ICA funds, particularly aviation.[97] The two governments responded differently to the looming budgetary crisis. While the U.S. country team hoped for additional funding, it counseled Kabul to accept a five-year schedule for the completion of the Kandahar and the regional airports. Aziz however insisted upon a three-year timetable, which the U.S. negotiators believed to be entirely infeasible. Should the United States be obligated to relinquish the unfinished airports in 1962, who might complete them?[98]

Nor did the Helmand Valley offer encouragement. Abdul Kayeum, the HVA's vice president, lamented the project's failure to improve government revenue or benefit the people of the valley. In spring 1959, Byroade reached the same conclusion as his predecessors: U.S. objectives remained bound to the project, "so much so in fact that our prestige and position in this general area . . . undoubtedly will . . . be influenced by the appearances of success or failure there." Reporting continued problems with agriculture, irrigation, and resettlement, Byroade observed, "I do not believe that any private engineering firm in the US has any record of success in a job of this character." He and his aid mission colleagues suggested enlisting advisors from the Bureau of Reclamation.[99]

The enduring Afghan dispute with Iran over the waters of the Helmand complicated matters further. The 1951 international commission had allocated to Iran twenty-two cubic meters per second of Helmand water. After Iran rejected the verdict, the issue continued to simmer, albeit without the violence sparked by Pashtunistan. Periodic nudges from Washington failed to sway Tehran. Echoing his government's views, Byroade described the Afghans as holding a "virtually impregnable negotiating position": the commission report had endorsed their position, and geography itself favored them as the upstream party.[100]

In August, while the latest round of Afghan-Iranian talks dragged on in Kabul, Naim solicited U.S. assistance toward the construction of flood-control dams along the lower Helmand River. Iranian officials expressed alarm that the Afghans contemplated further diversions from the river. The Shah believed that U.S. aid to Afghanistan had encouraged the downriver schemes. Daoud, meanwhile, remained determined to build on the lower Helmand, even expressing interest in a U.S. loan (despite his stated policy). "We do not like the philosophy of taking on a project merely to deny it to the Russians," Byroade wrote of the downriver proposal, ultimately concluding, "There seems little doubt that if we refuse RGA will ask for Russian assistance." This argument made little headway in Tehran, where a senior official observed: "We would rather have Russians than Americans build this dam."[101]

Apparent U.S. hesitancy toward the kingdom's latest major project could only solidify increasingly unfavorable assessments of the U.S. aid program. Commerce Minister Ghulam Mohammed Sherzad complained publicly and repeatedly that Washington was "deliberately going slow" in its Afghan aid program. Although angered, Byroade privately pondered the merits of the allegation. In early 1959, after consultation with the U.S. embassy, the Afghan Textile Company applied for DLF funding to support the completion of a mill at Gulbahar. DLF officials, although skeptical about the Afghan proposal, stopped short of turning it down outright, leaving the application in limbo. At year's end, the frustrated ambassador pleaded for news, even if negative. "It seems strange to us here," he wrote, "that we have been unable . . . to obtain any DLF assistance whatsoever while we hear frequently of DLF loans of magnitude to other nations in this part of the world."[102]

If such disparities between neighboring aid programs frustrated the U.S. mission, they vexed Afghan officials even more. Afghan criticisms of U.S. aid highlighted such comparisons. Afghan officials cited the aerial fleets of Iranian and Pakistani carriers when requesting turboprop airliners. The disparity between the extensive military assistance dispensed to either neighbor versus a small-scale Afghan pilot training program brought further complaints. This criticism escalated as the kingdom's neighborly relations worsened.[103]

Rising tensions with both eastern and western neighbors noticeably intensified a growing sense of grievance within Kabul. As Ayub pursued his reorganization program in the frontier areas, he responded pugnaciously to Afghan criticism. After Ayub and Daoud sparred rhetorically in the spring, an alarming new element entered the kingdom's Pashtunistan propaganda. Radio Kabul charged that a new U.S. communications facility in Peshawar could bring nuclear war to the borderlands and blamed Washington for Pakistani recalcitrance. Perhaps irreversibly, the kingdom's conflicts were becoming intertwined with the Cold War, forcing stark choices upon the Eisenhower administration.[104]

Amid reports of growing Soviet economic and military assistance throughout the Third World, Afghanistan emerged again as an object of concern for the National Security Council (NSC). The scope of Moscow's aid to the kingdom demanded attention, as did apparent shifts in Soviet tactics, especially the $80 million grant. CIA estimates placed 950 communist specialists within Afghanistan, a number only exceeded by those in India and the just-formed United Arab Republic.[105] By any reckoning, Afghanistan constituted a principal target of Moscow's economic assistance program. As before, the challenge appeared daunting. CIA director Allen Dulles observed in August that preventing the loss of Afghan independence would be "very difficult." An updated regional strategy statement, NSC 5909, echoed that assessment, yet reiterated familiar prescriptions: encouraging better ties with Pakistan and Iran; fostering better connections with the West: and employing development programs to provide "immediately visible evidence of U.S. friendship."[106]

Late-decade warnings of rising Soviet influence within Afghanistan did not incite hostility toward its government. Daoud and Naim retained the respect of the Eisenhower administration, which feared instead that they had gravely miscalculated in their pursuit of aid. NSC assessments expressed concern about the intermediate future but not the alarmism of the mid-decade. Moscow's presumed means of subversion, economic absorption, lacked applicable recent precedent and was perversely difficult to track. Consistent, however, were statements about South Asia's importance in the Cold War and Afghanistan's historic role as an invasion route. Assistant Secretary of State for Near Eastern and South Asian Affairs G. Lewis Jones wrote:

> We believe the USSR looks upon Afghanistan not only as a prize in itself but as a valuable political fulcrum for exercising political leverage on the Indian subcontinent and the Middle East. If the Russians were in effective control of Afghanistan they would have driven a wedge between Iran and Pakistan, be within three hundred miles of the port of Karachi, and be in a position to stir up trouble among all the tribal peoples of Pushtunistan. . . . Thus, the defenses of the entire Indian subcontinent would be gravely endangered.

Dillon designated the kingdom an "emergency area."[107]

In Kabul, Byroade nursed doubts about his government's capacity to wage the Cold War aid contest. Contemplating "ingratiating, flattering, correct, effective" Soviet efforts led Byroade to a difficult conclusion. "We must face fact that West is not well organized for type of contest we face here," he wrote. Unlike its adversaries, Moscow appeared able to change its Afghan commerce, in volume, type, and price, to suit its political objectives. Byroade knew better than to seek a dramatic increase in U.S. aid. Nor did he counsel abandonment—a policy course usually invoked for shock effect, in advance of proposing a palatable median option. Conceding that his government could not match the Soviets, bid for bid, Byroade endorsed initiatives able to achieve specific political and psychological goals: transit and aviation.[108]

When he descended from his high-altitude hunting excursion that year, with mounting, concealed impatience at every bounteous, leisurely display of local hospitality, Byroade sought to return to Kabul for the annual Jeshyn. Extensive communist exhibitions and performances awaited him. Moscow dispatched Tajik and Turkmen singers and dancers on a national tour. Beijing sent a troupe of acrobats, whose performances amazed audiences of elite and ordinary Afghans alike. A Soviet aircraft conveying dignitaries from the Central Asian republics executed the first ever jet-powered landing within Afghanistan, at the newly completed Bagram airfield. Beholding the bloc's vigorous counteroffensive, Byroade had to wonder whether his own government's efforts would ultimately suffice.[109]

Taking Stock of the Afghan Cold War

Years earlier, shortly after the announcement of the Kandahar airport project, Armin Meyer encountered Soviet ambassador Mikhail Degtyar at a Kabul cocktail party. Noting that his government had followed Moscow's $100 million loan with $15 million in aid, he jibed: "You put in another $100 million and we'll put in another $15 million. I think, at this game, we're ahead of you." Degtyar smiled and amicably replied that it was up to the Afghans to make that decision. Pausing, he added that the United States "wouldn't like it" if his government acted similarly in Mexico.[110]

Degtyar's reply lingered with Meyer, who conceded that it "was not without substance." His previous quantification of the aid contest, however, is worth examining. Western participants in the Afghan Cold War labored under the ominous shadow of Khrushchev's loan. Yet statements like Meyer's troubled Weston Drake, the ICA desk officer assigned to Afghanistan. As Drake noted in January 1957, the comparison treated Khrushchev's promise as aid delivered, when it actually represented a "line of credit," of which little had yet been allocated. "If all Soviet Bloc aid actually obligated equals $50 million at this point," Drake wrote, "it would be very surprising." The myriad forms of U.S. and allied assistance—including two Eximbank loans, other credits, and ICA grants—totaled $117.1 million: more than twice his maximal estimate of actual communist aid. Adding UN programs, which Moscow regarded as another U.S. instrumentality, would skew the ratio even further. This led Drake to an almost subversive conclusion: "Too many of us have allowed the thought to persist that U.S. aid is being built up in response to Russian challenges. In Afghanistan in particular I believe it would be useful to recognize perhaps only among ourselves that the Russians are responding to U.S. blandishments."[111]

Remarkably, Drake was not alone in ascribing defensive motivations to Moscow. NIE 53–59, the updated national assessment of Afghanistan, echoed his verdict. Even as it posited that Moscow perceived Afghanistan as "the gateway to ultimate expansion into the subcontinent," that statement conceded that "in 1953–55, the USSR's objective was probably to deny

Afghanistan to the West in the face of Western moves to create the 'northern tier' alliance."[112]

Such judgments could mostly only be made in hindsight. The difficulty of assessing adversary actions within Afghanistan fostered threat inflation. Had the Afghan Cold War been measurable only quantifiably or financially, the rival blocs still would have struggled to understand the battlefield. Much within the contest, of course, was intangible, while new fronts opened with jarring frequency. Perceptions of progress swung dramatically over time, hinging upon the uncertain advance of specific projects, the sudden emergence of new opportunities, and subjective assessments of Afghan opinion.

Afghan officials had, of course, knowingly stoked this competition. The congenial turn in U.S. diplomacy enabled a campaign of outreach by Daoud's government, which actively engaged the U.S. mission and the Eisenhower White House. Meyer's increasingly favorable views of Daoud contrasted sharply with words he had penned just after the Khrushchev visit.[113] Afghans engaged in their own campaign of reassurance, convincing Americans that aid represented a worthwhile endeavor. If they dabbled in "blackmail," they did so adroitly, usually averring a preference for Western aid. Concerned by the sudden ebbs and turns in the Afghan aid contest, Washington labored to keep pace. To their ultimate detriment, and that of their patrons, the Afghans insisted upon a rapid timetable that privileged aggressive bidding and discouraged careful analysis.

Overlooked in Washington, meanwhile, was the possibility that the bloc regarded the Afghan status quo as acceptable. Predictions of Afghanistan facing Soviet economic blackmail oddly failed to contemplate the broader consequences of such arm-twisting. An early exemplar of Asian self-determination, Afghanistan had numerous friends within the nonaligned world. Coercive Soviet action against Kabul risked sparking criticism elsewhere and would offer the capitalists a powerful parable of the dangers of accepting Soviet aid and commerce. Although they were determined competitors, the Soviets and their allies erred on the side of caution where Afghan sensitivities were concerned.

They had a compelling positive reason for doing so. Afghanistan could serve as a proving ground for Soviet theories of development; its poverty and isolation might add special significance to any ensuing triumphs. As a monarchy and neighbor, Afghanistan stood well apart from other major postcolonial recipients of Soviet largesse, offering Khrushchev a unique showcase for his propaganda theme of peaceful coexistence. The Soviets applied the phrase frequently to their relationship with Kabul, even backdating it to the 1920s. No other nonaligned state offered Khrushchev such an opportunity to rebuff Western claims of communist imperialism: to proclaim that Soviet beneficence came free of political strings. Often suspicious of the Soviet Union, Naim contended in autumn 1959 that Moscow's immediate goal within the kingdom was to impress other Asian states.[114]

As a nonaligned showcase of Soviet aid and neighborly amicability, Afghanistan would have given U.S. policymakers cause for irritation, not anxiety. Perceiving dangers to Afghan independence instead forced them to grapple with the limitations and inconsistencies of the beachhead concept. Despite vowing not to compete with Moscow, offer for offer, they rose regularly to the challenge. The stakes of each contest usually proved compelling in the moment. By itself, moreover, a beachhead could not suffice—not if the objective was to prevent the emergence of a hostile regime in Kabul, menacing Iran and Pakistan. The imperative of responding rapidly precluded detailed planning. In the south, this specifically entailed defending an ill-conceived irrigation scheme by rushing into a doubtful airport project.

Caveats should be appended when assessing the ambitious U.S. effort and, by extension, the success of Afghan entreaties. The late 1950s represented the apogee of the Afghan aid competition, as both blocs committed to the contest, encouraged by Daoud's government. Afghan-Pakistani détente enabled the free flow of material while removing a potent counterargument against aiding Kabul. As a Republican president, meanwhile, Eisenhower could marshal votes for aid from otherwise skeptical conservative legislators, persuasively describing a growing Soviet threat in the uncommitted world. Nevertheless, Washington could only do so much. Budgetary limits constrained Eisenhower, but so did domestic ideology and considerations of political economy. Domestic restrictions against aiding overseas cotton cultivation precluded assistance in one promising sector.[115] Washington also remained aloof from oil exploration, and Morrison-Knudsen obtained additional contracts, despite obvious Afghan animosity. Stubborn bureaucratic divisions obstructed action and withstood complaints from the field. Even at its height, Kabul's leverage had clear limits.

Despite such constraints, the U.S. mission in Afghanistan labored energetically and enthusiastically. Commitment, personal and ideological, made such persistence possible. The Afghan Cold War offered its share of trials and frustration, yet its frontline combatants visibly embraced the struggle. Mills, Byroade, Meyer, and Snyder worked exhaustively to oppose the Soviet challenge within the kingdom. Their correspondence reveals bureaucratic friction and interpersonal sniping but betrays no doubts that Afghanistan was worth contesting. Notions of duty and commitment to a global Cold War partially explain this, but so too does the particular affinity felt for Afghanistan by Americans. Born of necessity, accompanied by reminders of forsaken past entreaties, Afghan nonalignment elicited far more understanding than exasperation. The Eisenhower administration worried more about Afghan miscalculation than nascent socialism. Yet Washington and its adversaries were, themselves, taking additional chances—within the kingdom and on the global stage. Renewed friction along Afghanistan's flanks coincided with a worsening of Cold War tensions, risking the entanglement of the East-West struggle with the Durand Line conflict. Entering the new decade, the risks of calamitous misjudgment—whether in Central Europe, the Caribbean, or the Pashtun borderlands—mounted dangerously.

CHAPTER 6

The Crisis Era, 1959–1963

Under other circumstances, Dwight Eisenhower's December 1959 trip to Afghanistan might have been a success. Soviet-made MiG Afghan fighter jets escorted his aircraft from the Pakistani border to the Bagram airfield, where more MiGs sat parked, to Eisenhower's unease. An hour-long drive into Kabul took him within sight of the Soviet-built silo complex. Eisenhower only spent three hours in the capital, divided between events at the palace and brief formalities at the parade grounds. He expressed concern over the growing Soviet presence to King Zahir and Foreign Minister Mohammed Naim Khan, who in turn stressed the kingdom's poverty and their desire to remain independent. Eisenhower found his hosts sincere if not entirely realistic. He later described Afghanistan as "the poorest country" he had ever seen, yet the enthusiasm of Kabulites heartened him considerably. Secret Service agents had to restrain exuberant Afghans from reaching into the open vehicle to touch the president.[1]

The trip illuminated Washington's regional predicaments, on the eve of the new decade, without revealing any solutions. Eisenhower practiced presidential diplomacy with atypical, unaffected skill. Yet Afghans observed that the visit had been a quick interlude between lengthier stops in Pakistan and India. Pakistani President Mohammed Ayub Khan's hostility toward Prime Minister Mohammed Daoud Khan, whom he repeatedly derided as "stupid," and his complaints about U.S. aid to India offered scant encouragement for U.S. efforts to surmount regional rivalries. Daoud remained

Figure 6.1 Afghans awaiting Eisenhower's motorcade, December 9, 1959
Source: United States National Archives, College Park, Record Group 306

convinced of Afghanistan's need for rapid development and of his ability to balance between the blocs. On a subsequent stop in Tehran, Eisenhower found the Shah to be more concerned by the prospect of Soviet-inspired aggression from Afghanistan or Iraq than of a direct attack from the north. Assurances of solidarity and appeals for restraint made little impression on either ally.[2]

Less than two weeks later, on the morning of December 21, Kandahar erupted into a spasm of rioting. The uprising sprung from multiple causes. An earlier decree by Daoud, permitting the voluntary unveiling of women, had roiled religious sentiment. Local farmers chafed at regulations on water use from the Helmand Valley Authority, and landowners resented Daoud's efforts to collect taxes. Road building, conscription, and increased traffic into Kandahar's old airport contributed to regional unrest. Inevitably Americans, the largest foreign community present in Kandahar, suffered at the hands of the rioters. Aid workers, their families, and Afghan servants barricaded themselves inside their residences against the mob, which was, ultimately, violently dispersed by the arrival of Afghan soldiers in Soviet-made tanks.[3]

U.S. Ambassador Henry Byroade privately blamed Pakistan's incendiary Pashto-language propaganda for sparking the violence.[4] After Kabul boosted its own broadcasts into the Pakistani borderlands during the autumn, its neighbor had answered in kind, describing Daoud's unveiling decree as proof of atheistic tendencies in Kabul.[5] The barrage continued after the riots, in the new decade, as Radio Pakistan charged the Afghan government, including the royal family, with violating the tenets of Islam.[6] Daoud's expansive modernization agenda had already strained his government's tenuous relations with its citizenry; his festering conflict with Ayub drove each to attempt acts of subversion against the other. The conflict between the neighbors could be postponed no longer, nor could the contradiction between Kabul's development aspirations and its appeals for Pashtun self-determination.

As the Afghan-Pakistani conflict escalated unpredictably, it became entangled with an increasingly volatile Cold War. Daoud's continued appeals for aid alternated with challenges to Washington's regional policy, especially its military presence in the Pashtun borderlands. Nor were U.S. relations with Pakistan devoid of friction. Although Ayub promised staunch support for U.S. Cold War policies, deepening ambivalence afflicted ties between Washington and Karachi. Pakistani officials professed disappointment with U.S. military aid and alarm at growing U.S. assistance to India. For his part, dismayed by Pakistan's incessant requests for weaponry, Eisenhower occasionally expressed doubts about the alliance. He also held a growing conviction that the economic battle for India could decide the fate of Asia. U.S. regional policy teetered between engaging India and reassuring Pakistan, hoping to surmount the subcontinent's all-defining rivalry.

While Eisenhower sought an improbable balance in Afghanistan's immediate region, he enjoyed a phase of fleeting calm in his relations with the Soviet Union. First Secretary Nikita Khrushchev's conciliatory tone and festive autumn 1959 visit to the United States afforded some hope of reduced tensions. Yet concerns about the Soviet missile program festered and spurred Eisenhower along a different path. His country team in Afghanistan concurrently perceived and reacted to a mounting crisis of U.S. credibility, worsened by baffling logistical and bureaucratic impediments. Concurrently, Eisenhower's pursuit of conclusive intelligence on the Soviet missile arsenal shattered any late prospects for détente while drawing South Asia deeper into the Cold War.

Eisenhower's successor, John F. Kennedy, inherited an unsettled situation around the world—including along the Afghan-Pakistani frontier. Western anxiety about the Sovietization of Afghanistan peaked after Daoud's closure of the frontier in late summer 1961. While hardly prominent among the crises Kennedy faced, the impasse presented a far graver challenge than that of its shorter 1955 precursor. Kennedy's choices here proved both fateful and revealing. Amid fatalistic prognoses and nuclear crises, Kennedy achieved rare success, exploiting the growing contradiction between Afghan agendas through fruitful interaction with elements of the royal family. Daoud's fall from power in 1963 opened new possibilities as Cold War tensions waned.

"This Timetable Is Not Good Enough": 1960

Before Afghanistan policy became a matter of crisis management, the logic of the 1950s aid contest remained dominant. On the first day of the new decade, the U.S. country team wrote emphatically about the project posing the "most striking single opportunity to make [a] significant impact" within Afghanistan. They referred neither to the Helmand Valley, nor to aviation, nor to a new road, but rather to the field of education.[7]

As Soviet-made arms flowed into the kingdom, bloc technicians explored northern petroleum deposits, and as Moscow planned the Herat-Kandahar highway, education remained an anomalous field within the Afghan aid contest. Americans retained a visible advantage in that arena, dating back to the days of wayward teachers like Wilbur Harlan. Afghan elites had long preferred the pedagogical services of nationals from noncontiguous powers: educators less likely to pursue a subversive agenda. The University of Wyoming emerged in 1954 as the aid mission's primary partner in educational efforts. The university responded promptly to early appeals for Point Four assistance, convincing the Technical Cooperation Administration (TCA) that the Cowboy State enjoyed crucial geographic and climatic similarities with Afghanistan. During the 1950s, Wyoming dispatched agricultural instructors and other specialists to Kabul University and welcomed Afghan students at its campus in Laramie.[8] In a 1957 exchange, Daoud termed the university the most important contribution he could make to Afghanistan.[9]

As the Soviet presence grew, education remained a unique U.S. preserve. Increasingly anxious about the U.S. standing, Byroade and his International

Cooperation Administration (ICA) counterpart Stellan Wollmar argued emphatically in their New Year's Day cable for support of the expansion of Kabul University and the Afghan education system, citing the possibility to "influence [the] upcoming ranks" of Afghan leaders. Education constituted the "principal U.S. hope for [the] future." Upon an earlier commitment to fund the construction of five buildings, Byroade and Wollmar proposed financing a faculty of sciences and technology institute. Outside of Kabul, they proposed providing designs and materials for a network of model high schools, perhaps connected to capital schools via closed-circuit television, and expanded educational assistance to help staff and advise them.[10]

For all their symbolism, education programs in Afghanistan had previously been eclipsed by grandiose, capital-intensive endeavors. Seeking new advances on favorable terrain, Byroade and Wollmar now pursued ambitious, transformative objectives in this sector. Their revised program called for increased expenditures of aid dollars and locally generated afghanis; crucially, it also required multiyear funding and far greater certitude than the Eisenhower administration appeared able to provide. The ensuing intragovernmental debate about the education program more broadly reflected faltering U.S. efforts within Afghanistan.

Galvanized by Soviet advances, Eisenhower had developed an array of new aid programs, including PL-480, the Development Loan Fund (DLF), international aid consortia, and the Asian development fund. The ICA had shifted much of its aid toward a grant basis. Yet from Byroade's perspective, Washington appeared hamstrung, indecisive, even indifferent to Afghan requests. Daoud and Naim expressed puzzlement and frustration at Washington's inability to respond clearly to specific requests. Directly addressing Secretary of State Christian Herter, Byroade complained of unacceptable "delays, red tape, and frustrations of attempting to get foreign construction projects in [Afghanistan] completed or, in fact, even started." He likened the task of resolving impasses to that of solving a jigsaw puzzle, when half of the pieces could be found in Kabul and the others in Washington.[11]

Byroade knew a bit about construction projects; diplomatic service actually represented his second career. A 1937 West Point graduate, he spent much of the Second World War commanding U.S. Army Corps of Engineers (USACE) units, supervising efforts to pave airfields in India. He attained the rank of brigadier general in 1946, at thirty-two, before accompanying Gen. George Marshall on an ill-fated mediation mission to China. Afterward he branched out into diplomacy, heading the State Department's German desk while Eisenhower commanded NATO. Eisenhower's choice to retain Byroade as assistant secretary of state—the sole Truman appointee at that level to survive the party transition—conveyed his regard. So did high-profile, challenging ambassadorial assignments in Egypt and South Africa. Byroade's experience, prestige, and rapport with Eisenhower afforded him an unusual degree of latitude for an ambassador in Kabul.[12]

Separate developments in early 1960 impelled Byroade forward in an unusual effort to change both the focus of U.S. aid within Afghanistan and the means by which it was delivered. Worsening tensions between the kingdom and Pakistan amid the propaganda war and following the Kandahar riot offered one major impetus. Worse, Byroade reported, Daoud and Naim suspected that Washington had encouraged Ayub to take a hard line. Unyielding Pakistani policy appeared more likely to antagonize Afghanistan than would any Soviet initiative in the kingdom. Byroade's frustration led him toward a more sympathetic assessment of the Afghan viewpoint than that of any of his predecessors. Regardless of whether Ayub was willing to admit it, he wrote, a "genuine and practical issue exists over the status and welfare of the [Pakistani] Pashtuns." His embassy was "satisfied that Afghan emotional involvement [in] this issue [is] largely genuine."[13]

Khrushchev's second visit to Kabul, undertaken in March, suggested that Moscow might exploit the worsening conflict. Publicly, Khrushchev emphasized the tenet of peaceful coexistence, citing the Soviet-Afghan bond as evidence that "countries possessing different social systems" could "maintain the closest ties of friendship." The trip lent itself to ambiguities. Khrushchev appeared fatigued, and the visit did not yield any milestones comparable to his December 1955 loan. One of his gifts to his Afghan hosts, a crate of pungent Indonesian durian fruit, verged on prankishness. Another, however, held an ominous significance: the joint communique issued by Khrushchev and Daoud expressed agreement that the principle of self-determination should be accorded to the Pashtuns of Pakistan.[14]

Such ominous trends gave Byroade cause to visit Eisenhower on April 23. Byroade contended that the Soviets had made the country a testing ground for economic assistance programs. This made the failures of U.S.-funded efforts especially galling. The ICA's contracting process seemed "unworkable," and the agency appeared unable to supervise its own projects. Byroade recommended shifting further overseas work to the USACE. The complaint struck a sympathetic nerve. Eisenhower replied that he was tired of hearing about "waste, mistakes, and delays," especially as legislators used these episodes to attack his administration. Of Byroade's notion of using the USACE, he wrote, "I must say the idea has some appeal."[15]

Were it solely a matter of convincing Eisenhower, Byroade would have had cause for optimism. The president's complaint about appropriation committees, however, identified the real obstacle in Washington. Eisenhower's final foreign aid budget faced a rocky reception on Capitol Hill, where opponents spoke of cutting it by a quarter. In a May 2 national address, Eisenhower warned the public of a "crushing defeat" in the Cold War if his aid program was cut substantially. In this heated atmosphere, Afghan entreaties faced dim prospects.[16]

While one group of legislative opponents assailed Eisenhower's aid budget, another prodded him toward an action that would link Afghanistan's border conflict with the Cold War. On May 1, 1960, Soviet air defense forces shot down a U.S. spy plane over the Siberian city of Sverdlovsk. Attempting to assess the Soviet missile program, in response to domestic critics, Eisenhower had authorized a series of overflights. The ill-fated U-2 aircraft had launched from an airfield in Peshawar. Shortly before he trespassed over the Soviet Union, Capt. Francis Gary Powers had also violated Afghanistan's sovereign airspace. A Soviet prosecutor noted this fact at the pilot's Moscow trial—a neighborly gesture of sorts.[17]

The U-2 episode undermined Eisenhower's final summit with Khrushchev, intensifying Cold War tensions for the remainder of his presidency. Its effect on bilateral relations with Afghanistan was subtler. With Byroade away, Naim handed the acting chief of mission, Norman Hannah, an official protest. He appeared more flummoxed by Eisenhower's admission of the overflight than by the violation itself. Washington pledged not to repeat the offense, and the U-2 incident receded from the bilateral agenda. Kabul saw little purpose in straining relations with its second-greatest benefactor, particularly while it hoped that Washington might support the Second Five-Year Plan.[18]

More ominously, the incident risked turning the Pashtunistan conflict into a Cold War proxy battle. "Where is this place, Peshawar?" Khrushchev reportedly demanded of Pakistan's ambassador at a Moscow reception, "we have circled it in red on our maps." Standing nearby, the Afghan ambassador helpfully volunteered that it lay within "occupied Pashtunistan." "So, it is occupied Pashtunistan," Khrushchev agreed. His government threatened attacks on Pakistani air bases if further intrusions occurred. Notably, Kabul assailed Pakistan over the incident more vehemently than it had the United

States, subsequently terming its neighbor's (truthful) denial of prior knowledge further evidence of "ill will." The episode fit neatly into a mounting pattern of incursion and escalation between the two neighbors. Months earlier, Pakistan had accused Afghanistan of a similar aerial violation.[19]

The U-2 debacle meanwhile reinforced doubts in Karachi. Washington had acted recklessly, with little apparent consideration for its ally's safety, compounding Pakistani anxieties about Eisenhower's economic assistance to India, the limits of Washington's military aid program, and seeming U.S. equivocation on Pashtunistan. Ayub questioned his ally's resolve and judgment in late June and moved to mend fences with Moscow. Little time remained for Eisenhower to soothe Pakistani anxieties.[20]

Nor did the administration enjoy leeway to address Byroade's complaints. On May 6, Afghan ambassador Mohammed Hashim Maiwandwal asked Acting Secretary of State C. Douglas Dillon for U.S. support toward the Second Five-Year Plan, which would require roughly $500 million in foreign currency—four times as much as its predecessor. Concurrently, Byroade continued his advocacy in Washington, meeting with Dillon and ICA director James Riddleberger on May 13. The duo responded favorably to Byroade's notion of employing the USACE but could make no promises about long-term commitments. Byroade suggested mirroring the Soviet approach: extending Afghanistan a line of credit toward separate projects. Dillon opined that it could not be achieved during the current legislative term but promised to raise his concerns about Afghan aid at the National Security Council (NSC) level.[21]

In a political sense, Dillon was correct. By that point, Eisenhower's final foreign assistance bill faced the legislative gauntlet, and its survival in recognizable form was all that could be hoped for. Its expansion to include tens, perhaps hundreds of millions of dollars in support of centralized planning in Afghanistan lay well outside the realm of political possibility. Simultaneously, however, Byroade's complaints highlighted a new, invidious disparity between Afghan aid and other U.S. programs in the region.

Complaints about extensive U.S. assistance to Iran and Pakistan were a familiar Afghan refrain by the end of the Eisenhower years, lent greater feeling by escalating tensions with both neighbors. A new, more glaring contrast could be made with the rapidly changing U.S. aid program in India. Two years earlier, as Jawaharlal Nehru's own Second Five-Year Plan faced a debilitating foreign exchange shortage, Eisenhower had responded promptly. The Eximbank and DLF jointly extended a loan of $225 million.

Washington convened a lenders consortium, soliciting an additional $350 million in emergency assistance from allies. Toward Afghanistan, meanwhile, the Eximbank assumed the role of a hectoring creditor, while the DLF appeared aloof and unresponsive. Nor was a grand consortium of Western lenders likely to convene.[22]

Once again, the comparison begs for additional context. Obviously, Afghanistan could not command the same sense of urgency in Western capitals. Nehru's standing as the world's preeminent nonaligned statesman and his country's potential to act as a geopolitical and symbolic counterweight to China galvanized the Eisenhower administration to bend the rules of its foreign assistance policy and to invent new ones. Political heavyweights like Eleanor Roosevelt, Hubert Humphrey, Chester Bowles, and John F. Kennedy ardently supported aid to New Delhi. Their advocacy drew considerably from liberal enthusiasm for India and its charismatic leader, and the belief of theorists that the South Asian giant could serve as a crucial proving ground for Western, democratic models of development.[23]

Afghanistan did not enjoy the active interest of such proponents. While, unlike India, it lacked dedicated legislative opponents, the lack of passionate aid advocates outside of the State Department limited the possibilities available to it. That absence was unsurprising. Afghanistan lacked a vital or reliable export—karakul prices fluctuated distressingly—and had failed to attract Western investment. Its connections to the West were poor, even when Pakistan was in a congenial mood. An embryonic university system—the focus of Byroade's education program—limited opportunities to engage foreign experts. Development theorists had identified numerous other postcolonial polities with theoretically better prospects for attaining economic takeoff and acting as showcases for Western models. Most did not adjoin the Soviet Union. Thus, Afghanistan remained marginal within the development literature that influenced the Eisenhower administration and its successors. Whereas the kingdom's delicate geopolitics disqualified it from the alliance-building race of the early decade, its isolation, obscurity, and poverty disadvantaged it as the Cold War shifted toward more symbolic grounds.

Thus, even as Byroade received a sympathetic hearing and apparent endorsement from Eisenhower, his aid program remained mired by delays and disagreements between the country team and its parent agencies. Word that the USACE could consult on future Afghan projects gave Byroade rare cause for elation upon his return to Kabul. Three weeks later, however, the country team received instructions to redraft and downscale its education program. Byroade found the new, reduced budget preposterous, as Washington had seemingly already approved their expansive January 1 program. "This unhappy history typifies difficulty we have in competing effectively with the Soviets in Afghanistan," Byroade wrote. Khrushchev had promised the Afghans a technical institute during his March visit, and his government offered to fund laboratories at Kabul University. Furious, Byroade demanded that the Afghanistan Action Group in Washington account for the inexplicable delay, submitting its findings to the Kabul embassy "for review and accuracy, as we are confronted with statements in Washington . . . which lead us to wonder if such material was even thoroughly read, let alone studied."[24]

A sense of crisis emerged within the U.S. country team in the early summer, fueled by reports that Moscow had offered to cover the $500 million foreign exchange requirements of the Second Five-Year Plan. Acknowledging the difficulties posed by the unfolding presidential election, and the legislative timetable, Byroade exhorted his superiors to undertake dramatic action. Daoud remained intent on a crash program of development but required concrete promises of foreign assistance before finalizing it. Byroade appealed for a Western aid consortium able to cover half the costs, as well as expanded PL-480 and DLF support. Absent immediate action, he warned, "we cannot much longer be able accurately to refer to Afghanistan as neutral nation."[25]

In Washington, however, a sense of resignation prevailed. As promised, Dillon raised the question of Afghan aid at a May 31 NSC meeting. Remaining noncommittal, he noted that congressional limits on the DLF prevented that agency from extending long-term support. No meaningful prospect for revising the law remained during the current session, but the issue could perhaps be raised in 1961. Eisenhower lamented that the next year might be "too late for Afghanistan," adding that Soviet control over the country would endanger the entire Middle East. The discussion then turned to the aftermath of the U-2 affair.[26]

Byroade's superiors clearly believed that he was best handled delicately. A message approved by Dillon and Riddleberger affirmed the importance of the education program but cautioned that the U.S. government had "sometimes embarked on projects in Afghanistan under such great time pressure that certain aspects of their implementation have later returned to plague us." Nor could the U.S. government offer any preliminary commitments in advance of the Five-Year Plan, creating a maddening impasse. Whereas Kabul contended that it needed specific commitments to devise its plan, Washington insisted upon receiving a concrete plan before it ventured additional commitments. Byroade's suggestion of a consortium received no reply.[27]

Byroade's improbable effort had failed, but it had brought the Kabul embassy full circle: to a repudiation of the beachhead strategy adopted earlier. Commenting on the revised Operations Control Board program for Afghanistan, Byroade's embassy explicitly criticized paragraph 56-A of NSC 5409, which had cautioned against attempting to match the Soviets bid for bid. What had previously seemed a judicious balancing of ends and means struck them as woefully inadequate. The OCB plan called for demonstrating that Afghanistan need not rely solely on the Soviets and deemed present aid levels "probably sufficient" for that objective. "Logically, this is no doubt true," the embassy wrote, "and would be so even if U.S. aid were to fall to one hundred dollars per year, but it leaves unanswered the question of whether it is adequate to provide a successful 'alternative to Soviet sources of development assistance.' . . . Considering that total Soviet aid approaches $350 million whereas total American aid is approximately $150 million, the question arises: 'How can the lesser or weaker be an effective alternative to the greater or stronger?' " Having thus obtained the initiative, the Soviets appeared willing to raise their own bids, drawing the United States into "a costly holding operation at best with no end in sight." Rather—in a section provocatively titled "A new look?"—the embassy proposed a comprehensive program: a consortium; generous support of the Five-Year Plan; mediation of the Afghan-Iranian dispute over the Helmand waters; and improvement of the kingdom's overland connections to its western neighbor.[28]

The shift in geographic emphasis was telling. Improving roads in western Iran appeared to be the only way to ensure Western access to Afghanistan, as Afghan-Pakistani relations deteriorated. Daoud's commerce minister accused Pakistan of impeding cross-border traffic, thereby violating the 1958 transit agreement. In May, Kabul announced that it would not allow Pakistani citizens to remain in the kingdom. British and U.S. appeals failed to still the increasingly vituperative propaganda war. The conflict even overshadowed what should have been celebratory moments for the U.S. mission. A groundbreaking ceremony for the Kabul University campus came partly undone when Daoud used the occasion to denounce the Durand Line.[29]

On September 23, the borderlands witnessed the most serious violence in years. Pashtun nomads crossed the border in the Bajaur district but retreated before fierce resistance from their counterparts in Pakistan. Although the full extent of Afghanistan's involvement in the clash remained unclear—by some reports, Afghan Army regulars had taken part—signs of premeditation were unmistakable. Defeat in Bajaur and the pro-government solidarity displayed by Pakistani Pashtuns dealt Daoud a humiliating blow. Following the debacle, he asked Byroade's assistance in preventing Pakistani retaliation.[30]

Oddly enough, as gunfire echoed in Bajaur, Naim and Eisenhower met amicably in New York. Much of their exchange revolved around Pashtunistan, although neither appears to have known about the violence then under way. To Naim's evident elation, Eisenhower promised to "have another look at this question." News of the clash cast Eisenhower's offer in a very different light. When Zahir wrote to request presidential mediation, Herter cautioned Eisenhower against accepting any sort of mediating role. Naim received the news with evident disappointment, suggesting that worse hostilities could follow.[31]

He may have been in an exceptionally difficult position. Rumors circulated of a serious rift between Naim and Daoud, who had been humiliated in Bajaur. Naim likely hoped that Eisenhower's offer could ease the kingdom out of its predicament, sparing his brother from total defeat. U.S. reticence closed off that avenue. Daoud, meanwhile, was not one to compromise under external pressure. In late November, weeks after Eisenhower's reply, Kabul formally accused the Pakistani military of massacring civilians in Bajaur.[32]

Rebuffed by Washington, Kabul recommitted to Pashtunistan but tailored its appeal in a manner likely to please Khrushchev. By the late autumn, a new argument entered Kabul's propaganda campaign: that Pakistan's Cold War alignment endangered the Pashtuns of the borderlands. Kabul media repeatedly alleged that Pakistan hosted Western "atomic and rocket bases." Stoking neutralist sentiment within Pakistan, Afghan propaganda criticized Pakistan's choice to align in the Cold War, linking it to the repression of non-Punjabis, the loss of national sovereignty, and a bloated military budget. Questioned about such messaging, Foreign Ministry official Nur Ahmad Etemadi disavowed any intent of vilifying the United States. Certainly, Washington faced worse rhetorical assaults in the Third World. Nonetheless, Afghan propaganda now effectively challenged the integrity of the U.S.

alliance system. The problem of reconciling Afghan independence with regional security had grown knottier, as the Eisenhower administration concluded.[33]

Eisenhower departed office at a moment of profound tension in the Cold War. The worsening relationship between Afghanistan and its U.S.-allied neighbors can be situated alongside other potential crises he faced that winter: the familiar litany of Berlin, Indochina, and Cuba. Afghanistan did not constitute a problem of the same magnitude, but it clearly worried Eisenhower as well. His final years attest to his interest in the kingdom and his concern about its possible absorption into the bloc.

Eisenhower's Afghanistan policy offers a recognizable microcosm of the evolution of his Cold War strategy. As much as any state, Afghanistan bore the consequences of Eisenhower's pursuit of a global alliance system. Confronting the ensuing dilemma, Eisenhower clearly considered covert options, ultimately rejecting them. Instead, Afghanistan witnessed the emergence of a wide-ranging, often vigorous, adaptive aid program. Eisenhower employed his own formidable charm repeatedly on the Afghan elite. Nevertheless, his successes flowed on the uncertain currents of Afghan-Pakistani ties, and Ike only dabbled with efforts to resolve the border conflict. Like his nuclear doctrine, his aid offensive only remained viable so long as it did not draw a competitive counterbid from the Soviet bloc. The concept of a beachhead offered a reassuring mantra to Americans, who remained loath in practice to cede any sector entirely to the foe. Eisenhower's efforts within Afghanistan were considerable and yet could not ultimately be sufficient. He managed contradictions of his own making as best he could but ultimately bequeathed a baffling, deteriorating situation to Kennedy.

The New Frontier and the Durand Line: 1961

Welcome news reached the Afghan government on January 12, 1961, eight days before Kennedy assumed office. With Byroade away, the interim chief of mission, Norman Hannah, presented a detailed proposal to Naim providing Afghanistan with a five-year funding commitment of $16.8 million toward the education project. Revised in dialogue between the country team and Washington, the finalized agenda included the expansion of Kabul University, the development of vocational education, and the construction of additional schools. To secure the Bureau of the Budget's approval, Dillon had attested that education development served to "safeguard United States interests in what we consider a critical country." Naim offered his gratitude. Above all, he expressed the hope that Byroade, upon his return, might bring further news of long-term U.S. support for the Afghan development program.[34]

Considerable Afghan expectations awaited the new administration, somewhat reflecting local esteem for Kennedy. Afghan officials had expressed satisfaction at JFK's victory, predicting that his election would further the cause of peace, but also hoping that he would expand the U.S. aid program and support the Second Five-Year Plan. Byroade hoped that the new administration would prove more receptive to his mission's advocacy.[35]

The new administration took office determined to discard the Manichean outlook it ascribed to its Republican predecessors. Kennedy had no fundamental objection to nonalignment in Asia or Africa. He hoped to pursue a creative new offensive within the Third World: engaging nonaligned governments, promoting economic development, and consequently staving off the risk of communist expansion or subversion. These objectives were acceptable, even desirable to Daoud's government.[36]

Kennedy's campaign rhetoric suggested the possibility of a dramatic expansion of U.S. foreign assistance. Reform of the foreign aid program quickly emerged as a priority for the new administration. In a special address to Congress on March 22, Kennedy decried a system that was "bureaucratically fragmented, awkward and slow" with its administration "diffused over a haphazard and irrational structure." He proposed the consolidation of the ICA, the DLF, and the PL-480 program, among others, into a single agency. Noting that institutional consolidation would not suffice by itself, Kennedy argued that the "instrument of primary emphasis—the single most important tool" would be the ability to extend long-term loans. Moscow's ability to provide such aid, meanwhile, enabled it "to make developing nations economically dependent on Russian support." Kennedy did not specify Afghanistan, but he had effectively invoked it.[37]

Yet, even as one program partially eclipsed another, Afghanistan would struggle for visibility. Daoud's credentials as a nonaligned statesman were impeccable, but he could not claim the same prominence as Nehru, Nasser, or Sukarno. Although well-traveled, the New Frontiersmen mostly lacked firsthand experience with Afghanistan. Walt Rostow, the administration's foremost development proponent, had not written of Afghanistan during the 1950s. The president-elect had never visited the kingdom (although a blank visa application from 1951 in his congressional files suggests some prior interest).[38]

The New Frontiersmen regarded Moscow's progress in Afghanistan during the 1950s as a cautionary tale, particularly Eisenhower's lost opportunity to pave the streets of Kabul.[39] Kennedy's criticisms of the fragmented aid system and its emphasis on short-term allocations echoed laments heard in embassies throughout the Third World—including and especially Byroade's. Fundamentally, however, the new administration kept other states foremost in mind. Rostow described the administration as shifting from "a defensive effort to shore-up weak economies" toward a coordinated, multilateral effort "to move forward those nations prepared to mobilize their own resources for development purposes": countries possessing "the capacity to absorb capital productively." He excluded Afghanistan from that category, recommending instead that increased aid to the kingdom be conditioned on the development of "serious domestic programs." Rostow's target list featured regional powers, including India, Pakistan, and Nigeria, as well as major Latin American allies.[40]

Afghanistan presented difficulties in early 1961, but not with the urgency of a Cuba or Laos. Nor could it compete with the Indias or Brazils of the world as a showcase of development. However global priorities were considered and policy targets were ranked, the kingdom remained profoundly unlikely to come out ahead. Yet, in the end, Afghanistan policy proved as much of a challenge to Kennedy as it had been for his predecessors. Having forced the Eisenhower administration to reckon with the limits of a strategy founded around alliances, Afghanistan impelled the New Frontiersmen toward a different reckoning: approaching it as a symbolic battleground, despite its unlikelihood of attaining economic takeoff.

Early signals from the new administration appeared heartening to the Kabul government. Upon his return in February Byroade presented a status report on U.S. projects to Naim, noting the effective completion of the Kandahar airport and forward movement in border road projects. Delivering the offer of educational assistance, Byroade also promised an additional $10 million toward irrigation and drainage work in the Helmand. Although he could not offer funding for the next Five-Year Plan, he noted interest in Washington in supporting it and suggested that longer-term commitments might be possible in the future. As an interim measure, the State Department sought economic experts to assist the kingdom with its planning.[41]

The new administration had heightened expectations, although the expansion of its aid program remained an uncertain prospect. Daoud's lengthy convalescence in Italy delayed the government's response to Byroade's offer. The prime minister's return renewed Afghan entreaties. Naim requested $196 million toward the Five-Year Plan. The often-frustrated Byroade detected a "change for the better so obvious it cannot be ignored." Heartened by its initial reading of the new administration, Afghanistan sought to maintain "equilibrium" between its benefactors and had thereby limited the requests it had placed with the Soviets. Pashtunistan rhetoric had softened in the new year. Yet moods in Kabul often changed suddenly. Reports of long-term U.S. aid to India piqued Naim's interest, and Byroade asked for updated guidance on the future of U.S. aid.[42]

Washington's response dashed any hope of a policy change, laying the Rostovian agenda squarely on the table. Long-term assistance, Byroade was informed, would be afforded primarily to "those countries whose stage of development, planning and internal resources mobilization" afforded real hope of "self-sustained growth in [the] foreseeable future."[43] "To us it seems inconceivable," Byroade wrote, "that our policy of trying to preserve neutral nation on borders of USSR should be rendered ineffective and unresponsive to clear US interests in Asia by the application of pure economic theory alone, divorced from consideration of history of our relations with this country and its neighbors as well as from the realities of the international situation."[44] Emphasis on a "highly sophisticated" plan was "unrealistic. This country needs everything." Byroade wondered, moreover, which countries truly enjoyed the possibility of self-sustained growth. Applied globally, the criterion would limit U.S. aid to a few recipients, ceding all others to Soviet programs. No tactful way existed of informing his hosts that economic criteria excluded the kingdom from consideration. Better, he argued, to abandon Afghanistan than engage in an extended, miserly "retreat based on theoretical economics."[45]

Byroade could not change policy, but he could capture the attention of his superiors. His cables elicited messages from Assistant Secretary of State Phillips Talbot, who headed the department's Near East and South Asia bureau, and Under Secretary of State Chester Bowles, assuring him that Afghanistan was important to the new administration and suggesting that support for the Five-Year Plan could be forthcoming—if further details emerged from Kabul.[46] The core problem remained, however. Without concrete promises, the Afghan government was unable to finalize its plan, while Washington required a completed plan as a prerequisite to offering assistance. "We are indeed in [a] vicious circle," Byroade commented.[47]

The aid bill dashed his hopes. While Kennedy succeeded in consolidating existing programs into the new Agency for International Development, he could not alter the basis of foreign assistance. The final bill maintained congressional authority over development lending, precluding direct loans from the U.S. Treasury, also suggesting that the administration enjoyed no political honeymoon on aid questions. The outcome precluded the sort of flexible, generous assistance desperately sought by the Kabul government. By the time Kennedy signed the bill on September 4, a sharp deterioration in Afghan-Pakistani relations left even the future of the current U.S. aid program deeply uncertain.[48]

After its autumn 1960 victory, the Pakistani government stumbled in efforts to consolidate its hold in the frontier. As Elisabeth Leake argues, Ayub overplayed his hand. His militarization of the borderlands antagonized local Pashtuns.[49] The CIA reported in March that Afghanistan had smuggled rifles and plainclothes volunteers into the region.[50] Escalating conflict tested Washington's relations with both governments. Byroade noted "increasingly caustic" discussion of the use of U.S. military equipment in the North West Frontier Province within the Kabul press.[51] For his part, Ayub faulted Washington for failing to restrain the Afghans.[52] The conflict appeared to be assuming a Cold War valence. The Soviet daily *Pravda* condemned the Pakistani campaign while reiterating Moscow's support for Pashtun self-determination.[53] Pakistani officials expressed alarm at the use of Soviet-made arms by Pashtun insurgents, suggesting that Moscow and Kabul were acting in concert.[54]

Unrest in the borderlands and Ayub's belief that Washington coddled Afghanistan compounded earlier doubts about the U.S. alliance. As a well-known proponent of closer ties to India, Kennedy elicited great suspicion in the Pakistani capital. Ayub chafed at U.S. requests to show restraint in the border region, complaining in an interview, "Our American friends seem to question our right to defend our territory. . . . They seem to put right and wrong on an even level." Washington's generosity toward India likely provided the single greatest grievance. The sums promised to New Delhi by the Western consortium galled Pakistanis, whose own donors' association appeared to be making only halting progress (the Afghans, of course, would have quite liked to have a consortium).[55]

Seeking fundamental reassurance, Ayub visited Washington in July. In a White House meeting with Kennedy, he theatrically unfolded military maps depicting the threats his country purportedly faced from east and west. Ayub opined that once Afghanistan mastered its Soviet-made weaponry, Pakistan would be "up the gum tree," pinned between two hostile neighbors. Kennedy remained skeptical. He did not think India would attack Pakistan, and he resisted Ayub's suggestion that the United States administer "shock treatment" to Afghanistan by withdrawing or limiting its aid. Afghanistan, Kennedy replied, "was not a satellite." As long as "chances remained in Afghanistan," he informed Ayub, "we'd like to be in a position to move forward with them."[56]

To the extent that Ayub sought to curb U.S. engagement of either of his neighbors, he left Washington empty-handed. Nevertheless, he appeared to depart triumphantly, to the evident discomfort of Afghan officials. Ambassador Maiwandwal declared his government's interest in a peaceful solution and obtained a meeting with Kennedy. When they met, it was Maiwandwal's turn to gesture at a map when JFK asked him to define the location of Pashtunistan. Kennedy observed noncommittally that disputes among "nations that are friends of ours create difficult problems," but posited that he could do more to aid Afghan development. Afghan apprehension stirred hopes in Washington. The State Department considered advising Ayub that an "agonizing reappraisal" of Pashtunistan agitation was under way in Kabul; as such, it would be advisable to give the Afghans a "cooling off" period.[57]

Visibly boosted by the trip, Ayub saw little use in letting up. A subsequent U.S. inquiry about use of his territory to monitor Soviet missile launches could only have elevated his confidence. Since the spring, each country had subjected the other's diplomats to increasing restrictions and harassment. On August 23, Ayub shuttered Pakistan's consulates in Jalalabad and Kandahar and demanded the closure of Afghanistan's consulates and trade agencies within Pakistan. Pakistani police barred access to the facilities on the following morning. Lacking an obvious provocation, the timing of the move surprised observers. Ayub issued his decree on the eve of the Jeshyn holiday, when Afghan officials were seldom to be found in their offices. Distracted and unwilling to disrupt the festivities, Daoud and Naim took days to respond. On August 30, they issued a one-week ultimatum, threatening the full severance of diplomatic relations if the consulates and agencies were not reopened.[58]

Afghan officials appeared disconsolate, even fatalistic. Maiwandwal grimly noted that Afghans thought that Ayub had acted with U.S. approval, obtained during his visit. Crucially, while the Pakistanis had closed Afghan facilities, they had not voided the 1958 transit agreement, leaving the border notionally open to commerce. Afghanistan's border regime required only basic declarations from incoming vehicles, chiefly a cargo manifest. Nothing precluded the issuance of documents at new, improvised checkpoints within the border zone, but Afghan consular officials doubted that their government would be so obliging. Shipping delays soon afflicted U.S. development projects within Afghanistan. U.S. officials urged Daoud and Naim to ensure that traffic continued. Blaming Ayub, however, the brothers refused to devise alternative arrangements. One minister declared that he would rather forfeit overland trade than "come begging to Pakistan." Ayub's September 6 closure of his Kabul embassy effectively severed relations.[59]

With dismaying rapidity, a dispute over diplomatic rights and conduct had escalated into a border closure measurably worse than the 1955 episode. Ayub had acted rashly, without prior consultation, in a manner that appeared calculated to disrupt U.S. efforts within Afghanistan—thus thrusting it into greater dependence on the Soviet Union. He imposed a bitter choice on his western neighbor: humiliation or deprivation. Yet Afghan choices frustrated the White House as well. Daoud's refusal to adopt new customs procedures promised to inflict far more economic damage on the kingdom than on its antagonist. Compounding the mess further was the risk, perceived in Washington and Kabul, that the crisis could lead successively to war, a Pakistani invasion, and Soviet intervention.

One Crisis Among Many, 1961–1962

By September, Kennedy had significantly altered the U.S. foreign aid administration but only incrementally changed the U.S. program within Afghanistan. He had, however, transformed the national security policy-making apparatus. Little trace of the purely deliberative Eisenhower-era NSC remained. JFK's national security advisor, McGeorge Bundy, had instead created a small, agile body of ambitious staffers who coordinated policy around the world. The new NSC could respond quickly to crises but also gained its own voice, no longer serving as a mere conduit for debate. At times, it could circumvent or override more venerable bureaucratic actors, especially the State Department.

Bundy's NSC parceled out the world according to the interests of its analysts. Afghanistan fell squarely within the domain of an energetic deputy named Robert Komer, whose responsibilities encompassed a swath of terrain that Genghis Khan would have respected: extending from Morocco to the Indonesian archipelago. A senior CIA analyst of the Near East and South Asia during the Eisenhower years, Komer watched the Pashtunistan conflict closely.[60] He included it on a list of policy problems he submitted to Bundy, days before Kennedy's inauguration.[61] "We had better do something on new flare-up coming here," he wrote in March.[62] With Bundy's approval, he notified Kennedy of the crisis on September 2.[63]

Admittedly, the Kennedy administration faced far more severe problems in the world, including a complex civil war in Laos and a mounting communist insurgency in South Vietnam. Above all, U.S.-Soviet relations had worsened dramatically after Kennedy's failed invasion of Cuba in April. Khrushchev retaliated in June by threatening the Western presence in Berlin; three weeks after construction of a barrier dividing the city commenced, tensions remained dangerously high. The crisis reverberated far beyond Central Europe. The conference of nonaligned states in Belgrade—which Daoud attended as the border crisis dawned—felt compelled to express its fears about the risk of global war. Daoud's own address to the Belgrade Conference conveyed his government's concern. True to form, the Afghan leader refrained from signaling support of either bloc's stance.[64]

Like the U-2 incident, the Berlin crisis worsened relations between the Soviet Union and Afghanistan's other neighbors. Soviet radio broadcasts into Iran sought to incite unrest against the Shah's government, touting secret Baghdad Pact documents purportedly seized during the 1958 Iraqi revolution. Some of the broadcasts described an alleged Western scheme to partition Afghanistan between its eastern and western neighbors.[65] The CIA stopped short of concluding that Khrushchev intended to open a second front, but warned that, should unrest in Iran or the Pashtun borderlands intensify, "the USSR would probably be prepared to take strong measures to exploit them."[66]

Moscow's rhetorical offensive amid the crisis necessitated U.S. efforts to reassure Central Treaty Organization (CENTO) allies. Concurrently, however, the Kennedy administration hoped to sway nonaligned states—particularly India. More than any other attendee, Nehru could conceivably shape the outcome of the Belgrade Conference. Yet Kennedy's provision of advanced weaponry to Pakistan following Ayub's visit had irked the government in New Delhi. After Nehru suggested recognizing the status quo of two German states in Central Europe, JFK worried that the Indian prime minister did not grasp "the basic problem in Berlin."[67]

Kennedy's concurrent efforts to engage India and reassure Pakistan were inherently irreconcilable. The eruption of the second border crisis constituted an unwanted additional complication, holding a greater immediate likelihood of triggering war than that posed by South Asia's central rivalry. At war, Ayub would demand additional military support, which could only be fulfilled at further cost to the relationship with Nehru. Nor could the prospect of further escalation be dismissed. If Pakistan attacked Afghanistan, Khrushchev might construe his neighborly duties expansively and come to the kingdom's aid. Kennedy could no longer ignore the problem of Pashtunistan.

During the crisis, the Kennedy administration entertained four distinct approaches, which were neither entirely complementary nor mutually exclusive. The first and most straightforward was mediation. The severity of the crisis and its potential for escalation overrode traditional hesitation about direct U.S. involvement. On August 31, Secretary of State Dean Rusk directed Byroade and Ambassador William Rountree in Karachi to offer Washington's good offices in resolving the dispute.[68] A presidential letter to Zahir entreated the Afghans to reopen the border to commerce. A simultaneous message to Ayub implored the Pakistani leader to exercise restraint, citing the risk of Khrushchev exploiting the conflict to his own purposes.[69]

One senior official suggested the second option: confronting one of the disputants. Regarding the claims of both governments skeptically, Komer doubted that the proffered good offices alone might resolve the conflict. "I cannot believe," he wrote Bundy, "Afghans want to commit suicide or that Paks want Soviets on the Khyber Pass. *Hence each side's intransigence is basically aimed at forcing the U.S. to intervene on its behalf.*" He endorsed the presidential messages but predicted that "only strongest U.S. pressure on both sides will work." His frustration with and wariness toward both governments inclined him toward tougher measures.[70]

Under Secretary of State Chester Bowles espoused the third option: circumventing the closure through the development of an alternative route into Afghanistan. Like Komer, Bowles—formerly Truman's ambassador to India—boasted considerable regional experience. He had previously visited Kabul and regarded the kingdom as a key Third World battleground.

An outspoken critic of the alliance with Pakistan, Bowles opposed leaving Afghan commerce to Ayub's mercy. He had earlier proposed constructing a special port for Afghanistan at Bandar Abbas in eastern Iran. The eruption of the crisis galvanized Bowles to advance a version of this scheme. In consultation with Talbot, he authorized Byroade to suggest the possibility of developing a new route through eastern Iran, but in order to persuade Daoud to relent on the transit question. An Iranian route appealed considerably to Afghans. Shah Wali, the last surviving royal uncle, inquired independently with Byroade about the possibility. Prior experience inclined Byroade to doubt that an Iranian route offered any sort of near-term solution, but he dutifully passed along the idea, hoping to spur Daoud and Naim toward compromise.[71]

The attention accorded to the unlikely prospect of an Iranian route attested to growing concern as the crisis continued. Confusion reigned within the border region as the cumulative implications of Afghan and Pakistani decisions only gradually emerged. Afghan border guards acted inconsistently: stopping some trucks without the requisite documentation, while allowing others through. The U.S. embassy focused on the admission of supplies for development projects. The closure placed Afghanistan in the strange position of barring entry to foreign assistance it had earnestly sought, but a selective opening to aid shipments and foreign contractors risked angering local traders, thereby undermining the entire policy. The U.S. consulate in Peshawar counted 346 loaded freight wagons stuck at the city's train station. Citing the congestion, the Pakistani government asked exporters to withhold further shipments.[72]

Within Afghanistan, the closure bore immediate and disastrous implications, both for the local economy and U.S. development projects. Stranded in Pakistan were cement, windows, and scientific equipment for Kabul University; asphalt and steel for various highway projects, steel, spare parts, and prepared food for the Helmand Valley; and an estimated million pounds of items necessary to finish the Kandahar airport. Also held up were 5,635 metric tons of PL-480 wheat, with much more en route. The closure threatened the commerce of Afghan fruit growers, who traditionally exported to the subcontinent. It also stood to deprive Afghan consumers of prized Western goods. On September 9, the U.S. aid mission warned that impending fuel shortages would halt work on all major construction projects, and the embassy warned that the aid program would be "crippled," leaving the U.S. position in Afghanistan in doubt.[73]

To a White House strained by the Berlin crisis, mediation offered the safest, most straightforward option. Bowles's proposal was characteristically visionary but also impractical while cargo accumulated at the border. Rountree suggested the dispatch of a presidential emissary. Byroade countered that Afghans would not be swayed by a reiteration of past offers or pleas to restore normal traffic. Inclined by temperament toward dramatic and preventive action, Komer found the two diplomats insufficiently imaginative. He dabbled with an overarching solution to the conflict: a joint border commission, a common market, an alliance, or regular Afghan-Pakistani summits. "All this sounds like a slice of real pie in the sky," he allowed, adding: "Is it likely to be any more unprofitable than our current course?"[74]

Meanwhile, the notion of an alternative route had taken on a life of its own. U.S. diplomats had offered it as an inducement toward moderation, but the ploy backfired. Afghan officials cannily exploited the promise of an aid conduit free from Pakistani interference. Naim proposed the immediate diversion of shipments into Iran and urgent studies of how the route could be improved. By late September, the Afghan position had hardened; Etemadi suggested that the closure could last for years. Gloomily contemplating the imminent collapse of U.S. projects in Afghanistan, Byroade regarded paying the added shipping cost as preferable to confronting either state. He also worried that dispatching a presidential emissary would only squander Kennedy's prestige, given the overwhelming likelihood of failure.[75]

Urgency prevailed over pessimism, however. With Zahir's approval, Kennedy appointed his friend, Ambassador to Canada Livingston Merchant, as a special envoy. To his frustration, Komer failed in efforts to craft a broad ambit for the emissary, who was charged with addressing transit questions.[76] When Kennedy met his envoy on October 16, neither man expressed optimism about the mission's prospects. Most significant was a question Merchant asked in parting: whether he might offer Zahir an official visit to the United States as an inducement toward a transit agreement? Kennedy gave his approval. Although it received less emphasis and did not constitute a coherent policy by itself, interpersonal diplomacy toward the Afghan monarch became the fourth and ultimately most important option.[77]

The two-week Merchant mission represented the zenith of public U.S. efforts to address the second border crisis. Modest expectations attended it. "If Merchant can pull this one off," Komer wrote, "no one will be more surprised than he."[78] In his first meeting with Ayub, the Pakistani president blamed the crisis entirely on Daoud, claiming that the Afghan leader had been deeply inspired by Adolf Hitler and wanted to establish a Soviet-allied "Aryan empire." In Kabul, Daoud, Naim, and Zahir faulted Ayub as emphatically, if less luridly. Daoud linked the transit problem to the plight of the frontier Pashtuns. "Present auguries do not seem propitious," Merchant wrote on October 24, but a trip to the overwhelmed Peshawar rail yards underscored the severity of the crisis. The envoy dutifully undertook a second round of negotiations, proposing a new compromise transit arrangement, without success. Naim and Daoud insisted on a restoration of the precrisis status quo, unmoved by arguments about the effect of the closure on U.S. aid programs. In his words, "seriously disappointed but not greatly surprised," Merchant concluded his mission.[79]

Despite Merchant's best efforts, mediation had failed. U.S. projects in Afghanistan faced a difficult future. Byroade advised Washington to determine how to reduce its program in Afghanistan. An "irreparable loss" of U.S. prestige appeared inevitable. Bowles proposed a grand gesture: an emergency airlift of heavy equipment to assist with the Kabul-Kandahar road project and dispatching a "prominent figure" (Bowles suggested David Lilienthal) to survey the Iranian route. Byroade doubted that the route could be completed in time. Afghans had embraced the western route proposal to an alarming degree, disregarding the condition of the roads involved. Naim reacted suspiciously to news that the shipping costs associated with the western route would reduce the quantity of aid available to the kingdom.[80]

Moscow and its allies, meanwhile, moved to exploit the crisis. Afghan-Soviet commerce proceeded without interruption, facilitated by improvements to the kingdom's northern communications. In other instances, the Soviets improvised. In a dramatic gesture, Moscow purchased Afghanistan's entire grape and pomegranate crop and dispatched fifteen aircraft to airlift it. Westerners noted a visible increase in visits by bloc officials. If cosmonaut Yuri Gagarin represented the kingdom's most famous guest that autumn, a military advisory mission headed by Field Marshal Vasily Sokolovsky was for Westerners its most ominous. The French ambassador in Kabul perceived a "prodigious advance in all areas" by the Soviets.[81]

By the late autumn, hints of flexibility could be discerned in Kabul, as delays beset the university project and the Kabul-Kandahar road. Abdul Hai Aziz hinted that aid project shipments could be admitted, provided the Iranian route was developed for future use. After three months, any Afghan flexibility was welcome, but little enthusiasm existed in Washington for the

Iranian route. Its leading proponent, Bowles, lost his position in a November shakeup. Congress was unlikely to appropriate either the added shipping costs associated with the Iranian route or the sums required to make it an adequate substitute. Nonetheless, even a brief reopening of the border offered U.S. projects within the kingdom a lifeline. Naim formalized the offer at the end of December, offering an eight-week window to transport the stranded goods. Byroade strongly urged acceptance.[82]

Global and regional circumstances had changed considerably while the border standoff calcified. U.S.-Soviet tensions ebbed gradually over the autumn, and with them the prospect of Khrushchev staging a diversionary action against a CENTO state. U.S. engagement of India had advanced somewhat, although not as far as Kennedy had hoped. India's December invasion of the Portuguese colonies of Goa, Diu, and Daman irked Kennedy and alarmed Ayub. With customary vehemence, Ayub cited Goa as proof of India's fundamentally aggressive agenda and sought U.S. support to raise the Kashmir dispute at the United Nations. Even as global tensions had receded slightly, South Asia's central rivalry imposed its own complications on the Durand Line conflict.[83]

Outreach to India represented one of Komer's core projects, and he refused to let Ayub derail the endeavor. Yet, having counseled Bundy to "ask whether we are giving [Pakistan] too much and not getting enough in return," he approached the Afghan offer with similar skepticism. Talbot argued emphatically for utilizing the Iranian route as the price for reopening the border. Komer countered that doing so would "prolong the agony," reducing any Afghan incentive to compromise. Calling Daoud's bluff appeared more sensible than further indulging the Afghans. "The geographic odds are simply stacked against us in this particular corner of the world," he argued, "Therefore, why not gamble in a game we probably can't win anyway?"[84]

Surprisingly, Komer failed to persuade his boss. Kennedy shared Komer's reluctance to accept heightened shipping fees—estimates of the Iranian route's expenses ran triple those of Karachi—and mused at one point that he should let the Afghans stew. Talbot convinced him, however, to pledge a nominal amount for shipping, buying the U.S. program in Afghanistan two months of unimpeded commerce. A frustrated Komer deemed the compromise "[paying] baksheesh to the Afghans for the privilege of sending them U.S. aid." At most, fundamental decisions had been temporarily postponed.[85]

Conciliation, Confrontation, and the Fall of Daoud, 1962–1963

The roar of truck engines once again sounded in the Pashtun borderlands on January 29, 1962, when the frontier reopened. The opening had a limited eight-week duration, only applied to aid-related cargo, and had required sustained negotiations to secure the separate assents of both neighbors. Nor did the reopening come without hitches. Truckers in the Kandahar region had a fruitful day, conveying hundreds of tons of backlogged cargo. Afghan and Pakistani officials by the Torkham crossing initially acted less helpfully, necessitating further mediation by U.S. diplomats. Ad hoc efforts succeeded, and in the ensuing week 1,200 tons crossed at Torkham, bringing kerosene and asphalt for the highway project and cement for Kabul University.[86]

Despite its limitations and the difficulties in attaining it, the pause fostered serious hopes of ending the closure. It reinvigorated U.S. projects within Afghanistan; consequently, U.S. officials hoped that Daoud would prove reluctant to resume the closure after eight weeks. The reopening also altered the dynamic between the two neighbors. While neither wished to appear weak, obstreperous behavior carried its own risks. Frontier officials strove to appear helpful. When an Indian national employed by the Agency for International Development (AID) was mortally injured in a traffic accident in the Afghan border zone, Pakistani border guards admitted the unfortunate man for treatment, even though he lacked the necessary documentation.[87]

Heartened, the Kabul embassy entreated its host government to extend the arrangement. Visits by Bowles, who now served as a roving ambassador, and AID director William Gaud demonstrated U.S. willingness to investigate the Iranian route. Yet, as Komer contended, an offer intended to foster Afghan moderation could easily encourage retrenchment instead. Bowles did not promise immediate progress on the Iranian route, but his enthusiasm for the endeavor likely came through, encouraging the Afghans to gamble. As the end of the eight-week period loomed, newly arrived Ambassador John Milton Steeves entreated the Kabul government to keep the border open, noting that while 26,000 tons of supplies had entered Afghanistan, the completion of existing projects could require near ten times that quantity. Professing their gratitude for U.S. aid and pledges to investigate the alternate route, Naim and Daoud held to the deadline.[88]

The renewed closure might have dashed any further hope of maintaining the U.S. position in Afghanistan. Throughout 1962, noncommunist observers predicted that the closure would tip the kingdom irrevocably into the arms of the bloc. In the north, Soviet engineers continued work on the ambitious Salang Pass tunnel project. In April, Moscow and Kabul announced a new agreement, providing the kingdom with expertise, funding, and a concrete prefabrication factory to facilitate the expansion of Kabul's residential housing. The Soviets secured Daoud's assent to construct a polytechnic institute, thereby achieving entry into the education field.[89]

It was a discouraging situation. No policymakers advocated abandonment, however. In separate analyses, Bowles and analyst William R. Polk argued that Afghanistan remained vital to regional security and that its absorption into the bloc could still be forestalled.[90] Having previously sidelined Afghanistan, Rostow offered his own endorsement for waging the Afghan Cold War. Rostow likened Afghanistan, as "an area in which the U.S. seeks an 'equilibrium' " instead of preeminence, to Laos. As the site of a "peculiarly Russian" form of Soviet policy that did not employ subversive action or ideological appeals, Afghanistan also bore close study: "Some of our counter-measures are clearly not appropriate to this form of challenge and we must learn about it."[91] The newly arrived Steeves also emerged as a crucial advocate, arguing for the preservation of the U.S. stake in Kabul.[92]

Without arguments for retrenchment, three positions emerged within the Kennedy administration. Bowles remained Washington's foremost proponent of circumventing the closure through Iran and conciliating the Afghan regime. Directly opposed to him stood Komer, who increasingly believed in the necessity of calling Daoud's bluff. In between the two were Talbot, his bureau, and the Kabul embassy, arguing for continued efforts to reopen the frontier, perhaps through use of another mediator, and some interim use of the Iranian route. Bowles's position had little prospect of advancing but likely played a vital role in the debate, situating the State Department's incremental approach as the middle position. In consultation with AID, the department committed to explore development of the Iranian route, to maintain a commitment toward major development projects, and to undertake special aerial shipments where feasible. Citing the present inadequacy of the Iranian route, Steeves informed Daoud that heavier goods would need to be unloaded in Karachi.[93]

Steeves would have preferred to bear different news. Much like his recent predecessors, he opposed challenging Daoud directly. Steeves sought other options instead. Early in his mission, Steeves began meeting with the last surviving royal uncle, Shah Wali, and his family. Long critical of Daoud, Shah Wali appeared sympathetic to U.S. concerns about the viability of the Iranian route and anxious about Afghanistan's direction. He promised to raise them with Zahir, adding that the king would act as "more than a figurehead" if fundamental Afghan interests were at stake. The ambassador remained averse to actions that might corner Daoud and worried that unloading cargo in Karachi would send an unwelcome signal. But, if Washington chose to confront Kabul, he wrote, "I believe we should light as many fires as possible in all Afghan quarters to bring internal pressures to bear on Daoud."[94]

Conciliation, however, remained Steeves's preferred approach. The ambassador revived the earlier proposal of inviting King Zahir to visit the United States. Notably, he linked an invitation to the crisis, contending that Zahir, rather than serving as a mere figurehead, offered a potential stabilizing force in Afghan political life. The monarchy represented "an institution we should actively support and strengthen among those assets which act as a brake on Afghanistan drifting in directions inimical to our interests." An invitation could well have an "ameliorating effect" on Afghan foreign policy. Complementing his focus on the monarch, Steeves argued against an invitation to Daoud, contending it would "complicate or lessen" a royal visit.[95]

Engaging Zahir directly offered the Kennedy administration one potential lever in 1962. Iranian mediation provided another. The prospect of Soviet subversion in Afghanistan had long worried Mohammed Reza Pahlavi, while the possibility of playing peacemaker appealed to his sense of personal and national grandeur. Signs of Pakistani flexibility appeared by the summer. Ayub now appeared willing to contemplate the eventual, phased reopening of Afghan trade facilities. Steeves noted that his Afghan contacts, including Shah Wali, appeared "really anxious for [an] honorable settlement and way out of current difficulties."[96] August shuttle diplomacy by the Iranian monarch fell short, however. Fundamental differences about the reopening of the trade agencies remained unresolved. Naim termed the situation "more hopeless than ever." Both states, at least, assented to further dialogue in Tehran.[97]

Future mediation offered scant comfort to the beleaguered U.S. country team. Crises loomed again on U.S. aid projects, especially the Kabul-Kandahar road. Imminent winter conditions drove Steeves to request the immediate shipment of asphalt via eastern Iran. Without coating, completed surfaces might deteriorate, risking the entire project. Under such circumstances, the country team argued, it would be better to bear the expense of hauling asphalt through Iran. A different closure-related scarcity afflicted the Kabul University project, among others. Deprived of the usual customs revenue from Pakistani commerce, the Kabul government struggled with a worsening currency shortage, which in turn impeded it from fulfilling its own obligations. Seeking to retain the increasingly anxious West German contractor, the U.S. country team cast about for alternative sources of funds.[98]

Critical decisions on the future of U.S. aid in Afghanistan could no longer be delayed. Scheduled autumn trips to the United States by Ayub and Naim offered Kennedy his first personal opportunity to address the crisis with senior figures in either government. To no avail, JFK pressed his guests to relent. Ayub proclaimed that there was little use in dealing with Afghanistan so long as the royal family remained in power. Naim insisted upon the immediate reopening of facilities, while claiming that the Iranian route imposed no additional costs. Kennedy observed ruefully that each country "seemed to feel that the United States had the capacity to influence its neighbor, although not itself."[99]

Within weeks, two separate crises of far greater magnitude diverted the attention of the Kennedy administration and then rendered it intolerant of further prevarication. On the morning of October 16, Kennedy received word that Soviet missiles had been photographed in Cuba. Concurrently, fighting on the disputed Sino-Indian border intensified, peaking near the end of the month. Neither crisis directly involved Afghanistan, which practiced its characteristic reticence in both instances. Rather, the impact was felt in Washington. Two weeks spent contemplating Armageddon left little patience afterward for disputes such as Pashtunistan. The specter of Chinese aggression against India, meanwhile, galvanized the Kennedy administration to seek a common South Asian front against Beijing.[100]

By the time both crises had eased, the question of provisioning the Kabul-Kandahar highway could no longer be postponed. Warning of imminent stoppages and escalating costs, Steeves appealed for the Iranian route and requested an invitation for Zahir. Komer objected sharply, as Pakistani cooperation toward the creation of a regional anticommunist front appeared both necessary and obtainable. Arguing, "We can't fight a two-front war with Ayub," and hoping to bring Kabul to heel, Komer lobbied against any further consideration of the alternate route. Talbot warned Steeves of "growing" administration sentiment "that Afghans are being so inflexible" as to "bring into question [the] practicality and desirability" of the U.S. presence within the kingdom. Following the Sino-Indian War, it seemed "not inconceivable [that] we are on threshold [of a] major problem-settling era in South Asia." It behooved the Afghans, in other words, not to be left behind.[101]

One additional policy option cohered over the autumn, potentially complementing either Komer's confrontational course or a more conciliatory approach. In October, after contact with Wali Shah (son of Shah Wali), Steeves reported the existence of a dissident faction within the royal family. Alarmed by the long standoff and Afghanistan's growing economic dependence on the Soviets, the group sought Daoud's removal as a necessary precursor to a truce with Pakistan. Washington directed Steeves to maintain contact without providing any encouragement. Questioned about the likely Soviet reaction to Daoud's ouster, the U.S. embassy in Moscow predicted that any such event would draw "intense Soviet attention." A peaceful, legal change of regime would afford Moscow no grounds for action if Afghan neutrality was preserved. Violence in Kabul, however, could easily draw some form of intervention. In Kabul, Steeves disclaimed any inclination to seek Daoud's dismissal, noting that the dissidents had not requested U.S. support. While some possibility for violence existed, Steeves believed that Daoud might well resign peacefully if Zahir asked him to. He pointedly asked how Washington's "preference for maintenance [of] Daoud regime" could be reconciled with its reluctance to employ the Iranian route.[102]

The issue reached a head in December, as Daoud's government gave two separate indications of its continued rigidity. First, whereas Pakistan somewhat softened its stance in the Tehran talks, the Afghans still insisted upon a full restoration of precrisis arrangements. Second, Daoud and Naim rebuffed a final entreaty from Steeves to allow highway project supplies across the Pakistani border. Allusions to the recent Himalayan war made no difference; the Afghans felt unthreatened by China and encouraged by the possibility of a route to the sea free from Ayub's malice. Waging his own two-front struggle, Steeves lobbied for use of the Iranian route for the present time, observing that it was possible that the Afghan government could "be replaced by leadership less committed [to] cooperation [with the] bloc."[103]

Washington did not conceal its dismay—Steeves's colleagues termed the Afghan stance "unyielding and depressing"—but the ambassador's counsel could not be dismissed lightly. Steeves was summoned to Washington for consultations, while work on the highway continued in expectation of a final decision. The interrelated goals of aiding India, somehow reconciling Pakistan to this program, and mediating the Kashmir conflict now consumed much of Kennedy, Bundy, and Komer's time.[104] Komer's vehement opposition to indulging Daoud, his argument that Washington was already risking its ties to Rawalpindi, and his proximity to the president could easily have decided the issue when Kennedy met with his ambassador and advisors on the afternoon of January 18, 1963.

Remarkably, the ambassador emerged triumphant. No memorandum of the meeting has been found, but Steeves's recollections suggest that the discussion was spirited, even heated. Steeves could speak expertly on his conversations with the Kabul dissidents and enjoyed the support of Talbot, Gaud, and George McGhee, who now ranked third in the State Department hierarchy. Komer was most likely outmatched. Winning JFK's approval for continued use of the Iranian route, Steeves also achieved a second, equally pivotal victory. "When are you bringing that king over here?" Kennedy asked. Komer objected fruitlessly. "Listen, Komer," the president told him, "you lost that argument long ago, forget it." The ensuing policy directive called for maintaining U.S. aid programs via the Iranian route, observing: "This posture gives us an interval during which more favorable conditions may develop; it could make possible emergence of [a] more moderate government in Afghanistan more allergic to Soviet threat."[105]

The current Afghan government appeared unaware that such hopes were entertained in Washington. Upon his return, Steeves presented the updated U.S. program to Naim, and added, to his host's delight, that Kennedy would invite the king for a state visit in September. The State Department subsequently deemed its offer of good offices in the border conflict "inactive." Afghanistan received scant subsequent notice, as Washington's South Asia specialists focused on the complex, intertwined problems of Kashmir negotiations and Indian military aid. Five weeks later, on March 4, 1963, Daoud resigned his office, following an argument with the king. Naim accompanied his brother into retirement.[106]

A New Day in Kabul

Daoud's ouster was a necessary yet insufficient condition for resolving the crisis. His successor, Mohammed Yusuf, hoped to end the closure but could not act hastily, lest sudden concessions inflame Daoud's supporters.

Heartened by his adversary's downfall, but otherwise anxious, Ayub finally saw reason to exercise moderation. Bilateral talks reconvened in May, mediated by the Iranian government. In a calmer atmosphere, they advanced measurably, although not easily. Ayub assented to the reopening of Afghan facilities but required assurances that they would not be used for subversive purposes. The Afghans balked, believing this concession tantamount to forsaking Pashtunistan entirely. In a personal letter to Zahir, delivered forcefully by Steeves, Kennedy urged acceptance of the Pakistani language. The president pointedly added that he looked forward to Zahir's September visit. Wary of Daoud's loyalists, Zahir finally agreed to offer confidential assurance to Ayub.[107]

In those anxious weeks preceding the May 28 agreement, foreign observers sought to comprehend the remarkable transition in Kabul. U.S. diplomats especially hoped to ascertain and clarify the roles played by the border crisis and their own policy: both to rebuff rumors that they had played a hand in Daoud's dismissal and to understand the opaque internal politics of the Afghan royal family. Steeves cautioned against giving the "impression [of] undue approval" of the new regime.[108] Afghan sources, including Wali Shah and Maiwandwal, described a range of motivations behind the resignation. By early accounts, a dispute between the king and his cousin over constitutional reform provided the proximate cause. Undergirding the rupture, however, were Zahir's deepening worries about the border closure and the kingdom's increased dependence on Soviet commerce. Shah Wali's dissident faction, which had contacted U.S. diplomats during the preceding year, had shared these concerns.[109]

No extant evidence suggests close communication or coordination between the king, his relatives, and Steeves's embassy in early 1963. Following his instructions, the ambassador acted punctiliously, eschewing a direct role in the activities of the dissident faction, which sought merely to keep him informed. Steeves scarcely needed to tell Shah Wali that the border closure had disrupted U.S. aid programs, and Washington's concern about the kingdom's northern commerce went without saying.

Even so, these contacts proved consequential. Thus informed, Steeves worked to guide U.S. policy in ways that enhanced the prospects of Daoud's domestic critics. Chief among them was an unprecedented focus on King Zahir. The soft-spoken monarch had largely been eclipsed by his cousins yet made his concern about the closure known to the embassy. In October 1962 remarks later conveyed to Steeves, Zahir worried that the crisis could bring down the Afghan government. By Wali Shah's account, Washington's embrace of the king bolstered his willingness to act. Ironically, it also pleased Naim and Daoud, as did Kennedy's January offer to ship supplies through Iran. The brothers could take heart in the continuation of U.S. aid and the long-term promise of another route to the sea. Informed of the added shipping cost by Shah Wali and at least passingly aware of the troubled history of U.S. development projects in his country, Zahir could readily grasp that Afghanistan had no real alternative to Karachi.[110]

Paradoxically, policy choices made to placate Daoud and Naim also assisted their opposition. Sustained discussion of a possible change of government in Kabul in early 1963 indicates that the White House understood this fact. U.S. distance from the dissident faction allowed it to act with less fear of sparking a violent reaction from either Daoud or the Soviet Union. Conciliating Daoud with aid also freed Washington from the implication that it had worked to foment a crisis. The differences between the cousins remained civil. Consequently, Kabul experienced a peaceful transition of power. Before leaving office, Naim welcomed Steeves one final time, thanking the ambassador and his government for their assistance, and emphatically entreating him to be similarly supportive of the new government, "for this is most essential now and they need it very much."[111]

Such magnanimity suggests that he and his brother had accepted their dismissal. Neither man had enjoyed good health in recent years, and the long crisis had exacted its own toll on both. Pashtunistan agitation had offered the brothers one claim to legitimacy, as they balanced between blocs and pursued ambitious modernization programs. For years, they had conveyed an unusual confidence, born of Afghanistan's distinct history of neutrality, that they could manage the feat. They had benefited from a fortuitous coincidence. Escalating Cold War tensions gave the Eisenhower and Kennedy administrations renewed cause to vie for Afghanistan. Yet Western aid required a stable southern route, which Ayub's belligerence and the brothers' policy jeopardized. Surprised and angered by the closure of their facilities, Daoud and Naim adopted a response that inflicted far more injury on the kingdom than on its larger, more powerful neighbor. Ultimately the crisis created an explicit opposition between the delivery of U.S. aid and the pursuit of Pashtunistan, which the Afghans could neither deny nor evade.[112]

Even as the border closure hamstrung U.S. aid programs within Afghanistan, it also afforded them a political respite. The problems posed by supply shortages were self-evident, defusing complaints about slow progress. For nearly two years, debates about the delivery of aid to Afghanistan supplanted fundamental consideration of the U.S. program: the very questions that Byroade had labored to raise before the crisis. New projects could scarcely be contemplated when the completion of existing ones remained unlikely. Yet the auguries provided by Byroade's efforts and Kennedy's first aid bill had been poor. Well before the border crisis, Kabul's leverage in Washington had crested.

When the border finally reopened, the new Afghan government hoped for the reinvigoration of U.S. aid programs. Disappointment lay ahead, however. The era of Cold War crisis had passed, and with it the sense of urgency that had driven Washington's earlier responses to Afghan events, abetting entreaties from Kabul. Kennedy and Khrushchev now sought a nuclear test ban treaty and a general reduction of East-West tensions. Kennedy remained inclined to support the kingdom's aspirations but had limited sway in Congress, where a backlash against foreign assistance programs gathered momentum. Transforming the bureaucratic structure overseeing foreign aid had not diminished the political obstacles limiting its efficacy, while domestic opposition to aid had grown considerably.

Afghanistan and the United States had survived a period of exceptional danger. Observers in Kabul and Washington had separate cause, in spring 1963, to look forward to a reduction of tensions, if not peace itself. In both countries, projects of democratic reform held a growing urgency. Regrettably such endeavors faced unforeseen complications, the bilateral relationship still contended with mutual miscomprehension, and neither state could evade the sudden intrusion of tragedy.

CHAPTER 7

Reform and Retrenchment, 1963–1968

Rain fell steadily on the morning of September 5, 1963, as King Zahir's helicopter touched down just south of the White House. The downpour troubled neither President John F. Kennedy nor his guest, however. Both men—hatless—endured a thorough soaking during a fifteen-minute welcoming ceremony. Dismissing the weather, Kennedy promised that Zahir would find "a very warm welcome in the hearts of all my countrymen." Afterward, the two leaders could be observed passing a towel back and forth.[1]

A state dinner awaited the Afghan party, attended by Kennedy, Secretary of State Dean Rusk, and Judge Thurgood Marshall. Toasting Zahir, Kennedy pondered aloud the "remarkable" transformation of U.S. foreign policy over the preceding quarter century—so that the "security, independence, and well-being" of Afghanistan had become "a matter of such interest" to his government. He described the two states as linked by a "common desire" to maintain security, national independence, freedom, and peace. By all accounts, the dinner was a success. A fireworks show over the White House dazzled the Afghan guests but alarmed Washingtonians, who phoned police to ask whether the city was being bombed.[2]

The royal itinerary stretched well beyond the capital. Zahir and Queen Humaira visited former president Dwight D. Eisenhower at his Gettysburg farm. In Florida, they toured the facilities of the National Aeronautics and Space Administration. A ticker-tape parade greeted the Afghans in

Figure 7.1 (L-R) Dean Rusk, Eunice Kennedy Shriver, Queen Humaira, King Zahir, and President Kennedy in Washington, September 5, 1963
Source: John F. Kennedy Library

New York City, where the king disembarked from his car to shake the hands of friendly spectators. In Fort Bragg, North Carolina, the two were treated to a demonstration of airborne warfare by Gen. William C. Westmoreland. Out west, they visited the University of Wyoming, watched the opera *Aida* in San Francisco, and (inevitably) toured Disneyland.[3]

U.S. and Afghan observers deemed the visit to have been a remarkable success, suggesting the start of a new era in the bilateral relationship. Cold War tensions had eased remarkably since the previous year. Zahir congratulated Kennedy on concluding a nuclear test ban treaty with the Soviet Union.[4] Afghan-Pakistani relations, although still delicate, were much improved since the end of the border crisis. Afghan publications noted with satisfaction that Zahir had affirmed the kingdom's commitment to nonalignment throughout his visit, without drawing criticism from his hosts. Lastly, perhaps most significant to a people who ascribed paramount importance to courtesy and hospitality, Kennedy had proved a generous, sympathetic, and attentive host. Afghans could take satisfaction in the interpersonal bond between the two leaders.⁵

The visit unfolded at a fateful time for both countries. As Cold War tensions waned, the United States and Afghanistan each contemplated far-reaching domestic reform. Kennedy finally felt compelled to confront the problem of racial segregation. Zahir's earlier dismissal of Mohammed Daoud Khan and appointment of Prime Minister Mohammed Yusuf signaled a fundamental shift in Afghan governance away from absolute monarchy and potentially toward a constitutional system.

Neither government could fully predict the tragedies and complications that awaited, however. Kennedy's aid program foundered before withering congressional resistance. His subsequent assassination deprived Afghanistan of a president who regarded it with interest and understanding. Kabul could not forge a comparable bond with Kennedy's successor. Lyndon B. Johnson lacked his predecessor's sympathetic grasp of Afghan nonalignment or his interest in the kingdom. As the Afghan constitutional experiment began uncertainly, U.S. aid programs faltered before mounting red tape, heightened standards of efficiency, legislative restrictions, and presidential apathy. A nonaligned Afghanistan, in which popular sentiment was no longer muzzled, struggled to understand Johnson's war in Vietnam. A Cold War at low ebb undermined the urgency of Afghan appeals. The war and fundamental disputes about democratic governance destabilized domestic politics in both countries. Muted Afghan criticism of the war incensed LBJ, who sought to punish the kingdom. Little trace of the amity of 1963 could be found by the end of his presidency, and the Afghan constitutional project remained only partially fulfilled.

Changing Seasons, 1963

Weeks before Daoud's resignation, an unheralded exchange in Washington offered a far more accurate portent of the future of the relationship. On the afternoon of January 26, 1963, an array of officials testified before the Clay committee. Led by the famous Gen. Lucius Clay, the bipartisan panel of experts had been charged by Kennedy with assessing, adjusting, and affirming the embattled foreign aid program.⁶

Kennedy's plans notwithstanding, Clay held fundamental doubts about aid, anchored by a belief that it was profoundly overextended. As much as any recipient, Afghanistan bore the brunt of his criticism. Clay opined bluntly that it had "no strategic value" to the United States, adding that the U.S. balance of payments bore more importance than its position in Kabul. Committee witnesses Assistant Secretary of State Phillips Talbot and Assistant Administrator William S. Gaud defended the utility of maintaining Afghan independence, but Clay was unimpressed. At an estimated $450 million, the Afghan aid program, he maintained, was simply "not worth it."[7]

The dispute hinged on two key points of contention. First, Talbot, Gaud, and Robert Komer, who testified in February, maintained that South Asia constituted an indivisible unit. As Komer wrote to Kennedy: "To argue that we should help India, but not Nepal, Pakistan but not Afghanistan . . . is to ignore the direct relationship between the security of these smaller countries and those larger ones in which we have a major interest. If Afghanistan goes, our investment in Iran and Pakistan will have to go up."[8] Second, Komer and his colleagues objected to subjecting aid to uniform criteria of economic efficiency. The Afghan program, among others, served unabashedly political ends: preventing states "from sliding backwards, to buy time." That rationale fit Kennedy's Afghan aid program uncannily; indeed, Daoud had mere hours left in office as Komer composed his thoughts. Clay and his colleagues remained adamant. Although their final report defended foreign assistance in principle, it questioned aid appropriated according to political criteria: "to prove our esteem for foreign heads of state, hastily-derived projects to prevent Soviet aid, gambles to maintain existing governments in power."[9]

Afghanistan went unnamed in the Clay report, but it scarcely needed to be. Clay had effectively undermined the core justifications for U.S. aid to Kabul. Weeks before the report became public, Foreign Minister Mohammed Naim Khan expressed his government's concern. "Greatly disturbed" by suggestions that Afghanistan might be targeted, Ambassador John Milton Steeves subsequently argued that aid cuts would undermine efforts by the new Yusuf government to resolve the border conflict. The report cast an ominous shadow on the future of U.S. aid, even as the new government struggled to gain its footing, negotiate with Pakistan, and initiate broader processes of reform.[10]

Prime Minister Yusuf presented an ambiguous profile to foreign observers straining to discern Afghanistan's direction. Lacking a familial connection to Zahir, Yusuf held an advanced degree in physics from the University of Göttingen and had served as a professor and administrator at Kabul University. He appeared highly capable but lacking in popular standing, while his Cold War sympathies (if any) remained indistinct. The U.S. embassy termed him a "somewhat enigmatic figure." Yusuf's cabinet retained six of Daoud's ministers but no members of the royal family, offering neither an assurance of continuity nor a sharp break. Steeves predicted that Yusuf, lacking Daoud's "power and authority," would rely more on Zahir. The new government would face its "moment of truth" when the project of reform encountered royal resistance.[11]

Yet in the immediate wake of Daoud's dismissal, a changed mood could be discerned in Kabul. The feared, once omnipresent secret police now acted within a narrower jurisdiction. Newspapers were less closely censored or tendentious, according increased space to sometimes candid discussion of domestic issues. Yusuf opined that newspapers should serve as "a forum for reporting the views of the people."[12]

Beside resolving the border crisis, political reform represented the most critical project confronting the government. Daoud declared the need for a "true and stable democracy" and the separation of government powers in his farewell address. Yusuf subsequently affirmed that he intended to make Afghanistan's government responsive to popular sentiment. He assembled a commission to study revisions to the Afghan constitution in late March. The commission proceeded slowly, and its agenda remained unclear. Some Afghans, in government or on the commission, reportedly hoped to establish a republic.[13]

Nevertheless, formidable hurdles lay ahead. Even as some appeared eager for reform after twelve years of repression, Yusuf remained cautious, wracked by a stubborn tuberculosis infection that required treatment in Vienna. Abdul Hai Aziz, the dissenter turned minister, expressed optimism about the prospects of reform. Sadly, recent events had strained his health. Aziz died suddenly of heart failure at forty-nine—a grievous loss to the reformist camp. Dissidents who recalled the brief thaw and ensuing crackdown of the early 1950s expressed growing frustration. One U.S. embassy contact named Nur Mohammed Taraki professed skepticism that meaningful reform could be enacted.[14]

Zahir's concern about protecting the monarchy partially explained the slow pace of reform. Afghan anxieties about the Soviet Union provided another. Moscow and its allies watched the transition in Kabul closely but evinced little alarm. Two days after Daoud's resignation, a "relaxed" Soviet ambassador Sergey Antonov informed Americans that the change of government had unfolded through internal developments and was unlikely to affect Afghan nonalignment.[15] Soviet media hailed Yusuf's first address for its affirmation of nonalignment, and Khrushchev sent his congratulations.[16] Ardent communists could regard the elevation of a prime minister unrelated to the king as a positive development. As Daoud's minister of mines and industries, moreover, Yusuf was hardly an unfamiliar figure. A Czechoslovak analysis of his government posited that nonalignment would remain the kingdom's foreign policy for the foreseeable future.[17]

The Warsaw Pact's circumspect reaction also attested to shifts in Moscow's perception of both Afghanistan and the Cold War. A February exchange between a U.S. diplomat, Terrence Grindall, and the Soviet embassy's counselor, Anatoly Andreyev, suggested this new outlook. Andreyev complained that the United States had "abstained" from aiding Afghanistan. Startled, Grindall asked Andreyev why this concerned the Soviet Union. Because, Andreyev retorted, the dearth of U.S. aid brought further unwelcome requests to his own government's doorstep. Andreyev separately characterized Afghan policy in the borderlands as an act of aggression. He added that the threat of nuclear war—Andreyev was assuredly thinking of the recent Cuban crisis—compelled the two superpowers to prevent such acts around the world.[18]

Andreyev's views were not idiosyncratic. Other Soviets had privately expressed skepticism about the Pashtunistan campaign and fatigue toward unrelenting Afghan requests for assistance. Post-Cuba wariness toward peripheral conflicts constituted one reason for caution. The uncertain aftermath of the Himalayan war provides another explanation. While Andreyev privately criticized the Chinese assault on India, his government could not speak so bluntly. Khrushchev's relationship with Mao Zedong had already disintegrated, but bloc politics compelled the Soviets to support China nominally during the conflict. The act earned them no forgiveness in Beijing but jeopardized Soviet relations with India. Now contemplating the possibility of a new Indo-American alliance, Moscow had to hedge its bets. Mounting Pakistani disaffection toward the United States afforded an intriguing opportunity. Continued indulgence of Afghan calls for Pashtunistan, thus, served no constructive purpose.[19]

Concurrently, the communists wrestled with their own questions of economy. Like their adversaries, the Soviets struggled to reconcile Afghan aspirations with their own fiscal realities—and to deflect more grandiose requests. "You don't have enough cargo for a railroad," Khrushchev bluntly told one Afghan guest.[20] Kabul's entreaties continued, however, even as Moscow looked further afield. To the extent that Afghanistan had been intended to provide a showcase for the benefits of Soviet aid, it had done so. Soviet inroads elsewhere diminished the kingdom's symbolic importance. Afghanistan remained a crucial buffer state, of course, but the border crisis and the resulting setback to Western aid programs left scant prospect of the capitalists surpassing or displacing the bloc. To avoid acrimony or embarrassment, Moscow needed its foes to stay in the game. Strangely enough, Andreyev and his government offered stronger support for the U.S. aid program in Afghanistan than did the Clay committee.

As the border reopening loomed in summer 1963, Washington's Afghan aid program faced rising expectations. The border crisis had been felt unevenly across various projects. The faltering Kabul-Kandahar highway project had profoundly influenced the Kennedy administration's January 1963 deliberations. Other endeavors, however, either continued or reached fruition despite the closure. Kandahar International Airport had been completed the previous December. Although periodically hampered, work on Kabul University had advanced sporadically as well.[21]

Yet, as before, completed projects did not necessarily represent successes. Kandahar's airport was, indeed, an impressive, visually striking facility. Daoud called it "magnificent." Its graceful arches surely pleased local aesthetic sensibilities more than the Kabul airport's boxy terminal building. The airport boasted shops, restaurants, a hospital, and an attached hotel. Few international travelers were likely to patronize it, however, as the adoption of long-range jets rendered the field unnecessary as a way station. Nor did major airlines add routes to Kandahar. Agency for International Development (AID) figures submitted to Congress estimated that the airport served an average of eighty-five *weekly* passengers, most of them domestic. One British diplomat termed the airport "a white elephant of a size and grandeur that would have warmed the heart of a King of Siam" and "an object lesson in misplaced and badly planned foreign aid." Steeves called it "a monstrosity in the desert."[22]

Legislative foes of aid tended to agree. By the late spring, Kennedy's aid bill faced a ferocious bipartisan assault. Afghan aid programs did not evade hostile scrutiny. In May hearings, the Kandahar airport and Kabul-Kandahar road drew fire from critics on the House Foreign Affairs Committee. Hearing Gaud's estimate of the airport's passenger count, Ohio congressman

Wayne Hays remarked, "That is a lot of money for one hundred people." ("There are only a thousand people who use Dulles," interjected the committee chairman, Thomas Morgan.) Worse came from Otto Passman, a cantankerous Louisiana congressman who had elevated opposition to aid into something like religion. In June hearings, Passman wildly overstated Afghanistan's northern trade, mischaracterized Soviet assistance as "modest," and lambasted the administration for continuing deliveries despite the border closure. "It looks like we are going a long way to find a place to give away our money," he declared.[23]

Afghans, of course, felt differently. During 1963, their entreaties centered on road construction and food aid. The border closure had set back efforts to improve connections to Karachi, ideally by extending rail lines to the border towns of Spin Baldak and Torkham. Kabul also retained hopes of developing an Iranian route, through Herat. Poor snowfall and rising wheat and flour prices meanwhile lent heightened importance to the delivery of PL-480 grain. The border crisis forced Afghanistan to rely on Soviet grain donations, while thousands of tons of blocked U.S. surplus wheat rotted in Peshawar.[24]

Neither proposition came without complications. Kabul placed coequal emphasis on both rail lines. Regarding the Spin Baldak line as more economically feasible than the Torkham line, Washington sought to tamp down Afghan enthusiasm for the latter project. Yet the Afghan government contended that the United States had made a verbal commitment to Torkham during the border crisis. Citing tenuous relations with Pakistan, Yusuf asked that construction of both spurs move ahead immediately.[25]

Mounting opposition to Kennedy's foreign aid bill made the allocation of funds for the Torkham spur unlikely. Nor was the kingdom's request for a PL-480 wheat grant a simple proposition. Yusuf's earlier devaluation of the afghani had made grain comparatively inexpensive in Afghanistan. The U.S. country team believed, however, that an act intended to keep the cities tranquil had undermined planting incentives for farmers, thus fostering wheat shortages.[26] Afghanistan's unique status as a regular grant (Title II) recipient, meanwhile, stood to attract further unfriendly congressional scrutiny.

Kennedy's grand welcome to Zahir in September constituted his last major policy act toward Afghanistan. Other South Asian challenges, to say nothing of problems elsewhere, consumed the remaining weeks of his presidency. Throughout the autumn, the prognosis for his aid bill worsened.

While Afghanistan mercifully did not draw the same targeted, sustained attacks as other recipients, the onslaught boded poorly for its modest aid allocation. Aware of the dire outlook for aid, Afghans could take some solace in the recent demonstration of Kennedy's regard for their country.

News of the president's assassination reached the U.S. embassy in Kabul early on November 23. Awakened at 2:00 A.M., Steeves doubted many Afghans would receive the news immediately. By mid-morning, however, the embassy was deluged. A queue to sign the condolence book extended hundreds of feet, forcing staff to open additional books and lines. Yusuf decreed three days of official mourning. Protocol precluded Zahir from visiting the embassy, but virtually every other prominent figure did so, including Shah Wali, Daoud, and Naim. At a crowded outdoor memorial service on November 26, a cold, snowy day, Yusuf eulogized "a crusader for peace and a champion for human rights." In Kabul and in the countryside, Afghans expressed their sorrow to Americans.[27]

The bases of John F. Kennedy's approach to Afghanistan require conjecture. He did not speak of it voluminously, and his policy interventions were intermittent, albeit decisive. Yet JFK impressed advisors and Afghans alike with his interest in the kingdom. Talbot recalled, "I gained the strong impression that he was much attracted by the combination of a rugged country landlocked up against the Soviet border . . . just beginning the modernization process." Afghanistan's colorful past likely added something to the kingdom's appeal. His speech introducing Zahir referenced the conquests of Alexander the Great and the wars of the nineteenth century: episodes that likely fascinated him as a history enthusiast.[28] Although the fate of his final aid bill undermined Kennedy's ability to assist Afghanistan, his policy choices and personal diplomacy conveyed a degree of interest and sympathy that Afghans would find wanting from his successors.

Reform and "Self-Help," 1963–1964

In the traumatic aftermath of Kennedy's death, Afghanistan policy understandably received little conscious consideration in Washington. Two events in December offered starkly different suggestions of the direction of policy under Johnson. Yusuf received word on December 1 that Washington had approved a Title II grant of 100,000 tons of wheat. Yet Steeves received instructions to drive a harder bargain. His mission pressed its hosts to raise the price of wheat, thereby improving the planting incentives of Afghan farmers. Washington also advised that the December 1963 grant would be the kingdom's last Title II agreement.[29]

Generosity in December offered a partial salve against a coming austerity. Beleaguered and exasperated, the Johnson administration accepted defeat in the case of the fiscal year 1964 aid bill, which had been cut to $3 billion from $4.5 billion. Afterward, the administration sought to determine the distribution of aid cuts. Neither geography nor strategic utility favored Afghanistan: AID planned to shield major recipients and Latin American countries. In the near term, however, little damage was inflicted. The resumption of PL-480 assistance, unaffected by the aid cuts, swelled the kingdom's receipts, as did a onetime upsurge in lending. The fallout of the aid battle only emerged gradually, as a chastened White House sought to advance defensible aid bills on Capitol Hill.[30]

Three months later, the cycle began anew. Johnson's first aid bill sought a modest $3.4 billion. Bundy deemed it "the bare minimum which is essential to the national interest." LBJ defended foreign assistance as stoutly as Kennedy. He sought to deflect criticism similarly as well: stressing the need to expedite economic takeoff and describing several important, tightly defined classes of recipients. Johnson's aid message highlighted Latin American states, allies proximate to the communist bloc, and large recipients like India and Nigeria. That Afghanistan went unmentioned is unremarkable; more revealing was the kingdom's inapplicability to any of the major categories of recipient states. Afghanistan was neither large, nor an ally, nor in immediate danger of achieving takeoff. AID administrator David Bell neglected to list it in an early, influential effort at recipient categorization.[31]

The administration attached great urgency to revising the foreign aid program. Johnson, himself, was torn between the moral imperative of combating poverty and the baleful politics of aid. Entering an election year, he noted popular disaffection with foreign assistance. "Foreign aid is just so damned unpopular," he complained.[32] LBJ nursed his own doubts about the program but chiefly sought to advance a viable bill. Concurrently, his administration's reconsideration of foreign assistance embraced the related themes of recipient "self-help" and economic growth. Predicting increased demand for U.S. assistance, driven by population growth throughout the developing world, a presidential task force argued that aid was best used to encourage the recipient "to make better use of its own resources."[33] Bell advocated concentrating aid where economic "performance is good enough to enable our assistance to produce results." Neither notion was novel, but the fraught aid politics of Johnson's first year lent each real urgency.[34]

Johnson, meanwhile, inherited unresolved challenges in Afghanistan's vicinity. Alarmed by Kennedy's expansive Indian aid program, Pakistan had embarked on its own policy of engagement toward China. Johnson simultaneously nursed a more ambivalent view of India and responded cautiously to its appeals for further military assistance. Each of the South Asian giants afforded him cause for hesitance, and LBJ lacked his predecessor's long-standing interest in the subcontinent.[35] He had problems enough in the world as it was, particularly a deteriorating military and political situation in South Vietnam.[36]

Even so, an intriguing experiment was unfolding in the kingdom. The process of drafting a new constitution advanced considerably in 1964, as the appointed commission convened. The assemblage featured Abdul Majid Zabuli—who had recently returned from exile—as well as several former liberal political prisoners. Debate raged over a provision that barred members of the royal family from holding public office. The commission concluded its work in mid-May, and the draft constitution awaited the approval of a *loya jirga*.[37]

Contemporaneous U.S. documentation reveals that the endeavor received close attention from the U.S. embassy and records the names of Afghan sources. The cables and airgrams of 1964, however, do not suggest a direct U.S. advisory role. The composition of the constitutional commission nevertheless afforded grounds for optimism. So did an early draft, which established a constitutional monarchy, separated the royal family from direct rule, and established three branches of government including an independent judiciary. The omens looked encouraging.[38]

The enthusiasm felt by Western observers for the Afghan experiment can appear naïve more than half a century later. Setting hindsight aside, the anomalous nature of the endeavor should be noted. The mid-1960s was otherwise hardly a banner era for constitutionalism. Daoud's peaceful departure and conspicuous efforts to broaden political representation in Afghanistan rendered the kingdom a remarkable exception to currents of violence and authoritarianism elsewhere. Observers perceived obstacles—Zahir's ambivalence, Yusuf's shaky health, Daoud's plotting, and persistent budgetary problems—but also derived optimism from the open deliberations and the increasingly liberal character of the draft document.

A localized thaw in Cold War tensions further diminished U.S. concern about the direction of events in Afghanistan. Western documents record a striking degree of sociability between diplomatic antagonists in Kabul, who dined and drank together regularly. "I've never been in a post where you had as friendly relations with Soviets as we had in Kabul in those days," recalled diplomat Archer Blood. Steeves provides a revealing example of interpersonal détente. The staunchly anticommunist ambassador had received his appointment after clashing vociferously with colleagues over proposals to neutralize Laos. In Kabul, Steeves not only proved accepting of Afghan nonalignment but also developed warm friendships with several of his communist counterparts. He described Soviet ambassador Antonov as "one of the best friends I had in the country." Steeves posited that the rival blocs had adopted "an open door policy in Afghanistan, both respecting each other's position that exclusive domination of Afghanistan militarily, politically, and economically shall be mutually denied."[39]

If not détente, something of a collaborative spirit could be glimpsed within Afghanistan between the rival blocs. Increased sociability in the absence of serious Cold War tensions perhaps accounted partially for it. The haphazard distribution of projects within Afghanistan also doomed East and West to some level of cooperation. Aviation had forced the issue in the 1950s; in the 1960s, road construction played the same role. Antonov volunteered the assistance of Soviet work crews when U.S. engineers realized that a segment of the Kabul-Kandahar road had been omitted. When an explosion wracked a joint Czechoslovak-Afghan coal mine outside Pul-i-Khumri, U.S. personnel assisted in rescue efforts.[40]

Both blocs celebrated milestones in their respective Afghan aid programs that year. Zahir inaugurated the central Kabul University campus on May 31, 1964, bringing Washington's most visible project to fruition.[41] Three months later, joined by Alexei Kosygin, the king cut the ribbon at the southern entrance to the Salang Pass tunnel, connecting the capital with the northern provinces.[42]

Other major U.S.-funded projects continued afterward, notably the Kabul-Kandahar and the Herat–Islam Qala roads. The Helmand Valley remained a focal point. Seeking to maintain momentum, the U.S. country team advocated the long-delayed installation of hydroelectric generators at the Kajakai Dam.[43] Austerity in Washington limited the possibilities for future projects, however. Around the world, U.S. aid missions labored to articulate the rationales for continuance of their projects. Simultaneously, they exhorted host governments to enact "self-help" programs while envisioning the eventual conclusion of their efforts.

Neither the tenuous Afghan political experiment nor the kingdom's parlous economic state suggested that aid could be safely drawn down. Continued difficulties raising revenue, worsened by the local currency expenses of development projects, added inflationary pressure on the afghani, which plunged against the dollar. Repeated efforts to maintain an official exchange rate merely cost Afghanistan precious foreign currency, while the prices of imported goods increased. Anticipating a billion-afghani deficit, Yusuf's government pleaded for another Title II grant—months after Washington had forsworn future donations.[44]

Food for Peace had evaded neither legislative scrutiny nor LBJ's grandiose ambitions. Administration officials forecast a dismal future in which global hunger would outstrip U.S. surpluses. Johnson aspired to employ the PL-480 program to achieve agricultural reform in recipient states, fostering food security through the adoption of advanced (U.S.) methods. Title II grants remained a component of the envisioned program, but the overriding emphasis on "self-help" made them a less desirable instrumentality.[45]

Thus, AID and the State Department attempted to steer the Afghans toward a Title IV transaction (a dollar purchase), which would weaken the kingdom's foreign exchange reserves. Rising levels of Afghan debt also worried Washington. The U.S. country team did not waste effort reconciling Afghan food aid to the emerging criteria in Washington. "Purely economic justification for additional aid is nonexistent," Steeves and his AID counterpart Delmas Nucker admitted. Acknowledging the imperatives of fiscal reform and self-help, Steeves and Nucker argued that other goals should take precedence: that within Afghanistan "political objectives to be reached are still paramount."[46]

Meanwhile, the *loya jirga* convened to consider the draft constitution. The assembly met over eleven days, ultimately approving a somewhat revised but recognizable document. Article 24, which precluded the participation of members of the royal family in government, was approved. Another article, while affirming the principles of Islamic law, elevated laws passed by the parliament and signed by the king. French ambassador Georges Cattand wrote exuberantly that the country had entered "a new period of its existence—a truly revolutionary period."[47] British ambassador Arthur de la Mare termed the document a "necessary" and "courageous . . . leap in the dark."[48] The White House approved a congratulatory message to Zahir, expressing the hope that the Afghan experiment would be "an inspiration to the many countries and peoples around the world who share our ideals of building a better future for mankind."[49]

Afghanistan's evolution into a constitutional monarchy improved its case in Washington. So did Steeves, who flew home to lobby for aid. Steeves acknowledged concerns about Afghan fiscal practices and a low wheat price. In Washington, he could cite pledges by Afghan officials to improve revenue collection and limit waste. Kabul received notice in November that Washington would approve a 100,000-ton grant, subject to a higher wheat price and the continued pursuit of financial reforms.[50]

Paradoxically, even as the prospect of continued assistance became less certain, the U.S. country team grew more deeply involved in the minutiae of Afghan governance. U.S. officials conferred extensively with representatives of the International Monetary Fund (IMF) and economic consultants Robert Nathan and Arthur Paul. Here, too the West held no monopoly; communist bloc economists advised the Kabul government as well. Yet, remarkably, they did not provide significantly different counsel. Nathan was struck by the extent to which his Soviet counterparts agreed that Afghanistan needed to limit major projects and improve its finances. "Well, this is just what we've been saying all the time," remarked one of Nathan's consultants.[51]

Often agreeing with criticisms of past policies but believing that the task of improving Afghan finances would require years, Steeves worried that Washington had set arbitrary deadlines. Westerners found Yusuf's cabinet to be largely congenial, moderate, and accepting of criticism. The government's persistent afghani problems offered a useful, if blunt, illustration of Afghanistan's limited capacity to support large-scale projects. Steeves beheld a fundamentally different contest than that confronted by his predecessors. The blocs now acted with less urgency, greater outward congeniality, and a shared fatigue for the problems of Afghan development. Polish ambassador Edward Kolek lamented to Steeves the Afghan "penchant for plushness" in projects, musing that both blocs faced the same difficulties.[52]

Steeves remained optimistic. Indeed, Afghanistan represented "an almost classic example of . . . maintaining an effective presence for the achievement of political goals" despite great distance and logistical disadvantages. Yet the pursuit of political objectives had no specifiable end date. Washington's insistence on eventually reducing aid led Steeves to wonder "whether or not we are beginning to lose sight of the objectives and purposes for which the aid program was established." Washington appeared to be applying lessons from the reconstruction of industrial economies in Western Europe and Japan to the task of developing agrarian Afghanistan, where the challenges were "often more sociological than . . . technological" and, thus, "not subject to short-term treatment."[53]

Tenacious but not myopic, Steeves did not contemplate returning to the frenetic competition of the 1950s. While he advocated continued development of the Helmand, he advanced other, less grandiose efforts: paving simple rural roads and exploring light industrial projects to improve the kingdom's export trade. He suggested recasting the Helmand Valley as a site for demonstration farms, continued advisory work within the education system, and administrative assistance to provincial governing authorities. Steeves's program was ambitious but fiscally restrained, acknowledging some of the difficult lessons of the previous eighteen years. It somewhat resembled Truman-era technical assistance.[54]

Once again, Steeves waged a two-front battle, seeking fiscal reform in Kabul and continued attention in Washington. The latter proved more difficult; perversely, Afghanistan's quiescent state worked against it. Komer prevented Steeves from meeting Johnson during a spring 1964 visit, keeping the country off LBJ's agenda.[55] Komer contended that Afghanistan ranked as a "far lower priority than many other foreign policy matters." Magnanimously crediting Steeves with "doing a good job," the NSC staffer classified the kingdom as a success story, "one country where our influence is on the upgrade."[56] Subsequent events—in New York, Southeast Asia, and Kabul—suggested otherwise.

Faltering Aid and the Perils of Nonalignment, 1964–1965

The December 1964 conversation began agreeably. Yusuf, welcoming Steeves upon his return, congratulated Johnson on his landslide electoral victory and expressed satisfaction over the trend in U.S.-Afghan relations. The ambassador did not share the sentiment. Two weeks earlier, Belgian and U.S. soldiers had deployed against antigovernment Simba rebels in the Congolese city of Stanleyville, who held hundreds of Europeans and several Americans captive. Nonaligned states decried an act of aggression against the Congo. At the United Nations, Afghanistan joined its peers in protesting the U.S action. A livid Steeves excoriated Yusuf for the vote. Before departing, he asked the Afghan prime minister to imagine his own "lovely teenage daughter" as a captive of the Simbas.[57] His British colleague and friend, Arthur de la Mare, wrote that Steeves, "usually the mildest and gentlest of men," had returned with a "virulent anti-Afghan complex."[58]

Such episodes had been rare within U.S.-Afghan dialogue. To date, the kingdom had enjoyed esteem in Washington atypical for a nonaligned country. Understanding that Afghanistan could not afford to anger Moscow, U.S. officials accepted artfully evasive protestations of concern over Berlin or Cuba. Yet the Congo, not strictly a Cold War clash, had incendiary effects within the relationship. Steeves and Yusuf parted civilly, but flickers of mutual disaffection could be detected afterward, and the Afghan press did not refrain from criticizing the Stanleyville operation.[59] The question of how the Congo, a conflict far removed from Afghanistan, had jolted the relationship is a curious one.

Some factors were purely circumstantial. U.S. diplomats had been among the hostages, and State Department personnel took a dim view of governments that opposed their rescue. Yusuf suggested that Afghanistan's UN representative, Abdul Rahman Pazhwak, had exceeded his instructions. Yet Pazhwak chaired the Afro-Asian caucus at the UN, thus reflecting the esteem of other nonaligned delegations, and his choices likely conveyed the importance Afghanistan ascribed to these relationships. Afghanistan's commitment to nonalignment increasingly brought it into conflict with the United States.

As long-standing practitioners, Afghans understandably regarded nonalignment with an almost-proprietary air. Addressing the 1964 Cairo Conference, Yusuf declared that he represented "the oldest non-aligned country in the world." Larger countries led the Non-Aligned Movement (NAM), however, and Afghan diplomats sometimes betrayed unease or frustration with the deliberations and grandiose joint statements of the growing caucus. At major gatherings, Afghans largely strove to avoid critical scrutiny, particularly when Cold War issues led the agenda. To U.S. officials, they professed discomfort over Cuba's membership in the organization and wariness toward Chinese-backed efforts to remake the Afro-Asian grouping.[60]

Yet the NAM broadened the kingdom's diplomatic horizons, bringing Afghan officials into contact with peers from countries where Kabul lacked representation. The NAM also facilitated Afghan advocacy on a key concern: the rights of landlocked states. Amid the second border crisis, at a

1962 economic conference in Cairo, Afghan advocacy on the issue received vital support from Bolivia.[61] Two years later, the predicament of landlocked Zambia, at the economic mercy of white minority governments in Rhodesia and Portuguese Mozambique, dramatized the issue further. Working separately, Yusuf and Zambian president Kenneth Kaunda placed language on the rights of the landlocked into the closing declaration of the 1964 Cairo Conference, weeks before Stanleyville.[62]

Like other Afghan leaders before him, Yusuf likely hoped to employ the NAM to improve his government's international standing and his own domestic legitimacy.[63] Denunciations of colonialism also appealed to younger Afghans, whose passions had been engaged by Suez, Palestine, and Vietnam. Afghanistan had been bound to a shrinking world by improvements in education, broadcast communication, and aerial transportation. The release of political prisoners and press liberalization transformed domestic discourse. Afghans were freer than ever before to perceive and express feelings of solidarity.[64]

Fading Cold War tensions should have enabled Afghanistan to broaden its involvement with the NAM. Yet, unexpectedly, greater participation produced unprecedented friction with the United States. The same Cairo Conference declaration affirming the rights of landlocked states also condemned Washington's policy toward Cuba.[65] Afghanistan had not meaningfully shifted from its middle position between the blocs, but its greater anticolonial advocacy added an unexpected flashpoint in its relations with the Johnson administration, even as the latter's commitment to aiding the kingdom appeared increasingly shaky.

In other respects, Afghan foreign policy continued with modest course corrections, seeking expanded regional commerce and new U.S. aid initiatives. Although the low-level persistence of Pashtunistan rhetoric prevented full rapprochement, and Pakistani skepticism sidelined the proposed rail-spur projects, Afghanistan concluded a new transit agreement with its eastern neighbor in March 1965.[66] Hoping to boost regional exports and domestic revenue, the Yusuf government turned its eyes to the Helmand Valley, now connected to the world with modern roads and a grandiose (if somnolent) airport. Fruit and cotton cultivation made headway in the valley but faced intermittent difficulties. A Czechoslovak-built canning plant in Kandahar suffered from labor shortages, while power interruptions disrupted cotton ginning. Canal maintenance posed another challenge, as the Afghan staff of the Helmand Valley Authority (HVA) coped with aged, increasingly balky

Morrison-Knudsen machinery. Yet the fatalism discerned by U.S. observers in the 1950s no longer hovered over the operation. The Afghan HVA appeared resourceful and determined, if frustrated by a lack of personnel and resources.[67]

Unlike his immediate predecessors, Yusuf and his government embraced the Helmand. Fruit and cotton crops might improve export revenue. Beet sugar, refined domestically, could reduce costly imports. Abdul Wakil, the provincial governor, fought to rationalize and reconcile ambitious schemes emanating from Kabul. Afghan officials implored the U.S. country team to accelerate the development of the Helmand, bringing the intended 300,000 acres of land under cultivation within seven years. Such a speedup carried risks: added debt and increased local currency costs. The timeframe appeared wildly infeasible to the U.S. country team.[68]

Nevertheless, Steeves and his colleagues argued against rejecting Yusuf's appeal, lest the Afghans seek aid elsewhere. Yusuf, Steeves warned, believed that "the lion's share of economic support" would come from Moscow and was "quite willing to pay a certain price in subservience to maintain it." Citing a rival Soviet hydroelectric and irrigation project near Jalalabad—which he likened to a Cecil B. DeMille movie set—Steeves appealed for some meaningful effort to expedite work in the valley. Moscow, he noted, did not appear so focused upon the return on its original investment.[69]

At this point, Steeves received the impromptu assistance of Ambassador at Large Averell Harriman (ironically a past adversary on the question of neutralizing Laos). Harriman's instructions, cabled amid a previously scheduled trip, stressed the importance of forging new links with the Afghan government and assuring it of Washington's continued regard. While he came without specific new offers, Harriman pledged to investigate expediting assistance in the Helmand Valley. For good measure, he added some stern words on the Congo. Harriman found Yusuf "a bit too trustful" of Soviet intentions, but also wondered what Moscow intended in the kingdom. "The 64 dollar question," he wrote, "is why are Soviets so friendly and generous with aid, with no return demands and no evident communist subversive activity."[70]

Steeves considered the visit a success. Yet the kingdom's financial crisis worsened, as the budgetary deficit neared 1 billion afghani. Efforts to improve revenue collection and improve domestic productivity had not matched project expenditures. The budgetary crisis imposed a serious dilemma on the U.S. country team: extending loans toward further projects risked exacerbating the afghani shortage; deferring them could suggest abandonment. The different bases of aid to Afghanistan created further difficulties. Title II commodity assistance had eased afghani shortages on Washington's projects. Moscow could only cover an estimated 35 percent of the local currency expenses associated with their projects. To the Afghans, the distinctions between their creditors and the sources of budgetary deficits mattered little. Americans, however, fretted at being asked to ease financial problems they ascribed to Soviet-backed projects (while omitting Helmand-related debts from discussion).[71]

The growing desperation of the Yusuf government presented both perils and opportunities to the U.S. country team. Yusuf's avid interest in developing the Helmand and his government's willingness to publicize the valley contrasted starkly with the policies of the Daoud years. Steeves sought some assurance of further funding. Washington's reply, which merely reiterated the need for strict fiscal discipline, evoked an impassioned, frustrated reply, which he poured out in a personal letter to Talbot. Terming his instructions "unimaginative and sterile," Steeves warned that Afghanistan would not subsist on reminders of past U.S. generosity. Years of rebuffed or delayed aid proposals had dispirited Afghans friendly to the West. "We try to employ initiative, we try to develop new ideas," he wrote, "but . . . every approach has been either frustrated or turned down." Days earlier, as he expanded his commitment to the defense of South Vietnam, Johnson had promised extensive development aid to Southeast Asia. "I was very moved by the President's speech," Steeves wrote, adding bitterly that he doubted that "the very effective 'carrot'" of "huge economic assistance for largely political objectives" had to "wait for exhaustive feasibility studies."[72]

Weakening political support for aid had generated secondary effects by 1965, as other tendencies within the administration emerged. Officials in Washington tended increasingly to second-guess proposals from the field. Thus, even as Steeves perceived Afghanistan to be entering financial crisis amid the constitutional experiment, efforts to craft new initiatives foundered. Legislative hostility and bureaucratic torpor provided only a partial explanation. Advisors close to Johnson wondered about his commitment to foreign assistance.[73] Harold Saunders of the NSC staff wrote that LBJ "apparently belongs to the school that thinks every overseas mission would profit from being cut in half."[74] Johnson approached aid with a majority leader's sense of reciprocity, which only intensified as he plunged into the Vietnam War.

Desperation impelled the Afghan government to pursue attainable goals. The Afghans sought a seven-year continuation of Title II assistance, $20 million in commodity loans, and further Helmand aid. Concurrently, Yusuf's government pledged to undertake serious reforms. Admitting prior mistakes, the Afghan government pledged to enact a new income tax and restrain spending. Some elements of the crisis, especially a plunge in karakul export revenues, stemmed from factors outside of its control. Observing real "soul-searching" on the part of their host government, Steeves and his team were inclined to grant the Afghans much of their request.[75]

The Helmand Valley presented a more difficult problem. Yusuf's enthusiasm for it was undeniable, but his ambitions exceeded the country's team's sense of the possible. Informed that the U.S. government hoped to develop another 50,000 acres in seven years—one-sixth of his proposal—Yusuf lost patience. "This is the same old story," he said crossly. Doubting Yusuf's timetable, Steeves still had to conclude, "I believe that he really means business," and that the bilateral relationship would suffer if Washington could not expand its efforts in the valley.[76]

Intensifying Afghan entreaties galvanized Steeves to send Rusk one final extraordinary appeal for Helmand aid.[77] The State Department's noncommittal reply disavowed any wish to let bilateral relations deteriorate, but added, "neither can we ignore our own aid standards and political requirements."[78] While Washington deliberated, Yusuf's government welcomed an IMF advisory team. Over several difficult days, the Afghans and IMF reached agreement on a set of reform measures, facilitating a short-term loan and somewhat strengthening the country team's case for aid.[79] Acting separately, meanwhile, the Soviet Union granted a three-year moratorium on Afghan debt. In June, Washington approved a onetime 150,000-ton Title II grant, a $2 million commodity loan, and promises of further support for the Helmand, including a loan toward the completion of the Kajakai power plant. Observing that the United States had not met his requests in full, Yusuf nevertheless expressed his thanks.[80]

This was a satisfying victory for the Kabul government and its resident U.S. mission. It was also the last of its kind. Steeves and his predecessors had doggedly defended Afghan aid for years, but fundamental changes could not be averted. In the current climate, Afghanistan could not continue as the world's sole Title II recipient. Above all, deepening U.S. military involvement in Southeast Asia limited the future possibilities for Afghan aid. Johnson's war further weakened legislative support for foreign assistance.

Equally ominous was the war's effect on the president, who became increasingly intolerant of criticism from nonaligned states. Afghanistan's constitutional experiment, meanwhile, faced difficult, unexpected challenges.

Elections and Consequences, 1965

Concurrently, Afghanistan looked ahead to a historic vote. By June, governmental preparations had visibly intensified, as the government finalized lists of voters and established a rolling schedule for voting, from August 26 until September 25. The electoral process offered new challenges to the Afghan state. Much of the population, women, and nomads especially, were rarely available to be photographed for registration. High rates of illiteracy posed another hurdle, as did Afghanistan's lack of prior experience with the secret ballot.[81] Enthusiasm for the process varied considerably. Election fever ran highest in the capital, which featured several competitive, volatile legislative races. Travelers elsewhere in Afghanistan observed a comparative dearth of electoral activity and a popular apathy.[82]

A particular legal impediment further limited electoral mobilization: political parties remained illegal entities in Afghanistan. Zahir refused to sign legislation, the Political Parties Bill, authorizing their existence. As Faridullah Bezhan reasons, the monarch likely feared that parties could either abet Daoud or curb his family's power. In practice, this hardly precluded likeminded individuals from congregating and organizing. Inevitably some factions would organize, and their proclivity to do so increased proportionate to their political distance from the royal family and its chosen prime minister.[83]

One such organizer repeatedly met with U.S. diplomats in 1965. Political officer Frank Schmelzer occasionally drove to Kabul's old town, parked under a distinctive tree, and opened the back door for his contact, Nur Mohammed Taraki. Taraki lay furtively on the floor until the vehicle reached Schmelzer's house. Formerly an employee of the Afghan embassy in Washington, Taraki passed along information about the Afghan left. Schmelzer later recalled, "He had wonderful stories, a sharp mind, and sources of information in many parts of the government." Colleague William Piez termed Taraki "an honest and sincere man."[84] Taraki informed his American hosts in March that he intended to form a "slightly left of center" party to advocate for land reform and pledged to maintain Afghanistan's nonalignment.

While prizing his reports, U.S. diplomats found Taraki somewhat self-aggrandizing. He repeatedly described himself as a "future prime minister." Given Taraki's determination and experience, one analysis concluded, "it is probable . . . that his new party will play a significant role."[85]

If official sources are to be believed, the People's Democratic Party of Afghanistan (PDPA) emerged from the deliberations of thirty male dissidents in Taraki's house on New Year's Day, 1965. Afghan leftists, suppressed in the early 1950s, had met covertly in study groups during the Daoud years, emerging to seize the relative opportunity presented by the constitutional regime. Taraki and his future deputy—later nemesis—Hafizullah Amin had both spent significant time in the United States: the former as a press attaché at the Afghan embassy; the latter as a master's student at Columbia University Teachers College. Taraki's dialogue with the U.S. embassy may attest to his pragmatism, yet within the huddled counsels of the PDPA he and his allies emerged as firebrands, advocating the revolutionary overthrow of the Afghan state. The son of an Afghan general, Babrak Karmal advocated pursuing the party's goals via the parliamentary route. Class origin and personal ambition divided Karmal from his purported comrades, ensuring that the young party only briefly enjoyed meaningful cohesion.[86]

It was hardly in any danger of sweeping the parliament, although candidates of the left could thrive in Kabul, harnessing the mounting frustration of Afghan reformers and the capital's burgeoning student population. Scarcely a year old, Kabul University's central campus had emerged as a hub of student protest. Student activists initially focused on academic and quality of life issues—and their complaints appeared merited to embassy observers. Yet authorities expressed concern about student radicalism, and the PDPA and other nascent organizations perceived unprecedented opportunity on its grounds. Amid a precarious transition, politically minded students could exert influence beyond their numbers. The government adjusted the summer recess period to reduce Kabul's student population during balloting: "simply dodging the issue" in the prescient words of one U.S. observer.[87]

When they commenced, the Afghan elections received little foreign attention, overshadowed by the outbreak of war between India and Pakistan. The left fared well in Kabul precincts: Karmal and his ally Anahita Ratebzad each won seats. Yusuf's continued leadership appeared the most likely outcome of the balloting. Yet the work of forming a government remained, and some of the newly elected deputies to the lower house, the *Wolesi Jirga*, opposed Yusuf's bid to remain in power with his existing cabinet. Joined by other new legislators and cheered on by unruly students, Karmal and Ratebzad vociferously denounced Yusuf's cabinet, and the royal family by extension. On October 24, an uproarious performance by students in the gallery prevented Yusuf from presenting his cabinet to the house. The following day, after a closed parliamentary session confirmed the prime minister and his cabinet, Afghan soldiers opened fire on a group of young demonstrators marching toward Yusuf's house, killing several.[88]

Observers struggled afterward to comprehend the sudden, tragic turn of events. Nothing in the peaceful, even subdued election had presaged the ensuing tumult and bloodshed. The Kabul elite appeared, to British ambassador Gordon Whitteridge, "disturbed, saddened and utterly surprised." Whitteridge aptly blamed the absence of political parties, which otherwise might have imposed discipline on the incoming legislators. Zahir apparently faulted Yusuf and obtained his resignation, appointing Mohammed Hashim Maiwandwal in his place.[89]

Maiwandwal represented a curious and revealing choice. The longtime diplomat was a familiar, respected figure to Western governments, particularly after his service in Washington during the second border crisis. Maiwandwal enjoyed a reputation for personal integrity but was not a figure of great public renown. While poor health had been cited as the official cause for Yusuf's resignation, Maiwandwal was scarcely in better condition. His government, which Westerners placed somewhat to the political right of Yusuf's, appeared able to institute significant policy changes but unlikely to challenge Zahir and the monarchy.

After Yusuf's missteps with Washington, Maiwandwal's diplomatic background and popularity among Americans might have recommended him to Zahir. The State Department described his appointment as presenting "an unexpected opportunity."[90] Komer sent his personal congratulations.[91] Communist observers shared the assessment. "You Americans should be happy, at last your man got in," one Soviet diplomat remarked over drinks. Yet Maiwandwal suffered from the expectations placed upon him. Americans expected him to be sympathetic; communists regarded him skeptically. Afghans, above all, wondered whether he would enjoy any greater success than Yusuf in addressing sources of popular discontent and advancing the kingdom's constitutional experiment.[92]

The new prime minister immediately extended an olive branch to the students, paying his respects at a memorial service. Mourning students appeared to welcome the gesture, yet campus disputes over academic policy soon erupted again. "Political situation here fragile at best," Steeves warned. In December, after the arrest of a campus organizer, several hundred students staged a nonviolent march to Maiwandwal's office. Steeves concluded that Kabul's restive students posed a "serious and continuing problem to [the] Maiwandwal government." French ambassador Georges Cattand reflected that it was "bad luck for future governments" that Kabul University stood so close to the parliament.[93]

In Yusuf's downfall, Kabul's student protesters claimed a success that would elude their U.S. counterparts over the ensuing years. In the United States, opposition to Johnson's war had begun to coalesce in cities and on college campuses. While Maiwandwal sought to find his footing, the U.S. war escalated precipitously. The headlong descent into war boded poorly for U.S. diplomacy and aid programs elsewhere. Even without Vietnam, however, it is questionable how much consideration the Johnson administration was prepared to afford South Asia. Earlier that year, Johnson had abruptly canceled visits by both Ayub and Indian prime minister Lal Bahadur Shastri. In August, India and Pakistan plunged into war. Incensed, Johnson slapped an arms embargo on both combatants. To Johnson, the South Asian conflict underscored the limits of U.S. influence in the region. It also bolstered his determination to bring heedless aid recipients to heel. Preoccupied by its parliamentary elections, Afghanistan maintained a precarious neutrality but could not evade the ensuing undertow or the broader consequences of Johnson's war.[94]

Faltering Aid and the Shadow of Vietnam, 1966–1968

The Kabul-Kandahar highway opened to traffic on the afternoon of July 13, 1966. Along an especially scenic stretch twenty miles south of Kabul ("of great beauty and very typical of Afghanistan" in the words of one U.S. diplomat), King Zahir inaugurated the 483-kilometer road, completing a highway system that linked Afghanistan's major cities. The visiting U.S. secretary of agriculture, Orville Freeman, offered his government's congratulations. Afghanistan's senior-most U.S. visitor since Eisenhower, Freeman enjoyed the kingdom's usual warm hospitality, which included a royal dinner and palace accommodations. Outwardly, the Freeman visit and highway dedication offered the image of a healthy bilateral relationship.[95]

Yet the Freeman visit did not so much inaugurate a new phase of the aid relationship as to confirm the passage of the aid contest initiated by Eisenhower and continued by Kennedy. Funded largely by U.S. grant assistance, the highway represented Washington's last grand endeavor within Afghanistan. Freeman's speech alluded to coming changes. A central combatant in the U.S. campaign against global hunger, he warned ominously of population growth and rising demand for food, exhorting his hosts to improve domestic production. Privately, Freeman was shaken by what he saw, telling U.S. diplomats that Afghan agricultural efforts appeared "shockingly inadequate."[96]

Once again, Afghanistan expected shortages of grain. Freeman believed that repeated Title II grants had undermined planting incentives. That was certainly plausible, but Nathan Associates consultants believed that Freeman, applying universal yardsticks, especially fertilizer use, had neglected factors distinct to the kingdom.[97] Internal transportation difficulties had hitherto limited the development of a national market. Agricultural data, like other indicators of Afghan economic life, were not easily gathered. Reduced snowfall and anecdotal reports of wheat rust lent credence to Afghan entreaties. The U.S. country team believed that urban population growth suggested that another donation could be absorbed by local demand. Nevertheless, Washington held firm. Johnson's proposed reform of the PL-480 program faced an uncertain legislative reception, and Afghanistan's anomalous status as a perennial grant recipient could endure no longer. Freeman categorically stated that further Title II donations were impossible. Steeves, paying an end-of-mission visit to Maiwandwal days later, said the same.[98]

The inescapable fact remained that Afghan aid levels had little to do with anything done by the Kabul government. The domestic politics of aid remained determinative and precarious. Deepening unrest in American cities called attention to racial injustice and pervasive poverty, suggesting a reallocation of resources. The worsening U.S. balance of payments further hardened opposition to aid—even as overseas military commitments posed a far greater danger to the dollar. Kabul lacked arguments to overcome these obstacles.[99]

Johnson's fiscal year 1967 budget reflected the new austerity. The final bill notionally capped the number of countries able to receive development loans—a revision that boded poorly for Afghanistan. Quantifiably, the administration received $115 million more than it had initially requested, yet regional bureaus within the State Department fretted that the White

House was setting its sights too low. By the estimation of Harold Saunders and Howard Wriggins—the NSC staffers tasked with the Middle East and South Asia after Komer's reassignment to Vietnam policy—the planned fiscal year 1968 budget fell short of the program needs of the region's aid missions, which came to an estimated $979 million. Prospective cuts, ranging from $100 to $246 million, imperiled objectives in the bureau's largest aid missions: India, Pakistan, and Turkey. Other, smaller programs—Afghanistan's included—had little left to cut.[100]

Cuts still had to be made somewhere. Washington's spirit of austerity expressed itself on its last major Afghan road project: the Herat–Islam Qala highway. In one sense, the project was an anachronism, originating in promises made during the second border crisis. Nonetheless, the goal of improving connections between Herat and the Iranian border appealed to Kabul, which could neither entirely abandon Pashtunistan agitation nor take Pakistan's benevolence for granted. Well before 1966, the road had become an object of contention. Seeking to minimize costs, Washington insisted upon a narrower highway and a northern route: both against Afghan preferences. When, in May 1964, his superiors abruptly insisted that the Afghans assume more debt to fund a highway maintenance organization, Steeves complained that Washington was "changing the rules in the middle of the game."[101]

Awkward compromises between Afghan aspirations and American austerity risked a road that would satisfy neither party. Kabul had grand expectations for the road, which promised to connect the kingdom to a planned Asian highway system. At its inception, the road included 5.5 meters of lanes and another 1.2 meters of shoulder, making it narrower than the 10-meter Soviet-built road linking Herat to Kandahar or the 9-meter connecting segment in Iran. Maiwandwal complained vehemently to the U.S. chief of mission, Archer Blood. Warning that a narrow road would merely serve as a monument to U.S. frugality, Blood pleaded with his superiors to revisit the decision. Afghan entreaties ultimately widened the road by 0.7 meters.[102]

Maiwandwal had withstood the perilous period following Yusuf's resignation. A timely legislative adjournment and the end of the academic term gave him an interlude in early 1966. Yet once parliamentarians and students returned to Kabul, the capital regained its former volatility. Maiwandwal's attorney general ordered the closure of Taraki's publication *Khalq* in May. Relations between the legislature and government worsened by the summer. Within the parliament, animosity between conservatives and leftists erupted into violence on November 29. Angered by a speech by Karmal—whose relations with Taraki's Khalq faction had already frayed—several deputies assaulted him, Ratebzad, and an ally. Ratebzad sustained minor injuries; her male colleagues required hospitalization. Hundreds of sympathetic students demonstrated the following day. Maiwandwal also faced a fractious cabinet and his own health concerns. He received emergency surgery in October, requiring the postponement of a scheduled November visit to Washington.[103]

The delay likely cost Maiwandwal some of his political standing. He informed U.S. ambassador Robert Neumann that the trip, now scheduled for March, needed to yield "positive results." He regularly faced accusations of favoring the United States or even of being a U.S. agent. Maiwandwal sought a loan toward the completion of the Kajakai Dam, a debt moratorium, an Eximbank loan to Ariana, and some form of multiyear commitment to his Five-Year Plan. Neumann, who quickly apprehended the two-front nature of Kabul diplomacy, worked to ground the Afghan leader's expectations while exhorting his superiors to give Maiwandwal some favorable news.[104]

Washington, meanwhile, closely scrutinized the kingdom's circumspect position on Vietnam. In March 1965, Afghanistan had joined sixteen other nonaligned states in Belgrade, signing a cautious declaration that called for an immediate end to the hostilities and comprehensive peace negotiations. On joint Soviet-Afghan communiques, the Afghans resisted language condemning the war, limiting themselves to statements of concern. Members of the royal family privately expressed understanding of U.S. policy. Revealingly, India succeeded where the Soviets had failed. A February trip to New Delhi by Zahir produced a bilateral statement calling for an end to the bombing of North Vietnam.[105] Questioned by Neumann afterward, Maiwandwal alluded to Soviet and Chinese pressure as well as domestic sentiment, adding: "Please give us credit for doing it quietly."[106]

The point was valid. Other nonaligned governments had spoken far more critically about the war by early 1967. Yet the deepening quagmire and Johnson's increasingly frayed state left uncommitted governments scant room for maneuver. Maiwandwal was, if anything, in a worse position. Before his departure, a peculiar episode erupted within the Afghan student community in the United States. Abdul Latif Hotaki, a student facing deportation, alleged that the CIA had attempted to recruit him earlier in the decade. Hotaki also claimed, less plausibly, that Washington had engineered

Maiwandwal's appointment. The news had not yet reached Afghanistan, but it clearly worried Maiwandwal. Neumann predicted that the Hotaki case would make the Afghan leader "tougher to deal with." As the trip loomed nearer, Maiwandwal's wish list expanded considerably.[107]

Johnson's encounter with Maiwandwal on March 28 began amicably. LBJ welcomed Maiwandwal's promise to seek agricultural self-sufficiency and promised to dispatch experts to assist. Johnson could not offer a return to Title II but promised wheat sales on the best terms possible. Yet the tenor of the exchange shifted when Vietnam came up. As James Spain, the State Department's Afghanistan specialist, recalled, Johnson delivered an extensive "monologue" on the war to a "disconcerted and bored" Maiwandwal.[108] Maiwandwal praised Johnson afterward but appeared somewhat perturbed, fearful that he had been misunderstood by his host. The United States, he informed Spain, tended to be "unduly concerned" with different problems at different times: the northern tier of the Middle East, Korea, Central Europe, and now Vietnam. As a nonaligned country, Afghanistan's perception of its interests could not change as fluidly.[109]

Maiwandwal's own feelings about Vietnam emerged during a subsequent press conference at the National Press Club. Repeatedly questioned as to

Figure 7.2 President Johnson receives Prime Minister Mohammed Hashim Maiwandwal, March 29, 1967
Source: Lyndon Baines Johnson Library

what the United States should do, he finally, irritably called for an end to the bombing of North Vietnam. National Security Advisor Walt Rostow sought to contain the damage. Citing other Afghan statements and noting Maiwandwal's vulnerability to accusations of being "too pro-American," he suggested that the statement had been a "temporary aberration." Unappeased, Johnson wrote: "I don't want any action taken on Afghanistan either indirectly or directly until they talk to me about it."[110] Johnson did not explain his order, his most direct intervention in Afghanistan policy to date. He did not need to, as it fell within a pattern of actions his advisors immediately recognized. LBJ resented criticism of his war—particularly from aid recipients. When it occurred, he reacted punitively.[111]

Intended to facilitate further aid commitments, Maiwandwal's trip had backfired terribly. In his absence, Afghanistan faced a mounting grain shortage. Neumann reported in early March that Kabul's silos were nearly empty; rising prices in April sparked demonstrations. Citing constructive steps taken by Afghanistan, Freeman, joined by Gaud and Bureau of the Budget director Charles Schultze, supported a PL-480 sale of wheat and cooking oil.[112] Rostow endorsed the sale, noting that Maiwandwal had spoken moderately about the war in other U.S. appearances. LBJ remained unmoved, to the frustration of his aides. Wriggins wrote, "I think it puts the president in a bad light if he appears to hold up food because a Prime Minister from a little country up against the Soviet Union answers Press Club queries in a way to annoy us."[113] Ironically, the Hotaki case broke the logjam. News of the allegations finally reached Afghanistan in April, further weakening the government. Neumann argued emphatically that it behooved Washington to offer "proof of disinterested help": that far more than Maiwandwal's political survival was at stake. Johnson finally approved the sale—weeks after the Soviet Union pledged to sell the kingdom wheat.[114]

While essential, food assistance still constituted only one pillar of the aid relationship. Afghanistan still awaited word on loans for the Kajakai Dam and the Helmand. Saunders encouraged Rostow to forge ahead with the two loans. Cognizant of Johnson's mood, Rostow remained wary, writing: "We'd damned well better check it with the President." He waited until early June to seek LBJ's approval and did so, amid the upheaval of the Arab-Israeli War, once again backed by Schultze and Gaud. Remarkably, Johnson insisted on meeting with Rostow to discuss the loans but ultimately assented to both. LBJ could be swayed on individual issues, but his animus against Kabul lingered.[115]

Presidential hostility was merely the newest obstacle besetting the Afghan aid program. Bureaucratic parsimony and capricious nature offered more durable hurdles. Late April floods seriously damaged the Herat–Islam Qala road. Maiwandwal inquired whether additional funds were available to repair the roadbed. Washington declined the request with the acuity of a sharp-eyed insurance inspector, citing insufficient funds, and terming the floods an unpredictable "capricious act of nature/act of God." Cosmic malice notwithstanding, it bears recalling that Washington, not Kabul, had chosen the route. The Army Corps of Engineers, lacking climate data, had not designed the road with such events in mind.[116]

At Washington's suggestion, the Afghan government requested an additional loan to repair the road. Yet the State Department and AID soon retracted their advice. Johnson's unfriendly scrutiny of Afghan aid and legislative limitations on the number of borrowers likely made another loan a dubious proposition. A "baffled and disappointed" Neumann warned that his government risked appearing "confused, inefficient, and excessively penurious." Washington's suggestions only reinforced that image; the State Department proposed using a less expensive gravel surface or asking the Afghans to finish the road themselves. Mother Nature had already demonstrated the inadequacy of the former option; the latter would violate a standing commitment.[117]

The project's timetable made delay costly, compelling Neumann and his superiors to cast about wildly. A solution was ultimately reached locally. Farcically, it entailed shifting funds from another loan that had been intended to finance the fertilizer purchases. Reminding Neumann that the northern route had never been their idea and citing earlier promises by Freeman, the Afghan government nevertheless agreed. The diversion made earlier pious statements about self-help risible, and Neumann still faced the humiliating task of retracting the loan offer. Maiwandwal appeared especially shocked by the news.[118]

By that point, the prime minister had far greater concerns, including his own health. He underwent emergency surgery in late August to clear an intestinal blockage (fittingly, he received care from Canadian, American, and Soviet specialists). Ill feeling from the Hotaki affair lingered. Above all, as Amin Saikal writes, Maiwandwal had lost Zahir's support. While the Political Parties Bill languished in parliament, Maiwandwal attempted to create his own informal organization, to the king's apparent alarm. The apparent withdrawal of royal support fostered intrigue against the ailing prime minister, chiefly on the part of Foreign Minister Nur Ahmad Etemadi, whom Zahir found more pliable.[119] Maiwandwal resigned on October 11 and flew to New York for treatment. Etemadi emerged as his successor after a two-week interregnum. To Neumann the new prime minister appeared capable, unburdened by the charge of excessive pro-U.S. sympathies. Thomas Hughes, who headed the State Department's Bureau of Intelligence and Research, termed the new government "somewhat more conservative" and capable than its predecessor.[120]

Neumann sought to reassure the new government while encouraging further fiscal reform. He succeeded in arranging a second trip by Harriman, in November. As before, Harriman could only profess his government's interest in furthering Afghan development but had no additional offers to make. Throughout the short trip, Harriman strove to communicate the White House position on Vietnam. Etemadi's deputy prime minister, Abdullah Yaftali, pointedly stressed the importance of a low wheat price. Before his resignation, Maiwandwal's government had submitted a new PL-480 request. With grants unavailable, Neumann's embassy pursued a sale of 90,000 tons.[121]

The outlook for food aid had worsened, however, as the dollar gap widened. In early 1968, Johnson announced several drastic measures to reduce the dollar outflow. AID received a presidential directive to reduce foreign expenditures. Another potential obstacle jeopardized the sale. An amendment to Johnson's fiscal year 1968 foreign aid bill, authored by Senator Stuart Symington, barred aid and PL-480 sales to states engaged in "unnecessary" military expenditures: a criterion that might be applied against Kabul.[122]

Despite these concerns, an interagency consensus supported offering Afghanistan food aid. Once again, Freeman, Gaud, and Schultze endorsed the sale. Rostow urged approval, advising: "nothing is gained by immediate termination of technical assistance and food aid." Johnson overruled the sale, however, on March 29, 1968, without elucidating his reasons. Considering all that preoccupied him at the time, following the Tet Offensive and the New Hampshire primary, LBJ probably did not give the matter much thought. His rejection of recommendations from Rostow and Freeman, two advisors whose advice he esteemed, is worth noting.[123]

The Fates intervened, however, to Afghanistan's benefit. A chagrined Rostow reported to Johnson in April that a serious, bizarre miscommunication had occurred within the White House chain of command. During a telephone conversation, the NSC staffer assigned to Afghanistan had heard the word "approved" instead of the uttered "disapproved." Etemadi had already been informed of the sale's approval. "Thus due to our error," Rostow wrote, "I am afraid that there will be some broken crockery if we back out now." "No choice," Johnson replied, reversing his earlier decision. It was his final intervention in Afghanistan policy.[124]

The Slow Unraveling

The gradual waning of the U.S.-Afghan relationship was easily missed amid the tumult of Lyndon Johnson's final year. In a span marked by the Tet Offensive, the assassinations of Martin Luther King Jr. and Robert F. Kennedy, and another wave of urban riots, veteran commentators can be pardoned for the oversight. Yet the change from the halcyon months following the resolution of the border crisis and preceding Kennedy's assassination was unmistakable.

Any assessment of this decline must begin with Congress's deepening hostility toward foreign aid. Despite attaining some parting victories on aid issues over its five-year duration, the Johnson administration witnessed the inexorable decline of both the foreign assistance budget at large and the discretion available to the executive branch. Johnson's final aid bill sustained cuts comparable to Kennedy's fiscal year 1964 legislation: falling from $2.92 billion, as submitted, to $1.78 billion. Confronting such opposition, Washington officials shelved any hopes of expanding aid, focusing instead on limiting and managing its decline. Afghanistan could hardly escape the consequences.[125]

Incontestably also, Afghanistan had lost salience within the Cold War, as U.S.-Soviet tensions waned. Johnson did not achieve détente, but he inarguably narrowed the gap between Washington and Moscow, capitalizing upon the tentative progress made by Kennedy.[126] Improved relations between Iran and the Soviet Union and the frayed U.S.-Pakistani alliance defused previously compelling arguments for Afghanistan's strategic importance.[127] Candid, sometimes constructive exchanges between Americans and Soviets in Kabul further dispelled the tensions of the earlier decade. This trend is all the more striking when one considers growing upheaval in Kabul after 1965. Communist diplomats in Kabul communicated with the embryonic PDPA but refrained from close coordination. Karmal complained in 1967 that the socialist embassies failed to consult with the group.[128]

Wider shifts in U.S. strategic thought and perception allowed this change. The notion of Afghanistan providing forward defense for the subcontinent quietly vanished from the analyses of South Asia specialists. So, too, did the more dire predictions voiced during the earlier border crises. Cold Warriors still feared Afghan absorption into the Soviet economic sphere, but as a potential development in the intermediate future. Afghan leverage, having peaked in the late 1950s, now neared its Cold War nadir.

Did the relative absence of Cold War tensions make Johnson's disengagement from Afghanistan inevitable? Not necessarily. Johnson had a great capacity for empathy and dedicated his life's work to the alleviation of poverty. He pursued that mission domestically, through his Great Society reforms, and abroad, via a reimagined Food for Peace program. Congressional hostility posed a challenge, but not an insurmountable one. Johnson's most significant South Asian initiative, massive food assistance to India, won the support of the legislature. Nor does it strain credulity to imagine Johnson sympathizing with the Afghans: appreciating their hospitality, supporting their economic aspirations, and respecting their oft-professed desire to remain independent. Plenty of his countrymen had come to feel similarly.[129]

Emotion and interpersonal contact—in this case, the absence thereof—should be considered here. In addition to hosting Naim and Zahir, Kennedy met often with then-ambassador Maiwandwal, including a valedictory session before the diplomat returned to Kabul. Johnson's March 1967 meeting with Maiwandwal was the first substantive conversation he held, as president, with any Afghan official. To Afghans, the contrast with his two immediate predecessors was glaring and could not be remedied by high-level visits—especially not when the flow of aid diminished. For Johnson, whose 1962 trip to Pakistan fostered a lingering warmth toward that ally and its headstrong leader, Afghanistan remained obscure. He encountered it as a supplicant but never as a host.

The absence of an empathetic connection to Afghanistan is noteworthy when the kingdom is contrasted with the embattled state upon which Johnson staked his presidency. As Afghanistan undertook tentative steps toward more representative governance, South Vietnam descended into a demagogic, state-sponsored campaign of religious repression. While hardly ideal, the Afghan elections of 1965 easily outshone any comparable exercise to date in the former French colony. Even the tragedy of October 25 provides a revealing comparison. Rather than clamp down on the capital's unruly student population, Zahir and Maiwandwal sought some form of reconciliation. However imperfect the liberalization of politics in Kabul, dissent remained a riskier endeavor in Saigon.

Afghanistan, of course, did not require military aid, but it might have garnered sympathy. Nor were the sum totals of Kabul's entreaties what they once were. The post-Daoud governments confronted serious fiscal problems and, consequently, had to grapple with the accumulated expenses of capital-intensive projects. The emergence of food aid as the central pillar of the U.S. aid program attested to this shift. Afghan leaders asked for much but read the newspapers like everyone else—and paid close attention to the mounting backlash against aid in Washington. Undoubtedly, they understood a relaxed Cold War had diminished their leverage. Their core requests—highway completion, the Kajakai loan, and food aid—were not, in total, very expensive.

Afghan entreaties did, however, require two qualities in short supply within Washington: flexibility and patience. The cardinal rationale for Afghan aid remained fundamentally political: providing a meaningful show of support to relatively weak governments, principally by easing food prices and budgetary deficits. Past errors had made Washington and its representatives chary of grand projects, leading the country team back toward more modest, incremental ideas: persistent, if not bold, experimentation. Economic takeoff remained unlikely, but Afghanistan might have been understood in Washington as something other than a showcase for the transformative benefits of aid. Its anomalous constitutional experiment, however limited, held profound potential implications. Even if one posits that the kingdom needed to attain self-sufficiency, the timetable foisted upon it had nothing to do with Afghan realities or possibilities and everything to do with the politics of aid in Washington and Johnson's grand designs. As Maiwandwal lamented during his trip, Afghanistan could not pivot so quickly or capriciously.

Perhaps the opportunities before the kingdom were limited. A list of the daunting obstacles confronting the constitutional project is easily compiled. Nevertheless, it is lamentable, even tragic, that—while he undertook a reform program of breathtaking ambition—Lyndon Johnson did not perceive a similar process to be under way in Afghanistan. Even more so that his choices compounded the burdens faced by Afghan reformers. Whatever the opportunities were, observers agreed that reform had a limited window to meet rising expectations, and that if it failed, the Afghan kingdom faced an uncertain, perilous future.

CHAPTER 8

The Fall of the Monarchy, 1968–1973

For Kabul it was unprecedented; for Spiro Agnew it was unremarkable. Driving briskly along the road to Chihilsitoon Palace, the American vice president had yet another encounter with student militancy. Behind police barricades, youthful protesters waved various unwelcoming signs: "Agnew Go Home," "Hands Off Middle East," and "Peace, Freedom, and Independence for Viet Nam." Afghan police massed against the Khalq faction, which congregated on the Bagh-i-Omomi Bridge, spanning the Kabul River, while its Parcham rivals gathered in nearby Zarnegar Park. This proved a mistake. As the motorcade passed the park, the Parchamis surged, using a downward slope to gain momentum, momentarily breaching the police cordon. A hail of projectiles, ranging from produce to rocks, pelted the cars as they drove out of range, bearing Agnew toward a friendlier reception.[1]

Agnew had been dispatched to Afghanistan on a mission of reassurance. The previous July, President Richard Nixon had given a startling but ambiguous statement during a brief stop on Guam. He promised to "avoid other Vietnams" while insisting that Asian states assume the primary burden of their own defense—but qualified the statement by pledging continued economic and military support of U.S. allies. Remarks delivered informally by Nixon failed to dispel allied anxiety about an American withdrawal from Asia. It subsequently fell to Agnew to communicate that Washington remained committed to playing "a responsible role in helping the non–Communist nations and neutrals as well as our Asian allies to defend their independence."[2]

Afghanistan represented Agnew's outermost stop on a far-flung itinerary: a short visit between Nepal and Malaysia. A briefing memorandum provided by National Security Advisor Henry Kissinger advised him to offer his hosts reassurance of Washington's goodwill, its understanding of Afghan nonalignment, and support for the constitutional project. Agnew was instructed to speak vaguely about aid and to avoid discussion of Pashtunistan entirely. Reaching the palace unscathed, and seemingly unruffled, Agnew met with King Zahir, Prime Minister Nur Ahmad Etemadi, and numerous ministers. Improvising somewhat, he declared that his country's "admiration for Afghanistan" flowed from "a kindred spirit growing out of a common heritage where both have felt adversity in defending our freedom." The Vietnam War scarcely emerged within the conversation. Etemadi—described by Agnew as "by far one of the most impressive Asian leaders I have yet met"—praised Nixon's Asian policies and expressed his government's hopes for peace.[3]

Official hospitality had its intended effect. Agnew lauded his hosts, writing to Nixon afterward, "The Afghans seem to think and react more like Americans than any Asians I have thus far encountered."[4] Agnew and his administration gave the protests little subsequent thought. The actions of Americans in Kabul elicited a far greater response. Erroneous reports that Peace Corps members had participated in the demonstrations and in a limited protest prior to Agnew's arrival fueled an ongoing campaign within the administration to shutter the organization altogether.[5]

Such a narrow focus masked the episode's deeper implications. Nothing like the protest had happened before. Kabul had stage managed past visits, including Eisenhower's and Khrushchev's, without major mishap. If Washington's reaction conveyed a parochial fixation, the demonstrations suggested a growing volatility within Afghanistan: an increasingly militant left and a government caught flat-footed by events.

Far greater calamities unfolded in Afghanistan's vicinity during the Nixon era, while the constitutional project struggled. Afghan governments in this era were led by figures without great popular standing: Etemadi, Abdul Zahir, and Mohammed Moussa Shafiq. Unable to command the same interest in superpower capitals amid a general relaxation in Cold War tensions, they proved far more responsive to U.S. pressure. Aided by an energetic ambassador in Kabul, the Nixon administration sometimes responded vigorously to Afghan events, especially a serious drought in the early 1970s. In other regards, domestic politics and policies, especially Nixon's war on drugs and the continued imperative of fostering "self-help" among aid recipients, overrode Washington's professed concern for the constitutional project and even its long-standing regional security agenda. Uninvested in the kingdom's fitful democratic experiment, the Nixon administration proved willing to accept a return to autocracy in Kabul.

Afghanistan and the United States at Decade's End

Few Kabulis were likely to forget the end of August 1968. A time of profound upheaval elsewhere in the world, the late summer witnessed the kingdom's fiftieth celebration of its independence. By now Jeshyn veterans, the United States country team deployed an extensive and well-received pavilion on the theme of space exploration. Beside the U.S. exhibition, a playground drew the happy attention of Afghan families—until the merry-go-round "finally gave up under the pressure of intense adult use." Iranian and Pakistani exhibitions also graced the fair. Some signs of foreign tumult could be discerned at the fairground. Absent entirely was an exhibition from the People's Republic of China, usually a Jeshyn stalwart, but now in the throes of the Cultural Revolution. Incensed by the unfolding Soviet invasion of their homeland, the Czechoslovak exhibitors closed their pavilion for two hours as an act of protest.[6]

The fiftieth Jeshyn, of course, was intended to present Afghanistan's best face to the world. To U.S. ambassador Robert Neumann, the festivities provided an opportune moment to evaluate the five-year-old Afghan democratic experiment. Neumann gave the endeavor mixed marks. Afghanistan had achieved "fairly impressive progress in developing democratic institutions." A "zigzag course" had emerged in recent years, however, reflected especially by the rise and fall of Prime Minister Mohammed Hashim Maiwandwal. His successor, Etemadi, showed no inclination to dabble with electoral politics or to risk the king's disfavor. Yet Etemadi had his own faults, including recurrent health concerns. Neumann believed him to be indecisive by nature, "a shy, retiring man, a skilled diplomat but no strong leader."[7]

Nor had Afghanistan experienced a tranquil year. Student protests, backed by opposition legislators, erupted in April over Kabul University admissions exams. Government concessions failed to placate the activists. In May, a wave of industrial strikes erupted, ranging from petroleum workers in Sheberghan to Kandahar cannery workers. Legislative and academic recesses defused some of the accumulating pressure in Kabul, allowing Jeshyn to run its course uneventfully. Nevertheless, the confrontation strained Etemadi, who battled recurrent ulcers and evidently contemplated resigning. He spent the late summer in Paris, receiving medical treatment, thereby missing the festivities. French ambassador André Nègre described a "latent crisis" within the kingdom.[8]

Studiously noncommittal and verbally adept, Etemadi enjoyed greater success in maintaining Afghan nonalignment: evading the scrutiny drawn by Maiwandwal while placating both blocs. His expressions of support for negotiations in Vietnam aligned reasonably with the U.S. position. The Soviet invasion of Czechoslovakia clearly alarmed Afghan officials, but Kabul maintained its usual reticence. Afghan relations with China remained superficially cordial, bolstered by China's myriad projects within the kingdom, but tempered by quiet dismay toward the Cultural Revolution and concern about provoking Soviet suspicions. Yet, by 1968, the Chinese had receded from view. Beijing recalled its ambassador in 1967, and its few remaining diplomats rarely ventured beyond the red gate of their embassy. "Never have so few been missed by so many," Neumann wrote.[9]

Afghan foreign relations offered some grounds for optimism. Kabul secured another sale of U.S. wheat (and remained blissfully unaware of how the sale had been approved). The kingdom welcomed Soviet premier Alexei Kosygin, Yugoslav president Josip Broz Tito, West German chancellor Kurt-Georg Kiesinger, and French prime minister Georges Pompidou (whose May trip was cut short by student protests in Paris). Autumn visits by Etemadi to Tehran and by his Iranian counterpart, Amir-Abbas Hoveyda, to Kabul bolstered hopes of finally resolving the difficult Helmand waters question and of improved bilateral commerce and cooperation. Etemadi also initially enjoyed greater leeway to temper the kingdom's rhetoric on Pashtunistan.[10]

Thus, Jeshyn occurred amid a fleeting moment of calm. Within weeks of the festival's end, an ill-timed effort to overhaul the administration of Kabul University—too close to the October 25 anniversary—prompted further student demonstrations. The ensuing standoff lasted well into November. Concurrently, perhaps not incidentally, Afghan rhetoric on Pashtunistan intensified. Radio broadcasts charged Pakistan with repressing Pashtuns and drew attention to unrest in neighboring Baluchistan. The kingdom's UN representative, Abdul Rahman Pazhwak, explicitly raised the Pashtun question within the General Assembly in October. Tensions with Pakistan compounded Afghan anxieties about a U.S. withdrawal from Asia. On the eve of Nixon's inauguration, Etemadi sought assurance of Washington's continued aid.[11]

Unlike any of his predecessors, Richard Nixon already had visited Afghanistan, albeit briefly, in 1953. His conversations with Afghans convinced him of their determination to resist Soviet expansion. As vice president, he argued emphatically for contesting Afghanistan. Nothing in the extant record suggests that he nursed any animus against the kingdom. Indeed, Afghan hospitality likely impressed him. In the White House, he displayed a priceless, ancient Hellenistic Buddha sculpture, presented to him by Zahir. The same cultural affinities that inclined him favorably toward Pakistan probably benefited the Afghans as well—inasmuch as Nixon considered them. Plainly, he confronted more pressing policy questions.[12]

The entire South Asian region received very little White House attention before 1971. An uncertain equilibrium between India and Pakistan endured, and a regional U.S. arms embargo leveled during their 1965 war remained in effect. Although the military supply question merited some discussion, Nixon's NSC did not venture a broad reassessment of policy toward the subcontinent. Political turmoil in Pakistan and a serious challenge to Prime Minister Indira Gandhi's leadership in India offered further reason to move slowly.[13]

Nixon regarded aid skeptically, but also feared ceding political ground to critics intent on global retrenchment. He wrote scornfully to Kissinger of the "peacenik types" who believed that "the United States should reduce its world role and start taking care of the ghettoes instead of worrying about Afghanistan."[14] The domestic politics of aid remained acrimonious. "The U.S. foreign aid program is in major crisis," Kissinger warned in early 1969.[15] While Nixon ultimately intended to transform aid, he inherited a draft fiscal year 1970 budget from his predecessors and had no time to contemplate reinvention. Nixon affirmed his support for aid in March 1969 but, warning of "increasingly isolationist" sentiment in Congress, he advised emphasizing its "humanitarian aspect," as well as long-term benefits to the U.S. economy.[16]

A White House consumed by Vietnam, disengaged from South Asia, and daunted by the politics of foreign aid boded poorly for the U.S.

program within Afghanistan. One incidental factor somewhat improved the kingdom's visibility within Washington, however. Although Neumann had been appointed by Johnson, as a long-standing California Republican and a friend of Nixon, he enjoyed atypical access to the White House. Among the ambassadors discussed here, Neumann served in Kabul the longest, during a crucial period. His remarkable life story requires some examination.[17]

Born to a middle-class Viennese family in 1916, Neumann grew up amid the dislocation and breadlines of postwar Austria. Neumann's characteristic energy and optimism revealed themselves even in his childhood, especially in his education. By fourteen he had attained a rare fluency in English. He also felt called to political action, joining a socialist paramilitary group opposed to the dictatorship of Kurt Schuschnigg. By 1937, however, Neumann had begun to turn away from socialism, toward Catholic thought. He enrolled in the University of Vienna's law school. In the summer of 1937, while studying in Geneva, he fell in love with Marlen Eldredge, a well-educated, cosmopolitan classmate from the United States.

Disaster followed that happy summer. While Robert and Marlen exchanged loving correspondence, fragile Austria foundered, succumbing to Nazi Germany in March 1938. As a onetime socialist militant, Neumann should have fled immediately. By his own rueful recollection, he underestimated the savagery of the Nazis, felt loath to leave his parents, and—characteristically—wanted to complete his law degree. Someone informed on him to the Gestapo. Neumann was arrested, taken to Gestapo headquarters, and tortured. He witnessed the deaths of several fellow detainees. On June 2, 1938, he entered hell: a nightmarish twenty-hour train journey brought him to the concentration camp at Dachau. After several terrible months, he was transferred again to the camp at Buchenwald.

Neumann wrote later that life in the camps was "incredible in its depravity, its sickening inhumanity, the daily dosage of torture and death." Hope for release seemed faint, and inmates retained the option of suicide—by means of either the machine guns mounted in the guard towers or the electrified fence ringing the camps. Yet he did not succumb. Self-respect and self-preservation aligned in the camps. Dachau and Buchenwald taught Neumann of "the superiority of the spirit over the flesh." Survival, he later reasoned, "was not a matter of physical but of mental resistance." The experience also afforded him an unparalleled perspective; afterward, he was not one to complain.

Neumann was released in February 1939, probably because his mother courageously petitioned on his behalf. Yet he remained imperiled while he lingered in the Reich. Marlen enlisted her family to provide the U.S. authorities financial guarantees on his behalf—helping Robert to avoid rejection on the basis of poverty. He departed Vienna with "a tiny attaché case of dubious parentage" containing a few clothes and "a sturdy Austrian salami." Most of his pitiful funds went toward the purchase of a shirt in Genoa. Passing through the Straits of Gibraltar aboard the ocean liner *Conte di Savoia*, Neumann let his old Vienna apartment key slip beneath the waves. Disembarking in New York, he knelt and kissed the ground—"not precisely an original gesture," but an entirely heartfelt act.

Like other immigrants delivered from horror, Neumann felt an unquestioning and total love of his adoptive country. He married Marlen, resumed his studies at the University of Minnesota, and—after wartime military service—began work as a professor of political science, ultimately arriving at the University of California, Los Angeles. Neumann joked, "To be a good Republican, you have to have started as a Socialist." He initiated a friendly correspondence with then-congressman Richard Nixon, which he maintained into the 1960s. The rightward shift of the GOP in 1964 drove him to support Johnson. Unlikely consequences ensued. Neumann's friend and fellow anti-Goldwater Republican, Senator Thomas Kuchel, recommended him to LBJ in 1966, as the administration labored to find a replacement for John Steeves. Kuchel's intervention elevated Neumann to the top of the list.[18]

Neumann had long aspired to diplomatic service and embraced the belated opportunity to serve his adoptive country.[19] He assumed the Kabul post in February 1967. Nixon's inauguration bolstered his standing and hopes of continuing in diplomatic service. Neumann was broadly admired by his subordinates and respected by his superiors. He discerned a "definite advantage" in his political background, as the Washington agencies could "never quite make out how much power you have in the White House." He maintained an active correspondence with Nixon and his fellow émigré academic Kissinger.[20]

Neumann enjoyed partial success initially. After months of exasperating delay, he secured a new U.S. loan toward the purchase of fertilizer, replacing funds diverted to repair the Herat–Islam Qala road. The country team failed, however, to obtain U.S. backing for an initiative to support private enterprise in the kingdom. Informed that an aid pause might be desirable, diplomat Bruce Laingen retorted, "[The] last thing Afghans need is a 'cooling off period' for their fairly stagnant economy."[21]

If not an island of stability in a troubled region, Afghanistan did not elicit undue concern. Secretary of State William Rogers staged a friendly, uneventful visit to Kabul in May.[22] An August assessment approved by the NSC reaffirmed long-standing policy tenets. U.S. aid, while unable to equal Soviet aid, provided the Afghans vital room to maintain their independence while affording Washington "a significant level of influence." Most notably, the assessment made explicit an assertion that prior administrations had not elucidated:

> Given present conditions, the establishment of control over Afghanistan by means of direct intervention or by a major attempt at subversion to achieve an Afghan communist regime would not appear to be in the Soviet interest. Such action would cause serious damage to Soviet interests in other Afro-Asian areas where Soviet policy objectives currently have a higher priority than Afghanistan. For example, in its dealings with other neighboring states, such as Turkey, Iran and Pakistan, Moscow can represent the Soviet posture toward Afghanistan as a prototype of the kind of relationship it would like to establish with those states.

Yet Moscow remained attentive to Afghanistan and would react if its interests were threatened.[23]

Second, the document reaffirmed a continued "important" U.S. interest in Afghanistan. "Excessive Soviet influence in Afghan affairs" would worsen the "psychological and subversive vulnerability" of Iran and Pakistan. Yet Washington did not perceive an active contest to be under way: "We do not want Afghanistan to become a serious friction point in U.S.-Soviet relations and, it would appear, the Soviets share our view." The aid program, which now largely featured educational and agricultural assistance, could thus be maintained at its current level.[24]

Lastly, the NSC viewed the Afghan constitutional project ambivalently. Allowing that the United States was "in no way" behind the endeavor, it nonetheless posited that the Afghan public associated the experiment with the West. If "wisely directed," democratization was "clearly in our interest," since a representative government offered the "greatest flexibility and the best prospects" to Afghanistan for managing the stresses of modernization and resisting potential Soviet subversion. But Washington hedged its bets. Acknowledging the fragility of the endeavor, the August assessment contended that, even if Afghanistan reverted to "strict authoritarian rule," ties to Kabul should continue as before, so long as Afghan independence and nonalignment remained intact.[25]

Absent any imminent Soviet threat, the most pressing issues confronting the United States in Afghanistan arose from fundamentally domestic concerns. The Symington and Conte-Long amendments to the Foreign Assistance Act targeted states receiving sophisticated or "unnecessary" weaponry. Afghanistan's continued acquisition of Soviet-made arms risked triggering either amendment. Afghan representatives withstood repeated U.S. admonitions about military spending—eleven in 1968—as their government had its own conception of military necessity.[26]

The issue reached a head in summer 1969. Reports of the December 1968 purchase of Sukhoi-7 fighter-bombers received belated confirmation on August 20. Days later, three of the aircraft made a cameo appearance above the Jeshyn fairground. Aware of the legal complications, the Afghans claimed that the purchase predated the Conte-Long amendment. Whatever the merits of that defense, Washington was ill prepared to rebuff claims that Afghanistan needed the Sukhois. Noting recent borderland unrest, one analyst allowed: "The Afghans do, after all, have internal security problems." Legal analysis might deem the Sukhois to be "sophisticated"; finding them "unnecessary" was another matter entirely.[27]

While hardly tranquil, Afghanistan presented no clear signals of imminent distress. Student radicalism, economic sluggishness, and Soviet influence within the military posed at most hypothetical threats in the indeterminate future. The absence of major ongoing development projects and the unrelentingly grim outlook for aid appropriations further limited Washington's cause for direct engagement. Soviet restraint, a trusted ambassador, and a friendly government in Kabul concurrently afforded grounds for reassurance.

Nascent Crises, 1970–1971

The letter reached the U.S. embassy in Kabul on July 20, 1970. Citing poor winter snowfall, rising food prices, and expectations of a meager harvest, Afghan minister of planning Abdul Wahid Sarabi requested a Title I sale of

100,000 tons of wheat. The request's fate reveals much about the evolving aid relationship, as the kingdom faced a growing agricultural crisis.

Since the late 1960s, agriculture represented the core bilateral development and aid issue. Afghanistan had failed to adhere to the increasingly strict deposit schedules of previous PL-480 agreements (which had been influenced by U.S. balance of payment concerns). For their part, the Afghans complained that shipments of wheat dispatched under the 1968 agreement had been infested with weevils in transit.[28] Afghan agricultural reforms provided further grounds for disagreement. The Kabul government's insistence on a centralized fertilizer distribution system frustrated the U.S. country team, which regarded soil enhancement as fundamental to raising productivity.[29]

The U.S. country team scrutinized Sarabi's letter closely, gauging more than the Afghan grain market. Washington demanded concrete progress toward agricultural self-sufficiency, as measured by several criteria: improved water management, mechanization, adaptation of new seeds, and intensive use of fertilizers and insecticides. A steep learning curve loomed ahead, however. "Afghan farmers never have been obliged before to consider seriously the importance of rogueing, seed cleaning, and the avoidance of mixing varieties," the country team reported, allowing that successful adaptation required a "mammoth educational program." A dearth of educated personnel at the grassroots level—most agricultural extension agents had an eighth- or ninth-grade education—frustrated such efforts. The country team found Afghanistan's use of fertilizer, seeds, and insecticides "highly unsatisfactory" but hoped for a "gradual Green Revolution" if distributional problems were overcome.[30]

Yet such scrutiny ultimately stemmed from budgetary factors and strategic choices. Afghanistan had not asked for much grain, but a tight PL-480 budget imposed trade-offs. The Kabul embassy endorsed the full 100,000-ton request. Crucially, however, the U.S. aid mission placed the coming harvest 320,000 tons above the Afghan estimate. Better attuned to budgetary constraints, officials from the regional bureau argued for at least 80,000 tons. A draft agreement in late October only offered the Afghans 50,000 tons at $3 million—once again contingent on further self-help measures. Believing the financial terms to be unduly stringent, Neumann protested in vain.[31]

This response could seemingly illustrate the invidious politics of Vietnam-era aid. Days earlier, however, Nixon had endorsed a $72 million PL-480 program providing 800,000 tons of wheat to Pakistan, including a grant of 272,000 tons. Turkey received a 500,000-ton wheat sale in

September—despite U.S. concern about domestic opium cultivation. The Pakistani sale was intended to compensate for a poor harvest in the country's eastern wing. Defending it to an incredulous Neumann, the State Department cited Pakistani progress toward self-sufficiency. The reported resale of smuggled Pakistani wheat within Afghanistan, however, suggested that demand was higher on the other side of the Durand Line. Self-help criteria were inescapable but, under the embryonic Nixon Doctrine, Afghanistan could not compete with outright allies.[32]

Nonetheless, U.S. admonitions toward agricultural modernization offered Afghanistan some opportunities. Etemadi retained his predecessors' aspirations for the Helmand Valley and sought U.S. support for extending irrigation canals in the Shamalan district. While the Helmand generally remained troubled, as local authorities grappled with the related problems of water management, salinization, and retaining farmers, Shamalan posed a different challenge. The land there showed great promise, and actively cultivated plots dotted the region. These irregular holdings, however, fell short of their potential, as imagined by Afghan modernizers, the U.S. country team, and consultants from the Bureau of Reclamation. To them, the district suffered from poor roads, insufficient irrigation and drainage, and an overabundance of small subsistence farms unsuited to produce a surplus.[33]

To improve Shamalan, the Afghan authorities and their U.S. advisors proposed a wide-ranging program of road construction, canal extension, and land leveling. Afghan farmers would leap from subsistence-level cultivation to mass production, aided by new seed varieties, fertilizers, a credit system, and pest control measures. First, however, they would have to move. The planners envisioned larger farms: nearly double the five-hectare average size of existing plots. Shamalan's farmers would not be permanently displaced, but they would lose access to their lands and homes while the bulldozers did their work. Unsurprisingly, they evinced scant enthusiasm for the project. Anxious farmers feared dispossession or the loss of homes and fruit trees and remained unpersuaded by their government's promises. Productive by valley standards, they were not inclined to gamble for better harvests.[34]

Despite local resistance, the U.S. country team believed that Afghan farmers could learn to embrace capital-intensive methods. The Afghan constitution, however, posed a more fundamental problem, as the Shamalan project required the passage of amendments to the national water law. Etemadi's cabinet had approved the revisions, but parliamentary deputies from the drought-afflicted north and Hazarajat objected to further investment in the region. Neumann watched the legislative impasse with mounting alarm, as further delay jeopardized U.S. funding toward the project. The ambassador urged Zahir in December to enact the water law amendments by royal decree. Neumann informed Etemadi, in another meeting, that the kingdom had a "very poor" record of self-help, which made it difficult for his government to assist Afghanistan under the Nixon Doctrine.[35]

In reply, Etemadi cited the difficulties faced by embryonic democratic institutions. After seven years, however, such arguments carried less weight. Neumann had adopted a more skeptical view. Rather than "a novel and revolutionary approach to government," he wrote to Assistant Secretary of State Joseph Sisco, the experiment represented the latest variation of Zahir's balancing act, dividing the ranks of potential opponents. The repeated selection of politically weak prime ministers suggested that this objective superseded the goal of government efficiency. A fundamental choice thus existed between observing democratic procedures and advancing Afghan development. Neumann perceived the need to "press for speedier and more effective economic measures" than the "reluctant and inexperienced" Afghan government was willing to take. After a January 1971 parliamentary walkout prevented passage of the water law amendments, Zahir enacted them by decree, to Neumann's satisfaction.[36]

Stymied at home, the career diplomat Etemadi could claim greater success in his foreign policy, where his incremental, cautious nature dovetailed with the agendas of neighboring powers. Negotiations with Iran through 1970 yielded significant progress toward resolving the long-standing Helmand waters dispute. Accord seemed tantalizingly near at the end of the year. Relations with Pakistan also improved, after Gen. Mohammed Yahya Khan replaced Mohammed Ayub Khan in early 1969. Yahya's abolition of the "One Unit" system pleased Afghan officials, and Kabul indicated renewed interest in pursuing bilateral economic projects with its eastern neighbor, consciously downplaying Pashtunistan agitation.[37]

Nor did Afghan policy toward the Cold War evoke serious concern. Nixon's April invasion of Cambodia drew at most a muted response within Kabul. "They have never been more neutral," Neumann wrote. Other indicators remained constant. To the great frustration of the East German government, the Afghans still only maintained diplomatic relations with their archrivals in Bonn. When King Zahir visited Prague in September, the East Germans entreated their Czechoslovak comrades to argue their case. Zahir remained noncommittal. Generally satisfied with the bloc's position in Kabul, the Czechoslovaks concluded that their allies would have to wait a while longer.[38]

Improved ties with Tehran and Islamabad did nothing for Etemadi's domestic standing, meanwhile softness toward either neighbor offered his opponents, on either flank, a potential cudgel against the government. His relations with parliament remained poor. Attending the deliberations of the lower house on April 27, 1971, where he was goaded by attacks on his Iran and Pakistan policies, Etemadi bickered with the deputies on a seemingly procedural matter. Ultimately, he stormed out; the legislators responded by adopting a no confidence measure. Zahir attempted to save Etemadi but, finding the legislators obdurate, merely managed to stave off the humiliation of a public vote. Etemadi announced his resignation on May 16.[39]

In office since autumn 1967, selected largely for his loyalty to Zahir, Etemadi had clearly worn out his welcome. Yet some facets of his fall revealed the contours of greater crises confronting Afghanistan and its neighbors. Another winter of meager snowfall contributed to water scarcity throughout the kingdom, driving up grain prices and amplifying fears of famine. Etemadi's riparian negotiations, which would guarantee Tehran a portion of the Helmand's flow, exposed him to charges of betraying Afghan interests. Worse, the eruption of violence in East Pakistan that spring added fervor to the agitation of Pashtun nationalists, who glimpsed opportunity in the potential disintegration of the kingdom's eastern neighbor.[40]

Unlike Afghanistan's gradually building crisis, Pakistan's plunge toward civil war and mass violence unfolded with alarming rapidity. Yahya's inept response to a devastating November 1970 cyclone brought long-standing Bengali grievances to the surface just before national elections. After the separatist Awami League won nearly every eastern seat and an absolute majority in the national legislature, Yahya panicked. Negotiations with the victorious Awami League stalled, and Yahya could countenance neither eastern dominance nor revision of the constitution. Backed by Zulfikar Ali Bhutto, whose Pakistan People's Party emerged foremost in the western wing, Yahya unleashed the army against the Bengalis shortly before midnight on March 25. Three days later, the distraught U.S. consul in Dacca, Kabul alumnus Archer Blood, warned Washington that "selective genocide" was under way in East Pakistan.[41]

Publicly reticent about the unfolding calamity, Afghan officials privately worried and seethed. Etemadi spoke scathingly of Pakistani policy, remarking that Yahya had chosen the worst possible course. Afghans predicted the failure of the Pakistani campaign and the likelihood of Indian intervention. They could sympathize with the Bengalis; Zahir did in a summer conversation with Neumann. More pressing, however, was the growing risk of another Indo-Pakistani war, which could disrupt Afghanistan's access to the sea, just as the kingdom's own crisis reached critical mass.[42]

Elements of Afghanistan's drought manifested themselves alarmingly in early 1971. Helmand waters negotiations stalled as the flow into Iran dwindled, renewing suspicions of diversions in Tehran. Foreign Minister Ardeshir Zahedi threatened economic retaliation against Afghanistan if the flow did not improve. Before leaving office, Etemadi released water from the Helmand storage dams to placate the Iranians. Measurements provided by U.S. engineers confirmed a diminished outflow from major reservoirs. Returning from Hazarajat, British ambassador Peers Carter described a panicked atmosphere: "very little live vegetation left on the mountains, practically no snow on the tops, and irrigation water is already low." Frantic herders attempted to sell their sheep as feed ran out, glutting the local market.[43]

Although cognizant of the drought, U.S. experts within Afghanistan disagreed over the danger of famine. The aid mission maintained that the Afghans were underestimating the coming harvest. Richard Saunders, an agricultural economist employed by the Nathan consulting group, found that estimate unduly optimistic. Institutional and interpersonal rivalry precluded substantive discussion for months; the aid mission's agricultural specialist accused Saunders of exaggerating the problem to obtain a larger wheat sale. The inter-American split mirrored a division on the Afghan side: the Agency for International Development (AID) team dealt with the Agriculture Ministry, while the Nathan group collaborated with the Planning Ministry. Wheat became scarce as the squabble dragged on.[44]

By the time Etemadi's successor, longtime parliamentarian Abdul Zahir, had been appointed, Afghanistan's food crisis had become unavoidable. Urban wheat prices had grown precipitously since the previous July, threatening political upheaval. A shortage of animal feed, meanwhile, jeopardized the national economy, especially indispensable karakul export revenue. Four Afghan ministries conferred with representatives of AID, the Nathan team, UN officials, and representatives of the International Bank for Reconstruction and Development (IBRD) in June. Using Afghan Air Force helicopters, two eclectically composed teams hurriedly canvassed the country, compiling rough, often anecdotal data on herds, feed supplies, and water.[45]

The composite picture jolted the new government into action. Kabul had already asked for an emergency delivery of PL-480 wheat in mid-June. A second request, composed with the assistance of the U.S. aid mission, warned that up to 70 percent of Afghanistan's 22 million sheep might perish. The government also pleaded for feed, water pumps, drilling equipment, and vehicles. Kabul cast a wide net, appealing to its major patrons, to the United Nations and IBRD, and to major agricultural exporters ranging from Denmark to New Zealand.[46]

Fittingly, Afghanistan received a truly international response. The kingdom's resident UN mission hosted an all-expatriate meeting in late July. Present but relatively quiet was a Soviet diplomat, who tendered his government's regrets that it could not open its borders to starving Afghan sheep—its Central Asian republics faced drought as well. The participants grappled with fundamental limits in their collective capacity to respond. Pledges to the UN's World Food Program (WFP) had declined in 1971, and United Nations Development Programme representative Bjørn Olsen expressed pessimism that the WFP would be able to contribute. Aside from the European Economic Community, Afghanistan's relief would have to come from individual donors.[47]

The U.S. country team endorsed its host government's plea, adding that crop and livestock losses were probably worse than the Afghans believed.[48] A combination of urgency and transformative aspiration guided the mission. Neumann wrote: "I have long been convinced that only a major crisis could shake Afghanistan's ruler and government out of their paralysis, hopefully setting patterns for action which might last sufficiently long to become habit-forming."[49] Regarding a Title II grant as justified, but not immediately feasible, the U.S. mission proposed a 100,000-ton Title I sale along financial terms identical to its immediate predecessor (which they had previously described as onerous). They also advised retaining self-help language, observing "we are not satisfied with progress to date." Consultant Robert Nathan was troubled by the aid mission's apparent belief that the emergency presented an opportunity to seek further reforms. Nevertheless, the self-help provisions stood, obligating Afghanistan to expand the use of fertilizer and improved wheat seed.[50]

Whether the emergency offered the opportunity to pursue an agricultural revolution was questionable. Conditional aid had abetted Lyndon Johnson's earlier efforts to modernize Indian agriculture but at considerable cost to Washington's image. Afghanistan lacked India's powerful ministries, and Abdul Zahir, although politically adept (and the father of Afghanistan's leading pop star, Ahmad Zahir), was no Indira Gandhi. The Indian famine response had a preemptive character; Afghanistan's would-be benefactors five years later scrambled to make up for lost time. Landlocked, mountainous, and devoid of railroads, Afghanistan also imposed its own distinctive transportation challenges. Lastly, once again, the kingdom could not claim the spotlight. The East Pakistani catastrophe seized world attention and limited what an overstretched international community could provide. Even as the United States demanded more from the Afghans, it had comparatively less to offer.

Some acts of creativity and flexibility could be observed as Afghans, Americans, and others confronted the drought. Neumann employed his embassy's emergency funds to purchase Pakistani feed and water pumps. "Thus far, things have gone better than could be anticipated," he wrote to Sisco, describing the new government as "exceedingly active, beyond anything I have seen in 4½ years here." Under the energetic foreign minister, Mohammed Moussa Shafiq, Afghanistan secured relief from governments ranging from Iraq to Canada. Iran moved to purchase a million head of sheep. Even the beleaguered Pakistani government offered a nominal gift, equivalent to $1 million. Abdul Wakil, the minister without portfolio tasked with responding to the crisis, outlined an ambitious program: using the agricultural extension service to expand the use of new seeds and fertilizer, distribute feed, and to continue development projects by compensating workers with food. Observers nursed doubts. U.S. diplomat Samuel Lewis wrote that the government had "very limited capacity" to implement Wakil's program, predicting "serious managerial problems caused by red tape, ineptitude, and corruption."[51]

Shafiq and Wakil appeared gratifyingly open to self-help measures, but another problem lay well beyond their authority. Their colleague, Finance Minister Ghulam Haider Dawar, appealed for a moratorium on Afghanistan's debt payments.[52] Afghanistan's debts posed a complex problem. The Soviet Union held, by U.S. estimates, almost three-quarters of Afghanistan's debt. Obligations to international institutions, including the IMF and IBRD, further complicated matters. The drought had worsened Afghanistan's ability to pay for the foreseeable future, especially if karakul sheep perished en masse. Pakistan's crisis had reduced customs receipts, and Kabul still had not developed effective internal taxation. Nor was it likely to do so amid the emergency.[53]

Washington expressed willingness to discuss a postponement with Afghanistan's other creditors. On individual debts, however, the State Department and its peer agencies held firm. The Eximbank insisted upon prompt payment of a coming installment, unwilling to set a precedent exploitable by other borrowers. Nor was Washington willing to act unilaterally, lest its leniency abet repayments to a less charitable lender. U.S. officials called for a consistent policy, applicable to all the kingdom's debts. In other cases, the IBRD or IMF would have been able to coordinate between creditors, but Moscow belonged to neither institution. Soviet representatives in Kabul remained elusive on the question of a moratorium, while U.S. representatives continued to insist that the Afghans secure some form of Soviet participation.[54] Grappling with the drought and economic crisis, Abdul Zahir's government could not easily play middleman between its various, uncommunicative creditors. Soviet-American dialogue in Kabul had its purposes but was unlikely to work as expeditiously as circumstances required. The situation called for an improvisational approach and direct bilateral dialogue: either in Moscow or in Washington.

Nixon and Kissinger could, of course, claim to be fully preoccupied that summer. The latter had just undertaken his historic visit to Beijing, bringing to fruition years of efforts to forge contacts with China (an endeavor in which Neumann had played a peripheral role). Weeks later, responding to unremitting pressure on the dollar, Nixon suspended convertibility between the national currency and gold. The superpowers vied for influence in the Middle East, as Nixon sought to regain ground lost to the Soviet Union after the 1967 war. The August 9 announcement of a friendship treaty between Moscow and New Delhi, lastly, drove Nixon and Kissinger to worry that Moscow intended to exploit the East Pakistan crisis.[55] Consequently, the heated White House tapes contain no meaningful mention of Afghanistan. By the recollections of Samuel Hoskinson, an NSC South Asia specialist, Kissinger was happy to delegate emergency relief to the State Department and AID. Food aid lay well within their sphere of competency, but without a high-level approach to the Soviets, the knot obstructing a comprehensive solution to Afghan debt remained uncut.[56]

Afghanistan remained relatively quiescent, but the mounting drought and East Pakistan crises added discernible strains to its neighborly relations. Indo-Pakistani tensions and Islamabad's banning of the National Awami Party (which had split earlier from the Bengali-dominated Awami League) drew criticism in Kabul. Babrak Karmal assailed the government for failing to support the cause of Pashtunistan. The Helmand ceased flowing in late August, bringing further accusations from Tehran. Elements of Iran's lavish October celebration of the 2,500th anniversary of the Persian Empire added a further, symbolic point of friction. Depictions of their territory lying within the boundaries of Cyrus's domain and the perceived denigration or appropriation of figures venerated by Afghans stung—especially when the kingdom faced mounting hardships and its affluent neighbor engaged in a gaudy fête.[57] Afghanistan had little to celebrate that autumn, and indeed even the annual Jeshyn festivities were curtailed to a single day.

To date, the global response had left the kingdom an estimated 200,000 tons of wheat short of its requirements. Accordingly, the U.S. country team sought a Title II grant of 150,000 tons. A prompt response from Washington accorded Afghanistan an emergency donation of 100,000 tons.[58] Conveying the grain into Afghanistan did not pose the primary obstacle. Afghanistan's grain crisis was best monitored in the cities but most acute in the countryside, particularly the mountainous center and far west. Delivering thousands of tons of grain to remote areas over difficult terrain would have challenged a country with better infrastructure and a tradition of centralized governance. In Afghanistan, the task constituted a leap into the unknown.

Abdul Wakil's Food for Work program seemingly offered a solution: delivering grain into impoverished regions afflicted by famine. Himself an agronomist, past governor of Helmand Province, and president of the Helmand-Arghandab Valley Authority, Abdul Wakil impressed foreign observers with his initial dynamism and lent the program domestic legitimacy. Yet the program elevated the development-centered priorities of Afghans and foreign patrons above relief. Foreign advisors, including Richard Saunders, had long advocated rural public works programs as essential to raising farm productivity.[59] Concurrent trial efforts by the Afghan Planning Ministry and UN advisors to develop such a program foundered without adequate oversight.[60] The inexpensive West German–funded Paktia Development Authority (PDA), which employed Afghans on irrigation and land reclamation projects and compensated them with food, appeared to offer a promising model.[61] Spring and summer meetings of West German, AID, U.S. embassy, Nathan group, and WFP personnel produced a general consensus for developing a national program along the Paktia model.[62] Saunders and PDA project director Christoph Häselbarth advised Wakil as they struggled to launch the program, obtaining government approval in late August.[63]

The ensuing program shackled relief efforts to development imperatives in pursuit of what Saunders termed a "triple benefit": "food, jobs, and increased production" through development of Afghanistan's resources. In exchange for donated wheat, recipients would labor on transportation and irrigation projects, supervised by an impromptu cadre of technicians, including foreign volunteers and recent university graduates. Setting aside the inevitable logistical and administrative challenges, a basic problem loomed: those Afghans in greatest need might be those least able to pursue work opportunities. Caloric deprivation and development imperatives would not correspond neatly. Nor was the PDA necessarily a sound basis for a national program. West German agricultural projects had enjoyed some success but—as Timothy Nunan writes and the U.S. embassy observed—concurrent efforts to manage Paktia's forests failed abjectly.[64]

Food for Work launched rapidly but haphazardly. Four early pilot projects in the mountain provinces of Ghor, Faryab, Badghis, and Farah were intended to precede similar ventures in other regions. Small teams of U.S., West German, and Afghan volunteers—totaling a mere twenty-six individuals—raced to the four provinces in the late summer, while Wakil and his foreign allies frantically worked to manage the central organization. An early progress report tallied roads built, canals and irrigation tunnels (*karezes*) dug, and springs improved. Inevitably transportation and staffing problems hindered the program. Grain flowed unevenly to the hard-hit provinces of Ghor, Faryab, and Badghis, worsening scarcities. Winter conditions obstructed delivery and halted work in northern and mountainous regions. Isolated, understaffed administrators struggled to obtain reliable figures on the number of workers employed, the progress of projects, and the quantities of wheat distributed.[65]

The long-feared outbreak of war between India and Pakistan on December 3 added one more complication. Fearing the interruption of relief shipments should India blockade Karachi, Neumann inquired whether grain could be shipped through Iran or—in a novel form of superpower cooperation—delivered to the Soviet Union and effectively traded for Soviet grain shipments into Afghanistan. A Soviet diplomat in Kabul appeared to endorse the grain swap idea. Tehran helpfully offered to divert inbound wheat shipments into Afghanistan. Such improvisations proved unnecessary. India's rapid victory removed the specter of a blockade. Pakistan's railroads, meanwhile, maintained service between Karachi and Peshawar without serious interruption.[66]

The wartime continuation of service could attest to the professionalism of the Pakistani railways or to Yahya's need to keep a quiet western border. Afghan neutrality, maintained despite Pashtunistan agitation in parliament, elicited satisfaction in Islamabad. Shafiq and Zahir had each earlier expressed trepidation at the prospect of war. No responsible Afghan, Shafiq remarked, wished see Pakistan dismembered.[67] Their anxiety was probably genuine, rhetorically consistent with their policy throughout the crisis. The Soviet Union, meanwhile, had reportedly warned Shafiq against any irredentist statements.[68] After the ceasefire, Afghanistan confronted a transformed region, an unsettled neighbor, an unrelenting humanitarian crisis, and the capricious demands of its leading Western benefactor.

Restless Kingdom, 1972–1973

In rapid order, a ravaged Bangladesh attained its independence, Yahya was driven from power, replaced by Bhutto, and Pakistan grappled with the consequences of defeat. Nixon and Kissinger, whose conversations toward the war's end had tilted toward the apocalyptic, returned to other priorities afterward.[69] The president's historic trip to China loomed, as did a subsequent summit in Moscow. Overhanging all was the ongoing Vietnam War and the presidential election. Express consideration of South Asia receded once again from the White House agenda.

The region's reduced profile in Washington attested only to its diminished importance within the Cold War, not to any real postwar stability. Only a tenuous ceasefire prevented further fighting between India and Pakistan while critical issues between the combatants remained unresolved. Postwar Pakistan now resembled a greater Punjab to pessimistic observers. To the unease of restive border regions, Punjabis now composed 60 percent of the postwar population and 70 percent of the army. Bhutto faced a demoralized citizenry, high unemployment, rising opposition to the martial law regime he had inherited from Yahya, and an onerous debt burden.[70]

In Tehran, the Shah mournfully proclaimed that the Soviet Union was the war's principal victor. Iran had covertly, with Nixon's approval, transferred weaponry to its Central Treaty Organization (CENTO) ally, in a scheme far more clever than consequential. Already concerned by deepening Soviet ties to the regime in Iraq, the Shah now entertained a variety of nightmarish possibilities: a Soviet naval presence in India, the Soviet-sponsored disintegration of Pakistan through aid to regional separatists, even revolution in Islamabad. Afghanistan he deemed unable to resist Soviet pressure. He solicited arms from Washington, and Nixon gladly entrusted Iran with responsibility for policing its immediate region.[71]

Between ambitious, anxious Iran and volatile Pakistan, Afghanistan still struggled with the drought. Heavy winter snowfall offered a mixed blessing: promising a better harvest later in the year but obstructing food deliveries to remote areas and imperiling surviving livestock. Well before relief work could resume, a new policy goal had risen meteorically: one that would reshape Washington's approach to Afghanistan until the events of April 1978, rivaling even the Cold War imperative of preserving Afghan neutrality.

Nixon did not create the federal campaign against narcotics. Nevertheless, over his first term, that struggle assumed a central position within his policy agenda. Antinarcotics policy flowed irresistibly from the "law and order" themes of Nixon's 1968 campaign, providing an effective cudgel against the counterculture, as he vied to capture the political center. Nixon spoke early and vehemently of the drug problem and signed a sweeping revision of the national drug codes into law in October 1970. Shocked by rising rates of heroin addiction and by reports of widespread use among soldiers returning from Vietnam, he warned in June 1971 that the drug problem had "assumed the dimensions of a national emergency."[72]

Nixon's antidrug campaign was international from its inception. An October 1969 memorandum from Attorney General John Mitchell and Acting Secretary of State Elliot Richardson offered Nixon a topography of opium production, ranging from Mexico, to Turkey, to Southeast Asia's "Golden Triangle" region. Turkey and Mexico loomed as the preponderant sources of heroin.[73] Mexico faced exhortations from Washington to prosecute traffickers. Turkey contended with escalating U.S. pressure to ban the cultivation of the opium poppy. Two weeks after Nixon declared a national emergency, he proudly reported that Ankara had come aboard.[74]

Poppies grew elsewhere, of course. The anarchic Golden Triangle presented its own distinct difficulty. So did Iran, which had banned cultivation in 1959 but struggled to enforce the policy. Pressed by Washington to maintain the ban, the Iranians countered that little could be accomplished without Turkish and Afghan cooperation. "We are already working with Turkey," Kissinger wrote to Nixon, "but Afghanistan is a problem." The prospect of Afghan-grown opium reaching U.S. markets remained only hypothetical. It was, however, flooding across Iran's thinly policed eastern border, to Tehran's consternation. Mitchell and Richardson had predicted that the elimination of the Turkish crop would render Afghan opium production "a serious raw material threat."[75]

Opium was not a new issue within the U.S.-Afghan relationship, as historians James Tharin Bradford and Daniel Weimer chronicle. In 1944, U.S. minister Cornelius Engert had persuaded Prime Minister Hashim Khan to ban cultivation. Yet the ban went largely unenforced, and Afghanistan failed to persuade skeptical U.S. officials in its bid to become a legal opium exporter. The poppy question complicated pre-Nixon relations but remained a secondary issue until the early 1970s. Cold War concerns evoked far more anxiety, while the prospect of Afghan opium reaching the United States remained nebulous. The 1969 NSC policy statement discussed earlier in this chapter omitted any mention of opium.[76]

Whether Afghanistan could undertake an effective anti-narcotics policy under the constitutional experiment was questionable. A frustrated Interior Minister Abdul Kayeum complained in 1964 that poppies were grown openly in Herat, Badakhshan, and Jalalabad provinces, likely with the connivance of senior government officials.[77] A 1970 embassy assessment echoed his conclusion. Afghanistan lacked a specialized anti-drug police or explicit anti-trafficking laws. Too draconian a crackdown risked driving away Western tourists—beyond the subset visiting for drug-related reasons. Neumann cautioned against expecting dramatic change: Afghanistan's "limp performance in this area" was "little different from efforts in other fields."[78]

Even so, pressure on Afghanistan visibly escalated in late 1971, following the Turkish announcement. Neumann emphasized the importance of the narcotics issue to Abdul Zahir days after Washington approved the Title II wheat grant. Weeks later, in a New York meeting, Rogers primarily stressed the importance of drug policy to Shafiq, while the latter conveyed his concern about the drought and the kingdom's debt burden. Neither Neumann nor Rogers expressly connected food aid or a debt moratorium to narcotics policy, but emphasis carried its own implications. Kabul promised rapid action.[79]

Assisted by a representative of the Bureau of Narcotics and Dangerous Drugs, the U.S. country team crafted an extensive counter-narcotics agenda. They did so despite a panoply of obstacles. Scarce data on opium cultivation forced the team to rely on estimates from AID, Iran, and the Soviets. Finalized in December 1971, the plan called for conclusively locating centers of production, curtailing cross-border trafficking, a "crash" research program to select alternative crops for farmers, and establishing an effective national enforcement program. Seeking a united front, Washington pursued multilateral collaboration with its European allies, Turkey, Iran, and Pakistan.[80]

Washington and its allies enjoyed tremendous leverage within Kabul, and U.S. officials cannily exploited local vulnerabilities. Afghans appeared "unusually sensitive" to foreign press coverage, one U.S. diplomat observed. Citing the case of Turkey, Rogers warned Shafiq that "certain practices" could easily foster an undesirable image. Lurid newspaper articles about the fates of Western travelers who had visited Afghanistan for cheap opium amplified Afghan discomfort. They, a Turkish diplomat reported, felt themselves under "tremendous pressure from the Americans." So did members of the coalition. French ambassador Eugene Wernert worried about appearing to gang up on the Afghans but reasoned that it would be worse to arouse "the suspicion of the Americans." Privately, Wernert wrote that, while some elements of the U.S. approach appeared reasonable, others, intended to curtail drug-related travel, verged on the utopian.[81]

Perhaps so, but Washington left Afghanistan little room to maneuver. Absent explicit arm-twisting, the Nixon approach still presented the kingdom with the risk of angering its principal source of food aid. Kabul offered no resistance, seeking instead to assure itself of Washington's continued goodwill. Shafiq appeared especially earnest, emphatically affirming the need for greater enforcement of the kingdom's drug laws. Accordingly, Neumann suggested making the foreign ministry the "focal point" for narcotics-related entreaties.[82]

Like others before him, Shafiq benefited personally from a close relationship with the United States. "Energetic, ambitious, and extremely intelligent" in Neumann's evaluation, Shafiq's performance offered one basis among several for discerning a general improvement in both Afghan governance and the bilateral relationship. Citing Kabul's prudence during the recent war, the Food for Work program, and Abdul Zahir's handling of the legislature, Neumann reported that the "performance of Afghan government [has] considerably improved." Shafiq's outreach toward Tehran and Islamabad offered further grounds for satisfaction. Although its ability to implement its promises remained questionable, Kabul had responded constructively to U.S. pressure on narcotics. The present period, Neumann wrote, represented the "high point in [U.S.] standing in Afghanistan."[83]

If not rosy, the assessment was resoundingly positive. It rested entirely on early evaluations of relief efforts. Washington had provided two-thirds of the grain shipped after the emergency appeal. Within Kabul, the grain price had fallen somewhat. Assessing provincial relief efforts in winter remained a more speculative endeavor. Nevertheless, in March, the country team credited its hosts with "imaginative efforts to meet the drought-caused disaster." Employing the yardsticks of rural development and self-help, they looked ahead optimistically:

> For the first time, the RGA [Royal Government of Afghanistan] accepted as a responsibility . . . the relief of the people suffering from effects of a drought. They made structural changes within the government to promote rapid agricultural development and to an extent never previously achieved focused resources, human and material, on meeting specific goals. Through these efforts the RGA was able to increase the use of fertilizer and improved seed throughout the country, begin a Food for Work program that could have a major immediate and long term impact on rural development. . . . The country has come through the drought with a minimum amount of dislocation and hardship.[84]

Afghans—besides the elite Kabul milieu Americans usually encountered—were not as bullish. Kabul University remained wracked by unrest. Relations between Abdul Zahir and the parliament became acrimonious, and the government contrived to deprive the legislature of its necessary quorum. Political parties remained illegal entities. A less sanguine Neumann diagnosed an "ill-defined political crisis which appears deeper than available facts and known factors warrant," detecting an "atmosphere here of lassitude, of resignation, as if the *élan vital* of the government has become exhausted."[85]

One event in March suggested the imminent possibility of a fundamental rupture. In successive conversations with Neumann and a subordinate, a senior foreign ministry official, Wahid Abdullah, asked how Washington would react if Mohammed Daoud Khan returned to power. Abdullah's first inquiry, on March 11, was phrased vaguely. At a second meeting, on March 27, the intermediary sought more precise answers: would Neumann's government continue to aid Afghanistan and support its independence if Daoud assumed power?[86]

Daoud's return appeared improbable. He had largely receded from view, although his dissatisfaction with the constitutional project was no secret.

To Neumann, Daoud appeared more likely to act within the royal family than against it. The ambassador perceived peril in either encouraging Daoud or in alienating him. He therefore crafted a cautious reply, which his superiors approved. In a subsequent April 11 meeting, Neumann informed Wahid Abdullah that, while Washington could not comment on internal Afghan politics, the U.S. attitude toward Afghanistan would be governed by its "policies and actions, in particular toward U.S. interests and towards peace and stability in the region."[87]

What had Washington approved? The U.S. response offered an effective green light to Daoud. The message assumes a more sinister implication in light of later events, but Neumann clearly believed that Daoud would return via a prime ministerial appointment. Wahid Abdullah claimed during the second meeting that efforts were under way to reconcile Daoud and his rivals within the royal family. Neumann's superiors, doubtful that a Daoud restoration would occur so harmoniously, suggested reminding Abdullah of U.S. support for the constitutional experiment—should he ever reach out again. The emissary made no further contact, however, and Neumann's conditional acceptance remained Washington's standing word on the matter.[88]

In the intervening months, while Daoud remained elusive, other events drew the attention of the country team. Heavy snowfall had blanketed the kingdom, ironically compounding the drought's effects in isolated provinces such as Ghor. Poorly connected to Kabul in dry months, Ghor became inaccessible in winter. Spring floods washed out bridges, further isolating the province. Countless sheep drowned in the deluge, leaving their owners destitute. Many fled to the provincial capital, Chakcharan. Visiting Chakcharan in the late spring, *New York Times* correspondent James Sterba witnessed a calamity unfolding. He wrote subsequently of "the sounds of once-strong and proud men weeping and the sights of veiled women grazing like animals on field grass and of children lying like tiny rag heaps beside roads."[89]

Isolation, poverty, and the cruel sequence of drought and excess snowfall had afflicted Ghor. Yet much of the tragedy originated in choices made in Chakcharan, Kabul, and Washington. Like other provinces, Ghor served as a site for Abdul Wakil's Food for Work program. The Afghan government sold donated grain at concession prices, but Food for Work represented its only means of feeding truly destitute citizens. A hastily assembled cadre of foreigners, including Peace Corps Volunteers (PCVs), labored alongside Afghans to administer the program. Provincial governors selected projects, specified work schedules, and controlled the disbursal of grain as compensation.[90]

Figure 8.1 Afghans gather outside the governor's office in Chakcharan, 1972
Source: Photograph by Ron Dizon

Flying into Chakcharan that spring, PCV James Mathewson, an aspiring geologist from Kansas City, beheld a lovely red field of poppies alongside the grassy airstrip. Ghor's provincial governor, Abdul Razak Lala, received him enthusiastically and delighted in showing the American volunteer off to his constituents. Effort to jumpstart local Food for Work projects foundered, however. Chakcharan's central granary was nearly empty, and Lala remained reluctant to initiate projects. Without work, grain simply sat in the warehouse as Afghans starved outside.[91]

Mathewson and his Peace Corps colleagues, Ron Dizon and Tim McCormack, quickly apprehended that the situation was desperate. Food for Work assumed a basic relationship between hunger and labor supply. In fact, the drought had already driven able-bodied workers to seek employment in the cities. Many of those remaining were too young, old, or weak to work. Projects were devised according to preexisting development or political agendas and required malnourished people to walk miles for a day of hard labor. Workers occasionally died on the job. Shortages of equipment hindered efforts; Sterba encountered one Herat-area road project that equipped fifty men with four shovels and a pick. Workers lacked assurance that their coupons for grain would be honored afterward. Laborers in neighboring Badghis complained to PCV Jim Hicks that their wheat sacks, provided as compensation, contained stones; Hicks confirmed the report, to his horror. Meanwhile, grain, equipment, and supplies simply vanished from storehouses or in transit.[92]

Scarcity in Ghor drove tensions toward a breaking point. Idealistic and increasingly frustrated, the PCVs quietly rebelled. Dizon began distributing coupons freely. Mathewson urged his superiors to provide food on a relief basis. McCormack spoke extensively to Sterba, whose articles offered many Americans their first real news of the famine. Sympathetic readers subsequently donated $1,000 to care for the famine's orphans; Lala refused to accept the money. When McCormack was summoned to Kabul for consultations, he packed his bags, apprehending that he would not be invited back.[93]

To its credit, having reported optimistically about the drought earlier, the country team responded with alacrity in the spring. Neumann transmitted reports of hunger in Ghor, Faryab, Uruzgan, Badghis, and Herat, warning of government inaction. Neumann advised Washington in May that Food for Work had been stymied by poor local and central administration. Ghor's granary held 85 tons of wheat, but a lack of trucks prevented its distribution. A visiting government delegation, including Deputy Prime Minister Samad Hamed and Abdul Wakil, faced a food riot in Chakcharan in June. An angry crowd surrounded them in Lala's compound, only dispersing after Wakil pledged to open the warehouse and distribute grain, freely, to all who needed it.[94] As the PCVs had long contended, starving Afghans needed food, not additional work. The arrival of the harvest presented them with a cruel choice: between laboring on sometimes spurious projects or gathering their own crops. In June, Food for Work projects in Ghor and Uruzgan faltered for a lack of workers.[95]

By then, the failures of provincial relief had reinforced a growing consensus that the Afghan government and constitutional experiment were in crisis. "Is there a government?" Neumann asked Minister of the Interior Amanullah Mansuri in May. "I really don't know," Mansuri replied. A raucous May Day demonstration brought Kabul to a halt. Former prime minister Maiwandwal denounced the constitutional experiment as a fraud, adding some criticism of the U.S. war in Vietnam. Disaffection, audible within the government itself, extended to the constitutional system. "If the system does not change, what is [the] use of changing governments?" another minister complained. Government and parliament clashed bitterly over the maldistribution of wheat. Neumann now believed that Abdul Zahir's resignation was imminent.[96] In July, King Zahir admitted to the visiting Treasury secretary, John Connally, that the experiment might have been "premature."[97]

The fall of another prime minister constituted, by now, an unremarkable occurrence in the short history of Afghanistan's constitutional project. Increasingly, however, observers logged direct criticism of King Zahir. Stymied as prime minister, Abdul Zahir nonetheless proved adept at redirecting blame for the ongoing crisis. Nostalgic remarks by senior officials about the Daoud years reached the ears of Western diplomats.[98]

Earlier, such reports might have sparked alarm in Washington. But the U.S. investment in the democratic experiment remained moderate, weathered by years of frustration. Kabul's slow-moving crisis elicited no discussion within the White House, then grappling with détente diplomacy and the aftermath of the Easter Offensive in Vietnam. Externally, Afghanistan did little to call attention to itself. Even within the State Department, the prospect of constitutional upheaval did not elicit anxiety. Diplomat Robert Flaten, recently returned from Kabul, wrote, "In spite of this political uncertainty, the U.S. role in Afghanistan remains positive and welcome by almost all Afghans. . . . Our position in Kabul is probably as strong as it ever has been and would be cause for considerable optimism if we could be assured of a responsible government with which to continue to deal."[99] On this basis, the Connally visit principally served to bolster Washington's emphasis on self-help and cooperation on narcotics.[100] No further carrots were proffered. Asked about further aid by a reporter, Connally replied: "I don't want to be pessimistic, but I sure don't want to be optimistic."[101]

Concurrently, the government's failure to respond to the famine had become undeniable. After his own trip to Chakcharan, Deputy Prime Minister Hamed admitted that Kabul's relief efforts had been undermined by corruption and poor distribution. The aid mission presented its Afghan counterparts with a list of ongoing problems with Food for Work: inadequate rations, poor record keeping, and the misuse of wheat to pay for project expenses. Citing Ghor, and distilling the consensus views of his Western colleagues, Lewis pressed Abdul Zahir to develop a coordinated plan to address the famine. Without immediate action, the coming snowfall would once again close off the mountain provinces from relief.[102]

Within days, the Afghan government began to assemble an emergency effort, dubbed Operation Help. Although Kabul already faced considerable pressure, Lewis's intervention may have contributed to this outcome. Professed concern from foreign governments and agencies at least encouraged the Kabul government to expect and seek material support from its donors. Unlike Food for Work, which depended upon the capabilities and priorities of provincial governors, Operation Help was closely directed from Kabul. The Afghan Army trucked supplies into Herat, Badghis, Uruzgan, Faryab, Ghor, and Badakhshan. Armed soldiers supervised the distribution of grain.[103]

Operation Help received significant support from the international community, as numerous foreign donors pledged material support to Afghan relief. The commitment of an additional 20,000 tons of Title II wheat—no small feat after prices skyrocketed earlier in the year—established the United States as the program's most important contributor. The Soviet Union provided milk, rice, flour, and clothing; Iran shipped garments; Pakistan sent shoes; India, Poland, Switzerland, and the United Kingdom contributed vitamin pills and essential medicine.[104] Over its brief duration, Operation Help assisted an estimated 235,000 Afghans. Veterans of Food for Work, like Dizon, regarded it as a great success. Lewis termed it "truly extraordinary by any standards and unprecedented in Afghanistan." Operation Help was even more remarkable for occurring while Kabul underwent another change of government. Abdul Zahir tendered his resignation in late September, only to have the monarch reject it. A perplexing interregnum followed in which he soldiered on unhappily, only managing to step down in December. Long before then, U.S. officials had turned their attentions to his evident successor, Shafiq.[105]

Afghanistan's last prime minister contrasted conspicuously with his predecessors. Although another technocrat, Shafiq approached his office with ambition, energy, and seemingly a clean bill of health. A Columbia University alumnus and onetime Kissinger student (and reportedly something of a bon vivant), Shafiq had long enjoyed and benefited from the esteem of the U.S. country team. One analysis termed him "an outstanding choice" and "a bright intelligent young man with a quick agile mind that penetrates immediately to the core of issues before him." Shafiq appeared atypically willing to act decisively. On major bilateral issues, Americans found him understanding, even ingratiating. Visiting New York in October, Shafiq promised that his government would undertake a "crusade" against illicit drugs. "It's obvious he has learned his lines well!" Lewis wrote.[106]

Shafiq began with aplomb. His conspicuously youthful cabinet received near-unanimous legislative approval. His description of the parliament as a coequal branch won him a rare olive branch from the legislature. A December 11 policy address unveiled ambitious proposals, including enhanced domestic revenue collection, agricultural self-sufficiency within five years, an aggressive anti-narcotics program, and extensive educational reform. Questioning the program's feasibility, Neumann nonetheless termed it "impressive" and lauded the new prime minister's "contagious optimism."[107]

Shafiq also moved expeditiously to resolve one of Afghanistan's long-standing disputes. As foreign minister, he had continued dialogue with Tehran over the Helmand waters question, eliminating the major outstanding differences during the autumn. Tehran finally accepted the findings of the 1951 commission, allocating 22 cubic meters per second, while Kabul magnanimously offered another four cubic meters. For its part, Iran promised to accelerate road construction to the eastern port of Bandar Abbas, improving Afghanistan's alternate route to the sea. While parliamentary ratification of the agreement posed a further hurdle for Shafiq—"Iranophobia still strong here" the U.S. embassy warned—Tehran had conceded ground on the central issue. The Shah's deepening security concerns undoubtedly helped to facilitate the accord. Shafiq hosted his Iranian counterpart, Hoveyda, for a signing ceremony in March. Afterward, thousands of demonstrators—leftists prominent among them—marched in Kabul, denouncing the agreement as a betrayal.[108]

Relations with Pakistan further challenged Shafiq, especially after Bhutto abruptly dismissed the opposition-led provincial government in Baluchistan in February. Baluch insurgents commenced guerrilla attacks against the Pakistan Army within weeks. Bhutto's battles with the National Awami Party fostered suspicion of him in Kabul. Karmal's Parcham faction and its Khalqist rivals vied to outdo each other in appeals to Pashtun nationalism. Upheaval across the Durand Line further exposed Shafiq to nationalist attacks from either flank.[109]

The nationalist upsurge of early 1973 brought Shafiq's grace period to its inevitable end. Yet Neumann and other Western observers, who found the new prime minister both congenial and admirably energetic, detected faults in his approach to governance. By his own account a workaholic, Shafiq carried a daunting load on his shoulders and appeared reluctant to delegate. His efforts to professionalize the bureaucracy drew praise, but Neumann also detected an authoritarian streak. At times Shafiq acted abruptly. His government's sudden spring 1973 demolition of a church in Kabul, likely undertaken to appease fundamentalist sentiment, drew protests from American clergy, including the Rev. Billy Graham.[110]

Most of Shafiq's promises remained unfulfilled on July 11, 1973, when Lewis transmitted a half-year assessment. Applauding his dynamism, pragmatism, successful Iranian diplomacy, and noting improved U.S. dealings with the Afghan bureaucracy. Lewis wrote that Shafiq seemed to be the "best prime minister under constitution to date." Some unnamed observers viewed his centralization of power as "creeping Daoudism." Events six days later demonstrated that phrase to be a contradiction in terms.[111]

Experiment's End

The first inkling of trouble came at 2:30 A.M., when the sound of cannon fire echoed in Kabul. Sporadic bursts of gunfire followed, while tanks and helicopters closed in on the royal palace. The identity of the insurgents remained unclear for hours, as Radio Afghanistan played a mix of martial music and warnings to stay off the streets. Daoud took to the airwaves, sometime after 7:00 A.M. The detention of Shafiq, his cabinet, and members of the royal family, and the abolition of the 1964 constitution and the monarchy followed in short succession. British ambassador John Drinkall credited the conspirators with "remarkable efficiency and secrecy." King Zahir was recuperating from eye surgery in Italy.[112]

Afghanistan's ten-year experiment in constitutional democracy had come to a sudden, violent end. True, Daoud had advised the U.S. embassy of his plans in March 1972, sixteen months earlier. Evidently, he felt no need to ask twice. Washington's reply had given him all that he needed. In the intervening time, he provided no further hints of his intentions, and U.S. estimations of the situation in Kabul shifted away from the pessimism of the previous year. They remained close to their zenith in the early summer. Neumann and his government regarded Shafiq highly and assuredly did not prefer the headstrong Daoud. Nonetheless, they resolved to make do with him.

Named doctrines are often treated synonymously with a president's foreign policy—to the point where each president is expected to coin one. At times, the assumption is wildly reductive. In Nixon's case, the principles unfolded on Guam in July 1969 offer a meaningful synecdoche of U.S. policy worldwide during the final years of the Afghan constitutional experiment. One therefore might seek an explanation of Washington's Afghanistan policy from the Nixon Doctrine, but few White House fingerprints can be found in this era. Key decisions, especially on famine relief and governance in Kabul, unfolded beneath the presidential level.

Questions of timing present themselves as well. The Nixon Doctrine did not emerge fully formed on that July day. Nixon expressed a set of policy principles, but the painstaking work of selecting regional partners and determining the terms of collaboration lay ahead, competing for his scarce time with the Vietnam War and superpower diplomacy. Nixon's seminal partnership with the Shah of Iran only crystallized in spring 1972—by which point the Afghan constitutional experiment had scarcely a year remaining. Even then, the Nixon Doctrine did not apply to the kingdom. Greater U.S. support of the fragile but relatively neighborly government in Kabul would have pleased the Shah, who had made plain his concern about Afghan events.[113]

Instead, the dominant influences on U.S. policy during the Nixon era proved to be domestic in origin. Nixon inherited and partly shared popular skepticism toward foreign aid and a simmering frustration toward "ungrateful" recipients. Afghanistan never failed to express the requisite gratitude—Rogers told Shafiq as much—but could not escape repeated admonitions to practice self-help.[114] Even as a natural disaster called the entire objective into question, that imperative remained dominant. This emphasis, in turn, shaped how the Afghan government responded to the growing crisis in the second half of 1971. The disastrous Food for Work program received U.S. approval in its initial months and was co-administered by an American advisor. Its promise to expand rural roads and irrigation canals spoke to long-standing U.S. objectives. Attention to the program's serious conceptual flaws only came later. U.S. officials retained, throughout, a reflexive confidence in the applicability of Western agricultural methods to Afghan soil. Advocacy for the Shamalan project continued into 1973, as the country team called for regularizing holdings and physically leveling the land.[115]

The sudden ascendance of narcotics within the relationship further demonstrates the supreme importance of domestic imperatives. The prospect of Afghan-grown opium reaching U.S. shores remained merely hypothetical in 1971. The task of restricting poppy cultivation and local trafficking, meanwhile, imposed significant demands on Kabul. Neumann had warned in 1970 of "the limited Afghan capability for managing several crises at the same time." The political effects of Afghan adherence to Nixon's crusade are difficult to discern, as Bradford writes. It did, perhaps, stretch the already thin resources of the Afghan state, while diverting the U.S. country team from the unresolved problem of the drought.[116]

Meanwhile, the Afghan constitutional experiment continued to falter. Enthusiasm for it waned during its second half, as Afghan domestic politics grew increasingly vituperative. The struggles of nascent Afghan democracy—overseen by an anxious king, ready to stamp out independent centers of power—tired observers. Identifying stability and development as core objectives within the kingdom fostered an ambivalence toward the entire endeavor. Yet the Nixon administration undervalued a seemingly frustrating factor that worked to its benefit. The relative weakness of the final prime ministers rendered them more pliable to Washington's entreaties and less confrontational toward its allies. It left them, however, more vulnerable to a nationalist backlash, as Daoud formed a temporary coalition with the Parcham faction.

In this sense, the Afghan story runs parallel to others in the Nixon era. Nixon had stated, in 1967, that democracy was "not necessarily the best form of government for people . . . with entirely different backgrounds." While his White House tapes are mercifully free of remarks disparaging Afghanistan and its inhabitants, Nixon famously admired strongmen, including Yahya and the Shah. The nature of governance in Kabul was immaterial to him, inasmuch as he considered the question. His White House drew no significant lessons from Agnew's Kabul trip, whereas a similar earlier episode—befalling Nixon, himself, on a 1958 Latin American trip—had galvanized the Eisenhower administration. Tellingly, the White House expended more ink on microanalysis of the conduct of local PCVs—from the program that subsequently proved essential to drought relief. The preservation or fulfillment of a tenuous, flawed democratic process did not rank as a significant policy priority.[117]

Yet more had been lost than the shaky 1964 constitution. Daoud had ended four decades of peace within Kabul itself, bringing the increasingly well-armed Afghan Army into politics, and setting a fresh precedent for the violent seizure of power. Missteps and cynical manipulation had greatly tarnished the standing of the Afghan monarchy, so that Neumann and his colleagues detected little apparent regret at the king's ouster. Shots had been fired, and lives lost, but relatively few when set alongside subsequent events. Having ruthlessly thrust aside a flawed but long-standing sovereign institution, Daoud could not himself rest easily in power. His dethroned cousin understood this too. After the coup, the Shah proposed flying Zahir into Afghanistan to stage a counter-revolt. Prudent, if not always wise, Zahir declined the offer, accepting exile in Italy instead.[118] Three decades would pass before he returned to an Afghanistan ravaged by the choices of his successors and the interventions of others.

CHAPTER 9

Return to Engagement, 1973–1976

Long before he achieved international renown, Henry Kissinger attained notoriety in Afghanistan. In January 1962, the then–Harvard professor visited India and Pakistan to lecture on behalf of the United States Information Agency (USIA). In Peshawar, Kissinger was asked if he had seen any signs of Pashtun agitation—a pertinent, predictable question amid the ongoing border crisis. An earlier extemporaneous gibe about Kashmir had already gotten him into trouble, but Kissinger nursed "the theory that the subcontinent had been deprived of my wisecracks long enough." He replied: "I would not recognize Pashtun agitation if it hit me in the face." Mohammed Daoud Khan's government tendered a diplomatic protest. "There is no telling what else I might have achieved if I had followed my wanderlust to visit Afghanistan," Kissinger wrote afterward, but the USIA evidently had other ideas.[1]

Life afforded Kissinger second—and third—chances. Now secretary of state, he undertook a whirlwind six-hour Kabul trip on November 1, 1974. Meetings with Daoud and Mohammed Naim Khan preceded lunch at the palace and, memorably, a *buzkashi* match. His earlier faux pas went gracefully unrecalled. Predictably, the conversation largely revolved around difficult relations between the Afghan republic and Pakistan. Naim asked his guest to intercede with Islamabad. Experienced in shuttle diplomacy, Kissinger chuckled, "No one ever asks me to deal with problems that are less than a thousand years old."[2]

Humorous interjections speckled the conversation, and the Afghans appeared charmed by Kissinger and satisfied with the visit. Kissinger was equally affected. Kabul had not initially featured on his itinerary. A stream of reports cannily passed along by the Near East and South Asia Bureau piqued Kissinger's interest until, as one aide recalled, "His curiosity got the better of him." Afghanistan's perennial geopolitical balancing act between great powers intrigued Kissinger. "This is a fascinating country," he wrote to President Gerald Ford, "and a stalwart people whose geographic location has made them probably the world's oldest and most successful practitioners of non-alignment." Crediting his hosts for the "warmth of their reception" and their "legendary" hospitality, he pondered the afternoon's *buzkashi* match. Kissinger mused that the game explained "why these people have managed so well in maintaining their independence." He visited again in August 1976.[3]

Kissinger's brief Kabul visit goes unmentioned in his memoirs. Nor has his Afghan policy commanded great scholarly attention. Neither omission occasions lamentation, but Afghanistan's emergence on his political map remains noteworthy. As national security advisor, Kissinger had been detached from Afghanistan policy before Daoud's July 1973 coup. Afterward, following his confirmation as secretary of state, the U.S. approach to Kabul bore his distinctive fingerprints. Working with trusted envoys, Kissinger monitored Afghanistan and its simmering feud with Pakistan. A problem that he had derided as obscure and unrecognizable twelve years earlier now demanded his personal attention.

While concerns over Kabul's alignment mounted after the coup, the nature of U.S. policy toward Afghanistan during the late Nixon and Ford years remains subject to debate. Daoud faced several purported coup attempts, as well as a July 1975 uprising. Contemporary observers—notably the journalist Selig Harrison—discerned the involvement of the CIA and its Iranian and Pakistani counterparts in these episodes. Documentary corroboration of U.S. covert activity remains elusive, however. The extant record neither confirms nor refutes the claim, and thus this chapter cannot definitively assess its validity.

Available evidence and recent scholarship, however, indicate that engagement emerged as the principal U.S. policy toward Afghanistan during the détente era. Washington contended with a limited aid budget, and Afghan requests misaligned with new doctrines of foreign assistance, but Iran's Shah eagerly embraced his new role as regional hegemon. As Gregory

Winger writes, Afghanistan constituted a key proving ground for the Nixon Doctrine, long after its author departed unhappily for California. Concern over continued unrest in Pakistan and Daoud's uncertain trajectory galvanized the Shah toward extensive efforts there, with Washington's general approval.[4]

Superpower détente had reached Afghanistan well before the mid-1970s, and the period witnessed no upsurge in Cold War tensions over the country. Backchannel diplomacy defused the immediate risk posed by Daoud's coup. A general compatibility of aims between Washington and Moscow limited the possibility of renewed conflict over the Durand Line. Nevertheless, the coup fostered dynamics inimical to détente. Itself less perturbed by Afghan events, the United States endeavored to reassure regional allies and maintain influence in Kabul. Simultaneously, Moscow scrutinized U.S. actions closely, discerning another project of pact-building. Daoud's credentials as a nationalist and nonaligned statesman offered each superpower some reassurance, but his long-term ability to retain the office he had violently seized remained an open, troubling question. Heading an ungainly political coalition, he pursued ambitious, ultimately contradictory objectives: rapid economic development and self-determination for borderland Pashtuns and Baluchs. Ultimately, prodded by Washington and Tehran, he chose the former. An impressive diplomatic breakthrough in 1976 could not entirely alleviate the anxieties of regional and Cold War actors, however. Like the détente regime itself, regional stability and Kabul's nonalignment rested on fragile foundations.

A Republic, If You Can Keep It, 1973

Kabul appeared subdued but largely unscarred at daybreak on July 17. Helicopters buzzed overhead, an upended tank lay in the river, and soldiers halted outgoing cars. The post office and airport closed, and the telephone system went offline. "End of monarchy has been accepted by majority with philosophical calm," reported the Italian ambassador, noting that younger Kabulis appeared enthusiastic about the coup. Most government offices reopened within a day, and ubiquitous photos of Daoud appeared, as Louis Dupree wrote, "like magic." The lively independent newspapers of the constitutional era vanished.[5]

Predictably, Western observers pondered Moscow's role in the coup. U.S. ambassador Robert Neumann detected no evidence of Soviet involvement. His counterparts in Washington, Paris, and London concurred but considered the possibility that extensive Soviet contacts within the Afghan military had afforded Moscow some advance warning. Leonid Brezhnev's government hurriedly recognized Daoud's regime while its Western adversaries debated their options.[6]

Western governments saw little purpose in delaying recognition. No evidence existed of serious opposition to Daoud, although diplomats in Kabul strained, without domestic flights or telephone service, to report on the rest of the country. London evaluated whether the regime had attained control over national territory, the "obedience" of most citizens, and a "reasonable prospect of permanency." Washington attached an additional criterion: continued Afghan adherence to prior commitments.[7] Kissinger's aides, Harold Saunders and Henry Appelbaum, identified three core objectives: continued anti-narcotics efforts, the preservation of Afghan independence, and Kabul's commitment to regional stability.[8]

Although his coup had surprised Western governments, Daoud benefited from being familiar. His motivations for seizing power remained murky, but his politics invited little speculation. "He is basically a nationalist," Saunders and Appelbaum reasoned, liable to "lean a bit more toward the Soviets than his predecessors did," but likely to maintain Afghan nonalignment. Daoud might be "a little harder to deal with" than his predecessors and was "likely to be a bit more suspicious of U.S. motives." Nevertheless, neither they, nor the State Department's Bureau of Intelligence and Research (INR) expected abrupt changes in Afghan foreign policy, although the latter predicted increased tensions with Pakistan.[9] "With luck and delicate handling," Neumann advised, the "new regime need not necessarily present threat to any major U.S. interests." Hopefully Daoud had learned from experience.[10]

Wishful thinking, perhaps, but the absence of any challenge to Daoud's regime soon forced the issue. Afghan envoys impatiently requested U.S. recognition. West Germany abruptly recognized Daoud on July 20, prompting Neumann and British ambassador John Drinkall to warn that further delay risked their position in Kabul. "Everyone is trying to jump onto the Daoud bandwagon as soon as possible with little or no attempt to coordinate timing," Drinkall wrote. Washington favored a quiet statement of continuing relations. Too formal a declaration could prompt reexamination of Afghanistan policy across the government. Too long a hiatus risked making the choice an uncomfortably public affair, prompting "public debate . . . over our policy toward another military dictator abrogating a democratic constitution." Best not to add Afghanistan to an already extensive litany.[11]

Yet ascertainment of Daoud's hold on power could not occur overnight. Anxious about further delay and concerned that Daoud might nurse suspicions of U.S. involvement in his earlier dismissal, Neumann acted independently. He dispatched, through Daoud's nephew Ismail Osman, a friendly message, reminding the Afghan leader of his earlier covert contact with the embassy, and expressing the hope that his government would help to make early recognition possible. With Washington's approval, Neumann visited Naim at his home. Pledging a continued commitment to nonalignment, Naim entreated Neumann for immediate economic assistance.[12]

Only Pakistan opposed prompt recognition. Prime Minister Zulfikar Ali Bhutto remained at odds with the opposition National Awami Party (NAP), headed by Wali Khan, son of the famous Pashtun dissident Abdul Ghaffar Khan. Dominant in Punjab and Sindh, Bhutto's Pakistan People's Party (PPP) commanded little support in either the North West Frontier Province (NWFP) or Baluchistan. Bhutto's dismissal of opposition governments in both western provinces angered the NAP, which he tarred as a secessionist entity. Less than two years after the trauma of 1971, Pakistani politics retained a dangerously regional character. An INR study, released just after Daoud's coup, warned that the country's "prospects for stable constitutional government remain uncertain."[13]

Daoud's return further complicated Bhutto's predicament. Bereft of reliable reports from Kabul, Bhutto failed to communicate his own preferences before U.S. opinion solidified. His ambassador in Washington, Sultan Khan, proposed a delay in extending recognition. Assistant Secretary of State Joseph Sisco replied that his government felt a need to "move expeditiously" to preserve the Western position in Kabul. Sultan Khan subsequently telephoned with an official request to withhold recognition until Bhutto could confer with the Shah three days later, on July 23. Pakistan's appeal could not be rejected outright, but Bhutto's stalling ploy required Iranian cooperation. Cannily, Sisco undercut the Pakistani position. He spoke next to Iranian ambassador Ardeshir Zahedi, a consummate insider in both Tehran and Washington. Zahedi concurred and pledged to advise the Shah to extend recognition. Agreeing that further delay served no constructive purpose, the

Shah instructed his ambassador in Kabul to convey a statement of recognition on July 21.[14]

As intended, Iranian recognition broke the impasse. Neumann transmitted his government's wish to continue "long-standing warm relations" on the morning of July 22. A friendly afternoon meeting with Daoud followed, in which the latter promised to maintain a nonaligned foreign policy. Pakistani and British recognition followed that day. Neumann thanked his counterparts in Washington, especially Sisco, for their decisive action.[15]

Daoud's efficiency as a coup plotter and his credibility as a nonaligned statesman made recognition a foregone conclusion. While frustrating to Neumann and his peers, the five-day interval stemmed from prudence and uncertainty. Most revealing about the brief episode were the respective roles adopted by Pakistan, the United States, and Iran. Whereas Islamabad regarded the new Afghan republic warily, Washington argued for continued diplomatic engagement. Between the two stood Iran. Balancing the Shah's sense of geopolitical threat was his own distinctive sense of national grandeur and long-standing aspirations for the expansion of Iranian power and influence. The latter trait rendered Afghanistan a field of opportunity for Iran, its coffers glutted by rising oil revenues. Lastly, the brief scramble illuminated a fundamental lack of communication inside the Western camp. Drinkall complained afterward that the Iranians, Pakistanis, and Americans had each acted "pretty shabbily," failing to advise London of their decisions. Twenty years into the Afghan Cold War, coordination between the allies remained halting—even as each government felt an increased need to respond coherently to expanding Soviet influence in the region.[16]

Two months earlier, in National Security Study Memorandum (NSSM) 182, President Richard Nixon had solicited analysis of "Soviet strategy, policy, and actions" from the Eastern Mediterranean to South Asia. His administration still grappled with the implications of British withdrawal from the region, a growing Soviet naval presence in the Indian Ocean, Moscow's heightened influence in the Arab world, and increased U.S. dependence on Persian Gulf oil. Other allies specified their own concerns. Pakistan feared concerted Soviet action through India and Afghanistan, exploiting unrest in Baluchistan or the NWFP. Iran worried about Moscow flanking it from east and west. Saudi Arabia expressed trepidation about Soviet ties to Iraq and South Yemen. Visiting China in November, Kissinger found Premier Zhou Enlai to be "gravely concerned" about the Kabul coup.[17]

NSSM 182 posed a difficult question: Should the entire specified area be treated as a coherent whole, meriting a single policy? Regional allies clearly feared that a Soviet grand design was unfolding while Washington stood aside, chastened by defeat in Vietnam. "They see the area and believe the Soviets do also, as a strategic whole from India through Turkey," Kissinger stated in a July 12 meeting. "We don't see it as a cohesive unit and our policy is conducted more on a bilateral basis." Hardly hostile to the notion of grand strategy, Kissinger remained unconvinced that Moscow pursued a coherent project along its southern tier. The allies offered too stark a prognosis of imminent Soviet aggression, even employing the timeless myth of an advance toward a warm-water port. Their anxieties could not be dismissed outright, however. Sisco deemed Iranian and Pakistani warnings "somewhat exaggerated" but "fundamentally sound," adding, "It is important that we be responsive to these concerns." Gen. Vernon Walters of the CIA opined: "The fact that [the Soviets] are seeking détente in Western Europe doesn't mean that they want détente in the Middle East."[18]

The allies had convinced Washington to demonstrate its support—whether or not a grand Soviet southern design actually existed. Five days later, Daoud's coup offered the latest, perhaps most ambiguous portent of expanding Soviet influence. The Shah, shortly to arrive in Washington, had already expressed his anxiety about unrest in Baluchistan. "The Soviet strategy has succeeded in Afghanistan," he told Nixon and Kissinger on July 24. "Even if it was not a Russian coup, they must have known about it." He feared a renewed, Soviet-backed Afghan campaign for Pashtunistan, perhaps coupled with aid to Baluch rebels. This, in turn, would enable Moscow to advance toward the Persian Gulf. "We will not let the Pakistanis disintegrate," he vowed. Kissinger promised to discuss Afghanistan at the next opportunity with Soviet ambassador Anatoly Dobrynin.[19]

Dialogue with Moscow offered one means of clarifying the situation. In successive conversations with Dobrynin, Kissinger deemed the coup an internal Afghan affair, and thus not of direct concern to the United States, but warned that Washington could not remain indifferent if Afghanistan engaged in aggression against its neighbors. In a mid-August note, the Soviet Politburo responded civilly, noting its "satisfaction" at Nixon's pledge not to interfere in Afghanistan, and agreeing that the Kabul coup stemmed from domestic causes. Brezhnev's government also concurred that the two superpowers should work to prevent any escalation of the Pashtunistan conflict.

Yet Moscow noted another potentially destabilizing factor in the region: the Shah's ambitious armaments program.[20]

As elsewhere, communist views of the July coup bear consideration. Moscow had appeared content in its relations with the former regime. In May, Chairman of the Presidium Nikolai Podgorny had visited Kabul. Subsequent Soviet communiques to Prague and East Berlin expressed satisfaction with the visit and Afghan foreign policy.[21] The year 1973 had even brought progress on a front where the bloc had long been stymied. Seizing upon the consolidation of détente and the West German policy of *Ostpolitik*, Prime Minister Mohammed Moussa Shafiq wrote to East Berlin in May, requesting the establishment of relations.[22] The bloc did not visibly celebrate the end of the monarchy. "This was a military coup, not a revolution," the Czechoslovak embassy in Kabul wrote.[23] Post-coup Moscow press coverage appeared "positive but bland," praising Daoud's continued commitment to nonalignment. Indeed, his return to power stood to complicate the Soviet agenda, which included outreach to Pakistan and promotion of a regional nonaggression pact.[24]

Experienced analysts detected an ambivalent bloc response, yet allied notions of a grand Soviet design could not easily be refuted. The sudden emergence of a nationalist regime in Kabul underscored Pakistan's vulnerability, reinforcing Bhutto and the Shah's appeals. To a White House intent on demonstrating undiminished solidarity with regional partners, this accident of timing rendered Afghanistan policy a test of credibility. "We are going to be watching very carefully," Nixon assured the visiting Bhutto in September, "and will not be taking anything on faith."[25] Welcoming his guest, he publicly termed the preservation of Pakistan's independence and integrity "a cornerstone of U.S. foreign policy."[26]

Reassuring Pakistan required analyzing the new Afghan regime. Aside from Daoud and Naim, who served as an unofficial foreign minister, the republic's government presented few familiar faces. The conspirators appeared to have planned for a coup later in the year, only to advance the date hurriedly to exploit King Zahir's sudden absence or to prevent Shafiq's further consolidation of power. Having acted hastily, they seemed unprepared to staff the government. The British embassy noted a "general administrative confusion and lack of direction." The identities and motivations of the junior officers who had supported Daoud against the conservative, pro-monarchy army leadership remained unclear. Many had received training in the Soviet Union and affiliated with the Marxist Parcham faction.[27]

Afghan officials endeavored to reassure Americans of their continued nonalignment. Daoud proclaimed his desire for continued friendship and aid to the visiting Senator Charles Percy of Illinois. Senior Afghan diplomats Abdul Samad Ghaus and Wahid Abdullah pledged full cooperation with anti-narcotics efforts. Yet the early months of the republic offered troubling indications. Daoud described Shafiq's Helmand waters treaty with Iran skeptically, promising to study it closely before seeking its ratification. He spoke emotionally about Pashtunistan to Percy, warning that Bhutto might experience another "Vietnam" in the borderlands if he did not modify his policies. The August arrest of several senior NAP leaders by the Pakistani authorities further incensed the Afghan government. Wahid Abdullah requested U.S. good offices in resolving the situation, but Washington had other plans. Neumann received instructions to imply that the renewal of the Pashtunistan conflict could jeopardize U.S. aid. Naim's chilly response to that suggestion convinced the ambassador not to press his luck.[28]

Assertive nationalism represented a rare unifying thread for an otherwise eclectic government. Preparing to conclude his mission in late August, Neumann offered a somber closing assessment. Daoud's regime had made a "distinctly unfavorable impression on most observers." His appointments, seemingly intended to reward the junior officers who had catapulted him into power, had produced "a generally inferior and incompetent cabinet," and his public rhetoric had raised expectations of reform to dangerous levels. Heartened by Pakistan's apparent disarray and the precedent of Bangladesh, the junior officers appeared willing to take their chances against their eastern neighbor. Their own success against a vestigial monarchy, meanwhile, made them contemptuous toward the Shah's government.[29]

No single policy option came without risk. Neumann predicted that any further warnings to Kabul would endanger the U.S. position. His colleagues conceded the point but observed that reticence could allow the conflict to worsen, ultimately necessitating greater U.S. involvement. Deferring to Neumann, they asked him to make one final appeal for moderation during his farewell visit to Daoud. Characteristically, and atypically among Kabul's diplomats, the ambassador had cultivated ties with the Afghan leader during his decade in political exile. Bidding Neumann a warm farewell, Daoud received his guest's counsel graciously.[30]

Over six and a half years, Neumann had dealt energetically with five Afghan heads of government while coping with the decline of the constitutional experiment, the 1971 war, and the drought and ensuing famine.

Diplomacy inevitably hinges upon personality. Despite his lack of professional training, the gregarious Neumann had thrived in the challenging Kabul environment, no doubt bolstered in the eyes of his hosts by his friendship with Nixon. As it happened, upheaval and changes of personnel in autumn 1973 contributed to a sense of instability. Interim heads of mission led U.S. embassies in Kabul and Islamabad. The Watergate scandal crippled the Nixon administration. Bhutto continued his campaign against the opposition, while the specter of another coup appeared to surface in Kabul.

A bizarre, tragic series of events in the autumn simultaneously worsened regional relations and raised fundamental questions about the new regime. On the afternoon of September 20, Kabul radio announced the arrest of four "reactionaries" charged with plotting against the republic. The alleged plot precipitated hundreds of arrests and countless additional firings within the government. Foremost among the accused was the former prime minister, Mohammed Hashim Maiwandwal. Little about the purported plot made sense. A fierce critic of the constitutional experiment, Maiwandwal appeared supportive of the new regime. On the evening of October 1, official radio announced that Maiwandwal had hanged himself in his cell. A purported handwritten confession implicating Pakistan in the plot ran in the *Kabul Times*, and Wahid Abdullah shared photos of Maiwandwal's body with diplomats. Marked deterioration in Maiwandwal's handwriting, as evidenced in his "confession," lent credence to reports that he had undergone torture. A disgusted Drinkall wrote, "The whole affair reeks of incompetence, embarrassed improvisation and the seedy police state atmosphere that is growing here."[31]

He had good cause for skepticism. By Ghaus's surviving account, Maiwandwal and his peers had been targeted by leftists in the interior ministry, who strangled him to prevent Daoud from showing clemency. Enraged by the murder, Daoud nevertheless let the cover story stand. Whatever unfolded in Kabul that September, the ensuing purge revealed the instability of Daoud's government, as radical elements seized an apparent opportunity to neutralize potential rivals. Who truly held power, if Daoud could not restrain his subordinates?[32]

Ongoing efforts to implicate Islamabad added another worrisome element to the situation. The purported conspirators, previously regarded as Pashtun patriots, made unlikely foreign agents. Yet the Kabul rumor mill produced occasional whispers of involvement by another government, perhaps the United States. Afghan officials denied to U.S. diplomats that they blamed Washington for the plot, but by Ghaus's recollection Daoud entertained his own suspicions.[33] So did the Soviet bloc. The Czechoslovak embassy credulously transmitted Afghan claims that Maiwandwal had been recruited by the CIA while acting in league with monarchist elements.[34]

Bhutto chafed at the accusation. More inclined to dwell in the realm of conspiracy, the Shah opined that the Afghans could scarcely complain if Pakistan—exasperated with their meddling in the borderlands—returned the favor. Iran had already dispatched helicopters to assist the Pakistani military in Baluchistan. The mid-October arrival of a Soviet military delegation in Kabul afforded further cause for concern. Yet, even in autumn 1973, neither government beheld any real alternative to Daoud. Unpleasant as the new regime was, a worse alternative could easily emerge. Visiting Tehran, Bhutto conceded to U.S. ambassador Richard Helms that Daoud's leadership represented the best option available in Kabul.[35]

At most, this was faint praise. Daoud showed scant inclination toward conciliation on either flank. Diplomat Samuel Lewis found that the Afghan leader displayed an "obsessive preoccupation" with Pashtunistan during an October 13 meeting, neglecting to mention the war between Israel, Egypt, and Syria that had erupted days earlier. Subsequent events cast a strange light on that omission. Five days later, Lewis received sudden notice that Wahid Abdullah would depart for Washington the following day and sought personally to deliver a letter from Daoud to Nixon on the unfolding Arab-Israeli war.[36]

Even in normal circumstances, it would have been an odd gambit. Consumed by the war and the fallout from his clumsy interference with the Watergate investigation, Nixon was unprepared and unwilling to host a surprise guest. Kissinger, meanwhile, was away. Foisted upon Kissinger's deputy, Kenneth Rush, the flustered Abdullah declined to deliver Daoud's letter, although a copy eventually reached the State Department. The letter, an unremarkable appeal for U.S. intervention to end the war, does not suffice to explain the trip. Daoud likely hoped that the gesture would reforge an interpersonal tie with Nixon. Saunders and Appelbaum believed that Abdullah intended to reassure Nixon about the Soviet presence within Afghanistan. In any case, both Daoud and his envoy were stung by the apparent rebuff. "Surely four or five minutes could have been found," the latter complained after returning to Kabul.[37]

The Afghan republic lacked the leeway to nurse a grudge toward Washington. As a member of the royal family heading a putative republic, established violently, Daoud's legitimacy remained tenuous.[38] Even as he and Naim decried the purported snub, they sought a continued U.S. aid commitment toward major development projects. The tenor of bilateral exchanges largely remained civil, and developments within Kabul gradually led Western diplomats to revise some of their earlier, gloomier predictions. In an early, revealing volte-face, Daoud signaled that he intended to pursue ratification of the Helmand waters treaty. The government continued to cooperate with international and U.S. agencies to interdict the flow of opium. Above all, Western observers detected a shift within Kabul, as Daoud and his partisans gained leverage over the Parcham faction.[39]

The core problems remained, however. As INR reasoned, domestic factors propelled the neighbors toward confrontation. Daoud's adoption of the Pashtun and Baluch causes appeased nationalist sentiment in Kabul, and Bhutto treated the struggles against the NAP and secessionism as fundamentally indivisible. While both had shown some past capacity for compromise, present circumstances gave neither leeway to cede ground. Each had reason to fear the displeasure of his military. Neither could expect decisive action from the politically crippled Nixon administration. The alleviation of regional tensions would require effective coordinated diplomacy directed by Kissinger's State Department and implemented by embassies in Tehran, Kabul, and Islamabad in cooperation with their host governments.[40]

Engagement and Coordination, 1974

Among the ambassadors sent to Kabul during the Cold War, Theodore Eliot boasted the most impressive resume. A career diplomat, Eliot had worked as an assistant to C. Douglas Dillon. He served in Tehran from 1962 to 1966, and then directed Iran policy from Washington. In 1969, Eliot was appointed executive secretary of the State Department. The exacting work of coordinating with the White House was rendered more difficult by Nixon and Kissinger's penchant for secrecy and circumvention. A posting to Kabul provided a welcome escape from the Byzantine atmosphere of Nixon-era Washington. Coincidentally, Eliot had been the senior State Department official present, late on July 16, when reports of Daoud's coup reached

Washington. Reasoning that "there would be no great disaster if we went to sleep," he opted not to awaken his superiors.[41]

A confident, experienced diplomat with a ready laugh, Eliot enjoyed a reputation for plain speaking. His knowledge of Persian gave him some facility with Dari (although Afghans sometimes joked about his accent). He labored to earn Daoud and Naim's trust. "I had to go to them and say," he recalled in 2014, "we realize that Daoud is an Afghan nationalist, and we want to do business with you, and we have no intention of overthrowing the coup." Soon after his arrival, local officials once again raised and dismissed rumors of U.S. involvement in the Maiwandwal affair. Daoud and Naim emphasized their desire to maintain close relations with the United States.[42]

Effective coordination with colleagues in Tehran and Islamabad bolstered Eliot's efforts. Ambassador Helms in Tehran had been dispatched, not only to manage the crucial Iranian alliance but also to watch over developments between Iraq and the Indian subcontinent. His background as a former CIA director, while notorious within Iran, commended him to the Shah and his government. Kabul alumnus Henry Byroade assumed leadership of the Islamabad embassy at Kissinger's request—his sixth and last ambassadorial post—despite some State Department opposition. "They feel Byroade likes to have a good time a little bit too much," Nixon informed Bhutto, who did not hold the ambassador's conviviality against him.[43]

The Helms-Eliot-Byroade trio collaborated effectively and collegially. Each of the three, moreover, enjoyed entrée in one of the neighboring countries. Eliot benefited from prior experience in Iran. Helms was a welcome face in Islamabad, facilitating White House efforts to aid Pakistan covertly through the transfer of Iranian weapons. Daoud and Naim, meanwhile, applauded Byroade's appointment in Islamabad, recalling him fondly from his earlier Afghan mission. Lastly, perhaps most important, each of the three had at least a modicum of Henry Kissinger's respect.[44]

Of the three, Eliot's mission entailed the greatest ambiguity. Nixon had promised Iran and Pakistan stalwart support, and both relationships hinged upon military assistance. The Shah purchased prodigious quantities of weaponry, while Bhutto desperately sought the lifting of Washington's arms embargo. Economic assistance, however, had been the central, albeit crumbling pillar of U.S.-Afghan ties before the coup. High grain prices had undermined the Food for Peace program, while capital-intensive projects no longer enjoyed unqualified global acclaim. The nature of Daoud's republic, moreover, required thorough evaluation.

Thus, in early 1974, Eliot's embassy undertook the first comprehensive study of Afghanistan policy in five years. It was no exercise in groupthink. Eliot's deputy, Robert Curran, headed a review group that critically reexamined long-standing policy tenets. Curran's team argued that events in Afghanistan did not directly affect regional security and questioned whether U.S. policy could exert significant local influence. Crediting the dissenters for their "eloquence and tenacity," Eliot nonetheless disagreed. He maintained that, regardless of any material assessment of Afghanistan's military or economic potential, Pakistan, Iran, China, and the Soviet Union clearly perceived the country as important. Although détente had lessened Cold War tensions, a key tenet of the 1969 policy statement still applied: "Excessive Soviet influence in Afghan affairs would materially increase psychological and subversive vulnerability" of Iran and Pakistan. Daoud's coup had not fundamentally changed U.S. objectives or interests within Afghanistan.[45] Washington concurred.[46]

Daoud's June trip to Moscow yielded no evidence of a change in alignment. The Afghan president received the usual warm welcome, and his hosts promised an estimated $500 to $650 million in aid across the next five years. The Soviets remained noticeably circumspect on the Pashtun and Baluch issues, however. Indeed, after Daoud decried Pakistani policy, his hosts warned him to exercise restraint, pointedly observing that Afghan development required calm in the borderlands. Daoud, meanwhile, only vaguely supported Moscow's proposal for an Asian collective security system, alluding to certain unresolved problems of self-determination.[47]

Cautionary advice from Moscow also revealed concern for the republic itself. In February 1974, a Soviet diplomat lamented the state of the Afghan economy and disputes within the government. Repeated coup plots, meanwhile, suggested the breadth and potential power of conservative opposition. A Czechoslovak embassy analysis in early 1974 expressed alarm about growing anti-Daoud sentiment among the clergy but posited that a "certain balance" existed between the regime and its domestic opposition. Daoud's incremental approach to land reform, which eschewed direct confrontation with rural landholders, was thus understandable.[48]

Infighting within the Afghan left and the government offered special cause for concern and frustration. A blunt January appeal from the Communist Party of the Soviet Union's (CPSU) Central Committee expressed "deep alarm" at reports of bickering between the rival Khalq and Parcham factions. Acidly observing that internecine feuding could "gladden only the domestic [and] foreign enemies" of Afghanistan, the CPSU implored the dueling factions to "combine their efforts at giving comprehensive aid to the republican regime." The party reiterated the message after Daoud's Moscow trip.[49] Not only did Moscow see no alternative to Daoud, it could easily contemplate a worse government emerging in Kabul—particularly as Iranian influence expanded.

A sudden diplomatic thaw between Kabul and Tehran in 1974 astounded observers but also illustrated subtle differences in Daoud's statecraft. Past clashes with Pakistan had illuminated to him the necessity of maintaining a quiet western flank. To this end, Daoud craftily played upon his neighbor's anxieties. In a January visit, Wahid Abdullah informed his Iranian hosts that Daoud and Naim were the only force preventing a communist takeover in Afghanistan.[50] Having reached the same conclusion, the Iranians were prepared to promise their neighbors duty-free trade and commercial use of Iran's rails. A joint visit by Naim and Abdullah followed in May. "The sky is the limit," the Shah reportedly promised his Afghan guests.[51]

For once, he was scarcely exaggerating. In late July, an Iranian economic mission offered to finance an estimated $2 billion worth of projects within Afghanistan. No Cold War benefactor had ever promised Kabul as much. The list of projects included railroads connecting Kabul to Iran's train network via both Kandahar and Herat, a network of lower Helmand storage dams, and aid toward the construction of sugar, cement, and textile factories. Deferring to their hosts, the Iranians accepted the Afghan development proposals wholesale, tactfully eschewing discussion of the still-unratified Helmand waters treaty. To Eliot, it appeared a historic moment, likely to reduce dramatically Afghanistan's economic dependence on Moscow. "This development is good news to them, for this region, and for us," he enthused.[52] Interceding with ambassadors from oil-exporting states, he further sought to bolster investment in Afghanistan.[53]

U.S. aid to Afghanistan could not grow so dramatically. Daoud and Naim retained their passion for grandiose, capital-intensive projects, although general experience had called their feasibility into question. The difficulty of directly pursuing land reform, a cardinal objective obstructed by powerful rural landholders, perhaps reinforced the appeal of expanding industry and infrastructure.[54] A decade out of power had rendered the brothers somewhat out of step with the prevailing nostrums of foreign assistance. In February, Naim appealed to Lewis for U.S. assistance in completing the Helmand project. His guest attempted to steer the conversation to questions of "self-help," planning, and "priority setting." Undaunted, Naim renewed his appeal in a subsequent conversation with Eliot, arguing that no other project could do more to enhance U.S. standing within Afghanistan.[55]

Within the context of Naim's career, the statement was startling. In the early 1950s, the brothers had benefited from rising disaffection toward their predecessors' indulgence toward the Helmand project and Morrison-Knudsen. In office, they had mustered scant enthusiasm for the trouble-prone valley. Most likely, they succumbed to the same sunk-cost reasoning that repeatedly ensnared their U.S. counterparts. Whatever its merits, the Helmand remained inextricably tied to U.S. standing within Afghanistan. Washington was more likely to continue an existing project than to embark upon a new one. Above all, Naim's phrasing suggests the preeminence of political considerations. The United States should not "scatter [its] shots" in Afghanistan, he pleaded.[56]

By then, U.S.-supported efforts in the Helmand had all but ground to a halt, largely because of the embattled Shamalan project. Well before the coup, tensions had built within the district, as the project neared its commencement. Kept uninformed for months by the local authorities, farmers vehemently opposed the leveling of their land. Damage caused by construction vehicles to crops and property and the Helmand-Arghandab Valley Authority's (HAVA) frequent failure to compensate the farmers heightened grievances. Armed villagers met the arriving bulldozers with rifles. Frustrated, the aid mission blamed the impasse on HAVA, which, beset by local criticism, claimed that Shamalan was a purely American enterprise. Daoud's coup appeared to offer a new opportunity, and AID analyst Richard Scott suggested approaching the new government with a proposal focused on directly engaging the valley's farmers.[57]

Scott's initiative held the virtue of timeliness, as Washington now largely eschewed funding capital-intensive projects. Legislative frugality partly compelled this shift, but the prevailing objectives and instrumentalities of aid had also changed. Nixon had favored humanitarian, grassroots-level objectives while lessening the burden on the taxpayer through greater multilateralism and private investment. USAID director John Hannah promised a new focus on human necessities: "better food, more education, improved health, and more jobs." Hannah also envisioned aid as a smaller-scale, less obtrusive endeavor, enabling him to cut his agency's personnel by half from 1968 to 1975.[58]

Such changes hardly disadvantaged Afghanistan, where health, agriculture, and education had long been U.S. policy emphases. They did, however, augur a more diffuse program, oriented around rural development. For this, post-coup Afghanistan presented challenging terrain. Turnover within the government severed working relationships between local officials and the aid mission. Wary or inexperienced newcomers, often from a military background, sometimes acted to undermine individual projects. In March, Eliot sought an explanation for the sudden termination of Peace Corps teaching projects and the removal of U.S. medical personnel from Hazarajat and Jalalabad. The same administrative disorder and suspicion obstructed action in the Helmand, Naim's hopes notwithstanding. Lou Mitchell, the aid mission's rural development advisor, wrote in April: "The [Afghan government] does not know whether it wants continued U.S. assistance" in the valley.[59]

Another challenge confronted U.S. aid programs in Afghanistan, meanwhile. Section 32 of the 1973 Foreign Assistance Act called for withholding aid from any country detaining political prisoners.[60] The provision applied readily to Afghanistan, where Daoud's rivals remained in captivity. One released detainee recounted two weeks spent in "indescribably filthy conditions," with a meager diet of bread and tea, and no communication with fellow prisoners. The existence of political prisoners was undeniable, but the U.S. embassy endeavored to contextualize them. It contended that "severe definitional problems" precluded applying Section 32 to Afghanistan, where the state had long been free to jail individuals deemed dangerous to public order. While hope existed that Kabul might enact judicial reforms, linking aid to the release of prisoners would antagonize Daoud, lending credence to rumors of involvement in the Maiwandwal affair. "Yes, but never mind," one analyst wrote sardonically upon receiving the embassy's Section 32 assessment.[61]

The human rights revolution had not yet reached its political culmination, still the episode illustrated how human rights politics would interact with Afghanistan policy. Daoud's republic engaged in repressive acts, but these could be juxtaposed with others in the long sweep of Afghan history, while diplomats predicted the futility of direct intervention and the possibility of reform. Afghanistan's precarious geopolitical situation afforded it some benefit of the doubt, while its relative obscurity shielded it from the legislative or media scrutiny that befell more conspicuous offenders.

Afghan aid, however limited, proved durable and adaptable for changed conditions. Devoid of extravagance, it presented no obvious targets. Discerning the new trends in U.S. aid, Daoud's government tactically adapted its requests, temporarily shelving older capital-intensive notions. "Afghan government response has been very favorable to people-oriented programs," Eliot reported in October. Above all, Kabul emphasized the symbolic importance of U.S. aid. "We have always been of the opinion that the presence of the United States was needed," Naim informed Kissinger in November. Kissinger assured his host, "Our basic attitude is sympathetic."[62]

The chief obstacle to improved relations remained the nettlesome border question. The propaganda war between the two neighbors remained vitriolic, as each charged the other with undertaking acts of subversion. Bhutto offered the more elaborate indictment. India's explosion of a nuclear device on May 18, 1974, alarmed Islamabad, even as Bhutto contended with restive border provinces and religious upheaval. In a speech that Byroade found "rambling" and "highly emotional," the Pakistani leader linked the Indian explosion, Daoud's Moscow visit, and Afghan support of the NAP. A "foreign hand," he suggested, lay behind Pakistan's turmoil.[63]

Byroade watched Bhutto's rhetorical escalation with alarm. His government found scant evidence of a grand anti-Islamabad axis or of abnormal military deployments along Pakistan's borders. Prone to vituperating the Afghans in public, Bhutto often spoke more reasonably in private. He remained convinced, however, that Afghanistan had a hand in Pashtun and Baluch unrest and warned Byroade that he had been urged to retaliate in kind. "It is difficult to see how we can do very much about this worsening situation," Byroade reported.[64]

The August crash landing of a Pakistani helicopter on Afghan soil and the subsequent detention of its crew could have sparked a major crisis. "I do not like this, I do not like this," the Shah declared to Helms after receiving a list of complaints about Baluchistan from Daoud.[65] Fearing the spillover of unrest into his own Baluch region, he dispatched a senior diplomat, Sadegh Sadrieh, to Kabul and Islamabad while continuing to aid the Pakistani military. On Sadrieh's urging, Islamabad offered a qualified statement of regret, securing the return of the aircraft and its crew.[66] Bhutto, meanwhile, retreated somewhat from earlier rhetorical excesses. A successful September offensive in Baluchistan allowed him to declare the end of organized resistance, and a late October trip to Moscow brought reassurance that the Soviets recognized the Durand Line.[67] "We have put down the difficulties in Baluchistan," Bhutto informed Kissinger on October 31. "The Afghans know it."[68]

As before, he indulged in hyperbole, while Baluchistan and the NWFP remained restive. Daoud had likely moderated his government's rhetoric in advance of Kissinger's Kabul trip. As intended, the visit signaled U.S. acceptance of his regime, of Afghanistan's nonalignment, and a renewed interest in supporting Afghan development. Thereafter, Kabul renewed efforts to raise the Baluch question before the United Nations. A November 27 letter to the secretary-general condemned Pakistan for an "act of genocide and mass extermination" in the restive province.[69]

Fifteen years earlier, the smoldering border conflict would have occasioned greater concern in Washington. Cold War tensions remained at a lull, however. Soon after his Kabul trip, Kissinger joined Ford to negotiate with Brezhnev in Vladivostok. Arms control and the expansion of East-West trade dominated the summit agenda. Neither superpower raised South Asian issues. Although Afghanistan's neighbors still fretted about Daoud's agenda, U.S. assessments of Soviet policy in and around the republic avoided alarmism. U.S.-Soviet détente, however imperfect, limited the leverage of regional actors and gave both Washington and Moscow cause to counsel restraint. Events in the new year, however—in Afghanistan, Pakistan, and elsewhere—exposed stresses building within the détente system and between the Afghan republic and its neighbors.

Commitment, Credibility, and Crisis, 1975

"All I can say is that the visit has been a colossal failure," joked Zulfikar Ali Bhutto. "I'm only trying to help the Indians." His joviality strongly implied the converse. Several days into his February 1975 state visit to Washington, Bhutto had good cause for satisfaction. An Oval Office meeting with Ford, followed by a state dinner, had cemented his relationship with the new president. Ford had quadrupled his offer of concession grain to Islamabad, to 400,000 tons. Best of all, Bhutto received long-awaited word that the United States would lift the decade-long arms embargo. For his part, he held firm against U.S requests to forswear developing his own nuclear arsenal. His hosts had intended to withhold news of the embargo's end for at least a few weeks, but Bhutto's visible ebullience, while describing a "fruitful and constructive visit," gave away the game.[70]

Terrible news reached him days later: of the death of a prominent young PPP leader, Hayat Mohammed Khan Sherpao, in a February 8 bombing at Peshawar University. Pakistani officials blamed the Sherpao assassination on the NAP and the Afghan government. "Terrorism has become the pattern of political activity and Afghanistan has a hand in it," Bhutto declared. Sherpao had served as the indispensable de facto head of the NWFP government. Bhutto cut short his travels, returning home to shore up the fragile provincial government and escalate his campaign against the NAP. The mass arrests of the NAP leadership, including Wali Khan, commenced on February 9, before Bhutto's plane touched down. He banned the party and ordered the seizure of its property the next day. His government canceled scheduled bilateral talks with Afghanistan.[71]

Whatever lay behind Bhutto's response, the repression of the NAP and the imprisonment of Wali Khan shook Afghanistan and Pakistan out of their fragile stasis. Bhutto froze a program of diplomatic outreach that the Afghans, wary of their devious, dynamic adversary, had mistrusted. Islamabad's bill of indictment against its neighbor included hostile radio broadcasts, the presence in Kabul of former NAP leader Ajmal Khattak, and allegations that Afghanistan hosted training camps for terrorists. Khattak denied responsibility for the Sherpao killing to U.S. diplomats but implied that his partisans were willing to take up arms against the Pakistani authorities. The CIA reported that it could not corroborate Pakistani claims that Afghanistan was training and arming subversives.[72]

The situation presented many of the requisite conditions for another border crisis. The Sherpao assassination and a climate of mutual vituperation, coupled with the recent lifting of the arms embargo, could have quickly led to another disruption of commerce or diplomatic relations. Yet the road to confrontation was not nearly so direct in 1975. Alongside incendiary acts of provocation and retaliation came efforts at conciliation, encouraged by third parties. Nor did post-Sherpao tensions evoke the same Cold War concerns about the direction of Afghan foreign policy. Thus, a tense but often ambiguous situation developed over the ensuing months. The year witnessed violence in the borderlands and a Pakistani effort to foment unrest in its neighbor in July, but nothing so dire as a frontier closure. Why? Personalities, the interventions of third parties, and Washington's demonstrated willingness to aid Afghanistan afford a possible explanation.

Observers in 1975 justifiably feared a collision between Daoud and Bhutto. Both men were obdurate, troubled by domestic unrest, and prone toward confrontational rhetoric. Bhutto's demagoguery against the NAP unnerved the normally sympathetic Byroade. Repeated proclamations of foreign-backed conspiracies stoked national sentiment to the detriment of Islamabad's regional relationships. Yet Bhutto was no Ayub. He bore Afghanistan no fundamental animus and proffered grand proposals for regional economic cooperation, so long as Kabul respected his country's sovereignty. Bhutto's interest in securing U.S.-made arms—both to safeguard his borders and placate his military—afforded Washington some influence over him. He was as ready to play the peacemaker as the defender of an embattled nation.[73]

Daoud, meanwhile, could credibly deny involvement in Sherpao's murder. While he hosted dissidents like Khattak, he limited their activities. "[The Afghans] wish to make things difficult for Bhutto without going beyond a war of words," one British diplomat reported. CIA and embassy analyses predicted that prior experience with border closures and awareness of Afghanistan's military weakness would dissuade Daoud from escalation.[74] Nor did U.S. observers question his nonalignment. "We continue to think that [the Afghan government] over longer run appreciates U.S. presence as counterbalance to the USSR and therefore that President Daoud will not permit any serious erosion in U.S.-Afghan bilateral relations," the Kabul embassy reported.[75]

So did Afghanistan's reliance on Western and now Iranian aid. "Iran's improved relations with Afghanistan may be paying dividends in limiting Afghan options vis-à-vis Pakistan," a State Department analyst wrote in March. While anxious about violence in Baluchistan, the Shah did not change course. "There is no doubt that he feels [Daoud] is the best individual to head Afghanistan at the present time," Helms reported. The monarch hosted his Afghan counterpart in April, and Daoud pledged—undoubtedly after some prodding—that he would employ "peaceful and honorable" means in his quarrel with Pakistan. The trip yielded an Iranian commitment to lend Afghanistan $700 million.[76]

Thus, Kabul and Islamabad avoided headlong escalation, and the ensuing months witnessed sporadic efforts at negotiation. One promising early episode unfolded in February at a coronation ceremony in Nepal, where Senator Percy conferred separately with both Naim and Pakistani president Fazal Chaudhry. Each appeared willing to limit propaganda if the other did.[77] Efforts to secure a rhetorical ceasefire fell through in the late winter. Nebulous Pakistani transit problems afflicted Afghanistan in the early spring. Bhutto magnanimously promised to resolve the bottlenecks impeding Afghan goods, assuring an Afghan envoy that logistics not politics lay behind the delays.[78]

Kabul's response to the lifting of the arms embargo was similarly restrained. While the decision clearly frustrated Afghan officials, Daoud and Naim largely refrained from comment. Their March 9 recognition of the Provisional Revolutionary Government (PRG) of South Vietnam after a visit by its lead diplomat, Nguyen Thi Binh, struck Eliot as an Afghan "rejoinder." "You should realize that we, too, have our sensitivities," Wahid Abdullah retorted when Eliot inquired. Arguably, however, the act merely followed established practice within the Non-Aligned Movement, and Kabul could hardly be accused of acting in undue haste.[79]

Afghan nonalignment appeared otherwise unchanged. Daoud's government maintained relations with both Koreas and both Germanys. Seeking financial support, Afghanistan also continued to pursue closer relations with major oil exporters. Such outreach promised the further dilution of Soviet financial assistance as Iran, Saudi Arabia, and other oil powers offered to bankroll major projects. Their largesse eased Washington's problem of politely deflecting Afghan requests for project aid; the oil exporters appeared to have no political or conceptual objections against funding capital-intensive projects.[80] They also made plain their disapproval of continued Pashtunistan agitation.[81]

Loans from multilateral institutions offered Afghanistan another funding source—and Washington another aid instrument. The Asian Development Bank (ADB), launched in 1966 to support regional development, emerged by the mid-1970s as a vital instrumentality for U.S. policy, willing to fund capital-intensive projects after they had lost favor in Washington. Alongside Japan, the United States enjoyed preponderant influence within the ADB. With the full support of the U.S. delegation, and despite concerns about local administrative capacity, the ADB approved a $14 million loan toward the completion of the Kajakai Dam in December 1974.[82]

Events in early 1975 restored much of the earlier vitality of the bilateral aid relationship, even as Americans and Afghans entertained substantially different visions. Fulfilling a promise made by Kissinger, AID administrator Daniel Parker visited Kabul for talks in January. As before, the Helmand Valley remained the preponderant topic of discussion. Afghan officials termed the valley an "unfinished symphony"; Parker rejoined that it was an "Afghan symphony requiring an Afghan conductor." AID officials endeavored to steer the Afghans toward grassroots-level rural development. Afghan officials retained a preference for big projects but appeared willing to entertain U.S. counteroffers if doing so kept the United States in the valley.[83]

Kabul and Washington endeavored to reach a workable compromise. A program of drainage improvement seemingly addressed their respective agendas. To the aid mission, improved drainage would enhance soil quality and address the long-standing problem of salinization while potentially educating farmers and providing a source of labor income. Eschewing "grandiose schemes," the aid mission proposed a segmented approach. Phase I aspired not only to demonstrate the viability of enhanced drainage but also to establish "a different, more mature bilateral relationship," thus facilitating subsequent efforts to improve drainage throughout the valley. Noting his mission's earlier reluctance to "get back into the valley," Eliot endorsed both the drainage project and a concurrent soil and water survey, arguing that they made "good development sense" and served to advance U.S. objectives in Afghanistan. The Helmand hiatus had ended and—segmented approach notwithstanding—Washington once again entertained grand plans for the valley.[84]

Embassy and CIA analyses of Daoud's republic by the spring tended toward optimism. Although tensions with Pakistan remained worrisome, greater stability existed within Afghanistan. Daoud had firmly established control, appeared likely to pursue modernization more effectively than his predecessors, and remained committed to Afghan independence and nonalignment. Admittedly, his rule bore unpleasant traits: "Afghanistan is a suspicious, closed society, characterized by a fear of strangers and a police state atmosphere." Nevertheless, Eliot discerned a substantial improvement in U.S.-Afghan ties and lauded rapprochement between Kabul and Tehran as an event of transcendent significance. Widening Afghan ties to oil-rich Islamic states also promised to lessen Kabul's dependence on Soviet aid. Meanwhile, Daoud had slowly whittled down the influence of the Parcham faction within the government. The most prominent Parchamists remained in office, potentially able to seize control in the event of Daoud's overthrow or death, but at a clear, mounting disadvantage in the immediate term.[85]

Tense relations with Islamabad still posed a significant problem, but the spring brought some prospect of improvement. In May, the neighbors agreed to avoid ad hominem propaganda attacks. By July, Kabul appeared to have reassessed the utility of its campaign. Wahid Abdullah omitted direct mention of Pashtunistan at a conference of Islamic states in Saudi Arabia.[86]

Daoud's speech at Jeshyn (which had been moved to mark the anniversary of his coup) described his forthcoming First Seven-Year Plan, another characteristically ambitious economic program. He offered, meanwhile, only a perfunctory discussion of the border question.[87] The situation remained dangerous, however. Periodic violent episodes in the border region drew allegations and countercharges of subversive activities. Reporting the bombing of a police station in Jalalabad and a movie theater in Kandahar, Eliot warned, "Beneath all this smoke there may be a bit of fire." He was not wrong. Four days after Daoud's speech, revolt rocked Afghanistan.[88]

From its inception, Daoud's regime had drawn the antipathy of Afghanistan's burgeoning Islamist movement. Galvanized by transnational currents of Islamist thought, militarized by their earlier clashes with leftists, Afghanistan's Islamists perceived peril and opportunity after the coup. While Daoud quietly purged Parchamists, his government openly battled the religious opposition. Militants found sanctuary and support in Pakistan.[89] Bhutto had hinted earlier at his willingness to retaliate in kind for Afghan acts of subversion, and he was not the first Pakistani leader to assail Daoud in this fashion. A Pakistani diplomat later recalled: "The intention was not regime change in Kabul, but to demonstrate to Daoud that his anti-Pakistan posture carried a price tag, that two could play the game."[90]

The operational plan was strikingly ambitious, considering the limited resources and small numbers of the inexperienced insurgents. Universally, the rebels underestimated the response of the Afghan military and overrated their ability to rally the citizenry. Their unruly conduct alienated villagers, who denounced them to the advancing military. The insurrection wrought the most havoc in the provinces of Panjshir—where they were led by a young Tajik named Ahmed Shah Massoud—and Laghman. Nowhere were the Islamists able to hold ground or induce defections from the army. Those not killed or captured fled back to Pakistan.[91]

In retrospect, the events of July 1975 assume an outsized significance: in the evolution of Daoud's relations with Pakistan, in the life of his republic, and within the broader history of U.S. encounters with political Islam. In some accounts, the episode convinced an unnerved Daoud to seek rapprochement with Bhutto and to purge leftists from his cabinet, leading inexorably toward his fatal confrontation with the People's Democratic Party of Afghanistan (PDPA) in April 1978. Claims of covert U.S. backing for the rebels, in concert with Iran or Pakistan, render the episode a prelude of sorts to similar alliances of convenience during the 1980s.[92]

It appears more likely that the July uprising encouraged Daoud along courses that he had already adopted. He had already attempted dialogue with Bhutto, and Western observers noted a drop in official attacks on Pakistan in the early summer. Efforts to raise the Pashtun and Baluch causes in international forums had yielded meager results and scoldings from Afghanistan's oil-rich benefactors. Second, although Daoud's dismissal of leftists from his government noticeably accelerated after July 1975, it antedated the summer. By Ghaus's account, Daoud worked gradually to thin the Parchamists, biding his time during the shaky early months of his reign, even after such provocations as the Maiwandwal murder.[93]

The question of U.S. support for the July insurgency or other attempts against Daoud requires far more conjecture. No declassified evidence exists supporting claims of CIA backing for any of the subversive plots against Daoud: three alleged coup plots between September 1973 and summer 1974, in addition to the July uprising—even as contemporaneous efforts in Iraqi Kurdistan and Angola are now well documented. A comparative dearth of evidence does not disprove involvement, but it does suggest the absence of sustained official consideration.

Tacit U.S. support of Pakistani and Iranian policy would be a likelier scenario, given Tehran and Islamabad's profound concern with Daoud and their superior capacity to stage covert activities inside Afghanistan. Yet here, too, cause exists for skepticism. Nixon, Ford, and Kissinger had pledged their support to these allies and now relied upon them to a greater degree. Key differences of opinion, however, separated Washington from its partners in their perception of Afghan and Soviet foreign policy and events in Pakistan's borderlands. These, in turn, flowed from a distinct U.S. perception of Daoud and his state and of the détente system more broadly.

By July 1975, Washington had long since concluded that Daoud was indispensable. Daoud seemingly retained the esteem of the Afghan people as, in Eliot's words, "a wise and valuable leader whose rule is legitimate." His tightening grip on power afforded cause for comfort, not anxiety. Of Daoud, Eliot wrote before Jeshyn, "It seems increasingly clear that our own, United States, interests in Afghanistan will be preserved under his leadership." Daoud's troubled relationship with Pakistan remained an ongoing but familiar problem. The propaganda truce suggested that Daoud had set upper limits on Pashtunistan agitation and would endeavor to prevent outright conflict. Repeated CIA assessments agreed on this point. Nixon's NSC staff had regarded Daoud as somewhat stubborn but durably nonaligned; nothing suggests that Ford or Kissinger had adopted a more alarmist portrait. Kissinger's visit and the renewal of the aid program describe, instead, an ongoing project of engagement, coupled with what Eliot termed "quiet diplomatic suasion" on the borderlands problem.[94]

Preoccupied by problems elsewhere, conditioned by experience to regard the Durand Line as a baffling but manageable conflict, U.S. perception of Afghanistan departed fundamentally from those of allies. Washington did not subscribe to Bhutto's thesis of an anti-Pakistan axis. CIA and State Department assessments noted scant enthusiasm in both Moscow and New Delhi for another Pashtunistan campaign. Nor did U.S. officials credulously accept Pakistani claims about Afghan subversion in the borderlands. Kabul's conduct left much to be desired, but the bill of indictment presented after the Sherpao killing proved unconvincing. "We have no independent evidence to support Pakistani claims that the Afghans train and equip Pakistani subversives," the CIA reported.[95] Some of this disbelief reveals a quiet wariness toward Bhutto, who continued to pursue an expansive agenda with characteristic aplomb and, at times, recklessness. The Pakistani leader's support for the Afghan Islamists illustrates the disparity in perceptions and interests separating him from Washington. The latter could accept a limited degree of borderlands agitation as the price of a noncommunist Afghanistan. Pakistan could not.

Mercurial and confident to a fault, Bhutto was able to act independently, according to his own distinctive calculation of risk and reward. So, conceivably, was the Shah. Each ascribed greater urgency to the Afghan problem. U.S. diplomats appear to have been left uninformed, pursuing rumors of Pakistani involvement. The only apparent description of the episode within White House files, in a memorandum Kissinger sent to Ford the following year—"(possibly with some covert Pakistani support)"—implies that uncertainty lingered in Washington as well.[96]

In Kabul there was no doubt. Captured rebels confirmed that they had received sanctuary and material support in Pakistan. Pakistan's ambassador in Kabul, Ali Arshad, allowed to Curran that the Islamists might have found sanctuary in the NWFP but denied that his government had aided them. Bhutto unconvincingly denied responsibility as well. Any satisfaction enjoyed in Islamabad proved short-lived. Weeks later, alarmed Pakistani officials told Byroade that a Soviet diplomat in Kabul had asked Arshad's deputy, Tanvir Ahmad Khan, whether their country might cede some land to Afghanistan. When Khan rejected the brazen proposal, the Soviet rejoined,

"Then God alone knows what will happen." In another Kabul conversation, Soviet ambassador Alexander Puzanov derided the Durand Line as a vestige of the colonial era.[97]

Some skepticism was appropriate. Bhutto dabbled in alarmism, and his efforts to expand U.S. arms sales gave him incentive to pass along every ominous account that reached him. Yet, once again, a response was required. Pakistan remained insecure: troubled by internal unrest, hampered by aging weaponry, and pinned between two adversaries. Bhutto looked warily upon the formalization of the détente regime in Europe. In an August letter to Ford, he predicted that the recent Helsinki Accords, rather than lessening conflict, would channel Soviet aggression southward. "Assured of security in Europe," Moscow would "relentlessly exert pressure on the smaller states of Asia and on Pakistan." Bhutto coupled his dire prediction with the suggestion that Pakistan's foreign policy, and potentially its continued membership in CENTO, required "credible evidence of support" from the United States.[98]

Pakistan's insecurity was unrelenting. So were the demands for tangible support Bhutto and the Shah directed to Washington. Anxiety about the direction of Afghan foreign policy represented only one factor at play by the autumn of 1975. A military coup in Bangladesh and India's descent into authoritarianism offered fresh shocks alongside the familiar, tiresome borderland issues. Amid a generally unsettled climate following the July uprising, Daoud and his neighbors had separate incentives to pursue their own form of détente.

The "Spirit of Kabul," 1975–1976

"I have trouble grasping this issue. What do you want precisely?" Meeting Wahid Abdullah in September, a perplexed Kissinger sought clarification: "What do you want in Pashtunistan? Self-determination?" Abdullah contended that Afghanistan merely asked that Pashtuns and Baluchs receive their full rights under the Pakistani constitution: "We want Bhutto to treat them with love and affection." "Who treats anyone with love and affection in the subcontinent?" Kissinger retorted.[99]

By autumn 1975, the bitter truth confronted Daoud's government: its advocacy of Pashtun and Baluch rights had only yielded friction with Pakistan. While Moscow had obliquely challenged Pakistan following the

July uprising, the Soviets otherwise remained intent on promoting their Asian collective security scheme. Oil-rich donor states frowned upon the interminable dispute while courting Islamabad. Afghanistan and Pakistan, meanwhile, engaged in an ongoing letter-writing campaign at the United Nations. By Ghaus's recollection, Daoud asked in late 1975 whether the campaign had run its course. Ghaus allowed that it had. "We started it," Daoud remarked, "and it's up to us to end it." His foreign ministry let Bhutto have the last word.[100]

Daoud's reputation preceded him on the Pashtunistan question, yet the Afghan leader was capable of pragmatism. Foreign observers noted signs of diminished ardor for Pashtunistan by the end of the year.[101] In the following year he planned to launch his First Seven-Year Plan, which would rely heavily upon foreign financing, most likely from oil exporters, even as Afghanistan remained heavily indebted.[102] The shock of the July uprising offered Daoud some cause to change course, and it bears recalling that he had attempted détente with Pakistan two decades earlier, following another confrontation.

So did a change in the composition of his government. By the autumn, the diminution of Parcham influence was apparent. Daoud removed six provincial governors in August and announced a cabinet reshuffle in September. Perhaps most dramatically, Daoud extended an olive branch toward rivals associated with the former regime. In early October, on the eve of *Eid al-Fitr*, he released Shafiq, his cousin Abdul Wali, and his uncle Shah Wali from detention, along with nearly 300 others. Eliot described the amnesty and Daoud's cabinet changes as a quiet return to "a more traditional Afghan regime." Afghanistan would not act as a "Soviet catspaw," and it behooved Bhutto to offer "some gesture" that he recognized and appreciated the changes in Kabul.[103]

Such counsel was easier to offer outside of Pakistan. From Islamabad, Byroade argued that anything beyond informal discussion was bound to backfire. With Pakistan's Supreme Court due to rule on the legality of the NAP ban and the detention of opposition leaders, U.S. intercession could easily be regarded as an intrusion into internal affairs. Nor did Islamabad ascribe much significance to cabinet changes within Kabul.[104]

As such, only patient suasion in Kabul and Islamabad could advance U.S. aims. The Supreme Court's affirmation of the NAP ban gave Bhutto space for another grand gesture. In an October 31 address, he offered to host Daoud or to visit Kabul if the Afghans preferred. While he refused to discuss internal matters with Daoud, Bhutto suggested that successful talks would incline him to be "large-hearted" toward the imprisoned NAP leadership. The offer was not Bhutto's first stab at summitry with his western neighbor; a similar proposal at the end of 1974 had fallen through. Yet, while Daoud did not immediately accept, neither did he reject the offer, nor did his government rush to excoriate the court ruling. Kabul, Eliot reasoned, appeared constrained by fears of another uprising and by U.S. and Iranian opinion. Daoud could either risk another confrontation or appear to abandon the Pashtun and Baluch causes. He was in no visible hurry to choose.[105]

An uneasy stasis prevailed well into 1976. Ford and Kissinger contended with election-year challenges. Pakistani insecurity endured, but the border issue ebbed as a contributing factor. When Bhutto visited New York in February, his conversation with Kissinger ranged widely over the détente system and Washington's willingness to defend its allies. "Bhutto's general mood was subdued, with deep concern about growing Soviet power," reported one observer. Washington's failure to prevent the defeat of anti-communist forces in Angola troubled him, and he still sought arms sales. Afghanistan featured only slightly within the conversation. Bhutto subsequently agreed with Byroade that personnel changes in Kabul were promising. In April, after earthquakes and spring floods wracked Afghanistan, Bhutto finally broke through. His government offered its neighbor emergency aid and a statement of "heartfelt grief." An immediate propaganda ceasefire ensued. Early in May, Daoud invited his counterpart to visit Kabul to discuss their differences.[106]

The ensuing thaw was born of shared necessity. If Daoud saw little benefit in continued conflict, Bhutto had abundant cause to seek a calmer western border. Elements of the planned June summit in Kabul suggested haste on his part. Islamabad accepted a definition of the talks that appeared to encompass internal affairs: exactly what Bhutto had forsworn discussing. Successive conversations with U.S., Iranian, and Turkish emissaries had apparently impressed on the Afghans the need for dialogue. Bhutto and his diplomats had heard much the same from their allies. Iranian pressure was visibly acute. "Both sides seem to be drawn to the talks by the need to meet the Shah's wishes," wrote one British analyst.[107]

A season of summitry commenced in early June, when Bhutto landed at Kabul, extending through late August, when Daoud reciprocated by visiting Islamabad. Complementing and reinforcing the Afghan-Pakistani thaw were Naim's July visit to Washington and Kissinger's second trip to Kabul on

August 8. In between hosting Kissinger and visiting Bhutto, Daoud attended and addressed the NAM's summit in Colombo, Sri Lanka. Neither orchestrated nor entirely incidental, the spate of high-level meetings confirmed a tenuous détente across the Durand Line, Daoud's determination to expand his aid relationship with the United States and the petro-lenders, and his growing concern about subversion.

To observers jaded by years of weary experience with the Durand Line conflict, the warmth of the Daoud-Bhutto summits offered grounds for hope. Neither summit produced a comprehensive agreement addressing the linked issues of self-determination and Pakistan's policy in the borderlands, but the two sides appeared to inch toward a recognizable quid pro quo: Afghan affirmation of Pakistan's existing borders in exchange for Pakistani leniency toward the NAP leadership. Bhutto's government sought, during the first summit, Afghan adherence to the famous Five Principles of Peaceful Coexistence, thus binding Kabul to diplomatic channels. After some initial resistance, Daoud assented, reasoning to Ghaus: "The situation in the region and in the world is such that we cannot afford another stalemate in our relations. The vital interests of Afghanistan militate for an accommodation with Pakistan."[108]

What were those interests in summer 1976? In successive high-level conversations in Washington and Kabul, Daoud and Naim entreated Ford and Kissinger for renewed U.S. assistance: both open and covert. Naim's visit had been scheduled before his brother invited Bhutto to Kabul. In Washington, Naim conveyed his government's growing worry about Soviet influence: "We don't feel any results from U.S.-Soviet détente. In our country, we feel the antagonism has increased, not diminished." Expressing concern about the sympathies of military officers who had trained in the Soviet Union, Daoud's brother sought both a more visible U.S. presence and intelligence on Moscow's activities within Afghanistan.[109]

Like Bhutto, Daoud distrusted the détente regime. Diminished U.S. threat perception limited the persuasive power of his government's requests for aid. Inasmuch as it offered Moscow a free hand or implied a U.S. retreat from Asia, détente also evoked unease. However circumspect their government's public statements on the fall of South Vietnam or Cuban intervention in Angola, in private Afghan officials could sound much like their aligned neighbors. Some of this anxiety emerged when Daoud addressed the Colombo NAM summit. While much of his speech invoked familiar themes—the rights of landlocked states, anticolonialism, and economic justice—it also offered a revealing discussion of détente. Differentiating a détente "brought about by fear" from one truly based on the principle of coexistence, Daoud observed, "Détente must be universal."[110]

Yet détente also offered Daoud and Bhutto useful tactics in their respective quests for security and legitimacy. Afghanistan and Pakistan each grasped the possibilities attendant in a thaw. The "Spirit of Kabul" afforded both governments an opportunity to appeal to oil-rich donor states. Amid other ongoing efforts at political normalization—superpower détente, *Ostpolitik*, and Middle East shuttle diplomacy—Daoud and Bhutto adopted a similar program of incremental negotiations. Their own cold conflict could be lessened via the means employed by Kissinger and his Soviet counterparts. "It is premature for me to say the end results," Daoud told Kissinger in August, "but I am hopeful that if this atmosphere continues, we can solve it honorably." "For two years everyone was afraid of President Daoud, and now everyone speaks of you as such a gentle person," Kissinger joked, "Have you changed?"[111]

Undoubtably, he had. Ten years in political exile had not led Daoud to shelve his ambitions, both economic and national, but sustained reflection on his earlier fall surely informed his calculus, fostering a greater pragmatism. Returned to power, he again faced a fundamental contradiction between borderlands agitation and the promotion of rapid development. He could promote Pashtunistan and Baluchistan or he could court foreign aid, especially from petro-lenders. He could not do both. While his economic agenda remained statist and heavily dependent on unlikely or shaky foreign promises, this time he chose it decisively.[112] Thus his July 17 Republic Day address exhaustively detailed the Seven-Year Plan while affirming Afghan nonalignment and lauding the recent Bhutto visit.[113]

To the extent that Daoud hoped to gain U.S. approval, he succeeded. The extent of Washington's largesse remained undetermined. "We will do our best to help," Ford promised Naim in July. While in Kabul, Kissinger applauded Daoud's summitry with Bhutto and spoke sympathetically about Afghan nonalignment: "We don't consider ourselves in competition with the Soviet Union here. We think that for you, nonalignment is the best policy." Kissinger volunteered general assurances of support, coupled with caveats about budgetary limitations and the need to circumvent the foreign aid bureaucracy.[114]

Afghan aspirations had not diminished with time. In successive meetings, Planning Minister Ali Ahmad Khurram produced an extensive litany of new projects: an engineering school at Kabul University, an expanded rural development program, a power line connecting the Kajakai Dam to Kabul, and a 500-bed hospital, among others. "How do you answer the argument I get from my colleagues that you can't pay for it?" Kissinger asked. "I can't answer it," Khurram replied, adding to the list. Minister of Mines and Industries Abdul Tawab Assifi requested satellite surveys to help Afghanistan map its oil reserves. "Oil?" Kissinger exclaimed to general laughter, "All we need is an Afghan in OPEC!"[115]

The Limits of Détente

Such bonhomie attested, at least, to fundamental improvement in the U.S.-Afghan relationship and to the easing of tensions between Daoud and his neighbors. The two summits did not resolve the conflict. Nor did they entirely alleviate distrust between the two leaders. "Bhutto is certainly a statesman and an extremely intelligent person," Daoud said to Ghaus, en route back to Kabul, "but I don't know to what extent he can be trusted." In lieu of further contacts that year—an autumn visit by Bhutto to Kabul was postponed—improved cross-border commerce and the resumption of direct airline service afforded further cause for optimism.[116]

Bhutto and Daoud were, of course, the principal architects of the thaw. Each acted with domestic factors in mind: Bhutto appeared to have prevailed in the frontier provinces, and Western observers believed that Pashtunistan was a waning issue in Afghanistan. Yet external factors and expansive domestic agendas gave both reasons to heed U.S. and Iranian opinion. Both states sought foreign capital, and Iran, backed by the United States, stood ready to bankroll ambitious development projects.

In financial terms, the Shah's munificence far overshadowed U.S. efforts, and Iranian pressure, applied bluntly in both Kabul and Islamabad, probably constituted the single most important outside factor. Yet U.S. diplomacy played a necessary if inobtrusive role: coaxing and reassuring allies and Afghans alike. Kissinger's personal outreach augmented the efforts of his ambassadors in Tehran, Kabul, and Islamabad. The task of reassuring allies was more complex than that of engaging Daoud. Iranian and Pakistani threat perception raced well ahead of U.S. conceptions of the Soviet agenda. The Shah and Bhutto's ambitious arms agendas, extending into the nuclear realm, posed a growing problem. Prudently or otherwise,

Washington banked its regional diplomacy on three prominent, ambitious leaders, seemingly at the height of their power. Experienced, trusted representatives in Tehran and Islamabad managed the ensuing contradictions while coordinating with Eliot in Kabul. Like the détente system itself, the thaw hinged on personal relationships, and this reliance offered both immediate strength and long-term fragility.

Shuttle and local diplomacy could only achieve so much. At best, they papered over a widening disagreement about the future of U.S. aid to Afghanistan. Having notionally acceded to Washington's preference for grassroots-level aid, Kabul's pivot back toward capital-intensive projects, consistent with the Seven-Year Plan, was unmistakable. Within the Helmand, the drainage project appeared little different from previous efforts. HAVA remained uncommunicative and wracked by delays. Plans to educate farmers on water use or to enlist manual laborers remained embryonic.[117] Heartened by Washington's receptiveness to aid requests and by another $14 million loan from the ADB, Afghan officials turned to other fronts.[118] Stressing the need for Washington to offer a visible counter to Soviet projects, Wahid Abdullah suggestively mentioned the discovery of a new oilfield near Maimaneh.[119]

A renewed aid contest could serve Daoud's interests, but only if it did not undermine the tacit modus vivendi between the superpowers. The absence of sustained Cold War competition within the republic after the coup limited the danger of either the border conflict or upheaval in Kabul sparking a broader conflagration. Considering subsequent events, mid-1970s U.S. assessments of Soviet policy in Afghanistan were strikingly restrained. Aside from their jarring statements after the July uprising, the Soviets displayed little interest in overturning the local status quo. Moscow's chief regional initiative remained a nonaggression pact. "The Soviet Union clearly prefers good relations with Daoud's regime to adventuring with local admirers," Eliot wrote in early 1977.[120] Backchannel dialogue, meanwhile, enabled Washington and Moscow to communicate their respective stakes in Afghanistan. Suspicion, of course, lingered on the ground. Absent from the records of the mid-1970s are indications of the same collegiality that Soviets and Americans had enjoyed in Kabul earlier—perhaps because Puzanov discouraged fraternization with U.S. diplomats. Soviet bloc diplomats wrote warily of Iranian overtures and Durand Line summitry.[121]

Wariness was not alarmism, however. Other factors moderated communist threat perception. First, as noted, the bloc did not welcome conflict between Afghanistan and its neighbors, fearing the consequences for the republican regime and the implications for its own regional policy. Prudent Afghan diplomacy offers a second explanation. Daoud continued to solicit assistance from the bloc, and successive reports from Kabul expressed satisfaction about Afghan stances on a variety of international questions. "Afghanistan performs correctly on the main issues of principle," Puzanov observed. Third, even as the bloc accepted a limited thaw between Kabul and Islamabad, it did not expect rapprochement—the "Spirit of Kabul" might easily prove fleeting. Last, most fundamentally, Daoud personally retained the respect of the Soviet Union and a corresponding benefit of the doubt. Noting a "certain right-wing tendency" within the regime, Puzanov nevertheless praised Daoud for withstanding the July revolt, pursuing a "wise policy" of incremental land reform, and recognizing the danger of dependence on Iran. Consequently, the minutes of meetings between bloc ambassadors in Kabul have a remarkably mundane quality: recording discussions of economic assistance, the Afghan press, UN votes, and film screenings.[122]

Yet older Cold War dynamics and suspicions endured amid a more fluid and uncertain environment. Daoud's embrace of détente increased the risk of a clash with domestic nationalists, exploitable by an increasingly alienated left. Kissinger's project of reassurance and stabilization existed in tension with the détente system. U.S. encouragement of Iranian efforts in Afghanistan and of Afghan-Pakistani dialogue inevitably resembled pact-building to the Soviet leadership. Moscow, meanwhile, beheld a multiplicity of other actors within Afghanistan: Iran, Islamist insurgents, and even its nemesis China, which appeared to pay the country greater heed after the coup. The opaque, conspiratorial, often violent nature of politics under Daoud gave the foreign powers monitoring Afghanistan continual cause for vigilance. A Cold War at low ebb undercut alarmism; a rising wave of upheaval in and around the republic, however, augured a dangerous future.

CHAPTER 10

The End of Diplomacy, 1977–1979

The battle for Kabul commenced on April 27, 1978. Tanks bombarded the presidential palace, and the ensuing explosions echoed widely, punctuated by automatic weapons fire.[1] MiG-21 jet fighters screamed overhead, strafing an infantry encampment and military facilities at Kabul's airport. To foreign onlookers, the identity of besiegers and besieged remained unknown. "We do not know which side is which," U.S. ambassador Theodore Eliot wrote at 4:30 P.M.[2] Around 5:45 P.M., MiGs and Sukhoi-7 attack aircraft struck the palace compound, where, Eliot had learned, President Mohammed Daoud Khan and his supporters had barricaded themselves. The defenders' guns fell silent by dusk, around 6:30, as the palace burned.[3]

Within the darkened palace, an increasingly grim mood spread among the officials sheltering within. Daoud's ministers had arrived that morning for a weekly cabinet meeting, only to be trapped by the uprising. Daoud, his brother Mohammed Naim Khan, and several ministers sat silently in the palace reception room amid the gunfire. A small transistor radio carried insurgent claims that Daoud had been killed; Deputy Prime Minister Said Abdulillah switched the device off. Mining Minister Abdul Tawab Assifi recalls Daoud breaking the silence, stating firmly: "It is my mistake!" No one requested clarification, and Daoud did not elaborate further. The president balked at Foreign Minister Wahid Abdullah's suggestions that he leave the palace. Several members of Daoud's family attempted to flee, only to be killed or wounded by a machine gun just outside. When two of his ministers requested permission to surrender, Daoud assented and embraced them tearfully before they departed. As dawn neared, Daoud approved a general surrender and sheltered in a hallway with Naim, Abdulillah, and his family—perhaps forty people in all. Held captive in a nearby room, the ministers heard a sustained burst of gunfire, as the rebels brutally fulfilled their earlier claim.[4]

Smoke wreathed Kabul that morning as Eliot and others sought to make sense of the scene. Overnight battles in nearby neighborhoods belied earlier rebel claims of victory, and conditions outside of the capital remained unknown. "To seize Kabul is not to control Afghanistan," Eliot observed, "centrifugal forces abound in this multi-ethnic country."[5]

Inexorably, but not immediately, the April coup ended the long-standing U.S. policy of engaging Afghanistan. While the new government's ideological proclivities were readily discernible, established diplomatic practice and the tenuous constraints of the détente system preserved some rationale for outreach. The administration of President Jimmy Carter remained internally divided on Soviet policy and accorded no special emphasis to either Afghanistan or its region. The new Democratic Republic of Afghanistan (DRA) meanwhile proclaimed its continued interest in U.S. aid, even as it visibly broke with the nonaligned policy of its predecessors. Washington had some initial incentive to adopt a wait-and-see attitude.

Yet three concurrent processes of destabilization spelled disaster. Brutal, ill-conceived acts of policy undermined what scant legitimacy the DRA enjoyed. Unwise efforts to emulate prior Afghan nonalignment inflamed Moscow's suspicions. Nearby, sudden changes of government in Iran, Pakistan, and India created a fluid, unpredictable regional environment, spurring the two blocs to perceive both opportunities and risks. Lastly, independently, and crucially, the wider deterioration of U.S.-Soviet relations fostered mistrust and undermined any possibility of a renewed understanding about Afghanistan. As the DRA flailed, Moscow sought to aid its embattled leadership while growing increasingly disaffected with them. Soviet leaders comprehended the risks of military intervention but convinced themselves that they had no alternative. The mistake was theirs, but U.S. choices made it more likely and magnified its implications. Aware of Moscow's difficulties but embittered by the murder of Eliot's successor, Ambassador Adolph Dubs, and spurred by other states in the region, the Carter administration dabbled with alarmism and an old, maximalist view of Soviet intentions. Action and reaction compounded. To its enduring misfortune, Afghanistan came to represent a canvas upon which both superpowers projected their hopes and fears about the coming decade.

Uneasy Interregnum, 1977–1978

The preceding year presented few auguries of coming upheaval. As the Ford administration concluded, Daoud requested elections to another *loya jirga* to review and endorse his proposed constitution, his continuing nonalignment, and his outreach toward Pakistan. Kabul and Islamabad observed a diplomatic pause, awaiting the upcoming assembly and Pakistani national elections. The outlook of the incoming U.S. administration toward the republic and its immediate region also remained unknown.[6]

Like many other governments, Daoud's regime struggled to assess Jimmy Carter. Abdul Samad Ghaus tacitly admitted having preferred Ford's election but opined that Carter would have "no sensible alternative" to his predecessor's policies. Daoud dispatched congratulatory messages to Carter after both the presidential election and the inauguration. His brother, Naim, described a "need to reaffirm the relationship." Afghanistan could not receive its answers too soon, yet Carter had to situate the republic and its broader region within an ambitious global agenda.[7]

Carter held contradictory aspirations and impulses. He acknowledged and accepted growing American disaffection from the earlier Cold War consensus after the Vietnam War and Watergate. Carter also grappled with the relative diminution of U.S. power, economic interdependence, and the possibility that questions of global inequality had supplanted the superpower struggle. Largely devoid of Cold War themes, his inaugural address promised wars "against poverty, ignorance, and injustice" and pledged to pursue nuclear disarmament. In a foreign policy address at Notre Dame University, Carter decried an "inordinate fear of communism." An observation that "the unifying threat of conflict with the Soviet Union has become less intensive, even though the conflict has become more extensive" struck a tentative balance. Beholding what he perceived to be communist aggression, Carter could respond promptly and sharply, with a sense of righteous indignation that Soviet leaders came to deplore.[8]

Carter's dual approach to the Cold War stemmed from the inescapable fact that his administration was a house divided. Some caveats merit mention. The notorious disagreements between his secretary of state, Cyrus Vance, and his national security advisor, Zbigniew Brzezinski, did not surface immediately. Nor was Carter an intellectual lightweight; his energy, determination, and curiosity routinely impressed his subordinates. Nevertheless, presidents inevitably require a rigorous, balanced advisory process and suffer in its absence. Brzezinski's unparalleled access to Carter, control over policymaking, and warm rapport with his boss ultimately advanced his own hawkish views.[9]

Ambivalent toward the Cold War, Carter espoused universal goals: disarmament, shared prosperity, and human rights. Some regional issues, meanwhile, held immediate urgency. The Panama Canal Zone dispute, Rhodesian war, and Arab-Israeli peace process each took precedence over South Asian matters.[10] Events in 1977, moreover, gave the administration cause to act cautiously. After rescinding emergency rule, Indian prime minister Indira Gandhi lost power in a surprising March election. Simultaneously, Pakistani prime minister Zulfikar Ali Bhutto's efforts to rig elections provoked sustained upheaval, culminating in his overthrow and arrest by the military. Alongside its neighbors, Afghanistan appeared a veritable island of stability. "Daoud's control over Afghanistan is greater than anyone's has ever been," Eliot cabled on Inauguration Day, noting the "dispersed and cowed" state of the left.[11]

Within Carter's agenda, a proposed renewal of foreign aid held some potential for Afghanistan. One objective, however, directly affected Kabul. Carter's refinement of counter-narcotics policy brought a narrower focus on heroin and emphasized crop eradication. His drug advisor, Peter Bourne, identified Afghanistan as "the single most significant threat to our long-term narcotics efforts." Washington lacked evidence that Afghan-grown opium had reached North America but centered the issue within the relationship, using aid to obtain leverage. Eliot described opium cultivation as the only bilateral problem in his first post-inauguration meeting with Daoud. Others spoke more bluntly. Deputy Assistant Secretary Adolph Dubs advised Afghan ambassador Abdullah Malikyar that recent amendments could bar aid, should Kabul's counter-narcotics efforts prove wanting.[12]

Visibly anxious, Daoud and his government promised their cooperation, and an impromptu committee of Afghan, U.S., and UN narcotics personnel convened in the summer. Pressed by Washington, Daoud's government could wring its own benefits. Although Eliot's embassy balked at funding an addiction treatment clinic in Badakhshan, the United Nations and Western European donors proved more accommodating. Bourne, meanwhile, attempted to nominate his deputy, Charles O'Keeffe, to succeed Eliot, gaining Carter's tentative approval before Brzezinski intervened.[13]

The abortive nomination suggested an altered U.S. focus within Afghanistan and the recession of Cold War concerns about Daoud's orientation or his hold on power. Although Daoud protested his age and complained of fatigue, he enjoyed Eliot's confidence. Embassy assessments noted the less commendable aspects of Daoud's rule: enduring corruption, bureaucratic inefficiency, and political repression. Yet the *loya jirga's* approval of the constitution, Daoud's subsequent election as president, and the absence of meaningful opposition portended well for him. In April, as an apparent gesture of reconciliation, Daoud approved and attended Kabul memorial services for his uncle, Shah Wali, who had died in Italy. "I see little possibility that the stability of [Daoud's] regime will be seriously challenged in the next two to five years," Eliot wrote, days before the Afghan leader departed for Moscow.[14]

Daoud's April 1977 visit to Moscow holds a cardinal significance in accounts of his subsequent overthrow. By Ghaus's recollection, General Secretary Leonid Brezhnev abruptly berated Daoud about the increased number of Western and UN experts in Afghanistan—particularly in the north. Brezhnev declared that his government "took a grim view" of their presence, deriding them as "spies" and "imperialists." Daoud coldly rejected the statement, retorting: "We will never allow you to dictate to us how to run our country and whom to employ in Afghanistan." The Afghan delegation stood up, said a nominal farewell, and departed, rebuffing Soviet efforts to shelve the dispute and continue the meeting.[15]

Undeniably, subsequent events lend the episode an ominous cast. Ghaus suggests that the exchange marked "the beginning of the end for Daoud." Without disputing Ghaus's account, contemporaneous evidence suggests another, less sinister reading. Other Afghan officials were struck by Brezhnev's poor physical condition rather than his hostility. The Soviet leader spoke haltingly, appearing disoriented and heavily medicated. Ghaus noted that Brezhnev's outburst had embarrassed his Politburo colleagues. Experienced Kremlin watchers were familiar with Brezhnev's parlous health and erratic behavior—Anatoly Chernyaev scathingly described a Brezhnev address in March as a "dementia session." Daoud may well have been personally alarmed by the episode, but his subordinates did not mention it to

Western diplomats. They instead described a satisfactory, unremarkable visit, as did the Soviets in communications to their allies.[16]

As before, Afghanistan maintained a delicate balance: soliciting aid from antagonistic blocs. Brezhnev's complaint about foreign experts, however incoherently delivered, recalled a long-standing Soviet concern (although one that his ambassador in Kabul, Alexander Puzanov, does not seem to have raised).[17] Other geopolitical factors complicated Soviet-Afghan relations. Daoud's thaw with Pakistan and Iran's influence in the republic bore scrutiny, yet neither development necessarily endangered Afghan nonalignment. Earlier summitry had not resolved the Pashtunistan dispute, while upheaval in Pakistan made further progress uncertain. Recent events, meanwhile, called the extent of Iranian influence within Afghanistan into question.

Promises of Iranian aid had warmed relations between Tehran and Kabul. Having previously opposed the Helmand waters treaty, Daoud announced its ratification in January, seemingly resolving the perennial dispute. A new proposed Afghan floodwater retention dam on the Helmand, the Kamal Khan, threatened to reopen the issue. The migration of Afghans into Iran—500,000 by French and British estimates—in pursuit of better wages added another point of friction. Aid agreements, meanwhile, were more easily signed than fulfilled, as Iran had made financial commitments beyond its stated foreign aid budget. The overrun delayed credits to Afghanistan and other recipients, throwing Iranian-funded projects into doubt.[18]

Prominent among them was a proposed cement factory in Kandahar. The previous year, Daoud's government had nearly awarded the Iranian-backed project to a Czechoslovak bidder, before Washington objected. Planning Minister Ali Ahmad Khurram was apparently persuaded to select a different contractor. The U.S.-based Fuller Company bid successfully for the $50 million factory, but Iran failed to provide the promised funds, leaving the project in limbo. Afghan officials suspected Iran of retaliating for the Kamal Khan Dam. Other Iranian-supported projects ground to a halt, and Wahid Abdullah angrily declared that the Shah could keep his money.[19]

A May trip by Naim to Tehran resolved the dispute, reopening discussion of aid. Still, faced with a sudden decline in oil revenues, Iran had become frugal. A protocol signed in 1976 had committed Tehran to financing $700 million within Afghanistan. While finalizing the revised program, Khurram encountered Iranian claims of a budget deficit equivalent to $7 billion and was able to secure promises to fund only $51 million in projects. Even then, Iran demanded further study of the cement plant. The delay voided the Fuller Company contract. While Iran prevaricated, the State Department unsuccessfully tried to interest the Eximbank in the project, and the Czechoslovaks prepared a new bid with their own line of credit.[20]

While his government reneged on its earlier promises, the Shah kept one fretful eye on Afghanistan. Already unnerved by upheaval in Islamabad, he charged that Daoud planned to exploit his neighbor's distress. His diatribe listed Afghan ingratitude, "insidious" Soviet influence within Kabul, and the likelihood that Daoud's eventual successors would be "willing dupes for the Russian imperial drive to the Sea of Oman." No stranger to Iran or its anxious leader, Eliot responded irritably: Kabul continued to balance adroitly between its neighbors "in a traditional time-proved Afghan fashion," it had ceased significant agitation on the Pashtun and Baluch questions, and Moscow favored bilateral ties over the promotion of a small, disorganized left. Eliot countered, moreover, that Iran had hardly done all it could to aid Afghanistan. Rather than treating the Afghans "in a patronizing manner as bumpkin country cousins," the Shah could attempt to strengthen friendly factions in the republic.[21]

Reports of Afghanistan's absorption into an Iranian sphere of influence were greatly exaggerated. Whether the Shah's fears were similarly overblown was difficult to tell. A growing unease was apparent in Kabul that year. Having established Afghanistan as a presidential republic earlier in the year, Daoud moved sluggishly to solidify his government. Daoud, himself, receded from view. He minimized his role in the annual Jeshyn festivities, seeming "perfunctory and absent" when he appeared. He had recently undergone surgery and had been greatly distraught by the discovery of seventy-seven bodies at a mental asylum. Yet age and stress likely plagued him as well. Senior officials confided that Daoud had been inattentive and unfocused during deliberations on the constitution earlier in the year. Often optimistic about Daoud, Eliot allowed that "68 is old for an Afghan."[22]

Daoud had aged, but he had also learned from experience. Afghanistan remained publicly reticent during Bhutto's implosion, declining to exploit Pakistan's latest crisis. The prospect of another military regime in Islamabad led some Afghan officials to worry. Bhutto's successor, Gen. Mohammed Zia ul-Haq, pledged to maintain the "Spirit of Kabul," however, while Pakistani diplomats expressed satisfaction at Daoud's restraint and their government's sense that its interests were best served by stability in Afghanistan. A cordial visit by Zia to Kabul followed in October in which he promised leniency toward Pashtun and Baluch dissidents, and Daoud affirmed his recognition of Pakistan's borders. Unlike the mercurial Bhutto, Zia struck the Afghans as an honest statesman: "the most affable, well-disposed, and farsighted Pakistani leader we had ever met," in Ghaus's fond recollection.[23]

Maintaining détente with Pakistan served Daoud amid uneasy circumstances. He fretted about communist insurrections in Ethiopia and Thailand to Eliot, professing his belief in the domino theory. Afghanistan presented few signs of incipient revolution, but several unrelated events in the autumn fostered a general apprehension. Daoud faced a brief crisis within his cabinet, as six ministers, including Wahid Abdullah, submitted and then retracted their resignations. An unknown gunman assassinated Planning Minister Khurram on November 16. The regime detained a growing number of political prisoners, and construction of a new specialized prison began along the road to Jalalabad, at Pul-i-Charkhi. French ambassador Georges Perruche described a "deep malaise" within the country.[24]

In such circumstances, Eliot sought to provide clear signs of U.S. support. Presidential diplomacy and food aid afforded some leverage, yet neither could be employed easily. An invitation to Daoud in early 1978 could convey continued U.S. interest, but impending visits by the Shah and Indian prime minister Morarji Desai complicated Carter's calendar. An Afghan request for PL-480 grain posed a similar opportunity. Improved Afghan foreign currency holdings argued against a sale, as did the lateness of the request. Additionally, Washington was unenthusiastic about Kabul's request that it cover shipping costs. Yet in both cases, the Carter administration gave some ground. Daoud received an invitation to visit in summer 1978, and Washington approved a sale of 50,000 tons of wheat and the use of U.S.-held rupees to cover transshipment from Karachi.[25]

Much like its predecessors, the Carter administration endeavored to reconcile Afghanistan policy within broader regional and global objectives. The White House carefully engaged the Desai government in India while monitoring Pakistan. Although Carter's human rights rhetoric unsettled the Shah, the White House reaffirmed the special relationship, approving extensive arms sales to Tehran. Simultaneously, Carter also authorized negotiations with Moscow to limit the militarization of the Indian Ocean. At one point, Carter expressed a willingness to abandon the recently established U.S. base on the island of Diego Garcia, should the Soviets pledge a commensurate withdrawal. Afghanistan did not enter the conversation, yet the constructive tenor of superpower exchanges on the wider region attested to a relative lack of Cold War conflict in the republic's vicinity.[26]

Events on a different continent, thousands of miles away, fundamentally altered Washington's perception while amplifying Daoud's unease. Massive Tupolev and Antonov transport aircraft thundered over Afghanistan during the autumn, bound for the Horn of Africa. The Soviet Union had joined its ally, Cuba, in aiding a revolutionary government in Ethiopia, which was under attack by neighboring U.S.-backed Somalia. Moscow initiated an emergency airlift, apparently failing to inform Kabul of what was flying overhead.[27]

Born of local rivalries and colonial legacies, the Horn conflict need not have influenced any other part of the world. Concerned with negotiating a new SALT arms control treaty, and faulting the Somalis, Vance advised against interpreting the episode as proof of aggressive Soviet intent. He won the immediate argument, but the implications of the episode reverberated in ways inimical to the pursuit of détente. Moscow's perceived victory fostered alarmism in the wider region and in Washington. Brzezinski and his aides froze further superpower dialogue on the Indian Ocean, citing Moscow's intervention. Brzezinski also sought some means of admonishing the Soviets, observing: "They must understand that there are consequences in their behavior." The origins of the conflict were immaterial: what mattered were the lessons drawn by allies and adversaries alike about U.S. resolve and credibility.[28]

Afghan leaders agreed with Brzezinski. In early February 1978, the republic hosted Adm. Maurice Weisner, the most prominent U.S. officer to visit since the Second World War. Concerned about Afghan officers trained in the Soviet Union, Weisner had discussed expanding Afghan enrollment in U.S. military training programs. Daoud lamented the Soviet overflights, and Ghaus endorsed the U.S. naval presence in the Indian Ocean. Afterward, Naim bitterly asked Eliot what use "all of [your] admirals are" if the United States failed to prevent the communists from overrunning Angola and the Horn. The frequency and vehemence of such complaints far exceeded the usual efforts at balancing. Fear of both Soviet adventurism and internal subversion animated the Afghan government in its final year.[29]

Nevertheless, in contemplating the final weeks of Daoud's republic, the perils of hindsight loom: of reading backwards from a calamitous event and handpicking a litany of missed warnings. Taken in the aggregate, the auguries of early 1978 were at most ambiguous. To close observers, they presented no evidence of Soviet hostility. Regular Warsaw Pact ambassadorial meetings in Kabul during the winter and early spring had neither an air of confrontation nor one of crisis: merely the same familiar, incremental deliberations.[30] Daoud, meanwhile, embarked upon a series of foreign visits, including a friendly four-day trip to Islamabad. Upon his return, he conducted a speaking tour in three eastern provinces. Kabul looked ahead to hosting a ministerial meeting of the Non-Aligned Movement in May.[31]

Thus, by the spring, the United States regarded Afghanistan without great trepidation. The core political question remained Daoud's successor, yet his health and recent vigor made the matter hypothetical. No clear alternative to him appeared to exist. Eliot ascribed more political strength to Daoud's Islamist opposition than to the left. Despite Washington's recent postponement of Daoud's American visit, bilateral relations remained cordial. Daoud, Eliot wrote on April 15, appeared "increasingly confident in his own position, and in the merits of his overall program for the future of his country."[32]

Two days later, unknown gunmen assassinated Mir Akbar Khyber, a popular senior People's Democratic Party of Afghanistan (PDPA) leader, as he took his daily evening stroll. A raucous, outsized funeral march two days later featured soaring eulogies for Khyber and denunciations of Daoud's government by the combined leadership of the PDPA: Nur Mohammed Taraki and Babrak Karmal. In an April 20 report, the CIA allowed that the Marxists were a more powerful force than previously estimated but maintained that they still did not threaten Daoud. Eliot mused that Daoud may have authorized the march to shock his U.S. patrons and perhaps to allow leftist anger to vent. Initially, it appeared to work: "Kabul is calm and Daoud is still very much in charge," Eliot wrote. Two days later, Daoud ordered the arrest of the senior PDPA leadership—but not before they had set their own coup into motion.[33]

"What Are We Dealing With?"
Spring 1978–February 1979

"What happened?" a puzzled Zbigniew Brzezinski asked Thomas Thornton, the NSC's South Asia specialist, upon learning of the coup. Thornton had no idea. He later recalled experiencing disbelief, incredulous that Afghanistan had a viable communist party. Although the Cold War remained at a relative ebb, the shock of Daoud's overthrow, the exhortations of allies, and a rising alarmism in Washington inclined policymakers toward a changed view of

Afghan events. Jolted out of complacency by the bloodbath in Kabul, Americans and allies alike had less difficulty imagining its fearful implications—even as basic prudence and uncertainty about the new Afghan regime recommended restraint and even diplomatic engagement.[34]

Two questions now held paramount importance: the nature of the new Afghan regime and what role, if any, the Soviet Union had played in establishing it. Citing anecdotal evidence, Eliot postulated a degree of coordination between the rebels and Soviet military advisors. Washington was more skeptical. Neither the State Department nor the CIA detected direct Soviet involvement, although the latter suggested that Moscow might have had some forewarning.[35]

The passage of time and the opening of communist bloc archives have not refuted this assessment. Available evidence generally affirms the initial CIA thesis: a Soviet Union on the sidelines, with some ineffectual measure of prior knowledge. Czechoslovak diplomats in Moscow reported that the Kremlin had not expected the coup and knew little about the new government.[36] Taraki suggested to Czechoslovak ambassador Zdeněk Karmelita that his party had acted in the expectation that it would receive bloc support. Most significant are the accounts of KGB defectors. Vladimir Kuzichkin writes that the Soviet embassy received an eleventh-hour notice of the coup but was directed to respond vaguely: to "let them make their own decisions." By Kuzichkin's recollection, "not one Soviet organization" aided in Daoud's overthrow. Former KGB archivist Vasili Mitrokhin largely corroborates this account. In his telling, Moscow received word on April 26. Puzanov worried that the PDPA was being manipulated by government provocateurs, whereas the KGB in Moscow speculated bizarrely that the Israeli Mossad might be acting as puppetmaster.[37]

The question of Soviet culpability also requires consideration of the earlier reconciliation of the Khalq and Parcham factions in July 1977. Mediated by Moscow and the Iraqi and Indian communist parties, the shotgun marriage of the PDPA's feuding factions can be read as portending Soviet malice toward Daoud. It need not, however. Regardless of its attitude toward Daoud, and heeding recent experience in Chile and Ethiopia, Moscow had abundant cause to pursue party unity. A fractious Afghan party weakened its leverage within Kabul and, conceivably, risked one of the rival wings seeking Chinese support. Brezhnev's Politburo had every reason to cudgel the PDPA's factions into grudging collaboration. It had tried before, as early as January 1974.[38]

"The less turbulence there is in that part of the world, the better it is for us," remarked a Soviet diplomat in Washington on April 29, reflecting his government's instinctive view of Afghan affairs. Four decades later, the case for Soviet culpability remains unproven. The more important question is why Moscow embraced the DRA, despite doubting the credentials of its leadership and Afghanistan's suitability for socialism. If the Kremlin did not plot Daoud's overthrow, it had cause to worry about his trajectory and who might follow him. Afghan-Pakistani détente and Iran's regional ambitions complicated the picture further, while Warsaw Pact records suggest considerable, albeit exaggerated concern about Chinese influence. The coup had thrust Afghanistan into Moscow's arms; a conservative, wary mentality guided the Kremlin thereafter. They may not have sought an allied government in Kabul, but they dared not let it go.[39]

Meanwhile, the Carter administration endeavored to assess the new regime. Reporting from Kabul identified a majority of the announced cabinet as founding members of the PDPA: "a group of long-term and dedicated communists." An interdepartmental group chaired by Thornton concluded that "this regime will be bad news for us" but advised against precipitate action. Eliot reasoned that the new regime could slavishly render Afghanistan the de facto sixteenth Soviet republic—or strike out in its own direction, à la Yugoslavia.[40] A patient response made eminent sense, whereas militant reaction contravened the administration's broader program and public weariness with the Cold War. The extent of Kabul's alignment with Moscow remained undetermined, as did the stability of the regime itself. Washington followed a restrained policy after the revolution, but the shock of the event reverberated widely.

Notions of history offered policymakers long-term frameworks that both clarified and discomfited. "What the British fought to prevent for over one hundred years . . . has finally occurred," Eliot wrote: "Direct Russian influence appears to have moved south of the Oxus and the Hindu Kush." Brzezinski mused that for the first time since the Bolshevik Revolution, no buffer separated the Soviet Union from South Asia. His invocations of a long-standing imperial project accompanied predictions of Soviet action against either Iran or Pakistan.[41] With greater abandon, regional leaders invoked vivid images of empires past while imagining Moscow's next move. "The Afghan barrier has been breached and our country lies directly in the path of the flood which rolled out of Czarist Russia," Pakistan's Zia wrote, appealing for U.S. aid. The disconsolate Shah termed the coup another example of "the Soviet grand design" and part of a broader plot to encircle Iran. Writing to Carter, he alluded to "the pressure exerted from certain quarters to push forward towards the Indian Ocean."[42]

Broad-brush descriptions of Russian imperialism, coupled with near-term predictions of next steps, obscured the ambiguities of the coup: Moscow's role in it, the orientation of the new government, and its prospects. Although such alarmism did not immediately shape policy, it did influence planning. Discussion of covert action against the DRA commenced immediately. Notably, the CIA had to be prodded to consider it. Understaffed in Afghanistan, where the coup had endangered its station chief, humbled by recent failures in Southeast Asia, and beleaguered by congressional investigations, the agency lacked its erstwhile sense of adventure. Thornton worried that the CIA would be disinclined to evaluate the merits of covert action fairly.[43]

More pressing decisions loomed in Kabul, where tanks guarded key intersections, and air force jets swept overhead periodically. The airport and telephone network ceased operations. Moscow recognized the new regime on April 30, as the DRA solicited statements of recognition from other governments. Attendees of an emergency meeting of Western ambassadors on May 1 reluctantly agreed that delayed recognition risked retaliation. As in 1973, Washington consulted with Tehran and Islamabad but determined independently to extend recognition, even after Pakistan pleaded for delay (while an increasingly distracted Iranian government failed to offer substantial comment). A junior diplomat delivered a note conferring recognition early on May 6, hours before Eliot met amicably with a clearly "exhilarated" Taraki, now president of Afghanistan's Revolutionary Council.[44]

Taraki clearly intended that conversation, during which he declared his affinity for the United States and continued interest in aid, to reassure Eliot's superiors. It was not, however, his government's first exchange with U.S. diplomats. A week earlier, soldiers had briefly detained two senior aid mission officials in the Kabul zoo. One warned: "You Americans are being seen in more places than you need to get from home to the office." Days after Eliot met Taraki, Peace Corps Volunteer John Sumser, who taught English at a Kabul school, was seized by soldiers and accused of espionage. Held at gunpoint, he was struck repeatedly and threatened with execution before being abruptly released and treated to dinner by his captors.[45]

Such episodes raised fundamental questions about the DRA. The events of April 27–28 already demonstrated the ruthlessness of the ascendant

Marxists. Horrifying reports of the palace massacre circulated, followed by public announcements of the execution of senior officials, including Daoud's vice president, defense minister, and Wahid Abdullah. Other Afghan officials sought asylum. The U.S. air attaché briefly hid a senior Afghan colleague in his residence before the embassy decided that the risk was too great. The Afghan colonel stoically accepted a car ride to the Shar-i-Nau neighborhood, where he nonchalantly exited the vehicle.[46]

The executions, arrests, and flight of Afghan officials presented the Carter administration with the latest incarnation of a familiar dilemma. Washington had earlier declined to press Afghanistan on human rights. Its post-revolution concern could therefore appear opportunistic, yet the volume of abuses under the DRA far exceeded Daoud's. The regime's targets, moreover, were often the individuals most familiar to Western governments: diplomats, senior officials, and their families, whom Eliot termed "old and close friends of the United States." Western diplomats received sympathetically asylum requests from fearful Afghan officials and plaintive inquiries about the fates of loved ones. The DRA's detention of family members of former officials at the unfinished prison at Pul-i-Charkhi resembled hostage taking. Elite repression in Kabul had the incidental but powerful effect of transforming Afghan diplomats—usually the country's most important and dedicated advocates—into sympathetic, compelling witnesses to the cruelty of the new regime.[47] Kabul's small, capable, and invaluable diplomatic apparatus was collapsing.

Citing "gross violations of human rights," Eliot appealed for action from Washington. Tellingly, however, he urged a quiet approach to the DRA, ideally a presidential appeal to Taraki that might flatter him rather than a message linking further aid to human rights. A coercive approach would most likely backfire, and aid still held some potential to encourage Afghan nonalignment. Other governments reacted more directly. Representatives of other Muslim states, including Saudi Arabia and Egypt, tendered their concerns to the DRA, which responded indignantly, denying any unfair treatment. Not keen to be seen leading the charge, the State Department sought to enlist other states, including the Soviet Union, to make the case in Kabul.[48]

Initial U.S. policy toward the DRA observed a delicate balance, while Washington pursued fundamentally incompatible objectives. The Kabul embassy cautiously engaged the new regime, and strategists in Washington attempted to reassure allies. Strong signals, in either direction, on questions of aid or human rights jeopardized either goal. Taraki had informed Eliot that he would gauge foreign governments on their willingness to aid Afghanistan and promised to remain independent. Informed of the conversation by Brzezinski, Carter opined that the United States should build a "good relationship" with the DRA but proceed cautiously on aid. Having been stymied by Daoud's bureaucracy, U.S. aid workers within Afghanistan were surprisingly eager to take the new regime at its word. Just before the Sumser incident, the Peace Corps mission requested additional personnel.[49]

Accordingly, Eliot concluded his mission investigating possibilities for further bilateral collaboration. Meetings with Taraki's ministers yielded a decidedly mixed picture. Most received Eliot warmly. Only some appeared suited for their portfolio, however, and a coherent Afghan suggestion for the U.S. aid program did not emerge. "The new government is having difficulty getting its act together," Eliot cabled. Yet its development ambitions visibly exceeded even Daoud's lofty goals. In Eliot's farewell meeting with Taraki, the Afghan leader proposed that Washington provide Afghanistan with a lump sum: ideally between $100 and $300 million, averring an interest in capital-intensive projects. Informed that the lump sum was infeasible, Taraki reiterated the request.[50]

Eliot's final weeks in Kabul presented him with traumatic violence and unprecedented challenges. Although personally shaken by the bloodshed, his reporting remained measured, grappling with the ambiguities of the early DRA. Afghanistan now lay within the Soviet sphere, he reasoned, but could not yet be labeled a communist state. U.S. interests still called for a continued presence, which might encourage a return to nonalignment. "Even if that chance were only 10 percent, it would still be worth the effort," he argued. Eliot's parting contacts with the regime discouraged him, however. Predicting "rocky times may lay ahead," he counseled strong support of Iran and Pakistan, thereby encapsulating the dilemma confronting his government.[51]

Iranian and Pakistani frustrations had already surfaced in a June meeting of the moribund CENTO alliance. "Iran was told that Afghanistan would always be a buffer state," Tehran's representative declared bitterly. Declaring the existence of a "USSR-Afghanistan-India" axis, the Pakistani delegate threatened to leave the alliance "unless something is done." Ambassador Arthur Hummel in Islamabad discerned a "wave of gloom and trauma," amplified by dismay at India's prompt recognition of the DRA and Washington's cautious policy. Others expressed concern and demanded reassurance. In Ankara, Ambassador Ronald Spiers linked Afghan events to a broader Turkish crisis of confidence in its American ally and CENTO. China's ambassador in Kabul, Huang Ming-ta, warned that Washington would need to bolster its regional allies to prevent a Soviet drive to the Persian Gulf. Other expressions of concern could be heard: from local nonaligned states, such as Nepal and Bangladesh; from Arab allies including Jordan, Egypt, and Saudi Arabia; and even from governments friendly to Moscow, in Syria and Iraq.[52]

The collective anxieties of regional governments provided compelling motivation for Washington to confront the DRA. Other concerns, however, reinforced the Carter administration's cautious approach. Superpower negotiations toward a SALT II agreement continued. Carter sought, meanwhile, to consolidate recent Israeli-Egyptian dialogue, ideally as part of a wider Middle East peace process. Brzezinski, the policymaker most inclined to ascribe sinister implications to the Afghan revolution, pursued the more pressing goal of normalizing relations with China, visiting Beijing in late May (where Vice Premier Deng Xiaoping proclaimed that Moscow had orchestrated Daoud's ouster). Existing policy priorities, ambiguity in Kabul, and a prudent caution precluded a rapid or forceful response, instead recommending an evaluative approach. Irked by proxy conflicts elsewhere, Moscow took note. Perceiving the absence of significant U.S. activity, the Soviet desk officer for Afghanistan described a "wait and see" policy.[53]

U.S. forbearance also stemmed from a lack of options. The CIA had focused its limited Afghan efforts on Soviet bloc personnel and had thus been entirely surprised by the revolution. "Things are pretty tough in Afghanistan collection-wise," observed Thornton. "Covert action is not appropriate at this time," Brzezinski advised Carter.[54] Intelligence gathering in Afghanistan could scarcely be refined in short order, amid the oppressive, paranoid atmosphere of the DRA. Yet foes of the regime could not wait. Dr. Mir Ali Akbar, who headed Jamhuriat Hospital, conversed with the interim head of mission, Bruce Amstutz, in June. Representing a senior figure in the Afghan Army, Akbar sought U.S. advice on staging a countercoup, hoping that Washington would act to preclude Soviet intervention. Amstutz counseled supporting and advising the plotters. In Washington, Deputy Director of Central Intelligence Frank Carlucci argued against encouraging them but suggested maintaining contact with the embryonic resistance. "I guess . . . giving a helping hand is out of the question," Thornton reasoned, noting: "the result would likely be an invitation for massive Soviet involvement." Brzezinski concurred.[55]

Kabul was not the only potential locus of contact with anti-regime movements. Dissident Afghans presented themselves to Western officials outside the country but faced reticence and incredulity. Their claims could appear outlandish, and embassy officials feared being gulled by provocateurs. One repeat visitor in Islamabad sought U.S. aid against "red imperialism." Delivering a list of military requirements, he claimed that his organization had begun attacking government targets in Paktia and Jalalabad. Hummel cautiously directed the embassy to avoid further contacts with "Gul Badeen"—almost certainly Gulbuddin Hekmatyar—thereby closing the door on an early entreaty by the Hezb-i-Islami ("Party of Islam").[56]

Another Afghan conflict loomed larger by late June, however. Following rumors of renewed feuding between the Khalq and Parcham factions, the embassy reported on the imminent transfer of Babrak Karmal and other leading Parchamists to Afghan embassies. The Khalq's preeminence within the Afghan military had enabled the coup, and its triumphant leadership saw no need to share credit or rewards with longtime rivals. While state media lavished daily adulation upon the Khalqists—especially Taraki, the proud object of a cult of personality campaign—their rivals vanished from view. The as-yet bloodless purge of the Parchamists modestly encouraged advocates of engagement. More nationalist than Karmal, Taraki and his ambitious deputy, Hafizullah Amin, appeared likely to retain some autonomy from Moscow. A graduate of Columbia University Teachers College, Amin exhibited, in Selig Harrison's observation, an intense Pashtun nationalism and "a swaggering self-confidence."[57] Glad to facilitate the Parchamist exodus, Washington and its allies quickly accepted their inbound appointments.[58]

Eliot's replacement, Adolph Dubs, pondered the merits of engaging the DRA. A veteran diplomat with extensive experience in Moscow—more recently a senior official within the Near Eastern and South Asian Affairs bureau—Dubs sought to reinvigorate U.S. diplomacy in Kabul. Never bullish about the Khalq, he nevertheless argued persistently for a patient approach. His counsel contrasted starkly with the alarmism emanating from regional allies. Dubs's own initial assessment of the revolution emphasized the initiative of the Afghan left and the accumulated frustrations of the Daoud years. He credited the PDPA's success to its long-term cultivation of officers in the Afghan military. Defense Minister Abdul Qadir—who had played a singularly decisive role in the coup, bringing the air force into action against Daoud's palace—assured Dubs that his country would remain independent of the Soviet Union. Dubs's reporting notably declined to endorse the thesis of a Soviet drive toward the Indian Ocean.[59]

A July visit by Under Secretary of State David Newsom helped to bolster U.S. outreach. Meeting with Taraki and Amin, Newsom professed an interest in maintaining the aid relationship, particularly the Helmand project, while suggesting that other efforts could be ventured. His audience proved welcoming, although Taraki bristled at the suggestion that he treat political prisoners leniently. A mystified Newsom asked afterward: "What are we dealing with? Is it an inexperienced group of genuine reformers feeling their way? Are Amin and Taraki dedicated communists masking their intentions? Are they fronts for an unseen junta or committee?" Newsom was not "sanguine about the nature or intentions" of the DRA, but warned: "the situation is sufficiently fluid that it would be a mistake for us . . . to appear to be backing away."[60]

Thus, aid to Afghanistan continued—albeit diminished by U.S. hesitancy and administrative upheaval in Kabul. Washington disbursed $3.2 million toward continued Helmand Valley drainage efforts, and bilateral discussion of the project continued. "You started it, and we hope you are going to finish it," declared one minister. The U.S. delegation to the Asian Development Bank (ADB) endorsed a small agricultural development loan to the DRA, which the bank approved in July. Aviation collaboration also continued. Before leaving for Kabul, Dubs helped to persuade Pan American's chairman to maintain his airline's partnership with Ariana. The Afghan carrier subsequently asked to purchase a U.S.-made DC-10 aircraft and obtained an Eximbank loan to finance the transaction.[61]

Escalating violence rendered the effort hollow, however. Killings of government teachers north of Kabul in May preceded the eruption of revolt in the eastern province of Nuristan in July.[62] Credible reports reached the embassy soon afterward. Shots echoed around Kabul nightly, and Eliot's embassy reported one incident in which a mutinous tank crew shelled an army headquarters. The influx of Soviet personnel into the country produced audible public discontentment and rumors of disaffection within the Afghan military, including on the part of Defense Minister Qadir. Persistent unrest undermined the Khalq's efforts to launch an ambitious social program, as did brutal acts of repression. Mitrokhin records the arrest of 900 Afghans in Balkh and a subsequent series of mass executions; Dubs's embassy reported the destruction of villages by the air force in the east. Now imprisoned in Pul-i-Charkhi, Assifi observed an influx of military officers and religious figures. By the summer, its professions of respect for Islam to the contrary, the regime persecuted religious leaders en masse. "We are arresting hundreds of mullahs, but I do not know what is happening to them," one official admitted.[63]

The Khalq's ambitious program had collided with the skepticism and resistance of the countryside. As Elisabeth Leake argues, it was not consistently revolutionary. Its espoused programs sometimes resembled promises made earlier by Daoud. Its speed and heedless implementation, however, made resistance inevitable. A debt relief decree undermined existing forms of rural credit without providing an alternative. Carelessly enacted land reform failed to take water resources into account. Marriage regulations interposed the government into a profoundly local institution, overlooking its myriad political and economic dimensions. Unused to such exertion of state power, which undermined communal leaders, Afghans reacted with suspicion.[64] By one East German account, some peasants committed suicide after being coerced, via threats of imprisonment, into accepting confiscated land.[65]

The collision of the PDPA's schism with Afghanistan's nascent insurgency was inevitable. Late on August 17, Radio Afghanistan announced the arrest of Qadir, Army Chief of Staff Shahpur Ahmadzai, and Dr. Akbar on conspiracy charges. The latter two sustained severe torture and solitary confinement at Pul-i-Charkhi. Taraki subsequently claimed that the trio had plotted with the United States, China, Iran, Pakistan, and West Germany. Akbar had, of course, solicited Washington's aid. Whether his confession described his conversation with Amstutz or conformed to the demands of his torturer is probably immaterial. Further dismissals of Parchamists followed, and in early September Kabul abruptly revoked the diplomatic credentials of Karmal and his comrades.[66]

The violent, fractious tendencies of the PDPA had long concerned Moscow. Puzanov received instructions to endorse collective party leadership and to warn against "unjustified mass repression."[67] He advised Taraki in July that it was "politically unwise to bomb and eradicate a village just because some of its inhabitants had rebelled."[68] Now, fearful of returning to Afghanistan, Parchamists dispatched as ambassadors pleaded with host governments for sanctuary. "In the name of humanism, save us!" protested Karmal's brother, Mahmud Baryalai, to a Soviet diplomat.[69] For the second time in months, rash acts in Kabul had turned diplomats into antagonists, as the Khalq heedlessly destroyed one of its country's greatest geopolitical assets.

Moscow and its allies did not embrace the Parchamists, but neither did they deport or shun them. Karmal found improbable sanctuary in a western Bohemia forest lodge, guarded by the Czechoslovak secret police.[70] The surprising candor of communist representatives in Kabul, who promptly notified Western counterparts of the mass recall, offered another indication of the bloc's dismay.[71]

"Things in Afghanistan are deteriorating rapidly," Thornton wrote to Brzezinski, "the regime is devouring its children with amazing speed." By autumn, the NSC had discarded any lingering doubt as to the regime's orientation. It also contemplated the possibility of Soviet intervention but deemed it presently unlikely. Concerned with Middle East peacemaking, revolution in Central America, normalizing Sino-American relations, and unrest in Iran, the Carter administration declined to elevate Afghanistan policy onto the NSC's Special Coordinating Council (SCC) agenda.[72]

The absence of new directives from Washington afforded the Kabul embassy considerable discretion. Although committed to engagement, Dubs found little to praise in the foreign policy of the DRA. Taraki's government denounced the U.S. presence at Diego Garcia and signaled that it would vote against the United States in favor of Puerto Rican independence. Taraki and Amin were, Dubs concluded, "dedicated communists, although of an Afghan variety that defies precise description." While Kabul still welcomed U.S. assistance, most collaborative efforts in the country had faltered. Consequently, Dubs recommended efforts to shore up U.S. allies, especially Pakistan, while maintaining a "holding pattern" within Afghanistan until its direction clarified. Subsequent events only afforded further cause for pessimism. Fighting in eastern Afghanistan intensified, driving thousands of refugees into the Pakistani borderlands. Louis and Nancy Dupree, long-time fixtures of the American community, were detained by police, threatened, and effectively expelled from the country. A new all-red national flag debuted in October, and at year's end Taraki made his first official trip abroad to the Soviet Union.[73]

An unflinching assessment did not lead Dubs to advocate confrontation, however. He argued that efforts to overthrow the DRA would only bring civil war and Soviet intervention, suggesting instead "retaining a foot in the door in the hopes that the Soviets, as they have done elsewhere, would eventually alienate the Afghans." Modest, well-targeted aid could preserve some influence while awaiting better circumstances. His superiors agreed. A cable approved by Newsom and Thornton observed, "The most adverse development in terms of our interests would be the introduction of Soviet combat troops in Afghanistan."[74] Engagement remained Washington's policy in Afghanistan, albeit in diminished form.

The End of Diplomacy, February–December 1979

The first cable reached Washington shortly after midnight on February 14, 1979, reporting the abduction of Ambassador Dubs. Gunmen disguised as policemen had halted his car around 8:45 A.M., directing his chauffeur to drive to the Kabul Hotel, where they barricaded themselves and their captive in a second-story room. U.S. diplomats raced to the hotel, imploring Afghan police and Soviet advisors to avoid forceful action and to negotiate with the kidnappers. At the hotel, police asked diplomat Bruce Flatin to communicate with Dubs through the door. Flatin and Dubs conversed briefly in German before the suspicious gunmen silenced their captive. The police prepared to storm the room, even as Flatin and his colleagues protested. The embassy desperately attempted to reach Amin, as Afghan security forces swarmed the second-story hallway and snipers deployed across the street. Soviet and Afghan personnel commenced firing at 12:50 P.M., and a gunfight raged for forty seconds. "They went in and firing is over," Amstutz cabled despairingly from the embassy. Inside Room 117, the ambassador lay dead, killed by some combination of bullets from his kidnappers and purported rescuers.[75]

The killing of Adolph Dubs has prompted decades of investigation and speculation; it is questionable whether a definitive explanation will ever emerge. No plausible explanation does the DRA any credit. The most generous interpretation of the Afghan response, held by some in Washington, ascribed an appalling combination of arrogance and incompetence to the authorities. For Americans in Kabul, more sinister explanations came readily to mind. The subsequent behavior of Afghan officials compounded their distrust. Three kidnappers had been apprehended, one unharmed, but the authorities produced *four* bodies, two of whom Flatin did not recognize. The weapon that had killed Dubs remained unaccounted for. At best, the DRA compounded misjudgment with mendacity. At worst, Amin's suspicion of U.S. diplomacy yielded lethal results.[76]

Forty-five days into a tumultuous new year, the killing wrought profound consequences. Within the embattled republic, it reduced bilateral diplomacy to an empty exercise. Elevated in rank by the tragedy, understandably furious toward his host government, Amstutz continued to meet with Afghan officials, including the detested Amin. The exchanges became stale and repetitive. Striving to preempt Congress, meanwhile, the White House sharply reduced aid to Afghanistan.[77] Increasing safety concerns, driven by escalating violence and the apparent hostility of the DRA, augured a reduction in both personnel and purpose, as U.S. policy shifted toward confrontation, and rebellion erupted within Afghanistan. The collapse of local diplomacy—between Americans and Afghans, and between the superpowers in Kabul—removed a crucial restraint, allowing tensions and rhetoric to spiral further. Alarmism supplanted dialogue, as policymakers in Washington and Moscow peered anxiously at regional maps.

Widely felt outrage and feelings of failure served to initiate this cycle. The American media appended the Dubs murder to an ungainly, expanding list of Carter's purported failings. Carter's normalization of relations with China, achieved in December, had already inflamed domestic supporters of Taiwan. China's February 17 invasion of northern Vietnam aroused fears of a clash between Beijing and Moscow and criticism of Carter's policy. Events in Iran furthered the indictment. The disconsolate Shah had fled the country in January, effectively ceding power to an unruly coalition of opponents. Two hours after reports of Dubs's kidnapping reached Washington, another call notified the State Department of a large mob storming the embassy in Tehran. Bewildered officials wondered briefly if the two events were somehow connected. Critics assailed Carter as indecisive and weak. Several Republican presidential hopefuls invoked the murdered Dubs. "Both abroad and at home the United States is seen as indecisive, vacillating, and pursuing a policy of acquiescence," Brzezinski informed Carter in February.[78]

Public criticism only intensified anger within the administration toward the DRA and its Soviet sponsors. "Spike Dubs was simply sacrificed," fumed Brzezinski's deputy, David Aaron. A visibly distraught Carter consoled Dubs's wife and daughter at Andrews Air Force Base. His wife, Rosalynn, and Vice President Walter Mondale headed the official delegation of mourners at Dubs's funeral. While the White House did not immediately express its outrage, neither did the feeling lie dormant. The French embassy in Washington discerned an "immense and sincere wave of indignation."[79]

Such emotions spurred presidential concern about geopolitical currents in Afghanistan's region. On December 2, 1978, Brzezinski described to Carter a geographic "arc" from Bangladesh to the Arabian Peninsula as

Washington's area of "greatest vulnerability." Citing crises in Iran, Pakistan, India, Saudi Arabia, and Turkey, he predicted: "We are confronting the beginning of a major crisis, in some ways similar to the one in Europe in the late 40s," as "fragile social and political structures" fragmented, to Moscow's advantage. If Carter did not embrace the notion of a hazardous arc initially, others did after Brzezinski elucidated it publicly on December 20.[80] Shortly before the Shah abdicated, *Time* magazine's cover displayed a "Crescent of Crisis": a honey-hued swath of terrain from South Asia to the Horn eyed greedily by a ravenous bear. Revolution in Iran spurred efforts by policymakers to shore up a faltering security system. Looking past evidence of local disaffection with the Shah, Brzezinski and his aides searched for proof of Soviet instigation.[81] Opportunistic Soviet propaganda within Iran angered them. "I get the sense from Iran, Afghanistan, and Vietnam that the Soviets are feeling their oats," Brzezinski's aide, Michel Oksenberg, wrote.[82]

Moscow's mood was not so sanguine. China's invasion of Vietnam alarmed the Kremlin, which responded by deploying divisions along the Sino-Soviet border and airlifting military materiel to Hanoi.[83] A privileged position in the new Afghanistan, meanwhile, gave Moscow and its allies, if anything, a more disquieting perspective. One bracing autumn telegram that reached East Berlin reported the slaughter of party leaders and their families by insurgents in southern and central provinces.[84] Taraki's bellicose rhetoric toward Pakistan necessitated a scolding from Brezhnev.[85] Often delivered multiple times, to different governments, aid requests from the DRA strained notions of communist solidarity. "The Afghan comrades are only very seldom prepared to perceive the problems and difficulties of the socialist states," complained the East German embassy.[86] Yet Moscow provided generous support, in part because the DRA had cannily exploited Soviet anxieties about the revolution in Iran.[87]

Such fears preceded the first major challenge to the Khalqists. On March 15, antagonized by months of repressive policies, villagers outside of Herat revolted. The uprising spread to the city, drawing support from the local garrison.[88] The mutiny alarmed the Politburo, as did an initially blithe regime response. Taraki's subsequent request for the assistance of soldiers from the Central Asian republics stunned Soviet Premier Alexei Kosygin. "Hundreds of Afghan officers were trained in the Soviet Union. Where are they all now?" he asked. "Most of them are Muslim reactionaries," Taraki replied.[89]

Recounting the conversation, Kosygin sparked a cathartic Politburo exchange about the troublesome Khalqists. KGB chairman Yuri Andropov termed Afghanistan unready for socialism, opining: "We know Lenin's teaching about a revolutionary situation. Whatever situation we are talking about in Afghanistan, it is not that type of situation." Politburo member Andrei Kirilenko gave voice to the frustration in the room, exclaiming about the DRA, "We gave it everything. And what has come of it? It has come to nothing of any value." Opinion coalesced quickly against dispatching soldiers. Foreign Minister Andrei Gromyko rejected Afghan claims of external interference, terming the violence an "internal affair." With unnerving prescience, he predicted the consequences of military intervention:

> The army there is unreliable. Thus, our army, when it arrives in Afghanistan, will be the aggressor. Against whom will it fight? Against the Afghan people first of all, and it will have to shoot at them. . . . And all that we have done in recent years with such effort in terms of detente, arms reduction, and much more—all that would be thrown back. China, of course, would be given a nice present. All the nonaligned countries will be against us. In a word, serious consequences are to be expected from such an action.

The Politburo subsequently agreed to expand military and economic aid to Afghanistan while counseling Taraki and Amin against further repression. The March deliberations seemingly set firm limits on the use of Soviet power but also, fatefully affirmed a long-standing special relationship with Kabul. Gromyko observed: "Under no circumstances may we lose Afghanistan. For sixty years now we have lived with Afghanistan in peace and friendship."[90]

Confoundingly, that objective mandated rhetorical solidarity with Kabul. While the Politburo privately scorned Taraki's claim of foreign interference, the uprising illuminated fundamental problems with Khalqist governance. Addressing the latter through comradely suasion required granting the former public credence. Thus, Soviet publications accused the United States and Britain of training and supplying the rebels. The newspaper *Pravda* charged Washington with trying to create a new anti-DRA "Islamic bloc" to replace the now-defunct CENTO alliance. Moscow accused Pakistan of supporting the resistance, warning that it could not "remain indifferent" to further attacks against the DRA.[91]

Wittingly or otherwise, the Politburo elevated its relationship with the manipulative Khalq above its tenuous rapport with the Carter administration.

Spurious charges of U.S. involvement did not upend SALT II negotiations but did further inflame sentiment in Washington. An administration wounded by domestic criticism and concerned about Soviet influence in the Third World scarcely needed motivation to retaliate in kind. "Zbig, get CIA, [International Communication Agency], State, Congressional leaders to hit back," Carter wrote, urging emphasis of the "atheistic nature" of the Soviet and Afghan governments. "The President was angry over the Soviet allegations" read a draft memo written by Thornton. "What are we doing?" Mondale asked the NSC staff. "This is a case where the Russians have gotten themselves at odds with the Muslims and the point ought to be made." Depicting the Afghan conflict as a battle between Islam and atheism offered a wider message—especially in Iran, where Carter still hoped to salvage some influence. Lastly, it released some of the anger held personally by Carter and Mondale, accelerating a search for answers to the latter's question.[92]

Political warfare represented the first front of the escalating superpower contest over Afghanistan. Washington agencies strove to rebuff allegations of U.S. involvement in Herat while publicizing Moscow's deepening entanglement and the DRA's human rights abuses. Voice of America covered Afghan events closely, and the State Department advised regional governments of U.S. concern that Soviet accusations constituted "a smokescreen to cover their greater involvement in Afghanistan." "This Afghanistan issue poses a good opportunity for us," Mondale advised the SCC in a pivotal meeting on April 6: "It is embarrassing to them. It would be nice for us to be seen on the other side."[93]

Covert action presented a knottier problem. The uprising transformed CIA analyses of the nascent Afghan resistance. It did not resolve, however, questions of Soviet intentions in Afghanistan. As CIA analyst Arnold Horelick reasoned, U.S. support to the resistance could provide Moscow with an alibi to justify its own deepening role or it could galvanize them to do so. If the Kremlin already sought the Sovietization of Afghanistan, covert support of the rebels would increase the cost it sustained. This might afford some satisfaction and would certainly embarrass Moscow, but no program could keep the Soviets out. The dilemma of spring 1979 offered a bleak variation of that first confronted by Eisenhower a quarter-century earlier: insufficient action could embolden the Soviets; too great an effort would afford them either cause or pretext to act militarily. One's analysis hinged on what one thought Moscow wanted in Kabul—and elsewhere.[94]

Unsurprisingly, consensus did not reign. CIA analyses questioned Moscow's willingness to intervene; such action would "undermine Soviet influence and prestige" around the world. Similarly, the U.S. embassy in Moscow doubted that the Soviets would risk the SALT II talks, reporting accurately that senior officials distrusted, even "hated" the Khalqists. The factors cited by Gromyko when he warned against military action were readily identifiable in Washington. By Horelick's analysis, if Moscow was uncertain about Afghanistan, visible covert action risked forcing a decision: presenting the Kremlin with a clear "challenge on their periphery." Standing against these cautionary observations were arguments that rejected ambiguity or flowed from outrage. Brzezinski believed that Moscow intended military intervention and described, in the April 6 meeting, the ongoing "takeover of Afghanistan." Global perceptions of Soviet behavior afforded him certainty. He spoke of "[keeping] the situation boiling the way that they have kept it boiling for us" elsewhere. Asked what covert action achieved, Brzezinski countered, "If you don't do it, you lose an opportunity." He recognized the political benefits of a conflict between the Soviets and the Afghan resistance but declined to see them as factors capable of deterring intervention. Brzezinski's certitude simplified the problem: the only real question was what price Washington might extract from its irredeemably expansionist adversary. Mondale framed matters succinctly: "The Russians are getting away with murder and we should not take it."[95]

By Brzezinski's account, Mondale's "forceful pep talk" swayed the SCC to approve exploratory negotiations with Pakistan. Aiding the rebels would require a presidential finding, but even dialogue carried its own costs. Any expression of interest could encourage Zia to arm the rebels while rebalancing the shaky post-CENTO relationship with Islamabad. Washington had just terminated aid to Pakistan after having failed to stem Islamabad's nuclear ambitions. Zia's execution of Bhutto, two days earlier, raised concerns of further unrest. Washington faced the confounding problem of checking Pakistan's nuclear program while reassuring Zia that he otherwise enjoyed Washington's support. Tenuous ties to India further complicated matters. Vance observed that actions taken toward Islamabad should not "cause excessive hazards" to the relationship with New Delhi. Yet Zia promised to drive a hard bargain, most likely at the expense of his eastern neighbor.[96]

The nature of aid remained undetermined and hinged on the CIA's assessments. Early proposals had ranged widely, from propaganda to nonlethal or lethal support, to wildly improbable notions of encouraging a countercoup in Kabul. Carter's directives had already advanced some anti-DRA campaigns, but State Department opposition stalled a CIA-proposed campaign within Afghanistan. Contacts with resistance representatives convinced the CIA of the necessity of financial and material assistance, especially food, clothing, and medical supplies. Yet the White House moved incrementally. Sentiment in the April 6 SCC meeting favored the provision of nonlethal supplies, and Zia's fear of angering the Soviets set upward bounds. A subsequent meeting on June 26 led Carter to sign two presidential findings authorizing nonlethal assistance, support for radio broadcasts and other forms of insurgent propaganda, and exploration of humanitarian aid to the growing numbers of refugees in Pakistan. Carter authorized the action on July 3, two weeks after he and Brezhnev signed the SALT II agreement in Vienna.[97]

Carter's July 3 finding was more culmination than turning point. His order to respond to communist propaganda had already set his administration against the DRA. CIA analyst Samuel Hoskinson advised in April, "We are well into a war [of] words and propaganda with the Soviets and it's not clear who is going to win." Washington embraced a rare opportunity to depict Moscow as hostile to Islam. Publicizing Soviet involvement increased the prospective costs of further intervention, perhaps prohibitively, while placating allies. Aid to the resistance—$695,000 initially—was framed similarly and given in hopes of encouraging Pakistan, Saudi Arabia, and others to act in parallel. Absent from the discussions was any positive notion of drawing the Soviets into Afghanistan. Some policymakers perceived deeper involvement as foreordained, others as avoidable, but all deemed it undesirable and inimical to U.S. interests. Shared outrage, concerns about credibility, and the conviction that Moscow should pay a price for its Afghan policy offered easy points of consensus within a divided administration.[98]

Within Afghanistan, the United States had little to lose. The last Peace Corps personnel departed in mid-April. Counter-narcotics collaboration stalled. Textbooks supplied through the U.S. educational assistance program were destroyed by the Khalq, and Afghans who had collaborated with the program were imprisoned or executed. Recurrent violence necessitated the aerial evacuation of Americans from the Helmand Valley, the only remaining locus of aid activity. Amstutz proposed drawing down the mission and planned for its potential evacuation, along uncertain roads, to Peshawar. Safety and morale became daily concerns as the community contracted. The July evacuation of civilian dependents angered the DRA, which directed the embassy to reduce its staff. The routine harassment, arrest, and even torture of Afghans employed by the U.S. mission offered frequent reminders of the Khalq's hostility. "We show the flag, are trying to keep Washington informed, and are ready to duck when the shells fly over," Amstutz wrote stoically.[99]

Some activities gained urgency amid the grim atmosphere. Human rights reporting provided a revealing indictment of the Khalq, which—deeply conscious of its international image—proved highly sensitive to criticism. The teeming prison at Pul-i-Charkhi featured prominently in embassy reports. "It is a rare family at Kabul that does not have a relation or friend out there," Amstutz wrote. U.S. criticism drew an irate response from Taraki, who protested that his regime *only* held 1,356 political prisoners, not the thousands reported in Western media. U.S. officials countered by suggesting that Pul-i-Charkhi alone contained 15,000, estimating that 3,000 executions had been conducted. Citing mass abuses, the U.S. delegation to the ADB pivoted suddenly, now opposing all loans to the DRA.[100]

Figure 10.1 Afghan civilians amid the wreckage of civil war, April 1979
Source: Getty

The Kabul embassy also reported on the spreading insurgency. With hindsight, Amstutz and his peers performed remarkable work: disseminating credible eyewitness accounts of the Herat uprising, the temporary seizure of Pul-i-Khumri by rebels, and an army mutiny in Jalalabad. One scarcely needed to leave embassy grounds to observe the war. A barrage of midday gunfire on August 5 alerted the embassy to a mutiny within the garrison at Bala Hissar, a venerable hill fortress on the southern side of Kabul. Tanks and helicopter gunships shelled the mutineers into submission, but the battle highlighted the DRA's "growing shortage of trustworthy military manpower," calling the regime's viability into question.[101]

So, too, did a series of surprisingly candid conversations with Warsaw Pact officials. The bloc's waning esteem for the Khalq was no secret. Nor had its failure to deport the Parchamist diplomats home, to certain death, gone unnoticed. Soviet ambassador Anatoly Dobrynin admitted to some difficulties with Taraki in a winter conversation with Vance. Yet Kabul necessarily emerged as the nexus of inter-bloc communications about Afghanistan. Soviet diplomat Alexander Morozov complained vividly in May about the DRA to an American colleague, citing unrealistic goals, strained relations between Soviet advisors and their clients, and continued mass repression. He clearly feared that his government would become enmired in Afghanistan.[102]

More remarkable still were several summer conversations involving East German ambassador Hermann Schwiesau and Soviet diplomat Vasily Safronchuk. Their proximity to each other suggested some coordination between the communist allies, while variance in messaging likely derived from differences in outlook and personality. Dispatched to Kabul to supplant the faltering Puzanov, Safronchuk brought an open demeanor and a fresh perspective. He perceived easing Cold War tensions in Afghanistan as integral to his mission of stabilizing the DRA. Amstutz termed him "the most interesting Soviet diplomat I have ever met."[103]

On June 24, Safronchuk candidly described his stymied efforts to broaden the base of the DRA. Taraki and Amin were "very stubborn people": unwilling to tolerate opposition or share power. He rejected any possibility that Moscow would intervene militarily. "Every revolution must defend itself," he remarked, quoting Lenin. Sending troops, Safronchuk observed, would undermine SALT negotiations and his government's global standing. He and Amstutz agreed that the Red Army would face a difficult struggle in the mountains. Above all, Safronchuk invoked a bygone era, when superpower objectives in Afghanistan had coexisted. "Like your country," he said, "our main objective here is to promote regional stability."[104]

Safronchuk's composed presentation conveyed thorough preparation. Schwiesau's conduct, conversely, suggests some improvisation and personal frustration. Thrice in July, the affable East German informed U.S. colleagues about Safronchuk's efforts to broaden the government at Amin's expense. He derided Taraki as ineffectual and oblivious, preoccupied by his own personality cult. Unlike Safronchuk, Schwiesau spoke with evident anger and pessimism about the Khalq, echoing complaints he had made to his ministry. "We are now seeing the closing chapter of this government," he declared repeatedly, on July 17, seemingly predicting a change of regime in August. He agreed with Safronchuk that Moscow would not introduce troops while warning that his allies would require a friendly government in Kabul, whatever befell the Khalq. Afterward, Schwiesau sent Amstutz a bouquet of flowers.[105]

Safronchuk's admissions elicited interest, but the Schwiesau exchanges sparked conversation in Washington. Thornton pondered the meaning of the encounters: whether the impetus had been to improve relations, to protect U.S. citizens, or to secure U.S. acquiescence in a newly composed government. He and Brzezinski agreed that they could not accept "cosmetic changes" to the DRA, recommending the restoration of a neutral government in Kabul. In a later conversation, Safronchuk did not discuss ousting Amin or Taraki, but repeated that his government would not intervene while insisting that the revolution must be preserved. "The signals are, at the least, confusing." Thornton wrote.[106]

These were the most substantive inter-bloc exchanges on Afghanistan before December. Khalqist obstinacy doomed Safronchuk's mission, and problems of coordination and U.S. suspicion impeded his efforts at outreach. Schwiesau almost certainly said too much, heightening expectations that his colleague could not meet. Yet extant records reveal, at least retrospectively, honesty on the part of the communist envoys: an effort to signal accurately to their adversaries to avert calamity. On the question of military intervention, they could not say what was then unknowable. Schwiesau's conduct apparently rendered him unacceptable to the DRA. He departed Afghanistan suddenly in August, purportedly for medical reasons, but also after asking to speak to Flatin on an unspecified urgent matter.[107]

Separately, the U.S. intelligence community gauged the likelihood of Soviet intervention. Rebellion had spread to twenty of Afghanistan's twenty-eight provinces, dangerously straining the army. The regime only exerted control over major towns and cities, and travel between them grew uncertain. An estimated 142,000 Afghan refugees now resided in Pakistan. Moscow had exhausted all options short of committing its own soldiers, confronting an "unavoidable choice between defeat and some form of military intervention" in the assessment of CIA analyst Harry Cochran. Cochran reasoned, "Familiar great power anxieties over prestige and the credibility of commitments" could lead Moscow into an intermediate intervention, especially because it had not defended Vietnam in February. A phased intervention appeared likely to analyst Douglas MacEachin: perhaps through the deployment of combat forces to Kabul and other cities. Such a commitment could be undertaken quietly, thereby avoiding the political drawbacks of a mass deployment. Cochran, however, warned that Afghanistan represented a "special case" for the Soviets, distinct from others in the Third World. Proximity and the special history of Soviet-Afghan ties would lead Moscow to contemplate "strenuous measures" to maintain a friendly government, accepting a "temporary freeze" in relations with Washington if necessary. By his reckoning, a Kremlin wracked by indecision confronted its worst dilemma since the Cuban missile crisis.[108]

Allusions to 1962 proved jarringly pertinent that summer. Carter had reaped scant political benefit from the SALT II treaty, grappling with inflation and the aftermath of an ill-executed cabinet shake-up. Revolution in Nicaragua aroused concern about communist gains in the Caribbean just before a bizarre pseudo-crisis. Preempting leaks, the administration admitted the "discovery" of a Soviet combat brigade in Cuba, only to determine that the unit had been present since the early 1960s. Having previously deemed the brigade's presence "unacceptable," Carter subsequently sought to calm the public, pledging several steps, including the expansion of Indian Ocean naval patrols. He also urged Congress to approve the SALT treaty, whose ratification had been endangered by the furor. Carter's effort to straddle the issue irked both Brzezinski and Brezhnev. Determined to treat a seventeen-year deployment as a fresh offense, Brzezinski warned Carter that the speech risked encouraging Soviet adventurism. Baffled by the entire episode, meanwhile, the Politburo entertained the possibility that Washington was acting in bad faith.[109]

Moscow still fretted about the faltering Khalq. The KGB and Politburo faulted Amin for enacting repressive policies and for quashing efforts to create a national front government. Taraki's appearance at the September summit of the Non-Aligned Movement in Havana offered a chance to intercede with the Great Leader on a homebound Moscow stop. The notional head of the DRA would have been wise to skip the summit altogether, but he evidently felt some need to bolster his government's standing within the nonaligned world. While Brezhnev applied his powers of persuasion, urging Taraki to dismiss his subordinate, Amin feuded acrimoniously with four allies of Taraki. Upon his return, Taraki confronted an incipient crisis, as Amin demanded his rivals' arrest. The Soviets briefly considered detaining Amin but deemed it "direct interference" in Afghan affairs. A brokered meeting between the two leading Khalqists went violently awry; enraged, Amin seized control of the government late on September 14. Even as government newspapers heralded Taraki's Havana speech, the next morning, the longtime PDPA leader sat forlorn in a palace cell, and innumerable photographs of him disappeared from public view. Amin ordered his murder weeks later.[110]

Moscow's political intervention had backfired grievously, leaving Amin suspicious. The Kremlin hurriedly proclaimed its support of him, albeit without excess enthusiasm. "We must deal with the new leadership," the Politburo wrote to East Berlin, acknowledging Amin's "extreme lust for power" and "ruthlessness" toward fellow communists. Dependence on Soviet aid might constrain Amin while advisors limited his repressive tendencies.[111] Soviet assistance helped the DRA take the offensive in Paktia, but the inadvertent bombing of Soviet territory by Afghan aircraft during another campaign in Badakhshan—with some loss of life—illustrated the limits of fraternal solidarity.[112] Amin also brutally deprived his patrons of alternatives. Former prime minister Nur Ahmad Etemadi was executed in the autumn; the Khalq had already killed his successor, Mohammed Moussa Shafiq.[113]

Bizarrely, even as repression continued, Amin attempted to transfer blame for the regime's human rights abuses onto the shoulders of his murdered predecessor. On November 14, in a sudden shift away from Taraki's earlier denials, an interior ministry spokesman commenced a public reading of the names of the dead and imprisoned. Amstutz described a scene of "emotional pandemonium" as distraught Afghans gathered for news of missing family members. The public readings ended abruptly after one father committed suicide, upon learning of his son's death. At least ten thousand names had been pronounced, and the dead significantly outnumbered the imprisoned. The grotesque effort at deflection backfired, only further implicating Amin as the architect of the Khalq's brutality.[114]

Apprehending his shaky position, like other Afghan leaders before him, Amin attempted to widen his diplomatic horizons over the autumn. Like Taraki, he perceived some value in a performative nonalignment. He indirectly communicated interest in improving relations with Washington and perhaps apologizing for Dubs's death. A "loquacious," Amin received Amstutz on September 27, while his foreign minister, Shah Wali, met Newsom in New York. Much-publicized, token prisoner releases seemingly responded to Washington's human rights criticism. Having pieced together the events of September 14, Amstutz concluded that Amin had demonstrated some independence and nationalism. Nonetheless, he was unlikely to turn West, and Washington's moribund aid program afforded no leverage. After Amstutz departed for a much-needed vacation, his interim replacement, Archer Blood (a Kabul alumnus on temporary assignment), also met amicably but inconclusively with Amin in late October.[115]

Amin overrated his charms and the prospects of outreach. Neither Amstutz, who loathed him, nor Blood saw much likelihood of a thaw. Their superiors perceived greater benefits in publicly opposing the DRA than in treating privately with it. Amin's coup only further illustrated the regime's instability; an embassy confidant described the PDPA as a "bunch of scorpions biting each other to death." Of Amin's coup, Thornton observed: "Whatever the Soviet role in this, they should be made to look as if they had a hand in the operation." The influx of Soviet soldiers and their reported involvement in counterinsurgency operations suggested that an incremental intervention had already commenced. Thornton worried that a large-scale intervention would doom SALT and wondered how it might be prevented.[116]

Perversely, the humiliating Cuban brigade incident and uncertainty about Soviet intentions limited Washington's options. While earlier public statements and private conversations had conveyed U.S. disapproval, a public warning risked abetting the legislative opponents of SALT. Incremental escalation made the tipping point between an intermediate and a large commitment difficult to detect. To the State Department, this argued for rhetorical restraint. Vance's aide, Marshall Shulman, cautioned that a premature warning risked another charge of "crying wolf." The secretary did not mention Afghanistan during a September 27 meeting with Gromyko, who mused afterward to Shah Wali: "The Americans are still wavering and cannot come to a definite conclusion."[117]

Gromyko mistook reticence for indecision. Vance indeed hesitated to discuss Afghanistan, but his peers perceived opportunity and necessity in doing so. Citing the "prospect of an evolutionary intervention," Carter requested more frequent public commentary alongside efforts to advise allies and others in the DRA's neighborhood. Third countries could make Soviet intervention costlier, but the allure of a decisive regional reaction had an entrapping effect on the administration. To Brzezinski and his aides, rebukes from allies, meanwhile, offered validation and rhetorical ammunition as another decision loomed on covert action. Debating an additional allocation of funds, Newsom suggested waiting until the spring but was overruled. Brzezinski argued that demonstrating U.S. resolve to the Saudi government, which also stood ready to aid the rebels, held paramount importance.[118]

To the NSC and Defense Department, covert aid served a crucial symbolic purpose: helping to assemble a new coalition for containing Soviet power along the "arc of crisis." Distrust of the DRA offered a rare point of consensus between Washington and Islamabad. It even provided an illusory reed for renewing relations with the revolutionary Iranian government, which sometimes solicited U.S. views on Afghan affairs.[119] Although intrigued by the prospect of a Soviet Vietnam, Walter Slocombe of the Defense Department posited that one reason for aiding the rebels was "the beneficial effect on other countries (Iran, Pakistan, Saudi Arabia, even China) rather than our impact on events in Afghanistan itself." He advanced that argument after the November 4 seizure of the U.S. embassy in Tehran by student militants.[120]

The ensuing hostage crisis diverted Carter, taking immediate precedence over Afghan affairs. Concurrently, events in Tehran spurred the Politburo toward action. Senior officials feared U.S. retaliation against Iran and also the prospect of Washington seeking new signals intelligence facilities in Afghanistan to compensate for those it had recently abandoned. Andropov read fervidly into Amin's contacts with U.S. diplomats but wildly exaggerated their ramifications. When he, Gromyko, and Defense Minister Dmitri Ustinov castigated Amin for his repression and factionalism, they described reality. When they claimed that Afghanistan was shifting in "a direction which is pleasing to Washington," they engaged in unfounded projection.[121]

Admittedly, Amin recklessly stoked such speculation. He falsely told Safronchuk that Archer Blood had offered aid if Soviet troops were withdrawn. Such machinations only reinforced Andropov's image of "a power-hungry leader who is distinguished by brutality and treachery." The abrogation of the Soviet partnership with Egypt, and Cairo's subsequent swing to the West, remained a bitter, recent memory. Ailing and upset by Taraki's murder, Brezhnev proved susceptible to wilder suggestions from Andropov and

Ustinov: that Amin was a CIA agent, and that he might defect and host U.S. missiles—hundreds of rough miles from the nearest port, amid a bitter insurgency, and while U.S.-Pakistani relations remained visibly strained. Nor did the Politburo consider that the same concerns about credibility that compelled them to defend the DRA would preclude Washington from engaging it.[122]

Andropov and his fellow hawks imagined developments that would have struck anyone familiar with Washington's haphazard efforts in Afghanistan since 1942 as grossly infeasible. They did not, however, read the course of the Cold War unreasonably. The SALT II treaty remained mired in the U.S. Senate, while NATO debated the deployment of intermediate-range missiles to Western Europe. Worsening global tensions removed their prior inhibitions against action, and a shared animus against Amin tempted them to believe that his ouster could stabilize the situation and allow for a temporary intervention. The prospect of an intensifying superpower contest along their southern border, meanwhile, made most in the Politburo loath to risk a hostile regime in Kabul. Thus, they approved armed intervention on December 12, rebuffing earlier protests by senior generals that the Red Army was ill prepared to battle Afghan insurgents.[123]

Preoccupied by the hostage crisis, the Carter administration labored to gauge Moscow's intentions in Afghanistan. Satellite photography and reporting from Kabul quantified the acceleration of the Soviet deployment but did not clarify Moscow's purposes. Amstutz and the CIA station chief disagreed as to whether the Soviets contemplated Amin's removal. Cognizant of the distrust between Moscow and Kabul, the chargé posited that the Soviets had no alternative to Amin, who remained fundamentally supportive of their role in Afghanistan. In Washington, the CIA analyst MacEachin diagnosed a lingering refusal to believe that the Soviets would use their growing Afghan detachment to address their underlying problem in Kabul. An official inquiry to the Soviet embassy did not clarify matters. A Soviet diplomat observed that repeated questions about Afghanistan could be read as a U.S. effort to divert attention from Iran, shortly before Brezhnev entreated Carter to show restraint in the hostage situation.[124]

Contending with Soviet reticence and their own exhaustion, the Carter administration focused on publicizing Moscow's intervention. "Keep up PR re [Soviet] troops there," Carter instructed Vance on December 15. A December 21 SCC meeting featured brief discussion of the Afghan crisis, weighing the possibility of imminent military action against the danger of crying wolf. A rough consensus emerged: that "getting the story out" offered "the best pressure available to us to prevent the Soviets from going ahead." The policymakers most anxious about issuing a false warning were those most supportive of détente. Concern about misreading an ambiguous, albeit growing Soviet deployment fostered hesitancy among the doves, while Brzezinski and his peers perceived broad dividends in condemning an ongoing intervention.[125]

A veritable airbridge formed between the Soviet Union and the greater Kabul area before sunrise on Christmas Day, conveying around 7,700 soldiers into the capital by the following morning. Other units crossed the Amu Darya, advancing toward the Salang Pass. Attached to the theory of a gradual intervention, Brzezinski was initially skeptical that Moscow had changed course, until convinced otherwise by his aide, William Odom. Meeting on December 26, the SCC concluded that the "greatest risk we face is a quick, effective Soviet operation to pacify Afghanistan," which threatened Washington's regional standing and Carter's domestic image. It behooved the United States to "make the operation as costly as possible." The committee called for remedying the "slow" progress of covert aid but stopped short of other measures or even a public statement, deferring further deliberation until the following day.[126] Before they reconvened on the afternoon of December 27, Soviet commandos fought their way uphill, past dogged resistance, killing Amin in his palace. Battles between erstwhile socialist comrades raged throughout Kabul, a terrible portent of the decades to come.[127]

Cataclysm

Across three years, Afghanistan moved from comparative obscurity to the center of a reinvigorated Cold War. Far from exhibiting prescience, senior policymakers were repeatedly surprised by Afghan events: Daoud's overthrow, the Dubs killing, and the form if not the act of Soviet intervention. Initially obscure to Carter, chiefly significant because of its opium crop, Afghanistan came to represent the ultimate litmus test of Soviet conduct in the world. The president declared on December 31 that his opinion of the Soviets had "changed more drastically in the last week" than in the preceding time in office. Carter's deeply felt ire at Moscow's conduct explains much about his subsequent response.[128]

Afghan events from the overthrow of Daoud onward engendered shock, sympathy, anger, and suspicion. The plights of Afghans—exiles, political prisoners, and refugees—evoked outrage from an administration dedicated to advancing human rights. The Dubs killing compounded this sentiment while discrediting the DRA and its Soviet allies. Dangerous conditions and personal animus toward the Khalq debilitated diplomacy within Afghanistan, even as Amin's machinations backfired disastrously. At home, righteous indignation intertwined with unchecked alarmism, motivating pursuit of the newest Afghan opportunity.

Paradoxically, Afghanistan also held glinting possibilities amid the year's tumult. Contemplating a buckling alliance system, concerned by the prospect of Soviet aggression around the globe, the Carter administration seized the rhetorical offensive. Condemning the DRA and its Soviet patrons served diverse goals but with unequal efficacy. Vance's State Department and Thornton hoped to deter Moscow from intervening. Brzezinski, Mondale, and increasingly Carter sought to put Brezhnev on the defensive. Events in Iran animated the administration, while shared outrage and the principle of cost extraction afforded its factions a working consensus. Neither wished to see Moscow further ensconced in Afghanistan, but some believed that outcome was unavoidable and acted accordingly.

Prediction justified anticipatory action. Here, the Carter administration's factions drew apart. Brzezinski's conduct revealed his certainty; his memoranda after Christmas exhibited a sense of vindication. His counsel helped to establish policies that would endure long after he and Carter exited office. The decision to confront Moscow and Kabul entailed elevating regional priorities over the problem of Afghanistan. In the long arc of the Afghan-American relationship, the choice had ample precedent. For Americans, as for others, the country held enduring possibilities as a showcase. Afghanistan had previously been a peaceful stage for a very different type of superpower contest, and fears of provoking Soviet intervention had constrained U.S. policymakers. The fulfillment of that worst-case scenario in 1979 freed Washington's hand, rendering Afghanistan the proving ground of another, deadlier form of containment.

Conclusion

"Into the Jaws of Catastrophe"

> Woe, woe for England! Not a whit for me,
> For I, too fond, might have prevented this.
> —WILLIAM SHAKESPEARE,
> THE TRAGEDY OF KING RICHARD THE THIRD

> What happened that ruined our home?
> What unraveled the fabric of our nest?
> Do you not feel sorry that you caused this?
> —AHMAD ZAHIR, "CHE SUD"

Shaken and somber, President Jimmy Carter addressed the American public in a televised speech on the evening of January 4, 1980. After reiterating his "outrage and impatience" at the continued captivity of Americans in Iran and pledging to secure their release, the president turned to a less familiar topic: "another very serious development which threatens the maintenance of the peace in Southwest Asia." Condemning Moscow's Afghan intervention, rejecting its risible claims of having been invited, Carter announced a set of reprisals: the cessation of grain sales, the suspension of advanced technological exports, and, above all, the effective withdrawal of the SALT II treaty from consideration by the U.S. Senate. He hinted at the withdrawal of the U.S. Olympic team from the upcoming 1980 games in Moscow. Carter's response confirmed the effective end of U.S.-Soviet détente, signaling a dangerous escalation of tensions between the two superpowers. Notably, the president also endeavored, for the first time, to explain the geopolitical significance of Afghanistan to the American public at large.

The effort required geographic finesse, rhetorical alarmism, and a visual aid. Carter's address marked the first ever presidential mention of "Southwest Asia," a seldom-used but convenient term that encompassed Afghanistan,

Iran, and other lands to the west. Carter implicitly characterized the intervention as an act of "expansion." Building upon prior rhetorical efforts, he termed it "a deliberate effort of a powerful atheistic government to subjugate an independent Islamic people." He warned of the threat posed by a Soviet-held Afghanistan to its eastern and western neighbors and its potential to serve as a "steppingstone to control over much of the world's oil supplies." To illustrate the point, a colorful political map of the region appeared on-screen, gradually expanding to depict the Persian Gulf and Arabian Sea.[1]

Shock and outrage partially explain Carter's rhetoric. Yet his language attested to a maximal interpretation of Soviet objectives, one held by National Security Advisor Zbigniew Brzezinski. As much as any senior policymaker, Brzezinski ascribed imperial motivations to the Kremlin's actions. He had written, on December 26, of the "age-long dream of Moscow to have direct access to the Indian Ocean."[2] Brzezinski prudently left Peter the Great out of it, but an article he forwarded to Carter antedated this goal to the early nineteenth century.[3] In another memorandum, Brzezinski claimed, somewhat speciously, that Stalin had pursued southern expansion while he was tacitly allied with Nazi Germany.[4] A customarily broad-brush survey of postwar Soviet foreign policy he composed in early January described an unceasing expansionist pressure since 1945, limited only by the strategic balance and the strength of the U.S. reaction.[5]

Other analyses struck a more cautious tone in early 1980. Washington's prevailing assumptions, retired diplomat George Kennan advised, overlooked Moscow's long-standing concern with political stability in a neighboring state, which contained peoples also found within Soviet territory. Testifying alongside the historian Richard Pipes—who wholeheartedly endorsed the imperial thesis—Kennan proposed that the Soviet intervention had been "primarily defensive" in motivation. "They began to meddle in Afghan politics, and things went wrong for them, and they got sucked into it . . . rather involuntarily," he suggested, rebuffing any notion of further aggressive designs. Afghanistan made, he observed, a poor steppingstone for any advance into another country. Kennan contradicted Pipes at many points and enjoyed a characteristically fleeting sense that he had contributed positively to the policy debate. Yet within a year, Pipes would be ensconced in Washington, on the NSC staff of President Ronald Reagan, while Kennan fretted about "the present march of Western civilization . . . into the very jaws of catastrophe."[6]

Kennan's growing despair, evident in his post-invasion diary entries, drew heavily from his own sense of guilt. While Brzezinski encouraged Carter to enact a response commensurate to the 1947 Truman Doctrine, Kennan reexamined the counsel he had given at that time, arguing to himself that he had been misinterpreted.[7] However understandable, the effort showed. The impassioned Kennan of decades past, employing a teleological interpretation of Russian history, had depicted the Soviet Union as a relentlessly expansionist force. Kennan's 1980 pleas to ponder the peculiarities of the Afghan-Soviet relationship were overshadowed by universal, alarmist analyses that he had earlier helped set into motion. The architect of containment was left, once again, to ponder the doctrine's unforeseen but hardly improbable consequences.[8]

The Triumph of Alarmism

Kennan's original diagnoses, refined and modified by his successors up to Brzezinski, easily accommodated notions of Afghanistan succumbing to one or another form of Soviet intervention. Across three decades of Cold War competition within Afghanistan, Americans attributed one or another scheme to their adversary: Sudetenland-style dismantling; internal subversion; economic entrapment; and of course outright invasion, perhaps en route to somewhere else. Alarmism and misperception motivated U.S. policy at key junctures, leading them to ascribe maximalist ambitions to their communist bloc adversaries. Absent this sense of imminent danger, the case for diplomacy and aid appropriations would have lacked the requisite urgency. As would have the entreaties of sympathetic Afghan officials.

Throughout this period, Afghan diplomacy managed an improbable, remarkable balancing act. Consolidating their earlier successes in advancing the formalization of relations, they sought and maintained a vital tie with Washington. *Bi-tarafi*, Afghanistan's form of nonalignment, predated not just the Cold War but also the world wars. It lent successive Afghan leaders a shared framework, while its reputation preceded it into the capitals of great powers. It enabled leaders and representatives to convince

Americans of the sincerity of their Pashtunistan advocacy, if not of the merits of the case itself. Successive governments in Kabul maintained amicable relations with both blocs, practicing a reticent nonalignment while soliciting aid from all interested parties. Remarkably, Afghanistan appears to have enjoyed the benefit of the doubt from both blocs: from the first Daoud era, through the constitutional experiment, and during the first republic. The year of the first border crisis, 1955, witnessed the greatest risk of confrontation, but President Dwight D. Eisenhower ultimately decided upon a course of engagement.

He did so because his own representatives in Kabul, themselves influenced by contacts with Afghan officials, proved persuasive. From Cornelius Engert onward, diplomats in Kabul lobbied emphatically for the interests of their mission. The strength of their appeals constituted a key factor, even as their content varied considerably. Engert's advocacy meaningfully affected Afghan economic life, reducing the strains of wartime deprivation. Postwar churn limited the embassy's effectiveness during pivotal times, allowing disastrous decisions made elsewhere to proceed. Effective local diplomacy could serve as a vital check on ill-considered policies crafted elsewhere; its absence could and did prove disastrous. It was not the strongest factor in play; rather, it proved the most variable. At its most effective, it served to identify meaningful opportunities in Afghanistan while informing policymaker perceptions, thus mending the flaws in one or another grand strategy.

If Angus Ward's embassy helped convince Washington of Afghanistan's significance within the Cold War, his successors—influenced by their contacts with Afghan officials—argued persuasively that the struggle was not lost. Dedicated ambassadors from Sheldon Mills onward lobbied passionately for waging the Cold War within Afghanistan. Absent their appeals, Washington's regional strategy would have unfolded differently. The adoption of Iran and Pakistan as strategic allies made the continued reassurance of their governments a vital interest. That might have suggested confrontation with Kabul; Ward had at least dabbled with the possibility. But his successors held otherwise, attesting that their hosts valued their independence from the bloc. Thus, while the reassurance of allies galvanized an interest in Afghanistan, interactions within the country fostered a distinctive optimism. Washington shared Iranian and Pakistani concern but differed significantly in its assessments of what could be achieved, at times appearing indulgent to its frustrated allies. Afghanistan was not expressly incorporated into the U.S.

alliance system. Rather, it emerged as a Cold War buffer state that could neither be enlisted nor rejected.

This choice kept it in a kind of limbo. The problem of Afghanistan could at best be managed—and remarkably it was for perhaps a quarter century. Here, again, local diplomacy played a necessary role in the day-to-day management of a difficult situation, especially during the second border crisis. In early 1963, it worked to the detriment of Daoud's government and the benefit of its rivals within the royal family, even as it staved off a policy choice more outwardly confrontational toward the kingdom. Perceptive local diplomacy could forestall hazardous policy choices, but its ultimate success hinged on arbitrary factors within Washington.

Kabul was losing its geopolitical leverage. Peaceful, albeit anxious Cold War competition faded into tacit coexistence by the mid-1960s, and U.S. policymakers stopped speculating about a southward Soviet advance. Several interrelated factors contributed to the calm. The ebbing of U.S.-Soviet tensions after the Cuban missile crisis yielded a less fervid atmosphere, in which alarmist analyses wielded less persuasive power. Separately, inter-bloc dialogue within Afghanistan built upon interpersonal rapport, fostering an informal understanding of each other's minimum goals. It is doubtful that any other Third World arena witnessed the degree of dialogue or tacit collaboration seen within Afghanistan. The Afghans had encouraged the adversaries toward a constructive definition of peaceful coexistence. Ultimately, however, contacts forged among foreigners in Kabul undermined the host government's capacity to pit the blocs against each other.

So did fundamental doctrinal and political changes in Washington (and Moscow). If Daoud and Naim had escaped the personalized opprobrium heaped upon better-known nonaligned statesmen, Afghan aid allotments still hinged entirely on the fortunes of the foreign assistance budget. The politics that had abetted Eisenhower and Kennedy's aid advocacy changed capriciously by 1963, for reasons only somewhat related to the course of the Cold War. Thereafter a self-imposed frugality curbed the appeals of Afghans and the U.S. country team alike, even as the kingdom embarked upon an unprecedented if flawed constitutional project. Communist bloc fatigue with capital-intensive aid had also become unmistakable and a recurrent topic of inter-bloc conversations, compelling enough to help ardent Cold Warrior John Steeves reach concord with his Soviet counterpart.

They had ample cause for concern. The pursuit of opportunity in the early Cold War years was a largely Afghan story, resulting in a country strewn with major projects, in various stages of completion. If Afghan elites felt compelling cause to seek aid, the politics and consequences of rapid development proved destabilizing. The Helmand project alienated local Pashtuns and facilitated Daoud's covert campaign against Shah Mahmud. Daoud's runaway modernization fostered inflation, while his efforts at revenue collection drew violent resistance, including the 1959 Kandahar riots. The kingdom's diverse array of patrons inhibited planning and coordination and encouraged imprudent counterbidding. An inescapable conflict loomed between development and continued appeals for Pashtunistan. U.S. diplomacy helped to illuminate it; Zahir's ouster of his cousin confirmed that he perceived the choice.

The constitutional experiment acknowledged the decades-old desire for political reform, and successive prime ministerial governments sought aid—with far less success than their authoritarian predecessor. Yet the fractious parliament, further agitated by the capital's growing student population, balked at close collaboration with the king and his chosen prime ministers. Efforts to improve Afghanistan's position within the nonaligned world and to placate student sentiment drove a wedge between Prime Ministers Mohammed Yusuf and Mohammed Hashim Maiwandwal and President Lyndon Johnson. Development imperatives, driven by U.S. frugality, led to a disastrous early response to the famine of the early 1970s, which treated "self-help" as a coequal goal with relief.

In another sense, the aid race, while superficially beneficial, weakened the Afghan state. Once again, rival factions within the Afghan elite could employ contacts with foreign governments toward their parochial benefit. Such efforts could fail—Abdul Majid Zabuli and Mohammed Kabir Ludin suffered for their Morrison-Knudsen advocacy—but they continued, nevertheless. The Shah Wali faction's tacit contacts with Steeves aided their campaign against Daoud in early 1963. Mohammed Moussa Shafiq clearly benefited, amid the crisis of 1972, from Washington's good favor—yet Daoud's own contacts with foreign governments enabled his seizure of power in July 1973. Afghans, not foreigners, held the initiative in these episodes, but the ensuing churn hardly promoted effective governance, careful planning, or domestic legitimacy. In an era of diminished international leverage, after 1963, chastened by the second border crisis, Afghan governments could not employ Pashtunistan rhetoric to the same effect. Iran's increasing affluence as an oil exporter, meanwhile, weakened Kabul's position on the Helmand waters. Not able to deliver upon promises of modernization or to placate nationalist sentiment, Afghan leaders faced a growing crisis of legitimacy.

Daoud exploited and inherited the crisis. Partially dependent on the Parcham, initially more confrontational toward Afghanistan's neighbors, he, too, had to confront the limits imposed externally upon him. While local diplomacy enabled renewed U.S. engagement in Kabul, superpower détente limited the willingness of either Washington or Moscow to spend lavishly in Afghanistan or to ascribe great malevolence to the other. Doctrines of U.S. aid had shifted considerably from those of the 1950s. Richard Nixon and his successors, meanwhile, had become highly focused on the hitherto secondary question of narcotics. Retaining his grand designs, Daoud faced a choice between continued borderlands agitation or petro-lender largesse, ultimately opting for the latter.

Absent sustained attention from Washington, in the absence of elevated threat perception, local diplomacy preserved a useful tie to Daoud's republic and facilitated regional dialogue. Interpersonal dynamics in these years offered a local microcosm of the détente regime. Ambassador Theodore Eliot read Daoud's intentions correctly, but gauging the stability of his regime proved a far more difficult problem. In his defense, the success of the Marxist coup was hardly foreordained. The plotters benefited from the conditional assistance of nationalists like Abdul Qadir; even then, as Louis Dupree writes, it occurred "by a series of accidents."[9]

Did the bloodshed of April 1978 make a superpower confrontation in Afghanistan inevitable? Not by itself. Subsequent acts by the Khalq, undertaken against Soviet advice, heightened that possibility. Their purging of the diplomatic corps—once in spring 1978, again in the summer—undermined a crucial pillar of Afghanistan's international standing. In Kabul and foreign capitals, persecuted and grieving Daoudists and Parchamists attested to the new regime's brutality and erratic character. Whether inept or malicious, Hafizullah Amin's conduct in the Adolph Dubs incident in February 1979 wrought a comparable effect on the U.S. mission: embittering his successors and inhibiting their efforts. So, of course, did the spreading insurrection provoked by ill-conceived Khalqist policies.

Yet Afghanistan remained a lesser concern to President Jimmy Carter before that final, fateful year. Détente-era prudence and Dubs's counsel precluded a forceful response after the April coup. To understand his administration's pivot, one should consider a grim confluence of factors. Conflict in the Third World and regional upheaval abetted a resurgent alarmism, within both the White House and the U.S. electorate, even before the Dubs killing. The emotional effects wrought in Kabul were mirrored in Washington, strengthening the hands of Carter's more hawkish advisors. Dubs's death, meanwhile, silenced the diplomat best able and most inclined to rebut claims that Moscow's Afghanistan policy constituted creeping expansionism. Anxiety and outrage fostered opportunism—a widely felt desire to place the Soviets on the defensive as Washington struggled with revolution in neighboring Iran and a regional crisis of credibility. The ensuing rhetorical battle preceded wider efforts at cost extraction. Concurrently, a comparable alarmism spread in Moscow, worsened by a Politburo animus against Amin and his faction. Ascribing the worst of intentions to the defiant Khalqist and his imagined American patrons, disregarding sage predictions made earlier in the year, the Kremlin made a disastrous choice.

The Impact of U.S. Policy

A certain fatalism can attend this history. The difficult balancing act pursued by pre-1978 Afghan governments always faced a significant chance of failure. Détente was a fragile system, whether it was localized or global in scope. Nevertheless, it is useful to ask how U.S. policy influenced Afghanistan during its prewar era: whether acts commissioned in Washington diminished or increased the likelihood that the country would become ensnarled in the global conflict. Regrettably, but irrefutably, the conclusion must be that U.S. policy inadvertently and greatly complicated Afghanistan's difficult path through the Cold War years. Three principal failures occurred: of counsel, of consistency, and of diplomacy.

Aspiration and expectation defined the Afghan-American relationship from its inception. Afghan leaders, from Amanullah onward, sought closer ties to Washington and sought to leverage business relationships into a sturdier bilateral tie. This pursuit, however, left them susceptible to poor advice. Afghanistan's wartime dependence on U.S. exports wrought transformative consequences. The eviction of Axis technicians from the country opened space for American experts. Little resistance to their employment existed in Kabul, but the State Department's sustained advocacy on behalf of Morrison-Knudsen deepened the relationship and committed the U.S. government to the postwar project of development. Overlooking the obvious lessons of an earlier generation, disregarding prescient warnings from diplomats and experts tendered well before the contract was signed, Washington exercised no meaningful oversight over its chosen instrument, as MKA advanced recklessly and spent prodigiously. Seeking to salvage the Helmand project, to which they ascribed symbolic significance, and their position within the country, U.S. policymakers endorsed the ill-advised effort to develop northern oil, thereby arousing Moscow's suspicions.

Some counsel was irresponsible. Other advice was understandable but carried unavoidable risks. The establishment of alliances with Iran and Pakistan gave the United States cause for concern whenever Kabul feuded with either neighbor. At times, explicit efforts at mediation and conflict resolution appeared suitable. Washington could hardly do otherwise—unrestrained conflict over the borderlands or the Helmand waters posed its own dangers—but efforts at conflict resolution bore two undesirable consequences. Within Afghanistan, governments that appeared too deferential to either neighbor courted a nationalist backlash. The Soviet Union, meanwhile, nursed suspicions of a pact-building agenda, which waned and waxed according to the broader tenor of the Cold War.

Changes in U.S. aid policy, and in the Washington bureaucratic landscape meanwhile, repeatedly jolted the bilateral relationship. Washington shifted over time from lending, toward grant aid including relief grain, toward a Rostovian emphasis on economic takeoff, toward frugality accompanied by admonitions to practice "self-help," and lastly toward a notionally grassroots-focused program. Its willingness to support aid projects on political grounds varied widely over time. Afghans grappled with, at different times, the wartime import regime, Point Four, the Eximbank, the PL-480 program, the Development Loan Fund, and the Asian Development Bank. Hopeful statements made by U.S. representative in Kabul did not always correspond to the detached assessments of their superiors in Washington. Afghan requests were ambitious and not always feasible, but Kabul officials can be forgiven for their occasional expressions of bafflement, while the complaints of the U.S. mission form, in composite, an indictment of an aid program hamstrung by bureaucratic fragmentation and domestic politics. Some ambassadors proposed reforms: Henry Byroade called for multi-year lending; his successor, Steeves, suggested a low-cost advisory program focused on rural needs. Adopted and implemented deliberately and patiently, these measures could have added a valuable consistency to U.S. aid.

More vital, however, would have been a recognition that aid to Afghanistan served fundamentally political ends. Specifically citing the Soviet-paved streets of Kabul, the great political scientist Hans Morgenthau argued for that conception.[10] Afghan aid could not be rationalized primarily on a basis of cost-efficiency or a self-concluding timetable, so long as the Cold War raged, and Washington remained invested in its Iranian and Pakistani alliances. Aid was unlikely to generate economic takeoff, but food donations could limit the worst effects of drought and famine. Rural assistance programs, drawing upon the lessons of the Helmand, might have contributed to food security. The unstable nature, quantity, and implementation of U.S. aid served donor and recipient poorly. So did the sudden intrusions of other, unrelated concerns—the Vietnam War and counter-narcotics policy among them.

Hindsight, of course, imperils this argument. For much of the time chronicled, Afghans and Americans remained enamored of capital-intensive development. Indeed, it is clear that Daoud and Naim never set aside their penchant for grandiosity. A better aid program could not have offered a panacea against all forms of domestic upheaval. While Afghanistan enjoyed relative peace during the first quarter century of the Cold War, foreign diplomats confronted, by the early 1970s, the possibility of profound change in Kabul. Although it came via the return of the familiar Daoud, the violent overthrow of the constitutional regime augured further disorder. It is here that the final failure bears relevance.

Even considering the fragility of its governments, Afghanistan's arc, from a peripheral, symbolic venue of competition to military battleground remains bizarre and senseless. Neither superpower truly wanted to fight there. Whereas Washington drew cautionary lessons from early missteps and took quick measure of its disadvantages, Moscow primarily sought a quiet southern border. Soviet leaders held no illusions about the prospects for socialism in a rural, highly religious society, steeped in a historical suspicion of Russia. Rather, Afghanistan offered them a showcase within the nonaligned world. Both blocs discerned the willingness of successive Afghan governments to play them against each other, as frustrations with their development programs accumulated. After the missile crisis, each had incentive to limit the contest. Their failure to do so constitutes tragedy.

Congressman James Richards hit on the idea shortly after his 1957 visit to Kabul. Having fulfilled the Quixotic task of carrying the Eisenhower Doctrine to Afghanistan, he suggested formalizing Afghan neutrality, invoking the earlier case of Switzerland. The span of the Cold War witnessed numerous agreements between the superpowers to limit the scope of their competition. A pact that dictated Afghan neutrality and circumscribed U.S.

and Soviet involvement in the country would have addressed the respective concerns of all parties. Had it been a more pressing concern—a Berlin or a Cuba—Afghanistan might have been the object of sustained, high-level inter-bloc dialogue. In the comparative context, however, the escalation of the Afghan Cold War falls into another category. Like postwar Korea, Afghanistan held an ill-defined intermediate value, gauged primarily in terms of how neighboring powers would react to a sudden change in its alignment. Overshadowed by familiar areas of conflict, it thus escaped mention in superpower summits before 1979.

Afghan leaders would have resented superpower negotiations above their heads. At the least, such exchanges limited their diplomatic leverage; at worst, they could constitute insidious imperial bargaining. Yet Washington and Moscow could have formalized the tacit understanding reached by their Kabul representatives in the 1960s. The most important element of any bilateral agreement would have been a shared nonintervention pledge: a mutual commitment not to seek predominance in Afghanistan, thus capping the Afghan Cold War at a symbolic level. Instead, sporadic interpersonal contacts formed a necessary but insufficient restraint. Vasily Safronchuk and Hermann Schwiesau's summer 1979 approaches to a beleaguered U.S. mission represented the final meaningful exchange.

Diplomacy—in Kabul, Washington, Moscow, or elsewhere—had some prospect of curbing the escalation of the Afghan Cold War. In its absence, at moments of anxiety or anger, policymakers fell back on familiar, generalized images of their adversary. Afghanistan's internal complexity and nebulous geographic setting lent themselves to a variety of scenarios. So did the predilection of early Cold War analysts—Kennan among them—to ascribe traditional imperialist objectives to the Soviet state. Another interpretation, noting the wide chasm between Soviet notions of socialism and Afghan conditions, the frequent laments of communists in Kabul, and the historic special relationship between the Bolshevik state and the Afghan kingdom, could have advanced less alarmist conclusions.

Instead, the image of Russian imperialism in an altered guise shaped the expectations of Brzezinski and his successors in the Reagan administration. Contemplating Moscow's chances, both thought less of the Anglo-Afghan Wars than of the Red Army's successful campaigns against Basmachi rebels. The aid program initiated by Brzezinski and his peers—as an early effort at cost extraction rather than a Machiavellian entrapment scheme—was continued by his Republican successors, who nursed similar expectations of

Soviet behavior and who came, from afar, to affix their own symbolism to the war in Afghanistan.[11]

Afghanistan was not then known as a "graveyard of empires." Rather, it was a Cold War battlefield that boasted an array of mundane traits that combined ultimately and invidiously to its profound and lasting misfortune. If Afghan leaders stoked the competition to a degree, Afghanistan's deluge derived from the willingness of others to render it a canvas for grand designs on their own part, and menacing intentions on the part of others. It retained this characteristic long after the Soviet withdrawal, to the enduring sorrow of its inhabitants and countless others.

After One Century

Contemporary Afghanistan contains countless mementos of the pre-1979 Cold War—all marked and redefined by the twenty-year U.S. war with the Taliban. The irrigation ditches of the Helmand project offered the insurgents ideal sites for ambushes. The U.S.-led coalition labored to repair the Kajakai Dam, which entailed the hazardous transport of a massive 220-ton turbine across Helmand Province. Once delivered, it went uninstalled for years and sat gathering rust—like the wayward Morrison-Knudsen equipment of yore. Kandahar's airport, a major coalition air base, witnessed a pitched battle between government and infiltrating Taliban forces in December 2015, in which dozens were killed. Its Soviet-built counterpart in Kabul provided the scene for the American war's terrible final act—mere weeks after the centennial anniversary of Wali Khan's visit to the White House—as thousands of Afghans crowded the runway in a desperate bid to escape the advancing Taliban. The Panjshir Valley, where Myles Walsh once searched for silver, held out a while longer and remains a locus of resistance. Kabul University, perhaps the most consequential U.S. project within Afghanistan, reopened after the fall of the capital, devoid of its female faculty and students.[12]

The future of Afghanistan, at this writing, appears grim, and the United States does not appear poised to play a positive role in it. An atmosphere of mutual recrimination in the wake of failed state-building, unmet promises, and the abandonment of thousands bodes poorly. Contact between Washington and the Taliban may serve the interests of both, but it is unlikely to assume a productive tenor. Yet history cautions us against treating

Afghanistan's future as predetermined or its diplomacy as set in stone. The breadth, energy, and urgency of Afghan diplomacy once struck a chord with Americans. A far-flung, dynamic Afghan diaspora provides its own connective tissue. Foreign interests, some of them American, salivate over its extensive mineral resources. Afghanistan is distant from the concerns of many Americans but not as remote as it used to be. Wallace Murray–like attitudes may shape contemporary views of Afghanistan, but perhaps not indefinitely. The challenges of Kabul diplomacy may one day resume. "It makes a lot of difference whom we place in difficult spots like Afghanistan," President John F. Kennedy said in 1962. Six decades later, it still does.

Acknowledgments

Acknowledgments often have an autobiographical quality, and understandably so. While giving thanks, one also wants to communicate the combination of choices, interactions, acts, and circumstances that enabled a book to be written. This book took shape over a very long decade in which the global pandemic constituted the foremost but not the only intruding event. I have my pandemic-era thanks to give below, but one key fact, predating 2020, should be mentioned. In the project's early months, I was uncertain that I should write this book. A variety of factors, including a good look at two brilliant projects already under way on Afghanistan, left me deeply ambivalent, doubtful that there would be a story left to tell. That anxiety is commonplace but no less daunting for its ubiquity. I do not share this detail triumphally but rather in the hope that it affords someone some reassurance that they might be on the right track.

I would not have developed a sustained interest in Afghanistan had I not taken Thomas Simons's class in my final academic quarter in spring 2000. An early conversation with Alam Payind in spring 2009, during a fellowship at The Ohio State University's Mershon Center for International Security Studies, provided important assurance. The financial and intellectual support of the United States Studies Centre at the University of Sydney during 2011–2012 proved crucial: here I should thank Margaret Levi, Brendon O'Connor, and David Smith especially.

Mentors who were indispensable for my earlier book provided similarly invaluable aid. Mel Leffler provided his usual sage advice over the decade. Recent Californian Bob McMahon attended talks and was willing to review a late draft on short notice. He and Mel provided vital advocacy for this project, as did Fred Logevall, Nick Cullather, and Arne Westad.

Key early financial support came from two sources: the American Institute of Afghanistan Studies and the Hoover Institution. The former's early endorsement helped me to overcome my own doubts. In the case of the latter, I am especially grateful to David Brady, Heather Campbell, and Amy Zegart. Subventions from Stanford's Hamid and Christina Moghadam Program in Iranian Studies and Center for Russian, East European and Eurasian Studies facilitated its publication. I would like to give special thanks to Abbas Milani and Jovana Lazić Knežević.

Stanford has been a wonderful, enriching environment. Thanks go to IR Program chairs Judy Goldstein, Michael Tomz, and Kenneth Schultz for their support, as well as to Paul Festa, Jessica Michael, and Stephen Busse, as well as the SGS staff. Conversations with Stanford colleagues David Holloway, Scott Sagan, Norman Naimark, Asfandyar Mir, and Amir Weiner aided me considerably. Bart Bernstein brought his fierce scrutiny to bear. Bob Crews, author of a splendid book on Afghanistan, deserves special mention here for his expert advice and moral support. Benjamin Stone offered vital aid as Stanford's curator for British and American history.

The project has benefited from the insights and assistance of many Cardinal. Thanks go to the countless alums of IR 174 (where Henry Byroade's Wakhan travelogue found a wider audience). At Summer Research Colleges, stewarded by Mike Tomz, Becca Hall, and Brenna Boerman, Laura Marti (2015), and the immortal "Warsaw Pact" of 2020—Dagny Carlsson, Katherine Crandell, Anastasiia Malenko, and Elizabeth Sinyavin—offered crucial aid (and memes). Medina Husakovic provided sound editorial advice. Kyle Kinnie contributed his remarkable expertise. Molly Campbell provided stellar assistance. Many others offered encouragement of a sort by asking after the book. Alumna Mariam Amini was always keen to explain facets of Afghan history and culture. Tea given by Elena Wadden and Angela Zhang proved indispensable in staving off fatigue.

I would like to thank the authors of self-published works that often filled sizable gaps: Abdul Tawab Assifi, Jane Morrison Engert, Muhammad Khan Jallalar, Nancy Howland Washburne, and Wilbur Harlan. Wilbur's relatives, Sherry Harlan, Harry Harlan, and Ruth Harlan Lamb, helped me get to know Uncle Bill. I would also like to thank Ms. Engert for kindly according me permission to use one of her grandfather's photographs.

I would like to thank the staff at the National Archives, the Franklin Roosevelt, Truman, Eisenhower, Kennedy, Johnson, Nixon, Ford, and Carter presidential libraries, the British Library, the National Archives in Kew, the Ministry of External Affairs (MAE) archives in Paris and Nantes, the Bundesarchiv in Lichterfelde, the Auswärtiges Amt, the libraries at UCLA, the University of Nebraska Omaha, Georgetown, Boise State, Colorado State, Oklahoma University, the University of Virginia, the United Nations archives, the Idaho State Archives, and the American Heritage Center (AHC). Thanks to the State Department's Office of the Historian and David Zierler for making this possible in the first place.

I cannot hope to thank each individual archivist by name but am able to credit some who provided vital assistance, especially during the later stages of this book. Thanks go to: John Zarrillo, Jay Sylvestre, and Scott Taylor at Georgetown; Alex Meregaglia at Boise State; Susan Peschel at the University of Wisconsin-Milwaukee; Abby Cape and Amy Schindler at the University of Nebraska Omaha; Maryrose Grossman at the Kennedy Library; Chris Banks at the Johnson Library; Grégoire Eldin at the MAE; Sven Schneidereit at the Bundesarchiv in Lichterfelde; and Mary Beth Brown and Renah Miller at the AHC. Jim Duran offered valuable insights on the surviving Morrison-Knudsen records. In Cambridge, Mark Kramer made time amid a busy schedule and graciously excused a comedy of errors.

Intrepid research assistants performed essential work, especially as travel became much tougher. Special mention goes to Ondřej Pekáček in Prague, whose enthusiasm for the topic was inspiring. Sophie Stuber mastered the French diplomatic archives. Brice Bowrey offered key aid in Washington. Mattie Webb helped on very short notice. Malcolm Craig assisted in Kew.

The archives of the Czech Republic play an important role in this book. I would not have been able to employ them without the aid of Milada Polišenská, Oldřich Tůma, Jan Koura, and Francis Raska. Thanks go as well to Jara Dusatko, who endured my elephantine noun declensions.

Hospitality enabled me to visit numerous archives. I am grateful to Phil Haberkern and Danielle Dong, Todd and Judy Endelman, Landon Reid, and Allison Robbins and John Check. The Stanford-in-Washington house enabled sustained work in the National Archives—hearty thanks go to Adrienne Jamieson and the staff.

Colleagues have supported this project with sage advice and friendship. Asher Orkaby, Ali Olomi, Mejgan Massoumi, Brad Simpson, Salim Yaqub, Mary Dudziak, Sarah Cameron, Ned Richardson-Little, Matthew Jacobs, William Glenn Gray, Mario Del Pero, Kelly Shannon, Aaron O'Connell, Gregg Brazinsky, Jayita Sarkar, Sergey Radchenko, Gregory Brew, Daniel Bessner, Michael Koncewicz, Mitchell Lerner, Tim Nunan, Chris Dietrich, Susie Colbourn, Austin Jersild, Simon Miles, Conor Tobin, Christopher Lash, Mari Webel, Pierre Journoud, Matthieu Vallieres, Christian Ostermann, Artemy Kalinovsky, Jonathan Hunt, James Cameron, Paul Chamberlin, Jeff Byrne, Julia Irwin, Tanvi Madan, Marc Palen, Malcolm Jorgensen, and Chris Nichols each aided this project. Adam Dean supplied his fishing expertise. Thanks go to Mark Lawrence, Paul Miller, David Milne, C. Raja Mohan, and Lynn Eden for hosting early presentations of this material. Special thanks go to Roham Alvandi and Shah Mahmoud Hanifi for reading vital sections. As a good friend, Elisabeth Leake has been extraordinarily supportive of this endeavor. She read a complete draft, as did Ryan Irwin and Bob.

Special thanks go to colleagues who shared documents, especially during the pandemic. I'd like to credit Ben Allison, Andrew David, Karine Walther, Andrew Johnstone, Elisabeth, Tim, Sergey, and Gregory Winger.

Columbia University Press has been amazingly supportive, embracing an atypical manuscript and easing its road to publication. Thanks go to series editors Sarah Snyder and Jay Sexton. Within Columbia, Christian Winting, Michael Haskell, and Milenda Lee helped the book see print. Chris Curioli copyedited the manuscript, and Ben Kolstad at KGL served as project manager. Editor Stephen Wesley was a generous, insightful, and stalwart supporter. I would also like to thank the three anonymous readers for their careful attention, encouragement, and helpful suggestions.

Interviews helped me to fill gaps in the documentary record. I am grateful to the following people for sharing their recollections and insights: Margaret Blood and her family, Bruce and Kay Flatin, Ron and Diane Dizon, Jim Hicks, Jim Mathewson, Tim McCormack, Samuel Hoskinson, Cecil Uyehara, Howard and Teresita Schaffer, Thomas Thornton, Judge John True, and the alums of the American International School of Kabul. Ambassador Ronald Neumann and John Bergstrom assisted the biographical elements of this project. The late Ambassador Ted Eliot recounted his Kabul experiences fondly; it saddens me that we will not be able to discuss the finished book. Gary Sick, Denis Clift, and Bruce Riedel took time to correspond.

The Dizons also kindly accorded permission to use one of their remarkable photos from Afghanistan.

The 2016 Chicago Cubs provided enduring inspiration.

Family played an essential role. Roberta Rakove and Michael Plumpton welcomed me to Chicago, my home away from home. Stephen and Leslie Scharf hosted me in Los Angeles. Uncle Stevie passed away in September 2018; this book is co-dedicated to his memory. My parents, Jack and Helen Rakove, lovingly supported this project, even if their interest in hearing tales of the Helmand Valley flagged after a while. My brother and sister-in-law, Daniel and Hyesun Rakove, hosted me and kept my good cheer up. This book is co-dedicated to their children, Alex and Elliot.

Abbreviations

ADSTOH	Association for Diplomatic Studies and Training Oral History
AUFS	American Universities Field Service
SAS	South Asia Series
CF	Country Files
CIARR	CIA Reading Room
CWIHP	Cold War International History Project
DNSA	Digital National Security Archive
DOSB	Department of State Bulletin
FRUS	Foreign Relations of the United States
KT	Kabul Times
NAP	National Awami Party
NESA	Near East and South Asia
NSA	National Security Archive
NSC	National Security Council
NSF	National Security File(s)
NYT	New York Times
OCB	Operations Coordinating Board
OH	Oral History
PPP	Public Papers of the President
RGA	Royal Government of Afghanistan
SHA	Scott Helmand Archive
USDDO	United States Declassified Documents Online database
WP	Washington Post

Notes

Note: Numbered boxes and folders are denoted with colons (e.g., 1:8). Folder titles are provided when files are not arranged chronologically. Archival abbreviations can be found in the following section.

Introduction

1. Letter, Steeves to Talbot, April 15, 1965, SNF, POL AFG-US, USNA.
2. Melvyn P. Leffler, *For the Soul of Mankind: The United States, the Soviet Union, and the Cold War* (New York: Hill and Wang, 2007); Odd Arne Westad, *The Cold War: A World History* (New York: Basic Books, 2017); Lorenz M. Lüthi, *Cold Wars: Asia, the Middle East, Europe* (New York: Cambridge University Press, 2020); Jeremy Friedman, *Shadow Cold War: The Sino-Soviet Competition for the Third World* (Chapel Hill: University of North Carolina Press, 2015).
3. Leon B. Poullada and Leila Poullada, *The Kingdom of Afghanistan and the United States, 1828–1973* (Lincoln, NE: Center for Afghanistan Studies and Dageforde Publishing, 1995); Jeffery J. Roberts, *The Origins of Conflict in Afghanistan* (Westport, CT: Praeger, 2003); Rosanne Klass, ed., *Afghanistan: The Great Game Revisited* (New York: Freedom House, 1987); Tom Lansford, *A Bitter Harvest: US Foreign Policy and Afghanistan*, US Foreign Policy and Conflict in the Islamic World (Burlington, VT: Ashgate, 2003).
4. Nick Cullather, *The Hungry World: America's Cold War Battle Against Poverty in Asia* (Cambridge, MA: Harvard University Press, 2010); Timothy Nunan, *Humanitarian*

Invasion: Global Development in Cold War Afghanistan (New York: Cambridge University Press, 2016); Jenifer Van Vleck, "An Airline at the Crossroads of the World: Ariana Afghan Airlines, Modernization, and the Global Cold War," History and Technology 25, no. 1 (March 2009): 3–24; James Tharin Bradford, Poppies, Politics, and Power: Afghanistan and the Global History of Drugs and Diplomacy (Ithaca, NY: Cornell University Press, 2019); Daniel Weimer, "'It's That Difficult of a Terrain': Opium, Development, and Territoriality in US-Afghan Relations, 1940s–1970s," Social History of Alcohol and Drugs 33, no. 1 (March 2019): 113–44.

5. Lüthi, Cold Wars.
6. Gregg Brazinsky, Winning the Third World: Sino-American Rivalry During the Cold War, The New Cold War History (Chapel Hill: University of North Carolina Press, 2017); Friedman, Shadow Cold War.
7. Mohammed Kakar, Afghanistan: The Soviet Invasion and the Afghan Response, 1979–1982 (Berkeley: University of California Press, 1997), 106–9.
8. Letter, Kabul to London, June 23, 1965, FO 371/181509, UKNA.
9. Anatoly Dobrynin, In Confidence: Moscow's Ambassador to America's Six Cold War Presidents (1962–1986) (New York: Random House, 1995), 434.
10. Conor Tobin, "The Myth of the 'Afghan Trap': Zbigniew Brzezinski and Afghanistan, 1978–1979," Diplomatic History 44, no. 2 (April 2020): 237–64.
11. William C. Green, "The Historic Russian Drive for a Warm Water Port: Anatomy of a Geopolitical Myth," Naval War College Review 46, no. 2 (Spring 1993): 80–102.
12. Robert Jervis, Perception and Misperception in International Politics (Princeton, NJ: Princeton University Press, 1976).
13. G. H. Jansen, Nonalignment and the Afro-Asian States (New York: Praeger, 1966), 125.
14. Ernest F. Fox, Travels in Afghanistan, 1937–1938 (New York: Macmillan, 1943), vii.
15. Interview, Theodore Eliot with author, September 17, 2014.
16. See, among others, Jeffrey James Byrne, Mecca of Revolution: Algeria, Decolonization, and the Third World Order (New York: Oxford University Press, 2016); Thomas C. Field, From Development to Dictatorship: Bolivia and the Alliance for Progress in the Kennedy Era (Ithaca, NY: Cornell University Press, 2014); Elidor Mëhilli, From Stalin to Mao: Albania and the Socialist World (Ithaca, NY: Cornell University Press, 2017).
17. David C. Engerman, The Price of Aid: The Economic Cold War in India (Cambridge, MA: Harvard University Press, 2018).
18. Among others: Westad, The Global Cold War; Bradley R. Simpson, Economists With Guns: Authoritarian Development and U.S.-Indonesian Relations, 1960–1968 (Stanford, CA: Stanford University Press, 2008); Artemy M. Kalinovsky, Laboratory of Socialist Development: Cold War Politics and Decolonization in Soviet Tajikistan (Ithaca, NY: Cornell University Press, 2018).

19. Frank Costigliola, *Roosevelt's Lost Alliances: How Personal Politics Helped Start the Cold War* (Princeton, NJ: Princeton University Press, 2012); Barbara Keys, "The Diplomat's Two Minds: Deconstructing a Foreign Policy Myth," *Diplomatic History* 44, no. 1 (January 2020): 1–21.
20. Memorandum, David Wharton to Ely Palmer, May 4, 1948, OSAA, SFRA, box 9, "860.3 Post Report and Living Conditions," USNA.
21. Letter, Wharton to Richard Leach, July 13, 1949, ibid.
22. Henry Byroade, ADSTOH, September 19, 1988, 61.
23. Among others, Anne E. Blair, *Lodge in Vietnam: A Patriot Abroad* (New Haven, CT: Yale University Press, 1995); Natalia Telepneva, *Cold War Liberation: The Soviet Union and the Collapse of the Portuguese Empire in Africa, 1961–1975* (Chapel Hill: University of North Carolina Press, 2021); David Mayers, *FDR's Ambassadors and the Diplomacy of Crisis: From the Rise of Hitler to the End of World War II* (New York: Cambridge University Press, 2013).
24. James W. Spain, *In Those Days: A Diplomat Remembers* (Kent, OH: Kent State University Press, 1998), 192; John M. Steeves, *Safir (Ambassador)* (Hershey, PA: s.n., 1991), 142.
25. Daniel Bessner and Fredrik Logevall, "Recentering the United States in the Historiography of American Foreign Relations," *Texas National Security Review* 3, no. 2 (Spring 2020): 38–55.
26. Amin Saikal, *Modern Afghanistan: A History of Struggle and Survival* (London: I. B. Tauris, 2012); Robert D. Crews, *Afghan Modern: The History of a Global Nation* (Cambridge, MA: The Belknap Press of Harvard University Press, 2015); Faiz Ahmed, *Afghanistan Rising: Islamic Law and Statecraft Between the Ottoman and British Empires* (Cambridge, MA: Harvard University Press, 2017); Louis Dupree, *Afghanistan* (Princeton, NJ: Princeton University Press, 1973); Elisabeth Leake, *The Defiant Border: The Afghan-Pakistan Borderlands in the Era of Decolonization, 1936–65* (New York: Cambridge University Press, 2017); Ludwig W. Adamec, *Afghanistan's Foreign Affairs to the Mid-Twentieth Century: Relations with the USSR, Germany, and Britain* (Tucson: University of Arizona Press, 1974); Jonathan L. Lee, *Afghanistan: A History from 1260 to the Present* (London: Reaktion, 2022).
27. Artemy M. Kalinovsky, *A Long Goodbye: The Soviet Withdrawal from Afghanistan* (Cambridge, MA: Harvard University Press, 2011); Vasiliy Mitrokhin, "The KGB in Afghanistan," CWIHP Working Paper 40 (Washington, DC: Woodrow Wilson Center, 2009); Odd Arne Westad, *The Global Cold War: Third World Interventions and the Making of Our Times* (New York: Cambridge University Press, 2005); Rodric Braithwaite, *Afgantsy: The Russians in Afghanistan, 1979–1989* (London: Profile, 2011); V. M. Zubok, *A Failed Empire: The Soviet Union in the Cold War from Stalin to Gorbachev* (Chapel Hill: University of North Carolina Press, 2007); Nunan, *Humanitarian Invasion*; Paul Robinson and Jay Dixon,

Aiding Afghanistan: A History of Soviet Assistance to a Developing Country (London: Hurst, 2013).
28. Poullada and Poullada, *Kingdom of Afghanistan*; Roberts, *Origins of Conflict*.
29. Nivi Manchanda, *Imagining Afghanistan: The History and Politics of Imperial Knowledge* (New York: Cambridge University Press, 2020), 27–40.

1. A Game of Hide-and-Seek

1. "Two Royal Afghans Are Not Acquainted," *NYT*, July 13, 1921.
2. "Rattle of City Streets Ruins Afghan Envoy's Sleep," *WP*, July 31, 1921.
3. "Prince Wali Khan Sails with Staff," *NYT*, July 31, 1921.
4. Thomas J. Barfield, *Afghanistan: A Cultural and Political History* (Princeton, NJ: Princeton University Press, 2010), 24–31; Barnett R. Rubin, *The Fragmentation of Afghanistan: State Formation and Collapse in the International System* (New Haven, CT: Yale University Press, 2002), 22–32.
5. Jonathan L. Lee, *Afghanistan: A History from 1260 to the Present* (London: Reaktion, 2022), 387–90, 526–28.
6. Rubin, *Fragmentation of Afghanistan*, 32–44; Barfield, *Afghanistan*, 32–35.
7. Afghan Government, *First Seven Year Economic and Social Development Plan*, vol. 1 (Kabul: Ministry of Planning, 1976), 2.
8. Abdul Ghafoor Arefi, "Urban Policies, Planning and Implementation in Kabul, Afghanistan" (PhD diss., Indiana University Bloomington, 1975), 120.
9. Amin Saikal, *Modern Afghanistan: A History of Struggle and Survival* (London: I. B. Tauris, 2012), 19–37; Barfield, *Afghanistan*, 96–146.
10. Robert D. Crews, *Afghan Modern: The History of a Global Nation* (Cambridge, MA: The Belknap Press of Harvard University Press, 2015), 63.
11. B. D. Hopkins, "The Bounds of Identity: The Goldsmid Mission and the Delineation of the Perso-Afghan Border in the Nineteenth Century," *Journal of Global History* 2, no. 2 (July 2007): 233–54; Pirouz Mojtahed-Zadeh, *Small Players of the Great Game: The Settlement of Iran's Eastern Borderlands and the Creation of Afghanistan* (London: Routledge, 2007), 178–90.
12. B. D. Hopkins, *The Making of Modern Afghanistan* (New York: Palgrave Macmillan, 2008); Shah Mahmoud Hanifi, *Connecting Histories in Afghanistan: Market Relations and State Formation on a Colonial Frontier* (Stanford, CA: Stanford University Press, 2011); Zalmay Gulzad, *External Influences and the Development of the Afghan State in the Nineteenth Century*, American University Studies, vol. 161 (New York: Peter Lang, 1994), 67–84.
13. M. Hassan Kakar, *A Political and Diplomatic History of Afghanistan, 1863–1901* (Boston: Brill, 2006), 171–92; Ludwig W. Adamec, *Afghanistan, 1900–1923: A Diplomatic History* (Berkeley: University of California Press, 1967), 20–27;

Lee, *Afghanistan*, 384–404; Francesca Fuoli, "Colonialism and State-Building in Afghanistan: Anglo-Afghan Co-Operation in the Institutionalisation of Ethnic Difference, 1869–1900" (PhD diss., SOAS University of London, 2017).

14. Saikal, *Modern Afghanistan*, 42–51; Crews, *Afghan Modern*, 114–18; Vartan Gregorian, *The Emergence of Modern Afghanistan; Politics of Reform and Modernization, 1880–1946* (Stanford, CA: Stanford University Press, 1969), 163–80.
15. A. C. Jewett, *An American Engineer in Afghanistan*, 2nd ed., ed. Marjorie Jewett Bell, (Kabul: Irajbooks, 2004).
16. Adamec, *Afghanistan, 1900–1923*, 86–96; Barfield, *Afghanistan*, 178–79; Faiz Ahmed, *Afghanistan Rising: Islamic Law and Statecraft Between the Ottoman and British Empires* (Cambridge, MA: Harvard University Press, 2017), 138–60.
17. Jon Jacobson, *When the Soviet Union Entered World Politics* (Berkeley: University of California Press, 1994), 69–78; Adamec, *Afghanistan, 1900–1923*, 142–44.
18. Ludwig W. Adamec, *Afghanistan's Foreign Affairs to the Mid-Twentieth Century: Relations with the USSR, Germany, and Britain* (Tucson: University of Arizona Press, 1974), 53–55; Erez Manela, *The Wilsonian Moment: Self-Determination and the International Origins of Anticolonial Nationalism* (New York: Oxford University Press, 2007).
19. Adamec, *Afghanistan's Foreign Affairs*, 60–64.
20. Despatch 2701, Paris to Washington, June 24, 1921, CDF, 033.90H11/1, USNA; Letter, Hardinge to Wallace, June 23, 1921, ibid.
21. Telegram 418, London to Washington, July 9, 1921, IOR/L/PS/10/975-1, BL.
22. Telegram 472, Washington to London, July 11, 1921, ibid.
23. Memorandum, Hughes to Harding, July 18, 1921, *FRUS, 1921, I*: 258–59.
24. Memorandum, Hughes to Harding, July 21, 1921, *FRUS, 1921, I*: 259–60.
25. Letter, Harding to Amanullah, July 29, 1921, *FRUS, 1921, I*: 261.
26. "Harding Receives Fatima with Formal Ceremony," *NYT*, July 26, 1921; St. Clair McKelway, *The Big Little Man from Brooklyn* (New York: Houghton Mifflin, 1969).
27. Adamec, *Afghanistan's Foreign Affairs*, 64–65.
28. "Prince Wali Khan Sails with Staff," *NYT*.
29. Adamec, *Afghanistan, 1900–1923*, 157–66.
30. Adamec, *Afghanistan's Foreign Affairs*, 98–112; Saikal, *Modern Afghanistan*, 66–68.
31. See, for example, Despatch 947, London to Washington, December 17, 1924, CDF, 701.90H11/2, USNA; Despatch 5671, Paris to Washington, November 4, 1925, *FRUS, 1926, I*: 557; Telegram 177, Rome to Washington, September 19, 1931, *FRUS, 1931, I*: 825–26.
32. Replies include Despatch 511, Washington to London, January 20, 1925, CDF, 701.90H11/2, USNA; Despatch 1839, Washington to Paris, January 26, 1926, ibid. (/6); Telegram 143, Washington to Rome, September 24, 1931, *FRUS, 1931, I*: 826.

33. Emily S. Rosenberg, *Spreading the American Dream: American Economic and Cultural Expansion, 1890–1945* (New York: Hill and Wang, 1982), 122–37; Frank Costigliola, *Awkward Dominion: American Political, Economic, and Cultural Relations with Europe, 1919–1933* (Ithaca, NY: Cornell University Press, 1987), 140–66.
34. Michael J. Hogan, *Informal Entente: The Private Structure of Cooperation in Anglo-American Economic Diplomacy, 1918–1928* (Columbia: University of Missouri Press, 1977).
35. Francis R. Nicosia, "'Drang Nach Osten' Continued? Germany and Afghanistan During the Weimar Republic," *Journal of Contemporary History* 32, no. 2 (1997): 235–57; Adamec, *Afghanistan's Foreign Affairs*, 101–5.
36. Letter, Phillips to Engert, February 6, 1923, CDF, 890H.927/5, USNA; Despatch 869, Washington to Paris, February 26, 1924, in *FRUS, 1924, I*: 753–54.
37. Despatch 9082, Paris to Washington, October 29, 1928, CDF, 711.90H12-Antiwar/5, USNA.
38. Adamec, *Afghanistan's Foreign Affairs*, 90–113; Leon B. Poullada, *Reform and Rebellion in Afghanistan, 1919–1929: King Amanullah's Failure to Modernize a Tribal Society* (Ithaca. NY: Cornell University Press, 1979), 233–56.
39. Gregorian, *Emergence of Modern Afghanistan*, 256–58; Adamec, *Afghanistan's Foreign Affairs*, 113–32.
40. Four royal visits had occurred: two by the king of Hawai'i, one by the emperor of Brazil, and recently, one by the king of Belgium. Emily Bishko, "Of Dinners and Diplomacy: What White House State Dinners Reveal About Relationship Building and Goodwill Signaling in U.S. Foreign Policy" (undergraduate thesis, Stanford University, 2020), 143.
41. Telegram, Bombay to Washington, December 30, 1927, CDF, 890.001 Am1/7, USNA; Telegram 1, Rome to Washington, January 13, 1928, ibid. (/11); Telegram 6, Washington to Rome, January 20, 1928, ibid.
42. Ahmed, *Afghanistan Rising*, 254–73; Poullada, *Reform and Rebellion*, 160–79.
43. Poullada, *Reform and Rebellion*, 201–3; Saikal, *Modern Afghanistan*, 99–109.
44. Gregorian, *Emergence of Modern Afghanistan*, 334–38; Adamec, *Afghanistan's Foreign Affairs*, 192–212.
45. Despatch 1016, Tehran to Washington, January 20, 1932, CDF, 890H.001/34, USNA.
46. Letter, Murray to White, September 27, 1937, CDF, 124.90H/36A, USNA.
47. Memorandum, Murray to Sumner Welles, April 8, 1940, CDF, 124.90H/49, USNA.
48. Memorandum, Murray to Castle, November 30, 1929, CDF, 890H.01/6, USNA.
49. Memorandum, Murray to Castle, September 22, 1931, CDF, 890H.01/15, USNA.

50. Despatch 1960, London to Washington, May 19, 1931, CDF, 890H.01/13, USNA; Memorandum, Murray, October 20, 1931, ibid. (/17).
51. Letter, Ashurst to Hull, April 19, 1933, CDF, 890H.01/23, USNA; Letter, John Barrett to Roosevelt, June 1, 1933, ibid.; Memorandum, Murray to Phillips, June 16, 1933, ibid. (/24).
52. Letter, Grew to Murray, October 26, 1933, CDF, 890H.01/34, USNA.
53. Memorandum, Murray to Phillips, November 16, 1933, ibid.
54. Letter, Murray to Grew, November 21, 1933, ibid.
55. Lee, *Afghanistan*, 524–29.
56. Despatch 256, Karachi to Washington, November 28, 1933, CDF, 890H.00/147, USNA.
57. Despatch 10, Moscow to Washington, March 28, 1934, CDF, 701.90H11/26, USNA.
58. Despatch 580, Calcutta to Washington, January 17, 1934, CDF, 890H.00/152, USNA; Despatch 415, Karachi to Washington, November 8, 1934, CDF, 890H.607 Kabul/2, USNA.
59. Despatch 10, Tehran to Washington, March 27, 1934, CDF, 890H.01/41, USNA; Despatch 95, Tehran to Washington, June 5, 1934, ibid. (/46); Despatch 10, Moscow to Washington, March 28, 1934, CDF, 701.90H11/26, USNA.
60. Daily Report, Near East Division, July 2, 1934, CDF, 890H.001 Zahir/6, USNA; Telegram 493, Paris to Washington, June 30, 1934, *FRUS, 1934, II:* 747; Letter, Zahir to Roosevelt, April 24, 1934, *FRUS, 1934, II:* 748; Letter, Phillips to Roosevelt, August 21, 1934, *FRUS, 1934, II:* 748–49; Letter, Roosevelt to Zahir, August 21, 1934, *FRUS, 1934, II:* 750.
61. Despatch 61, Kabul to London, May 24, 1935, IOR/L/PS12/1611, BL; Despatch 10, Tehran to Washington, June 22, 1935, CDF, 124.90H/16, USNA; Memorandum, Murray to Phillips and Hull, June 19, 1936, ibid. (/21); Despatch 15, Tehran to Washington, July 9, 1935, CDF, 890H.00/162, USNA.
62. Memorandum, Alling to Barnes, November 12, 1934, CDF, 711.90H/25, USNA.
63. Telegram 257, Paris to Washington, March 26, 1936, *FRUS, 1936, III:* 7.
64. Telegram 85, Moscow to Washington, March 15, 1936, CDF, 711.90H/51, USNA; Telegram 94, Moscow to Washington, March 28, 1936, ibid. (/56); Letter, Hare to Marriner, February 11, 1936, ibid. (/41).
65. Telegram 8, Tehran to Washington, February 9, 1921, CDF, 890H.6363, USNA.
66. Despatch 459, London to Washington, October 26, 1925, CDF, 890H.6363/4, USNA.
67. Despatch 6078, Paris to Washington, February 20, 1926, CDF, 701.90H11/9, USNA.
68. Letter, A. C. Hearn to the Undersecretary, January 24, 1927, POWE 33/422, UKNA.

69. Despatch 140, Tehran to Washington, August 23, 1930, CDF, 390H.1163/3, USNA; Despatch 172, Tehran to Washington, September 23, 1930, ibid. (/7).
70. Despatch 30, Washington to Tehran, September 26, 1930, ibid. (/5).
71. Despatch 830, Tehran to Washington, September 2, 1931, CDF, 890H.032/2, USNA.
72. Letter, Tehran to Washington, February 3, 1933, CDF, 123H 255/141, USNA.
73. Despatch 48, Tehran to London, January 31, 1934, FO 416/92, UKNA; Chester W. Washburn, "Frederick Gardner Clapp," *Bulletin of the American Association of Petroleum Geologists* 29, no. 3 (March 1945): 402–9.
74. Letter, Tehran to Washington, July 25, 1934, CDF, 890H.6363/27, USNA.
75. Daily Report, Murray, September 11, 1934, ibid. (/31).
76. Despatch 1252, Berlin to Washington, November 20, 1936, *FRUS, 1937, II*: 598–99.
77. Letter, Ogden Mills to Cordell Hull, August 23, 1937, CDF, 124.90H/31, USNA; Memorandum, Murray, July 27, 1937, *FRUS, 1937, II*: 607–10.
78. Report R-39-45, Kabul to Washington, June 20, 1945, CDF, 890H.6363/10-745, USNA.
79. Memcon, April 26, 1938, CDF, 891.6363 Amiranian Oil Co./71, USNA; Memcon, May 5, 1938, ibid. (/73).
80. Report R-39-45; Telegram 74, Tehran to Washington, June 21, 1938, *FRUS, 1938, II*: 756.
81. Hornibrook described Shir Ahmad Khan, Afghan minister to Iran, as: "A lovable personality, a colorful character, and a Near Eastern diplomat of more than average humor, honesty, and intelligence." Despatch 254, Tehran to Washington, November 2, 1934, CDF, 711.90H/24, USNA. Diplomat Loy Henderson wrote of Afghanistan's ambassador in Moscow, "He is an extremely interesting person and the whole Diplomatic Corps is fond of him." Letter, Henderson to Murray, March 17, 1938, CDF, 890H.00/174, USNA.

2. "We Have a Rare Opportunity"

1. Letter, Wilbur Harlan to Augusta Harlan, n.d., CDF, 1940–1944, 890H.00/192, USNA; Bill Harlan and Susan Shumway, *Looking Back at My Life* (Corvallis, OR: Franklin Press, 2001), 135–36.
2. Ella Maillart and Jessa Crispin, *The Cruel Way: Switzerland to Afghanistan in a Ford, 1939* (Chicago: University of Chicago Press, 2013).
3. Letter, Harry Harlan to Raymond Hare, August 22, 1940, CDF, 890H.00/192, USNA.
4. Ernest F. Fox, *Travels in Afghanistan, 1937–1938* (New York: Macmillan, 1943), 18; Maillart and Crispin, *Cruel Way*, 192–93.

5. Eunan O'Halpin, "The Fate of Indigenous and Soviet Central Asian Jews in Afghanistan, 1933–1951," *Holocaust and Genocide Studies* 30, no. 2 (August 2016): 306.
6. Jonathan L. Lee, *Afghanistan: A History from 1260 to the Present* (London: Reaktion, 2022), 535–37; Robert D. Crews, *Afghan Modern: The History of a Global Nation* (Cambridge, MA: The Belknap Press of Harvard University Press, 2015), 140–44; Amin Saikal, *Modern Afghanistan: A History of Struggle and Survival* (London: I. B. Tauris, 2012), 106–11; Vartan Gregorian, *The Emergence of Modern Afghanistan; Politics of Reform and Modernization, 1880–1946* (Stanford: Stanford University Press, 1969), 342–53.
7. Despatch 151, Kabul to London, November 16, 1938, IOR/L/PS/12/1689, BL; Milan L. Hauner, "Afghanistan Between the Great Powers, 1938–1945," *International Journal of Middle East Studies* 14, no. 4 (November 1982): 481–99.
8. O'Halpin, "Fate of Indigenous and Soviet Central Asian Jews in Afghanistan," 302–3.
9. Eunan O'Halpin, "Afghanistan, 1937–1945: From Lynchpin to Backwater," in *Neutral Countries as Clandestine Battlegrounds, 1939–1968: Between Two Fires*, ed. André Gerolymatos (Lanham, MD: Lexington, 2020), 212–13.
10. Ludwig W. Adamec, *Afghanistan's Foreign Affairs to the Mid-Twentieth Century: Relations with the USSR, Germany, and Britain* (Tucson: University of Arizona Press, 1974), 233–34.
11. Extract from Despatch 31, Kabul to London, March 7, 1936, IOR/L/PS/12/1689, BL.
12. Telegram, Kabul to Delhi, March 25, 1937, IOR/L/PS/12/1689, BL; Adamec, *Afghanistan's Foreign Affairs*, 219–27; Milan Hauner, *India in Axis Strategy: Germany, Japan, and Indian Nationalists in the Second World War* (Stuttgart: Klett-Cotta, 1981), 76–80.
13. Despatch 44, Kabul to Paris, July 28, 1938, A-O(A) 1918–1940, 44, MAE/P.
14. Despatch 85, Kabul to London, June 28, 1938, IOR/L/PS/12/1689, BL; Despatch 151, Kabul to London, November 16, 1938, ibid.; Adamec, *Afghanistan's Foreign Affairs*, 224–25.
15. Despatch 59, Kabul to London, July 7, 1939, FO 402/20, UKNA.
16. Despatch 104, Kabul to London, November 17, 1939, FO 402/20, UKNA.
17. Despatch 113, Kabul to London, December 22, 1939, FO 402/21, UKNA; Despatch 86, Kabul to Paris, December 18, 1939, A-O(A) 1918–1940, 45, MAE/P.
18. Telegram 77, London to Kabul, April 27, 1940, FO 402/21, UKNA; Hauner, *India in Axis Strategy*, 136–54.
19. Despatch 54, Kabul to London, June 28, 1940, FO 402/21, UKNA.
20. Hauner, *India in Axis Strategy*, 213–16.
21. Faridullah Bezhan, "The Second World War and Political Dynamics in Afghanistan," *Middle Eastern Studies* 50, no. 2 (March 2014): 175–91.

22. Adamec, *Afghanistan's Foreign Affairs*, 243–50.
23. Telegram 94, Kabul to London, March 24, 1941, IOR/L/PS/12/1778, BL; Adamec, *Afghanistan's Foreign Affairs*, 245–55.
24. Telegram 227, Kabul to London, July 11, 1941, IOR/L/PS/12/1778, BL; Telegram 4134, Simla to London, August 8, 1941, ibid.
25. Telegram 212, London to Kuibyshev, September 7, 1941, FO 181/962/1, UKNA; Minute, Churchill to Eden, September 6, 1941, PREM 3/5, UKNA; Adamec, *Afghanistan's Foreign Affairs*, 255–58; Hauner, *India in Axis Strategy*, 321–27.
26. Telegram 252, Kabul to London, August 1, 1941, IOR/L/PS/12/1778, BL.
27. Memorandum, Welles to Murray, March 30, 1940, CDF, 124.90H/49, USNA; Memorandum, Murray to Welles, April 8, 1940, ibid.; Memorandum, Welles to Murray, April 10, 1940, ibid.
28. Letter, Murray to Dreyfus, January 28, 1941, CDF, 711.90H/69, USNA.
29. Letter, Dreyfus to Murray, July 12, 1941, CDF, 124.90H/58, USNA; Afghan Series No. 6, Tehran to Washington, June 29, 1941, CDF, 711.90H/72, USNA.
30. Memorandum, Murray to Welles and Shaw, December 2, 1941, CDF, 124.90H/70, UNSA.
31. Letter, Henderson to Murray, March 17, 1938, CDF, 890H.00/174, USNA; Memorandum, Murray to Hull and Phillips, June 10, 1936, CDF, 124.90H/21, USNA.
32. Franklin D. Roosevelt, Orville H. Bullitt, and William C. Bullitt, *For the President, Personal and Secret: Correspondence Between Franklin D. Roosevelt and William C. Bullitt* (Boston: Houghton Mifflin, 1972), 531.
33. Telegram 157, Washington to Tehran, December 13, 1941, *FRUS, 1942, IV*: 44; Telegram 265, Tehran to Washington, December 26, 1941, ibid.; Memcon, March 6, 1942, *FRUS, 1942, IV*: 46–47; Telegram 64, March 12, 1942, *FRUS, 1942, IV*: 47–48.
34. Memorandum, Murray to Shaw, January 8, 1942, *FRUS, 1942, IV*: 44–45.
35. Memorandum, Roosevelt to Welles, March 16, 1942, *FRUS, 1942, IV*: 48.
36. Memorandum, Alling to Welles, April 28, 1942, CDF, 124.90H/75½, USNA; Memorandum, Welles to Alling, May 4, 1942, ibid.
37. Despatch 3, Kabul to Washington, June 22, 1942, CDF, 124.90H/80, USNA; Telegram 7, Kabul to Washington, June 6, 1942, *FRUS, 1942, IV*: 50; Diary, CTP, box 7, "Kabul, Afghanistan—May 7–June 22, 1942," HSTL.
38. See also Jane Morrison Engert, *Tales from the Embassy: The Extraordinary World of C. Van H. Engert* (Westminster, MD: Eagle Editions, 2006).
39. Leon B. Poullada and Leila Poullada, *The Kingdom of Afghanistan and the United States: 1828–1973* (Lincoln, NE: Center for Afghanistan Studies and Dageforde Publishing, 1995), 15–17; John J. Harter, "Diplomacy and War in the Twentieth Century: The Foreign Service Career of Cornelius Van H. Engert," *Foreign Service Journal* 58, no. 1 (January 1981): 53–54.

40. Engert, "Memorandum on Afghanistan," December 1, 1922, CDF, 890H.00/7, USNA.
41. Memorandum, Murray, March 30, 1937, CDF, 701.90H11/27, USNA.
42. Harter, "Diplomacy and War," 52.
43. Telegram 39, Kabul to London, March 1, 1942, IOR/L/PS/12/1789, BL; Telegram 41, Kabul to London, March 6, 1942, ibid.
44. Telegram 69, Kabul to London, April 21, 1942, IOR/L/PS/12/1789, BL.
45. Hauner, *India in Axis Strategy*, 511–23; Adamec, *Afghanistan's Foreign Affairs*, 257–59.
46. Telegram 40, Kabul to Washington, July 30, 1942, *FRUS, 1942, IV*: 52–53; Telegram 54, Kabul to Washington, August 16, 1942, *FRUS, 1942, IV*: 54–57; Bezhan, "Second World War and Political Dynamics," 176.
47. Telegram 54.
48. Telegram 174, Kabul to London, September 12, 1942, IOR/L/PS/12/1789, BL; Telegram 120, Kabul to Washington, November 14, 1942, CEP, 8:12, GUSC.
49. Telegram 41, Kabul to Washington, July 31, 1942, CEP, 8:10, GUSC; Telegram 43, Kabul to Washington, August 2, 1942, ibid.; Despatch 35, Kabul to Washington, September 20, 1942, CEP, 8:36, GUSC; Telegram 80, Kabul to Washington, September 21, 1942, CEP, 8:19, GUSC; Letter, Engert to George Merrell, September 9, 1942, CEP, 7:67, GUSC.
50. Telegram 47, Kabul to Washington, August 5, 1942, CDF, 890H.24/40A, USNA; Memorandum, Merchant to Alling, November 23, 1942, ibid.; Telegram 74, Washington to Kabul, July 3, 1943, ibid. (/76); Memorandum, Lewis to Alling, April 6, 1943, CDF, 890H.50/8, USNA; Telegram 19, Kabul to Washington, January 28, 1943, ibid. (/9).
51. Memorandum, Lewis to Alling, April 6, 1943, CDF, 890H.50/8, USNA.
52. Letter, Thayer to George, September 28, 1943, CTP, box 10, "Afghanistan correspondence," HSTL.
53. Despatch 39, Kabul to Washington, October 2, 1942, CDF, 890H.24/42, USNA.
54. Airgram A-23, Kabul to Washington, December 15, 1943, CDF, 890H.24/146, USNA; Telegram 93, Kabul to Washington, October 11, 1942, ibid. (/37).
55. Despatch 39, Washington to Kabul, June 19, 1943, CDF, 890.24H/81, USNA.
56. Telegram 143, Kabul to Washington, December 13, 1942, CDF, 890H.24/49, USNA; Letter, Omar to Alling, December 29, 1942, ibid. (/56); Letter, Girja Bajpai to Acheson, January 30, 1943, ibid. (/61); Kevin Smith, *Conflict over Convoys: Anglo-American Logistics Diplomacy in the Second World War* (New York: Cambridge University Press, 1996), 156–64.
57. Letter, Omar to Alling, February 2, 1943, CDF, 890H.24/63, USNA; Letter, Alling to Aziz, December 7, 1943, ibid. (/140A); Airgram A-10, Washington to Kabul, April 24, 1944, ibid. (/165).

58. Telegram 18, Kabul to Washington, January 27, 1943, *FRUS, 1943, IV*: 20–21.
59. Telegram 93, Kabul to Washington, October 11, 1942, CDF, 890H.24/37, USNA; Telegram 76, Washington to Kabul, July 16, 1943, ibid. (/91); Telegram 77, Washington to Kabul, July 16, 1943, ibid. (/97A).
60. Telegram 157, Kabul to Washington, July 31, 1943, CDF, 890H.24/104, USNA; Telegram 88, Washington to Kabul, July 31, 1943, ibid.; Airgram A-21, Kabul to Washington, December 10, 1943, ibid. (/142).
61. Memcon, August 3, 1943, CDF, 890H.24/105, USNA; Despatch 240, Kabul to Washington, July 22, 1943, CDF, 890H.24/107, USNA; Telegram 95, Washington to Kabul, October 2, 1943, ibid.
62. Despatch 393, Kabul to Washington, February 11, 1944, CDF, 890H.24/160, USNA; Airgram A-82, Washington to Kabul, November 2, 1943, ibid. (/127B).
63. Letter, Beecroft to William Bissell, February 25, 1944, CDF, 890H.24/164, USNA.
64. Despatch 140, Kabul to Washington, April 4, 1943, CDF, 890H.24/81, USNA.
65. Despatch 393, Kabul to Washington, February 11, 1944, CDF, 890H.24/160, USNA; Letter, Beecroft to William Bissell, February 25, 1944, ibid. (/164).
66. Letter, Beecroft to Foreign Economic Administration, February 17, 1944, CEP, 7:52, GUSC.
67. Memorandum, Allen to Merchant, September 26, 1944, *FRUS, 1944, V*: 51–52.
68. Memorandum, Oakes, August 28, 1942, CDF, 890H.24/51½, USNA.
69. Telegram 75, Engert to Washington, March 31, 1943, *FRUS, 1943, IV*: 56.
70. Telegram 83, Kabul to Washington, May 15, 1944, CDF, 890H.42/28, USNA. Frye and Ingalls later enjoyed distinguished academic careers: Frye as a historian of Iran, and Ingalls as a scholar of Sanskrit.
71. Telegram 70, Washington to Kabul, June 21, 1943, CEP, 8:17, GUSC.
72. Telegram 127, Engert to Washington, June 24, 1943, CEP, 8:17, GUSC.
73. Memcon, July 1, 1943, CDF, 103.918/1864, USNA. I thank Frank Costigliola for sharing this document.
74. Telegram 107, Washington to Kabul, November 15, 1943, *FRUS, 1943, IV*: 61–62; Memorandum, Oakes, February 15, 1944, CDF, 890H.42A/52, USNA; Letter, Alling to Herrick Young, April 5, 1944, ibid. (/56).
75. Memorandum, Allen, April 27, 1944, CDF, 890H.42A/59, USNA; Letter, Fluker to NED, April 24, 1944, ibid. (/4-2444); Despatch 546, Kabul to Washington, September 14, 1944, ibid. (/9-1444).
76. Telegram 205, Kabul to Washington, October 26, 1943, CDF, 890H.64A/17, USNA.
77. Despatch 476, Kabul to Washington, June 22, 1944, CEP, 9:2, GUSC; Letter, Squire to Caroe, April 27, 1944, IOR/L/PS/12/1595, BL; Report, Savage, May 8, 1944, ibid.; Letter, Foy, June 27, 1944, ibid.

78. Despatch 607, Kabul to Washington, December 4, 1944, CDF, 890H.64A/12-444, USNA; Despatch 6, Kabul to London, February 2, 1945, FO 371/45215, UKNA.
79. Telegram 90, Kabul to Washington, October 1, 1942, CEP, 8:11, GUSC.
80. Despatch 565, Kabul to Washington, October 26, 1944, CEP, 9:6, GUSC; Letter, Engert to Cook, September 12, 1944, CEP, 8:3, GUSC; Despatch 199, Kabul to Washington, June 10, 1943, CEP, 8:48, GUSC.
81. Telegram 130, Kabul to Washington, August 5, 1944, CEP, 8:24, GUSC; Telegram 135, Kabul to Washington, August 12, 1944, ibid.; Telegram 79, Washington to Kabul, August 17, 1944, ibid.; Despatch 544, Kabul to Washington, September 12, 1944, CDF, 890H.48/9-1244, USNA.
82. Telegram 3630, New Delhi to London, May 8, 1943, IOR/L/PS/12/1798, BL.
83. Letter, Wylie to Caroe, May 29, 1943, IOP/L/PS/12/1789, BL; Telegram 107, Kabul to Washington, May 24, 1943, *FRUS, 1943, IV*: 35–37.
84. Telegram 63, Washington to Kabul, June 5, 1943, *FRUS, 1943, IV*: 38–39; Telegram 117, Kabul to Washington, June 8, 1943, *FRUS, 1943, IV*: 39–40; Telegram 3953, London to Washington, June 11, 1943, *FRUS, 1943, IV*: 40–42; Telegram 3716, Washington to London, June 16, 1943, *FRUS, 1943, IV*: 43–44.
85. Minute, Ivor Pink, June 18, 1943, IOR/L/PS/12/1798, BL.
86. Letter, Wylie to London, July 3, 1943, FO 371/34936, UKNA; Minutes, E4500/G, August 3, 1943, ibid.; Letter, Squire to R. R. Burnett, October 6, 1944, IOR/L/PS/12/165, BL; Maximilian Drephal, *Afghanistan and the Coloniality of Diplomacy: The British Legation in Kabul, 1922–1948* (Cham, Switzerland: Palgrave Macmillan, 2019), 212–16.
87. Telegram 184, Kabul to Washington, September 29, 1943, CEP, 8:19, GUSC; Telegram 144, Kabul to Washington, July 20, 1943, *FRUS, 1943, IV*: 25–27; Despatch 54, Kabul to London, October 2, 1943, IOR/L/PS/12/163, BL.
88. Telegram 34, Kabul to Washington, February 14, 1943, *FRUS, 1943, IV*: 21–22; Telegram 90, Kabul to Washington, April 29, 1943, *FRUS, 1943, IV*: 22–23; Memcon, October 22, 1943, *FRUS, 1943, IV*: 29–30; Telegram 224, Kabul to Washington, November 22, 1943, *FRUS, 1943, IV*: 32–34.
89. Telegram 217, Kabul to Washington, November 6, 1943, *FRUS, 1943, IV*: 30–32.
90. Despatch 376, Kabul to Washington, January 17, 1944, CEP, 8:56, GUSC; Letter, Squire to Caroe, January 14, 1944, FO 371/39960, UKNA; Letter, Squire to Caroe, January 22, 1944, ibid.
91. Letter, Roosevelt to Hurley, October 12, 1943, PJHC, 8:6, OU; Letter, Roosevelt to Zahir, October 13, 1943, ibid; Letter, Hurley to Roosevelt, December 21, 1943, ibid.
92. Frederick Clapp, "Preliminary Notes on Northern Afghanistan," August 22, 1936, PJHC, 8:7, OU; Letter, Clapp to Frederick Sharp, July 25, 1942, ibid.; Minute, November 19, 1943, IOR/L/PS12/1644, BL; David S. Painter, *Oil and*

the American Century: The Political Economy of U.S. Foreign Oil Policy, 1941–1954 (Baltimore, MD: Johns Hopkins University Press, 1986), 76–81; Russell D. Buhite, *Patrick J. Hurley and American Foreign Policy* (Ithaca, NY: Cornell University Press, 1973), 126–33; George J. Hill, *Proceed to Peshawar: The Story of a U.S. Navy Intelligence Mission on the Afghan Border, 1943* (Annapolis, MD: Naval Institute Press, 2013), 70–74.

93. Telegram, Hurley to Roosevelt, January 14, 1944, PJHC, 84:4, OU; Memorandum, Alling to Hull, August 8, 1944, CEP, 9:22, GUSC.
94. Despatch 705, Kabul to Washington, April 22, 1945, CEP, 9:14, GUSC; Telegram 45, Kabul to Washington, April 16, 1945, CEP, 8:28, GUSC.
95. Despatch 48, Kabul to London, June 1, 1945, IOR/L/PS/12/990B, BL.
96. Gregorian, *Emergence of Modern Afghanistan*, 389–92.
97. Despatch 7, Kabul to London, February 1, 1946, FO 406/84, UKNA; Despatch 784, Kabul to Washington, July 17, 1945, CEP, 9:17, GUSC.
98. Mark A. Stoler, *Allies and Adversaries: The Joint Chiefs of Staff, the Grand Alliance, and U.S. Strategy in World War II* (Chapel Hill: University of North Carolina Press, 2000), 53–54.
99. Despatch 612, Kabul to Washington, December 8, 1944, CEP, 9:9, GUSC.

3. Preeminence and Peril

1. See Letter, Walsh to Richard Koenig, April 23, 1947, MWP, box 9, "Subject File 1947–51 Afghanistan (2)," AHC.
2. Memcon, September 20, 1946, CDF, 890H.64A/9-2046, USNA; Memcon, November 18, 1946, ibid. (/11-1846); Letter, Minor to Ghulam Mohammed, December 4, 1946, ibid. (/12-246).
3. Letter, Myles Walsh to Richard Leach, April 12, 1948, CDF, 890.63/4-1248, USNA; Letter, Walsh to Gholam Mohamed Khan, April 8, 1948, ibid.; Despatch 64, Kabul to Washington, April 15, 1946, ibid. (/4-1546).
4. Telegram 48, Washington to Kabul, June 25, 1945, CDF, 890H.24/6-1645, USNA; Memcon, June 20, 1945, ibid. (/6-2045); Despatch 821, Kabul to Washington, September 13, 1945, ibid. (/9-1345).
5. Memcon, November 21, 1945, CDF, 890H.24/11-2145, USNA; Summary of Action, February 5, 1946, ibid. (/3-2546); Telegram 45, Washington to Kabul, April 5, 1946, ibid. (/3-2546).
6. Telegram 102, Kabul to Washington, July 16, 1945, CDF, 890H.24/7-1645, USNA; Letter, Minor to Aziz, October 15, 1945, ibid. (/9–745).
7. Despatch 724, Kabul to Washington, May 6, 1945, CDF, 890H.64A/5-645, USNA.

8. James David Duran, "Building the Modern World: The Morrison-Knudsen Construction Company" (master's thesis, Boise State University, 2013), 31.
9. Memcon, June 2, 1945, CDF, 890H.64/6-245, USNA; Letter, Dunn to Aziz, June 30, 1945, CDF, 890H.64A/6-3045, USNA; Memcon, October 18, 1945, CDF, 890H.6463/10-1845, USNA; Letter, Dunn to Alexander, June 11, 1945, OSAA, SFAA, box 10, "820.8 Morrison-Knudsen, Afghanistan 1945–48," USNA.
10. Despatch 727, Engert to Washington, May 10, 1945, CEP, 9:15, GUSC.
11. Telegram 120, Kabul to Washington, August 9, 1945, CDF, 890H.6363/8-945, USNA. Letters are at ibid. (/9-1145).
12. Telegram 96, Kabul to Washington, July 5, 1945, CDF, 761H.90H/7-545, USNA; Despatch 841, Kabul to Washington, October 20, 1945, CDF, 890H.00/10-2045, USNA.
13. Report to State-War-Navy Coordinating Committee 202/2, March 21, 1946, *FRUS, 1946, I*: 1157.
14. Ibid.
15. Memorandum, Merriam, January 4, 1946, *FRUS, 1946, VII*: 6–7.
16. Harry S Truman, Radio Address, April 19, 1946, *PPP, 1946*, 215.
17. Memcon, April 30, 1946, CDF, 890H.61311/4-3046, USNA; Memcon, August 8, 1946, ibid. (/8-846).
18. Letter, Acheson to Anderson, October 11, 1946, CDF, 890H.61311/4-3046, USNA.
19. Telegram 151, Washington to Kabul, October 24, 1946, CDF, 890H.61311/10-2446, USNA; Letter, R. W. Shields to Acheson, October 28, 1946, ibid. (/10-2846); Telegram 3, Kabul to Washington, January 7, 1947, ibid. (/1-747); Telegram 50, Kabul to Washington, February 28, 1947, ibid. (/2-2847); Despatch 168, Kabul to Washington, November 27, 1946, CDF, 890H.00/11-2746, USNA.
20. Despatch 57, Kabul to London, June 28, 1947, FO 402/23, UKNA.
21. Despatch 168, Kabul to Washington, November 27, 1946, CDF, 890H.00/11-2746, USNA.
22. Memorandum, MEI to NEA, March 28, 1947, CDF, 890H.00/3-2847; Despatch 6, Moscow to London, January 4, 1947, FO 402/23, UKNA.
23. Memcon, October 18, 1945, CDF, 890H.6463/10-1845, USNA; Telegram 1, Kabul to Washington, January 4, 1946, CDF, 890H.64A/1-446, USNA.
24. Memcon, January 26, 1946, CDF, 890H.64/1-2646, USNA; Memcon, February 26, 1946, CDF, 890H.64A/2-2646, USNA. The timing of the divulgence is unclear.
25. Memcon, July 17, 1946, OSAA, SFAA, box 10, 820.8 Morrison-Knudsen, Afghanistan 1945–48, USNA.

26. Telegram 17, Washington to Kabul, February 8, 1946, KCR, 1946, 864, USNA; Memorandum, ME to MEA, June 15, 1946, CDF, 890H.796/7-1346, USNA.
27. Memcon, September 6, 1947, KGR, 1947, 864 M-K, USNA.
28. Memcon, November 18, 1946, CDF, 890H.64A/11-1846, USNA.
29. Telegram 198, Kabul to Washington, November 15, 1946, CDF, 890H.64A/11-1546, USNA; Despatch 200, Kabul to Washington, January 11, 1947, ibid. (/1-1147); Telegram 14, Kabul to Washington, January 13, 1947, ibid. (/1-1347); Telegram 34, Washington to New Delhi, January 17, 1947, ibid. (/1-1347); Telegram 77, New Delhi to Washington, January 31, 1947, ibid. (/1-3147).
30. Telegram 53, Washington to Kabul, March 24, 1947, CDF, 890H.64A/3-2447, USNA; Memcon, March 18, 1947, ibid. (/3-1847).
31. Despatch 26, Kabul to London, March 22, 1947, IOR/L/PS/12/1595, BL.
32. Telegram 1053, Tehran to Washington, August 1, 1946, CDF, 890H.6461/8-146, USNA; A. H. McMahon, Seistan Arbitral Award, April 10, 1905, ibid. (/10-3047).
33. Despatch 467, Tehran to Washington, August 11, 1947, CDF, 890H.6461/8-1147, USNA; Telegram 671, Washington to Tehran, August 9, 1946, ibid. (/8-346).
34. William Kerr Fraser-Tytler and Michael Cavenagh Gillet, *Afghanistan: A Study of Political Developments in Central and Southern Asia* (London: Oxford University Press, 1967), 305.
35. Telegram 97, Kabul to Washington, June 15, 1944, CDF, 761.90H/55, USNA; Telegram 98, Kabul to Washington, July 7, 1945, ibid. (/7-745); Memcon, November 18, 1946, CDF, 890H.64A/11-1846, USNA; Telegram 242, Tabriz to Washington, September 3, 1946, CDF, 711.90H/9-346, USNA; Despatch 169, Kabul to Paris, July 31, 1947, A-O(A) 1944–1972, 14, MAE/P.
36. Despatch 2202, Cairo to Washington, February 8, 1947, CDF, 890H.796/2-847, USNA.
37. Despatch 46, Kabul to London, May 29, 1947, FO 371/61487, UKNA; Letter, Squire to Baxter, May 29, 1947, ibid.; Telegram 78, Kabul to Washington, April 10, 1947, CDF, 890H.796/4-1047, USNA.
38. Louise L'Estrange Fawcett, *Iran and the Cold War: The Azerbaijan Crisis of 1946* (Cambridge: Cambridge University Press, 1992), 83–107.
39. Memcon, June 6, 1946, fond, 558, opis 11, dela 251, Russian State Archive of Socio-Political History (RGASPI), Moscow. I thank Sergey Radchenko for sharing this record.
40. Letter, Washington to London, May 12, 1947, FO 371/61470, UKNA; Statement, undated, *FRUS, 1947, V*: 607–8.
41. Elisabeth Leake, *The Defiant Border: The Afghan-Pakistan Borderlands in the Era of Decolonization, 1936–65* (New York: Cambridge University Press, 2017), 85–95; Timothy Nunan, *Humanitarian Invasion: Global Development in Cold War Afghanistan* (New York: Cambridge University Press, 2016), 58–59.

42. Jeffery J. Roberts, *The Origins of Conflict in Afghanistan* (Westport, CT: Praeger, 2003), 74–75.
43. Letter, Squire to Allen, September 3, 1947, FO 371/63260, UKNA; Letter, Washington to London, July 31, 1947, FO 371/63247, UKNA; Memcon, March 22, 1948, CDF, 745F.90H/3-2248, USNA.
44. Memcon, March 8, 1948, CDF, 745F.90H/3-848, USNA; Memorandum, Fox and Leach to Mathews, April 19, 1948, ibid. (/4-1948); Letter, London to Washington, September 12, 1947, FO 371/63247, UKNA.
45. Despatch 78, Kabul to Washington, May 20, 1946, CDF, 890H.6363/5-2046, USNA; Telegram 176, Kabul to Washington, October 15, 1946, ibid. (/10-1546).
46. Telegram 159, Kabul to Washington, July 7, 1947, CDF, 890H.6363/7-747, USNA; Airgram A-192, New Delhi to Washington, August 21, 1947, ibid. (/8-2147); Despatch 149, Karachi to Washington, September 27, 1947, ibid. (/9-2747).
47. Airgram A-2, Kabul to Washington, January 8, 1948, CDF, 890H.50/1-848, USNA.
48. Despatch 337, Kabul to Washington, October 1, 1947, CDF, 890H.6363/10-147, USNA; Despatch 149, Karachi to Washington, September 27, 1947, ibid. (/9-2747); Telegram 281, Kabul to Washington, November 3, 1947, ibid. (/11-347); Despatch 222, Karachi to Washington, November 14, 1947, ibid. (/11-1447); Memcon, April 28, 1948, OSAA, SFAA, box 10, "820.8 Morrison-Knudsen, Afghanistan 1945–48," USNA.
49. Memorandum, Walter MacLennan to MEI, August 19, 1947, CDF, 890H.001/8-1947, USNA; Telegram 166, Washington to Kabul, August 9, 1947, CDF, 890H.002/8-947, USNA.
50. Memcon, October 24, 1947, CDF, 890H.51/10-2447, USNA; Memcon, October 29, 1947, CDF, 890H.50/10-2947, USNA.
51. Zabuli, "Why Afghanistan Has Remained Backward," in Despatch 356, Kabul to Washington, November 5, 1947, CDF, 890H.51/11-547, USNA.
52. Telegram 228, Washington to Kabul, October 29, 1947, CDF, 890H.6461/10-2947, USNA; Memcon, December 4, 1947, ibid. (/12-447); Telegram 61, Washington to Tehran, January 21, 1948, ibid. (/1-2148); Despatch 132, Tehran to Washington, May 13, 1948, ibid. (/5-1348); Telegram 159, Kabul to Washington, June 26, 1948, ibid. (/6-2448).
53. Telegram 109, Kabul to Washington, May 12, 1947, CDF, 890H.64A/5-1247, USNA; Memorandum, February 15, 1947, KCR, 1947, 864, USNA.
54. Telegram 157, Kabul to Washington, June 25, 1948, CDF, 890H.64A/6-2448, USNA; Memcon, June 25, 1948, ibid. (/6-2548); Memcon, August 3, 1948, ibid. (/8-348); Letter, Gilsinn to Palmer, November 25, 1947, ibid. (/11-2547); Letter, Fred Huber to R. D. Gatewood, June 2, 1948, OSAA, SFAA, box 10, "820.8 Morrison-Knudsen, Afghanistan 1945–48," USNA.

55. Despatch 37E, Squire to Bevin, March 27, 1948, FO 371/69948, UKNA; Letter, Squire to Grey, July 24, 1948, FO 371/69449, UKNA; Letter, P. F. Grey to Squire, July 5, 1948, FO 983/13, UKNA; Memcon, August 3, 1948, CDF, 890H.64A/8-348, USNA; Minutes, December 26, 1949, in Despatch 20, Kabul to Washington, January 25, 1950, CDF, 890.2614/1-2550, USNA.
56. Letter, Ludin to Morrison, May 5, 1949, OSAA, SFAA, box 10, 820.8 Morrison-Knudsen, Afghanistan 1949, USNA; Agenda, Naim, March 28, 1949, ibid.; Despatch 105, Kabul to Washington, September 27, 1950, CDF, 889.10/9-2750, USNA.
57. Memcon, March 28, 1949, OSAA, SFAA, box 10, 820.8 Morrison-Knudsen, Afghanistan 1949, USNA; Agenda, Naim, March 28, 1949, ibid.; Despatch 109, Kabul to Washington, April 26, 1950, CDF, 889.00/4-2650, USNA.
58. Letter, Huber to Gatewood, June 2, 1948, OSAA, SFAA, box 10, 820.8 Morrison-Knudsen, Afghanistan 1945–48, USNA.
59. Memorandum, C. P. Schoeller to the Department of Commerce, December 11, 1947, KGR, 1947, 864 M-K, USNA.
60. Memcon, December 23, 1947, KCR, 1947, 864, USNA.
61. Telegram 95, Washington to Kabul, April 23, 1948, CDF, 890H.51/4-2348, USNA; Agenda, Naim, March 28, 1949, OSAA, SFAA, box 10, 820.8 Morrison-Knudsen, Afghanistan 1949, USNA.
62. Despatch 87, Kabul to London, June 22, 1948, FO 371/69449, UKNA.
63. Letter, Walsh to Dreyfus, October 8, 1949, MWP, box 9, "Subject File, 1947–51 Afghanistan (2)," AHC; Letter, Walsh to Ghulam Mohammed, May 12, 1948, MWP, box 9, "Subject Files 1947–48, Afghanistan Reports," AHC; John Hlavacek, *United Press Invades India: Memoirs of a Foreign Correspondent, 1944–1952* (New York: iUniverse, 2006), 126–27.
64. Despatch 131, Kabul to Washington, August 19, 1948, CDF, 890H.6363/8-1948, USNA; David Wharton, Annual Economic Report, February 19, 1949, CDF, 890H.50/2-1949, USNA; Telegram 301, Kabul to Washington, November 8, 1948, CDF, 890H.63/11-848, USNA; Letter, Walsh to Leach, April 7, 1948, ibid. (/4-748); Despatch 192, Kabul to Washington, December 28, 1948, ibid. (/12-2848); Letter, Paris to Kabul, April 20, 1948, A-O(A) 1944–72, 21, MAE/P.
65. Letter, Symon to Foreign Office, March 20, 1948, FO 371/69449, UKNA; Telegram 13, London to Kabul, January 20, 1948, FO 371/69948, UKNA; Memcon, March 3, 1948, CDF, 890H.24/3-348, USNA.
66. Telegram 170–03, Prague to Washington, June 3, 1947, CDF, 890H.24/6-347, USNA; Memorandum, Kent to Palmer, July 4, 1948, ibid. (/7-448); Telegram 193, July 30, 1948, CDF, 890H.20/7-2948, USNA; Memcon, November 19, 1948, *FRUS, 1948, V-1*: 491–92.

67. Telegram 141, Washington to Kabul, August 22, 1949, CDF, 890H.24/8-1249, USNA; Telegram 280, Kabul to Washington, December 6, 1949, ibid. (/12-649); Memcon, June 8, 1949, CDF, 745F.90H15/6-849, USNA; Robert David Johnson, *Congress and the Cold War* (New York: Cambridge University Press, 2006), 28–29.
68. Leon B. Poullada and Leila Poullada, *The Kingdom of Afghanistan and the United States: 1828–1973* (Lincoln, NE: Center for Afghanistan Studies and Dageforde Publishing, 1995), 133–37.
69. Ludwig W. Adamec, *Afghanistan's Foreign Affairs to the Mid-Twentieth Century: Relations with the USSR, Germany, and Britain* (Tucson: University of Arizona Press, 1974), 265–66.
70. CIA Report SR-32, "Afghanistan," October 21, 1948, CIARR.
71. Letter 36/9/49, Kabul to London, April 30, 1949, FO 983/44, UKNA.
72. Memorandum, Jernegan to Thurston, October 11, 1948, *FRUS, 1949, VI*: 1–8; SANACC 360/14, April 19, 1949, *FRUS, 1949, VI*: 8–31.
73. Harry S Truman, Inaugural Address, January 20, 1949, in *Public Papers of the Presidents, 1949* (Washington, DC: GPO, 1950), 112–16; Amanda Kay McVety, *Enlightened Aid: U.S. Development as Foreign Aid Policy in Ethiopia* (New York: Oxford University Press, 2012), 91–103.
74. Olav Stokke, *The UN and Development: From Aid to Cooperation* (Bloomington: Indiana University Press, 2009), 43–52; David Webster, "Development Advisors in a Time of Cold War and Decolonization: The United Nations Technical Assistance Administration, 1950–59," *Journal of Global History* 6, no. 2 (July 2011): 249–72.
75. Aide Memoire, December 29, 1949, Owen Lattimore Papers, box 20, "United Nations," LOC.
76. Telegram 82, Washington to Kabul, April 26, 1949, CDF, 745F.90H15/4-1949, USNA; Despatch 63, Kabul to Washington, May 11, 1949, ibid. (/5-1149); Telegram 55, Washington to Kabul, March 28, 1949, ibid. (/2-2349); Telegram 109, Washington to Kabul, June 17, 1949, ibid. (/6-1549); Telegram 68, Kabul to Washington, March 24, 1949, CDF, 890H.00(W)/3-2449, USNA.
77. Telegram 90, Kabul to Washington, April 13, 1949, CDF, 890H.51/4-1349, USNA; Peter G. Franck, *Obtaining Financial Aid for a Development Plan; the Export-Import Bank of Washington Loan to Afghanistan* (Washington, DC: Government Printing Office, 1954), 11–32.
78. Franck, *Obtaining Financial Aid*, 27–34.
79. Telegram 217, Kabul to Washington, September 19, 1949, *FRUS, 1949, VI*: 1778; Telegram 207, Kabul to Washington, September 5, 1949, CDF, 890H.51/9-549, USNA; Telegram 232, Kabul to Washington, September 28, 1949, ibid. (/9-2849); Franck, *Obtaining Financial Aid*, 27–34.

80. Airgram A-122, Kabul to Washington, November 2, 1949, CDF, 890H.51/12-249, USNA; Telegram 142.541, Kabul to Prague, October 13, 1949, TO-O(A) 1945–59, 1:8, AMZV; Telegram 6344/49, Kabul to Prague, October 24, 1949, TO-O(A), 1945–59, 1:12, AMZV; Franck, *Obtaining Financial Aid*, 34–35.

81. Louis Dupree, *Afghanistan* (Princeton, NJ: Princeton University Press, 1973), 494–96; Faridullah Bezhan, "The Pashtunistan Issue and Politics in Afghanistan, 1947–1952," *Middle East Journal* 68, no. 2 (2014): 197–209; Amin Saikal, *Modern Afghanistan: A History of Struggle and Survival* (London: I. B. Tauris, 2012), 116–17; Thomas Ruttig, "Flash from the Past: The 1950 Kabul Students Union and Its Impact on the Post-WWII Opposition Movement," Afghan Analysts Network, April 26, 2020, https://www.afghanistan-analysts.org/en/reports/context-culture/flash-from-the-past-the-1950-kabul-students-union-and-its-impact-on-the-post-wwii-opposition-movement/.

82. Telegram 45, Kabul to Washington, February 15, 1950, CDF, 789.00/2-1550, USNA.

83. Minute, "Petrol from Pakistan," December 19, 1949, FO 983/45, UKNA; Telegram 288, Kabul to Washington, December 22, 1949, CDF, 890H.00 (W)/12-2249, USNA.

84. Telegram 41, Kabul to Washington, February 14, 1950, CDF, 689.90D/2-1450, USNA; Telegram 55, Washington to Kabul, March 3, 1950, ibid. (/3-350); Letter P/41, Karachi to Kabul, March 3, 1950, FO 983/60, UKNA.

85. Memcon, February 1, 1950, CDF, 689.90D/2-150, USNA; David Ekbladh, *The Great American Mission: Modernization and the Construction of an American World Order* (Princeton, NJ: Princeton University Press, 2010), 119–20.

86. Letter, Jessup to McGhee, March 6, 1950, CDF, 689.90D/3-650, USNA; Letter, Karachi to Kabul, April 14, 1950, FO 983/60, UKNA; Depeche 120, Kabul to Paris, March 22, 1950, A-O(A) 1944–72, 14, MAE/P.

87. Telegram 52/53, Kabul to Paris, March 6, 1950, A-O(A) 1944–72, 14, MAE/P; Letter, Jessup to McGhee, March 6, 1950, CDF, 689.90D/3-650, USNA; Despatch 33, Kabul to London, March 9, 1950, FO 371/83043, UKNA.

88. William S. White, "Clashes Highlight M'Carthy Hearing," *NYT*, March 10, 1950; Robert P. Newman, *Owen Lattimore and the "Loss" of China* (Berkeley: University of California Press, 1992), 217–18.

89. Jonathan L. Lee, *Afghanistan: A History from 1260 to the Present* (London: Reaktion, 2022), 548.

90. Telegram 106, Kabul to Washington, September 30, 1950, RG-469, Administrative Services Division, Communications and Records Unit, Geographic Files, box 1, "Afghanistan—Projects," USNA; Despatch 104E, Kabul to London, August 2, 1950, FO 371/83069, UKNA.

91. Discussions between Iran and Afghanistan, August 1950, RRSA, SFPAA, box 12, "Helmand River Negotiations, 1950," USNA.

92. Ibid.
93. NSC 68, April 7, 1950, *FRUS, 1950, I*: 238.
94. NSC 98/1, January 22, 1951, *FRUS, 1951, VI-2*: 1650–52; Robert J. McMahon, *The Cold War on the Periphery: The United States, India, and Pakistan* (New York: Columbia University Press, 1994), 123–26.
95. Policy Statement, "Afghanistan," February 21, 1951, *FRUS, 1951, VI-2*: 2004–12.
96. Ibid.
97. Telegram 117, Washington to Kabul, November 2, 1950, *FRUS, 1950, V*: 1455; Telegram 167, Kabul to Washington, November 13, 1950, *FRUS, 1950, V*: 1456–57; Memcon, November 16, 1950, OSAA, SFAA, box 12, "Pakistan-Afghanistan Relations," USNA.
98. Telegram 63, Kabul to London, May 13, 1951, FO 371/92095, UKNA; Telegram 494, Karachi to London, May 10, 1951, ibid.
99. Memcon, March 12, 1951, *FRUS, 1951, VI-2*: 1948–51; George McGhee, *Envoy to the Middle World: Adventures in Diplomacy* (New York: Harper & Row, 1983), 310; McMahon, *Cold War on the Periphery*, 131–35.
100. Memcon, April 23, 1951, *FRUS, 1951, VI-2*: 1965–67; Memcon, June 8, 1951, *FRUS, 1951, VI-2*: 1980–82; McGhee, *Envoy to the Middle World*, 314–15.
101. Memcon, June 8, 1951, *FRUS, 1951, VI-2*: 1980–82; Telegram 111, Kabul to Washington, August 20, 1951, CDF, 789.5/8-2051, USNA; Telegram 178, Washington to Kabul, November 27, 1951, ibid. (/9-651); Telegram 232, Kabul to Washington, November 8, 1951, ibid. (/11-851); Telegram 279, Kabul to Washington, December 8, 1951, ibid. (/12-851).
102. Memcon, April 23, 1951, *FRUS, 1951, VI-2*: 1965–67; Despatch 362, Kabul to Washington, May 22, 1951, CDF, 789.00/5-2251, USNA; Telegram 383, Kabul to Washington, May 28, 1951, ibid. (/5-2851).
103. Faridullah Bezhan, "The Rise and Fall of the Liberal Hezbe Watan or Homeland Party in Afghanistan, 1949–52," *British Journal of Middle Eastern Studies* 42, no. 4 (October 2015): 401–26.
104. Telegram 81, Kabul to London, May 23, 1951, FO 371/92096, UKNA; Telegram 2745, London to Washington, May 31, 1951, ibid.; Letter, Kabul to London, July 10, 1951, FO 371/92084, UKNA; Despatch 362, Kabul to Washington, May 22, 1951, CDF, 789.00/5-2251, USNA; Telegram 184–186, Kabul to Paris, September 12, 1951, A-O(A) 1944–72, 18, MAE/P.
105. Depeche 50, Kabul to Paris, January 22, 1951, A-O(A) 1944–72, 18, MAE/P; Telegram 270, Kabul to Washington, December 5, 1951, CDF, 889.10/12-551, USNA.
106. Despatch 358, Kabul to Washington, May 22, 1951, CDF, 889.00TA/5-2251, USNA; Memcon, February 1, 1952, ibid. (/2-1452).
107. Despatch 102, Kabul to Washington, September 7, 1951, CDF, 889.00TA/9-751, USNA; Amanda Kay McVety, *The Rinderpest Campaigns: A Virus, Its Vaccines, and*

Global Development in the Twentieth Century (New York: Cambridge University Press, 2018), 152–62; Ritchie Calder, *Men Against the Jungle* (London: Allen & Unwin, 1954), 169–84; Kathleen McLaughlin, *New Life in Old Lands* (New York: Dodd, Mead, 1954), 168–96; Howard M. Teaf and Peter G. Franck, *Hands Across Frontiers: Case Studies in Technical Cooperation* (Leiden: Sijthoff, 1955), 13–64.

108. Despatch 102, Kabul to Washington, September 7, 1951, CDF, 889.00TA/9-751, USNA.
109. Norman M. Naimark, *Stalin and the Fate of Europe: The Postwar Struggle for Sovereignty* (Cambridge, MA: The Belknap Press of Harvard University Press, 2019), 231–66.
110. Ilya V. Gaiduk, *Divided Together: The United States and the Soviet Union in the United Nations, 1945–1965* (Stanford, CA: Stanford University Press, 2012), 195.
111. Despatch 35, Kabul to Washington, March 24, 1950, FO 371/83069, UKNA.
112. Despatch 268, Kabul to Washington, March 12, 1951, CDF, 889.00TA/2-1551, USNA; Despatch 43, Kabul to Washington, July 29, 1950, CDF, 889.2553/7-2950, USNA.
113. Letter, Kabul to London, March 28, 1951, FO 371/92089, UKNA.
114. Telegram 52/53, Kabul to Paris, March 6, 1950, A-O(A) 1944–72, 14, MAE/P; Depeche 120, Kabul to Paris, March 22, 1950, ibid.; Kabul to London, March 28, 1951, FO 371/92089, UKNA.
115. Telegram, Prague to Kabul, February 28, 1951, TO-T(A) 1945–54, 1:9, AMZV; Telegram 358/51, Kabul to Prague, January 15, 1951, TO-O(A) 1945–59, 3:1, AMZV.
116. Telegram 54/57, Kabul to Paris, March 16, 1951, A-O(A) 1944–72, 14, MAE/P.
117. Depeche 110/AS, Kabul to Paris, March 19, 1951, A-O(A) 1944–72, 14, MAE/P.
118. Letter, Kabul to London, March 28, 1951, FO 371/92089, UKNA; Letter, New York to London, May 15, 1951, FO 371/92121, UKNA; Airgram A-6, Washington to Kabul, July 12, 1951, CDF, 889.2553/6-1251, USNA.
119. Despatch 61, Kabul to Washington, August 9, 1951, CDF, 889.2553/8-951, USNA; Despatch 89, Kabul to Washington, August 21, 1951, ibid. (/8-2151).
120. Letter, Kabul to London, December 28, 1951, FO 371/100986, UKNA; Letter, London to Kabul, October 9, 1951, FO 371/92121, UKNA; Memcon, March 14, 1952, CDF, 889.2553/3-1452, USNA; Telegram 223, Kabul to Washington, November 2, 1951, CDF, 889.10-A/11-151, USNA.
121. Telegram 26, Washington to Kabul, July 14, 1951, CDF, 889.2553/7-1451, USNA; Despatch 132, Kabul to Washington, October 13, 1951, ibid. (/10-1351); Telegram 110, Kabul to London, July 6, 1951, FO 371/92120, UKNA; Memorandum, "Persian-Afghan Oil Agreement," September 18, 1951, ibid.; Despatch 111E, Kabul to London, October 13, 1951, ibid.

122. Despatch 121, Kabul to London, October 31, 1952, FO 371/92112, UKNA; Letter, Kabul to London, December 28, 1951, FO 371/100986, UKNA; Radio excerpt, May 4, 1952, ibid.; Letter, Kabul to London, January 11, 1952, ibid, UKNA; Despatch 138, Kabul to London, December 29, 1951, FO 371/100979, UKNA.
123. UNTAM Working Paper, January 14, 1952, FO 371/100979, UKNA; Despatch 43E, Kabul to London, April 1, 1952, ibid.
124. Despatch 632/52, Kabul to Prague, May 21, 1952, TO-T(A) 1945–54, 1:6, AMZV; Telegram 9548/52, Kabul to Prague, October 7, 1952, ibid.; Despatch 753/52, Kabul to Prague, June 18, 1952, TO-O(A) 1945–59, 2:24, AMZV.
125. Despatch 42E, Kabul to London, March 31, 1952, FO 371/100986, UKNA.
126. Despatch 90E, Kabul to London, August 31, 1952, FO 371/100986, UKNA; Depeche 959, Moscow to Paris, August 27, 1952, A-O(A) 1944–72, 21, MAE/P; Telegram 125, Kabul to Washington, September 9, 1952, *FRUS, 1952–54, XI-2*: 1449–50.
127. Report 39–45, Ernest Fox, June 20, 1945, CDF, 890H.6363/10-745, USNA.
128. Letter, Palmer to Leach, April 16, 1949, OSAA, SFAA, box 9, "Leach-Palmer Correspondence," USNA.

4. "We Might Be Willing to Take a Chance"

1. Telegram 620, Kabul to Washington, December 15, 1955, CDF, 033.6189/12-1555, USNA; Despatch 70, Kabul to London, December 23, 1955, FO 371/123282, UKNA; Despatch 460, Kabul to Paris, December 1955, A-O(A) 1944–72, 12, MAE/P.
2. Telegram 652, Kabul to Washington, December 21, 1955, CDF, 033.6189/12-2155, USNA; Despatch 157, Kabul to Washington, December 22, 1955, ibid. (/12-2255); Despatch 70, Kabul to London, December 23, 1955, FO 371/123282, UKNA; Despatch 460, Kabul to Paris, December 1955, A-O(A) 1944–72, 12, MAE/P.
3. Nikita Khrushchev and Sergei Khrushchev, *Memoirs of Nikita Khrushchev*, vol. 3, *Statesman, 1953–1964* (University Park: Pennsylvania State University Press, 2013), 763–67.
4. Ibid., 763–67, 849–51.
5. Telegram 146, Kabul to Washington, September 23, 1952, CDF, 661.89/9-2352, USNA; Telegram 147, Kabul to Washington, September 23, 1952, *FRUS, 1952–54, XI-2*: 1452–54.
6. Despatch 317, Kabul to Washington, March 3, 1952, CDF, 789.00/3-352, USNA; Despatch 57, Kabul to London, May 3, 1952, FO 371/100961, UKNA; Faridullah Bezhan, "The Rise and Fall of the Liberal Hezbe Watan or Homeland

Party in Afghanistan, 1949–52," *British Journal of Middle Eastern Studies* 42, no. 4 (October 2015): 401–26.

7. Telegram 485, Moscow to Washington, September 13, 1952, CDF, 889.2553/9-1352, USNA.
8. Intel Despatch 246, London to Various Posts, November 6, 1952, DO 35/6627, UKNA; Telegram 88, London to Kabul, October 9, 1952, ibid.
9. Telegram 112, Washington to Kabul, September 29, 1952, *FRUS, 1952–54, XI-2*: 1454–56; Memorandum, Byroade to David Bruce, October 10, 1952, *FRUS, 1952–54, XI-2*: 1458–62.
10. Telegram 176, Kabul to Washington, October 2, 1952, *FRUS, 1952–54, XI-2*: 1456–58; Telegram 141, Washington to Kabul, October 11, 1952, *FRUS, 1952–54, XI-2*:1462–63.
11. Telegram 254, Kabul to Washington, November 5, 1952, CDF, 889.2311/11-552, USNA; Telegram 313, Kabul to Washington, December 2, 1952, ibid. (/12-252).
12. Memcon, December 24, 1952, *FRUS, 1952–54, XI-2*: 1464.
13. Memorandum, Harriman to Truman, December 30, 1952, ONESAD/AB, PF, 1952–58, box 13, "Afghan Wheat Loan 1953," USNA.
14. Airgram A-51, Kabul to Washington, January 8, 1953, CDF, 611.89/1-853, USNA.
15. Russell Baker, "Career Diplomat 31 Years Retires," *NYT*, March 21, 1956; James McCargar, ADSTOH, 38–43; Kennan, November 29, 1945, George F. Kennan Papers, Writings: Diaries, 231:13, Princeton University Library.
16. "Merit in Acheson's Eyes," *Chicago Daily Tribune*, October 24, 1950; "State Dept. Denies 'Exiling' of Angus Ward," *New York Herald Tribune*, October 11, 1950; "Ward Urged as Envoy," *NYT*, July 14, 1950.
17. Memcon, May 24, 1950, CDF, 123-Ward, USNA.
18. Memorandum, May 6, 1954, JFDP, Personnel Series, box 1, "Evaluation of Chiefs of Mission (2)," DDEL.
19. Ibid.; William Lehfeldt, ADSTOH, April 29, 1994, 15–16; Ralph Lindstrom, ADSTOH, October 28, 1994, 9–12.
20. William I. Hitchcock, *The Age of Eisenhower: America and the World in the 1950s* (New York: Simon & Schuster, 2018), 94–102; Melvyn P. Leffler, *For the Soul of Mankind: The United States, The Soviet Union, and the Cold War* (New York: Hill and Wang, 2007), 95–113; Robert R. Bowie and Richard H. Immerman, *Waging Peace How Eisenhower Shaped an Enduring Cold War Strategy* (New York: Oxford University Press, 1998), 83–88.
21. Peter L. Hahn, *The United States, Great Britain, and Egypt, 1945–1956: Strategy and Diplomacy in the Early Cold War* (Chapel Hill: University of North Carolina Press, 1991), 131–59; Robert J. McMahon, *The Cold War on the Periphery: The United States, India, and Pakistan* (New York: Columbia University Press, 1994), 124–52.

22. 147th NSC Meeting, June 1, 1953, *FRUS, 1952–54, IX-1*: 379–86.
23. NSC 155/1, July 14, 1953, *FRUS, 1952–54, IX-1*: 399–405.
24. 147th NSC Meeting, June 1, 1953, *FRUS, 1952–54, IX-1*: 379–86; 153rd NSC Meeting, July 9, 1953, *FRUS, 1952–54, IX-1*: 394–98; McMahon, *Cold War on the Periphery*, 158–65.
25. NSC 162/2, October 30, 1953, *FRUS, 1952–54, II-1*: 578–96.
26. NSC 5402, January 2, 1954, *FRUS, 1952–54, X*: 867–89; Memcon, January 5, 1954, *FRUS, 1952–54, XI-2*: 1838–39; NSC 5409, February 19, 1954, *FRUS, 1952–54, XI-2*: 1089–96.
27. Mark Gasiorowski, *U.S. Foreign Policy and the Shah: Building a Client State in Iran* (Ithaca, NY: Cornell University Press, 1991), 85–92; McMahon, *Cold War on the Periphery*, 154–88; Abbas Milani, *The Shah* (New York: Palgrave Macmillan, 2011), 193–97.
28. Leon B. Poullada and Leila Poullada, *The Kingdom of Afghanistan and the United States: 1828–1973* (Lincoln, NE: Center for Afghanistan Studies and Dageforde Publishing, 1995); Jeffery J. Roberts, *The Origins of Conflict in Afghanistan* (Westport, CT: Praeger, 2003).
29. Letter, Kabul to London, March 21, 1953, FO 371/106650, UKNA; Letter, Kabul to London, June 26, 1953, ibid. (/15); Despatch 70, Kabul to London, August 22, 1953, ibid. (/17). See also Leffler, *Soul*, 120–22.
30. Despatch 785/52, Kabul to Prague, July 3, 1952, TO-O(A) 1945–59, 3:2, AMZV; Despatch 169/53, Kabul to Prague, February 11, 1953, TO-O(A) 1945–59, 2:8, AMZV; Quarterly Report, Kabul to Prague, (winter 1953), TO-O(A) 1945–59, 3:6, AMZV; Minute, W. B. J. Ledwidge, October 23, 1953, FO 983/101, UKNA.
31. Telegram 71617/52, Kabul to Prague, August 6, 1952, TO-T(A) 1945–54, 1:5, AMZV; Telegram 1016/51, Kabul to Prague, February 5, 1951, TO-T(A) 1945–54, 1:6, AMZV; Telegram 8886/50, Kabul to Prague, October 31, 1950, TO-O(A) 1945–59, 2:28, AMZV; Despatch 35(S), Kabul to London, April 15, 1953, FO 371/106650, UKNA.
32. Despatch 55, Kabul to Washington, September 8, 1953, CDF, 789.13/9-853, USNA; Amin Saikal, *Modern Afghanistan: A History of Struggle and Survival* (London: I. B. Tauris, 2012), 117–18.
33. Saikal, *Modern Afghanistan*, 112–25.
34. George McGhee, *Envoy to the Middle World: Adventures in Diplomacy* (New York: Harper & Row, 1983), 306.
35. Despatch 6, Kabul to London, January 25, 1954, FO 402/30 (DA 1011/1), UKNA.
36. Despatch 510/51, Kabul to Prague, December 13, 1951, TO-O(A) 1945–59, 2:11, AMZV.

37. Hafizullah Emadi, *Dynamics of Political Development in Afghanistan: The British, Russian, and American Invasions* (New York: Palgrave Macmillan, 2016), 58–61; Mir Tamim Ansary, *Games Without Rules: The Often Interrupted History of Afghanistan* (New York: PublicAffairs, 2012), 144–45.
38. Despatch 140, Kabul to Paris, May 2, 1954, A-O(A) 1944–72, 18, MAE/P; Despatch 10, Kabul to Washington, July 20, 1954, CDF, 789.00/7-2054, USNA.
39. Despatch 604, Kabul to Washington, May 14, 1957, CDF, 989.72/5-1457, USNA.
40. Despatch 282, Kabul to Washington, February 5, 1952, CDF, 889.2614-Helmand/2-552, USNA.
41. Telegram 252, Kabul to Washington, November 27, 1951, CDF, 889.2614-Helmand/11-2651, USNA; Despatch 321, Kabul to Washington, March 4, 1952, ibid. (/3-452); Despatch 330, Kabul to Washington, March 10, 1952, ibid. (/3-1052); Memcon, April 16, 1952, CDF, 889.00-TA/4-1652, USNA.
42. Telegram 56, Kabul to Washington, August 1, 1952, CDF, 889.2614-Helmand/8-152, USNA; Telegram 75, Kabul to Washington, August 13, 1952, ibid. (/8-1352).
43. Despatch 104, Kabul to Washington, November 13, 1952, CDF, 889.2614-Helmand/11-1352, USNA.
44. Despatch TOTEC 4, Kabul to Washington, November 24, 1952, CDF, 889.2614-Helmand/11-2452, USNA.
45. Despatch 48, Kabul to London, May 16, 1953, FO 371/106669, UKNA.
46. Harper, Notes on Afghanistan & India Trips Aug-Oct 1945, Sinclair O. Harper Papers, box 57, "India and Afghanistan Projects 1945–53," AHC; Letter, Harper to W. L. Powers, August 9, 1945, CDF, 890H.611/8-945, USNA; Letter, Minor to Oregon State College, October 12, 1945, CDF, 890H.611A/10-445, USNA; Despatch 824, Kabul to Washington, September 19, 1945, KCR, 1945, 864, USNA.
47. Despatch TOTEC 4; Despatch 25, Kabul to Washington, March 2, 1949, CDF, 890H.50/3-249, USNA; Nick Cullather, *The Hungry World: America's Cold War Battle Against Poverty in Asia* (Cambridge, MA: Harvard University Press, 2010), 118–22.
48. Despatch TOTEC 4; Memorandum, Hayes to Haldore Hanson, December 27, 1952, ONESAD/AB, PF, box 8, "Letters: Hayes and Lazaroff I," USNA; Letter, Hayes to Lou Lazaroff, October 3, 1952, ibid.
49. Despatch TOTEC 4; Memorandum, Taylor to Lazaroff, July 22, 1953, ONESAD/AB, PF, box 1, "Cables and Correspondence 1954," USNA; Louis Dupree, *Afghanistan* (Princeton, NJ: Princeton University Press, 1973), 499–502; Cullather, *The Hungry World*, 123–25.

50. Letter, Kabul to London, February 20, 1953, FO 371/106669, UKNA; Despatch 48, Kabul to London, May 16, 1953, ibid.
51. Peter G. Franck, *Obtaining Financial Aid for a Development Plan; the Export-Import Bank of Washington Loan to Afghanistan* (Washington, DC: Government Printing Office, 1954), 48–49.
52. Memorandum, Hays to Hanson, December 27, 1952, ONESAD/AB, PF, box 8, "Hayes and Lazaroff I," USNA
53. Letter, Kabul to London, February 20, 1953, FO 371/106669, UKNA.
54. Memorandum, Hays to Lazaroff, February 7, 1953, ONESAD/AB, PF, box 8, "Hayes and Lazaroff II," USNA.
55. Despatch TOTEC 48, Kabul to Washington, September 30, 1953, ONESAD/AB, PF, box 1, "Cables and Correspondence 1954," USNA.
56. Dennis Kux, *The United States and Pakistan, 1947–2000: Disenchanted Allies* (Washington, DC: Woodrow Wilson Center Press, 2001), 62–63.
57. Telegram 324, Kabul to Washington, April 3, 1954, CDF, 661.89/4-354, USNA; Telegram 327, Kabul to Washington, April 5, 1954, ibid. (/4-554); Telegram 326, Kabul to Washington, April 3, 1954, CDF, 789.5-MSP/4-354, USNA.
58. Despatch 7, Kabul to London, February 6, 1954, FO 371/111949, UKNA.
59. Despatch 23, Kabul to Paris, February 1, 1954, A-O(A) 1944–72, 12, MAE/P; Paul Robinson and Jay Dixon, *Aiding Afghanistan: A History of Soviet Assistance to a Developing Country* (London: Hurst, 2013), 6–8, 48–51; Timothy Nunan, *Humanitarian Invasion: Global Development in Cold War Afghanistan* (New York: Cambridge University Press, 2016), 60–64.
60. Telegram 210, Kabul to Washington, December 15, 1953, *FRUS, 1952–54*, XI-2: 1407; Telegram 202, Washington to Kabul, February 20, 1954, CDF, 889.2311/12-953, USNA; Letter, Naim to Eximbank, January 12, 1953, KCR, 1953, "501 Eximbank Loan," USNA.
61. Letter, Arey to Glendenning, April 19, 1954, *FRUS, 1952–54*, XI-2: 1472–74; Burton I. Kaufman, *Trade and Aid: Eisenhower's Foreign Economic Policy, 1953–1961* (Baltimore, MD: Johns Hopkins University Press, 1982), 29–32; William H. Becker and William M. McClenahan, *The Market, the State, and the Export-Import Bank of the United States, 1934–2000* (New York: Cambridge University Press, 2003), 92–99.
62. Peter G. Franck, "Economic Progress in an Encircled Land," *Middle East Journal* 10, no. 1 (January 1956): 47–50.
63. Memcon, April 13, 1954, CDF, 889.10/4-1354, USNA; Telegram 330, Kabul to Washington, April 5, 1954, ibid. (/4-554); Despatch 185, Kabul to Washington, April 13, 1954, CDF, 889.00/4-1354, USNA; Despatch 193, Kabul to Washington, April 20, 1954, ibid. (/4-2054); Letter, Kabul to London, February 20, 1954, FO 371/111937, UKNA.

64. NSC 5409, February 19, 1954, *FRUS, 1952–54, XI-2*: 1089–96.
65. Memcon, January 5, 1954, *FRUS, 1952–54, XI-2*: 1407–9; Memcon, January 15, 1954, CDF, 789.5-MSP/1-554, USNA.
66. Letter, Washington to London, March 4, 1954, FO 371/111942, UKNA.
67. Fred I. Greenstein, *The Hidden-Hand Presidency: Eisenhower as Leader* (Baltimore, MD: Johns Hopkins University Press, 1994); Anna Kasten Nelson, "The 'Top of Policy Hill': President Eisenhower and the National Security Council," *Diplomatic History* 7, no. 4 (October 1983): 307–26.
68. Airgram A-73, Washington to Kabul, May 14, 1954, CDF, 889.00/5-1454, USNA; Memorandum, Smith to Kennedy, June 23, 1954, *FRUS, 1952–54, XI-2*: 1474–75.
69. Letter, Kabul to London, June 12, 1954, FO 371/111936, UKNA; Letter, Kabul to London, October 13, 1954, ibid.; Despatch 243, Kabul to Paris, September 15, 1954, A-O(A) 1944–72, 20, MAE/P; Czechoslovak-Afghan Credit Agreement, August 22, 1954, TO-T(A) 1945–54, 1:5, AMZV.
70. NIE 53–54, "Outlook for Afghanistan," October 19, 1954, CIARR.
71. Telegram 192, Kabul to Washington, December 2, 1953, CDF, 689.90D/12-253, USNA; Telegram 227, Bombay to Washington, February 10, 1954, *FRUS, 1952–54, XI-2*: 1411; Letter, Karachi to London, February 17, 1954, FO 371/111942, UKNA.
72. Telegram 350, Kabul to Washington, April 16, 1954, CDF, 689.90D/4-1554, USNA; Despatch 868, Karachi to Washington, June 25, 1954, ibid. (/6-2554); Despatch 152, Karachi to Washington, September 20, 1954, ibid. (/9-2054); Telegram 470, Kabul to Washington, June 23, 1954, CDF, 789.00/6-2354, USNA; Letter, Kabul to London, March 5, 1954, FO 371/111943, UKNA; Telegram 623, Karachi to London, May 11, 1954, ibid.
73. Memcon and Memorandum, October 8, 1954, CDF, 689.90D/10-854, USNA; Memcon, October 8, 1954, *FRUS, 1952–54, XI-2*: 1421–22; Telegram 257, New York to Washington, October 12, 1954, *FRUS, 1952–54, XI-2*: 1423–24.
74. Telegram 257; Letter, Dulles to Lodge, November 22, 1954, *FRUS, 1952–54, XI-2*: 1433–34; Telegram 203, Kabul to Washington, December 2, 1954, *FRUS, 1952–54, XI-2*: 1434; Despatch 297, Karachi to Washington, November 19, 1954, CDF, 689.90D/11-1954, USNA.
75. Memorandum, December 10, 1954, PPAWF, NSC Series, box 6, 228th NSC Meeting, DDEL.
76. Ibid.
77. Ibid.
78. Memcon, December 13, 1954, *FRUS, 1952–54, XI-2*: 1435–36; Telegram 186, Washington to Kabul, December 16, 1954, *FRUS, 1952–54, XI-2*: 1437–38; Telegram 242, Kabul to Washington, December 25, 1954, *FRUS, 1952–54, XI-2*: 1441.

79. Ayesha Jalal, *The State of Martial Rule: The Origins of Pakistan's Political Economy of Defense* (New York: Cambridge University Press, 2008), 195–202.
80. Telegram 3998, Washington to London, February 4, 1955, *FRUS, 1955–57, VIII*: 163–64; Letter, Dulles to Lodge, February 15, 1955, *FRUS, 1955–57, VIII*: 165–66; Letter, Washington to London, February 3, 1955, FO 371/116992, UKNA; Letter, London to Washington, February 19, 1955, ibid.
81. Telegram 22, Kabul to London, March 30, 1955, FO 371/116995, UKNA; Telegram 29, Kabul to London, April 1, 1955, ibid.; Telegram 34/38, Kabul to Paris, March 31, 1955, A-O(A) 1944–72, 17, MAE/P.
82. Telegram 25, Kabul to London, March 31, 1955, FO 371/116995, UKNA; Telegram 30, Kabul to London, April 2, 1955, ibid.
83. Telegram 33, Kabul to London, April 2, 1955, FO 371/116995, UKNA; Telegram 1467, Karachi to Washington, April 12, 1955, *FRUS, 1955–57, VIII*: 173n; Letter, Kabul to London, May 5, 1955, FO 371/116992, UKNA.
84. Telegram 397, Washington to Kabul, April 12, 1955, *FRUS, 1955–57, VIII*: 170–72; Telegram 536, Kabul to Washington, April 26, 1955, *FRUS, 1955–57, VIII*: 175–77; Telegram 62, Kabul to London, April 27, 1955, FO 371/116997, UKNA; Telegram 99/104, Kabul to Paris, May 17, 1955, A-O(A) 1944–72, 17, MAE/P.
85. Telegram 635, Kabul to Washington, May 24, 1955, CDF, 689.90D/5-2455, USNA.
86. Telegram 87, Kabul to London, May 14, 1955, FO 371/116998, UKNA; Despatch 84, Karachi to London, May 13, 1955, FO 371/116999, UKNA; Telegram 954, Karachi to London, June 29, 1955, FO 371/117000, UKNA.
87. Despatch 117, Karachi to London, July 18, 1955, FO 371/117000, UKNA; Despatch 201, Kabul to Paris, June 4, 1955, A-O(A) 1944–72, 17, MAE/P.
88. Telegram 1911, Karachi to Washington, June 6, 1955, CDF, 689.90D/6-655, USNA; Telegram 133, Kabul to Washington, August 7, 1955, ibid. (/8-755); Telegram 193, Kabul to Washington, August 25, 1955, ibid. (/8-2555); NIE 52-55, March 15, 1955, CIARR.
89. Telegram 696, Kabul to Washington, June 20, 1955, CDF, 689.90D/6-2055, USNA; Telegram 627, Washington to Kabul, June 24, 1955, *FRUS, 1955–57, VIII*: 187–88; Telegram 74, Washington to Karachi, July 12, 1955, *FRUS, 1955–57, VIII*: 188–89.
90. Telegram 74; Memcon, July 9, 1955, CDF, 689.90D/7-955, USNA; Memcon, July 11, 1955, ibid. (/7-1155); Despatch 3, Kabul to Washington, July 12, 1955, ibid. (/7-1255); Memorandum, Jones to Allen, August 4, 1955, ibid. (/8-455).
91. Telegram 81, Karachi to Washington, July 15, 1955, CDF, 689.90D/7-1555, USNA; Telegram 1030, Karachi to London, July 27, 1955, FO 371/117001, UKNA; McMahon, *Cold War on the Periphery*, 199–204; Kux, *United States and Pakistan*, 80–82.

92. Telegram 141, Kabul to London, August 8, 1955, FO 371/117001, UKNA; Telegram 145, Kabul to London, August 11, 1955, ibid.; Telegram 112, Kabul to Washington, August 2, 1955, CDF, 689.90D/8-255, USNA; Telegram 259, Washington to Karachi, August 5, 1955, ibid. (/8-355).
93. Letter, Kabul to London, September 24, 1955, FO 371/117003, UKNA; Letter, Kabul to London, September 24, 1955, ibid.; Telegram 30, Lahore to Washington, September 16, 1955, CDF, 689.90D/9-1655, USNA.
94. Despatch 48, Kabul to London, September 24, 1955, FO 371/117003, UKNA.
95. Undated report (early 1956), TO-T(A) 1955–59, 1:3, AMZV.
96. Despatch 660/55, Kabul to Prague, April 5, 1955, TO-O(A) 1945–59, 2:29, AMZV; Letter, Kabul to London, July 16, 1955, FO 371/117008, UKNA; Despatch 44, Kabul to London, August 27, 1955, ibid.; Report 387/55, Kabul to Bonn, July 17, 1955, PA, B11/1379, AA; Telegram 194, Kabul to Washington, August 25, 1955, CDF, 889.2614-Helmand/8-2555, USNA.
97. Telegram 399, Kabul to Washington, October 22, 1955, CDF, 689.90D/10-2255, USNA; Telegram 192, Kabul to London, October 10, 1955, FO 371/116993, UKNA; Telegram 203, Kabul to London, October 19, 1955, ibid.; Report 586/55, Kabul to Bonn, October 22, 1955, PA, B11/1379, AA.
98. Telegram 399; Memorandum, J. J. Jones to Raymond Hare, October 6, 1955, *FRUS, 1955–57, VIII*: 191–93.
99. Despatch 384, Kabul to Paris, October 28, 1955, A-O(A) 1944–72, 5, MAE/P.
100. Letter, Lascelles to W. D. Allen, December 17, 1955, FO 371/117006, UKNA.
101. Despatch 93, Kabul to Washington, October 17, 1955, CDF, 661.89/10-1755, USNA.
102. Telegram 442, Kabul to Washington, November 5, 1955, CDF 689.90D/11-555, USNA; Telegram 444, Kabul to Washington, November 5, 1955, ibid.; Telegram 453, Kabul to Washington, November 7, 1955, ibid. (/11-755); Telegram 474, Kabul to Washington, November 14, 1955, ibid. (/11-1455); Telegram 281, Washington to Kabul, November 14, 1955, ibid.; Telegram 502, Kabul to Washington, November 19, 1955, ibid. (/11-1955).
103. Despatch 427, Kabul to Paris, November 27, 1955, A-O(A) 1944–72, 18, MAE/P; Telegram 512, Kabul to Washington, November 21, 1955, CDF, 689.90D/11-2155, USNA; Telegram 242, Kabul to London, November 29, 1955, FO 371/116990, UKNA; Report 672/55, Kabul to Bonn, November 28, 1955, PA, B11/1379, AA.
104. Memorandum, December 2, 1955, PPAWF, NSC Series, box 6, 228th NSC Meeting, DDEL.
105. Telegram 612, Kabul to Washington, December 14, 1955, *FRUS, 1955–57, VIII*: 208–11. Ward was not in Kabul when this cable was written. He reportedly departed to avoid having to shake Bulganin's hand.

106. Telegram 1066, Washington to Karachi, November 17, 1955, CDF, 689.90D/11-1755, USNA; Telegram 1036, Karachi to Washington, December 2, 1955, ibid. (/12-255); Telegram 1079, Karachi to Washington, December 8, 1955, ibid. (/12-855).
107. Andrew Jon Rotter, *Comrades at Odds: The United States and India, 1947–1964* (Ithaca, NY: Cornell University Press, 2000), 217–19, 243–48; Kux, *United States and Pakistan*, 70–74.
108. Memcon, March 7, 1956, *FRUS, 1955–57, VIII*: 220–25.
109. Richard H. Immerman, *John Foster Dulles: Piety, Pragmatism, and Power in U.S. Foreign Policy* (Wilmington, DE: Scholarly Resources, 1999), 147–52, 192–97.
110. NIE 53–56, January 10, 1956, CIARR; OCB, "Analysis of Internal Security Situation in Afghanistan," November 16, 1955, NSC Staff Papers, OCB Central File Series, box 22, "OCB 091 Afghanistan (1)," DDEL.
111. Memorandum, May 18, 1956, PPAWF, NSC Series, box 7, "285th NSC Meeting," DDEL.
112. Ibid.
113. Ibid.
114. Ibid.

5. Anxious Coexistence

1. Letter, Byroade to Ben Schoeman, September 5, 1959, Henry Byroade Papers, box 1, "Correspondence, Sept. 5 1959," DDEL.
2. Ibid.
3. Ibid.
4. Philip Nash, *Breaking Protocol: America's First Female Ambassadors, 1933–1964*, Studies in Conflict, Diplomacy, and Peace (Lexington: University Press of Kentucky, 2020), 14–16.
5. Despatch 196, Kabul to Washington, February 7, 1956, CDF, 789.5-MSP/2-756, USNA; Telegram 892, Kabul to Washington, February 23, 1956, CDF, 661.89/2-2356, USNA.
6. Despatch 205, Kabul to Washington, February 15, 1956, CDF, 661.89/2-1556, USNA; Letter, Poullada to Smith, January 31, 1956, CDF, 789.5-MSP/1-3156, USNA.
7. Despatch 41, Kabul to Washington, August 31, 1956, CDF, 889.00/8-3156, USNA; Maxwell J. Fry, *The Afghan Economy: Money, Finance, and the Critical Constraints to Economic Development* (Leiden: Brill, 1974), 69–81.
8. Telegram 863, Kabul to Washington, February 14, 1956, CDF, 789.5-MSP/2-1456, USNA.

9. Telegram 863; Telegram 600, Washington to Kabul, March 14, 1956, *FRUS, 1955–57, VIII*: 228–29.
10. 285th NSC Meeting, May 17, 1956, *FRUS, 1955–57, VIII*: 235.
11. Letter, George Blowers to Rountree, March 19, 1956, CDF, 889.2614-Helmand/3-1956, USNA; Memcon, March 14, 1956, ibid. (/3-1456).
12. Memcon, October 24, 1955, CDF, 889.2612/10-2455, USNA; Telegram TOICA 486, Kabul to Washington, May 20, 1956, CDF, 889.2614-Helmand/5-2056, USNA.
13. Memcon, July 11, 1955, CDF, 889.2614-Helmand/7-1155, USNA; Telegram TOICA 263, Kabul to Washington, January 10, 1956, ibid. (/1-1056).
14. Memcon, August 26, 1955, CDF, 889.2614-Helmand/8-2655, USNA; Telegram 553, Kabul to Washington, December 2, 1955, ibid. (/12-255); Despatch 144, Kabul to Washington, December 7, 1955, ibid. (/12-755).
15. Despatch 158, Kabul to Washington, December 22, 1955, CDF, 889.2614-Helmand/12-2255, USNA.
16. Telegram 377, Washington to Kabul, March 6, 1956, CDF, 889.2614-Helmand/3-656, USNA; Despatch 229, Kabul to Washington, March 14, 1956, ibid. (/3-1456); Telegram TOICA 433, Kabul to Washington, April 24, 1956, ibid. (/4-2456); Memorandum, Whatley to Strong, May 7, 1956, ibid. (/5-756); Telegram ICATO 517, Washington to Kabul, May 22, 1956, ibid. (/5-2256); Louis Dupree, *Afghanistan* (Princeton, NJ: Princeton University Press, 1973), 505–6.
17. Despatch 295, Kabul to Washington, February 18, 1952, CDF, 989.52/2-1852, USNA; Despatch 112, Kabul to Washington, November 22, 1952, ibid. (/11-2252); Despatch 87, Kabul to Washington, December 28, 1954, ibid. (/12-2854).
18. Telegram 230, Kabul to Washington, December 18, 1954, CDF, 989.52/12-1754, USNA; Despatch 87; Telegram 701, Kabul to Washington, June 21, 1955, CDF, 889.2612/6-2155, USNA; Jenifer Van Vleck, *Empire of the Air: Aviation and the American Ascendancy* (Cambridge, MA: Harvard University Press, 2013), 232–33.
19. Despatch 196; Telegram 892; Telegram 240, Kabul to Washington, September 10, 1955, CDF, 889.2614-Helmand/9-1055, USNA; Memorandum, Jones to Allen, March 20, 1956, CDF, 989.72/3-2056, USNA; Telegram 779, Washington to Kabul, April 3, 1956, ibid. (/4-356); Telegram 1131, Kabul to Washington, April 6, 1956, ibid. (/4-656); Telegram 1208, Kabul to Washington, ibid. (/4-1856).
20. Jenifer Van Vleck, "An Airline at the Crossroads of the World: Ariana Afghan Airlines, Modernization, and the Global Cold War," *History and Technology* 25, no. 1 (2009): 3–24.
21. Telegram 1268, Kabul to Washington, April 26, 1956, CDF, 989.72/4-2656, USNA; Telegram 1279, Kabul to Washington, April 30, 1956, ibid. (/4-3056);

Telegram 1340, Kabul to Washington, May 8, 1956, ibid. (/5-856); Telegram ICATO 480, Washington to Kabul, May 8, 1956, ibid.; Memorandum, Barnes to Hoover, May 21, 1956, ibid. (/5-2156); Memorandum, Hoover to Hollister, May 24, 1956, ibid. (/5-2456); Memorandum, Allen to Hoover, June 29, 1956, CDF, 789.5-MSP/6-2756, USNA.

22. Despatch 223, Kabul to Washington, March 8, 1956, CDF, 889.2612/3-856; David C. Engerman, *The Price of Aid: The Economic Cold War in India* (Cambridge, MA: Harvard University Press, 2018).

23. Richard T. Davies, ADSTOH, November 9, 1979, 52–58.

24. Despatch 39, Kabul to Washington, August 22, 1956, CDF, 989.724/8-2256, USNA; Memorandum, Witman to Rountree, September 17, 1956, ibid. (/9-1756).

25. Bruce Flatin, ADSTOH, January 27, 1993, 8; Despatch 73/56, Kabul to Prague, December 14, 1956, TO-T(A) 1955–59, 2:8, AMZV.

26. Despatch 204, Kabul to Washington, February 15, 1956, CDF, 611.89/2-1556, USNA.

27. Despatch 598, Kabul to Washington, April 22, 1958, CDF, 511.89/4-2258, USNA.

28. Telegram 974, Kabul to Washington, March 8, 1956, CDF, 889.191-KA/3-856, USNA; Telegram 750, Kabul to Washington, January 17, 1956 (/1-1756); Andrew James Wulf, *U.S. International Exhibitions During the Cold War: Winning Hearts and Minds Through Cultural Diplomacy* (Lanham, MD: Rowman & Littlefield, 2015), 70–77.

29. Telegram 176, Kabul to Washington, August 1, 1956, CDF, 889.191-KA/8-156, USNA; Telegram 223, Kabul to Washington, August 7, 1956, ibid. (/8-956).

30. Telegram 356, Kabul to Washington, August 30, 1956, CDF, 889.191-KA/8-3056, USNA; Telegram 391, Kabul to Washington, September 5, 1956, ibid. (/9-556); Despatch 204, Kabul to Washington, October 2, 1957, ibid. (/10-257); Survey PMS-10, United States Information Agency, December 30, 1956, RG-306, Office of Research, Program and Media Studies 1956–62, box 1, USNA.

31. Telegram 626, Washington to Kabul, June 24, 1955, CDF, 889.2311/6-155, USNA.

32. Telegram 178, Kabul to Washington, August 2, 1956, ibid. (/8-256).

33. Kristin L. Ahlberg, *Transplanting the Great Society: Lyndon Johnson and Food for Peace* (Columbia: University of Missouri Press, 2008).

34. Despatch 22, Kabul to Washington, August 2, 1956, CDF, 889.2311/8-256, USNA; Telegram 200, Washington to Kabul, August 10, 1956, ibid. (/8-856); Despatch 31, Kabul to Washington, August 14, 1956, ibid. (/8-1456).

35. Memorandum, Prochnow to Hollister, September 7, 1956, CDF, 889.2311/9-756, USNA.

36. Despatch 3, Kabul to Washington, July 1, 1957, CDF, 889.00/7-157, USNA.

37. Despatch 512, Karachi to Washington, January 13, 1956, CDF, 689.90D/1-1356, USNA.
38. Telegram 2247, Karachi to Washington, April 26, 1956, ibid. (/4-2656), USNA; Telegram 2510, Karachi to Washington, May 22, 1956, ibid. (/5-2256); Telegram 269, Kabul to Washington, August 13, 1956, ibid. (/8-1456); Telegram 837, Washington to Karachi, October 10, 1956, ibid. (/10-156); Telegram 2729, Washington to Karachi, May 17, 1956, *FRUS, 1955–57, VIII*: 238–40; Letter, Kabul to London, August 12, 1956, FO 371/123292, UKNA; Letter, Karachi to London, August 20, 1956, FO 371/123293, UKNA; Despatch 273, Kabul to Paris, August 13, 1956, A-O(A) 1944–72, 55, MAE/P.
39. Despatch 512; Telegram 299, Washington to Kabul, August 31, 1956, CDF, 689.90D/8-3156, USNA; Telegram 385, Kabul to Washington, September 4, 1956, ibid. (/9-456); Telegram 589, Kabul to Washington, October 19, 1956, ibid. (/10-1956); Telegram 683, Kabul to Washington, November 14, 1956, ibid. (/11-1456).
40. Telegram 692, Kabul to Washington, November 16, 1956, CDF, 689.90D/11-1556, USNA.
41. Salim Yaqub, *Containing Arab Nationalism: The Eisenhower Doctrine and the Middle East* (Chapel Hill: University of North Carolina Press, 2004), 80–81.
42. Memcon, January 9, 1957, CDF, 611.89/1-957, USNA; Despatch 455, Kabul to Washington, March 6, 1957, ibid. (/3-657); Telegram 1101, Kabul to Washington, March 7, 1957, ibid. (/3-757); Telegram 2220, Washington to Karachi, March 9, 1957, *FRUS, 1955–57, VIII*: 246–48.
43. Telegram 893, Washington to Kabul, March 16, 1957, *FRUS, 1955–57, VIII*: 250; Yaqub, *Containing Arab Nationalism*, 119–21.
44. Telegram 1264, Kabul to Washington, April 2, 1957, *FRUS, 1955–57, VIII*: 252–54; Despatch 522, Kabul to Washington, April 16, 1957, CDF, 120.1580/4-1657, USNA.
45. Telegram 1264; Despatch 522.
46. Telegram 969, Kabul to Washington, February 9, 1957, CDF, 689.90D/2-957, USNA; Despatch 550, Kabul to Washington, April 25, 1957, ibid. (/4-2557); Telegram 3265, Karachi to Washington, May 31, 1957, ibid. (/5-3157); Telegram 1564, Kabul to Washington, June 11, 1957, ibid. (/6-1157); Telegram 1578, Kabul to Washington, June 13, 1957, ibid. (/6-1357); Telegram 24, Kabul to London, February 9, 1957, FO 371/129383, UKNA; Despatch 204, Kabul to Paris, June 17, 1957, A-O(A) 1944–72, 55, MAE/P.
47. Burton I. Kaufman, *Trade and Aid: Eisenhower's Foreign Economic Policy, 1953-1961* (Baltimore, MD: Johns Hopkins University Press, 1982), 107–10; Engerman, *Price of Aid*, 172–75.
48. Tudor Engineering Co., *Report on Development of Helmand Valley* (Washington, DC: Tudor, 1956).

49. Letter, Mills to Jones, March 3, 1957, GSFSAA, box 22, "Afghanistan 1957," USNA; Letter, Mills to Jones, May 6, 1957, ibid.; Memcon, April 1, 1957, CDF, 889.2614-Helmand/4-157, USNA; Memcon, April 17, 1957, ibid. (/4-1757).
50. Memorandum, Jones to Rountree, June 12, 1957, 889.2614-Helmand/6-1257, USNA; Memorandum, Jones to Rountree, June 18, 1957, ibid.; Memorandum, July 31, 1957, ibid. (/7-3157); Letter, Jones to Mills, April 22, 1957, GSFSAA, box 22, "Afghanistan 1957," USNA.
51. The Eximbank was also financing Morrison-Knudsen projects in Iran and Peru.
52. Despatch 410, Kabul to Washington, January 13, 1958, CDF, 889.2614-Helmand/1-1358, USNA; Telegram 431, Kabul to Washington, November 19, 1958, ibid. (/11-1958); Memcon, December 20, 1958, ibid. (/12-2058); Telegram 320, Washington to Kabul, December 19, 1958, CDF, 789.5-MSP/12-1958, USNA; Telegram 515, Kabul to Washington, December 24, 1958, ibid. (/12-2458).
53. Memorandum, Murphy to Hollister, CDF, 989.72/11-856, USNA; Memorandum, Hollister to Murphy, December 5, 1956, ibid. (/12-556); Despatch 565, Kabul to Washington, April 30, 1957, ibid. (/4-3057); Despatch 419, Kabul to Washington, February 18, 1957, CDF, 789.5-MSP/2-1857, USNA; Van Vleck, "Crossroads," 13–14.
54. Telegram 1510, Kabul to Washington, May 29, 1957, CDF, 989.724/5-2957, USNA; Telegram 1583, Kabul to Washington, June 15, 1957, ibid. (/6-1557); Telegram TOICA 199, Kabul to Washington, August 29, 1957, ibid. (/8-3057).
55. Letter, Mills to Bartlett, September 7, 1957, GSFSAA, box 22, "Afghanistan 1957," USNA; Telegram 649, Kabul to Washington December 16, 1957, CDF, 789.5-MSP/12-1657, USNA.
56. Letter, Snyder to Seager, August 23, 1956, ONESAD/AB, PF, box 9, "Administration—Mission Contract," USNA.
57. Memcon, August 18, 1958, CDF, 789.5-MSP/9-658, USNA.
58. Despatch 340, Kabul to Washington, June 8, 1956, CDF, 889.2553/6-856, USNA; Telegram TOICA 490, Kabul to Washington, March 7, 1957, ibid. (/3-657); Despatch 1214/54, Kabul to Prague, September 12, 1954, TO-T(A) 1945–54, 1:5, AMZV.
59. Telegram 928, Kabul to Washington, January 29, 1957, CDF, 889.2553/1-2957, USNA; Telegram 1215, Kabul to Washington, March 26, 1957, ibid. (/3-2657); Despatch 671, Kabul to Washington, June 20, 1957, ibid. (/6-2057); Telegram 159, Kabul to Washington, August 11, 1957, CDF, 661.89/8-1157, USNA; Despatch 91, Kabul to Washington, August 12, 1957, ibid. (/8-1257).
60. Telegram 163, Kabul to Washington, August 12, 1957, CDF, 889.2553/8-1257, USNA; Memorandum, Bartlett to Rountree, September 5, 1957, ibid. (/9-557).
61. Letter, Jones to Mills, June 1, 1957, GSFSAA, box 22, "Afghanistan 1957," USNA; Letter, Meyer to Mills, October 25, 1957, ibid.

62. Telegram 316, Kabul to Washington, September 16, 1957, CDF, 889.10/9-1657, USNA; Telegram 635, Kabul to Washington, December 11, 1957, CDF, 789.5-MSP/12-1157, USNA; Telegram 668, Kabul to Washington, December 23, 1957, ibid. (/12-2357).
63. Telegram 697, Kabul to Washington, January 3, 1958, *FRUS, 1958–60, XV*: 215–18.
64. Telegram 798, Kabul to Washington, January 25, 1958, CDF, 789.5-MSP/1-2558, USNA.
65. Despatch 691, Kabul to Washington, June 9, 1958, CDF, 989.7190D/6-958, USNA.
66. "Missiles and Fantasy Mix for Afghan Chief," *Los Angeles Times*, July 2, 1958; "Afghan Premier Sees Eisenhower," *NYT*, June 25, 1958, 4; Armin Meyer, ADSTOH, February 8, 1989, 23–24; Telegram 30, Washington to Kabul, July 12, 1958, CDF, 033.8911/7-1258, USNA; Despatch 123, Washington to London, July 22, 1958, FO 371/135707, UKNA.
67. Memcons, June 24, 1958, *FRUS, 1958–60, XV*: 225–29; Memcon, June 25, 1958, *FRUS, 1958–60, XV*: 229–31; Memcon, June 26, 1958, *FRUS, 1958–60, XV*: 232–34.
68. Telegram 986, Washington to Kabul, June 27, 1958, CDF, 033.8911/6-2758, USNA.
69. Telegram 30; Despatch 36, Kabul to Washington, July 17, 1958, CDF, 789.5-MSP/7-1758, USNA.
70. Memorandum, Rountree to Herter, June 9, 1958, *FRUS, 1958–50, XV*: 224–25; Telegram 1219, Kabul to Washington, May 19, 1958, CDF, 989.72/5-1958, USNA; Memcon, August 1, 1958, CDF, 889.2614-Helmand/8-158, USNA; Letter, Mills to Parker Hart, November 24, 1958, *FRUS, 1958–60, XV*: 250–53.
71. Letter, Snyder to Dillon, September 6, 1958, CDF, 789.5-MSP/9-658, USNA.
72. Telegram 195, Kabul to Washington, August 27, 1958, CDF, 689.90D/8-2758, USNA; Letter, Snyder to Dillon, September 6, 1958, CDF, 789.5-MSP/9-658, USNA.
73. Memcon, June 28, 1958, GSFSAA, box 22, "Afghanistan 1958," USNA.
74. Telegram 827, Karachi to Washington, October 8, 1958, *FRUS, 1958–60, XV*: 670–72; Memorandum, Bartlett to Rountree, October 7, 1958, *FRUS, 1958–60, XV*: 668–70; Ayesha Jalal, *The Struggle for Pakistan: A Muslim Homeland and Global Politics* (Cambridge, MA: Harvard University Press, 2014), 96–102.
75. Robert J. McMahon, *The Cold War on the Periphery: The United States, India, and Pakistan* (New York: Columbia University Press, 1994), 254–56.
76. Memcon, October 15, 1958, *FRUS, 1958–60, XV*: 242–44; Elisabeth Leake, *The Defiant Border: The Afghan-Pakistan Borderlands in the Era of Decolonization, 1936–65* (New York: Cambridge University Press, 2017), 206–13.

77. Telegram 1049, Karachi to Washington, October 29, 1958, *FRUS, 1958–60, XV*: 244–45; Telegram 406, Kabul to Washington, November 3, 1958, *FRUS, 1958–60, XV*: 245–47; Telegram 1589, Washington to Karachi, January 9, 1959, *FRUS, 1958–60, XV*: 259–61; Telegram 1581, Karachi to Washington, January 6, 1959, CDF, 689.90D/1-659, USNA.
78. Telegram 195, Kabul to London, December 29, 1958, FO 371/135705, UKNA.
79. Telegram 1404, Moscow to Washington, January 10, 1959, CDF, 661.89/1-1059, USNA; Telegram 589, Kabul to Washington, January 15, 1959, ibid. (/1-1559).
80. Telegram 595, Kabul to Washington, January 18, 1959, ibid. (/1-1859); Telegram 47/50, Moscow to Paris, January 7, 1959, A-O(A) 1944–72, 52, MAE/P.
81. Letter, Ankara to London, November 16, 1956, FO 371/123282, UKNA; Telegram 368, Kabul to Washington, September 1, 1956, CDF, 789.56/9-156, USNA; Telegram 500, Tehran to Washington, September 30, 1956, ibid. (/9-3056); Despatch 391, Kabul to Washington, February 2, 1957, ibid. (/2-257); Telegram 1371, Washington to Tehran, December 2, 1958, ibid. (/11-2558); Telegram 790, Kabul to Washington, January 26, 1956, CDF, 789.5612/1-2556, USNA; Despatch 499, Kabul to Paris, September 24, 1958, A-O(A) 1944–72, 52, MAE/P.
82. Despatch 73/56, Kabul to Prague, December 14, 1956, TO-T(A) 1955–59, 2:8, AMZV; Despatch 08/59, Kabul to Prague, January 22, 1959, TO-T(A) 1955–59, 1:1, AMZV; Report, December 7, 1959, TO-T(A) 1955–59, 1:10, AMZV.
83. Despatch 36/57, Kabul to Prague, May 21, 1957, TO-T(A) 1955–59, 1:2, AMZV; Despatch 61/58, Kabul to Prague, July 17, 1958, TO-T(A) 1955–59, 1:3, AMZV; Telegram 4101, Kabul to Prague, April 1, 1958, ibid.; Despatch 5128/58, Washington to Prague, July 7, 1958, TO-O(A) 1945–59, 2:31, AMZV; Paul Robinson and Jay Dixon, *Aiding Afghanistan: A History of Soviet Assistance to a Developing Country* (London: Hurst, 2013), 53–55.
84. Despatch 57/57, Kabul to Prague, July 20, 1957, TO-T(A) 1955–59, 2:3, AMZV; Telegram 342/56, Kabul to Bonn, May 3, 1956, B12/922, AA.
85. Memcon, October 14, 1957, CDF, 861.0089/10-1457, USNA.
86. Letter, Kabul to Prague, July 1, 1956, TO-T(A) 1955–59, 2:5, AMZV; Letter, Kabul to Prague, August 20, 1958, TO-T(A) 1955–59, 1:3, AMZV; Minute, December 10, 1958, TO-O(A) 1945–59, 1:20, AMZV.
87. Report on Široký visit, undated, TO-T(A) 1955–59, 1:3, AMZV.
88. A. A. Fursenko and Timothy J. Naftali, *Khrushchev's Cold War: The Inside Story of an American Adversary* (New York: Norton, 2006), 81–82.
89. Despatch 360, Kabul to Washington, March 10, 1959, CDF, 789.5-MSP/3-1059, USNA.
90. Despatch 499, Kabul to Paris, September 24, 1958, A-O(A) 1944–72, 52, MAE/P; Philip Nash, *The Other Missiles of October: Eisenhower, Kennedy, and the Jupiters, 1957–1963* (Chapel Hill: University of North Carolina Press, 1997), 35–75.

91. Memcon, January 16, 1959, *FRUS, 1958–60, X-1*: 232–36.
92. Roham Alvandi, "The Shah's Détente with Khrushchev: Iran's 1962 Missile Base Pledge to the Soviet Union," *Cold War History* 14, no. 3 (July 2014): 423–44.
93. Memcon, April 7, 1959 fond 52, opis 1, dela 547, 25-40, Russian State Archive for Contemporary History (RGANI), Moscow; Nash, *Other Missiles of October*, 36–41. I thank Sergey Radchenko for supplying both RGANI documents cited here.
94. Airgram G-36, Kabul to Washington, April 14, 1959, *FRUS, 1958–60, XV*: 263–67; Telegram 1047, Kabul to Washington, June 16, 1959, *FRUS, 1958–60, XV*: 273–76; Memcon, May 20, 1959 fond 52, opis 1, dela 547, 41-54, RGANI.
95. Telegram 1035, Kabul to Washington, June 11, 1959, CDF, 611.89/6-1159, USNA.
96. Airgram A-26, Washington to Kabul, September 19, 1958, CDF, 989.72/9-1958, USNA; Despatch 195, Kabul to Washington, October 14, 1958, ibid. (/10-1458); Van Vleck, "Crossroads," 16–17.
97. Despatch 414, Kabul to Washington, April 21, 1959, CDF, 889.00/4-2159, USNA; Barnett Rubin, *The Fragmentation of Afghanistan: State Formation and Collapse in the International System* (New Haven, CT: Yale University Press, 2002), 62–65.
98. Airgram TOICA A-798, Kabul to Washington, January 20, 1959, CDF, 989.73/1-2059, USNA.
99. Memcon, August 1, 1958, CDF, 889.2614-Helmand/8-158, USNA; Telegram 888, Kabul to Washington, April 25, 1959, ibid. (/4-2559); Telegram TOICA 982, Kabul to Washington, May 14, 1959, ibid. (/5-1459).
100. Airgram G-33, Kabul to Washington, March 26, 1959, CDF, 889.2614-Helmand/3-2659, USNA.
101. Telegram 180, Kabul to Washington, August 31, 1959, CDF, 889.2614-Helmand/8-3159, USNA; Despatch 78, Kabul to Washington, September 10, 1959, ibid. (/9-1059); Telegram 229, Kabul to Washington, September 15, 1959, ibid. (/9-1559); Telegram 231, Kabul to Washington, September 16, 1959, ibid. (/9-1659); Telegram 698, Tehran to Washington, October 3, 1959, ibid. (/10-359).
102. Despatch 267, Kabul to Washington, December 22, 1958, CDF, 789.5-MSP/12-2258, USNA; Despatch 362, Kabul to Washington, March 12, 1959, ibid. (/3-1259); Despatch 477, Kabul to Washington, June 2, 1959, ibid. (/6-259); Telegram 584, Kabul to Washington, December 31, 1959, ibid. (/12-3159).
103. Telegram 1219, Kabul to Washington, May 19, 1958, CDF, 989.72/5-1958, USNA; Memcon, April 15, 1959, CDF, ibid (/4-1559), USNA.
104. Telegram 768, Kabul to Washington, March 18, 1959, CDF, 689.90D/1-659, USNA; Telegram 2245, Karachi to Washington, April 3, 1959, ibid. (/4-359); Telegram 85, Kabul to Washington, July 30, 1959, ibid. (/7-3059).

105. Report EIC-R14-S7, "Sino-Soviet Bloc Economic Activities in Underdeveloped Areas," August 28, 1959, CIARR.
106. Editorial Note, *FRUS, 1958–60, XV*: 279; NSC 5909, August 21, 1959, *FRUS, 1958–60, XV*: 29–46.
107. Memorandum, Jones to Herter, September 12, 1959, *FRUS, 1958–60, XV*: 280–85; NIE 53-59, September 22, 1959, *FRUS, 1958–60, XV*: 287–92; Afghanistan Action Group Meeting Notes, October 14, 1959, *FRUS, 1958–60, XV*: 306–8.
108. Telegram 432, Kabul to Washington, November 18, 1959, CDF, 120.171/11-1859, USNA.
109. Despatch 578/59, Kabul to Bonn, September 10, 1959, PA, B12/908, AA; Despatch 580, Kabul to Paris, September 10, 1959, A-O(A) 1944–72, 37, MAE/P.
110. Armin Meyer, ADSTOH, February 8, 1989, 19–20.
111. Letter, Drake to Snyder, January 30, 1957, ONESAD/AB, PF, box 9, "Administration—Mission Contract," USNA.
112. NIE 53-59, "The Outlook for Afghanistan," September 22, 1959, *FRUS, 1958–1960, XV*: 287–92.
113. Telegram 652, Kabul to Washington, December 21, 1955, CDF, 033.6189/12-2155, USNA.
114. Despatch 688, Kabul to Washington, June 26, 1957, CDF, 661.891/6-2657, USNA; Memcon, October 12, 1959, *FRUS, 1958–60, XV*: 297–300.
115. Memorandum, Arthur Paul, December 1961 (unsent), Arthur Paul Papers, box 2, "1961 Afghan Affairs," UNO.

6. The Crisis Era, 1959–1963

1. Editorial Note, *FRUS, 1958–60, XV*: 327; Dwight D. Eisenhower, *Waging Peace, 1956–1961: The White House Years* (Garden City, NY: Doubleday, 1965), 497–99; Clint Hill and Lisa McCubbin, *Five Presidents: My Extraordinary Journey with Eisenhower, Kennedy, Johnson, Nixon, and Ford* (New York: Simon & Schuster, 2016), 31–32.
2. Memcon, December 8, 1959, *FRUS, 1958–60, XV*: 781–92; Memcon, December 14, 1959, *FRUS, 1958–60, XII*: 658–59; Memorandum, Herter to Eisenhower, December 31, 1959, *FRUS, 1958–60, XII*: 660–61; Despatch 3, Kabul to Paris, January 4, 1960, A-O(A) 1944–72, 51, MAE/P.
3. Despatch 152, Kabul to Washington, January 4, 1960, CDF, 789.00/1-460, USNA; Despatch 1, Kabul to Paris, January 4, 1960, A-O(A) 1944–72, 38, MAE/P; Letter, Kabul to London, December 31, 1959, FO 371/152205, UKNA; Louis Dupree, *Afghanistan* (Princeton, NJ: Princeton University Press, 1973), 536–37.

4. Telegram 168, Kabul to London, December 23, 1959, FO 371/143811, UKNA.
5. Telegram 319, Kabul to Washington, October 11, 1959, CDF, 689.90D/10-1159, USNA.
6. Despatch 174, Kabul to Washington, February 23, 1960, CDF, 689.90D/2-2360, USNA.
7. Telegram 594, Kabul to Washington, January 1, 1960, CDF, 889.432/1-160, USNA.
8. "Afghanistan Agricultural Problems to Be Studied," *DOSB* 703, December 15, 1952, 951; "The Development of United States Policy in the Near East, South Asia, and Africa During 1955, Part III," *DOSB* 876, April 9, 1956, 599.
9. Telegram 1511, Kabul to Washington, May 29, 1957, CDF, 889.432/5-2957, USNA.
10. Telegram 594.
11. Telegram 612, Kabul to Washington, January 6, 1960, *FRUS, 1958–60, XV*: 328–29; Telegram 848, Kabul to Washington, March 8, 1960, CDF, 789.5-MSP/3-860, USNA; Telegram 894, Kabul to Washington, March 21, 1960, CDF, 611.89/3-2160, USNA.
12. Henry Byroade, ADSTOH, September 19, 1988.
13. Telegram 263, Kabul to Washington, February 14, 1960, *FRUS, 1958–60, XV*: 332–33; Telegram 896, Kabul to Washington, March 23, 1960, *FRUS, 1958–60, XV*: 339–42; Letter, Karachi to London, January 28, 1960, FO 371/152213, UKNA.
14. Khrushchev's Speech, March 4, 1960, FO 371/152211, UKNA; Editorial Note, *FRUS, 1958–60, XV*: 335–36; Nikita Khrushchev and Sergei Khrushchev, *Memoirs of Nikita Khrushchev*, vol. 3, *Statesman, 1953–1964* (University Park: Pennsylvania State University Press, 2013), 796–97.
15. Memcon, April 23, 1960, *FRUS, 1958–60, XV*: 346–48; Memorandum, Eisenhower to Herter, April 23, 1960, *FRUS, 1958–60, IV*: 497.
16. Burton I. Kaufman, *Trade and Aid: Eisenhower's Foreign Economic Policy, 1953–1961* (Baltimore, MD: Johns Hopkins University Press, 2019), 197–206.
17. Francis Gary Powers and Curt Gentry, *Operation Overflight: A Memoir of the U-2 Incident* (Washington, DC: Potomac Books, 2003), 144; Chester J. Pach and Elmo Richardson, *The Presidency of Dwight D. Eisenhower* (Lawrence: University Press of Kansas, 1991), 211–16; William Hitchcock, *The Age of Eisenhower* (New York: Simon & Schuster, 2018), 456–62.
18. Memorandum on U-2 Incident, August 12, 1960, CK2349701838, USDDO; Michael R. Beschloss, *MAYDAY: Eisenhower, Khrushchev, and the U-2 Affair* (New York: Harper & Row, 1986), 268; Norman B. Hannah, "Afghanistan: History as Obituary," *Asian Affairs* 7, no. 5 (1980): 301–2.
19. Memorandum on U-2 Incident; Memcon, June 2, 1960, *FRUS, 1958–60, XV*: 810–13.

20. Dennis Kux, *The United States and Pakistan, 1947–2000: Disenchanted Allies* (Washington, DC: Woodrow Wilson Center Press, 2001), 112–14; Elisabeth Leake, *The Defiant Border: The Afghan-Pakistan Borderlands in the Era of Decolonization, 1936–65* (New York: Cambridge University Press, 2017), 196–97; Robert J. McMahon, *The Cold War on the Periphery: The United States, India, and Pakistan* (New York: Columbia University Press, 1994), 268–70.
21. Memcon, May 6, 1960, CDF, 789.5-MSP/5-660, USNA; Memcon, May 13, 1960, *FRUS, 1958–60, XV*: 348–50; Maxwell J. Fry, *The Afghan Economy: Money, Finance, and the Critical Constraints to Economic Development* (Leiden: Brill, 1974), 70–72.
22. Dennis Merrill, *Bread and the Ballot: The United States and India's Economic Development, 1947–1963* (Chapel Hill: University of North Carolina Press, 1990), 141–48; David C. Engerman, *The Price of Aid: The Economic Cold War in India* (Cambridge, MA: Harvard University Press, 2018), 159–91.
23. Nick Cullather, *The Hungry World: America's Cold War Battle Against Poverty in Asia* (Cambridge, MA: Harvard University Press, 2010), 134–58; Tanvi Madan, *Fateful Triangle: How China Shaped U.S.-India Relations During the Cold War* (Washington, DC: Brookings Institution Press, 2020), 85–131.
24. Telegram 1200, Kabul to Washington, June 3, 1960, CDF, 889.2612/6-360, USNA; Telegram 1296, Kabul to Washington, June 24, 1960, CDF, 789.5-MSP/6-2460, USNA.
25. Telegram 4, Kabul to Washington, July 3, 1960, *FRUS, 1958–60, XV*: 350–53.
26. 446th NSC Meeting, May 31, 1960, PPAWF, box 12, DDEL.
27. Telegram 29, Washington to Kabul, July 6, 1960, CDF, 789.5-MSP/6-2460, USNA; Telegram 33, Washington to Kabul, July 11, 1960, ibid.; Telegram 30, Washington to Kabul, July 9, 1960, CDF, 789.5-MSP//7-360, USNA; Telegram 188, Washington to Kabul, August 30, 1960, ibid.
28. Despatch 26, Kabul to Washington, August 13, 1960, CDF, 611.89/8-1360, USNA.
29. Despatch 202, Kabul to Paris, May 18, 1960, A-O(A) 1944–72, 55, MAE/P; Letter, Kabul to London, June 3, 1960, FO 371/152218, UKNA; Letter, Kabul to London, July 23, 1960, ibid.; Despatch 438/60, Kabul to Bonn, May 25, 1960, PA, B12/923, AA.
30. Telegram 317, Kabul to Washington, September 22, 1960, CDF, 789W/9-2260, USNA; Letter, Kabul to London, October 7, 1960, FO 371/152219, UKNA.
31. Memcon, September 23, 1960, *FRUS, 1958–60, XV*: 355–58; Memorandum, Herter to Eisenhower, October 18, 1960, *FRUS, 1958–60, XV*: 365–66; Telegram 461, Kabul to Washington, October 27, 1960, *FRUS, 1958–60, XV*: 367–70.

32. Despatch 34, Kabul to London, October 25, 1960, FO 371/152220, UKNA; Letter, Kabul to London, November 12, 1960, ibid. Telegram 248, Kabul to London, December 2, 1960, ibid. Telegram 407, Kabul to Washington, October 12, 1960, CK2349061131, USDDO.
33. Telegram 657, Kabul to Washington, December 31, 1960, CDF, 689.90D/12-3160, USNA; Despatch 158, Kabul to Washington, January 31, 1961, CDF, 611.89/1-3161, USNA.
34. Letter, Dillon to Stans, December 16, 1960, CDF, 889.43/12-1660, USNA; Telegram 468, Washington to Kabul, December 30, 1960, ibid. (/12-2060); Telegram 686, Kabul to Washington, January 12, 1961, ibid. (/1-1261).
35. Telegram 526, Kabul to Washington, November 16, 1960, CDF, 789.00W/11-1660, USNA; Despatch 53, Kabul to Paris, February 1, 1961, A-O(A) 1944–72, 51, MAE/P.
36. Robert B. Rakove, *Kennedy, Johnson, and the Nonaligned World* (New York: Cambridge University Press, 2012).
37. Kennedy, "Special Message to the Congress on Foreign Aid," March 22, 1961, in *PPP, 1961*, 203–12.
38. Afghan Visa Application, undated, John F. Kennedy Personal Papers, box 10, "Washington office, 1951," JFKL.
39. "Foreign Aid: The Most Thankless Job," *Time*, November 23, 1962.
40. Memorandum, Rostow to Kennedy, February 28, 1961, *FRUS, 1961–63, IX*: 204–9.
41. Airgram G-40, Kabul to Washington, February 21, 1961, *FRUS, 1961–63, XIX*: 12–15.
42. Telegram 1000, Kabul to Washington, April 26, 1961, CDF, 789.5-MSP/4-2661, USNA; Telegram 1040, Kabul to Washington, May 10, 1961, ibid. (/5-1061); Telegram 1048, Kabul to Washington, May 12, 1961, ibid. (/5-1261); Telegram 1053, Kabul to Washington, May 14, 1961, ibid. (/5-1361).
43. Telegram 715, Washington to Kabul, May 18, 1961, *FRUS, 1961–63, XIX*: 43–44.
44. Telegram 1066, Kabul to Washington, May 22, 1961, *FRUS, 1961–63, XIX*: 51.
45. Telegram 1072, Kabul to Washington, May 25, 1961, CDF, 789.5-MSP/5-2561, USNA.
46. Telegram 739, Washington to Kabul, June 2, 1961, CDF, 789.5-MSP/6-261, USNA; Telegram 34, Washington to Kabul, July 22, 1961, ibid. (/6-2161).
47. Telegram 1130, Kabul to Washington, June 20, 1961, CDF, 789.5-MSP/6-2061, USNA; Airgram A-5, Kabul to Washington, July 21, 1961, ibid. (/7-2161); Telegram 71, Kabul to Washington, July 27, 1961, ibid. (/7-2761).
48. E. W. Kenworthy, "Congress Passes Aid Bill with Five-Year Loan Plan," *NYT*, September 1, 1961.
49. Leake, *Defiant Border*, 221–23.
50. CIA Memorandum 18–61, March 10, 1961, NSF, box 145, JFKL.

51. Telegram 812, Kabul to Washington, March 2, 1961, CDF, 689.90D/3-261, USNA.
52. Telegram 1832, Karachi to Washington, April 20, 1961, *FRUS, 1961–63, XIX*: 34–35.
53. Telegram 2294, Moscow to Washington, March 27, 1961, CDF, 689.90D/3-2761, USNA.
54. Telegram 1686, Karachi to Washington, March 30, 1961, CDF, 689.90D/3-3061, USNA; Memcon, May 23, 1961, ibid. (/5-2361).
55. Paul Grimes, "Pakistan Leader Critical of U.S.," *NYT*, May 30, 1961, 3; Telegram 2187, Karachi to Washington, June 15, 1961, NSF, box 145, JFKL.
56. Memcon, July 11, 1961, *FRUS, 1961–63, XIX*: 66–74; Srinath Raghavan, *Fierce Enigmas: A History of the United States in South Asia* (New York: Basic Books, 2018), 239–40.
57. Memcon, July 11, 1961, NSF, box 145, JFKL; Telegram 481, Washington to New Delhi, August 5, 1961, ibid.; Memcon, July 21, 1961, *FRUS, 1961–63, XIX*: 75–76.
58. Telegram 337, Karachi to Washington, August 24, 1961, NSF, box 145, JFKL; Telegram 358, Karachi to Washington, August 29, 1961, ibid.; Telegram 340, Karachi to Washington, August 24, 1961, CDF, 689.90D/8-2561, USNA; Telegram 4, Peshawar to Washington, August 25, 1961, ibid. (/8-2561); Telegram 131, Kabul to Washington, August 26, 1961, ibid. (/8-2661); Telegram 144, Kabul to Washington, August 30, 1961, ibid. (/8-3061).
59. Telegram 134, Kabul to Washington, August 29, 1961, CDF, 689.90D/8-2961, USNA; Telegram 135, Kabul to Washington, August 29, 1961, ibid. (/8-2961); Telegram 136, Kabul to Washington, August 29, 1961, ibid.; Telegram 89, Washington to Kabul, September 3, 1961, ibid. (/9-361); Telegram 13, Peshawar to Washington, September 5, 1961, ibid. (/9-561); Telegram 155, Kabul to Washington, September 5, 1961, ibid. (/9-661); Telegram 164, Kabul to Washington, September 7, 1961, ibid. (/9-761).
60. Frank L. Jones, *Blowtorch: Robert Komer, Vietnam, and American Cold War Strategy* (Annapolis, MD: Naval Institute Press, 2013), 19–29.
61. Memorandum, Komer to Bundy, January 9, 1961, NSF, box 321, "Staff Memoranda: Komer, Robert, 1/1-3/14," JFKL.
62. Komer, Notes for Planning Group Meeting, March 14, 1961, ibid.
63. Memorandum, Komer to Kennedy, September 2, 1961, *FRUS, 1961–63, XIX*: 87–88.
64. *The Conference of Heads of State or Government of Non-Aligned Countries: Belgrade, Sept. 1–6, 1961* (Belgrade: Yugoslav Foreign Ministry, 1961), 80–84.
65. Roham Alvandi, "Flirting with Neutrality: The Shah, Khrushchev, and the Failed 1959 Soviet–Iranian Negotiations," *Iranian Studies* 47, no. 3 (February 2014): 437–39.

66. Memorandum, Sherman Kent to McCone, September 20, 1961, CIARR.
67. Telegram 596, New Delhi to Washington, August 23, 1961, NSF, box 106, JFKL; Cablegram, Kennedy to Galbraith, August 24, 1961, ibid.
68. Telegram 411, Washington to Karachi, August 31, 1961, CDF, 689.90D/8-3161, USNA.
69. Telegram 113, Washington to Kabul, September 17, 1961, *FRUS, 1961–63, XIX*: 101–3; Telegram 534, Washington to Karachi, September 17, 1961, *FRUS, 1961–63, XIX*: 103–4.
70. Memorandum, Komer to Bundy and Rostow, September 12, 1961, NSF, box 145, JFKL. Emphasis in original.
71. Telegram 100, Washington to Kabul, September 11, 1961, CDF, 689.90D/9-1161, USNA; Telegram 187, Kabul to Washington, September 12, 1961, ibid. (/9-1261); Chester Bowles, *Promises to Keep: My Years in Public Life, 1941–1969* (New York: Harper & Row, 1971), 251, 277, 369–71; Howard B. Schaffer, *Chester Bowles: New Dealer in the Cold War* (Cambridge, MA: Harvard University Press, 1993), 133, 158–60.
72. Telegram 203, Kabul to Washington, September 15, 1961, CDF, 689.90D/9-1561, USNA; Despatch 18, Peshawar to Washington, September 21, 1961, ibid. (/9-2161); Telegram 576, Karachi to Washington, September 27, 1961, ibid. (/9-2761); Telegram 604, Karachi to Washington, September 30, 1961, ibid. (/9-3061).
73. Telegram TOICA 295, Kabul to Washington, September 9, 1961, NSF, box 145, JFKL; Despatch 45, Kabul to Washington, September 13, 1961, CDF, 689.90D/9-1361, USNA.
74. Telegram 575, Karachi to Washington, September 26, 1961, CDF, 689.90D/9-2661, USNA; Telegram 240, Kabul to Washington, September 25, 1961, ibid. (/9-2561); Memorandum, Komer to Bundy and Rostow, September 28, 1961, NSF, box 322, JFKL.
75. Telegram 203; Telegram 240; Telegram 116, Washington to Kabul, September 18, 1961, CDF, 689.90D/9-1861, USNA; Telegram 253, Kabul to Washington, September 28, 1961, ibid. (/9-2861); Telegram 271, Kabul to Washington, October 3, 1961, ibid. (/10-361).
76. Memorandum, Komer to Rostow, October 2, 1961, NSF, box 406, "Afghanistan-Pakistan," JFKL.
77. Memcon, October 16, 1961, *FRUS, 1961–1963, XIX*: 114–15.
78. Memorandum, Komer to Kennedy, October 16, 1961, *FRUS, 1961–1963, XIX*: 116.
79. Telegram 314, Kabul to Washington, October 24, 1961, CDF, 689.90D/10-2461, USNA; Despatch 281, Karachi to Washington, October 26, 1961, ibid. (/10-2661); Despatch 282, Karachi to Washington, October 27, 1961, ibid. (/10-2761); Telegram 772, Karachi to Washington, October 27, 1961, ibid.; Telegram 798,

Karachi to Washington, November 2, 1961, ibid. (/11-261); Telegram 336, Kabul to Washington, November 4, 1961, ibid. (/11-461).

80. Telegram 349, Kabul to Washington, November 9, 1961, CDF, 689.90D/11-961, USNA; Telegram 359, Kabul to Washington, November 17, 1961, ibid. (/11-1661); Telegram 204, Washington to Kabul, November 21, 1961, ibid. (/11-2161); Telegram 369, Kabul to Washington, November 24, 1961, ibid. (/11-2461).
81. Despatch 527, Kabul to Paris, December 25, 1961, A-O(A) 1944–72, 53, MAE/P; Letter, Kabul to London, November 3, 1961, FO 371/157427, UKNA.
82. Telegram 376, Kabul to Washington, November 28, 1961, CDF, 889.432/11-2861, USNA; Telegram 224, Washington to Kabul, December 9, 1961, ibid.; Telegram 430, Kabul to Washington, December 30, 1961, CDF, 689.90D/12-3061, USNA.
83. Paul M. McGarr, *The Cold War in South Asia: Britain, the United States and the Indian Subcontinent, 1945–1965* (New York: Cambridge University Press, 2013), 144–48.
84. Memorandum, Komer to Bundy, January 6, 1962, *FRUS, 1961–63, XIX*: 179–81; Memorandum, Komer to Bundy, January 11, 1962, NSF, box 230, "South Asia," JFKL.
85. Memorandum, Komer to Bundy, January 12, 1962, *FRUS, 1961–63, XIX*: 190–91; Telegram 256, Washington to Kabul, January 12, 1962, *FRUS, 1961–63, XIX*: 193; Memorandum, Komer to Bundy, January 12, 1962, NSF, box 322, JFKL.
86. Telegram 482, Kabul to Washington, January 30, 1962, CDF, 989.7190D/1-3062, USNA; Despatch 50, Peshawar to Washington, February 6, 1962, ibid. (/2-662).
87. Despatch 50, Peshawar to Washington, February 6, 1962, CDF, 989.7190D/2-662, USNA.
88. Airgram A-274, Cairo to Washington, February 17, 1962, NSF, box 116, JFKL; Telegram 529, Kabul to Washington, March 3, 1962, *FRUS, 1961–63, XIX*: 216–19; Telegram 565, Kabul to Washington, March 28, 1962, *FRUS, 1961–63, XIX*: 227–29.
89. Despatch 176, Kabul to Washington, March 31, 1962, CDF, 889.432/3-3162, USNA; Despatch 196, Kabul to Paris, April 13, 1962, A-O(A) 1944–72, 53, MAE/P.
90. Memorandum, Bowles to Rusk, April 26, 1962, NSF, box 1, JFKL; Polk "Elements of U.S. Policy Toward Afghanistan," March 27, 1962, ibid.
91. Memorandum, Rostow to Rusk, March 30, 1962, CDF, 611.89/3-3062, USNA.
92. Airgram A-359, Kabul to Washington, March 6, 1962, CDF, 611.89/3-662, USNA.
93. Telegram 346, Washington to Kabul, May 4, 1962, NSF, box 1, JFKL; Memorandum, Komer to Bundy, May 8, 1962, *FRUS, 1963–63, XIX*: 238–40; Telegram 559, Kabul to Washington, March 26, 1962, CDF, 689.90D/3-2662, USNA.

94. Telegram 572, Kabul to Washington, April 2, 1962, CDF, 611.89/4-262, USNA; Telegram 617, Kabul to Washington, May 1, 1962, NSF, box 1, JFKL; Telegram 624, Kabul to Washington, May 6, 1962, ibid.
95. Telegram 639, Kabul to Washington, May 16, 1962, NSF, box 1, JFKL; Telegram 663, Kabul to Washington, May 25, 1962, ibid.
96. Telegram 52, Tehran to Washington, July 12, 1962, CDF, 689.90D/7-1262, USNA; Telegram 37, Kabul to Washington, July 23, 1962, NSF, box 1, JFKL.
97. Telegram 278, Karachi to Washington, August 7, 1962, CDF, 689.90D/8-762, USNA; Telegram 74, Kabul to Washington, August 9, 1962, ibid. (/8-962); Telegram 286, Karachi to Washington, August 9, 1962, ibid. (/8-962).
98. Telegram 130, Kabul to Washington, September 14, 1962, NSF, box 1, JFKL; Telegram 175, Kabul to Washington, October 12, 1962, CDF, 889.2612/10-1262, USNA; Telegram TOAID 403, Kabul to Washington, September 17, 1962, CDF, 889.432/9-1762, USNA.
99. Memcon, September 24, 1962, *FRUS, 1961–63, XIX*: 326–31; Memcon, September 27, 1962, *FRUS, 1961–63, XIX*: 334–38.
100. Madan, *Fateful Triangle*, 141–48; McMahon, *Cold War on the Periphery*, 287–94.
101. Telegram 217, Kabul to Washington, November 20, 1962, NSF, box 1, JFKL; Memorandum, Komer to Talbot, November 23, 1962, ibid.; Telegram 149, Washington to Kabul, December 1, 1962, ibid.
102. Telegram 172, Kabul to Washington, October 11, 1962, NSF, box 1, JFKL; Telegram 110, Washington to Kabul, October 17, 1962, ibid.; Telegram 1017, Moscow to Washington, October 20, 1962, ibid.; Telegram 187, Kabul to Washington, October 21, 1962, ibid. The group also contacted the British embassy. Letter, Kabul to London, October 30, 1962, FO 371/164000, UKNA.
103. Telegram 152, Washington to Kabul, December 6, 1962, NSF, box 1, JFKL; Telegram 240, Kabul to Washington, December 9, 1962, ibid.; Telegram 264, Kabul to Washington, December 20, 1962, ibid.; Telegram 261, Kabul to Washington, December 19, 1962, *FRUS, 1961–63, XIX*: 443–47.
104. McGarr, *Cold War in South Asia*, 192–201.
105. Memorandum, Rusk to Kennedy, January 17, 1963, *FRUS, 1961–63, XIX*: 472–76; Telegram 196, Washington to Kabul, January 25, 1963, in *FRUS, 1961–63, XIX*: 483–85; Letter, Steeves to McGhee, January 30, 1963, CDF, 789.11/1-3063, USNA; John M. Steeves, OH, June 17, 1970, JFKL.
106. Telegram 324, Kabul to Washington, January 29, 1963, NSF, box 1, JFKL; Telegram 382, Kabul to Washington, March 5, 1963, ibid.; Telegram 201, Washington to Kabul, January 30, 1963, *FRUS, 1961–63, XIX*: 486–87; Telegram 14–15, Kabul to Paris, March 4, 1963, A-O(A) 1944–72, 38, MAE/P.
107. Telegram 330, Washington to Kabul, May 27, 1963, *FRUS, 1961–1963: XIX*: 605; Telegram 1782, Karachi to Washington, March 20, 1963, SNF, POL 15 AFG, USNA.
108. Telegram 392, Kabul to Washington, March 9, 1963, NSF, box 1, JFKL.

109. Telegram 398, Kabul to Washington, March 11, 1963, NSF, box 1, JFKL; Telegram 420, Kabul to Washington, March 18, 1963, ibid.
110. Telegram 398; Despatch 23, Kabul to London, October 14, 1962, FO 371/164000, UKNA; Telegram 2287, London to Washington, December 17, 1962, NSF, box 1, JFKL.
111. Telegram 394, Kabul to Washington, March 10, 1963, NSF, box 1, JFKL.
112. Despatch 7, Kabul to London, April 1, 1963, FO 371/170194, UKNA.

7. Reform and Retrenchment, 1963–1968

1. Warren Unna, "Rain Dampens Welcome for Afghan Royalty," *WP*, September 6, 1963; John F. Kennedy, Remarks, September 5, 1963, *PPP, 1963*, 654.
2. Dorothy McCardle, "Sky's the Limit for Afghans," *WP*, September 7, 1963; Kennedy and Zahir, Toasts, September 5, 1963, *PPP, 1963*, 655–56.
3. "NASA Officials Present His Majesty with Space Photo Album," *KT*, September 9, 1963; "Their Majesties in New York," *KT*, September 11, 1963.
4. Press Release, September 5, 1963, NSF, box 1, "Visit of King and Queen," JFKL.
5. Airgram A-152, Kabul to Washington, September 22, 1963, SNF, POL 15–1 AFG, USNA; Telegram 265, Kabul to Washington, October 15, 1963, ibid.
6. Andrew David and Michael Holm, "The Kennedy Administration and the Battle over Foreign Aid: The Untold Story of the Clay Committee," *Diplomacy & Statecraft* 27, no. 1 (January 2016): 65–92.
7. Clay Committee, Summary of Proceedings, January 26, 1963, NSF, box 412, "Clay Committee (2/2)", JFKL.
8. Memorandum, Komer to Kennedy, March 2, 1963, NSF, box 412, "Clay Committee (2/2)", JFKL.
9. Ibid; Clay Committee, Report to President, March 20, 1963, NSF, box 412, "Clay Committee (1/2)," JFKL.
10. Telegram 399, Kabul to Washington, March 11, 1963, NSF, box 1, JFKL; Telegram 384, Kabul to Washington, March 6, 1963, SNF, AID AFG (US), USNA.
11. Telegram 78, Kabul to London, March 14, 1963, FO 371/170194, UKNA; Telegram 424, Kabul to Washington, March 20, 1963, SNF, POL 15 AFG, USNA; Airgram A-386, Kabul to Washington, March 18, 1963, SNF, POL 6–1 AFG, USNA; Despatch 94, Kabul to Paris, March 15, 1963, A-O(A) 1944–72, 38, MAE/P.
12. Letter, Kabul to London, April 6, 1963, FO 371/170194, UKNA; Letter, Kabul to London, April 6, 1963, ibid.; "Sardar Daoud's Proposals," *KT*, March 11, 1963.
13. Telegram 421, Kabul to Washington, March 20, 1963, NSF, box 1, JFKL; Telegram 424; Airgram A-415, Kabul to Washington, April 1, 1963, SNF, POL 15–5 AFG, USNA; Airgram A-550, Kabul to Washington, June 23, 1963, ibid.

14. Telegram 601, Kabul to Washington, June 5, 1963, SNF, POL 15–1 AFG, USNA; Telegram 405, Kabul to Washington, March 12, 1963, ibid.; Letter, Kabul to London, November 1, 1963, FO 371/170195, UKNA; Airgram A-200, Kabul to Washington, October 27, 1963, SNF, POL 2 AFG, USNA.
15. Telegram 403, Kabul to Washington, March 12, 1963, SNF, POL 15 AFG, USNA.
16. Telegram 2340, Moscow to Washington, March 19, 1963, ibid.
17. Letter, Kabul to Prague, December 21, 1963, TO-O(A) 1960–64, 2:9, AMZV.
18. Airgram A-339, Kabul to State Department, February 18, 1963, SNF, POL AFG-USSR, USNA; Airgram A-340, Kabul to State Department, February 18, 1963, SNF, AID AFG (US), USNA.
19. Lorenz M. Lüthi, *The Sino-Soviet Split: Cold War in the Communist World* (Princeton, NJ: Princeton University Press, 2008), 224–31; Sergey Radchenko, *Two Suns in the Heavens: The Sino-Soviet Struggle for Supremacy, 1962–1967* (Stanford, CA: Stanford University Press, 2009), 25–33.
20. Memcon, April 7, 1959, fond 52, opis 1, dela 547, 25-40, Russian State Archive for Contemporary History (RGANI).
21. Airgram A-221, Kabul to Washington, December 7, 1962, CDF, 889.2612/12-762, USNA.
22. Airgram A-221; Despatch 9, Kabul to London, April 2, 1963, FO 371/170194, UKNA; U.S. House Committee on Foreign Affairs, *Hearings on HR 5490*, May 1, 1963, 447; John M. Steeves, *Safir (Ambassador)* (Hershey, PA: s.n., 1991), 156.
23. U.S. House Committee on Foreign Affairs, *Hearings on HR 5490*, May 1, 1963, 447.
24. Airgram A-332, Kabul to Washington, February 11, 1963, SNF, AID (US) 7–1 AFG, USNA; Airgram A-375, Kabul to Washington, March 11, 1963, SNF, AID (US) 15–6 AFG, USNA; Louis Dupree, *Afghanistan* (Princeton, NJ: Princeton University Press, 1973), 551.
25. Telegram 76, Washington to Kabul, August 16, 1963, SNF, AID (US) 9 AFG, USNA; Telegram 82, Kabul to Washington, August 2, 1963, SNF, AID (US) 9 AFG, USNA; Telegram 241, Kabul to Washington, October 3, 1963, ibid.
26. Telegram 237, Kabul to Washington, October 3, 1963, SNF, AID (US) 15–6 AFG, USNA.
27. "Afghanistan Mourns Kennedy's Death," *KT*, November 24, 1963; "Prominent Afghans Offer Condolences," *KT*, November 25, 1963; "Kennedy Memorial Meeting Held by U.S. Ambassador," *KT*, November 26, 1963; John M. Steeves, OH, June 17, 1970, 76–77, JFKL; Despatch 567, Kabul to Paris, December 2, 1963, A-O(A) 1944–74, 51, MAE/P; Steeves, *Safir*, 175–76.
28. Phillips Talbot, OH, July 27, 1965, 13–14, JFKL; Toast Speech, Kennedy, September 5, 1963, *PPP, 1963*, 655.
29. Telegram 345, Kabul to Washington, December 2, 1963, SNF, AID (US) 15–9 AFG, USNA; Telegram 390, Kabul to Washington, December 21, 1963, ibid.

30. Memorandum, Bell to Bundy, January 7, 1964, *FRUS, 1964–68,* IX: 1–4; Mark Atwood Lawrence, *The End of Ambition: The United States and the Third World in the Vietnam Era* (Princeton, NJ: Princeton University Press, 2021), 96–98.
31. Memorandum, Bundy to Johnson, April 2, 1964, *FRUS, 1964–68,* IX: 13–14; Memorandum, Bell to Bundy, January 7, 1964, *FRUS, 1964–68,* IX: 1–4.
32. Johnson Conversation with Bundy, May 13, 1964, Tape WH6405.06/3446, LBJL.
33. Report of the President's Task Force, undated, *FRUS, 1964–68,* IX: 42–61.
34. Memorandum, Bell to Gordon, December 4, 1964, *FRUS, 1964–68,* IX: 61–70.
35. Paul M. McGarr, *The Cold War in South Asia: Britain, the United States and the Indian Subcontinent, 1945–1965* (New York: Cambridge University Press, 2013), 278–84; Robert J. McMahon, *The Cold War on the Periphery: The United States, India, and Pakistan* (New York: Columbia University Press, 1994), 305–17.
36. Fredrik Logevall, *Choosing War: The Lost Chance for Peace and the Escalation of War in Vietnam* (Berkeley: University of California Press, 1999), 75–107.
37. Airgram A-357, Kabul to Washington, February 12, 1964, SNF, POL 15–5 AFG, USNA; Airgram A-377, Kabul to Washington, February 22, 1964, ibid.
38. Airgram A-346, Kabul to Washington, February 1, 1964, SNF, POL 15–5 AFG, USNA; Airgram A-402, Kabul to Washington, March 14, 1964, ibid.; Airgram A-424, Kabul to Washington, April 4, 1964, ibid.; Telegram 140, Kabul to Washington, September 16, 1964, ibid.
39. Chester Bowles, OH, July 1, 1970, 25, JFKL; John Steeves, ADSTOH, March 27, 1991, 37; Airgram A-229, Kabul to Washington, December 16, 1962, CDF, 789.001/12-1662, USNA; Despatch A-41, Kabul to Washington, July 28, 1963, SNF, AID (US) 10 AFG, USNA; Archer Blood, ADSTOH, June 27, 1989, 30.
40. John M. Steeves, ADSTOH, March 27, 1991, 39; Telegram 709, Kabul to Washington, June 13, 1964, SNF, SOC 10 AFG, USNA; Telegram 717, Kabul to Washington, June 17, 1964, ibid.; Dupree, *Afghanistan,* 529–30.
41. Airgram A-518, Kabul to Washington, June 13, 1964, SNF, AID (US) 8 AFG, USNA.
42. "His Majesty Opens Highway of Salang," *KT,* September 5, 1964.
43. Airgram A-131, Kabul to Washington, September 22, 1964, SNF, AID (US) 1 AFG, USNA.
44. Airgram A-437, Kabul to Washington April 11, 1964, SNF, FN 1–1 AFG. USNA; Telegram 60, Kabul to Washington, July 30, 1964, ibid.
45. Kristin L. Ahlberg, *Transplanting the Great Society: Lyndon Johnson and Food for Peace* (Columbia: University of Missouri Press, 2008), 42–58; Cullather, *The Hungry World: America's Cold War Battle against Poverty in Asia* (Cambridge, MA: Harvard University Press, 2010), 205–13.
46. Telegram 75, Kabul to Washington, August 10, 1964, SNF, FN 1–1 AFG, USNA; Telegram 39, Washington to Kabul, August 14, 1964, ibid.; Telegram 84, Kabul to Washington, August 15, 1964, ibid.

47. Despatch 745, Kabul to Paris, September 18, 1964, A-O(A) 1944–72, 37, MAE/P.
48. Despatch 44, Kabul to London, October 21, 1964, FO 371/175583, UKNA.
49. Telegram 71, Washington to Kabul, September 25, 1964, SNF, POL 15–5 AFG, USNA.
50. Telegram 74, Washington to Kabul, September 29, 1964, SNF, AID (US) 15–9 AFG, USNA; Telegram 262, Kabul to Washington, November 12, 1964, ibid.
51. Airgram A-355, Kabul to Washington, April 10, 1965, SNF, AID 6 AFG, USNA; Diary, Robert Nathan, March 13, 1965, RRNP, 1:34, CUSC; Diary, Robert Nathan, November 11, 1965, RRNP, 1:38, CUSC; Timothy Nunan, *Humanitarian Invasion: Global Development in Cold War Afghanistan* (New York: Cambridge University Press), 73-82. I thank Tim Nunan for his generous assistance with the Nathan Papers.
52. Airgram A-366, Kabul to Washington, February 12, 1964, SNF, AID (US) AFG, USNA.
53. Airgram A-131, Kabul to Washington, September 22, 1964, SNF, AID (US) 1 AFG, USNA.
54. Airgram A-131.
55. Memorandum, Komer to Bundy, April 23, 1964, NSF, RKP, box 10, "Afghanistan," LBJL.
56. Memorandum, Komer to Bundy, September 21, 1964, NSF, RKP, box 10, "Afghanistan," LBJL.
57. Telegram 310, Kabul to Washington, December 8, 1964, SNF, POL 15–1 AFG, USNA.
58. Letter, Kabul to London, December 9, 1964, FO 371/175588, UKNA.
59. Despatch 70, Kabul to Paris, January 20, 1965, A-O(A) 1944–72, 47, MAE/P.
60. Airgram A-339, Kabul to Washington, December 9, 1964, SNF, POL 32–1 AFG-PAK, USNA.
61. *The Conference on the Problems of Economic Development* (Cairo: General Organisation for Government Printing Offices, 1962), 134, 305, 356.
62. Airgram A-108, Kabul to Washington, September 5, 1964, SNF, POL 8, USNA.
63. Elisabeth Leake, "Afghan Internationalism and the Question of Afghanistan's Political Legitimacy," *Afghanistan* 1, no. 1 (April 2018): 68–76.
64. Airgram A-166, Kabul to Washington, October 29, 1964, SNF, POL 8, USNA; Crews, *Afghan Modern: The History of a Global Nation* (Cambridge, MA: Harvard University Press, 2015), 183–99.
65. Airgram A-160, Kabul to Washington, October 20, 1964, SNF, POL 8, USNA.
66. Airgram A-350, Kabul to Washington, April 10, 1965, SNF, POL 33–7 AFG-PAK, USNA.
67. Airgram A-34, Kabul to Washington, August 1, 1964, SNF, POL 33–1 AFG-IRAN/HELMAND, USNA.

68. Airgram A-34; Memorandum, Handley to Harriman, March 12, 1965, SNF, AID (US) AFG, USNA.
69. Letter, Steeves to Handley, January 30, 1965, SNF, POL 33–1 AFG-IRAN/HELMAND, USNA.
70. Telegram 481, Kabul to Washington, March 3, 1965, *FRUS, 1964–68, XXV*: 1050–52; Telegram 225, Washington to Kabul, February 26, 1965, AHP, box 544, LOC; Telegram 2485, New Delhi to Washington, March 4, 1965, ibid.
71. Telegram 522, Kabul to Washington, March 18, 1965, SNF, FN 1–1 AFG, USNA; Telegram 552, Kabul to Washington, March 31, 1965, ibid.
72. Letter, Steeves to Talbot, April 15, 1965, SNF, POL AFG-US, USNA.
73. Memorandum, Komer to Bundy, May 29, 1965, NSF, Name File, box 6, "Robert Komer, Vol. 1 (2/3)," LBJL.
74. Memorandum, Harold Saunders to Robert Komer, March 30, 1965, NSF, RKP, box 10, "Aid 2," LBJL.
75. Telegram 563, Kabul to Washington, April 2, 1965, SNF, FN 1–1 AFG, USNA; Telegram 576, Kabul to Washington, April 5, 1965, ibid.
76. Telegram 659, Kabul to Washington, May 6, 1965, SNF, POL 33-1 AFG-IRAN/HELMAND, USNA.
77. Telegram 660, Kabul to Washington, May 6, 1965, *FRUS, 1964–68, XXV*: 1054–55.
78. Telegram 326, Washington to Kabul, May 11, 1965, SNF, POL 33-1 AFG-IRAN/HELMAND, USNA.
79. Telegram 679, Kabul to Washington, May 13, 1965, *FRUS, 1964–68, XXV*: 1055–56.
80. Telegram 734, Kabul to Washington, June 12, 1965, *FRUS, 1964–68, XXV*: 1056–61.
81. Airgram A-408, Kabul to Washington, June 5, 1965, SNF, POL 14 AFG, USNA.
82. Letter, Kabul to London, October 2, 1965, FO 371/180677, UKNA; Airgram A-46, Kabul to Washington, August 10, 1965, SNF, POL 14 AFG, USNA; Report 732/65, Kabul to Bonn, September 8, 1965, PA, B36/177, AA.
83. Faridullah Bezhan, "The Emergence of Political Parties and Political Dynamics in Afghanistan, 1964–73," *Iranian Studies* 46, no. 6 (November 2013): 921–41.
84. Frank Schmelzer, ADSTOH, December 1, 1992, 8; William Piez, ASDTOH, September 11, 2009, 38.
85. Airgram A-329, Kabul to Washington, March 20, 1965, SNF, POL 12 AFG, USNA; Airgram A-10, Kabul to Washington, July 13, 1965, SNF, POL 14 AFG, USNA.
86. Elisabeth Leake, *Afghan Crucible: The Soviet Invasion and the Making of Modern Afghanistan* (New York: Oxford University Press, 2022), 14–20; Raja Anwar, *The Tragedy of Afghanistan: A First-Hand Account* (London: Verso, 1988); Henry S. Bradsher, *Afghanistan and the Soviet Union* (Durham, NC: Duke University Press, 1985), 36–49.

87. Airgram A-346, Kabul to Washington, April 6, 1965, SNF, POL 23-7 AFG, USNA; Airgram A-30, Kabul to Washington, July 31, 1965, SNF, POL 13-2 AFG, USNA.
88. Telegram 188, Kabul to Washington, October 14, 1965, SNF, POL 15-2 AFG, USNA; Airgram A-78, Kabul to Washington, September 22, 1965, SNF, POL 14 AFG, USNA; Dupree, *Afghanistan*, 589–92.
89. Letter, Kabul to London, October 27, 1965, FO 371/180677, UKNA; Despatch 32, Kabul to London, November 17, 1965, ibid.; Despatch 1115, Kabul to Paris, November 3, 1965, A-O(A) 1944–72, 37, MAE/P.
90. Memorandum, Read to Bundy, November 9, 1965, NSF, RKP, box 10, "Afghanistan," LBJL.
91. Letter, Komer to Maiwandwal, November 2, 1965, ibid.
92. Dupree, *Afghanistan*, 593–94.
93. Telegram 236, Kabul to Washington, November 5, 1965, SNF, POL 23-8 AFG, USNA; Telegram 274, Kabul to Washington, December 14, 1965, ibid.; Telegram 259, Kabul to Washington, November 29, 1965, NSF, RKP, box 10, "Afghanistan," LBJL; Despatch 1181, Kabul to Paris, November 18, 1965, A-O(A) 1944–72, 37, MAE/P; Despatch 1115, Kabul to Paris, November 3, 1965, ibid.
94. McGarr, *Cold War in South Asia*, 324–36; Srinath Raghavan, *Fierce Enigmas: A History of the United States in South Asia* (New York: Basic Books, 2018), 261–65.
95. Airgram A-19, Kabul to Washington, July 28, 1966, SNF, POL 7 US/FREEMAN, USNA; Telegram 415, Kabul to Washington, July 27, 1966, ibid.
96. "His Majesty Opens New Highway," *KT*, July 14, 1966; Telegram 379, Kabul to Washington, July 25, 1966, *FRUS, 1964–68, XXV*: 1064–65.
97. Letter, Rutillus Allen to Glenn Craig, August 21, 1966, NAR, box 4, "Correspondence General 1966 (3)," UNO; Letter, Craig to Allen, August 25, 1966, ibid.
98. Telegram TOAID 1724, Kabul to Washington, June 23, 1966, SNF, AID (US) 15 AFG, USNA; Telegram 379; Telegram 274, Kabul to Washington, July 16, 1966, SNF, AID (US) 15 AFG, USNA; Ahlberg, *Transplanting the Great Society*, 84–90.
99. Francis J. Gavin, *Gold, Dollars, and Power: The Politics of International Monetary Relations, 1958–1971* (Chapel Hill: University of North Carolina Press, 2004).
100. Robert Albright, "$3.5 Billion Foreign Aid Agreed Upon," *WP*, August 31, 1966; Memorandum, Saunders and Wriggins to Rostow, November 4, 1966, CK2349542462, USDDO.
101. Telegram 673, Kabul to Washington, May 30, 1964, SNF, AID (US) 9 AFG, USNA.

102. Telegram 1722, Kabul to Washington, October 25, 1966, SNF, AID (US) AFG, USNA; Telegram 2015, Kabul to Washington, November 19, 1966, ibid.
103. Airgram A-271, Kabul to Washington, June 30, 1966, SNF, POL 15-2 AFG, USNA; Telegram 2183, Kabul to Washington, December 1, 1966, SNF, POL 23-8 AFG, USNA; Anwar, *Tragedy of Afghanistan*, 49-54.
104. Telegram 3370, Kabul to Washington, February 23, 1967, SNF, POL 7 AFG, USNA; Telegram 3714, Kabul to Washington, March 16, 1967, ibid.; Telegram 3703, Kabul to Washington, March 15, 1967, SNF, AID (US) AFG, USNA.
105. Telegram 11328, New Delhi to Washington, February 8, 1967, SNF, POL 7 AFG, USNA.
106. Telegram 3383, Kabul to Washington, February 24, 1967, SNF, POL 27 VIETS, USNA.
107. Telegram 3704, Kabul to Washington, March 16, 1967, NSF, CF, "Afghanistan (1)," LBJL.
108. Memcon, March 28, 1967, *FRUS, 1964-68, XXV*: 1070-72; Memcon, March 29, 1967, *FRUS, 1964-68, XXV*: 1072-73; James W. Spain, *In Those Days: A Diplomat Remembers* (Kent, OH: Kent State University Press, 1998), 192-93.
109. Memcon, March 29, 1967, *FRUS, 1964-68, XXV*: 1072-73.
110. Memorandum, Rostow to Johnson, March 31, 1967, NSF, CF, box 116, "Afghanistan, Maiwandwal Visit," LBJL; Note, Lyndon Johnson, March 31, 1967, ibid.
111. Memorandum, Saunders to Wriggins, April 3, 1967, NSF, HHSF, box 1, LBJL; Memorandum, Rostow to Johnson, April 6, 1967, ibid.
112. Memorandum, Gaud and Freeman to Johnson, April 7, 1967, NSF, CF, box 116, "Afghanistan Cables," LBJL; Memorandum, Schultze to Johnson, April 15, 1967, ibid.
113. Memorandum, Wriggins to Rostow, April 19, 1967, NSF, CF, box 116, "Afghanistan Cables," LBJL; Memorandum, Rostow to Johnson, April 17, 1967, *FRUS, 1964-68, XXV*: 1074.
114. Telegram 4366, Kabul to Washington, April 28, 1967, *FRUS, 1964-68, XXV*: 1075-76; Telegram 185010, Washington to Kabul, April 29, 1967, SNF, AID (US) 15-8 AFG, USNA; Airgram A-177, Kabul to Washington, April 27, 1967, SNF, E 2-2 AFG, USNA.
115. Memorandum, Saunders to Rostow, May 2, 1967, *FRUS, 1964-68, XXV*: 1076-77; Memorandum, Rostow to Johnson, June 7, 1967, *FRUS, 1964-68, XXV*: 1077-78.
116. Telegram 218931, Washington to Kabul, June 29, 1967, SNF, AID (US) 9 AFG, USNA; Telegram 3023, Washington to Kabul, July 7, 1967, ibid.; Memorandum, Raymond Pagan to Walter Ramsay, November 14, 1967, NESA, OPAB/RRA, "AID 1 General, 1968," USNA.
117. Telegram 26, Kabul to Washington, July 28, 1967, SNF, AID (US) 9 AFG, USNA; Telegram 14362, Washington to Kabul, July 31, 1967, ibid.; Telegram

301, Kabul to Washington, August 1, 1967, ibid.; Telegram 14728, Washington to Kabul, August 1, 1967, ibid.

118. Telegram 366, Kabul to Washington, August 9, 1967, SNF, AID (US) 8–1 AFG, USNA.

119. Telegram 566, Kabul to Washington, August 28, 1967, SNF, POL 15–1 AFG, USNA; Telegram 689, Kabul to Washington, September 6, 1967, ibid.; Letter, Kabul to London, August 23, 1967, FCO 17/137, UKNA; Amin Saikal, *Modern Afghanistan: A History of Struggle and Survival* (London: I. B. Tauris, 2012), 156–59; Jonathan L. Lee, *Afghanistan: A History from 1260 to the Present* (London: Reaktion, 2022), 570.

120. Telegram 1166, Kabul to Washington, October 9, 1967, SNF, POL 15–1 AFG, USNA; Telegram 1205, Kabul to Washington, October 11, 1967, ibid.; Memorandum, Hughes to Rusk, November 14, 1967, ibid.

121. Telegram, Kabul to Washington, November 27, 1967, *FRUS, 1964–68, XXV*: 1078–81.

122. Memorandum, Johnson to Gaud, January 11, 1968, *PPP, 1968, 1*, 22–23; Letter, Neumann to Edward Hamilton, December 21, 1967, NSC, Edward Hamilton Papers, box 1, LBJL; Gavin, *Gold, Dollars, and Power*, 177–80.

123. Memorandum, Zwick to Johnson, March 27, 1968, *FRUS, 1964–1968, XXV*: 1083–85; Memorandum, Rostow to Johnson, March 29, 1968, NSF, CF, box 116, "Afghanistan, Vol. 1, Cables," LBJL.

124. Memorandum, Rostow to Johnson, April 22, 1968, *FRUS, 1964–1968, XXV*: 1085–86.

125. Message to Congress, Johnson, February 8, 1968, *PPP, 1968, 199–208*; Public Law 90–581, October 17, 1968, 82 Stat. 1137–43.

126. Thomas Alan Schwartz, *Lyndon Johnson and Europe: In the Shadow of Vietnam* (Cambridge, MA: Harvard University Press, 2003), 225–27; Jonathan Colman, *The Foreign Policy of Lyndon B. Johnson: The United States and the World, 1963–1969* (Edinburgh: Edinburgh University Press, 2010), 115–24.

127. Rouhollah K. Ramazani, *Iran's Foreign Policy, 1941–1973: A Study of Foreign Policy in Modernizing Nations* (Charlottesville: University Press of Virginia, 1975), 329–39; Dennis Kux, *The United States and Pakistan, 1947–2000: Disenchanted Allies* (Washington, DC: Woodrow Wilson Center Press, 2001), 169–77.

128. Despatch 0133/67, Kabul to Prague, September 19, 1967, TO-T(A) 1965–1969, 1:12, AMZV.

129. Randall Woods, *LBJ: Architect of American Ambition* (New York: Free Press, 2006), 448–58; Robert Dallek, *Flawed Giant: Lyndon Johnson and His Times, 1961–1973* (New York: Oxford University Press, 1998), 6–7; Cullather, *The Hungry World*, 205–31.

8. The Fall of the Monarchy, 1968–1973

1. Memorandum, Dunbar to Nass, January 7, 1970, NESA, OPAB, RRA, box 1, "Vice President's Trip to Afghanistan, 1970," USNA; Despatch 20, Kabul to Paris, January 14, 1970, A-O(A) 1944–72, 84, MAE/P.
2. Richard Milhous Nixon, *RN: The Memoirs of Richard Nixon* (New York: Grosset & Dunlap, 1978), 394–95; Daniel J. Sargent, *A Superpower Transformed: The Remaking of American Foreign Relations in the 1970s* (New York: Oxford University Press, 2014), 48–55.
3. Memorandum, Kissinger to Agnew, December 17, 1969, NSCF, HAKOF, box 81, "V.P. Agnew's Trip (1/3)," RMNL; Memorandum, Agnew to Nixon, January 21, 1970, NSCF, CF-ME, box 591, "Afghanistan (2/2)," RMNL; Telegram 24, Auckland to Washington, January 16, 1970, *FRUS, 1969–76, E-7:* #333.
4. Memorandum, Agnew to Nixon, January 21, 1970, NSCF, CF-ME, box 591, "Afghanistan (2/2)," RMNL.
5. Memorandum, Joseph Blatchford to Rogers, March 13, 1970, SNF, AID (US) 14 AFG, USNA; Interview, John True with author, October 14, 2022; Elizabeth Cobbs Hoffman, *All You Need Is Love: The Peace Corps and the Spirit of the 1960s* (Cambridge, MA: Harvard University Press, 1998), 217–34.
6. "His Majesty's Address," *KT*, August 26, 1968; Telegram 16, USIS Kabul to Washington, September 28, 1968, SNF, CUL 8 AFG(KA), USNA; Telegram 6227, Kabul to Washington, August 24, 1968, ibid.
7. Telegram 6410, Kabul to Washington, September 6, 1968, SNF, POL 15 AFG, USNA.
8. Airgram A-199, Kabul to Washington, May 1, 1968, SNF, POL 23–8 AFG, USNA; Telegram 5133, Kabul to Washington, June 18, 1968, ibid.; Telegram 5429, Kabul to Washington, July 5, 1968, SNF, POL 15–1 AFG, USNA; Telegram 5428, Kabul to Washington, July 5, 1968, ibid.; Telegram 5804, Kabul to Washington, July 29, 1968, ibid.; Telegram 5740, Kabul to Washington, July 24, 1968, SNF, POL 15 AFG, USNA; Louis Dupree, "Afghanistan: 1968, Part IV: Strikes and Demonstrations," *AUFS, South Asia Series* XII, no. 7, August 1968, 1–6; Despatch 200, Kabul to Paris, July 30, 1968, A-O(A) 1944–72, 64, MAE/P.
9. Airgram A-321, Kabul to Washington, November 20, 1968, SNF, POL 2–3 AFG-COMBLOC, USNA; Airgram A-198, Kabul to Washington, May 1, 1968, SNF, POL 2–3 AFG-CHICOM, USNA; Despatch 217, Kabul to Paris, August 28, 1968, A-O(A) 1944–72, 86, MAE/P; Despatch 259, Kabul to Paris, November 5, 1968, A-O(A) 1944–72, 85, MAE/P.
10. Airgram A-295, Kabul to Washington, September 23, 1968, SNF, POL 32–1 AFG-PAK, USNA; Telegram 6826, Kabul to Washington, October 1, 1968, SNF, POL 15–1 AFG, USNA.

11. Telegram 7501, Kabul to Washington, November 14, 1968, SNF, POL 23–8 AFG, USNA; Airgram A-613, Rawalpindi to Washington, October 21, 1968, SNF, POL AFG-PAK, USNA; Telegram 8085, Kabul to Washington, December 19, 1968, SNF, POL 15–1 AFG, USNA.
12. Meeting with the Vice President, January 8, 1954, USDDO (CK2349126097); Despatch 111, Kabul to Washington, December 19, 1953, CDF, 033.1100NI/12-1953, USNA; Conversation 578–9, Oval Office, September 24, 1971 (~1:24:45), nixontapeaudio.org/chron2/rmn_e578b.mp3.
13. Srinath Raghavan, *1971: A Global History of the Creation of Bangladesh* (Cambridge, MA: Harvard University Press, 2013), 82–84.
14. Memorandum, Nixon to Kissinger, February 10, 1970, *FRUS, 1969–76, I*: 186–87.
15. Memorandum, Kissinger to Nixon, undated, *FRUS, 1969–76, IV*: 10–17.
16. Memorandum, Kissinger, April 3, 1969, *FRUS, 1969–76, IV*: 18–20.
17. The following account is drawn from Neumann, "Reflections Out of My Life," April 1968, ADSTOH.
18. Ibid.; Memorandum, Howard Wriggins to Walt Rostow, July 18, 1966, USDDO (CK2349638363); Marlen Neumann, ADSTOH, January 15, 1988, 6–7.
19. Interview, Ronald Neumann with author, August 18, 2022.
20. Letter, Neumann to Karl Loewenstein, October 28, 1969, NFP, box 3, CEYL; Samuel Hoskinson, interview, May 1, 2018; L. Bruce Laingen, ADSTOH, January 9, 1993, 39–40; Archer K. Blood, ADSTOH, June 27, 1989, 32–33.
21. Telegram 219, Kabul to Washington, January 14, 1969, SNF, AID (US) 9 AFG, USNA; Telegram 732, Kabul to Washington, February 12, 1969, ibid; Telegram 4138, Kabul to Washington, August 12, 1969, SNF, AID (US) AFG, USNA.
22. Telegram 2080, Tehran to Washington, May 26, 1969, *FRUS, 1969–76, E-7*: #325.
23. Country Policy Statement on Afghanistan, August 6, 1969, *FRUS, 1969–76, E-7*: #326.
24. Ibid.
25. Ibid.
26. Memorandum, Walter Ramsay, August 21, 1969, NESA, OPAB, RRA, AID 1–12 1969, USNA; Telegram 142540, Washington to Kabul, April 5, 1968, SNF, AID (US) 15–8 AFG, USNA.
27. Memorandum, William Spengler to Davies, August 27, 1969, *FRUS, 1969–76, E-7*: #327; Letter, Ramsay to Naas, October 10, 1968, NESA, OPAB, RRA, AID 1–12 1969, USNA.
28. Airgram A-18, Kabul to Washington, February 19, 1970, SNF, AID (US) 15–8 AFG, USNA; Airgram A-31, Kabul to Washington, March 30, 1970, ibid.
29. Airgram TOAID A-375, Kabul to Washington, September 2, 1970, SNF, AID (US) 15–8 AFG, USNA.
30. Airgram TOAID A-375; Airgram A-72, Kabul to Washington, June 8, 1970, SNF, E 2–4 AFG, USNA.

31. Airgram A-375; Memorandum, Flaten to Spengler, September 1, 1970, BNESA, OPAB, RRA, box 1, "AID 15 PL-480," USNA; Memorandum, Spengler to Langmaid, undated, ibid.; Telegram AIDTO A2370, Washington to Kabul, October 24, 1970, SNF, AID (US) 15–8 AFG, USNA; Telegram 7482, Kabul to Washington, December 8, 1970, ibid.
32. Memorandum, Kissinger to Nixon, undated, *FRUS, 1969–76, E-7*: #82; Memorandum, Davis to Eliot, September 10, 1970, *FRUS, 1969–76, E-1*: #181; Telegram 6597, Kabul to Washington, October 28, 1970, SNF, AID (US) 15–8 PAK, USNA.
33. Airgram A-06, Kabul to Washington, January 17, 1970, SNF, E 5 AFG, USNA; Shamalan Unit Draft Feasibility Report, September 1967, i-2, SHA; Timothy Nunan, *Humanitarian Invasion: Global Development in Cold War Afghanistan* (New York: Cambridge University Press, 2016), 88–89.
34. Airgram A-97, Kabul to Washington, August 29, 1970, SNF, E 12 AFG, USNA.
35. Telegram 7635, Kabul to Washington, December 16, 1970, SNF, POL 15–1 AFG, USNA; Telegram 7540, Kabul to Washington, December 11, 1970, ibid.
36. Letter, Neumann to Sisco, December 29, 1970, *FRUS, 1969–76, E-7*: #337; Telegram 970, Kabul to Washington, February 3, 1971, SNF, AID (US) 9 AFG, USNA; Letter, Kabul to London, February 7, 1971, FCO 37/767, UKNA.
37. Telegram 7534, Kabul to Washington, December 10, 1970, SNF, POL 33–1 AFG-IRAN/HELMAND, USNA; Telegram 5896, Rawalpindi to Washington, July 22, 1970, SNF, POL AFG-PAK, USNA; Despatch 379, Kabul to Paris, December 7, 1969, A-O(A) 1944–72, 85, MAE/P.
38. Letter, Neumann to Nathan, May 20, 1970, NFP, box 4, CEYL; Telegram 7582, Kabul to Washington, December 14, 1970, SNF, POL AFG-USSR, USNA; Letter, Prague to Berlin, October 2, 1970, MfAA, C 1150/73, AA; Despatch 032/71, Kabul to Prague, March 28, 1971, TO-T(A) 1970–74, 3:2, AMZV; Report on King's Visit, October 8, 1970, KSČ-ÚV-02/1, 219, Czech National Archives, Prague.
39. Airgram A-57, Kabul to Washington, May 27, 1971, SNF, POL 15 AFG, USNA.
40. Telegram 1934, Kabul to Washington, March 18, 1971, SNF, POL 23–8 PAK, USNA.
41. Gary J. Bass, *The Blood Telegram: Nixon, Kissinger, and a Forgotten Genocide* (New York: Alfred A. Knopf, 2013), 49–66; Raghavan, *1971*, 28–53.
42. Telegram 63, Kabul to London, April 8, 1971, FCO 37/882, UKNA; Despatch 120, Kabul to Paris, April 25, 1971, A-O(A) 1944–72, 85, MAE/P; Telegram 5071, Kabul to Washington, August 17, 1971, SNF, POL INDIA-PAK, USNA; Telegram 2712, Kabul to Washington, April 21, 1971, SNF, POL 23–9 PAK, USNA; Letter Kabul to London, July 23, 1971, FC 37/767, UKNA.

43. Telegram 1876, Tehran to Washington, April 13, 1971, SNF, POL AFG-IRAN, USNA; Telegram 2619, Kabul to Washington, April 15, 1971, ibid.; Letter, Kabul to London, June 26, 1971, FCO 37/771, UKNA.
44. Diary, Robert Nathan, July 27, 1971, RRNP, 2:15, CUSC; Diary, Robert Nathan, August 7, 1971, ibid.; James P. Sterba, "Staving Afghan Children Await Death Along Roads," *NYT*, June 16, 1972.
45. Livestock Survey Mission Report, undated (July 1971), KASB, 10, "La Secheresse en Afghanistan," CADN; Letter, Cohn to Flaten, July 6, 1971, SNF, POL AFG-US, USNA.
46. Aide Memoire, Afghan Embassy, June 14, 1971, SNF, SOC 10 AFG, USNA; Aide Memoire, Afghan Embassy, July 19, 1971, ibid.; Minutes of Meeting, UN Information Centre, July 26, 1971, KASB, 10, "La Secheresse en Afghanistan," CADN; Arnold Schifferdecker, ADSTOH, May 14, 1996, 20–21; John P. Harrod, ADSTOH, March 1, 1999, 28.
47. Ibid.
48. Telegram 4311, Kabul to Washington, July 12, 1971, *FRUS, 1969–76, E-7*: #338.
49. Letter, Neumann to Sisco, August 12, 1971, *FRUS, 1969–76, E-7*: #343.
50. Airgram Circular A-1632, July 31, 1971, SNF, AID (US) 15–8 AFG, USNA; Robert Nathan, Diary, July 28, 1971, RRNP, 2:15, CUSC.
51. Telegram 4851, Kabul to Washington, August 7, 1971, *FRUS, 1969–76, E-7*: #341; Telegram 4961, Kabul to Washington, August 12, 1971, SNF, SOC 10 AFG, USNA; Telegram 5301, Kabul to Washington, August 30, 1971, ibid.; Telegram 5413, Kabul to Washington, September 2, 1971, ibid.; Telegram 5414, Kabul to Washington, September 2, 1971, SNF, POL AFG-IRAN, USNA.
52. Letter, Neumann to Sisco, August 12, 1971, *FRUS, 1969–76, E-7*: #343; Telegram 5041, Kabul to Washington, August 16, 1971, *FRUS, 1969–76, E-7*: #344.
53. Telegram 166666, Washington to Kabul, September 10, 1971, *FRUS, 1969–76, E-7*: #346.
54. Telegram 153803, Washington to Kabul, August 20, 1971, SNF, FN 14 AFG, USNA; Telegram 5417, Kabul to Washington, September 4, 1971, ibid.; Telegram 166666, Washington to Kabul, September 10, 1971, *FRUS, 1969–76, E-7*: #346.
55. Craig Daigle, *The Limits of Détente: The United States, the Soviet Union, and the Arab-Israeli Conflict, 1969–1973* (New Haven, CT: Yale University Press, 2012), 168–202; Raghavan, *1971*, 108–30; Salim Yaqub, *Imperfect Strangers: Americans, Arabs, and U.S.–Middle East Relations in the 1970s* (Ithaca, NY: Cornell University Press, 2016), 44–49. Neumann had sought contacts with the Chinese ambassador in Kabul in 1970.
56. Interview, Samuel Hoskinson with author, May 1, 2018.
57. Telegram 5414, Kabul to Washington, September 2, 1971, SNF, POL AFG-IRAN, USNA; Telegram 6603, Kabul to Washington, October 27, 1971, ibid.;

Telegram 6141, Tehran to Washington, October 29, 1971, ibid.; Despatch 310, Kabul to Paris, November 14, 1971, A-O(A) 1944–72, 79, MAE/P.

58. Telegram 5641, Kabul to Washington, September 13, 1971, SNF, SOC 10 AFG, USNA; Telegram 6010, Kabul to Washington, September 28, 1971, *FRUS, 1969–76, E-7*: #348; Despatch 229, Kabul to Paris, September 1, 1971, A-O(A) 1944–72, 64, MAE/P.
59. Saunders, Agriculture Sector Fourth Plan, July 23, 1970, NAR, box 2, "Agriculture General 1967/70," UNO.
60. Food for Work Program Analysis, USAID, February 1973, NAR, box 2, "Food for Work 1973," UNO.
61. Airgram A-8, Kabul to Washington, January 27, 1971, SNF, POL 18 AFG, USNA.
62. Letter, Cohn to Flaten, May 27, 1971, SNF, POL AFG-US, USNA; Memorandum, June 28, 1971, NAR, box 4, "Correspondence, June 1971," UNO.
63. Letter, Saunders to Nathan, August 23, 1971, NAR, box 4, "Correspondence, August 1971," UNO.
64. Airgram A-90; Nunan, *Humanitarian Invasion*, 106–16.
65. Telegram 5936, Kabul to Washington, September 25, 1971, SNF, SOC 10 AFG, USNA; Telegram 6737, Kabul to Washington, November 4, 1971, ibid.; Telegram 6986, Kabul to Washington, November 18, 1971, ibid.; Memorandum, Saunders, November 1, 1971, NAR, box 2, "Food for Work, 1971–1972," UNO; Progress Report, November 15, 1971, ibid.
66. Telegram 7543, Kabul to Washington, December 14, 1971, SNF, SOC 10 AFG, USNA; Telegram 7077, Tehran to Washington, December 14, 1971, ibid.; Telegram 2586, Karachi to Washington, December 15, 1971, ibid.; Telegram 7683, Kabul to Washington, December 20, 1971, ibid.
67. Telegram 7281, Kabul to Washington, December 4, 1971, *FRUS, 1969–76, E-7*: #352; Telegram 12582, Islamabad to Washington, December 15, 1971, SNF, POL AFG-PAK, USNA.
68. Telegram 12712, Washington to Moscow, January 22, 1972, SNF, POL AFG-PAK, USNA.
69. Raghavan, 1971, 235-63; Bass, Blood Telegram, 289-324.
70. Ayesha Jalal, *The Struggle for Pakistan: A Muslim Homeland and Global Politics* (Cambridge, MA: Harvard University Press, 2014), 177–92.
71. Telegram 7151, Tehran to Washington, December 17, 1971, NSCF, CF-ME, box 602, RMNL; Bass, *The Blood Telegram*, 293–303; Roham Alvandi, *Nixon, Kissinger, and the Shah: The United States and Iran in the Cold War* (New York: Oxford University Press, 2014), 59–64.
72. Nixon, Message to Congress, June 17, 1971, *PPP, 1971*; Kathleen J. Frydl, *The Drug Wars in America, 1940–1973* (New York: Cambridge University Press, 2013), 1–11; Daniel Weimer, *Seeing Drugs: Modernization, Counterinsurgency, and*

U.S. Narcotics Control in the Third World, 1969–1976 (Kent, OH: Kent State University Press, 2013), 50–58.

73. Memorandum, Mitchell and Richardson to Nixon, October 20, 1969, *FRUS, 1969–76, E-1*: #146.
74. Nixon, Statement, June 30, 1971, *PPP, 1971*; Weimer, *Seeing Drugs*, 58–61.
75. Memorandum, Mitchell and Richardson to Nixon, October 20, 1969, *FRUS, 1969–76, E-1*: #146; Memorandum, Kissinger to Nixon, October 23, 1969, *FRUS, 1969–76, E-4*: #37.
76. Country Policy Statement—Afghanistan, August 6, 1969, *FRUS, 1969–76, E-7*: #326; James Tharin Bradford, *Poppies, Politics, and Power: Afghanistan and the Global History of Drugs and Diplomacy* (Ithaca, NY: Cornell University Press, 2019), 74–82; Daniel Weimer, "'It's That Difficult of a Terrain': Opium, Development, and Territoriality in US-Afghan Relations, 1940s–1970s," *Social History of Alcohol and Drugs* 33, no. 1 (March 2019): 113–44
77. Airgram A-196, Kabul to Washington, November 21, 1964, SNF, SOC 11–5 AFG, USNA.
78. Telegram 4783, Kabul to Washington, August 6, 1970, SNF, SOC 11–5 AFG, USNA.
79. Telegram 5567, Kabul to Washington, September 9, 1971, SNF, SOC 11–5 AFG, USNA; Telegram 6178, Kabul to Washington, October 5, 1971, ibid.; Telegram Secto 157, USUN to Washington, October 14, 1971, *FRUS, 1969–76, E-7*: #350.
80. Airgram A-21, Kabul to Washington, February 28, 1972, SNF, SOC 11–5 AFG, USNA.
81. Telegram 1021, Kabul to Washington, February 22, 1972, SNF, SOC 11–5 AFG, USNA; Telegram 884, Kabul to Washington, February 12, 1972, *FRUS, 1969–76, E-7*: #355; Telegram Secto 157; Despatch 34, Kabul to Paris, February 15, 1972, A-O(A) 1944–72, 79, MAE/P.
82. Telegram 2055, Kabul to Washington, April 15, 1972, SNF, SOC 11–5 AFG, USNA; Telegram 1705, Kabul to Washington, March 27, 1972, ibid.
83. Telegram 616, Kabul to Washington, February 1, 1972, *FRUS, 1969–76, E-7*: #353.
84. Airgram TOAID A-71, Kabul to Washington, March 20, 1972, *FRUS, 1969–76, E-7*: #357.
85. Despatch 100, Kabul to Paris, April 27, 1972, A-O(A) 1944–72, 64, MAE/P; Telegram 1806, Kabul to Washington, March 31, 1972, *FRUS, 1969–76, E-7*: #359.
86. Telegram 1806, Kabul to Washington, March 31, 1972, SNF, POL AFG, USNA.
87. Telegram 1806; Telegram 2042, Kabul to Washington, April 13, 1972, SNF, POL AFG, USNA; Telegram 56321, Washington to Kabul, April 1, 1972, ibid.

88. Telegram 2042; Telegram 74767, Washington to Kabul, April 29, 1972, SNF, POL AFG, USNA.
89. Sterba, "Starving," 10; Memorandum, Rahim Ghosnowi to Lou Mitchell, May 25, 1972, AMA, AD/FPR, box 2, "Peace Corps Reports," USNA.
90. Telegram 6986, Kabul to Washington, November 18, 1971, SNF, SOC 10 AFG, USNA.
91. Interview, Jim Mathewson with author, September 7, 2020.
92. Ibid.; Interview, Ron and Diane Dizon with author, September 1, 2020; Interview, Tim McCormack with author, September 8, 2020; Interview, Jim Hicks with author, September 25, 2020; James Sterba, "Famine Relief in Afghanistan Hindered by Inertia and Corruption," *NYT*, June 21, 1972, 3; Sterba, "Starving," 10.
93. McCormack, Interview; Mathewson, Interview; Memorandum, Ron Dizon and Don Condon to Abdul Wahid Mansury, June 21, 1972, AMA, AD/FPR, box 2, "Peace Corps Reports," USNA.
94. Telegram 2294, Kabul to Washington, April 28, 1972, SNF, POL 6 AFG, USNA; Telegram 2941, Kabul to Washington, May 25, 1972, SNF, SOC 10 AFG, USNA; Telegram 3517, Kabul to Washington, June 21, 1972, ibid.; Interview, Tim McCormack.
95. Memorandum, Ron Dizon and Don Condon to Abdul Wahid Mansury, June 21, 1972, AMA, AD/FPR, box 2, "Peace Corps Reports," USNA; Situation Report, June 19, 1972, AMA, AD/FPR, box 2, "Situation Reports," USNA.
96. Telegram 2565, Kabul to Washington, May 10, 1972, SNF, POL 15 AFG, USNA; Telegram 2400, Kabul to Washington, May 3, 1972, ibid.; Telegram 3016, Kabul to Washington, May 30, 1972, ibid.
97. Telegram 4008, Kabul to Washington, July 12, 1972, SNF, POL 7 US/CONNALLY, USNA.
98. Telegram 2565; Airgram A-54, Kabul to Washington, May 17, 1972, SNF, POL 15 AFG, USNA.
99. Memorandum, Flaten to Laingen, May 31, 1972, *FRUS, 1969–76*, E-7: #362.
100. Telegram 4039, Kabul to Washington, July 13, 1972, SNF, POL 7 US/CONNALLY, USNA.
101. "Nixon's Envoy Meets Premier, Foreign Minister," *KT*, July 8, 1972.
102. Telegram 3653, Kabul to Washington, June 27, 1972, SNF, SOC 10 AFG, USNA; Telegram 4884, Kabul to Washington, August 22, 1972, *FRUS, 1969–76*, E-7: #364; Memorandum, A. D. Dominguez, August 5, 1972, AMA, AD/FPR, box 2, "Letters 1972," USNA; Memorandum, Ron Dizon and Don Condon to Abdul Wahid Mansury, June 21, 1972, AMA, AD/FPR, box 2, "Peace Corps Reports," USNA.
103. Telegram 5741, Kabul to Washington, September 2, 1972, SNF, SOC 10 AFG, USNA; Telegram 5348, Kabul to Washington, September 14, 1972, *FRUS, 1969–76*, E-7: #365.

104. Telegram 5348, Kabul to Washington, September 14, 1972, *FRUS, 1969–76, E-7*: #365; Operation Help, Final Report, March 15, 1973, provided to the author by Ron Dizon; Telegram 5741, Kabul to Washington, September 2, 1972, SNF, SOC 10 AFG, USNA; Letter, Lewis to Flaten, October 26, 1972, SNF, POL 15 AFG, USNA.

105. Telegram 5597, Kabul to Washington, September 25, 1972, SNF, POL 15–1 AFG, USNA; Telegram 5636, Kabul to Washington, September 27, 1972, ibid.

106. Memorandum, Sisco to Rogers, December 12, 1972, *FRUS, 1969–76, E-7*: #371; Telegram 3836, USUN to Washington, October 12, 1972, *FRUS, 1969–76, E-7*: #369; Letter, Lewis to Flaten, October 26, 1972, SNF, POL 15 AFG, USNA.

107. Telegram 7289, Kabul to Washington, December 13, 1972, SNF, POL 15–1 AFG, USNA; Telegram 7580, Kabul to Washington, December 27, 1972, SNF, POL 15 AFG, USNA; Report 72/73, Kabul to London, December 27, 1972, FCO 37/1006, UKNA; Bradford, *Poppies*, 165–66.

108. Telegram 6816, Tehran to Washington, November 14, 1972, SNF, POL 33–1 AFG-IRAN/Helmand, USNA; Telegram 1335, Kabul to Washington, February 24, 1973, ibid.; Airgram A-18, Kabul to Washington, March 22, 1973, SNF, POL AFG-IRAN, USNA.

109. Telegram 1606, Islamabad to Washington, February 24, 1973, *FRUS, 1969–76, E-8*: #109; Telegram 1121, Kabul to Washington, February 16, 1973, *FRUS, 1969–76, E-8*: #2; Telegram 2132, Kabul to Washington, April 2, 1973, SNF, POL 15 AFG, USNA; Selig S. Harrison, *In Afghanistan's Shadow: Baluch Nationalism and Soviet Temptations* (Washington, DC: Carnegie Endowment for International Peace, 1981), 34–36.

110. Telegram 1098, Kabul to Washington, February 15, 1973, SNF, POL 15 AFG, USNA; Telegram 1927, Kabul to Washington, March 26, 1973, ibid.; Telegram 123475, Washington to Kabul, June 25, 1973, SNF, SOC 12–1 AFG, USNA.

111. Telegram 5096, Kabul to Washington, July 11, 1973, AAD.

112. Telegram 5188, Kabul to Washington, July 17, 1973, AAD; Telegram 5193, Kabul to Washington, July 17, 1973, AAD; Telegram 5222, Kabul to Washington, July 17, 1973, AAD; Telegram 4728, Kabul to Washington, June 26, 1973, SNF, POL 15–1 AFG, USNA; Report 372/73, Kabul to London, July 31, 1971, FCO 37/1218, UKNA; Despatch 219, Kabul to Paris, July 17, 1973, KASB, 10, "Coup d'état du 17 Juillet 1973," CADN.

113. Alvandi, *Nixon, Kissinger, and the Shah*, 59–64; James A. Bill, *The Eagle and the Lion: The Tragedy of American-Iranian Relations* (New Haven, CT: Yale University Press, 1988), 200–204.

114. Telegram 3836, USUN to Washington, October 12, 1972, *FRUS, 1969–76, E-7*: #369.

115. Telegram 988, Kabul to Washington, February 9, 1973, SNF, POL 15–1 AFG, USNA.
116. Letter, Neumann to Sisco, December 29, 1970, *FRUS, 1969–76*, E-7: #337; Bradford, *Poppies*, 175–79.
117. Richard Nixon, Address to the Bohemian Club, July 29, 1967, *FRUS, 1969–76*, I: 2–10.
118. Abbas Milani, *The Shah* (New York: Palgrave Macmillan, 2011), 328.

9. Return to Engagement, 1973–1976

1. Henry Kissinger, *White House Years* (Boston: Little, Brown, 1979), 846–47.
2. Memcon, November 1, 1974, *FRUS, 1969–76*, E-8: #15; Peter W. Rodman, *More Precious than Peace: The Cold War and the Struggle for the Third World* (New York: C. Scribner's Sons, 1994), 201.
3. Telegram 5956, Kabul to Washington, September 18, 1974, AAD; Arnold Schifferdecker, ADSTOH, May 14, 1996, 34; Telegram 6921, Kabul to Washington, November 2, 1974, AAD; Telegram HAKTO 76, Kissinger to Brent Scowcroft, November 1, 1974, *FRUS, 1969–76*, E-8: #14; Abdul Samad Ghaus, *The Fall of Afghanistan: An Insider's Account* (Washington, DC: Pergamon-Brassey's International Defense Publishers, 1988), 153–55.
4. Diego Cordovez and Selig S. Harrison, *Out of Afghanistan: The Inside Story of the Soviet Withdrawal* (New York: Oxford University Press, 1995), 15–16; Gregory Winger, "The Nixon Doctrine and U.S. Relations with the Republic of Afghanistan, 1973–1978: Stuck in the Middle with Daoud," *Journal of Cold War Studies* 19, no. 4 (December 2017): 4–41.
5. Telegram 281, Kabul to London, July 17, 1973, FCO 37/1217, UKNA; Telegram 5249, Kabul to Washington, July 18, 1973, AAD; Telegram 5305, Kabul to Washington, July 19, 1973, AAD; Louis Dupree, "A Note on Afghanistan: 1974," *AUFS* XVIII, no. 8 (September 1974): 1–23.
6. Note, G. B. Chalmers to Eric Norris, July 18, 1973, FCO 37/1217, UKNA; Memorandum, Ray Cline to Kissinger, July 19, 1973, NSCF, CF-ME, box 591, "Afghanistan (1)," RMNL.
7. Telegram 262, London to Kabul, July 18, 1973, FCO 37/1217, UKNA; Telegram 302, Kabul to London, July 19, 1973, FCO 37/1219, UKNA.
8. Memorandum, Saunders and Appelbaum to Kissinger, July 17, 1973, NSCF, CF-ME, box 591, "Afghanistan (1)," RMNL.
9. Ibid.; Intelligence Note, INR, July 17, 1973, NSCF, CF-ME, box 591, "Afghanistan (1)," RMNL.
10. Telegram 5222, Kabul to Washington, July 18, 1973, *FRUS, 1969–76*, E-8: #4.

11. Telegram 5319, Kabul to Washington, July 20, 1973, AAD; Draft Memorandum, undated, NESA, OPAB, RRA, box 3, "Afghanistan Coup," USNA; Telegram 312, Kabul to London, July 21, 1973, FCO 37/1219, UKNA.
12. Telegram 5257, Kabul to Washington, July 18, 1973, AAD; Telegram 5325, Kabul to Washington, July 20, 1973, *FRUS, 1969–76, E-8*: #5; Telegram 143450, Washington to Kabul, July 20, 1973, *FRUS, 1969–76, E-8*: #6.
13. Research Study RNAS-15, INR, July 17 1973, *FRUS, 1969–76, E-8*: #138; Ayesha Jalal, *The Struggle for Pakistan: A Muslim Homeland and Global Politics* (Cambridge, MA: Harvard University Press, 2014), 188–92.
14. Telegram 5809, Islamabad to Washington, July 18, 1973, AAD; Telegram 142393, Washington to London, July 20, 1973, AAD; Telegram 143876, Washington to Kabul, July 21, 1973, AAD; Telegram 143877, Washington to Kabul, July 21, 1973, AAD; Telegram 5110, Tehran to Washington, July 21, 1973, AAD.
15. Telegram 5368, Kabul to Washington, July 22, 1973, AAD; Telegram 5397, Kabul to Washington, July 23, 1973, AAD; Telegram 321, Kabul to London, July 22, 1973, FCO 37/1219, UKNA.
16. Letter, Drinkall to Chalmers, July 24, 1973, FCO 37/1219, UKNA.
17. NSSM 182, May 10, 1973, *FRUS, 1969–76, E-9-II*: #3; NIE 30-1-73, June 7, 1973, *FRUS, 1969–76, E-9-II*: #5; Memorandum, Saunders and Richard Kennedy to Kissinger, July 12, 1973, *FRUS, 1969–76, E-9-II*: #6; Telegram 821, Beijing to London, July 26, 1973, FCO 37/1217, UKNA; Henry Kissinger, *Years of Upheaval* (London: Weidenfeld & Nicolson, 1982), 687.
18. Summary of Conclusions, July 13, 1973, *FRUS, 1969–76, E-9-II*: #7.
19. Memorandum, Kissinger, July 24, 1973, *FRUS, 1969–76, XXVII*: 84–85; Memcon, July 24, 1973, *FRUS, 1969–76, XXVII*: 95–96.
20. Memcon, July 27, 1973, *FRUS, 1969–76, XXVII*: 118–29; Note, Soviet Government, undated, NSCF, HAKOF, box 68, RMNL. I thank Gregory Winger for sharing this record.
21. Note, Soviet Embassy, June 8, 1973, MfAA, ZR 1944/79, AA.
22. Letter, Shafiq to Willi Stoph, May 30, 1973, MfAA, DC 20/16983, AA.
23. Despatch 4/73, Kabul to Prague, August 18, 1973, TO-T(A) 1970–74, 3:2, AMZV.
24. Telegram 9119, Moscow to Washington, August 1, 1973, AAD.
25. Memcon, September 18, 1973, *FRUS, 1969–76, E-8*: #147.
26. Nixon, Remarks to Bhutto, September 18, 1973, *PPP, 1973*, 795–96.
27. Telegram 148856, Washington to Colombo, July 28, 1973, AAD; Telegram 5685, Kabul to Washington, July 31, 1973, AAD; Letter, Kabul to London, August 15, 1973, FCO 37/1216, UKNA.
28. Telegram 5887, Kabul to Washington, August 8, 1973, AAD; Telegram 6030, Kabul to Washington, August 14, 1973, AAD; Telegram 164400, Washington to Kabul, August 17, 1973, AAD; Telegram 6176, Kabul to Washington, August

20, 1976, AAD; Telegram 376, Kabul to London, September 18, 1973, FCO 37/1216, UKNA.
29. Telegram 6377, Kabul to Washington, August 29, 1973, AAD.
30. Telegram 6377; Telegram 172577, Washington to Islamabad, August 29, 1973, *FRUS, 1969–76*, E-8: #7; Telegram 6660, Kabul to Washington, September 12, 1973, AAD.
31. Telegram 6844, Kabul to Washington, September 21, 1973, AAD; Telegram 7462, Kabul to Washington, October 22, 1973, AAD; Telegram 389, Kabul to London, October 4, 1973, FCO 37/1216, UKNA; Letter, Kabul to London, October 17, 1973, ibid.
32. Ghaus, *Fall of Afghanistan*, 188–89; Amin Saikal, *Modern Afghanistan: A History of Struggle and Survival* (London: I. B. Tauris, 2012), 177–78.
33. Ghaus, *Fall of Afghanistan*, 152.
34. Telegram 8798, Islamabad to Washington, October 10, 1973, AAD; Telegram 6995, Kabul to Washington, September 28, 1973, AAD; Despatch 1167/73, Kabul to Prague, October 30, 1973, TO-T(A) 1970–74, 1:1, AMZV.
35. Telegram 8798, Islamabad to Washington, October 10, 1973, AAD; Telegram 7326, Tehran to Washington, October 17, 1973, AAD.
36. Telegram 7332, Kabul to Washington, October 16, 1973, AAD.
37. Telegram 210797, Washington to Kabul, October 25, 1973, AAD; Telegram 211738, Washington to Kabul, October 26, 1973, AAD; Memorandum, Saunders and Appelbaum to Kissinger, October 23, 1973, NSCF, CF-ME, box 591, "Afghanistan (1)," RMNL; Telegram 7725, Kabul to Washington, November 5, 1973, AAD. See also Winger, "Nixon Doctrine," 20–22.
38. Saikal, *Modern Afghanistan*, 174–75.
39. Telegram 8539, Kabul to Washington, December 18, 1973, AAD.
40. Note RNAN-51, INR, November 5, 1973, *FRUS, 1969–76*, E-8: #9.
41. Theodore Eliot, ADSTOH, April 24, 1992.
42. Interview, Theodore Eliot with author, September 17, 2014; Robert Curran, ADSTOH, November 6, 1998; Telegram 8449, Kabul to Washington, December 12, 1973, AAD; Telegram 8495, Kabul to Washington, December 15, 1973, AAD.
43. Memorandum, Kissinger to Ford, September 6, 1974, *FRUS, 1969–76*, XXVII: 234–35; Memcon, September 19, 1973, *FRUS, 1969–76*, E-8: #148; Telegram 115, Karachi to Washington, January 17, 1974, AAD; James A. Bill, *The Eagle and the Lion: The Tragedy of American-Iranian Relations* (New Haven, CT: Yale University Press, 1988), 213; Roham Alvandi, *Nixon, Kissinger, and the Shah: The United States and Iran in the Cold War* (New York: Oxford University Press, 2014), 90–91. Byroade cabled ruefully one night, after leaving his host's residence at two A.M., that he was "no match for Bhutto at the brandy game." Telegram 115, Karachi to Washington, January 17, 1974, AAD.

44. Telegram 7033, Kabul to Washington, October 1, 1973, AAD.
45. Telegram 1090, Kabul to Washington, February 21, 1974, AAD.
46. Telegram 72260, Washington to Kabul, April 10, 1974, AAD.
47. Telegram 8987, Moscow to Washington, June 11, 1974, AAD; Letter, Kabul to London, June 19, 1974, FCO 37/1417, UKNA; Despatch 1092/74, Kabul to Prague, July 24, 1974, TO-T(A) 1970–74, 3:2, AMZV; Note, Cde Gloede, June 18, 1974, MfAA, ZR 1944/79, AA; Ghaus, *Fall of Afghanistan*, 162–66.
48. Despatch 1024/74, Kabul to Prague, February 27, 1974, TO-T(A) 1970–74, 2:1, AMZV; Despatch 1006/74, Kabul to Prague, January 28, 1974, TO-T(A) 1970–74, 3:2, AMZV.
49. CPSU Decree, January 8, 1974, CWIHP, #112505; KGB Cipher, June 2, 1974, CWIHP, #112503.
50. Telegram 1006, Tehran to Washington, February 6, 1974, AAD.
51. Telegram 2985, Kabul to Washington, May 16, 1974, AAD; Telegram 878, Tehran to London, May 13, 1974, FCO 37/1417, UKNA; Letter 3/9, Tehran to London, August 8, 1974, FCO 37/1420, UKNA.
52. Telegram 4681, Kabul to Washington, July 29, 1974, AAD.
53. Ghaus, *Fall of Afghanistan*, 158.
54. Anthony Hyman, *Afghanistan Under Soviet Domination, 1964–91* (Houndmills, UK: Macmillan, 1992), 66–67.
55. Telegram 953, Kabul to Washington, February 14, 1974, AAD; Telegram 1717, Kabul to Washington, March 20, 1974, *FRUS, 1969–76, E-8*: #11.
56. Telegram 1717.
57. Timothy Nunan, *Humanitarian Invasion: Global Development in Cold War Afghanistan* (New York: Cambridge University Press, 2016), 89–92.
58. Memorandum, Louis Mitchell, April 8, 1974, SHA; Stephen J. Macekura, *Of Limits and Growth: The Rise of Global Sustainable Development in the Twentieth Century* (New York: Cambridge University Press, 2016), 150–54; David Ekbladh, *The Great American Mission: Modernization and the Construction of an American World Order* (Princeton, NJ: Princeton University Press, 2010), 220–25.
59. Telegram 1717; Louis Dupree, "The New Look in American Aid to Afghanistan," *AUFS* XVIII, no. 6 (June 1974): 1–9.
60. Barbara J. Keys, *Reclaiming American Virtue: The Human Rights Revolution of the 1970s* (Cambridge MA: Harvard University Press, 2014), 136–40; Sarah B. Snyder, *From Selma to Moscow: How Human Rights Activists Transformed U.S. Foreign Policy* (New York: Columbia University Press, 2018), 161–62.
61. Telegram 68545, Circular, April 4, 1974, AAD; Telegram 654, Kabul to Washington, February 4, 1974, AAD; Telegram 2407, Kabul to Washington, April 22, 1974, *FRUS, 1969–76, E-8*: #13.
62. Telegram 6416, Kabul to Washington, October 7, 1974, AAD; Memcon, November 1, 1974, *FRUS, 1969–76, E-8*: #15.

63. Telegram 5734, Islamabad to Washington, June 14, 1974, AAD; Telegram 4410, Kabul to Washington, July 15, 1974, AAD; Feroz Hassan Khan, *Eating Grass: The Making of the Pakistani Bomb* (Stanford, CA: Stanford University Press, 2012), 117–23; Malcolm M. Craig, *America, Britain and Pakistan's Nuclear Weapons Programme, 1974–1980: A Dream of Nightmare Proportions* (Cham, Switzerland: Palgrave Macmillan, 2017), 18–30.
64. Telegram 153807, Washington to Kabul, July 16, 1974, AAD; Telegram 7872, Islamabad to Washington, August 16, 1974, AAD.
65. Telegram 7617, Tehran to Washington, September 11, 1974, AAD.
66. Telegram 8120, Tehran to Islamabad, September 25, 1974, AAD.
67. Telegram 2081, Karachi to Washington, October 17, 1974, AAD; Telegram 10248, Islamabad to Washington, October 30, 1974, AAD; Selig S. Harrison, *In Afghanistan's Shadow: Baluch Nationalism and Soviet Temptations* (Washington, DC: Carnegie Endowment for International Peace, 1981), 37–39, 95–99.
68. Memcon, October 31, 1974, *FRUS, 1969–76, E-8*: #183.
69. Letter, Daoud to Waldheim, November 27, 1974, FCO 37/1419, UKNA.
70. William Gildea, "Joviality Among 'Good Friends,' " *WP*, February 7, 1975; Memcon, February 5, 1975, *FRUS, 1969–76, E-8*: #188; "US Lifting Embargo Confirms Bhutto," *Times of India*, February 7, 1975; Craig, *America, Britain and Pakistan's Nuclear Weapons Programme*, 40–43.
71. Telegram 1223, Islamabad to Washington, February 9, 1975, AAD; Telegram 1256, Islamabad to Washington, February 10, 1975, AAD; Telegram 1302, Islamabad to Washington, February 12, 1975, AAD; Telegram 1333, Islamabad to Washington, February 12, 1975, AAD.
72. Telegram 1088, Kabul to Washington, February 20, 1975, AAD; CIA, National Intelligence Bulletin, February 19, 1975, CIARR.
73. Telegram 3176, Islamabad to Washington, April 11, 1975, AAD; Telegram 3216, Islamabad to Washington, April 11, 1975, AAD.
74. Letter, Kabul to London, February 26, 1975, FCO 37/1553, UKNA; CIA, National Intelligence Bulletin, February 19, 1795, CIARR; CIA, OCI 0682/75, "Prospects for Pakistan," May 30, 1975, CIARR.
75. Telegram 14347, Manila to Washington, December 6, 1974, AAD; Telegram 1155, Kabul to Washington, February 23, 1975, NSA, CF/MESA, box 2, "Afghanistan EXDIS," GRFL.
76. Telegram 71657, Washington to Tehran, March 29, 1975, AAD; Telegram 3547, Tehran to Washington, April 17, 1975, AAD; Telegram 3867, Tehran to Washington, April 27, 1975, AAD; Telegram 4419, Tehran to Washington, May 12, 1975, AAD.
77. Telegram 981, Kathmandu to Washington, February 28, 1975, AAD.
78. Telegram 3341, Islamabad to Washington, April 16, 1975, AAD.
79. Telegram 1534, Kabul to Washington, March 11, 1975, AAD.

80. Letter, Kabul to London, July 22, 1975, FCO 37/1552, UKNA; David M. Wight, *Oil Money: Middle East Petrodollars and the Transformation of US Empire, 1967–1988*, The United States in the World (Ithaca, NY: Cornell University Press, 2021), 125–28.
81. Telegram 1155, Kabul to Washington, February 23, 1975, AAD.
82. Telegram 14347, Manila to Washington, December 6, 1974, AAD; Stephen D. Krasner, "Power Structures and Regional Development Banks," *International Organization* 35, no. 2 (1981): 317–22; Robert Wihtol, *The Asian Development Bank and Rural Development: Policy and Practice* (Basingstoke, UK: Macmillan, 1988), 42–50.
83. Telegram 279, Kabul to Washington, January 14, 1975, AAD; Telegram 459, Kabul to Washington, January 24, 1975, AAD; Memoranda, Curran, February 3, 1975, SHA.
84. Mitchell, Staff Paper, April 8, 1974, SHA; USAID/Afghanistan, "Central Helmand Drainage," April 8, 1975, SHA; Telegram 2283, Kabul to Washington, April 14, 1975, AAD.
85. Telegram 778, Kabul to Washington, February 5, 1975, AAD; Telegram 1837, Kabul to Washington, March 26, 1975, AAD; Airgram A-24, Kabul to Washington, April 30, 1975, RG-59, P-Reels, P750080-0063, USNA; CIA, Staff Notes, MEASA, February 7, 1975, CIARR.
86. Telegram 4914, Islamabad to Washington, May 31, 1975, AAD; Telegram 4441, Kabul to Washington, July 9, 1975, AAD; Despatch 190, Kabul to Paris, July 7, 1975, A-O(A) 1973–80, 1987, MAE/P.
87. "President Addresses the Nation," *KT*, July 20, 1975; Telegram 4639, Kabul to Washington, July 17, 1975, AAD.
88. Telegram 4526, Kabul to Washington, July 15, 1975, AAD.
89. S. Fida Yunas, *Afghanistan: A Political History*, vol. 3 (Peshawar: s.n., 2002), 195–98; Olivier Roy, *Islam and Resistance in Afghanistan* (New York: Cambridge University Press, 1990), 71–75.
90. Ahmad M. Siddiqi, *From Bilateralism to Cold War Conflict: Pakistan's Engagement with State and Non-State Actors on its Afghan Frontier, 1947–1989* (PhD diss., Oxford University, 2013), 137–38.
91. Chris Sands and Fazelminallah Qazizai, *Night Letters: Gulbuddin Hekmatyar and the Afghan Islamists Who Changed the World* (London: Hurst, 2019), 86–89; Barnett R. Rubin, *The Fragmentation of Afghanistan: State Formation and Collapse in the International System* (New Haven, CT: Yale University Press, 2002), 103–4.
92. Greg Grandin, *Kissinger's Shadow: The Long Reach of America's Most Controversial Statesman* (New York: Metropolitan Books, 2015), 128–30; Cordovez and Harrison, *Out of Afghanistan*, 16–17.
93. Report 41/75, Kabul to London, January 2, 1975, FCO 37/1550, UKNA; Ghaus, *Fall of Afghanistan*, 188–92.

94. Telegram 1837, Kabul to Washington, March 26, 1975, AAD; Telegram 4439, Kabul to Washington, July 10, 1975, AAD; CIA, Staff Notes, MEASA, February 7, 1975, CIARR; CIA, Staff Notes, MEASA #454/75, March 27, 1975, CIARR.
95. National Intelligence Bulletin, February 19, 1795, CIARR, 4–5; CIA, Staff Notes, MEASA #651/75, April 7, 1975, CIARR; CIA, Staff Notes, MEASA #657/75, April 17, 1975, CIARR; Telegram 1446, Islamabad to Washington, February 18, 1975, AAD.
96. Memorandum, Kissinger to Ford, July 1, 1976, CF/MESA, box 2, "Afghanistan 2," GRFL.
97. Telegram 5002, Kabul to Washington, August 3, 1975, AAD; Telegram 5219, Kabul to Washington, August 11, 1975, AAD; Telegram 7433, Islamabad to Washington, August 13, 1975, NSF, CF/MESA, box 27, "To SecState NODIS (2)," GRFL.
98. Telegram 5307, Kabul to Washington, August 15, 1975, AAD; Letter, Bhutto to Ford, August 17, 1975, NSA, Presidential Correspondence, box 3, "Bhutto (1)," GRFL.
99. Memcon, September 6, 1975, *FRUS, 1969–76, E-8*: #18.
100. Ghaus, *Fall of Afghanistan*, 124.
101. Despatch 337, Kabul to Paris, November 9, 1975, A-O(A) 1973–80, 1987, MAE/P; Letter 3/1, Kabul to London, December 6, 1975, FCO 37/1554, UKNA.
102. Jonathan L. Lee, *Afghanistan: A History from 1260 to the Present* (London: Reaktion, 2022), 587–88.
103. "Prisoners Released on Eid Occasion," *KT*, October 11, 1975; Telegram 6594, Kabul to Washington, October 6, 1975, AAD; Telegram 6955, Kabul to Washington, October 22, 1975, AAD; Saikal, *Modern Afghanistan*, 180–81.
104. Telegram 9921, Islamabad to Washington, October 25, 1975, AAD.
105. Telegram 10144, Islamabad to Washington, November 1, 1975, AAD; Telegram 7327, Kabul to Washington, November 10, 1975, AAD; Telegram 7695, Kabul to Washington, November 26, 1975, AAD.
106. Letter, Islamabad to London, April 29, 1976, FCO 37/1688, UKNA; Telegram 4837, Islamabad to Washington, May 11, 1976, AAD; Telegram 4935, Islamabad to Washington, May 14, 1976, AAD.
107. Telegram 020/3, Islamabad to London, June 5, 1976, FCO 37/1688, UKNA.
108. Despatch 196, Kabul to Paris, June 23, 1976, A-O(A) 1973–80, 1987, MAE/P; Ghaus, *Fall of Afghanistan*, 132–33.
109. Memcon, June 30, 1976, *FRUS, 1969–1976, E-8*: #24; Memcon, July 1, 1976, *FRUS, 1969–1976, E-8*: #26.
110. "President Calls for World Consideration to Landlocked," *KT*, August 17, 1976.
111. Memcon, August 8, 1976 (12:35 P.M.), *FRUS, 1969–76, E-8*: #27.
112. Lee, *Afghanistan*, 587–88.

113. "President's Republic Day Broadcast," *KT*, July 20, 1976.
114. Memcon, July 1, 1976 (4:50 P.M.), *FRUS, 1969–76, E-8*: #26; Memcon, August 8, 1976 (12:35 P.M.), ibid.: #27.
115. Memcon, August 8, 1976 (12:35 P.M.), ibid.: #27; Memcon, August 8, 1976 (3:30 P.M.), ibid.: #28.
116. Ghaus, *Fall of Afghanistan*, 139–40.
117. Memorandum, Scott to Ronald Rogers, June 9, 1976, SHA.
118. Telegram 16411, Manila to Washington, October 22, 1976, AAD.
119. Telegram 8965, Kabul to Washington, December 8, 1976, AAD.
120. Telegram 503, Kabul to Washington, January 20, 1977, AAD.
121. Memcon, July 6, 1976, TO-T(A) 1975–79, 1:2, AMZV.
122. Note, East German Embassy in Iran, December 2, 1975, MfAA, ZR 1944/79, AA; Note, East German Embassy in Iran, July 5, 1976, ibid.; Despatch 1066/76, Kabul to Prague, May 26, 1976, TO-T(A) 1975–79, 1:2, AMZV.

10. The End of Diplomacy, 1977–1979

1. Telegram 3223, Kabul to Washington, April 27, 1978, AAD.
2. Telegram 3225, Kabul to Washington, April 27, 1978, AAD; Telegram 3229, Kabul to Washington, April 27, 1978, AAD.
3. Telegram 3233, Kabul to Washington, April 27, 1978, AAD.
4. Muhammad Khan Jalallar, *Rumi Tomato: Autobiography of an Afghan Minister*, ed. Babur Rashidzada (n.p.: CreateSpace, 2011), 1995–205; Tawab Assifi, *My Three Lives on Earth: The Life Story of an Afghan American* (Bloomington, IN: AuthorHouse, 2015), 137–54.
5. Telegram 3247, Kabul to Washington, April 28, 1978, AAD.
6. Telegram 199, Kabul to Washington, January 9, 1977, AAD; Telegram 260, Kabul to Washington, January 11, 1977, AAD.
7. Report, Tehran to East Berlin, November 14, 1976, MfAA, ZR1939/79, AA; Telegram 8132, Kabul to Washington, November 6, 1976, AAD; Telegram 32771, Washington to Kabul, February 13, 1977, AAD; Telegram 2243, New Delhi to Washington, February 15, 1977, AAD.
8. Carter, Inaugural Address, January 20, 1977, *PPP, 1977*:1, 1–4; Carter, Notre Dame Address, May 22, 1977, ibid., 954–62; Nancy Mitchell, *Jimmy Carter in Africa: Race and the Cold War* (Stanford, CA: Stanford University Press, 2016).
9. Betty Glad, *An Outsider in the White House: Jimmy Carter, His Advisors, and the Making of American Foreign Policy* (Ithaca, NY: Cornell University Press, 2009), 22–40; Kai Bird, *The Outlier: The Unfinished Presidency of Jimmy Carter* (New York: Crown, 2021), 128–32.

10. Daniel J. Sargent, *A Superpower Transformed: The Remaking of American Foreign Relations in the 1970s* (New York: Oxford University Press, 2014), 231–37; Scott Kaufman, *Plans Unraveled: The Foreign Policy of the Carter Administration* (DeKalb: Northern Illinois University Press, 2008), 28–55.
11. Telegram 503, Kabul to Washington, January 20, 1977, AAD.
12. Telegram 1186, Kabul to Washington, February 16, 1977, AAD; Telegram 1512, Kabul to Washington, March 5, 1977, *FRUS, 1977–80, XII*: 1–3; Telegram 102795, Washington to Kabul, May 5, 1977, AAD; Telegram 2401, Kabul to Washington, April 10, 1977, PBP, box 30, "Afghanistan, 2/9/77-7/31/77," JCPL; Daniel Weimer, "'It's That Difficult of a Terrain': Opium, Development, and Territoriality in US-Afghan Relations, 1940s–1970s," *Social History of Alcohol and Drugs* 33, no. 1 (March 1, 2019): 135–36.
13. Memcon, April 17, 1977, PBP, box 30, "Afghanistan, 2/9/77-7/31/77," JCPL; Memorandum, Bourne to Carter, August 19, 1977, *FRUS, 1977–80, XII*: 7–8; Telegram 8732, Kabul to Washington, December 14, 1977, AAD; Weimer, "'It's That Difficult of a Terrain,'" 137–38.
14. Telegram 2144, Kabul to Washington, March 30, 1977, AAD; Telegram 2685, Kabul to Washington, April 20, 1977, AAD; Letter, Kabul to London, April 20, 1977, FCO 37/1843, UKNA.
15. Abdul Samad Ghaus, *The Fall of Afghanistan: An Insider's Account* (Washington, DC: Pergamon-Brassey's International Defense Publishers, 1988), 174–80.
16. Telegram 2778, Kabul to Washington, April 24, 1977, AAD; Telegram 5953, Moscow to Washington, April 30, 1977, AAD; Report, Moscow to East Berlin, May 3, 1977, MfAA, ZR 1944/79, AA; Despatch 1050/77, Kabul to Prague, April 27, 1977, TO-T(A) 1975–79, 2:11, AMZV; Despatch 155, Moscow to Paris, April 19, 1977, A-O(A) 1973–80, 1986, MAE/P; Chernyaev Diary, March 22, 1977, NSA; Ghaus, *Fall of Afghanistan*, 180.
17. Abdul Tawab Assifi's detailed memoirs discuss conversations with Puzanov but no Soviet complaints about foreign experts. Assifi, *My Three Lives*, 111–30.
18. Telegram 10789, Tehran to Washington, October 28, 1976, AAD; Letter, Kabul to London, November 20, 1976, FCO 37/1689, UKNA; Despatch 340, Kabul to Paris, November 7, 1976, A-O(A) 1973–80, 1988, MAE/P.
19. Telegram 135, Tehran to Washington, January 6, 1976, AAD; Telegram 513, Kabul to Washington, January 21, 1976, AAD; Telegram 609, Kabul to Washington, January 26, 1976, AAD; Telegram 2111, Kabul to Washington, March 29, 1977, AAD; Telegram 3104, Tehran to Washington, April 11, 1977, AAD; Telegram 2495, Kabul to Washington, April 12, 1977, AAD; Henry S. Bradsher, *Afghanistan and the Soviet Union* (Durham, NC: Duke University Press, 1985), 61–62.
20. Telegram 4176, Tehran to Washington, May 11, 1977, AAD; Telegram 4022, Kabul to Washington, June 9, 1977, AAD; Telegram 184700, Washington to

Kabul, August 6, 1977, AAD; Telegram 7627, Kabul to Washington, November 2, 1977, AAD.

21. Telegram 5358, Tehran to Washington, June 19, 1977, AAD; Telegram 4387, Kabul to Washington, June 26, 1977, AAD.
22. Teleletter 51, Kabul to London, March 20, 1977, FCO 37/1843, UKNA; Letter, Kabul to London, August 1, 1977, ibid.; Telegram 5531, Kabul to Washington, August 10, 1977, AAD; Telegram 5746, Kabul to Washington, August 18, 1977, AAD; Ghaus, *Fall of Afghanistan*, 193.
23. Telegram 4752, Kabul to Washington, July 10, 1977, AAD; Telegram 6058, Kabul to Washington, August 29, 1977, AAD; Telegram 7208, Kabul to Washington, October 13, 1977, AAD; Ghaus, *Fall of Afghanistan*, 140–47.
24. Telegram 5732, Kabul to Washington, August 17, 1977, AAD; Despatch 500, Kabul to Paris, December 12, 1977, A-O(A) 1973–80, 1976, MAE/P; Letter, Kabul to London, September 10, 1977, FCO 37/1843, UKNA.
25. Telegram 4445, Kabul to Washington, June 27, 1977, AAD; Telegram 153281, Washington to Kabul, July 1, 1977, AAD; Telegram 4975, Kabul to Washington, July 20, 1977, AAD; Telegram 8072, Islamabad to Washington, August 8, 1977, AAD; Telegram 238361, Washington to Kabul, October 3, 1977, AAD.
26. Memcon, June 17, 1977, *FRUS, 1977–80, XVIII*: 367–68; James A. Bill, *The Eagle and the Lion: The Tragedy of American-Iranian Relations* (New Haven, CT: Yale University Press, 1988), 226–32.
27. Mitchell, *Jimmy Carter in Africa*, 261–83; Odd Arne Westad, *The Global Cold War: Third World Interventions and the Making of Our Times* (New York: Cambridge University Press, 2005), 273–79; Ghaus, *Fall of Afghanistan*, 182.
28. Memcon, February 23, 1978, *FRUS, 1977–80, XVII-1*: 149–60; Memorandum, Gary Sick and Reginald Bartholomew to Brzezinski, February 21, 1978, *FRUS, 1977–80, XVIII*: 403; Mitchell, *Jimmy Carter in Africa*, 382–97; Louise Woodroofe, *"Buried in the Sands of the Ogaden": The United States, the Horn of Africa, and the Demise of Détente* (Kent, OH: Kent State University Press, 2013), 83–105.
29. Telegram 1070, Kabul to Washington, February 6, 1978, AAD; Telegram 1206, Kabul to Washington, February 12, 1978, AAD.
30. Despatch 1019/78, Kabul to Prague, February 14, 1978, TO-T(A) 1975–79, 1:5, AMZV; Despatch 1028/78, Kabul to Prague, April 4, 1978, ibid.; Despatch 1041/78, Kabul to Prague, April 23, 1978, ibid.
31. Telegram 2046, Kabul to Washington, March 16, 1978, AAD; Ghaus, *Fall of Afghanistan*, 141–47.
32. Telegram 69795, Washington to Kabul, March 18, 1978, AAD; Telegram 2715, Kabul to Washington, April 10, 1978, *FRUS, 1977–80, XII*: 12–15; Telegram 2838, Kabul to Washington, April 15, 1978, AAD.

33. Telegram 3019, Kabul to Washington, April 19, 1978, AAD; National Intelligence Daily Cable, April 20, 1978, CIARR; Telegram 3142, Kabul to Washington, April 24, 1978, AAD.
34. Interview, Thomas Thornton with author, January 8, 2016.
35. Telegram 3419, Kabul to Washington, May 1, 1978, AAD; State Department Paper, April 29, 1978, *FRUS, 1977–80, XII*: 16–17; Memorandum RPM-78-10208, CIA, May 5, 1978, *FRUS, 1977–80, XII*: 26–32.
36. Telegram 049.433, Moscow to Prague, May 4, 1978, fond I, správy SNB—operativní svazky, "Operativní rozpracování americké a západoněmecké rozvědky," 10787/011, ABS.
37. Telegram 01036/78, Kabul to Prague, May 2, 1978, TO-T(A) 1975-79, 2:5, AMZV; Vladimir Kuzichkin, *Inside the KGB: Myth and Reality* (London: Deutsch, 1990), 311; Vasili Mitrokhin, "The KGB in Afghanistan," CWIHP Working Paper 40 (Washington, DC: Woodrow Wilson Center, 2009), 26.
38. CPSU appeal to PDPA, January 8, 1974, CWIHP, #112505.
39. Telegram 110015, Washington to Moscow, April 29, 1978, AAD.
40. Telegram 3419, Kabul to Washington, May 1, 1978, AAD; Telegram 3536, Kabul to Washington, May 3, 1978, AAD; Memorandum, Thornton, May 3, 1978, *FRUS, 1977–80, XII*: 23–25.
41. Telegram 3419, Kabul to Washington, May 1, 1978, AAD; Telegram 3856/63, Washington to Paris, May 4, 1978, A-O(A) 1973–80, 1986, MAE/P.
42. Letter, Zia to Carter, May 9, 1978, *FRUS, 1977–80, XII*: 37–40; Telegram 4062, Tehran to Washington, April 30, 1978, AAD; Telegram 129180, Washington to Tehran, May 21, 1978, AAD; Telegram 4355, Tehran to Washington, May 8, 1978, AAD.
43. Memorandum, Thornton, May 3, 1978, *FRUS, 1977–80, XII*: 23–25.
44. Telegram 3310, Kabul to Washington, April 29, 1978, AAD; Telegram 3343, Kabul to Washington, April 30, 1978, AAD; Telegram 3397, Kabul to Washington, May 1, 1978, AAD; Telegram 4342, Islamabad to Washington, May 3, 1978, AAD; Telegram 113280, Washington to Kabul, May 4, 1978, AAD; Telegram 3619, Kabul to Washington, May 6, 1978, AAD.
45. Owen Cylke, ADSTOH, November 6, 1996, 32–33; John Sumser, *A Land Without Time: A Peace Corps Volunteer in Afghanistan* (Chicago: Academy Chicago, 2006), 173–96.
46. Telegram 3300, Kabul to Washington, April 29, 1978, AAD; Telegram 3323, Kabul to Washington, April 29, 1978, AAD.
47. Telegram 3837, Kabul to Washington, May 11, 1978, AAD; Telegram 3933, Kabul to Washington, May 15, 1978, AAD.
48. Telegram 3934, Kabul to Washington, May 15, 1978, AAD; Telegram 4069, Kabul to Washington, May 20, 1978, AAD; Telegram 4094, Kabul to

Washington, May 20, 1978, AAD; Telegram 126022, Washington to Various Posts, May 18, 1978, AAD; Telegram 4425, Kabul to Washington, May 31, 1978, AAD.

49. Telegram 3619; Memorandum, Brzezinski to Vance, May 8, 1978, *FRUS, 1977–80, XII*: 37–38.
50. Telegram 4717, Kabul to Washington, June 12, 1978, AAD; Telegram 4752, Kabul to Washington, June 12, 1978, AAD.
51. Telegram 4422, Kabul to Washington, May 31, 1978, AAD; Telegram 4752; Telegram 4801, Kabul to Washington, June 13, 1978, AAD.
52. Telegram 4264, Ankara to Washington, June 6, 1978, AAD; Telegram 4980, Islamabad to Washington, May 18, 1978, *FRUS, 1977–80, XII*: 42–46; Telegram 4547, Tehran to Washington, May 14, 1978, AAD; Telegram 3828, Ankara to Washington, May 18, 1978, AAD; Telegram 2943, Damascus to Washington, May 23, 1978, AAD; Telegram 2049, Baghdad to Washington, October 4, 1978, AAD.
53. Memcon, May 21, 1978, *FRUS, 1977–80, XIII*: 446–47; Note, Moscow to Berlin, May 25, 1978, SAPMO, DY30-IVB2-20-229, B-L.
54. Memorandum, Thornton to Brzezinski, May 25, 1978, NSABM, Country Chron., box 1, "Afghanistan, 1978," JCPL; Memorandum, Brzezinski to Carter, May 22, 1978, *FRUS, 1977–80, XII*: 48–49.
55. Editorial Note, *FRUS, 1977–80, XII*: 57–58; Memorandum, Thornton to Brzezinski, July 14, 1978, NSABM, CF, box 1, "Afghanistan 1/77-3/79," JCPL.
56. Telegram 4758, Islamabad to Washington, May 14, 1978, AAD; Telegram 5717, Islamabad to Washington, June 11, 1978, AAD.
57. Diego Cordovez and Selig S. Harrison, *Out of Afghanistan: The Inside Story of the Soviet Withdrawal* (New York: Oxford University Press, 1995), 29.
58. Telegram 5048, Kabul to Washington, June 22, 1978, AAD; Telegram 5170, Kabul to Washington, June 26, 1978, AAD; Telegram 5276, Kabul to Washington, June 29, 1978, AAD.
59. Telegram 6127, Kabul to Washington, July 30, 1978, AAD; Telegram 6154, Kabul to Washington, July 30, 1978, AAD.
60. Telegram 5670, Kabul to Washington, July 14, 1978, *FRUS, 1977–80, XII*: 61–65; Telegram 5671, Kabul to Washington, July 14, 1978, AAD.
61. Telegram 4620, Kabul to Washington, June 7, 1978, AAD; Telegram 4965, Kabul to Washington, June 20, 1978, AAD; Telegram 167743, Washington to Kabul, July 1, 1978, AAD; Telegram 5981, Kabul to Washington, July 24, 1978, AAD; Telegram 12924, Manila to Washington, July 28, 1978, AAD; Telegram 208106, Washington to Kabul, August 16, 1978, AAD.
62. Elisabeth Leake, *Afghan Crucible: The Soviet Invasion and the Making of Modern Afghanistan* (New York: Oxford University Press, 2022), 137–38; Olivier Roy,

Islam and Resistance in Afghanistan (New York: Cambridge University Press, 1990), 98–101.
63. Telegram 6159, Kabul to Washington, July 30, 1978, AAD; Mitrokhin, *KGB in Afghanistan*, 37; Assifi, *My Three Lives*, 200–204.
64. Barnett R. Rubin, *The Fragmentation of Afghanistan: State Formation and Collapse in the International System* (New Haven, CT: Yale University Press, 2002), 115–20; Thomas J. Barfield, *Afghanistan: A Cultural and Political History* (Princeton, NJ: Princeton University Press, 2010), 229–32; Leake, *Afghan Crucible*, 45–62.
65. Telegram 5470, Kabul to Washington, July 19, 1979, AAD.
66. Mitrokhin, *KGB in Afghanistan*, 36–38; Assifi, *My Three Lives*, 205–13.
67. Instructions to Puzanov, spring 1978, CWIHP, #113042.
68. Memorandum, July 14, 1978, SAPMO, DY30-IVB2-20-229, B-L.
69. Mitrokhin, *KGB in Afghanistan*, 34–35.
70. Frud Bezhan and Petr Kubalek, "The Afghan President (to Be) Who Lived a Secret Life in a Czechoslovak Forest," *Radio Free Europe/Radio Liberty*, November 3, 2019, https://www.rferl.org/a/that-time-an-afghan-president-(to-be)-was-secretly-hiding-in-a-czechoslovak-forest/30250494.html.
71. Telegram 179/78, Belgrade to Berlin, September 8, 1978, SAPMO, DY30-IVB2-20-229, B-L; Telegram 7193, Kabul to Washington, September 9, 1978, AAD; Robert D. Crews, *Afghan Modern: The History of a Global Nation* (Cambridge, MA: Harvard University Press, 2015), 238–39.
72. Memorandum, Thornton to Brzezinski, September 11, 1978, *FRUS, 1977–80, XII*: 70–72.
73. Telegram 7328, Kabul to Washington, September 13, 1978, AAD; Telegram 7370, Kabul to Washington, September 14, 1978, AAD; Telegram 7560, Kabul to Washington, September 20, 1978, AAD; Telegram 9511, Kabul to Washington, December 2, 1978, AAD.
74. Telegram 10067, Kabul to Washington, December 24, 1978, AAD; Telegram 10082, Kabul to Washington, December 24, 1978, AAD; Telegram 304356, Washington to Kabul, December 1, 1978, AAD.
75. Telegram 1060, Kabul to Washington, February 14, 1979, AAD; Telegram 1074, Kabul to Washington, February 14, 1979, AAD; Telegram 1098, Kabul to Washington, February 14, 1979, *FRUS, 1977–80, XII*: 93–102.
76. Telegram 1444, Kabul to Washington, February 26, 1979, AAD; Telegram 4243, Kabul to Washington, June 3, 1979, AAD; Memorandum, Thornton to Brzezinski, February 16, 1979, RAC, NLC-24-100-4-4-6, JCPL.
77. Charles Mohr, "U.S. to Slash Aid to Afghanistan," *NYT*, February 23, 1979.
78. Bernard Gwertzman, "A Night of Tension Across Washington," *NYT*, February 15, 1979; Adam Clymer, "G.O.P. Presidential Aspirants Tour Nation to Denounce Carter's Foreign Policy," *NYT*, February 20, 1979; Memorandum, Brzezinski to Carter, February 24, 1979, *FRUS, 1977–80, I*: 567.

79. Telegram Sitto 19, White House to Brzezinski, February 14, 1979, RAC, NLC-4-17-5-1-3, JCPL; Telegram 1601–08, Washington to Paris, February 23, 1979, A-O(A) 1973–80, 1985, MAE/P.
80. Memorandum, Brzezinski to Carter, December 2, 1978, *FRUS, 1977–80*, I: 486–90.
81. W. Taylor Fain, "Conceiving the 'Arc of Crisis' in the Indian Ocean Region," *Diplomatic History* 42, no. 4 (September 2018): 694–719.
82. Memorandum, Oksenberg to Brzezinski, February 16, 1979, *FRUS, 1977–80*, XIII: 800–801.
83. Sergey Radchenko, *Unwanted Visionaries: The Soviet Failure in Asia at the End of the Cold War* (New York: Oxford University Press, 2014), 126–28.
84. Telegram 83/78, Kabul to Berlin, November 29, 1978, SAPMO, DY30/IVB2/20/229, B-L.
85. Report on Taraki Visit, December 18, 1978, SAPMO, DY30/13909, B-L.
86. Annual Report, Kabul to Berlin, January 2, 1979, MfAA, ZR 632/82, AA.
87. Paul Robinson and Jay Dixon, *Aiding Afghanistan: A History of Soviet Assistance to a Developing Country* (London: Hurst, 2013), 95–99; Westad, *Global Cold War*, 296–306.
88. C. P. W. Gammell, *The Pearl of Khorasan: A History of Herat* (London: Hurst, 2016), 289–94; Roy, *Islam and Resistance*, 107–9.
89. Politburo Meeting, March 17, 1979, CWIHP, #113260; Kosygin and Taraki, March 18, 1979, CWIHP, #113141.
90. Politburo Meetings, March 17–19, 1979, CWIHP, #113260.
91. "Iranian Infiltrators in Herat Wiped Out," *KT*, March 24, 1979; Telegram 6840, Moscow to Washington, March 20, 1979, AAD; Telegram 3713, Islamabad to Washington, March 28, 1979, *FRUS, 1977–80*, XIX: 774–78; Teleletter 74, Moscow to London, April 12, 1979, FCO 37/2131, UKNA.
92. Reuters Report, March 29, 1979, NSABM, CF, box 1, "Afghanistan 1/77-3/79," JCPL; Telegram MONTO 8, Mondale to White House, March 23, 1979, ibid.; Draft Memorandum, NSC to Vance, undated, ibid.
93. Telegram 93724, Washington to Various Posts, April 14, 1979, AAD; Editorial Note, *FRUS, 1977–80*, XII: 123–24; SCC Meeting, April 6, 1979, *FRUS, 1977–80*, XII: 139–41.
94. CIA Memorandum, undated, *FRUS, 1977–80*, XII: 134–38; Robert M. Gates, *From the Shadows: The Ultimate Insider's Story of Five Presidents and How They Won the Cold War* (New York: Simon & Schuster, 1996), 145.
95. CIA Memorandum, undated, *FRUS, 1977–80*, XII: 134–38; CIA Analysis Paper, March 23, 1979, ibid., 111–14; Telegram 8384, Moscow to Washington, April 5, 1979, ibid., 130–34; Editorial Note, ibid., 123–24; SCC Meeting, April 6, 1979, ibid., 139–46; Justin Vaïsse and Catherine Porter, *Zbigniew Brzezinski: America's Grand Strategist* (Cambridge, MA: Harvard University Press, 2018), 307–8.

96. Zbigniew Brzezinski, *Power and Principle: Memoirs of the National Security Adviser, 1977–1981* (New York: Farrar, Straus and Giroux, 1983), 426–27; Malcolm M. Craig, *America, Britain and Pakistan's Nuclear Weapons Programme, 1974–1980: A Dream of Nightmare Proportions* (Cham, Switzerland: Palgrave Macmillan, 2017), 197–202.
97. SCC Meeting, April 6, 1979, *FRUS, 1977–80, XII*: 139–46; SCC Meeting Conclusions, June 26, 1979, *FRUS, 1977–80, XII*: 155–57.
98. Memorandum, Hoskinson to Brzezinski, April 11, 1979, RAC, NLC-27-3-5-5-9, JCPL; Conor Tobin, "The Myth of the 'Afghan Trap': Zbigniew Brzezinski and Afghanistan, 1978–1979," *Diplomatic History* 44, no. 2 (April 2020): 243–55.
99. Telegram 3025, Kabul to Washington, April 18, 1979, AAD; Telegram 2340, Kabul to Washington, March 27, 1979, AAD; Telegram 3682, Kabul to Washington, May 13, 1979, AAD; Telegram 5544, Kabul to Washington, July 23, 1979, AAD; Telegram 5631, Kabul to Washington, July 25, 1979, AAD; J. Bruce Amstutz, *Afghanistan: The First Five Years of Soviet Occupation* (Washington DC: National Defense University Press, 1986), 303–4.
100. Telegram 3559, Kabul to Washington, May 8, 1979, AAD; "Every Penny to Be Spent for People's Welfare," *KT*, March 11, 1979; Don Oberdorfer, "Human Rights in Afghanistan Stir State Department Concern," *WP*, July 22, 1979.
101. Telegram 4051, Kabul to Washington, May 24, 1979, AAD; Telegram 5967, Kabul to Washington, August 6, 1979, AAD; Telegram 6060, Kabul to Washington, August 9, 1979, AAD.
102. Memorandum, January 15, 1979, CIARR; Telegram 3984, Kabul to Washington, May 22, 1979, AAD; Despatch 393, Prague to Paris, May 29, 1979, A-O(A) 1973–80, 1988, MAE/P.
103. Telegram 4888, Kabul to Washington, June 25, 1979, DNSA.
104. Telegram 4888; Telegram 4889, Kabul to Washington, June 25, 1979, DNSA.
105. Telegram 5246, Kabul to Washington, July 11, 1979, AAD; Telegram 5459, Kabul to Washington, July 18, 1979, AAD; Telegram 5470, Kabul to Washington July 19, 1979, AAD; Teleletter 158, Moscow to London, August 2, 1979, FCO 37/2125, UKNA; Telegram 11/79, Kabul to Berlin, July 25, 1979, SAPMO, DY30-IVB2-20-229, B-L.
106. Memorandum, Thornton to Brzezinski, July 19, 1979, *FRUS, 1977–80, XII*: 160–62; Telegram 6152, Kabul to Washington, August 13, 1979, AAD; Memorandum, Thornton to Brzezinski, July 18, 1979, RAC, NLC-10-22-3-2-1, JCPL; Memorandum, Thornton to Brzezinski, August 13, 1979, RAC, NLC-24-100-5-33-3, JCPL.
107. Telegram 6309, Kabul to Washington, August 20, 1979, AAD.
108. Intelligence Appraisal, Defense Department, August 21, 1979, *FRUS, 1977–80, XII*: 170–72; Editorial Note, *FRUS, 1977–80, XII*: 162–68; Memorandum,

Cochran to Lehman, June 18, 1979, CIARR; Memorandum to Lehman, July 11, 1979, CIARR; Memorandum, MacEachin to Lehman, August 10, 1979, CIARR; Memorandum, Cochran to Lehman, August 10, 1979, CIARR; Michael Kaufman, "Afghan Refugees Tell Why They Fled Taraki's Regime," *NYT*, August 15, 1979.

109. Melvyn P. Leffler, *For the Soul of Mankind: the United States, the Soviet Union, and the Cold War* (New York: Hill and Wang, 2007), 319–25; Brzezinski, *Power and Principle*, 346–52; Burton Ira Kaufman and Scott Kaufman, *The Presidency of James Earl Carter, Jr* (Lawrence: University Press of Kansas, 2006), 174–79.

110. Politburo Decision, September 13, 1979, CWIHP, #111561; Telegram 202, Kabul to London, September 18, 1979, FCO 37/2125, UKNA; Mitrokhin, *KGB in Afghanistan*, 49–61.

111. Letter, Central Committee to Honecker, October 1, 1979, CWIHP, #111571.

112. Telegram 33/79, Kabul to Berlin, November 22, 1979, SAPMO, DY30-IVB2-20-229, B-L.

113. Telegram 7063, Kabul to Washington, September 22, 1979, AAD; Telegram 7502, Kabul to Washington, October 15, 1979, AAD.

114. Telegram 8059, Kabul to Washington, November 19, 1979, AAD.

115. Telegram 7062, Kabul to Washington, September 22, 1979, AAD; Telegram 7218, Kabul to Washington, September 27, 1979, AAD; Telegram 256809, Washington to Kabul, September 29, 1979, *FRUS, 1977–80, XII*: 191–94; Telegram 7392, Kabul to Washington, October 9, 1979, ibid., 202–5; Telegram 7726, Kabul to Washington, October 28, 1979, ibid, 218–22.

116. Memorandum, Thornton to Brzezinski, September 17, 1979, *FRUS, 1977–80, XII*: 182–83; Telegram 6978, Kabul to Washington, September 18, 1979, *FRUS, 1977–80, XII*: 184–85; Memorandum, Robert Murray to McGiffert, September 21, 1979, *FRUS, 1977–80, XII*: 185–87.

117. Memorandum, Shulman to Vance, October 3, 1979, *FRUS, 1977–80, XII*: 196–98; Gromyko and Shah Wali, September 27, 1979, CWIHP, #111570.

118. Memorandum, Brzezinski to Vance, October 4, 1979, *FRUS, 1977–80, XII*: 201. SCC Meeting, October 23, 1979, *FRUS, 1977–80, XII*: 206–13; Telegram 193, Brussels to London, September 25, 1979, FCO 37/2126, UKNA.

119. Christian Emery, *US Foreign Policy and the Iranian Revolution: The Cold War Dynamics of Engagement and Strategic Alliance* (New York: Palgrave Macmillan, 2013), 93–103.

120. Telegram 10801, Tehran to Washington, October 9, 1979, AAD; Memorandum, Slocombe to Murphy, November 21, 1979, *FRUS, 1977–80, XII*: 226–27; Memorandum, William Odom to Brzezinski, November 28, 1979, *FRUS, 1977–80, XVIII*: 118–22.

121. Report, Andropov et al. to Central Committee, November 29, 1979, CWIHP, #111576.

122. Report, Andropov et al. to Central Committee; Safronchuk and Amin, October 24, 1979, NSA; Cordovez and Harrison, *Out of Afghanistan*, 44–49; Vladislav M. Zubok, *A Failed Empire: The Soviet Union in the Cold War from Stalin to Gorbachev* (Chapel Hill: University of North Carolina Press, 2007), 262–64; Artemy M. Kalinovsky, *A Long Goodbye: The Soviet Withdrawal from Afghanistan* (Cambridge, MA: Harvard University Press, 2011), 19–24.
123. Kalinovsky, *A Long Goodbye*, 21–24; Yaacov Ro'i, *The Bleeding Wound: The Soviet-Afghan War and the Collapse of the Soviet System* (Stanford, CA: Stanford University Press, 2022), 11–18; Sarah E. Mendelson, *Changing Course: Ideas, Politics, and the Soviet Withdrawal from Afghanistan* (Princeton, NJ: Princeton University Press, 1998), 54–62.
124. CIA Intelligence Cable, December 13, 1979, *FRUS, 1977-80, XII*: 233–36; Memorandum, MacEachin to Lehman, December 13, 1979, ibid., 237–40; CIA Alert Memorandum, December 19, 1979, ibid., 248–49; Telegram 323581, Washington to Moscow, December 15, 1979, *FRUS, 1977–80, VI*: 699; Message WH92270, Aaron to Carter, December 24, 1979, *FRUS, 1977–80, VI*: 704–7.
125. Memorandum, Vance to Carter, December 15, 1979, RAC, NLC-128-14-14-12-6, JCPL; Record, Carter and Thatcher, December 17, 1979, FCO 37/2132, UKNA; SCC Meeting, December 21, 1979, RAC, NLC-132-107-9-1-6, JCPL.
126. Telegram 8592, Kabul to Washington, December 26, 1979, *FRUS, 1977–80, XII*: 260–62; SCC Meeting, December 26, 1979, *FRUS, 1977–80, XII*: 262–63; Memorandum, Odom to Brzezinski, January 13, 1981, Zbigniew Brzezinski Papers, Series II, box 97, "Persian Gulf Security Framework," LOC.
127. Mohammed Kakar, *Afghanistan: The Soviet Invasion and the Afghan Response, 1979–1982* (Berkeley: University of California Press, 1997), 21–27; Rodric Braithwaite, *Afgantsy: The Russians in Afghanistan, 1979–1989* (London: Profile, 2011), 84–102.
128. David Binder, "Carter Says Soviet Isn't Telling Facts About Afghan Coup," *NYT*, January 1, 1980.

Conclusion

1. W. Taylor Fain, "Conceiving the 'Arc of Crisis' in the Indian Ocean Region," *Diplomatic History* 42, no. 4 (September 2018): 714–16.
2. Memorandum, Brzezinski to Carter, December 26, 1979, *FRUS, 1977–80, XII*: 265–67.
3. Memorandum, Brzezinski to Carter, February 13, 1980, NSABM, CF, "Afghanistan 2/80," JCPL.
4. Memorandum, Brzezinski to Carter, March 28, 1980, *FRUS, 1977–80, XII*: 661–63. The Soviet government had averred an interest in territory south of

the Caucasus, but only after much prodding by the Third Reich through 1940. See Milan Hauner, *India in Axis Strategy: Germany, Japan, and Indian Nationalists in the Second World War* (Stuttgart: Klett-Cotta, 1981), 183–86.

5. Memorandum, Brzezinski to Carter, January 9, 1980, *FRUS, 1977–80, XII*: 441–45.
6. George F. Kennan and Frank Costigliola, *The Kennan Diaries* (New York: Norton, 2014), 523–26.
7. Kennan and Costigliola, *Kennan Diaries*, 526–27.
8. Frank Costigliola, *Kennan: A Life Between Worlds* (Princeton, NJ: Princeton University Press, 2023), 284–89; Hannah Gurman, *The Dissent Papers: The Voices of Diplomats in the Cold War and Beyond* (New York: Columbia University Press, 2012), 53–59.
9. Louis Dupree, "Afghanistan Under the Khalq," *Problems of Communism* 28 (August 1979): 34–50.
10. Hans Morgenthau, "A Political Theory of Foreign Aid," *American Political Science Review* 56, no. 2 (1962): 301–9.
11. Robert B. Rakove, "The Central Front of Reagan's Cold War," in *The Reagan Moment: America and the World in the 1980s*, ed. Jonathan R. Hunt and Simon Miles (Ithaca, NY: Cornell University Press, 2021), 324-44
12. Rajiv Chandrasekaran, *Little America: The War Within the War for Afghanistan* (New York: Alfred A. Knopf, 2012), 301–6; Carter Malkasian, *The American War in Afghanistan* (New York: Oxford University Press, 2021), 241–72.

Archives

Czech Republic

ABS Archiv bezpečnostních složek (Archive of the Security Services), Prague
AMZV Archiv Ministerstvo zahraničních věcí) Archive of the Ministry of Foreign Affairs, Prague
TO-O(A) Teritorialní odbory—Obyčejné (Territorial Department—Regular) Afghanistan
TO-T(A) Teritorialní odbory—Tajné (Territorial Department—Secret) Afghanistan
CZNA National Archives, Prague
KSČ-ÚV Komunistické strany Československa—Ústřední výbor (Czechoslovak Communist Party—Central Committee)

France

CADN Centre des Archives Diplomatiques de Nantes
KASB Kabul Ambassade Serie B
MAE/P Archives Diplomatiques, La Courneuve
A-O(A) Asie-Oceanie, Afghanistan

Germany

AA	Auswärtiges Amt (Foreign Office), Berlin
PA	Politisches Archiv
MfAA	Ministerium für Auswärtigen Angelegenheiten
B-L	Bundesarchiv-Lichterfelde
SAPMO	Stiftung Archiv der Parteien und Massenorganisationen der DDR (Foundation for the Archives of the GDR's Parties and Mass Organizations)

United Kingdom

BL	British Library, London
IOR	India Office Records
UKNA	The National Archives, Kew
DO	Defense Office
FCO	Foreign and Commonwealth Office
FO	Foreign Office
POWE	Ministry of Power
PREM	Prime Minister's Office

United States

AHC	American Heritage Center, Laramie, WY
MWP	Myles Walsh Papers
CEYL	Charles E. Young Library, University of California, Los Angeles
NFP	Neumann Family Papers
CUSC	Cornell University Special Collections
RRNP	Robert R. Nathan Papers
GRFL	Gerald R. Ford Library, Ann Arbor, MI
CF/MESA	National Security Advisor, Country File, Middle East and South Asia
GUSC	Georgetown University Special Collections
CEP	Cornelius Engert Papers
DDEL	Dwight D. Eisenhower Presidential Library, Abilene, KS

JFDP		John Foster Dulles Papers
PPAWF		Papers as President, Ann Whitman File
HSTL		Harry S Truman Library, Independence, MO
	CTP	Charles Thayer Papers
JCPL		Jimmy Carter Presidential Library, Atlanta, GA
	NSABM	National Security Affairs, Brzezinski Material
	PBP	Peter Bourne Papers
	RAC	Remote Archive Capture
JFKL		John F. Kennedy Presidential Library, Boston MA
LBJL		Lyndon Baines Johnson Presidential Library, Austin, TX
	HHSF	Harold H. Saunders Files
	RKP	Robert Komer Papers
LOC		Library of Congress, Washington, DC
	AHP	Averell Harriman Papers
OU		Oklahoma University Special Collections, Norman, OK
	PJHC	Patrick J. Hurley Collection
RMNL		Richard M. Nixon Library, Yorba Linda, CA
	NSCF	National Security Council Files
	CF-ME	Country Files—Middle East
	HAKOF	Henry A. Kissinger Office Files
UNO		University of Nebraska Omaha
	NAR	Nathan Associates Records
	USNA	United States National Archives, College Park, MD

United States National Archives (USNA)

Record Group 59

CDF	Central Decimal File (1910–1963)
SNF	Subject Numeric File (1963–1973)
AAD	Archive of American Diplomacy (1973–1979)
OSAA	Records of the Office of South Asian Affairs, 1939–1953
SFAA	Subject Files Relating to Afghan Affairs, 1943–1953
SFRA	Subject Files Relating to South Asian Regional Affairs
RRSA	Records Relating to South Asia, 1947–1959
SFPAA	Subject File of the Officer in Charge of Pakistan-Afghanistan Affairs 1950–1956

GSFSAA	General Subject Files Relating to South Asian Affairs, 1957–1959
BNESA	Bureau of Near Eastern and South Asian Affairs
OPAB	Office of Pakistan, Afghanistan and Bangladesh Affairs, Records
RRA	Records Relating to Afghanistan, 1960–1974

Record Group 84

KCR	Kabul Classified General Records, 1942–1962
KGR	Kabul General Records, 1941–1955

Record Group 286

AMA	USAID Mission to Afghanistan
AD/FPR	Agriculture Division, Food Program Records, 1966–1975

Record Group 469

ONESAD/AB	Office of Near East and South Asia Division, Afghanistan Branch
PF	Project Files, 1952–1958

Index

Page numbers in *italics* refer to figures.

Aaron, David, 327
Abdali, Ahmad Shah, 15, 16
Abdul Ghaffar Khan, 150, 157, 276; Daoud Khan and, 158
Abdulilah, Said, 306–7
Abdullah, Wahid, 262, 263; Daoud Khan coup and, 306–7; execution of, 319; Iran and, 286; Kissinger and, 298; Maiwandwal and, 281; Nixon and, 282; Pashtunistan and, 294, 298; Percy and, 280; petroleum and, 304; resignation of, 313; South Vietnam and, 293
Abdullah Khan, 112–14
Abdur Rahman, 16
Acheson, Dean, 69, 91, 104, 105
Adamec, Ludwig, 10
ADB. *See* Asian Development Bank
Afghanistan. ——*See specific topics*
Afghanistan Airline Company, 74
Afghan Textile Company, 164–65

Agency for International Development (AID), 196, 197, 211, 214, 217, 234, 235, 252, 255; antinarcotics campaign and, 260; HAVA and, 287; Helmand Valley and, 293–94; Kissinger and, 293
Agnew, Spiro, 239–40, 271
Ahmad Khan, Shir, 372n81
Ahmadzai, Shahpur, 324
Ahmed, Faiz, 10
AID. *See* Agency for International Development
Akbar, Mir Ali, 321, 324
Alexander, John B., 55, 66, 72–73, 74, 79, 81
Ali Khan, Liaquat, 108
Ali Mohammed, 56, 74–75, 85, 90, 92, 111, 112; Boghra Canal and, 79–80; A. Dulles and, 131; UNTAM and, 97
Alling, Paul, 59

[449]

Amanullah, 16–17, 19–27, 32, 37, 86; Stalin and, 75
American Relief Administration, 104
Amin, Hafizullah, 226; Amstutz and, 338; CIA and, 341; coup by, 337–38; DRA and, 322, 326–27; Dubs and, 349; killing of, 341; Safronchuk and, 335, 339; Soviet Union and, 329, 337, 339, 341; Taraki and, 337
Amstutz, Bruce, 321, 326, 327, 332–35; Amin and, 338
Anderson, Robert, 131–32
Andreyev, Anatoly, 210
Andropov, Yuri, 328–29; DRA and, 339–40
Anglo-Iranian Oil Company, 96
Anglo-Persian Oil Company, 29
Angola, 300, 314; Cuba in, 301
antinarcotics campaign, 3; J. Carter and, 309–10; of Nixon, 259–61, 275, 349
Antonov, Sergey, 211; Steeves and, 216
Appelbaum, Henry, 275, 282
Ariana, 141, 142, 144, 163; Pan Am and, 152, 323
Arif, Mohammed, 111, 129
Arshad, Ali, 297
Ashurst, Henry, 26
Asian Development Bank (ADB), 293, 304, 351; DRA and, 323, 333
Assifi, Abdul Tawab, 303; Daoud Khan coup and, 306; DRA and, 323–24
aviation, 10, 74–75, 137–38, 140–43, 152–54, 163; Kandahar International Airport, 211–12; MiG-21 jet fighters, 306; pilot training program for, 165; Sukhoi-7 fighter-bombers, 247, 306; U-2 and, 177–78, 180–81. *See also specific airlines*
Ayub Khan, Mohammed, 158–59, 165, 250; Daoud Khan and, 171–72, 173, 189; Kennedy and, 188, 190–91; Komer and, 193–94; Naim Khan and, 189; Pashtuns and, 187; U-2 and, 178; in U.S., 199; Zahir (King) and, 202
Aziz, Abdul Hai, 142, 143, 161, 209; Iran and, 194–95
Aziz, Mohammed, 26–27
Azizullah Khan, 29

Badakhshan, 63, 260, 267, 310, 337
Baghdad Pact, 125, 130, 161, 190
Bagram, 2, 138, 163, 167, 171
Baikal, Lake, 62
Bakulin, Ivan, 60, 67, 74
Baluchistan, 274, 276, 277; Daoud Khan and, 283, 289, 290, 298–99, 300, 302; Pakistan in, 282; Pashtuns in, 242–43; UN and, 290; Zia and, 312
Bangladesh, 280; coup in, 298; DRA and, 321
Bank-i-Milli (National Bank), 95, 118
Barbier, Jean Baptiste, 37
Baryalai, Mahmud, 324
Beck, Philip, 93, 94, 97
Beecroft, Eric, 51, 52
Belgium, 23
Belgrade Conference, 190, 231
Bell, David, 214
Berlin crisis, 190, 193
Berthelot, Marcel, 95, 96
Bessner, Daniel, 8
BEW. *See* Bureau of Economic Warfare
Bezhan, Faridullah, 10, 39
Bhutto, Zulfikar Ali, 251, 258, 281, 429n43; Byroade and, 289, 300; Daoud Khan and, 276–77, 282, 291–92, 295, 299–301, 302, 303; Ford and, 290, 298; India and, 289,

290; Islamists and, 297; Kissinger and, 289, 300; Naim Khan and, 301; NAP and, 291–92; Nixon and, 279, 284; overthrow of, 308, 312; Pashtunistan and, 298; Shah of Iran and, 298, 303–4; Sherpao and, 291

bi-tarafi, 6, 345

Blood, Archer, 216, 230, 251, 338, 339

Boghra Canal, 54–55, 66, 70–73, 79–80, 112; Czechoslovakia and, 125; leakage along, 109; optimistic estimates for, 85; problems with, 113–18, 139–40, 151–52; revenue shortage from, 163–64; revised timeline for, 150; supply shortages for, 125; Tudor Engineering Company and, 140, 150, 151

Bohlen, Charles, 105

Bolsheviks, 18, 20

Bose, Subhas Chandra, 39

Bourne, Peter, 309

Bowles, Chester, 179, 186, 191–92, 194, 196, 197

Bradford, James Tharin, 2, 260, 270

Braithwaite, Rodric, 10

Brazinsky, Gregg, 3

Brezhnev, Leonid, 5, 278; Daoud Khan and, 275, 310–11, 316; DRA and, 339–40; Ford and, 290; SALT II and, 332, 336; Taraki and, 337

Briere, François, 100, 101

Britain, 10, 23; Afghan independence from, 17–18; in Cold War, 68–70, 73, 75–78, 94, 96–97, 124; after First World War, 17–19; in India, 16, 74; Nadir Khan and, 24; Operation Help and, 267; Russia and, 15; in Second World War, 33–62

Brzezinski, Zbigniew, 308; antinarcotics campaign and, 310; China and, 321;

Daoud Khan coup and, 315–16, 317; DRA and, 320, 321, 325, 327–28; Kennan and, 345; SALT II and, 336; Shah of Iran and, 328; Soviet Union and, 331, 339, 344, 353; Truman Doctrine and, 345

Buddhas of Bamiyan, 7, 33

Bukharans, 56–57, 58

Bulganin, Nikolai, 100–101

Bullitt, William, 27, 32, 43

Bundy, McGeorge, 189–90, 214

Bureau of Economic Warfare (BEW), 49, 50, 51

Bureau of Intelligence and Research (INR), 275, 276, 283

Bureau of Reclamation, 55, 113, 164, 249

buzkashi, Khrushchev and, 101; Kissinger and, 272–73; Ward and, 128

Byroade, Henry, 8, 103, 119, 120–21, 135–37, 166, 169–70, 173, 176–81, 186–87, 191, 204, 299, 351; Bhutto and, 289, 300, 429n43; Boghra Canal and, 163–64; education and, 174–75, 179–80, 183–84; Eliot and, 284; Helmand River dams and, 164; Islamists and, 297; Naim Khan and, 135–36, 162–63, 185

CAB. *See* Civil Aeronautics Board

Cambodia, Nixon and, 250

Capehart, Homer, 105

Carlucci, Frank, 321

Carter, Jimmy, 307–8; alarmism of, 349–50; antinarcotics campaign and, 309–10; China and, 327; Daoud Khan and, 308, 313, 317; DRA and, 319, 320, 325, 327–32, 339; Dubs and, 327, 349–50; India and, 308,

Carter (*continued*)
313; Iran and, 313, 327, 339; Iran hostage crisis and, 343; Israel and Egypt and, 321; Khalq and, 329–30; Naim Khan and, 308; NSC of, 330, 339; Pakistan and, 313; SALT II and, 332, 336; Shah of Iran and, 313, 317–18; Soviet Union and, 308–9, 313, 340–41, 343–45, 350; Truman Doctrine and, 345
Carter, Peers, 252
Carter, Rosalynn, 327
Castle, William, 25
Cattand, Georges, 217, 228
Central Treaty Organization (CENTO), 190, 258; DRA and, 320–21, 329; Khrushchev and, 195; Pakistan and, 298
Chakcharan, 263–66
Chaudhry, Fazal, 292
Chernyaev, Anatoly, 310
"Che Sud" (Zahir, Ahmad), 343
China, 3; Brzezinski and, 321; Byroade in, 175; J. Carter and, 327; Cultural Revolution in, 241, 242; Daoud Khan coup and, 316; Eliot and, 285; Engert in, 45; India and, 179, 199; Jeshyn festival and, 144; Kissinger and, 255, 277; NAM and, 220; Nixon and, 255; Pakistan and, 215; Soviet Union and, 328; in Vietnam, 327, 328; Ward in, 104–5
Churchill, Winston, 40, 49
CIA, 187; Amin and, 341; assassination of M. A. Khyber and, 315; in Cold War, 84, 120, 122; coups and, 273; Daoud Khan and, 282, 294, 296, 316, 318; DRA and, 318, 321, 330–32, 336, 340; Eliot and, 284; Hotaki and, 231–32; on Khrushchev,

190; Pakistan and, 291; Pashtunistan and, 297; Soviet Union and, 165, 278, 331
Civil Aeronautics Board (CAB), 152
Clapp, Frederick, 30
Clay, Lucius, 208–9, 211
Cochran, Harry, 336
Cold War. *See specific topics*
Cold War International History Project, 10
Communist Party of the Soviet Union (CPSU), 285–86
Congo, 219–20
Connally, John, 265, 266
Coolidge, Calvin, 23
Costigliola, Frank, 7
coups: of Amin, 337–38; in Bangladesh, 298; of Daoud Khan, 269–71, 273, 274, 278–79, 281–82, 306–8, 315–25, 352; in Iran, 108; by Marxists, 5, 12, 279; in Pakistan, 137, 158
CPSU. *See* Communist Party of the Soviet Union
Crews, Robert, 10, 16
Cuba: in Angola, 301; Ethiopia and, 314; failed invasion of, 190; missile crisis of, 199, 210, 347; in NAM, 220, 221; Soviet Union in, 336, 338, 347
Cullather, Nick, 2, 115
Cultural Revolution, in China, 241, 242
Curran, Robert, 285, 297
Czechoslovakia, 10, 91, 120, 159–60; Boghra Canal and, 125; canning plant of, 221; coal mine of, 216; Daoud Khan and, 127, 129, 161, 279, 282, 285, 316; East Germany and, 250–51; Egypt and, 131; Helmand Valley and, 311; Jeshyn festival and, 144, 241; Karmal and, 325; liberation

of, 73; MEDO and, 109; MKA and, 94–95; Soviet Union in, 241, 242; UNTAM and, 97; Yusuf and, 210; Zabuli and, 86

Czech Republic, 10

Daoud Khan, Mohammed, 11–12, 37, 60, 61, 65, 99, 110–12, 133–34, 165–66, 347; antinarcotics campaign and, 309–10; assassination of M. A. Khyber and, 315; aviation and, 141, 142, 152; Ayub Khan and, 171–72, 173, 189; Baluchistan and, 283, 289, 290, 298–99, 300, 302; at Belgrade Conference, 190; Bhutto and, 276–77, 291–92, 295, 299–301, 302, 303; Boghra Canal and, 151–52; Brezhnev and, 310–11; Byroade and, 284; J. Carter and, 308, 313; CIA and, 282, 294, 296, 316, 318; coup against, 281–82, 306–8, 315–25; coup of, 269–71, 273–75, 278–79, 352; Czechoslovakia and, 127, 129, 161, 279, 285; Durand Line and, 181; East Germany and, 293; Eisenhower and, 102; Eisenhower Doctrine and, 148, 149–50; Eliot and, 284, 296–97, 299, 307, 310, 312, 313, 315, 316, 349; Five-Year Plan and, 138–39; Ford and, 297; Ghaus and, 301; Helmand Valley and, 283, 311; Iran and, 286, 311; Islamists and, 295, 315; at Jeshyn festival, *145*, 295; Jessup and, 87; Kennedy and, 174, 184–85; Khrushchev and, 100–101, 162, 168, 176; killing of, 306–7; Kissinger and, 272, 297, 302; Maiwandwal and, 281; J. Mills and, 155, 156, 159; Mirza and, 158; Naim Khan and, 182, 188; NAM and, 301–2, 315; nationalism of, 110–11, 274; Neumann and, 262–63, 275, 276, 277, 280; Nixon and, 282–83, 296–97; NSC and, 131; overthrow of, 122–25, 127, 196–201; in Pakistan, 150, 285, 295, 311, 312–13; Parchamists and, 271, 283, 294, 296, 299, 349; Pashtunistan and, 76, 92, 110, 111, 122, 126, 130, 162, 173, 194, 282, 283, 298–99, 300, 302, 311; political prisoners of, 288, 313; return of, 269–71; Shafiq and, 299; Shah Mahmud and, 348; Shah of Iran and, 274, 292; South Korea and, 293; Soviet Union and, 126–27, 129, 131, 200, 282, 285–86, 304–8, 310–11, 316–18; at Stalin's funeral, 109; taxes and, 163, 172; in U.S., 156–58; West Germany and, 293; Zahir (King) and, 129, 132, *145*, 200

Dawar, Ghulam Haider, 254

Dawes, Charles G., 26

Degtyar, Mikhail, 116, 123, 167

DeLaive, Anton, 96, 97

Démarche (1952), from Soviet Union, 97, 102–4, 108–9, 115

DeMille, Cecil B., 222

Democratic Republic of Afghanistan (DRA), 307; ADB and, 323, 333; American evacuation from, 332–33; Brzezinski and, 320, 321, 325, 327–28; J. Carter and, 319, 320, 325, 327, 332, 339; CENTO and, 320–21, 329; CIA and, 318, 321, 330, 331–32, 336, 340; detention of families by, 319; Dubs and, 325–26, 327; East Germany and, 324, 328, 334, 335; Eliot and, 319–20; Helmand Valley and, 323; India and, 320; Islamists and, 324; Karmal and, 322, 324–25; KGB and, 336–37; Khalq and, 322,

Democratic Republic of Afghanistan
(DRA) (*continued*)
323, 324, 328–30, 333, 335, 336–37;
Marxists of, 318–19; NSC and, 325;
Pakistan and, 331, 332; Pan Am
and, 323; Parchamists and, 322, 325;
PCVs and, 318, 320; PDPA and,
324–25, 338; Soviet Union and, 307,
317, 318, 322–25, 328–31, 334–41;
Turkey and, 320–21; Warsaw Pact
and, 334; Zia and, 331, 332

Deng Xiaoping, 321

Desai, Morarji, 313

détente: in Cold War, 273–74, 278,
301–5; with Durand Line, 274,
301; between Afghanistan and
Pakistan, 12, 137, 147, 150, 157–58,
298, 313, 317

Development Loan Fund (DLF),
150, 161, 175, 178, 351; Afghan
Textile Company and, 164–65;
congressional limits on, 180;
Kennedy and, 184

Dillon, C. Douglas, 153–54, 156, 166,
178, 180; Eliot and, 283

Dixon, Jay, 10, 160

Dizon, Ron, 264, 267

DLF. *See* Development Loan Fund

Dobrynin, Anatoly, 5, 278–79; Taraki
and, 334

DRA. *See* Democratic Republic of
Afghanistan

Drake, Weston, 167

Dreyfus, Louis, 43, 80, 87–88, 90,
95, 98; 1941 visit to Kabul, 41–42;
Eximbank loan advocacy of, 85–86

Drinkall, John, 269, 275, 277;
Maiwandwal and, 281

drought, 12, 68–69, 73, 144, 280, 352; in
1970–1971, 247–56, 260–62

Dubs, Adolph, 309, 322–23; Amin and,
349; J. Carter and, 327, 349–50;
DRA and, 325–26, 327; murder of,
307, 326, 327; Pakistan and, 325

Dulles, Allen: as CIA director, 122, 129,
132, 165; as Near East Division head,
21, 22

Dulles, John Foster, 105, 106, 108, 118,
125, 131–32, 150, 156, 158; Daoud
Khan and, 156; Helmand Valley and,
139; views of proposed federation
120–21

Dupree, Louis, 10, 114, 274, 325, 349

Dupree, Nancy, 325

Durand Line, 11, 14, 16, 47; in Cold
War, 64, 74, 90, 119, 137; Daoud
Khan and, 181; détente with, 274,
301; Kennedy and, 183–89; Shafiq
and, 268; Soviet Union and, 289,
298, 304

earthquakes, 160, 300

East Germany, 161; Afghanistan and,
250–51; Daoud Khan and, 293;
DRA and, 324, 328, 334, 335;
Shafiq and, 279

education, 17, 53, 54, 174–75, 179–80,
183–84; Soviet Union and, 180, 197.
See also Kabul University

Egypt: Czechoslovakia and, 131; DRA
and, 321; Israel and, 282, 321;
revolution in, 161; Soviet Union and,
128, 339

Eid al-Fitr, 299

Eisenhower, Dwight D., 5, 11, 102,
116, 130, 134, 139, 168, 346; in
Afghanistan, 171–72, *172*; budgetary
limits of, 169, 177; Daoud Khan and,
122, 124, 156, 161, 165–66; departure
from office by, 183; Khrushchev

and, 177; Ludin and, 129; Naim Khan and, 165–66, 171, 182; on nationalism, 132, 148; national security strategy of, 106–9; NATO and, 176; NSC and, 119, 121; on Pakistan coup, 158; Soviet Union and, 173; Suez Canal and, 148; Zahir (King) and, 205

Eisenhower Doctrine, 148–50, 352–53

Eliot, Theodore, 7, 283–85; antinarcotics campaign and, 309–10; assassination of M. A. Khyber and, 315; J. Carter and, 309; CIA and, 284; Daoud Khan and, 296–97, 299, 307, 310, 312, 313, 315, 316, 317, 349; DRA and, 319–20; Iran and, 300, 312; Naim Khan and, 314; PCVs and, 288, 318; South Vietnam and, 293; Taraki and, 318, 319–20

Engerman, David, 7

Engert, Cornelius, 11, 32, 35, 98, 260, 346; background of, 43–45; Boghra Canal and, 66; cultural diplomacy of, 52–56; economic policy of, 47–52; inter-Allied diplomacy and, 56–58

Ertegun, Mehmet Münir, 43

Etemadi, Nur Ahmad, 182, 236, 241–43; Agnew and, 240; execution of, 337; Helmand Valley and, 249, 250; Iran and, 251; Pakistan and, 251–52; resignation of, 251; Zahir (King) and, 251

Ethiopia: Cuba and, 314; Daoud Khan and, 313; Engert in, 45; Italy in, 36; Soviet Union and, 314

Eximbank. *See* Export-Import Bank

Expanded Program for Technical Assistance, of UN, 85

Export-Import Bank (Eximbank), 78–79, 81, 94, 97, 98, 125, 167, 178, 231, 255, 351; first loan from 82, 85–86; second loan from, 112–18; MKA and, 151; Nixon and, 117

Faisal (King), 161

Fakir of Ipi, 39–40

famine, 12, 146, 247–58, 263–67, 280, 352

FAO. *See* Food and Agriculture Organization

Farah, 44, 257

Faryab, 257, 265, 267

Finland, 38

First Anglo-Afghan War, 16

First Five-Year Plan, 138–39

First Seven-Year Plan, 295, 299, 302, 304

First World War, 16–19

Five Principles of Peaceful Coexistence, 301

Flaten, Robert, 266

Flatin, Bruce, 326, 335

floods, 44, 56, 144, 234, 263, 300

Fluker, J. Robert, 54

Fly, Claude, 113, 114

Food and Agriculture Organization (FAO), 93, 95

Food for Peace, 217 *See also* Public Law 480

Food for Work, 256–57, 263–66

Ford, Gerald, 273, 296, 300; Bhutto and, 290, 298; Brezhnev and, 290; Daoud Khan and, 297; Ghaus and, 308; Naim Khan and, 302

Foreign Assistance Act, 247; political prisoners, 288

Fox, Ernest, 6–7, 34, 67, 69–70, 97–98

Foy, T. A. W., 55
France, 10, 14, 23; archeological mission by, 20, 36; in Cold War, 73, 94, 96–97
Franck, Peter, 115
Fraser-Tytler, William K., 36, 37–38, 40, 41, 73
Freeman, Orville, 228–29, 233, 235
Friedman, Jeremy, 3
Fry, Maxwell, 138
Fuller, R. Buckminster, 144
Fuller Company, 311, 312

Gabor, Zsa Zsa, 156
Gagarin, Yuri, 194
Gaiduk, Ilya, 94
Gandhi, Indira, 243, 308
Gardener, John, 94, 95
gasoline, 77–80; for Engert, 44; importation of, 47; from India, 72, 77; rationing of, 77, 86; shortages of, 40, 61, 77
Gaud, William S., 196, 201, 233, 235; Clay and, 208; on Kandahar International Airport, 211–12
Geddes, A. C., 19
Germany, 3, 10, 14, 16, 23; Amanullah and, 26–27, 37; Boghra Canal and, 54–55; Byroade in, 175–76; departure of, 40; after First World War, 18; India and, 39; Nadir Khan and, 24; in Second World War, 33–62; strained relations with, 22; technical assistance from, 20; U-boats of, 47, 51. *See also* East Germany; West Germany
Ghaus, Abdul Samad, 282, 296, 310; Daoud Khan and, 301; Ford and, 308; Maiwandwal and, 281; Percy and, 280

Ghor, 257; famine in, 263–67
Ghulam Mohammed, 82, 125
Girishk, 44, 72, 80, *111*, 113
Graham, Billy, 268
grain. *See* wheat
Greece, 75, 79; Marshall Plan for, 78; MSA and, 83
Grew, Joseph, 26, 32
Grindall, Terrence, 210
Gromyko, Andrei, 329, 331, 338–39

Habibia College, 17, 53
Habibullah, 16–17
Hakimi, Abdul Karim, 152–53, 160
Hamed, Samad, 265, 266
Hannah, John, 287
Hannah, Norman, 177, 183
Harding, Warren G., 11, 13, 19–20, 23
Hardinge (Lord), 19
Hare, Raymond, 29
Harlan, Wilbur, 33–34, 174
Harper, Sinclair O., 113–14
Harriman, Averell, 104, 222, 235
Harrison, Selig, 273, 322
Hart, Charles Calmer, 29–31, 32, 54
Häselbarth, Christoph, 256
Hashim Khan, Mohammed, 27, 35–41, 57, 58, 61, 67, 260; Engert and, 46–47, 62
HAVA. *See* Helmand-Arghandab Valley Authority
Havlin, Václav, 159–60
Hayes, William J., 112, 114, 115–16
Hays, Wayne, 212
Hays Organization, 55
Hazaras, 14–15; Khan, Abdul Rahman and, 16
Hekmatyar, Gulbuddin, 322
Heller, Joseph, 4

Helmand-Arghandab Valley Authority (HAVA), 287, 304. *See also* Helmand Valley Authority

Helmand Valley, 2, 3, 5; AID and, 293–94; American evacuation from, 332; Czechoslovakia and, 221, 311; dams on, 164; Daoud Khan and, 283, 311; DRA and, 323; in drought, 256; J. Dulles and, 139; Engert at, 44; Etemadi and, 249, 250; Iran and, 79, 252, 286, 311–12, 348; irrigation system in, 11; Kajakai Dam in, 216, 224, 231, 293, 303, 354; Kamal Khan Dam, 311; Naim Khan and, 286–87; Pashtuns and, 348; Poullada, Leon, and, 137–38; Steeves and, 219; Taliban in, 354; Yusuf and, 221–22, 224. *See also* Boghra Canal

Helmand Valley Authority (HVA), 112–13, 152, 163–64, 221–22; farmers' problems with, 172. *See also* Helmand-Arghandab Valley Authority

Helms, Richard, 282, 292; Eliot and, 284; Shah of Iran and, 289

Helsinki Accords, 298

Henderson, Loy, 105

Henson, Edwin, 87–88

Hentig, Werner Otto von, 40

Herat, 74, 286; aviation development around; famine in, 265, 267; oil in vicinity of, 29–30; opium cultivation around, 260; road construction around 162, 174, 212, 264; uprising in 328–29, 330, 334

Herat-Islam Qala Highway, 216, 230, 234, 245

Herat-Kandahar Highway, 162, 174, 230

heroin. *See* antinarcotics campaign

Herter, Christian, 175

Hezb-i-Islami ("Party of Islam"), 322

Hicks, Jim, 264

Hildreth, Horace, 130, 147

Hitler, Adolf, 34, 36, 194

Hoover, Herbert, 59

Horelick, Arnold, 330

Horner, John Evarts, 102–3

Hornibrook, William, 28, 32; on Ahmad Khan, 372n81

Hotaki, Abdul Latif, 231–32, 233

Hoveyda, Amir-Abbas, 242

Huang Ming-ta, 321

Hughes, Charles Evans, 13, 19–20, 21

Hughes, Thomas, 235

Humaira (Queen), 205, *206*

Hummel, Arthur, 320, 322

Humphrey, Hubert, 179

Hurley, Patrick, 59–60, 87

HVA. *See* Helmand Valley Authority

IBRD. *See* International Bank for Reconstruction and Development

ICA. *See* International Cooperation Administration

ICAO. *See* International Civil Aviation Organization

IMF. *See* International Monetary Fund

Indamer. *See* Indian-American Airlines

India, 4, 243; Bhutto and, 290; Britain in, 16, 74; Brzezinski on, 328; J. Carter and, 308, 313; China and, 179, 199; in Cold War, 67; DRA and, 320; gasoline from, 72, 77; Germany and, 39; Kennedy and, 190–91, 195, 215; Kissinger in, 272; Komer and, 208; Korean War and, 92; Naim Khan and, 186; NSC 98/1 on, 89; nuclear weapons of, 289; Operation Help and, 267; Pakistan and, 228, 257–58, 289; Pashtunistan and,

India (*continued*)
297; Second Five-Year Plan in, 178;
Soviet Union and, 277; Zahir (King)
in, 231
Indian-American Airlines (Indamer),
141
India Supply Mission, 49, 51, 66
Indonesia, 4
Indo-Pakistani War, in 1965, 228; in
1971, 251–52, 257–58
inflation, 61, 155, 217
Inland Exploration Company, 30, 34,
36, 45, 59
INR. *See* Bureau of Intelligence and
Research
International Bank for Reconstruction
and Development (IBRD), 252–53,
254, 255
International Civil Aviation
Organization (ICAO), 141, 142, 143
International Cooperation
Administration (ICA), 137, 140, 142,
143, 161, 167; contracting process
of, 176; education and, 174–75;
Kennedy and, 184; MKA and, 151;
Pan Am and, 152–53
International Monetary Fund (IMF),
218, 224, 254, 255
Iran, 4, 18, 303–4; Abdullah and, 286;
Anglo-Iranian Oil Company in,
96; antinarcotics campaign and,
261; Boghra Canal and, 73, 164;
Brzezinski on, 328; J. Carter and,
313, 327, 339; in Cold War, 89,
107–8; Daoud Khan and, 276–77,
286, 311; Eliot and, 285, 300, 312;
Etemadi and, 251; Helmand waters
and, 73, 79, 88, 140, 164, 181, 242,
250, 251, 252, 256, 268, 280, 283,
286, 311–12, 348; hostage crisis,
339, 343; Marshall Plan for, 78;
MSA and, 83; Naim Khan and,
286, 311–12; Nixon and, 258–59;
NSC 155/1 on, 107; NSC 5402
on, 107; oil in, 21, 30; Pakistan
and, 284, 292; roads to, 181, 192,
194–201, 212, 230; Soviet Union
and, 190, 258–59; U.S. aid to,
178–79; U.S. views of Afghanistan
and, 4, 297, 346. *See also specific
individuals*
Iraq, 39, 137, 264, 316; DRA and, 321;
revolution in, 161, 190
Islah, 109
Islamists: Bhutto and, 297; Daoud Khan
and, 295, 315; DRA and, 324; in
NWFP, 297
Israel: Daoud Khan coup and, 316;
Egypt and, 282, 321
Italy, 14; departure of, 40; in Ethiopia,
36; after First World War, 19; in
Second World War, 58; strained
relations with, 22; technical
assistance from, 20; Zahir (King) in,
269, 271
Izvestiya, 109

Jalalabad, 17, *117*, 144, 188, 222, 260,
288, 295; attack on Pakistani
consulate in, 123–24; uprising in
322, 334
Jansen, G. H., 6
Japan, 14; ADB and, 293; invasion of
Manchuria, 36; Nadir Khan and, 24;
in Second World War, 45, 54
Jeshyn festival, 143–44, *145*, 159, 241,
242–43; Daoud Khan at, 295; in
drought, 256
Jessup, Philip, 87, 94, 97, 108
Jewett, A. C., 16

Johnson, Lyndon B., 8, 11–12, 213–19, 221, 236–38, 348; India-Pakistan conflict and, 228; Maiwandwal and, *232*, 232–33; in Pakistan, 237; PL-480 and, 217; Vietnam War and, 207, 215, 223, 228–36
Jones, Lewis, 166
Jordan, 321

Kabul, 2, 22, 56, 354; 1973 coup in, 269, 271, 274–75; 1978 coup in, 306–7, 315–16; attack on Pakistani embassy in, 123, 124, 138; aviation in, 37, 72, 141–43; church in, 268; civil war in, 323, 334; development in, 101, 116, 120, 160, 161, 171, 197, 303; during 1928–1929 civil war, 23–24; education in, 53–54; elections in, 226; growth of, 15–17; protests in, 92, 103, 227–28, 230, 239, 241–42, 262; shortages in, 50, 233; Soviet invasion of, 341
See also Jeshyn festival, Kabul University, Radio Kabul, *various individuals*
Kabul-Kandahar Highway, 194, 198–200, 211–12, 216, 228
Kabul Times, 281
Kabul-Torkham Highway, 80
Kabul University, 175, 181, 183, 192, 196, 199, 209, 211; engineering school at, 303; protests at, 226, 241–42, 262; Zahir (King) and, 216
Kaiser Engineering, 113
Kajakai Dam, 216, 224, 231, 303, 354; ADB and, 293
Kalakani, Habibullah, 23
Kalinovsky, Artemy, 10
Kamal Khan Dam, 311

Kandahar, 63, 80, 91, 144, 162, 174, 196, 211; 1959 riot in, 172–73, 348; airport in, 141, 151–54, 163, 172, 185, 192, 211–12, 354; cement factory project in, 311–12; MKA in, 72, 74, 94; Pakistani consulate in, 123, 188; unrest in, 242, 286
Kandahar-Girishk Highway, 80
karakul, 41, 46; currency reserves from, 73; in drought, 252–56; price fluctuations for, 81, 179; in Second World War, 48–49, 53
Karmal, Babrak, 226–27, 231, 255–56; assassination of M. A. Khyber and, 315; Czechoslovakia and, 325; DRA and, 322, 324–25
Karmelita, Zdeněk, 316
Kashmir, 150, 201, 272; UN and, 195
Kaunda, Kenneth, 221
Kayeum, Abdul, 152, 163–64, 260
Kellogg-Briand Pact, 22
Kennan, George, 103, 104, 344–45; Brzezinski and, 345
Kennedy, John F., 8, 11, 212–13, 355; assassination of, 213; Ayub Khan and, 188, 190–91, 199; Clay and, 208; Daoud Khan and, 174, 184–85; India and, 179, 190–91, 195, 215; Maiwandwal and, 237; nuclear test ban treaty and, 204; Pakistan and, 187, 191; policy toward second border crisis, 189–201; Zahir and, 193, 198; Zahir (King) and, 205–7, *206*
Keys, Barbara, 7
KGB: Daoud Khan coup and, 316; DRA and, 336–37; Maoists and, 3
Khalq: J. Carter and, 329–30; Daoud Khan coup and, 316; DRA and, 322, 323, 324, 328–30, 333, 335, 336–37;

Khalq (*continued*)
　Parchamists and, 239, 268, 285–86; Soviet Union and, 349; of Taraki, 230
Khalq, 230
Khan, Tanvir Ahmad, 297–98
Khattak, Ajmal, 291, 292
Khattak, M. A. K., 123, 125
Khrushchev, Nikita, 105, 127–28, 129; in Afghanistan, 100–102, 176; aid policy, 138, 161, 162, 167–69, 211; Berlin crisis and, 190; CENTO and, 195; CIA on, 190; Daoud Khan and, 162, 168, 176; education and, 180; Eisenhower and, 177; nuclear test ban treaty and, 204; Pashtunistan and, 162, 182; in U.S., 173; Yusuf and, 211
Khurram, Ali Ahmad, 302–3, 311; assassination of, 313
Khyber, Mir Akbar, 315
Khyber Pass, *42*, 63; Soviet Union and, 191
Kiesinger, Kurt-Georg, 242
King, Martin Luther, Jr., 236
Kirilenko, Andrei, 329
Kissinger, Henry, 240, 243, 245, 283, 296; Abdullah and, 298; in Afghanistan, 272–73, 300–303; AID and, 293; Bhutto and, 289, 300; Byroade and, 284; China and, 255, 277; Daoud Khan and, 297, 302; Eliot and, 284; Helms and, 284; Naim Khan and, 289; Pashtunistan and, 298; Pashtuns and, 272; petroleum and, 303; Shah of Iran and, 278; Soviet Union and, 278–79, 290, 302
KLM, 142
Knowland, William, 105

Kolek, Edward, 218
Komer, Robert, 219; Ayub Khan and, 193–94; Clay and, 208; India and, 195; second border crisis and, 190–201; Vietnam War and, 230
Korea, Afghanistan compared to, 137–39, 353
Korean War, 88, 139; India and, 92; UN in, 94
Kosygin, Alexei, 216, 242, 328–29
Kuchel, Thomas, 245
Kuzichkin, Vladimir, 316

Lala, Abdul Razak, 264
Lancaster Plan, 76, 83
Lascelles, Daniel, 100, 110, 123, 126, 128, 147; Pashtunistan and, 150
Lattimore, Owen, 87–88, 94, 97
Leach, Richard, 88
League of Nations, 36
Leake, Elisabeth, 10, 158, 187, 324
Lebanon, 44, 148
Lee, Jonathan, 10
Lend-Lease program, 42, 46, 50
Lenin, Vladimir, 18, 334
Lewis, Samuel, 254, 268–69; Daoud Khan and, 282; Naim Khan and, 286–87
Life, 55
Lilienthal, David, 112, 194
Lingeman, Eric, 96–97, 115
Lodge, Henry Cabot, 121
Logevall, Fredrik, 8
loya jirga, 23, 40, 129, 131, 215, 217–18, 308, 310
Ludin, Mohammed Kabir, 64, 70, 72, 78–79, 81, 85, 118–19, 122, 348; Eisenhower and, 129
Lüthi, Lorenz, 3
Lynch, Robert J., 70

MacEachin, Douglas, 336, 340
Maillart, Ella, 33–34
Maiwandwal, Mohammed Hashim, 8, 143, 188, 189, 202, 227–28, 230–32; Daoud Khan coup and, 281–82; Eliot and, 284; Johnson and, *232*, 232–33; Kennedy and, 237; resignation of, 235; Zahir (King) and, 234–35, 237–38
Makowski, Waclaw, 141, 143
Malaysia, 3
Malenkov, Georgi, 109
Malik, Abdul, 111, 127; Five-Year Plan and, 138–39; wheat and, 146–47
Malikyar, Abdullah, 309
Mann, Thomas, 1
Manchuria, Japanese invasion of, 36
Mansuri, Amanullah, 25
Maoists, 3
Marco Polo sheep, 135–36
Mare, Arthur de la, 217, 220
Marshall, George, 78, 175
Marshall, Thurgood, 205
Marshall Plan, 81
Marxists: assassination of M. A. Khyber and, 315; coup by, 5, 12, 279; of DRA, 318–19
Masey, Jack, 144
Massoud, Ahmed Shah, 295
Mathews, Elbert, 60, 114
Mathewson, James, 264–65
McCarthy, Joseph, 87–88, 105
McCormack, Tim, 264–65
McGhee, George, 88, 90, 91, 94, 108, 110, 201
MEDO. *See* Middle East Defense Organization
Merchant, Livingston, 193–94
Merrell, George, 95, 98, 112
Mesopotamia, 21

Mexico: antinarcotics campaign and, 259; oil in, 31
Meyer, Armin, 137, 149, 167, 168, 169–70; Daoud Khan and, 156, 157–58
Middle East Defense Organization (MEDO), 105, 109
MiG-21 jet fighters, 306
Mikoyan, Anastas, 162
Miller, Ralph, 154
Mills, Ogden, 30
Mills, Sheldon, 136, 137, 141, 142, 169–70, 346; aviation and, 152, 153; Daoud Khan and, 155, 156, 157, 159; Jeshyn festival and, 144, *145*; Pashtunistan and, 150; petroleum and, 154; Ward and, 143; wheat and, 146–47
Mirza, Iskander, 125, 132, 147; Daoud Khan and, 158
Mitchell, John, 259–60
Mitchell, Lou, 288
Mitrokhin, Vasili, 10, 316, 323
MKA. *See* Morrison-Knudsen Afghanistan
Mohammed, Faiz, 13, 20, 24, 37, 40, 43
Mohammedzai dynasty, 14
Mondale, Walter, 327, 330, 331
monopolies *(shirkat)*, 36, 72, 86
Morgan, Thomas, 212
Morgenthau, Hans, 352
Morozov, Alexander, 334
Morrison, Harry, 80, 85, 139–40
Morrison-Knudsen Afghanistan (MKA), 9, 63, 90, 98, 109; advocacy for, 350–51; for aviation project, 141, 152–53; cost overruns by, 80–81; Eximbank and, 151; gasoline and, 77–78, 79–80; in Helmand Valley, 63; ICA and, 151; irrigation dam by, *111*, 112; Naim Khan and, 287;

Morrison-Knudsen Afghanistan (MKA) (*continued*)
   Soviet Union and, 74, 109–10, 127, 129; UNTAM and, 94–95. *See also* aviation, Boghra Canal, Helmand Valley, Kandahar
Mossadegh, Mohammed, 96, 107, 129
movies, in Second World War, 55–56
MSA. *See* Mutual Security Act
Murray, Wallace, 32, 41, 43, 355; Engert and, 45; policy of distance and, 21, 22, 25–26, 27; Seaboard Oil Company and, 30–31
Musahibans, 16–17, 23–34
Mutual Security Act (MSA), 83
Mutual Security Administration, 104
Mylnikov, Georgi, 67

Nadir Shah (King, formerly Nadir Khan), 21, 23–24, 27, 29–35
Naim Khan, Mohammed, 37, 60, 66–67, 80, 81, 111–12, 126, 165–66, 347; Ayub Khan and, 189; Bhutto and, 301; Byroade and, 135–36, 162–63, 185, 284; J. Carter and, 308; Clay and, 208; Daoud Khan and, 182, 188; J. Dulles and, 120–21; Eisenhower and, 171, 182; Eisenhower Doctrine and, 149–50; Eliot and, 284, 314; Ford and, 302; Helmand River dams and, 164; Helmand Valley and, 286–87; India and, 186; Iran and, 286, 311–12; Kennedy and, 199; Khrushchev and, 100–101; killing of, 306–7; Kissinger and, 272, 289; Lewis and, 286–87; MKA and, 287; Neumann and, 276; Percy and, 292; petroleum and, 154; railroads and, 154–55; Steeves and, 203; UNTAM and, 96; in U.S., 199

NAM. *See* Non-Aligned Movement
NAP. *See* National Awami Party
narcotics. *See* antinarcotics campaign
Nasser, Gamal Abdel, 131
Nathan, Robert, 218, 253, 256
National Awami Party (NAP), 255–56, 268, 276, 283, 289; ban of, 299; Bhutto and, 291–92
National Bank *(Bank-i-Milli)*, 95, 118
nationalism, 36, 39, 76, 132, 148, 251, 280; of Daoud Khan, 274; of the Khalq, 322, 338; of Qadir, 349; Shafiq and, 268
National Security Archive (NSA), 10
National Security Council (NSC), 89, 129, 178; antinarcotics campaign and, 260; of Carter, J., 330, 339; Daoud Khan and, 131; DRA and, 325; Eisenhower and, 119, 121; of Kennedy, 189–90; of Nixon, 243, 245–46, 296–97; NSC 68, 88, 98–97; NSC 98/1, 89; NSC 155/1, 106–7; NSC 162/2 (New Look), 107; NSC 5402, 107; NSC 5409, 118, 132–33, 142, 181 Pakistan and, 132; of Reagan, 344; Soviet Union and, 165–66
National Security Study Memorandum (NSSM) 182, 277–78
NATO: Eisenhower and, 176; SALT II and, 340; Sputnik and, 162; UNTAM and, 96
Nazimuddin, Khawaja, 108
Nègre, André, 242
Nehru, Jawaharlal, 178, 179, 190–91
Nepal: Agnew in, 240; DRA and, 321; Komer and, 208; Percy in, 292
Neumann, Marlen Eldredge, 244, 245
Neumann, Robert, 231–34, 241, 242, 246, 248–50, 252, 270; antinarcotics

[462] INDEX

campaign and, 260, 261; background of, 244–45; Daoud Khan and, 262–63, 275, 276, 277, 280; Food for Work and, 265; Naim Khan and, 276; Nixon and, 281; Shafiq and, 268
New Frontier, 183–89
New Look (NSC 162/2), 107
Newsom, David, 323, 325–26; Wali, Shah and, 338
New York Herald Tribune, 24–25
Nguyen Thi Binh, 293
Nicaragua, 336
NIE 53–56, 131, 132
NIE 53–59, 167–68
Nixon, Richard M., 12, 117–18, 121–22, 239–41, 287, 296; antinarcotics campaign of, 259–61, 275, 349; Bhutto and, 279, 284; Cambodia and, 250; China and, 255; Daoud Khan and, 156, 271, 282–83, 296–97; Iran and, 258–59; initial Afghan policy of, 247–58; Neumann and, 245, 281; NSC of, 243, 245–46, 296–97; NSSM 182 of, 277–78; PL-480 and, 248–49; Shah of Iran and, 278, 284; Soviet Union and, 277; Vietnam War and, 243–44, 270; Watergate and, 281, 282, 308; Zahir (King) and, 243
Nixon Doctrine, 239–40, 249, 250, 269–70
Non-Aligned Movement (NAM), 220–21, 231; Daoud Khan and, 301–2, 315; South Vietnam and, 293; Taraki and, 336–37
North Korea, Daoud Khan and, 293
North West Frontier Province (NWFP), 276, 277, 290, 291; Islamists in, 297

NSA. *See* National Security Archive
NSC. *See* National Security Council
NSC 68, 88, 98–97
NSC 98/1, 89
NSC 155/1, 106–7
NSC 162/2 (New Look), 107
NSC 5402, 107
NSC 5409, 118, 132–33, 142, 181
NSSM. *See* National Security Study Memorandum
Nucker, Delmas, 217
nuclear test ban treaty, 204
Nunan, Timothy, 2, 10, 257
NWFP. *See* North West Frontier Province

Oakes, Calvin, 53
OCB. *See* Operations Control Board
Office of Economic Warfare, 51
Office of Strategic Services (OSS), 53–54
O'Halpin, Eunan, 36
oil. *See* petroleum
O'Keeffe, Charles, 310
Oksenberg, Michael, 328
Olympics, in Soviet Union, 343
Omar, Mohammed, 50
One Unit plan, of Pakistan, 121, 122, 126, 127, 250
Open Door, 22
Operation Barbarossa, 39, 42
Operation Help, 266–67
Operations Control Board (OCB), 181
Osman, Ismail, 276
OSS. *See* Office of Strategic Services
Ostpolitik, 279, 302
Ottoman Empire, Young Turks in, 16–17

Pahlavi, Mohammed Reza, 198
Pakistan, 4; antinarcotics campaign and, 261; in Baluchistan, 282; border closure by, 126; Brzezinski on, 328; J. Carter and, 313; CENTO and, 298; China and, 215; CIA and, 291; civil war in, 251–52; in Cold War, 64, 67, 74, 76–77, 81, 85, 87, 89, 107–9, 118–19, 123–26, 130–31; coup in, 137, 158; Daoud Khan and, 150, 282, 285, 295, 311, 312–13; détente with, 12, 137, 157, 298, 313, 317; DRA and, 331, 332; Dubs and, 325; J. Dulles in, 105; Eisenhower and, 107–9; Eliot and, 285; Etemadi and, 251–52; federation between Afghanistan and, 120–22; India and, 228, 257–58, 289; Iran and, 284, 292; Johnson in, 237; Kennedy and, 187, 191; Kissinger in, 272; Komer and, 208; martial law in, 158; military assistance to, 118–19; NSC 98/1 on, 89; NSC 155/1 on, 107; NSC 5402 on, 107; NSC and, 132; One Unit plan of, 121, 122, 126, 127, 250; Operation Help and, 267; Pashtuns of, 3, 11, 14, 182, 251; political turmoil in, 243, 312; propaganda from, 173, 176; railroads and, 221, 258; roads to, 155–56; Shafiq and, 268; Shah of Iran and, 274, 278, 282, 284, 289, 312; Soviet Union and, 130, 191, 258–59, 277, 298–99, 329; Taraki and, 328; U-2 and, 177–78; in UN, 76; U.S. aid to, 178–79; U.S. views of Afghanistan and, 4, 289, 297, 346; Wakhan Corridor and, 136; wheat to, 248–49. *See also specific individuals and topics*

Pakistan People's Party (PPP), 251, 276; assassination of Sherpao, 290–92
Paktia, 322, 337
Paktia Development Authority (PDA), 256, 257
Palestine, 221; oil in, 21
Palmer, Ely, 69, 75, 76, 98; Ludin and, 78–79
Pan American World Airways (Pan Am), 3, 141–42; Ariana and, 152, 323; ICA and, 152–53
Parchamists: Daoud Khan and, 271, 283, 294, 296, 299, 316, 349; DRA and, 322, 325; Khalq and, 239, 268, 285–86; Soviet Union and, 279, 285–86, 325
Paris Peace Conference, 18
Parker, Daniel, 293
"Party of Islam" (Hezb-i-Islami), 322
Pashtunistan, 75–77, 82, 86–92, 120, 150, 157, 203; Abdullah and, 294, 298; Bhutto and, 298; CIA and, 297; Daoud Khan and, 76, 92, 110, 111, 122, 126, 130, 162, 173, 194, 282, 283, 298–99, 300, 302, 311; Eisenhower and, 108; India and, 297; Khrushchev and, 182; Kissinger and, 298; Soviet Union and, 95, 187, 210, 278, 297; U-2 and, 177–78; U.S. views of, 87, 91, 176, 199, 278, 297, 346; Zia and, 312
Pashtuns: Ayub Khan and, 187; in Baluchistan, 242–43; in Cold War, 65, 66; Germany and, 39; Helmand Valley and, 348; Khan, Abdul Rahman and, 16; Kissinger and, 272; of Pakistan, 3, 11, 14, 182, 251; in Waziristan, 22
Passman, Otto, 212
Pasteur, Louis, 55–56

Paul, Arthur, 218
Pazhwak, Abdul Rahman, 220, 243
PCVs. *See* Peace Corps Volunteers
PDPA. *See* People's Democratic Party of Afghanistan
Peace Corps Volunteers (PCVs), 240, 263–65, 271; departure of, 332; DRA and, 318, 320; Eliot and, 288, 318
People's Democratic Party of Afghanistan (PDPA), 226, 236, 295; assassination of M. A. Khyber and, 315; Daoud Khan coup and, 316, 317, 322; DRA and, 324–25, 338; Soviet Union and, 324–25, 328–30, 334–37, 339–41
Percy, Charles, 280; Naim Khan and, 292
Perruche, Georges, 313
Persian Empire, 15, 256
Peshawar, 40, 59; and 1950 energy crisis, 86–87; and 1960 U-2 incident, 177; attack on Afghan consulate in, 123, 124, 126; during second border crisis, 192, 194, 212; Kissinger in, 272; Sherpao assassination in, 290–91
Peter the Great, 6, 344
petroleum (oil), 154; Abdullah and, 304; Anglo-Iranian Oil Company, 96; Anglo-Persian Oil Company, 29; in Iran, 21, 30; Kissinger and, 303; in Mexico, 31; in Palestine, 21; Seaboard Oil Company, 30–31; Sinclair Oil Company, 59; Soviet Union and, 174; Standard-Vacuum Oil Company, 66. *See also* gasoline
Philippines, the, 83
Phillips, William, 22, 26, 28
Piez, William, 225–26

Pilger, Hans, 38, 46, 58
Piperno, Dario, 22
Pipes, Richard, 344–45
PL-480. *See* Public Law 480
Podgorny, Nikolai, 279
Point Four Program, 84–85, 174, 351
Poland, 23, 58; Operation Help and, 267
Political Parties Bill, 225, 234
political prisoners, of Daoud Khan, 288, 313; of DRA, 319, 323, 332, 333, 337, 338
poppies. *See* antinarcotics campaign
Poullada, Leila, 10
Poullada, Leon, 10, 128–29, 137–40; Daoud Khan and, 156; Helmand Valley and, 137–38
Powers, Francis Gary, 177
PPP. *See* Pakistan People's Party
Pravda, 187
"Princess Fatima," 13, 19–20
Provisional Revolutionary Government (PRG), of South Vietnam, 293
Public Law 480 (PL-480), 145–46, 175, 180, 192, 214, 224, 351; Freeman and, 229; Johnson and, 217; Kennedy and, 184; Maiwandwal and, 235; Nixon and, 248–49; Operation Help and, 267; for wheat, 212, 247–49, 253, 256
Pul-i-Charkhi, 313, 319, 323, 324, 333
Pul-i-Khumri, 34, 216, 334
Puzanov, Alexander, 298, 304, 305, 311, 324, 334, 435n17; Daoud Khan coup and, 316

Qadir, Abdul, 322–23, 324; nationalism of, 349
Qavam, Ahmad, 73, 75
Quaroni, Pietro, 58

Radford, Arthur, 121–22, 132
Radio Afghanistan, 269, 324
Radio Kabul, 110, 165
Rafik, Attik, 120
railroads, 149, 154–55, 163; Pakistan and, 221, 257–58
Ratebzad, Anahita, 226–27, 231
Rathbone, Basil, 112
Reagan, Ronald, 156; NSC of, 344; Soviet Union and, 353
Revolutionary Council, Taraki of, 318
Richards, James, 148–49, 151, 154–55, 352–53
Richardson, Elliot, 259–60
Riddleberger, James, 178
roads, 15, 80, 216; for American evacuation, 332–33; construction delays for, 194; flooding of, 234; to Iran, 181, 194–201, 212, 230; to Pakistan, 155–56; *versus* railroads, 155; Soviet Union and, 138, 147, 162, 174
Roberts, Jeffery, 10
Robinson, Paul, 10, 160
Rogers, William, 245, 260, 261, 270
Roosevelt, Eleanor, 179
Roosevelt, Franklin D., 26, 27, 28, 35, 41, 43; death of, 60; Hurley and, 59–60; Lend-Lease program of, 42, 46, 50
Rostow, Walt, 185–86, 197, 233, 235, 351
Rountree, William, 191
Rubin, Barnett, 10, 163
Rush, Kenneth, 282
Rusk, Dean, 191, 205, *206*, 224
Russia: Bolsheviks of, 18, 20; Britain and, 15. *See also* Soviet Union

al-Sadat, Anwar, 124
Sadrieh, Sadegh, 289

Safis, 61
Safronchuk, Vasily, 334–35, 353; Amin and, 335, 339; Taraki and, 335
Saikal, Amin, 10, 110, 234–35
Salang Pass tunnel, 2, 138, 216, 341
SALT II, 314, 321, 330, 331, 332, 336, 341; NATO and, 340; withdrawal from, 343
Sarabi, Abdul Wahid, 247–48
Saturday Evening Post, 55
Saudi Arabia, 142, 277, 293, 294; Brzezinski on, 328; DRA and, 319, 321, 332, 339
Saunders, Harold, 223, 230, 233, 275, 282
Saunders, Richard, 252, 256–57,
Savage, John Lucian, 55, 66, 71, *71*
SCC. *See* Special Coordinating Council
Schmelzer, Frank, 225
Schultz, Charles, 233, 235
Schuschnigg, Kurt, 244
Schwarzenbach, Annemarie, 33–34
Schwiesau, Hermann, 334, 335, 353
Scott, Richard, 287
Scripps-Howard, 105
Seaboard Oil Company, 30–31
Second Anglo-Afghan War, 15, 16
Second Five-Year Plan, 177, 178, 180, 184–86
Second World War, 33–66; U.S. cultural diplomacy in, 52–56; supply problems in, 47–52; inter-Allied diplomacy in, 56–59
September 11, 2001 terrorist attack, 1
Shafiq, Mohammed Moussa, 240, 254, 258, 267–69, 348; antinarcotics campaign and, 261; Daoud Khan and, 299; East Germany and, 279; execution of, 337; overthrow of, 269–71

Shah, Ahmad, 16
Shah, A. S. B., 120, 126, 127
Shah Mahmud Ghazi, 27, 60, 61, 67, 81, 86, 90–92, 99; Boghra Canal and, 112; in Cold War, 64, 65; Daoud Khan and, 348; Henson and, 88; Jessup and, 87; Pashtunistan and, 76; resignation of, 110; Truman and, 78, 91; TWA and, 74; UNTAM and, 96, 97
Shah of Iran, 159, 164, 172, 258–59, 270, 273–74, 286, 297, 312; abdication by, 328; Afghan aid program of, 286, 292, 300, 303, 311–12; Bhutto and, 298, 303–4; Brzezinski and, 328; J. Carter and, 313, 317–18; Daoud Khan and, 276–77, 282, 292, 317–18; Eliot and, 284; Helms and, 284, 289; Kissinger and, 278; Nixon and, 278, 284; overthrow of, 327; proposed Afghan countercoup and, 271
Shah Wali (uncle of King Zahir), 23, 27, 28, 192, 213, 299, 310, 348; and Daoud, 123, 198, 200, 202–3
Shah Wali (DRA foreign minister), 338
Shakespeare, William, 343
Shastri, Lal Bahadur, 228
Shaw, G. Howland, 21, 22, 23
Sheberghan, 82, 94, 242
Sher Ali, 16
Sherpao, Hayat Mohammed Khan, 290–92
Sherzad, Ghulam Mohammed, 164
Shiites, 14–15
shirkat (monopolies), 36, 72, 86
Shriver, Eunice Kennedy, *206*
Shulman, Marshall, 338
Sinclair Oil Company, 59
Sino-Indian War, 200

Široký, Viliam, 161
Sisco, Joseph, 250, 276, 277, 278
Slocombe, Walter, 339
Snyder, Robert, 143, 153–54, 155, 157, 169–70
Sokolovsky, Vasily, 194
Somalia, 314
South East Asia Treaty Organization, 130
South Korea: Daoud Khan and, 293; MSA and, 83; UN in, 92. *See also* Korean War
South Vietnam: compared to Afghanistan, 238; fall of, 301; PRG of, 293. *See also* Vietnam War
Soviet Union, 23; Amin and, 329, 337, 339, 341; aviation and, 142–43, 163; Berlin crisis and, 190, 193; Brzezinski and, 331, 339, 344, 353; J. Carter and, 308–9, 313, 340–41, 343–45, 350; China and, 328; CIA and, 165, 331; in Cuba, 336, 338, 347; in Czechoslovakia, 241, 242; Daoud Khan and, 126–27, 129, 131, 200, 275, 282, 285–86, 304–8, 310–11, 316–18; démarche of, 97, 102–4, 108–9, 115; DRA and, 307, 317, 318, 322–25, 328–31, 334–41; Durand Line and, 289, 298, 304; education and, 180, 197; Egypt and, 128, 339; Eisenhower and, 173; Eliot and, 285; Ethiopia and, 314; in Finland, 38; after First World War, 18; hydroelectric project of, 222; India and, 277; Iran and, 190, 258–59; Jeshyn festival and, 144, 159; Khalq and, 285–86, 316, 324–25, 328–30, 334–37, 339–41, 349; Kissinger and, 278–79, 290, 302; Lend-Lease program to, 42; loans from, 100–101,

INDEX [467]

Soviet Union (*continued*)
116; MKA and, 109–10, 127, 129; Nadir Khan and, 24; Nixon and, 277; NSC and, 165–66; Olympics in, 343; Operation Help and, 267; Pakistan and, 130, 191, 258–59, 277, 298–99, 329; Parchamists and, 279, 285–86, 325; Pashtunistan and, 95, 187, 210, 278, 297; PDPA and, 324–25; petroleum and, 154, 174; Reagan and, 353; roads and, 138, 147, 162, 174; in Second World War, 33–62; Steeves and, 1, 216; Taraki and, 322, 329; U-2 and, 177–78, 180–81; wheat and, 233; Yusuf and, 222; Zahir (King) and, 154, 210–11. *See also* Cold War; *specific individuals*
Special Coordinating Council (SCC), of NSC, 325, 330, 331, 332, 340–40
Spiers, Ronald, 320–21
Sputnik, 161–62
Squire, Giles, 58, 60, 69
Stalin, Joseph, 68, 72, 75; death of, 102, 105, 109; on UN, 94
Standard-Vacuum Oil Company, 66
Steeves, John Milton, 1–2, 8, 213–14, 218–19, 230, 347, 351; AID and, 217; Antonov and, 216; Clay and, 208; Naim Khan and, 203; in second border crisis, 196–201; Yusuf and, 219–20, 222–24; Zahir (King) and, 202–3
Stettinius, Edward, 70
Stevenson, Adlai, 130
Stratil-Sauer, Gustav, 22
Straus, Jesse Isidor, 28
Suhrawardy, Huseyn Shaheed, 150
Sukhoi-7 fighter-bombers, 247, 306
Sultan-Galiev, Mirsaid, 18
Sultan Khan, 276

Sumser, John, 318, 320
Sunni Islam, 14
Switzerland, 23; as potential model for Afghan neutrality, 149, 352; Operation Help and, 267
Symington, Stuart, 235, 247
Syria: DRA and, 321; Israel and, 282; in Second World War, 39

Tajikistan, 136, 337
Talbot, Phillips, 186, 213, 223; Clay and, 208; in second border crisis, 192, 195, 199–200, 201
Taliban, 354
Taraki, Nur Mohammed, 209, 230–31, 325; Amin and, 337; assassination of M. A. Khyber and, 315; Brezhnev and, 337; Dobrynin and, 334; early contacts with U.S. diplomats, 225–26; Eliot and, 318, 319–20; Khalq of, 230; murder of, 339; NAM and, 336–37; Newsom and, 323; Pakistan and, 328; of Revolutionary Council, 318; Safronchuk and, 335; Soviet Union and, 322, 329
Tarzi, Habibullah, 26
taxes, 16, 163, 224, 254; Daoud Khan and, 163, 172
Taylor, Carl, 114
Technical Cooperation Administration (TCA), 174
Tennessee Valley Authority (TVA), 112, 156
Texas Company (Texaco), 30
Thailand, 313
Thayer, Charles, 44, 48, 53
Third Anglo-Afghan War, 17–18
Thornton, Thomas, 315, 317–18, 321, 325–26, 330, 335, 338, 342

Time, 328
Title I and II. *See* Public Law 480
Tito, Josip Broz, 242
Tobin, Conor, 5
Torkham, 196, 212
Tragedy of King Richard the Third, The (Shakespeare), 343
Transcontinental & Western Air (TWA), 74
Trans-Ocean, 141
Treaty of Gandamak, 16
Treaty of Kabul, 20
Truman, Harry S, 68, 78, 81, 103–4; Byroade and, 176; Shah Mahmud and, 91; UN and, 84–85; Ward and, 105
Truman Doctrine, 345
Tudor Engineering Company, 140, 150, 151
Turkey, 14, 16, 18, 43; antinarcotics campaign and, 259–60, 261; Brzezinski on, 328; DRA and, 320–21; J. Dulles in, 105; Marshall Plan for, 78; MSA and, 83; technical assistance from, 20; U.S. arms in, 162; wheat to, 248–49
TVA. *See* Tennessee Valley Authority
TWA. *See* Transcontinental & Western Air

U-2, 177–78, 180–81
U-boats, of Germany, 47, 51
United Kingdom, *See* Britain
United Nations (UN), 87–88; antinarcotics campaign and, 310; Baluchistan and, 290; in Cold War, 68; Congo and, 219–20; Kashmir and, 195; in Korean War, 94; letter writing campaign to, 299; Pakistan in, 76; Pashtuns and, 243; in Second World War, 48, 57; in South Korea, 92; Stalin on, 94; Truman and, 84–85; WFP of, 253, 256
United Nations Educational, Scientific and Cultural Organization, 93
United Nations International Children's Emergency Fund, 93
United Nations Technical Assistance Mission (UNTAM), 93–97, 109
United States (U.S.). *See specific topics*
United States Information Agency (USIA), 272
University of Wyoming, 174
UNTAM. *See* United Nations Technical Assistance Mission
USAID, 287
U.S. Army Corps of Engineers (USACE), 176–77, 178, 179, 234
USIA. *See* United States Information Agency
Ustinov, Dmitri, 339, 340
Uzbekistan, 120

Vance, Cyrus, 308, 331, 338
Van Vleck, Jenifer, 2, 141–42, 152
Vietnam: China in, 327, 328. *See also* South Vietnam
Vietnam War, 11–12, 190, 266; J. Carter and, 308; defeat in, 278; Johnson and, 207, 215, 223, 228–36; 1966–1968, 228–36; Nixon and, 243–44, 270
Voice of America, 330

Wakhan Corridor, 136
Wakil, Abdul, 222, 254; Food for Work of, 256–57, 263–66
Wali, Abdul, 299
Wali Khan, Mohammed, 13, 14, 18–19, 24, 29, 31, 354
Wali Khan (NAP leader), 276, 291

Wallace, Hugh, 19
Walsh, Myles, 63–64, 82, 94, 354
Walsh, Ruth, 63
Walters, Vernon, 278
Ward, Angus, 102, 106, 109, 118, 137, 346; articulation of Afghanistan's Cold War significance, 116, 119–20, 128–29, 134; background of, 104–5; in first border crisis, 123–24, 126; S. Mills and, 143
War Production Board (WPB), 48, 49, 50
Warsaw Pact, 210, 314–15; DRA and, 334
Watan, 92
Watergate, 281, 282; J. Carter and, 308
Watson, J. H., 69
Waziristan, 22
weevils, 248
Weimer, Daniel, 2, 260
Weisner, Maurice, 314
Welles, Sumner, 41
Wernert, Eugene, 261
Westad, Odd Arne, 10
West Germany, Daoud Khan and, 275, 293
Westmoreland, William C., 206
Weyman, Stanley Clifford, 20
WFP. *See* World Food Program
Wharton, David, 7
wheat (grain), 50, 68, 117, 242; cessation of sales, 343; grant for, 144–47, 213–14; loan for, 104; PL-480 for, 212, 247–49, 253, 256, 313; Soviet Union and, 233
Whitteridge, Gordon, 227
WHO. *See* World Health Organization
Wilson, Woodrow, 18
Winged Scourge, The, 56
Winger, Gregory, 273–74

Wolesi Jirga, 226–27
Wollmar, Stellan, 175
World Food Program (WFP), of UN, 253, 256
World Health Organization (WHO), 93, 95
WPB. *See* War Production Board
Wriggins, Howard, 230, 233
Wylie, Francis, 45, 57–58

Yahya Khan, Mohammed, 250, 251–52, 258
Yaqub, Salim, 148
Youngs, Frank, 114
Young Turks, in Ottoman Empire, 16–17
Yusuf, Mohammed, 201–2, 207, 218, 348; Helmand Valley and, 221–22, 224; 1965 elections and, 225–28; resignation of, 230; Soviet Union and, 211, 222; Steeves and, 219–20, 222–24; Zahir (King) and, 208–9, 227

Zabuli, Abdul Majid, 64, 72, 83, 113, 215, 348; Afghan National Bank and, 95; Czechoslovakia and, 86; and Eximbank loan, 79, 81, 85–86; Henson and, 88; National Bank and, 118; Pashtunistan and, 92; TWA and, 74; wartime diplomacy of, 36–39
Zachystal, František, 97, 109, 116
Zafrullah Khan, 90
Zahedi, Ardeshir, 252, 276
Zahedi, Fazlollah, 108
Zahir Shah, Mohammed (King), 11, 27, 28, 110, 123, 124, 128; Agnew and, 240; Ayub Khan and, 202; Daoud Khan and, 129, 132, *146*, 200; Eisenhower and, 171; Etemadi and, 251; Hurley and, 59; in India, 231;

in Italy, 269, 271; at Jeshyn festival, *145*; Kabul University and, 216; Kennedy and, 193, 198, 205–7, *206*; Maiwandwal and, 234–35, 237–38; Neumann and, 250; Nixon and, 243; petroleum and, 154; Political Parties Bill and, 225, 234; Soviet Union and, 154, *206*, 210–11; Steeves and, 202–3; UNTAM and, 96; Yusuf and, 208–9, 227

Zahir, Abdul, 252–55, 258; antinarcotics campaign and, 260; Connally and, 25; resignation of, 267
Zahir, Ahmad, 254, 343
Zhou Enlai, 277
Zia ul-Haq, Mohammed, 312–13; borderlands policy of, 312; Daoud Khan coup and, 317; DRA and, 331, 332
Zubok, Vladislav, 10

GPSR Authorized Representative: Easy Access System Europe, Mustamäe tee
50, 10621 Tallinn, Estonia, gpsr.requests@easproject.com

www.ingramcontent.com/pod-product-compliance
Lightning Source LLC
Chambersburg PA
CBHW031227290426
44109CB00012B/191